NETWORKS

2nd Edition

Timothy S. Ramteke
DeVry Institute of Technology

Prentice
Hall

Upper Saddle River, New Jersey
Columbus, Ohio

Library of Congress Cataloging-in-Publication Data
Ramteke, Timothy
      Networks/Timothy S. Ramteke.--2nd ed.
         p. cm.
      ISBN 0-13-901265-6
      1. Telecommunication. 2. Computer networks. I. Title

TK5101 .R36 2001
621.382'--dc21

                                  00-031346

Vice President and Publisher: Dave Garza
Editor in Chief: Stephen Helba
Assistant Vice President and Publisher: Charles E. Stewart, Jr.
Production Editor: Tricia Huhn
Design Coordinator: Robin G. Chukes
Cover Image: Marjorie Dressler
Cover Designer: Becky Kulka
Production Manager: Matthew Ottenweller
Marketing Manager: Barbara Rose

This book was set in Times New Roman and was printed and bound by R. R.Donnelley & Sons Company. The cover was printed by Victor Graphics, Inc.

Copyright © 2001 by Prentice-Hall, Inc., Upper Saddle River, New Jersey 07458. All rights reserved. Printed in the United States of America. This publication is protected by Copyright and permission should be obtained from the publisher prior to any prohibited reproduction, storage in a retrieval system, or transmission in any form or by any means, electronic, mechanical, photocopying, recording, or likewise. For information regarding permission(s), write to: Rights and Permissions Department.

10 9 8 7 6 5 4 3 2 1

0-13-901265-6

Jesus Christ said,
   "Come unto me,
   all you who are weary and burdened,
   and I will give you rest and peace."

Overview

(Numbers in parentheses are page counts.)

Contents

Contents

Contents   vii

Contents

9/28/93

Preface

This text is organized into three layers. The first layer, consisting of Chapters 1 and 2, provides a broad overview of voice and data networking. The second layer, consisting of Chapters 3 through 8, discusses the fundamentals that are required for later chapters and introduces communications services, LANs (Local Area Networks), and the TCP/IP protocols used in the Internet. The final layer, consisting of Chapters 9 through 27, details the nuts and bolts of networking. This layer, because of its size, is divided into three parts called Voice Networking, WANs, and LANs and Internetworking.

The structure of this second edition is very much like that of the first edition except for the expansion of the first four chapters into eight chapters. These chapters give the advantages, purposes, and basic workings of networking protocols without delving into the bits and bytes or the fields and frames of protocols. Much of that is left for Chapters 9 through 27. Students don't need the details when they are first introduced to networks; they want to have a bird's eye view. Once they appreciate what these protocols can do, then they are ready to discover how their objectives are accomplished.

Figure A outlines the organization of the textbook. There is flexibility in the order in which the chapters can be covered. Notice that Chapter 6 can be covered after studying the first four chapters and that it is not a prerequisite to studying Chapter 7 or any other chapter. On the other hand, the suggested prerequisites for Chapter 17 are Chapters 1 through 5 and Chapter 16. The text is written roughly in the order that the different technologies evolved over time, and if possible, it should be covered in the same order. That is not necessary, however. Note that voice and data networks are converging and that the chapters relating to them may overlap.

Throughout the text, I have avoided the use of the phrase "at the time of this writing" because that is understood and technologies and solutions must continually change. Also, I have used "he" and "him" for personal pronouns throughout.

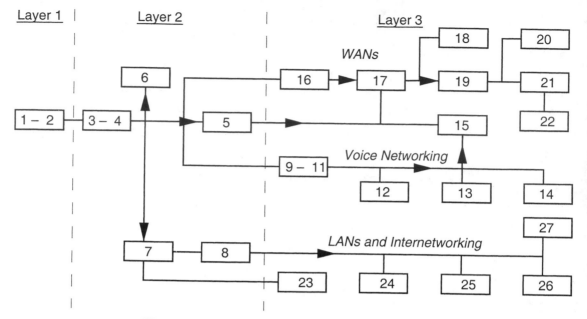

Figure A Suggested sequence of paths for chapters.

My thanks go to the technical editors of the first edition. I won't forget their invaluable assistance. They were Wally Bartus, Eric Harvie, Joseph Mastriani, David Drosdick, Dan Lawler, Ronald Mitchell, Robert Przybysz, Peter DePrima, Terry Henry, Al Hukle, Michael Zboray, Gary Morgenstern, Rick Wallerstein, Diane Pozefsky, Atul Kapoor, Peter Locke, Robert Fishel, Ted Haller, Annabelle Soper, Steve Silva, Radia Perlman, Tony Eldridge, Rory Pope, and Thomas P. Brisco.

I think of myself primarily as a teacher. Every teacher, however, has to be a student at one time or another, and I am no exception. For this edition I have had some fabulous teachers. Some of them include Alan Y. Schaevitz for frame relay and basic networking, Michael F. Finneran for xDSL and other access technologies, Darryl Schick (darryl@3Gtraining.com) for CDMA, and Gary Kessler for VPNs. Bill Yodlowsky, Jay Pear, and John Goswick, who were once my students, became my teachers in Linux and Windows 98 networking. Bhupinder Sran provided a great deal of support, not to mention my dear family, Jonathan, Sarah, Daniel, and Beth. Because English is not my mother tongue, I also appreciate Bret Workman's precise cye on the details of editing.

I hope that you will enjoy reading and studying this text as much as I have enjoyed writing it. I find the material fascinating and, given the time, I can assure you that you will too. I have just created a web page for possibly making available network-related resources at http://members.bellatlantic.net/~slickk. For comments, positive and especially negative, I am always glad to get e-mail. See you at slickk @bellatlantic.net and keep on networking!

Tim Ramteke

Chapter 1

Welcome to Telecommunications

Telecommunications is a very dynamic field. There are always new technologies being developed and adopted on all fronts. These first eight chapters take the view that the reader is new to telecommunications and so set the groundwork that is needed for the chapters which follow. This chapter, in particular, provides a historical perspective that gives reasons as to why things are the way they are today. It provides fundamental concepts of how a simple telephone call is made, through which points a call is processed, and which kinds of carriers are responsible for handling which segments of the call path. The elements that make up the Internet are also discussed. The chapter concludes by pointing out some recent developments in the industry and giving an introduction to the various standard organizations. Each topic presented here is essential for a person who needs to know the advanced elements of networking.

First a word about acronyms: Unfortunately, I will have to use many acronyms as networking topics are uncovered. Please don't be discouraged if you can't remember what the letters of an acronym stand for. On several occasions I have noticed that an expert in a field who uses a particular acronym daily ends up not being able to give its correct equivalent in words. The words of an acronym are not as important as its meaning. Of course, knowing the words of an acronym will help you remember its meaning better. However, it is more important to know how an acronym is used and where it fits in the overall picture of telecommunication terms. An appendix at the end of the book on acronyms should prove helpful for those who really want to know what words their letters represent.

1.1 HISTORICAL SURVEY

1.1.1 The 1800s

Telecommunications means communications at a distance just as telescope refers to a device which enables one to see objects at a distance. Telecommunications as we know it today started with the telegraph. It was invented by a physicist named Henry

1

in 1831. Samuel Morse made its use practical by inventing the repeater, which allowed transmissions over longer distances.

In 1845, the Western Union Telegraph Co. was formed and by 1861, the first telegraph lines spanning the continent were installed. The first Trans-Atlantic cable was installed in 1865 and the world was on its way to interconnecting itself with networks.

It was as early as 1854 when Philip Reise was able to send sound over wires. Many consider him to be the inventor of the telephone. It wasn't until 1876, however, that Alexander Bell obtained the patent for it. On the same day that Bell invented the telephone, Eliza Gray also invented the telephone, independently. Bell was working with the deaf, trying to convert voice into electrical energy and then have it somehow connect it to the brain so deaf people could "hear." He was successful in the first phase of the project, but unfortunately today, the rest is still unfinished.

Bell tried to sell his invention to Western Union, but was laughed at and was turned down. This was similar to when the inventors of the first digital computer, John Atanasoff and Clifford Berry, approached IBM and were told that IBM would never be interested in electronic computers. Bell formed his own company in June of 1877 and called it the Bell Telephone Company. In 1879, he bought out Western Electric and in 1885, Bell incorporated AT&T (American Telephone & Telegraph).

1.1.2 The Independents

When, in 1893, the telephone patent ran out, many independent telephone companies were formed. They were mostly interested in serving the rural areas which AT&T didn't find profitable. Soon the independents were also bringing their services into the cities. It became necessary for a home to have several phones if access to all surrounding areas was needed, one for each telephone company. This was necessary because the Bell system didn't interconnect with them and so the network services had to be duplicated, at least in urban areas.

Soon AT&T was buying up the independents. The Department of Justice insisted that AT&T violated the Sherman Anti-Trust Act. In response, Nathan Kingsbury, a vice president of AT&T, issued a unilateral letter, rather than a consent decree, called the Kingsbury Commitment in 1913. It ensured that AT&T would not buy out any more independents and would allow the independent networks to be interconnected with its own and would dispose of its Western Union stock. This meant that now homes needed only one telephone and that today we still have the existence of these independents. Currently, there are approximately 1400 independents.

Realizing the monopolizing nature of AT&T, Congress signed the Communications Act of 1934. From this the FCC (Federal Communications Commission) was created to protect the public from high prices and poor service.

Today, the FCC regulates interstate and international communications. "Inter" means between places while "intra" means within a place. For instance an interstate highway exists between states and an intrastate highway exists within a state. The PUCs (Public Utility Commissions), which come under the jurisdiction of each state, control and regulate intrastate communications.

1.1.3 The Road to Divestiture

Moving up to 1968, the Carterfone Decision allowed private devices to be connected to the telephone network. In this decision, the FCC decreed that AT&T could not prohibit connections, but could establish standards that must be met by connecting devices. This stimulated companies to buy PBXs from companies other than the local telephone companies.

In the same year, William McGowan met Jack Goeken. McGowan was a Harvard Business School graduate. He found out that Goeken's company, called MCI (Microwave Communications, Inc.), was not permitted to build a microwave link for truckers operating between Chicago and St. Louis. MCI was opposed by AT&T, General Telephone, Illinois Bell, Southwestern Bell, and Western Union.

Everyone who was in the telecommunications industry believed that it was nonsense to try to fight the FCC and AT&T. However, McGowan knew nothing about telecommunications. He set up his office close to the FCC in Washington, D.C. and within three years was able to provide this service not only to the truckers but also to other businesses. Needless to say, soon other cities were being served and other carriers were being established. In 1974 McGowan filed a lawsuit against AT&T for antitrust violations and in 1975, the Department of Justice did the same, which eventually led to the divestiture of the Bell System in 1984. Divestiture means creating separate independent companies out of one. Even Robert Allen of AT&T said that McGowan, more than anyone else, reshaped the monopolistic telecommunications industry to be a highly competitive one.

As far back as 1949, the Justice Department tried to break up the Bell System by making Western Electric independent. In 1956, however, a consent decree was signed that allowed Western Electric to be part of AT&T as long as it only furnished common carrier communication services.

As a modification to this decree, the MFJ (Modified Final Judgment) was approved by Judge Harold Green in 1982 and took effect on January 1, 1984. It created eight independent companies out of the Bell system. These were AT&T and seven RBOCs (Regional Bell Operating Companies).

At that time there were 23 local BOCs (Bell Operating Companies), out of which SNET (Southern New England Telephone) and Cincinnati Bell remained with AT&T, while the other 21 BOCs were divided among the RBOCs. The RBOCs were Ameritech, Bell Atlantic, Bell South, Nynex (NY and New England eXchange), Pacific Telesis, Southwestern Bell, and US West. Bellcore (Bell Communications Research) was created for all the RBOCs and the Bell Labs remained with AT&T. They serve as research and development facilities.

1.2 HANDLING OF CALLS (1984-1996)

1.2.1 LATAs, IXCs, and LECs

At the time of divestiture, the country was divided into 184 LATAs (Local Access and Transport Areas). These areas were divided so as to define the share of the business between the BOCs and the long distance companies. In 1993, there were 189

LATAs, out of which 161 were Bell LATAs and 28 were independent LATAs. In 2000, there are 196.

LATA boundaries are determined by the community of interest and usually don't change. Although LATA boundaries follow state boundaries and area code boundaries in many cases, they don't have to. Area code boundaries don't cross state boundaries, but LATA boundaries do in many cases. Figure 1.1 shows the LATA boundaries of California and the area codes as they were located in 1993. Today, there are many more area codes. Here, the area codes for Pasadena and Los Angeles are different, but they are in the same LATA, whereas the area code for Santa Cruz and Monterey is the same, but they are in different LATAs. In other words, a LATA can have more than one area code and an area code can have more than one LATA.

When most phone numbers available in an area code become assigned, it becomes necessary to split it into two area codes, thereby doubling the number of

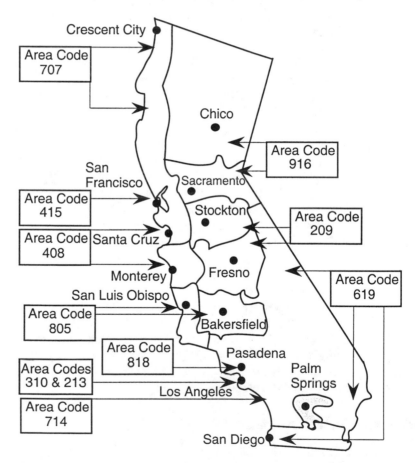

Figure 1.1 This map from 1993 shows the ten LATAs of California. Today, there are many more area codes, but the LATA boundaries are the same. Notice that an area code such as 916 once spanned two LATAs, and one LATA, such as the San Francisco LATA, had several area codes.

available phone numbers. Americans today are using more phone numbers than they did before, because of the proliferation of modems, cellular phones, and fax machines. Theoretically, the seven digits of each phone number in a given area code can vary from 000-0000 to 999-9999. This provides one area code with 10^7 or 10 million phone numbers. The only reason a new area code is introduced is to increase the number of available phone numbers. Nationwide we are running out of area codes and we will soon have to change our numbering system. To find which area codes and 3-digit exchanges are assigned to which states and cities, search the www.nanpa.com web site.

The term telco (telephone company) is used to refer to the operating company in the local area, whether it be a BOC or an independent. The telco is also called the LEC (Local Exchange Carrier). Here, the term "exchange" refers to a LATA and not the 3-digit number that comes after an area code in a phone number. Most telecommunications traffic within a LATA is handled by the telco, with increasing inroads made by cellular carriers.

Long distance carriers, such as AT&T, MCI, and Sprint (originally Southern Pacific Railroad Internal NeTwork for communications), which haul traffic between LATAs, are called IECs or IXCs (InterEXchange Carriers). In Figure 1.1, 11 LATAs are shown, out of which 10 are Bell LATAs served by Pacific Bell. The one independent LATA is served by GTE. There are many independent companies operating within these LATAs. Regardless of who the telcos are, however, if the call is being made within a LATA, it is usually handled by the LECs. Calls that cross a LATA boundary must be handled by an IXC. In this case, there may be more than two carriers that handle the call: the LEC that connects the caller to the IXC, the IXC itself, and the LEC that connects the IXC to the person being called. The LEC of the caller and the LEC of the person being called may or may not be the same.

For example, in Figure 1.1, we see that Santa Cruz and Crescent City, although far from each other and having separate area codes, are part of the same LATA, and calls between them are handled by the LECs. This call doesn't require the services of an IXC, because the call is within the same LATA. This will be a long distance call, but the bill will come from the LEC.

But if a person in Santa Cruz makes a call close by to Monterey, using the same area code does require the services of an IXC. This is because the call is an inter-LATA call. The bill for this call will come from the IXC — AT&T or whoever your long distance carrier may be. The LECs include not only the RBOCs but also independent phone companies, the largest of which here is GTE.

1.2.2 Defining Terms and Call Routing

Let us first define some terms, using Figure 1.2, which are necessary in order to examine how calls are routed.

A line is a link which connects a terminal (such as a telephone) to a network. A switch is typically an electronic device that provides a connection between two lines or trunks. A trunk is a connection between two switches and a trunk group is a collection of trunks between one pair of switches.

A CO (Central Office) is a building where the telco terminates all telephone lines from the local area and connects these lines to the switches that are inside the CO.

When you pick up your phone to call your neighbor, the switch at the CO detects that you have gone off-hook and sends you a dial tone. After you dial the phone number, the switch will ring your neighbor's phone. Although you are neighbors, the connection has to be made through your local CO.

A PBX (Private Branch eXchange) is a switch that provides switching between extensions in one facility such as a building. A CO is for the use of the public but a PBX is primarily for the use of the building occupants. Chapters 11 and 13 discuss COs and PBXs further.

Figure 1.2 shows an example of how these items may be interconnected. Let us see how various types of calls are handled. When phones that are attached to the same CO connect, it is called an intra-office call. The term "office" here refers to a CO. For example, a call between 356-2512 and 356-9199 is an intra-office call, while a call between 356-2512 and 718-1212 is an interoffice call.

The phones inside a building are considered to be phones in a private network, while all the remaining ones are considered to be part of the public network. The formal name for the public network is the PSTN (Public Switched Telephone Network). The PSTN is also referred to as the DDD (Direct Distance Dialing) cloud. DDD implies that the network can allow a person to make long distance calls without the assistance of operators. IDDD (International DDD) refers to the PSTN, which extends around the globe.

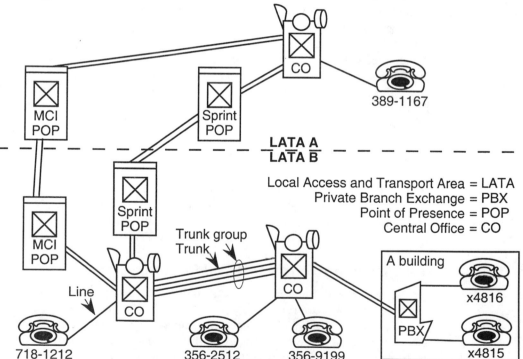

Figure 1.2 Calls within a building can be handled by a PBX, calls within a LATA generally require the services of COs, and calls between LATAs require the services of POPs belonging to a particular IXC.

Welcome to Telecommunications

When a phone from the PSTN calls the main number of the building, the attendant (previously referred to as the switchboard operator) may answer the call and transfer it to an extension in the building.

Private telephones in the building simply dial an extension to reach someone else in the building. To reach someone in the PSTN, the person at an extension must first get a dial tone from the PBX. Then that person must dial a special digit called an access code, such as 9, and then receive a dial tone from the CO. Now the person may dial anywhere in the public network, depending on the privileges granted by the PBX.

As we have said, IXCs must handle inter-LATA calls. In order to do that, IXCs must have locations where calls to and from COs can be connected to their nationwide networks. Such locations are called POPs (Point Of Presence) and at these locations the IXCs interface with the local telcos. For an IXC to have coverage in all parts of the country, it must have at least one POP in every LATA, and several may exist. Of course, these POPs must be networked. When a CO hands off a call from a customer to an IXC, it usually has predefined that customer's primary IXC. This is called pre-subscription.

Now, if extension 4816 in Figure 1.2 dials 389-1167 over the public network, the telco's network knows to which POP it must hand over the call. If the call is pre-subscribed to Sprint, then the Sprint POP on the egress side (receiving side) will hand the call over to the CO belonging to the local telco, which then connects the call to 389-1167.

Hence, intrafacility calls are typically handled by a PBX and intra-LATA calls by the COs. Finally, inter-LATA calls are handled by two or more COs, POPs, and possibly PBXs.

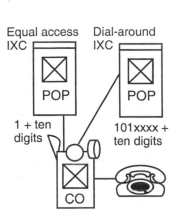

Equal access IXC   Dial-around IXC

POP   POP

1 + ten digits   101xxxx + ten digits

CO

When the presubscribed IXC handles your inter-LATA calls, that is called *equal access dialing*. The MFJ prevented the LECs from providing a faster and easier connection (say, having to use fewer digits) to AT&T than to other IXCs. For that reason, this is called equal access dialing. You simply dialed a "1" and then the ten digits.

If you want to try out an IXC other than your default or pre-subscribed IXC for a particular call, you are allowed to do that. Simply dial "101xxxx" first, then the ten numbers. The xxxx digits identify a specific IXC. For instance, AT&T's xxxx digits are 0288 and Sprint's are 0333. When you precede your out-of-LATA calls with these digits, the call gets forwarded to the appropriate IXC. This type of inter-LATA dialing procedure is called "dial around" because you are "dialing around" the IXC to which you are subscribed. For equal access or dial-around calls, the IXC can ask the LEC to bill you or the IXC can obtain your home address from the LEC, and bill you directly.

1.3 A CLOSER LOOK AT THE PSTN

1.3.1 The Cellular System

So far we have seen how PBXs, COs, and POPs are deployed in our PSTN. Unfortunately, other components are being added to make the picture more compli-

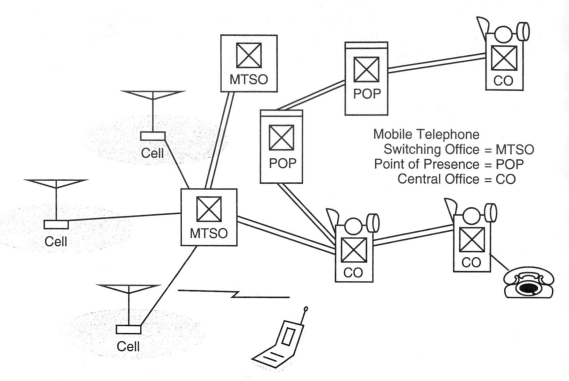

Figure 1.3 Connecting wireless services to "wire-line" services.

cated. One such component is the wireless cellular system. Figure 1.3 shows an MTSO (Mobile Telephone Switching Office) of a cellular company connected to a CO of an LEC. The MTSO is also directly connected to other MTSOs and each MTSO is connected to its own set of cell sites. The path from the COs to the MTSOs and their cell sites uses direct "wire-line" connections. Wireless communication occurs only from the cell sites to the mobile phones.

The MTSO is a switch that determines which cell site receives the strongest signal from a given mobile phone and establishes the connection via that cell site. If the mobile phone travels from one area to another, the signal from the current cell site fades out and another cell would be more appropriate to handle its communication. The MTSO determines this and "hands over" the call to a new cell site.

In Figure 1.3, when the phone connected to the CO calls the cellular customer, the CO, from the dialed phone number, determines that this call has to be switched over to that particular cellular company. Just as a CO hands over inter-LATA calls to the appropriate POP, here the CO will hand over the call to the MTSO of this cellular carrier. Then the MTSO finds out if the cellular customer is available from the various cell sites and makes the connection if possible. The MTSO is part of a cellular company's network just as a POP is part of an IXC's network. MTSOs belonging to one cellular company can be interconnected between LATAs and across states, but they are

Welcome to Telecommunications

not as much regulated by the government as other carriers are. The cellular companies can handle calls between LATAs and can connect calls across many states. They are not restricted by the MFJ as are the LECs and IXCs.

1.3.2 Signaling System 7

One of the unsung heroes of our PSTN is the SS7 (Signaling System 7) network. If we were still using the old electro-mechanical switches, we would be wasting a lot of our PSTN resources, such as switch capacity and trunks. The carriers would require more switches and more trunking capacity to provide us the same level of service which we enjoy today.

In Figure 1.4, if we were still using the old method of completing a call, when a phone called another phone, the connections to each switch along the way would have to be established one by one. Each switch would have to wait to make its connection along the voice path until the previous switch made its connection. This would take a long time. If 5 switches were needed to complete a call, first a connection with the first switch would have to be established, then with the second one, and so on until all the

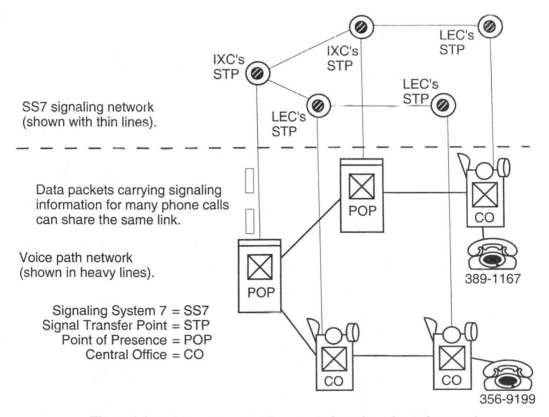

Figure 1.4 The signaling network, separate from the voice path network, determines how a call should be routed before the actual connection is made.

switches were connected. After all that trouble, if the number being called happened to be busy at that time, then all these connections which were reserved for this call would have to be dropped and although this attempt was unsuccessful, it would require networking resources and the phone company could not generate any revenue from it. The only service we received was a transmission of a busy tone along this path.

With SS7, the PSTN is divided into two networks: a voice-path network and a signaling network. The voice-path network is used only if necessary; otherwise signaling information is passed over the SS7 network using data packets. That is why the chapter on SS7, although part of the voice network, is located in the data networking portion of this text. The packet switches used in SS7 are STPs (Signal Transfer Points). They communicate with the COs, POPs, MTSOs, and each other using data packets over the signaling links. Each of these links carries signaling information for many telephone calls. Also, since the signaling information is needed for short durations, the same signaling links can be shared among many callers.

When a phone dials a number, that number is stored in a data packet by the local CO and sent to its STP, which then finds out the best way to connect this call using the other STPs. Once a voice path is determined for that call, all the voice switches are signaled in unison to make the connection using the trunk numbers determined by the STPs, and the voice path is established. The ringback tone comes from the distant CO and the network is ready to connect the two parties. SS7 has allowed us to bring the connect time for a cross-country call from 15 seconds down to almost 2 seconds.

If the distant phone is busy when its number is dialed, no voice path is established and the busy tone is provided by the local CO. There is no waste of switching and trunking capacity. Each signaling link can carry data packets for many connections, but each voice trunk can carry voice for only one conversation.

The SS7 network is the "nervous system" of our PSTN. Without it, all the switches would prove useless, just as without our nervous system, our body parts couldn't do anything either. Because of the importance of the SS7, there is a lot of redundancy built into it. Because of SS7, we are now developing what is called the AIN (Advanced Intelligence Network). SS7 allows us to use calling credit cards, 800 number dialing, and other features on our phone network. Databases used in the SS7 network allow the implementation of such services. Most important is that, if someone wants the phone network to provide a new type of service that no one has ever thought of before, that service is very simply provided by modifying the software for SS7. SS7 gives the PSTN flexibility.

1.3.3 PCS

At the time of this writing, if I want to give my phone number to someone else to get in touch with me, giving one number is not sufficient. If I want others to reach me, on my business card, I should provide my home number for when I am at home, my work number for when I am at work, and my cellular number for when I am driving. However, that is not enough. I must also provide my daily schedule so that they can reach me at the proper time at the proper number. Hopefully, my schedule will stay pretty much stable each day. But when I provide my e-mail address on my business card, I only have to give one address. Why then, when I give my phone number, should

I have to give several numbers and also provide a "good time" to use each of these numbers!

PCS (Personal Communications System) is a user-friendly concept which will achieve one phone number for each person. Along with having only one phone number, each person would only need one phone set. As long as my phone set is with me and it is turned on, it doesn't matter where I go, PCS will know where I am and how to make a connection.

When I come home, the base station at my home detects that I have come home and signals the databases in the SS7 network that I can be reached through my home telephone's base station. Then my phone would be like a cordless phone. If I go into someone else's home, that base station would register my presence with the PCS network. When I am at work, the wireless PBX would be my connection point. This way if anyone calls me using my one and only phone number, the SS7 network would know where I am and get me connected properly.

You might say that I can use my current phone as my only phone. However, at the time of this writing, all PCS communications occurs with PCS antennas at PCS cell sites. You have to pay for the air time as well as sacrifice on the quality of the signal at times. If, instead, you are using the cordless base station at home or the wireless PBX at work, chances are that you will get a better signal at a lower cost.

In order to get such wireless coverage around the world, consortiums of large corporations are building complex satellite systems called LEOS (Low-Earth Orbit Satellites). The LEOS will prevent us from having to install cell site antennas on every mountain and every valley. They will orbit close to the earth, providing a low-delay connection which is crucial to voice communications. Because of their proximity to the mobile phones, they would require lower power than traditional satellites do. Also, the handsets would require lower power.

1.4 THE INTERNET

1.4.1 A Data Network

In the last two sections we saw how our PSTN network is evolving. This network, originally designed to transfer voice, can now be used to transfer data, video, and other kinds of information. In this section, we will take a bird's eye view of the Internet. Originally, it was designed to transfer digital data, but now it can be used to transfer all kinds of information, including voice. The PSTN was designed to carry voice, while the Internet was designed to carry data.

The Internet today is an interconnection of networks. It is the largest data network in the world. These networks are so seamlessly connected that they appear as a single network to us, the users of the Internet. For a computer to communicate directly with other computers on the Internet, it must have its own IP (Internet Protocol) address. This IP address must be unique in the entire Internet and is used for host identification. A device on the Internet with its own IP address is called a host or a node. For a host to communicate with another host, it must know the IP address of the target host. Devices called routers transfer information between hosts in the Internet, but let us keep our view of the Internet simple by not considering routers.

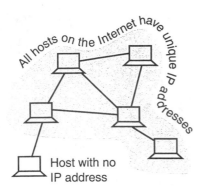

All hosts on the Internet have unique IP addresses

Host with no
IP address

In the side figure, we see a computer that does not have its own IP address. This is true of some PCs which are connected through certain ISPs (Internet Service Providers), such as AOL (America On-Line). All data from such computers must go through the ISP's server before they are sent to the routers on the Internet. Such ISPs provide specialized services such as protecting customers from indecent sites. All other computers in this figure are directly connected to the routers of the Internet and hence have a faster response time than the computer with no IP address.

1.4.2 The TCP/IP Protocol Suite

All hosts on the Internet, those with IP addresses, run a set of simple data protocols, two of which are called TCP (Transmission Control Protocol) and IP (Internet Protocol). Collectively, the family of these Internet protocols is called the TCP/IP protocol suite. A protocol is an agreed method of handling a particular communications task. As we will see in later chapters, there is a protocol for sending mail, another one for transferring a file, and so forth. The TCP/IP suite of protocols, which define a standard method of communications between Internet hosts, is implemented in virtually all kinds of computer systems. This means that it doesn't matter what kind of computer hardware you have, or what kind of operating system it is running, or what kind of connection you have, if it implements TCP/IP, then it can be directly on the Internet.

In 1970, when I was in a Tokyo train station, I could not find anyone who knew English. If I had known some Japanese, I would have been able to communicate with anyone because the communications protocol used in Tokyo was Japanese. Similarly, a computer that wishes to be a host on the Internet must "understand and speak" TCP/IP protocols. It wouldn't have mattered if my physical features (i.e., hardware) were different from those of the Japanese or that my cultural background (i.e., operating system) was different from theirs. The reason I couldn't communicate was because I couldn't "operate" in the Japanese language. This is how important TCP/IP is for the operation of the Internet.

1.4.3 The Client-Server Model

Now all the hosts on the Internet communicate with each other using the client-server model. This means that when events occur on the Internet, there is a host that acts as a client and a host that acts as a server. The host requesting a specific service is called the host and the host providing that service or a reply is the acting server.

In the side figure, if host X requests a file transfer from host Y, then host X becomes the client and host Y becomes the server. Both of these hosts will be communicating with each other using ftp (File Transfer Protocol). However, host X will be running the ftp client software while host Y will be running the ftp server software. After these two hosts close their connection, they could switch their roles and then host X would be the server and host Y would be the client.

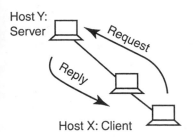

Host Y: Server

Request

Reply

Host X: Client

In the Microsoft Windows environment, typically a PC would be assigned an IP address when it goes on the Internet. Here, the PC could become an ftp client but not an ftp server since typically, PCs don't come with ftp server software.

There are servers on the Internet that provide different types of services. Mail servers accept and send e-mail. They have to be on all the time because they have to be able to process mail at any time. In fact, servers in general are on all the time because they have no way of knowing when someone might request them to do some work. Telnet is another example of a service provided by hosts on the Internet. It allows users to log onto servers from remote locations.

One host can provide a wide variety of services. Servers have special programs that are continuously running in the background. They "listen" for requests from clients and when a service is requested, they start a copy of the server software for that connection and continue to "listen" for other requests. Such programs are called daemons.

1.4.4 Sending E-mail

People find it awkward to use IP addresses when sending someone e-mail. For example, it is easier to remember an e-mail address of ramteke@pilot.njin.net than ramteke@[165.230.224.139]. Words are easier to remember than just random numbers. In my e-mail address, "ramteke" is the name of the account, "pilot" is the name of the e-mail server, and "njin.net" is the domain in which pilot is a member. "net" is the top-level domain. "pilot.njin.net" is the complete address of the e-mail server where "ramteke" has an e-mail account. pilot's IP address, in this example, is 165.230.224.139.

Since hosts on the Internet communicate with each other by specifying their IP addresses and we find it more convenient to use descriptive addresses such as pilot.njin.net, we need some way to convert descriptive addresses to IP addresses. Special servers on the Internet, called DNS (Domain Name Service) servers, provide the conversion from hostname addresses to IP addresses. These servers use the DNS protocol. Every time your host needs to do a hostname to IP address conversion, it requests this service from a primary DNS server. If that server doesn't know the IP address of the host which is requested, then it asks other DNS servers. There is a hierarchy of DNS servers in the Internet which provide this service.

If you send e-mail to me at ramteke@pilot.njin.net, your primary DNS server will find out pilot's IP address for you. After this, using pilot's IP address, the server will transfer your e-mail to pilot using data packets. This step would not be necessary if you sent e-mail to me using pilot's IP address. That is, if you use ramteke@[165.230.224.139] instead of ramteke@pilot.njin.net, the e-mail will be sent directly without you requiring the services of DNS servers.

1.4.5 The WWW

The WWW (World Wide Web) is a collection of servers on the Internet that provide web pages to the clients that request to receive them. A web server can also

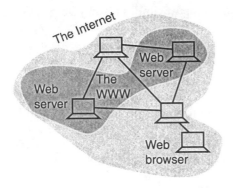

provide a link to other web servers. Hence, the WWW is a subset of the hosts on the Internet as shown in the side figure. Web pages are usually written in HTML (HyperText Markup Language) and web servers and clients run http (HyperText Transfer Protocol).

When you go on the Internet, or more accurately on the web, you are using a WWW client software called a web browser. Netscape is an example of a web browser. A browser can communicate with servers running http in order to request web pages. Apache is an example of a web server software which uses http.

1.5 INDUSTRY DEVELOPMENTS SINCE 1984

1.5.1 CAPs (Competitive Access Providers)

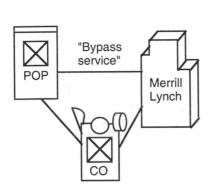

In 1984, Merrill Lynch realized that to gain access to the IXC's POPs, it would have to go through the LEC's COs. In order to avoid charges from the LEC, Merrill Lynch created the Teleport Communications Company to install and maintain fiber directly to the POP. This was the beginning of bypass services provided by CAPs (Competitive Access Providers).

In 1987, there was a fire in a CO in Hinsdale, Illinois near Chicago. This paralyzed telecommunications for two weeks. In order to provide a backup to the local phone company or the LEC, MFS (Metropolitan Fiber Systems) was created.

CAPs, in general, compete with the local operating telephone companies by providing transmission facilities directly to the IXC's POPs in metropolitan areas. Customers who use bypass carriers then don't have to pay charges from the local telephone company. CAPs generally provide services over fiber optic networks with duplicate routes between network locations to provide superior service quality and security compared to the local telephone companies. They also price themselves competitively to attract large-volume users away from the telcos.

In many cases, the bypass carriers' networks cross LATA boundaries because, in most states, they are not regulated and a customer may be able to not only bypass the LECs in both LATAs but also bypass the IXCs as well. Of course, the RBOCs don't like to lose large-volume customers to these carriers.

The RBOCs must file for approval with the PUC (Public Utility Commission) for providing specialized innovative services. Whereas the bypasses are not so regulated. CAPs also provide LAN interconnections and advanced services over mostly fiber backbone networks.

One of the most attractive reasons why managers like CAPs is the added reliability they provide to their network. This is done by alternative routes provided by these carriers. And in case a disaster strikes the established local carrier network, alternate routing is possible. CAPs also provide network management functions such

Welcome to Telecommunications

as rerouting and remote testing of circuits. This adds flexibility also by being able to switch routes through more than just one POP. CAPs provide competition to LECs, improving the quality of service and lowering prices from both the LECs and the CAPs.

1.5.2 Resellers and ISPs

Resellers buy telecommunications services wholesale from the main carriers such as AT&T, Sprint, and the RBOCs and resell them to end-users. Some resellers actually lease fiber cable runs and switch capacity from the primary carriers. They only provide this reselling service on circuits where they can get a large volume of traffic from customers where it would be cost effective for them.

ISPs (Internet Service Providers) are becoming more important as more people use the Internet. Basically, they provide connectivity to the Internet. ISPs can provide email service, web page service, and other types of Internet services. Some ISPs provide you a connection directly on the Internet while others require you to be connected via their servers. Being directly connected to the Internet enables information to be transferred faster, while going through an ISP's server can give you added bulletin boards and services such as filtering out indecent web sites.

1.5.3 The Telecommunications Act of 1996

Because the CAPs were starting to cut into the RBOC share of the local market, the RBOCs wanted to get into the inter-LATA market share. The Telecommunications Act of 1996 allows RBOCs to provide inter-LATA service on the condition that they allow IXCs to connect to their switches in the COs and provide local service. In 1984, the distinction was clear as to who provided which services. The IXCs provided inter-LATA services and the LECs provided intra-LATA services. Because of this act, the distinction is becoming blurred. This reminds me of two children who are served their dinner plates, and then want to eat from the other child's plate. The cable companies or whoever may come along are now also allowed to provide local access.

The MFJ created competition in the long distance, inter-LATA market place. The Telecommunications Act of 1996 is bringing competition to the local, intra-LATA market place. The RBOCs are required to prove that they have met a 14-point checklist, proving the existence of local area competition. In return the RBOCs would be allowed to provide inter-LATA services. This 14-point checklist does not apply to the independent telephone companies' LECs but only to the RBOC LECs.

The 14-point checklist includes such things as number portability. That is, if a customer changes his carrier from an RBOC to a CLEC (Competitive Local Exchange Carrier, pronounced *seelek*), they wouldn't have to change their phone number. It includes co-location of equipment or the right of a CLEC to place his equipment in the CO of the RBOC. It also includes fair access to their network, including telephone poles, white pages, 911 access, and so on. To differentiate the CLECs from the existing LECs, the existing LECs are called ILECs (Incumbent LECs).

The MFJ was handled by the courts, but the Telecommunications Act was an act of Congress. The MFJ opened up long distance competition, but the Act opened up local competition. The results of it backfired, however, and many carriers regrouped,

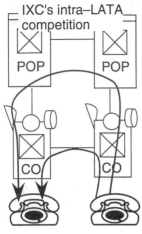

IXC's intra–LATA competition

POP   POP

CO   CO

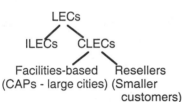

LECs

ILECs   CLECs

Facilities-based   Resellers
(CAPs - large cities) (Smaller customers)

reducing the number of players in the industry. In the side figure, we see that a particular IXC can have several POPs within the same LATA. The Act allows the IXC to handle intra-LATA traffic that would normally be charged as a long-distance call by the LEC. The LEC has an incentive to allow IXCs to compete in the local arena because they will then be allowed to compete in the long distance arena. As you can see, the distinctions between IXCs, LECs, and LATA boundaries are slowly beginning to disappear.

There are basically two kinds of CLECs: facilities-based and the resellers. See the side diagram. The CAPs of yesterday are known as facilities-based CLECs today. The two most important CAPs, MFS and TCI, have been bought out by MCI and AT&T, respectively. These are the carriers who own switching equipment and/or fiber runs through metropolitan areas. They attract the large customers in big cities while the resellers will take on smaller customers. Because the profit margins for resellers are low, however, they are not as prevalent. AT&T and MCI both stopped being resellers of local service, primarily for this reason. Back in the 1980's, long distance carriers were always calling at dinner time to get new customers. Today, even after the Telecommunications Act, the competition in the local area is not as serious.

1.5.4 Mergers and Acquisitions

Since the passing of the Telecommunications Act of 1996, the introduction of local market competition, the telecommunications industry has gone through drastic changes. Out of the original seven RBOCs, Bell Atlantic merged with NYNEX and SBC with Pacific Telesis and Ameritech. Bell Atlantic then purchased GTE, the largest independent telephone company. AT&T purchased McCaw Communications, enabling it to provide wireless services. AT&T has since spawned a company called Lucent to provide equipment such as CO switches and PBXs. This made it easy for Lucent to sell their equipment to competitors of AT&T such as Sprint and the RBOCs. Teleport Communications Group, a CAP in 66 cities, and TCI (Tele-Communications Inc.), a cable provider, were also acquired by AT&T. Worldcom also purchased WilTel and then MCI. All these mergers totaling more than 200 billion dollars in assets have created quite an uproar. One is never sure what will happen next in the telecommunications arena. An increase in wireless services, Internet usage, and international markets have also been reasons for such scrambling for opportunities within the telecommunications big players.

1.5.5 ASICs (Application-Specific Integrated Circuits)

While megacompanies were being created in the telecommunications market place, engineers have been creating "micro-sized mergers" on silicon chips. I remember the days when the active components in electronics were vacuum tubes. They were large, bulky, susceptible to breaking, gave off large amounts of heat, required very high voltage supplies, and needed to be replaced quite often. The introduction of transistors practically eliminated all these disadvantages.

Later, the CPU, the heart of a computer, reduced a cabinet full of vacuum tube circuitry into a single IC (Integrated Circuit) chip. Millions of transistors could be fabricated into one IC chip. Today, microprocessors fall into two basic categories: CISC (Complex Instruction Set Computing) and RISC (Reduced Instruction Set Computing). CISC processors have many complex machine-level instructions they can understand, while RISC processors have fewer elementary machine-level instructions. Several RISC instructions may be needed to perform one CISC instruction because one CISC instruction can do the equivalent of several RISC instructions. Because the number of CISC instructions is greater than the number of RISC instructions, however, it takes longer for the processor to look up one CISC instruction in the lookup table. Today, the trend is to use RISC processors, although the Intel Pentium uses CISC architecture.

Traditionally, networking devices like routers used RISC processors. These devices, of course, operate under software programs that are loaded in RAM. If a protocol is changed by a standards committee, one would just need to download the new version of the software which operates that router. Software provides flexibility to devices, such as routers.

As protocols have become fully defined and stable over the years, it is no longer necessary to update the software in network devices as often. Equipment vendors have now implemented software in ICs called ASICs and the logic is "burned into" the chip. This makes the ASIC a hardware-oriented, rather than a software-oriented device. The advantage of this is that the ASIC is now a special-purpose chip, and it runs about three times as fast as a RISC-based processor with software. The ASIC is very inexpensive to manufacture and uses much less space. The disadvantage of ASICs, of course, is that their function is "carved in stone" and cannot be updated by a software download. They take about a year to design and require highly skilled engineers. Sometimes, the entire piece of equipment has to be replaced because the ASIC built into it cannot be modified.

Because of this, vendors are creating a new breed of processors called *network processors*. These devices combine the advantages of both RISC and ASIC chips. The general-purpose RISC architecture is used to perform nonstandardized tasks and the ASIC architecture to perform tasks that are well established. When the new 56-kbps modems became available, they were actually network processors. The new modem standard had not yet been defined. When the standard was ratified, however, the modem was simply upgraded using the new software.

Because of these technological advances, as an example, the price of a network card has dropped from $300 to about $50. Also, they have contributed to how small the new cellular phones are.

1.6 STANDARDS

1.6.1 Open Systems

Traditionally, computer and communications companies tried to commit their customers to their own specific product line. Because of the investment made in the vendors' products, the customers were locked in. If the customer received poor service, the vendor wasn't much concerned, because the chance that the customer would scrap his/her investment and switch to another vendor was slim. Also, from the customer's perspective, the new vendor might prove to be the same or even worse than the previous one.

Today, vendors are still trying to keep customers using proprietary solutions, but customers are starting to look for open systems. An open system, although difficult to define, means that the customer can use his existing product on any computer or network. Also, open system products can be purchased from several vendors—the customer is not locked in with one vendor.

Let's look now at some examples of proprietary and open products. The Intel Pentium microprocessor is a relatively proprietary product, whereas the SPARC (Scalable Processor ARChitecture) chip is an open solution or a standard. Other vendors can manufacture it freely. Similarly, mainframe computers and their operating systems, such as IBM's MVS, are proprietary solutions, while IBM's PC and Unix are standards or open systems.

The PC is open, since many companies are allowed to make it. This is because initially, IBM didn't expect it to sell as well as it did. On the other hand, the Macintosh is a proprietary product. In the networking arena, OSI (Open Systems Interconnection) is an open network architecture. An application that is written to operate on OSI can run on any hardware, operating system, or network as long as it is OSI-based. On the other hand, IBM's SNA (Systems Network Architecture) is neither completely open nor completely proprietary.

There are many reasons why customers are choosing open system products, the most important one being the protection of their investment. If the system is open and the customer doesn't like the vendor he/she can switch vendors and still protect his investment. When there is competition, service from all vendors improves and prices go down, even when the vendor with which a customer is dealing provides good service. It is easier to hire skilled personnel. Many vendors claim that their product is open, but one should be careful that they are not misled into a proprietary system, although there may be reasons to go that route. One reason to use proprietary solutions is perhaps a standard has not been defined yet and the customer needs an immediate solution. Many times a proprietary solution will prove to be efficient or provide features which are not available with a standards-based solution.

1.6.2 Organizations

Figure 1.5 shows many of the standard organizations. The hierarchical structure relating the various organizations does not hold true that rigidly. They all interface with one another to some degree.

In the UN (United Nations), there is the ITU (International Telecommunications Union) which is based in Geneva. It primarily consists of ITU-T (Telecommunications standardization sector) and ITU-R (Radio communication sector). Previously these were called CCITT (Consultative Committee for International Telegraph and Telephone) and CCIR (Consultative Committee for International Radio). ITU-R assigns radio frequencies that affect international boundaries similar to what the FCC does domestically.

ITU-T receives its input from various organizations. PTTs (Post, Telegraph, and Telephones) are government monopolies similar to the postal system in the United States. Most countries in the world have their own PTTs which provide their telecommunications services. The only voting members of ITU-T are the PTTs and the US State Department.

ANSI (American National Standards Institute) is probably the next most important organization for us. It is the dominant one in setting American standards.

The ISO (International Standards Organization) sets standards for nuts, bolts, film type, and a wide range of other fields. In telecommunications it is noted for setting the OSI reference model.

IEEE (Institute of Electrical and Electronic Engineers) is a professional society. It is responsible for setting many of the LAN (Local Area Network) standards.

Aside from these organizations, there are many carriers and equipment manufacturers which are represented in the ITU-T.

Bellcore, now Telcordia, also has been very active in recommending standards such as SONET and SMDS. SONET (Synchronous Optical NETwork) is a standard used to transport digital signals over fiber, and SMDS (Switched Multi-megabit Data Services) is used to interconnect LANs over a wide geographical region.

Since standards take a relatively long time to become established, many vendors and users are creating forums which help a new technology get off its feet quickly. The frame relay forum is a good example of such a forum. It was able to move a concept to reality in a matter of two years. Currently, the ATM forum is very active.

One comment should be made about de facto standards. They are standards not because any agency has approved them, but they are standards solely on the fact that they exist and are used. Sometimes official standards are first approved, then the engineers try to make them work. On the other hand, de facto standards are not accepted by the industry until they are proved to work. An example of such a standard is TCP/

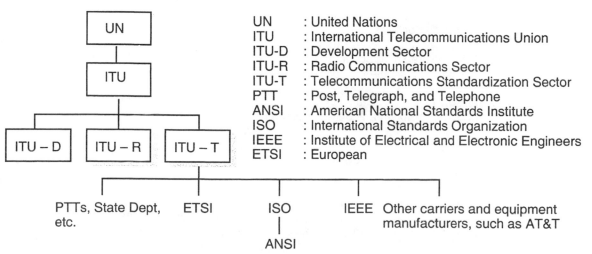

Figure 1.5 Some important standards organizations.

IP (Transmission Control Protocol/Internet Protocol), which is only documented in a large number of RFCs (Request For Comments). Although no standards body originally approved this set of internetworking protocols, it became more popular than OSI simply because it works.

Today the international Internet is governed by the IAB (Internet Architecture Board). It is divided into the IRTF (Internet Research Task Force) and IETF (Internet Engineering Task Force). The IRTF is a small group that does research on long-term Internet issues. The IETF is a much larger group which is divided into 20 or so working groups. It is very active and works on current Internet Engineering problems. The ISOC (Internet SOCiety) is a society that promotes the Internet's growth and research. The InterNIC (Internet Network Information Center) is an organization that manages the assignment of IP addresses and domain names. See www.internic.net for information. It also provides documents relating to the Internet such as RFCs. RFCs can be downloaded from www.ietf.org.

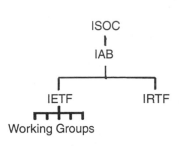

EXERCISES

Section 1.1:
1. Who received the patent for the telephone?
   - a. Reise
   - b. Morse
   - c. Bell
   - d. Gray
2. Who was probably the most responsible for breaking up the Bell System?
   - a. Judge Green
   - b. McGowan
   - c. Robert Allen
   - d. FCC
3. Who were some of the inventors of the telephone?
4. To protect the public interest from AT&T's monopoly, what did Congress do?
5. What was the MFJ modifying?
6. Describe the Kingsbury Commitment and its effects.
7. What historical event was similar to when Western Union showed no interest in Bell's telephone?
8. List some key events that led to the breakup of the Bell System and their dates.
9. What are some advantages that one can give about the Bell breakup? Disadvantages?

Section 1.2:
10. What prefix means between places?
    - a. inter
    - b. intra
    - c. intro
    - d. pre
11. Which system provides intrafacility switching?
    - a. CO
    - b. POP
    - c. PBX
    - d. trunk group
12. Within what area may an LEC handle the entire call?
13. When more phone numbers need to be made available, what is done?
14. Describe how an inter-LATA call is made and what points the call goes through.
15. Theoretically, within one area code, how many phone numbers are possible?
16. Who owns each of the following offices or switches? CO, POP, PBX, and MTSO

Welcome to Telecommunications

Section 1.3:
17. Which location of a cellular company provides a connection to the COs?
    a. POP   b. cell site
    c. MTSO   d. STP
18. Which network in the PSTN uses data packet switching?
    a. lines   b. trunks
    c. SS7   d. STP
19. Wireless communication in a cellular network occurs between which two points?
20. Name the packet switches used in SS7.
21. If the distant phone which is being dialed is busy, will any trunks between the COs and the POPs be utilized?
22. Give two advantages of LEOs.
23. What type of communication system will eventually allow the use of only one phone set and one phone number?

Section 1.4:
24. The Internet is based on which family of protocols?
    a. TCP/IP   b. Microsoft
    c. IBM   d. WWW
25. All hosts that are directly connected to the Internet must be assigned which address?
    a. LAN address   b. modem address
    c. IP address   d. connection address
26. In the client-server model, which host does the requesting and which one does the replying?
27. Describe how a host name is converted to an IP address.
28. All web servers must be running which protocol?
29. What is the difference between the Internet and the WWW? Or are they the same network?

Section 1.5:
30. Most residential users use which of the following to get connected to the Internet?
    a. CAPs   b. ISPs
    c. resellers   d. IXCs
31. Which legislation created competition in the local telecommunications area?
    a. MFJ   b. Telecom Act of 1996
    c. Carterfone Decision   d. Sherman Anti-Trust Act
32. Give two reasons why CAPs came into being.
33. Describe how resellers benefit customers as well as the big carriers from whom they buy services wholesale.
34. Describe the purpose of the Telecommunications Act of 1996 and how it hopes to achieve it.
35. What are the tradeoffs between using RISC-based versus ASIC-based equipment?

Section 1.6:
36. What was the previous name for ITU-T?
    a. ISO   b. IEEE
    c. ITU   d. CCITT

37. When would you want to use a proprietary solution?
    a. When a low-cost solution is an issue.
    b. When dependence on one vendor is not desired.
    c. When standardization with other companies is preferred.
    d. When a more efficient solution is available and necessary.
38. Who are some of the members who provide input to the ITU-T?
39. How is the IETF divided?
40. Give two examples of a de facto standard not mentioned in the chapter.
41. What is the opposite of an open system?
42. Describe the advantages from a user point of view of having an open system and a proprietary system.

Chapter 2

Basics of Data Networking

Foundational concepts dealing with data networks will be covered in this chapter. It is imperative that we understand these concepts thoroughly to appreciate the advanced issues covered in the later chapters. The use of layers in network architectures and how they are implemented in real physical networks, the role that routers and packet switches play, the difference between packet switched networks and datagram networks, and other essential topics in networking will be discussed here. The OSI (Open System Interconnect) reference model will be explained as well. This network architecture was originally intended to connect any kind of computer, running any operating system, using any kind of data communication connection, and providing a wide variety of services. This challenge was instead met by a low-profile network architecture called TCP/IP. Although at first glance studying the OSI reference model seems to be purely an academic exercise, it is the basis from which all other architectures are explained. The networking problems that we will point out while studying the OSI model will be the same problems that other networking options will need to solve. Hence, learning the OSI reference model becomes the starting point in understanding the basis of data networking.

2.1 WHAT IS A NETWORK?

In the early days when computers came into existence, most businesses had only one large computer to do their processing. Because of the expense, processing was even sent off to large computer facilities and the charges were based on CPU time and other items. The computer was located in one room where workers brought their computer jobs, coded in stacks of punched cards. These were then read by a card reader.

Today, although we still have data centers, much of the processing is being off-loaded to smaller computers, many times located on desktops. So instead of depending on one computer to do all the work, we have many smaller computers at our disposal. And instead of us having to walk down the hall to submit our jobs to the computer, the computer has come to the workers and their desktops.

Furthermore, since the combined power of many small systems (or computers) is greater than the power of one large system, these smaller systems are tied together using data communication links. These interconnections of computers, which are self-governing and not controlled by one another, are called networks. An internet is a network of networks.

Currently, just as it is necessary for a computer to be properly powered, so has it become necessary for a computer to be connected in a network to be useful. Hence, we have a "marriage" of communications and computers. Data communications is not possible without computers, and computers are almost useless without data communications.

So what is a network? A network can simply be defined as the interconnection of two or more independent computers or switches. A modern voice switch is nothing more than a special-purpose computer. A "good network" should be a network that doesn't look like a network at all to the end user. The end user should not have to specify the route through which data is acquired; that should be the concern of the networking software.

There are primarily two types of networks; LANs (Local Area Networks) typically provide networking capabilities within a facility (or a building). They can also extend to adjacent facilities in a campus environment and can span distances of two or three miles. WANs (Wide Area Networks) span much greater distances and even go around the globe. There are also MANs (Metropolitan Area Networks), which are difficult to classify as either WANs or LANs.

The reason to classify networks into LANs and WANs is because the protocols which drive networks generally fall into these two categories. LANs, because they use smaller distances, carry data at higher rates than WANs. WANs generally require the services of telephone carriers and, because of longer distances, are more expensive to transfer data. Hence, WAN speeds are usually low. Because the characteristics of WANs and LANs differ substantially, the last half of the text is divided into these two sections.

2.2 WHY NETWORK?

One reason to network is that the sharing of resources can be done easily. Resources are application programs (such as word processing packages), data, printers, modems, etc. In a LAN environment, instead of needing to install a word processing package on each and every station, we need only to install it once on a file server. Of course, we must have the necessary license. This makes the package available to all. Similarly, instead of buying each computer a low-cost printer, we can buy a few high-speed, high-quality printers that are accessible to all.

Networks also provide reliability. In the 1960s, if the central computer was down, then no one could process any jobs. But today, with multiple computers available, if one goes down, we still have many others to fall back on.

It is much easier to do backups of critical data over a network at night when the traffic is low than to rely on computer operators to mount tapes and hard drives, although that is done as well. In a college computer lab, for instance, if one PC is down, a student can move over to another one and get his files and applications, using the same working environment, from a network server. On the other hand, if all his work were stored on one PC, and someone were already there, he would have to ask that person to move so he could access his work. Of course, now we are more dependent on the network server, which becomes a common point of failure for all students. It is much easier, however, to mirror a few servers and have them continually back themselves up than for us to mirror each and every PC.

In the 1960s and the 70s, all data had to be accessed through a mainframe computer located in one data center. This created a phenomena called a "bottleneck," like water rushing through a neck of a bottle when being emptied. Similarly, the data center bottleneck also congested all the jobs that had to be processed through it. Today, processing can be distributed over a network. Jobs can run at several locations and do not depend on the performance of a single location. If one host is down, jobs can be redirected to others. Networks today give local departments more say in specifying what is important and what is not. They know more about local issues than corporate headquarters which may be miles away.

Network Advantages
1. Easier management
2. Reliability
3. Better price/performance ratio
4. Easier backups
5. Mobility
6. Resource sharing
7. More local control

Network Disadvantages
1. Security
2. Lack of skilled workers
3. Costlier to operate

It is true that one large mainframe (computer) has about ten times the processing power of a high-end microcomputer. However, the mainframe costs at least 1000 times as much. So for the same money spent on a mainframe, we could buy 1000 microcomputers and, after networking them, we could have 100 times more processing power than a mainframe.

Networks also allow us to be mobile. If we have an account on a computer in Dallas, and happen to be in San Francisco one week, we can still log on to the computer in Dallas from San Francisco, if the two sites are part of a network. We are not forced to be in the same place where our computing facility happens to be.

In a LAN environment, we don't have to depend on every worker to back up their work each day. From one central computer, an operator can back up everyone's work on a regular basis. Basically, networking makes administration of the computer systems more manageable.

Networks make the management of computers much easier. For those who have to administer and maintain networks on a daily basis, no matter what fancy functions their network provides, it is difficult to manage. Imagine having to manage 100 PC stations that are not networked. Every time software has to be upgraded, it must be done 100 times. Maintenance of printers has to be done continuously. If the PCs need connectivity using modems, 100 modems and 100 lines would have to be installed and maintained. With a network, these tasks become more manageable. We don't have to depend on the workers to back up their work. They may do it for a while, but then they may forget its importance. Backup can be automatic.

Now networking has become a Trojan horse. Administration has become simpler. However, security has emerged as the primary issue. Security of networks is a moving target. As soon as one security hole is fixed, others appear. Also, qualified networking specialists are difficult to find. Skilled workers demand high pay and require constant training. Furthermore, network installations are always changing. People find reasons to keep changing an existing network — adding and moving nodes, updating software, upgrading hardware, etc. Hence, even though the initial cost of networks and distributed systems may be lower than a mainframe setup, the ongoing costs of networks are generally higher and harder to itemize.

2.3 NETWORK ARCHITECTURES

2.3.1 What is a Network Architecture?

Let us now explore the concepts of network architectures, which, although not that complicated, are difficult for the beginner to grasp. Since every chapter on WANs and LANs in this book is based on this one, it is imperative that the reader gain a good understanding of this material. To reinforce the concepts and ideas presented, there is a liberal use of analogies.

When building a house, although it is possible for one person to do so alone, a contractor will usually have teams of workers specializing in their fields do their part of the job. The excavators dig the ground, the masons lay the foundation, the carpenters put up the frame, etc. Each team does its own part of the job more skillfully and efficiently than if one person was doing the entire project by himself. This way the functions of building a house have been divided into distinct components.

Similarly, when designing a network, because this is also a complex task, it is designed using distinct components called layers. Of course, the network could be designed viewing it as one large entity or task, but such an approach would be unwieldy, inflexible, and difficult to manage and implement. Just as a team of special contractors is better when building a house, so is a set of layers better when designing a network architecture. Each layer serves a certain function or purpose in the entire networking scheme. These functions could be, for instance, to check for errors in transmission or to encrypt (scramble) data, or a number of other tasks which are necessary to make a network work.

By designing a network in layers, we can isolate such networking functions into modules, which individually become easier to design than if the entire network were designed as one whole piece. Separating the design of a network into layers allows us to divide the big problem into smaller ones. This way we can do research and development on each layer independently from the others. Solutions for the smaller problems can then be recombined to obtain the solution for the entire network. Smaller problems are easier to solve than bigger ones.

By separating a network into layers, we can also make the network more flexible to implement changes in the future. That is, if a new method of performing the services of a layer is invented, we can swap it with the old method used in that layer. Then we can see if the network performance improves. If it does, good; if not, we can revert back to the old method easily. The set of methods and rules used in a particular layer is called that layer's *protocol*.

For example, if the protocol used by the excavators was to use picks and shovels, and now we want to change that protocol to using a steam shovel, or later, a backhoe, we can try changing it and see if it works better. To the masons, it doesn't matter how the excavators dig the hole. The excavators provide their services to the masons who continue the job from there. The services provided by a layer to the upper adjacent layer are called an *interface*.

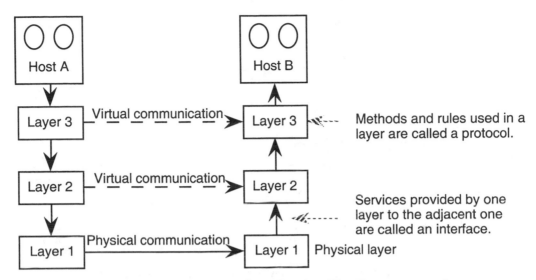

Figure 2.1 Transmission of data from Host A to Host B over a network is shown in solid arrows. There is no direct communication between peer layers except at the physical layer.

Figure 2.1 shows a computer called Host A transmitting data to Host B, with the computers made by different manufacturers running different operating systems over a network. Of course, communication may also occur in the opposite direction. This network is shown as using only three layers. The definitions of the layers and the interfaces between them are called a network architecture. A network architecture differs from our builders in the sense that the builders are always going up the layers, i.e., from the excavators to the roofers. In data communication, this is called a *simplex* transmission in which data only goes one way, as to a printer.

A network architecture should be able to handle transmission in both directions, using either half-duplex or full-duplex methods. *Half-duplex* is the transmission of data in one direction at a time and *full-duplex* is the simultaneous transmission of data in both directions. In the figure, Host A sends data, and it is processed by layer 3 and sent to layer 2. The protocol at layer 2 processes what layer 3 has forwarded to it and sends the data to layer 1.

Layer 1 then sends the data over a physical communication link to layer 1 of Host B. This same process is done in reverse, until the data reaches Host B. Layer 1 is always called the physical layer, because over this layer, the actual data is sent and received. Hence, the communication between layer 1s is called *physical communication* and communication between the upper layers is called *virtual communication*. The protocol for all the layers except the first one is implemented in software.

2.3.2 Another Analogy

Let us review the basic concepts underlying network architectures as explained using Figure 2.1 before we go into more detail.

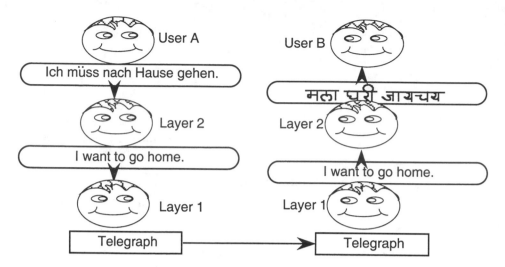

Figure 2.2 An analogy of a network architecture is a person in Germany communicating with a person in India, which requires the message to be transformed in various ways.

In Figure 2.2, we have two users, A and B, representing the two hosts in Figure 2.1. However, here we have only two layers shown instead of three. User A is in Germany and user B is in India. They want to communicate with each other using Morse code. We don't have translators between German and Marathi (an Indian language), but we do have English translators to each language. So when a person in Germany says in German that he wants to go home, the protocol used in the second layer translates it into English. This message is then forwarded to the telegraph operator who converts it to morse code.

The telegraph operator who is part of the physical layer in India receives the message and forwards it to its second layer, which translates it for the person in India.

If we change the protocol used in the first layer from a telegraph system to a telephone system or a postal system, all we need to do is to replace that one protocol. This does not affect the second layer. The services the second layer receives are the same. Likewise, network architectures provide specific networking services between their layers. The protocol used in a specific layer is a concern for that layer and does not concern any other, although the overall performance of the network is dependent on the protocols used in each layer.

2.3.3 Examples of Network Architectures

There are many network architectures that are defined. Some are proprietary and so are used by one particular vendor, while others are standards used by more than one vendor.

SNA (Systems Network Architecture) is the architecture defined by IBM. Originally, it used only one host or mainframe. See Figure 2.3. This was locally connected by a FEP (Front End Processor), which handled all the communications-related

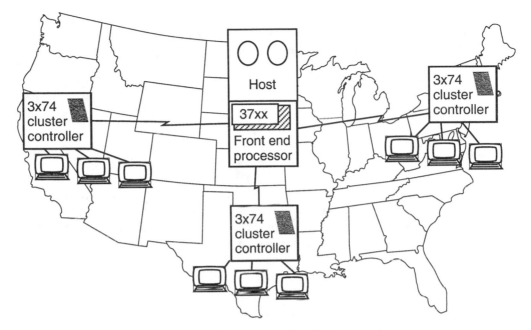

Figure 2.3 An example of an SNA network.

processing for the host. The FEP was then connected to cluster controllers, possibly in many different cities using communication links. The cluster controllers were then connected to dumb (without a CPU) terminals.

The terminals depended on cluster controllers to operate, which in turn depended on the FEP to operate. If the host or the FEP went down, the entire network went down. Even though the data on the host may have been backed up at another location, all terminals depended on the host.

The cluster controllers received all the data for the terminals and properly distributed it. SNA was run on such networks, but today it has evolved into a much more sophisticated network called APPN (Advanced Peer to Peer Networking). There are others such as DECnet and AppleTalk that are proprietary architectures.

OSI (Open Systems Interconnection) Reference Model is an international standard set forth by ISO (International Standards Organization). It allows for networking

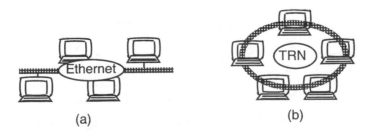

Figure 2.4 (a) An Ethernet LAN. (b) A Token Ring Network.

between hosts made by any vendor. TCP/IP, which we mentioned in Chapter 1 and will be covered throughout the text, is also an example of a network architecture.

The family of LAN architectures, which is a subset of OSI, includes IEEE 802.3 and IEEE 802.5. These architectures are run on Ethernet and TRN (Token Ring Network) networks, respectively. Figure 2.4(a) shows an Ethernet LAN where stations are connected to one cable called a bus and Figure 2.4(b) shows a TRN where stations are connected in a ring.

2.4 OSI

In the analogy of communication between people with different languages, the entire message at each layer was transformed. In network architectures, however, although this can happen, headers and trailers can also be added by the protocol at each layer. Let us now look at the layers of OSI, the architecture that other architectures are compared against in data networking.

2.4.1 Overview of OSI

Figure 2.5 shows the seven layers of the OSI reference model. They are physical, data link, network, transport, session, presentation, and application. Each layer serves its own set of functions which we will outline later on, but for now let us see how these layers are interrelated.

When a host transmits data over the network, it is first handed over to the protocol used in the application layer. The application layer will process this data and may add

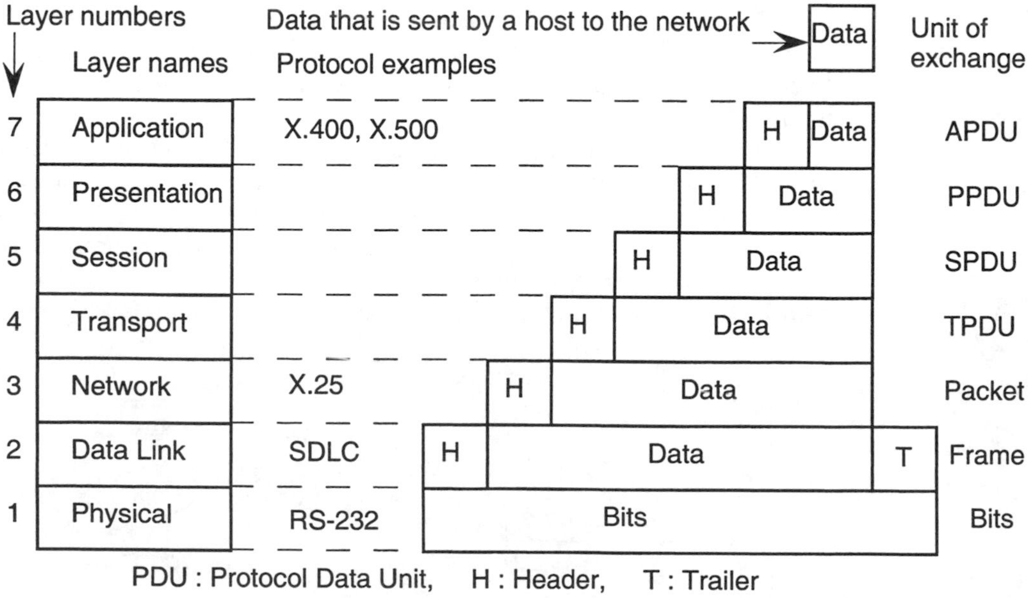

Layer numbers	Layer names	Protocol examples	Data that is sent by a host to the network → Data	Unit of exchange
7	Application	X.400, X.500	H Data	APDU
6	Presentation		H Data	PPDU
5	Session		H Data	SPDU
4	Transport		H Data	TPDU
3	Network	X.25	H Data	Packet
2	Data Link	SDLC	H Data T	Frame
1	Physical	RS-232	Bits	Bits

PDU : Protocol Data Unit,   H : Header,   T : Trailer

Figure 2.5 The OSI reference model. Layers 1, 2, and 3 make up the communications subnet.

Basics of Data Networking

some control information in a field called the header. This header is intended for the application layer on the receive end and forms the means for the two peer application layers to communicate virtually. The data, along with the application header, is called an APDU or an application PDU (Protocol Data Unit).

This APDU is then forwarded by the application layer to the presentation layer in the transmitting host. The APDU, including the application header, becomes the data portion for the PDU at the presentation layer. This is called the PPDU (Presentation PDU). The presentation header is the means for this presentation layer to communicate with its peer presentation layer at the receive end. The PPDU is handed over to the session layer.

This process is repeated for each layer, until at the data link layer, a trailer is added as well. Finally, the physical layer transmits the second layer's frame using a bit stream.

On the receive side, this process is done in reverse. The first layer receives the bits and hands over a frame to its second layer protocol. It then strips off the header and trailer, processes whatever is encoded in them, such as a check for data errors, and hands off the data portion of the frame to the third layer.

The third layer considers the data portion of the frame as a packet, so it strips off the header and processes it. The data portion of the packet is then handed over to the fourth layer. This process is repeated until the application layer forwards its data to its user for whom the data is intended. And if all the protocols are implemented properly, the receiving host can interpret the transmitting host's message. This is done despite the differences that exist between the hosts, regardless of their vendors, operating speeds, sizes, and so on. The obvious inherent tradeoff is a large increase in overhead for the flexibility of communicating with diverse systems.

2.4.2 The Layering Process

To gain a better insight into the working of OSI's network architecture, let us discuss how the protocols in the layers function as data is sent from one host to another. We will use Figures 2.6(a) through 2.6(h) to illustrate.

In Figure 2.6(a), the user is sending data for the network. It could be part of an email message, for example. All the 1's and 0's of the data are shown as a simple block. The protocol at the application layer adds a header to this data; together we call this unit of exchange an APDU (Application Protocol Data Unit) or simply a message. This is seen in Figure 2.6(b). The application header codes in information which is meant for the application layer at the receive host.

In Figure 2.6(c), the presentation layer adds its own header to the APDU. This layer treats the APDU as data as it does the user data. The presentation layer doesn't know or care about the application header's existence. It treats it as part of its data field. The information provided in the presentation header is intended for the presentation layer at the receive host. This process is continued at each layer as the protocols at each layer add their own headers until at the data link layer, a trailer is also added. The purpose of the trailer is to provide a means for checking for errors. The data link layer then passes this stream of bits to the physical layer, which in turn sends them over the network link.

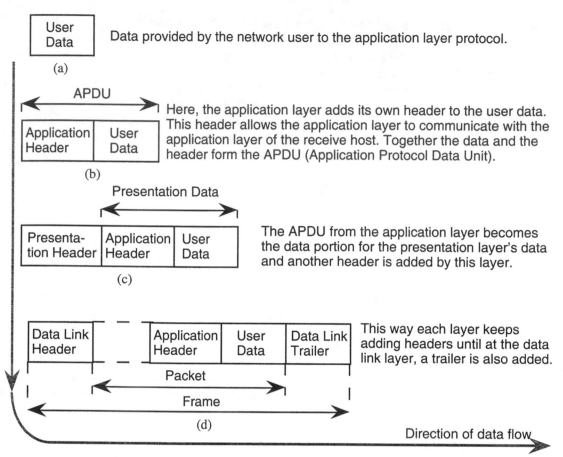

Figure 2.6 Each layer adds its own header in the transmitter.

In Figure 2.6(e), this data stream of 1's and 0's arrives at the receiver. Here the data link layer figures out within these 1's and 0's where the frame begins, where each header and its fields exist, where the data begins and ends, and where the trailer exists. It also checks for errors. If an error occurs in the frame, it will request the transmitter to retransmit the frame which the transmitter must keep in a buffer until an acknowledgment is received. The data link layer then strips off the data link header and trailer, and forwards the data portion to the network layer protocol. The network layer calls this unit a packet and processes its own header and forwards the remainder of the data to the transport layer.

This process continues until we come to the presentation layer. See Figure 2.6(f). Here, the protocol processes the presentation header and removes it. The data portion is forwarded to the application layer in Figure 2.6(g). Finally, the data arrives at the user in Figure 2.6(h) after going through all seven layers at the transmitter and then going through all the seven layers in reverse order at the receiver. In the transmitter, each layer adds a header as data goes down the protocol stack. In the receiver, each

Basics of Data Networking

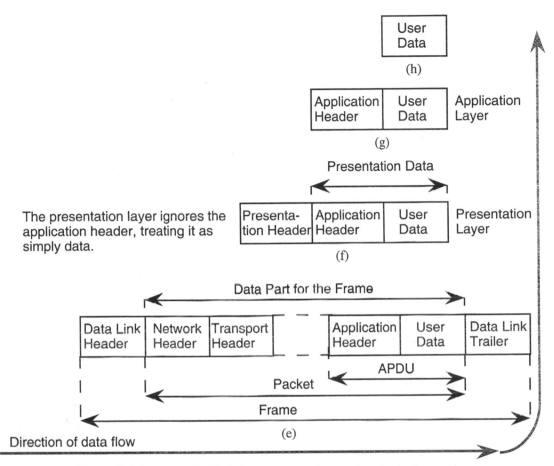

The presentation layer ignores the application header, treating it as simply data.

Figure 2.6 (continued) Each layer removes its own header in the receiver.

layer processes its own header and removes it and sends the data up to the layer above. The layers in the receiver disregard other headers that may be within its data field.

2.4.3 The Communication Subnetwork

Now that we have seen how data is sent by the transmitting host and how it is received by the receiving host, let us turn our attention to how the data gets transported over the network nodes to reach its destination. The transmitting host and the receiving host of data are called the *end points* of the network. For data to arrive at its destination, it may have to travel over several links, hopping from one intermediate point to another. The collection of these links and their intermediate nodes is called the *communication subnetwork*. At the end points of the network, all seven OSI layers are needed. However, over the communication subnetwork

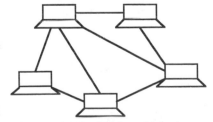

Data may need to hop through many midpoints to reach its destination.

only the first three layers are used. (The communications subnetwork described here has nothing to do with TCP/IP subnets as we will see in Chapter 8.)

The lower three layers of the model serve a set of functions that differ from those served by the upper four layers. The lower three layers are concerned about getting the data to the correct node in the network using the available communication links and packet switches. A packet switch is a generic term used for processors that route packets to the correct network node using these three layers. It can also be thought of as a *router*. A *bridge*, on the other hand, as we will see in Chapter 7, forwards frames using only the lower two layers of the OSI model.

The upper four layers are processed by the host and pertain to how the end users are using their applications. Although all seven layers can be implemented in a host, the function of the lower three layers is to route packets to the correct node. Before we study the subnetwork any further, an analogy may prove helpful.

2.4.4 An Analogy for a Subnetwork

In Figure 2.7, a person who lives in San Diego is sending a birthday card to her cousin in Chicago. The postal distribution center, acting as the fourth layer in this example, sends it off in a bag labeled for Chicago.

The postal workers at the airport performing layer 3 services decide the bag must go via Denver. The workers performing layer 2 services place this bag in an aircraft

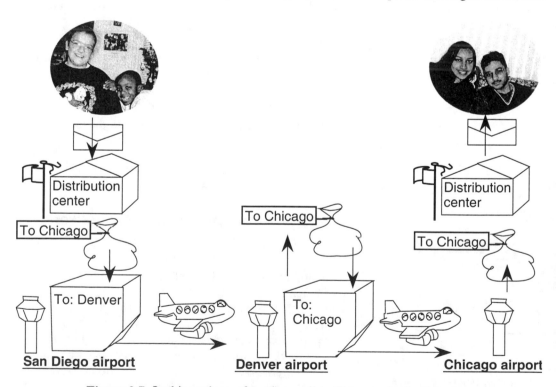

Figure 2.7 In this analogy of routing mail to Chicago, the facilities in Denver are acting as a layer 3 packet switch.

Basics of Data Networking

container headed for Denver. The airplane, our physical layer transportation system, gets the container to the Denver airport. Here, the layer 2 personnel take the bags out of the container and give them to the layer 3 personnel to sort them out.

The layer 3 personnel sort out these bags. The ones that go to the distribution center in Denver are sent there. The one with the birthday card in it is sent to Chicago. Others that are going to other cities are properly routed by these 3rd layer personnel. The 2nd layer personnel then place our bag in a container headed for Chicago.

This mechanism is repeated at Chicago and the 3rd layer personnel there send the bag to its distribution office and the card reaches its destination. Here, layers 1, 2, and 3 get the bag to the destination end point by using the intermediate points. The implementation of these three layers in the network is the subnetwork. Only Denver was used as a midpoint, but other cities or hops could also have been used for the subnetwork to get the bag to Chicago.

2.4.5 The OSI Subnetwork

We have three hosts (also called end systems) that are connected to each other using three communication links as shown in Figure 2.8. Each of the three hosts is concurrently processing several jobs or applications. In order for them to communicate with one another they must use the three layers of the subnet.

Here, Host A is sending data to Host C. The 3rd layer in Host A encodes its packet with the DA (Destination Address) of Host C. Although the communication link labeled Link 1 would be more direct, let us say that there is other traffic on it from other applications and it is therefore getting congested. The network layer then chooses to send the packet via link 2. The 2nd layer encodes the DA of Host B in its frame and sends it over the first layer.

Host B's second layer strips off the header and the trailer, processing them, and possibly checking for transmission errors. If there were transmission errors, it will use

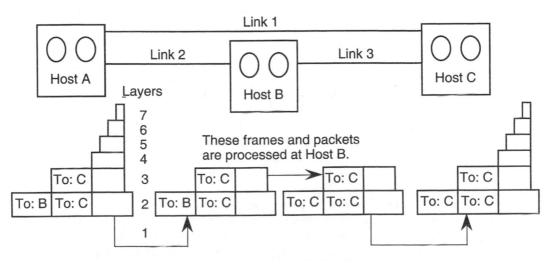

Figure 2.8 Host B is acting as a packet switch as Host A sends a message to Host C. The arrows show how the data is moved.

the headers of frames going to Host A to request Host A to retransmit the frames. Once an error-free frame is received, it will hand over its data portion, which is a packet, to layer 3. Layer 3 looks at the DA of Host C and doesn't hand over the data portion of the packet to its layer 4, but instead reconstructs the packet and sends it back down to layer 2. This layer encodes a DA of Host C and sends the frame over link 3.

The data link layer at Host C may ask Host B to retransmit any frames that were corrupted with errors. The network layer at host C detects its own DA and doesn't reroute the packet like Host B did. Instead, the packet's data is sent to Host C's 4th layer whose data then reaches the user there. Host B has acted as a packet switch, also called an intermediate system. On the other hand, Hosts A and C have behaved as end systems.

2.4.6 Description of the Layers

Follow Figure 2.5 as we describe the layers from 1 to 7 in the OSI model. All layers except the physical layer are implemented in software.

The Physical Layer: The physical layer primarily concerns moving bits from one node to the next over a physical link, whether it be a copper wire, satellite, microwave, etc. How many volts are a logical 1 and how many are a logical 0, what is the clock rate, is the transmission full-duplex or half-duplex—all are issues that concern this layer. Variations of RS-232 are examples of protocols which are used here. In essence, the mechanical, electrical, functional, and procedural characteristics are addressed here.

The Data Link Layer: The data link layer takes the bits that are received by the physical layer and detects errors. For transmission where errors have occurred, the data link layer will request its peer entity to retransmit the data until it is received error-free. Error detection and correction is simply called error control. If the acknowledgment sent by the receiver gets lost, transmission of data may be duplicated. Eliminating duplicate frames is also part of error control.

Besides error control, the data link layer also provides *logical synchronization*, flow control, and addressing of network nodes. After a receiver synchronizes its clock with the incoming data stream, it must establish where a data frame starts, where it ends, and so on. This is called logical synchronization or framing.

Data flow control is the process by which a receiving node controls the transmitter by making sure it does not send more data than it can receive. Sometimes, flow control is achieved by the receiver not sending an acknowledgment to the transmitter, thereby forcing the transmitter to wait before sending the next transmission. However, a core objective of this layer is the reliable transfer of information.

The Network Layer: When the data link layer forwards data packets to the network layer, the network layer doesn't have to be concerned about errors in the data. As was covered in Section 2.4.3, this layer performs routing.

Referring again to Figure 2.8, when the third layer in Host A is sending a packet to Host C, via Host B, the data link layers between each host pair detect errors and retransmit frames if necessary. The network layer has no knowledge if any frames had to be retransmitted over any links or not. But the network layer at Host B determines if the packet goes to Host C or if it goes to the application at Host B.

In addition to routing, this layer is also responsible for establishing and maintaining connection, while controlling congestion in a network and creating billing information where necessary. X.25 is a protocol used at this layer which is an implementation of packet switched networks. This is described in the next section.

The Transport Layer: As seen in Figure 2.8, the transport layer is not invoked for data passing through a node, such as Host B. Only a data source node (Host A) or a destination node (Host C) uses this layer. All the upper layers from 4 to 7 are called end-to-end layers.

This layer divides up a transmitting message into packets and reassembles them at the receiving end. It can send packets via multiple connections to Host B, enabling it to achieve a high bandwidth, without concerning the session layer. When a connection is established, this layer can request a quality of service that specifies the acceptable rate of errors, the amount of delay, security, and so on. It can also provide data flow control while performing this function on an end-to-end basis.

In Figure 2.7, San Diego's postal distribution center places letters going from many people to Chicago into one bag. The transport layer can send data from many terminal dialogues over one channel. The process of placing many messages using one channel is called *multiplexing*.

The Session Layer: The session layer manages logging in and logging off procedures. It manages dialogues between two users/applications. If a certain operation is allowed to be performed by only one user at a time, the protocol in this layer manages such operations, for example, preventing two users from updating the same set of data in a database simultaneously.

Suppose a user is transferring 100 dollars from database A to database B over a network. If the 100 dollars were deducted from database A but the transaction to add the 100 dollars to database B were lost, it would be the session layer's responsibility to either roll back database A to what it was and send an "unsuccessful transfer" message to the user or, otherwise, attempt to complete the transfer again.

The Presentation Layer: The sixth layer is responsible for converting file record formats. It performs conversions between ASCII and EBCDIC character codes, does data compression, and encrypts data if necessary. It can also do terminal type conversion.

The Application Layer: What is an application? A software application for a PC is the software which determines how the user is using the PC. If one says that he wants to buy a pickup truck so he can do odd jobs and make some money on the side, then doing odd jobs for others is the application for which the truck is being purchased.

Similarly, a network application is the reason for using the network in the first place, whether it is to transmit a video conference, send a medical image, or simply send voice. All of these are examples of network applications.

In OSI, which addresses data networks, the protocol used in the application layer determines how the user is using the data network.

This could be X.400, which provides e-mail (electronic mail), or it could be X.500, which provides directory services for directories that are distributed over a network. The application in this layer may also perform problem partitioning, which requires the task of one large job to be performed by several hosts. It could manage distributed databases. Basically, the application layer allows the user to use the network for whatever purpose he/she needs it for.

2.5 PACKET SWITCHED NETWORKS

As we have said, X.25 is a protocol used with the lower three layers of the OSI model, which is an implementation of packet switched networks. In this section we will explore such networks, which will help us also to understand frame relay networks, ATM, SS7, and other networking technologies that are the basis of forthcoming chapters. In the telecommunications industry there is so much talk about emerging technologies that we may otherwise lose sight of the basic principles on how networks are put together.

2.5.1 The Operation of a Packet Switched Network

Figure 2.9(a) shows a generalized packet switched network. Here four hosts are interconnected using a network of four packet switches. Host X has some data to transmit to Host Z so it sends a special-purpose packet to PSwitch A (Packet Switch A), to which it is connected. PSwitch A then decides to use PSwitch B instead of PSwitch D to find a path to Host Z. Similarly, PSwitch B uses PSwitch C to complete the path. When these three switches are set up to accept data for Host X, PSwitch A sends a special-purpose packet to Host X, signaling that it may start transmission. This completes the connection phase and begins the data transfer phase.

Figure 2.9(b) shows the switching tables for PSwitch A and PSwitch B, which were updated when this connection was established. An entry in PSwitch C is also added but it is not shown here. We see that PSwitch A transfers data packets from its port 1 to port 2 and in the packet header codes in a channel number, of say, 30. There may be other connections that must be supported on this link, and each connection will be using a different channel number. Several users from Host X and other hosts may require connections to various points that require this link. However, the channel numbers on this link identify to which connection the particular packet belongs.

Consequently, when PSwitch B sees this packet arriving on its port 1, it checks the header to find its channel number of 30. Then it will look up its switching table and find out that this packet must be switched to port 3 and be assigned a channel of 11. In the same fashion, PSwitch C will recognize this packet and switch it to Host Z, where the channel number helps Host Z to identify to which connection this packet belongs. Remember, there may be several connections opened on this host that use the link from PSwitch C to Host Z.

Figure 2.10(a) continues with this example and shows a connection being established from Host W to Host Y. The switching table in PSwitch A sends packets from the original connection and the new connection over port 2 to PSwitch B. The

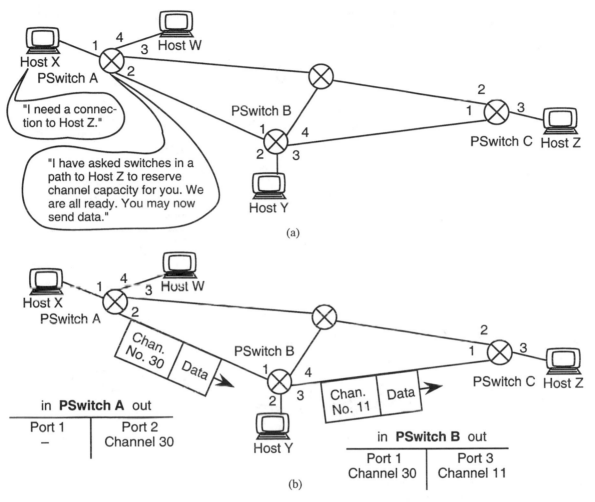

Figure 2.9 (a) Special-purpose packets are sent when Host X requests a connection with Host Z. (b) The packet switches A, B, and C update their tables to provide this connection.

only way for PSwitch B to identify which packet belongs to which connection is by the channel numbers coded in the headers. The use of channel numbers allows one link to support many connections. This is also one type of *multiplexing*. In X.25, there could be up to 4096 channels multiplexed over each link.

2.5.2 Virtual Circuits

The collection of channel numbers and links used to complete a connection in a switched network is called a *virtual circuit*. The two connections that we have established in our example form two virtual circuits. This is illustrated in Figure 2.10(b). In this figure, we are not interested in the actual packet switching tables and

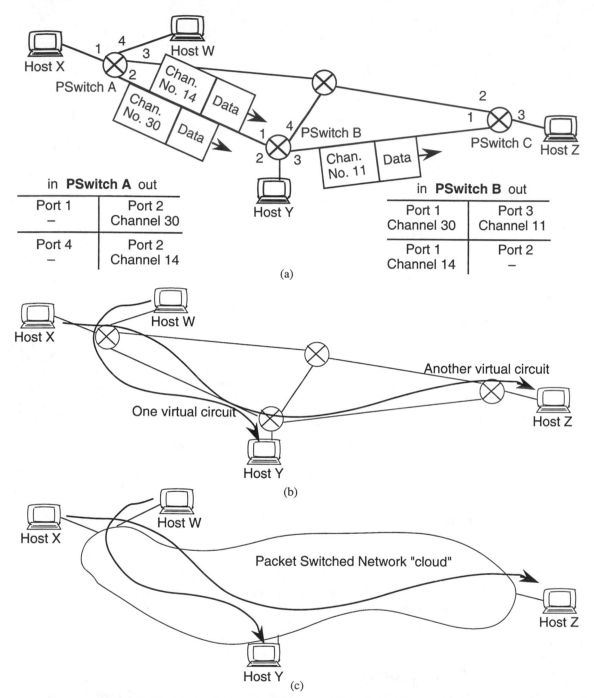

Figure 2.10 (a) Another connection is established. (b) Virtual circuit is another name for a connection. (c) The term "cloud" is used to disregard the working details of any network.

Basics of Data Networking

the channel numbers which are needed to complete each connection. We are only showing paths of the two connections or the two virtual circuits.

Suppose that you were flying from New York City to San Francisco and you had to change planes in Chicago. The seats in the planes where you were sitting are like *channel numbers* and the airplanes are like the *physical links* of a packet switched network. Each plane can *multiplex* many passengers having a separate seat number or channel number.

At Chicago, the airline worker would give you a boarding pass with a new seat assignment for the next leg of the journey. That worker is acting like a *packet switch* who is transferring you from one seat number to another one. The pair of airplanes you took to go to San Francisco and the corresponding seat numbers define a *virtual circuit*, in a sense.

In Figure 2.10(c) we simplify our view of the packet switched network by omitting the representation of the actual links and the switches. We do this by drawing a cloud. Only the hosts and the virtual circuits are depicted.

There are two kinds of virtual circuits: permanent and switched. A PVC (Permanent Virtual Circuit) is reserved for a connection which is always on whether there is traffic going over it or not, and an SVC (Switched Virtual Circuit) is more like the example we have described above. An SVC's connection is established when needed, then data is transferred, and when done, the SVC is disconnected. A PVC also uses these three phases; however, a technician has to establish a connection by entering it on a terminal and when the customer doesn't need it any more, days or months later, the connection is removed.

2.5.3 The Responsibilities of Packet Switches

In packet switched networks, layer 4 processes in the transmitting hosts are responsible for breaking up the messages into packets and the layer 4 processes in the receiving hosts are responsible for reassembling them. The order in which the packets are transmitted is the order in which they are received, because they are going over one path. In Figure 2.10(a), all layers are implemented in the hosts, but only layers 1 through 3 are implemented in the packet switches. If a link goes down or a switch crashes, the connection has to be reestablished via another path and the data has to be retransmitted.

Packet switches are responsible for handling error control, data flow control, acknowledgment of packets, time-outs, and other tasks on a link-by-link basis. Error control means detection and correction of errors. If one packet switch receives a corrupted frame, it will not be forwarded to the next packet switch until the frame is recovered. Data flow control means that if one packet switch cannot receive frames as fast as they are arriving, it can throttle back the transmitter. If frames have been lost and have not arrived in a given time, the receiving packet switch has a procedure to resolve the time-out problem with the transmitting switch.

2.6 DATAGRAM DELIVERY NETWORKS

Another approach to transferring data over a network is called datagram delivery. This approach is relatively simple. We will need only one diagram instead of five to

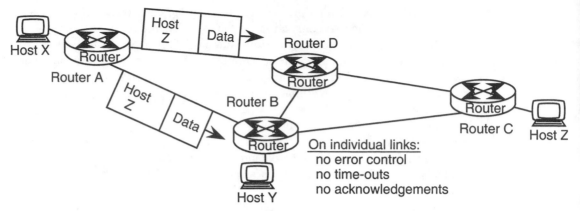

Figure 2.11 Transmission of data through a datagram delivery network is simple. The datagram contains the address of the final destination.

explain its operation. A datagram is just a packet, but differs in how it is used in a network. Datagrams when transferred over a network are usually called packets.

In the datagram delivery network of Figure 2.11, Host X has divided a message into two datagrams using its transport layer process. There are no channel numbers or virtual circuits. The destination address of Host Z is encoded in the headers of the datagrams. Because of this, the datagrams can travel on different routes and still arrive at Host Z, but may be out of order. There is no connection established. Hence, such a network is called a *connectionless* network. Data is simply fired into the network and the network nodes, usually called routers, route the data to its destination. Routers use special protocols, called *routing protocols,* which enable them to find out how the network is physically laid out. They also allow them to dynamically know which links went down, which were added, which became more error-prone, etc.

There is no checking of errors *in the data* from router to router as was the case in the packet switched network. The functions of the routers correspond to the first three layers of the OSI model. If the data in a datagram arrives corrupted into router B, that corrupted datagram will continue through the network and arrive at Host Z. Now the upper layers at Host Z, or layers 4 through 7, will have to detect and correct those errors.

If there are errors *in the headers* of the datagrams, or if there is a data flow control problem (datagrams are arriving too fast), or if they are undeliverable, then routers can discard such datagrams. Again, the upper layers at the end points will have to recover from such problems. They also must be able to reassemble the message from datagrams which may be arriving out of sequence. Notice how network intelligence is being removed from the network nodes (switches or routers) and is being added to only the end points. Consequently, datagram delivery networks are called unreliable networks. With fiber links becoming more common and error rates becoming lower, it isn't as important to check for errors on a point-to-point basis anyway. Why check for errors on all the links when the probability of finding errors is very low! For the few errors that do appear, we can check and correct them only once at the end points. This makes the routers faster and the network itself more efficient.

Integrity of data is an end-to-end issue and not a point-to-point issue. When it is decided that data has to be transferred to a destination, the upper layers make the connection. The lower three layers don't realize that the datagrams traveling in the network are all part of the same message, session, or connection. However, layers 4 and up at the end points sort the messages and keep track of the various existing connections and their integrity.

What we have just been describing is the Internet. The Internet uses this datagram delivery approach. One can appreciate its operation better by contrasting it with packet switched networks. IP (Internet Protocol) is the protocol used to deliver datagrams. Routers are based on IP. TCP (Transmission Control Protocol) is a layer 4 protocol that runs at the end points or hosts, which ensures the reliability and sequencing of data, establishment of connections, and so forth. More on that in Chapter 8.

2.7 NETWORK SERVICES

When we make a phone call, we have to first establish a connection; then we can talk or transfer information. And when we are done, we hang up or drop the connection. Then the network disconnects all the trunk and switch capacities which were allocated for our call. This type of network service is called a connection-oriented service and it always uses three phases to transfer information. Packet switched networks provide *connection-oriented* services.

Conversely, when we drop a letter in the mail box, we don't have to first establish a connection. Just as an IP datagram contains the IP address of the destination, so would our letter contain the destination address. But two letters dropped in the same mail box going to the same destination may quite likely take different routes and arrive out of order. This is a called connectionless service. Datagram delivery networks, such as the ones on which the routers of the Internet operate, are examples of *connectionless* service. TCP, an end-to-end protocol on the other hand, provides a connection-oriented service to the network user. It uses an underlying connectionless network (the IP routers) to provide a connection-oriented service.

In Figure 2.12, we see a list of protocols that we will study later in this text. These fall into either the connectionless or the connection-oriented services. LANs are connectionless because when data frames are sent from one host to another, no previous connection is set up; they are just sent on their way on the LAN cabling with the destination address encoded in the frame header.

When units of data, such as packets, are sent through a network, where channel numbers on each link identify to which connection the packets belong, we have virtual connections as we have discussed before. Whereas when a connection uses particular links and each link or trunk is reserved for a given connection over the path of a circuit, we have a physical connection. On a physical link, we can share the time periods between several connections; then we have a TDM (Time Division Multiplexed) connection. We will go over TDM in the next chapter and SMDS (Switched Multi-megabit Digital Service), ATM (Asynchronous Transfer Mode), and other technologies in later chapters.

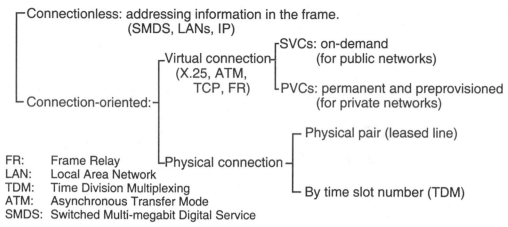

Figure 2.12 Types of communication services.

Quality of Service: QoS is a term which characterizes a network. It is a major issue being discussed in modern, emerging networks. The degree of consistency in delay determines the QoS a network provides. Another name for it is isochronous transmission service.

Technically, delay itself does not indicate QoS but the relation of it to other parts of the message. In a video satellite transmission of a sports event, there is a certain amount of delay from the time an event occurred to the time when it is displayed on a TV. Such traffic must have a good QoS. However, if the delay between successive events were erratic, then the transmission would have a poor QoS. Voice and video transmission are sensitive to inconsistent delays but a few errors in the transmission are acceptable. Data, on the other hand, does not require a high QoS but bit errors are unacceptable.

Tunneling and Encapsulation: A network can also provide a service called tunneling. Tunneling uses a mechanism called encapsulation where a data transfer unit of one protocol is enclosed inside a different kind of protocol.

Many times we may need to build a certain type of network, but we already have a different type of network that is available to us. How can we use an existing network to deploy incompatible equipment on it? One answer is tunneling or encapsulation. Tunneling allows us to transport one kind of frames using a network that uses a different kind of frame.

In Figure 2.13(a), we see a normal X.25 link between two hosts. On the left, an X.25 transmitter is sending application data by enclosing it inside a X.25 packet. Then the packet is enclosed inside a frame and sent over a normal X.25 link. In Figure 2.13(b), we don't happen to have X.25 links available, but only Internet links. We can make the X.25 hosts think that they have the same underlying X.25 links as before by encapsulating the X.25 frames into IP datagrams. Here, the X.25 frame is encapsulated or enclosed into an IP datagram and sent over the Internet to the receiving X.25 host. As far as the X.25 hosts are concerned, they don't care that the X.25 protocol is tunneled through IP; they only transmit and receive X.25 packets. As far as the X.25

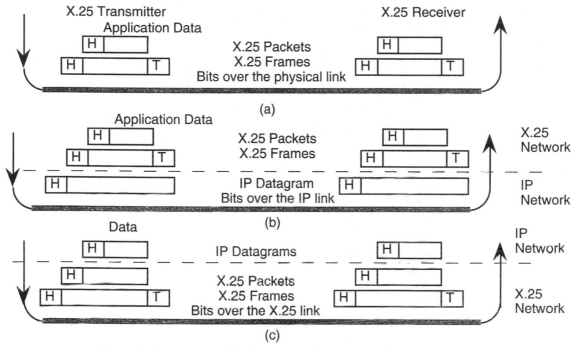

Figure 2.13 (a) A pure X.25 network. (b) Tunneling X.25 through IP or encapsulating X.25 frames inside IP datagrams. (c) Encapsulating IP inside of X.25.

network is concerned, the IP network is only used to transport its frames. And as far as the IP network is concerned, the X.25 frames are just application data.

Of course, we need special software to encapsulate the X.25 frames into IP datagrams. This software, which adds an extra layer of network protocol processing in the transmitting and receiving of information, causes the X.25 network to run slower than the one in Figure 2.13(a). But if no additional links have to be installed to carry just the X.25 traffic, the slower response may well be worth it. If we can get away without the data link layer of X.25 and encapsulate the X.25 packets directly into IP datagrams, then we would be replacing network layers instead of adding them. This would improve the overall network performance. Tunneling one protocol through another one is commonly done in many areas of networking. Figure 2.13(c) shows the reverse. Here IP traffic is sent over an X.25 network. IP datagrams are encapsulated in X.25 packets or IP is tunneled through X.25.

EXERCISES

Sections 2.1 and 2.2:

1. Which of the following is NOT a reason to network?
   a. easy access to resources
   b. increased reliability
   c. better security
   d. mobility of personnel

2. Being able to distribute the workload over a network reduces which problem?
   a. autonomous hosts   b. security
   c. bottle neck   d. easier connection to hosts
3. Define a network in your own words.
4. How are networks categorized? Describe the categories.
5. Describe the advantage of networking which someone may call "better price-to-performance ratio."
6. When a piece of software is available to all users on a LAN, which advantage of networking is being utilized?
7. When someone comes into my office and checks the files on his computer from mine, what advantage of networking is he utilizing?
8. Discuss why networks are cheaper to install but costlier to operate.

Section 2.3:
9. The services provided by adjacent layers are called what?
   a. interface   b. protocol
   c. virtual communication   d. network architecture
10. Which of the following is NOT an example of a network architecture?
    a. SNA   b. DECnet
    c. FEP   d. APPN
11. A set of rules used in a layer is called what?
12. Designing networks using layers must be important, because all networks are designed that way. Why?
13. What type of communication is done at the upper layers of a network architecture?

Section 2.4:
14. Which layer is responsible for dividing a message into packets?
    a. network   b. transport
    c. session   d. presentation
15. Which layer is responsible for correcting errors and establishing framing?
    a. data link   b. network
    c. transport   d. session
16. Which layer uses a frame for its PDU?
    a. data link   b. network
    c. transport   d. physical
17. What is the unit of transfer used in the network layer?
18. X.400 is an example of a protocol used in which layer?
19. As data is sent down from the application layer into the physical network, do the PDUs become larger or smaller?
20. What is the name for the network that uses only the lower three layers in the OSI model?
21. How something is being used is said to be the _____ .
22. Describe the process as data moves up and down the OSI layers and virtual communication occurs horizontally between the peer layers.
23. Describe the communications subnet.
24. List the functions which are the responsibility of the data link layer.

Section 2.5:
25. Which type of network does not use a form of packet switching?
    a. ATM   b. LANs
    c. X.25   d. SS7

26. Before data can be transferred in a packet switched network, what must be done?
    a. A connection has to be established.
    b. The recipient of the data must first request a connection.
    c. The data packets must be inserted in the tables of the packet switches.
    d. The same channel number has to be decided upon between each link of the network.
27. In a packet switching network, communication for several connections can travel over the same link. What is this called?
28. When PSwitch B receives a packet on its port 1, what are the steps it must perform to process that packet?
29. Describe virtual circuits, PVCs, and SVCs.
30. In Figure 2.10(a), show the contents of the tables if the connection between Host X and Host Z is dropped and a new connection is established between Host X and Host Y using channel number 22 on each link that is used.
31. Using the tables shown in Figure 2.14 and the network given in Figure 2.10(a), describe the virtual circuits that are established.

Section 2.6:

32. Datagram delivery networks provide which type of network service?
    a. fixed path   b. connection-oriented
    c. quality of service   d. connectionless
33. What is an example of a datagram delivery network?
    a. Internet   b. SS7
    c. PSTN   d. ATM
34. Can datagrams travel on different paths in a network? Yes or no.
35. What do routers do with datagrams that are arriving too fast?
36. What do datagram delivery networks use that correspond to the functions of packet switches used in packet switched networks?
37. What are the differences between a datagram and a packet used in X.25?

Section 2.7:

38. Which of the following is a connection-oriented protocol?
    a. ATM   b. LANs
    c. dropping a letter in a mail box   d. IP
39. Which network service has become important in emerging network solutions?
    a. connectivity   b. tunneling
    c. encapsulation   d. quality of service
40. Describe the purpose of tunneling.

in **PSwitch A** out	
Port 4	Port 1
–	Channel 10
Port 2	Port 4
Channel 30	–
Port 1	Port 2
–	Channel 50

in **PSwitch B** out	
Port 3	Port 1
Channel 20	Channel 30
Port 1	Port 2
Channel 50	–

in **PSwitch C** out	
Port 3	Port 1
–	Channel 20

Figure 2.14 Tables for Exercise 2.31.

Chapter 3

Analog and Digital Signals

In upcoming chapters we will be studying different transmission methods and the various types of services available to network users. To understand and appreciate what their limitations and benefits are, we need to learn the basic characteristics of analog and digital signals. Knowing these concepts will help us determine the "whys" of communications principles. Many network professionals are disadvantaged because they have never understood the basic concepts behind the technology that drives their bits over network links. We will be covering many terms in this chapter which are derived from the concepts of analog and digital signals. These terms will reappear throughout the text and so we take some time here to define them.

3.1 SIGNAL TYPES

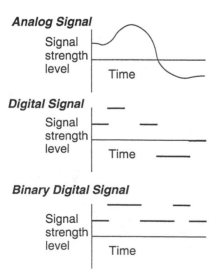

Analog Signal

Signal strength level

Time

Digital Signal

Signal strength level

Time

Binary Digital Signal

Signal strength level

Time

Analog signals have a continuous set of signal strengths. The strength of an analog signal can increase or decrease by any amount. This is not true of a digital signal. Its signal strength can increase and decrease only by fixed amounts. It can have only discrete levels of signal strengths. A discrete set of numbers is a set of numbers that are separate and distinct from each other and that we can count. A continuous set of numbers is a set that we can't count, such as the infinite number of analog signal levels.

For example, the number of digits (notice, the relation to the word "digital") between 0 and 9 is ten. However, the number of fractional numbers between 0 and 9 is infinite; we can't count them. Between 0 and 9, there is a discrete number of digits but there is a continuous number of real numbers or fractional numbers. Physicists say that the levels of energy that an electron can possess are discrete. When an electron is excited, its energy level jumps from one level to another one; its energy level cannot be increased gradually. We can think of energy levels for particles as being digital in nature. However, our eardrums can sense air pressure waves which are continuously changing in their strength. Hence, our eardrums are analog devices. In fact, the term "analog signal" comes from the fact that such an electrical signal is *analogous* to air pressure waves created by voice and heard by our ears.

In the side figure on the previous page, we first see the strength of an analog signal plotted against time. The changes in strength are continuous. A dimmer light in a dining room is an example of an analog device. Immediately below the analog signal, we see a digital signal that has several different signal strength levels. A headlight switch on a car is an example of a digital switch with 3 levels: on, off, and high beams. Last, we see a binary digital signal with only two signal strengths. We always mistake a binary digital signal for a digital signal. however, Theoretically, however, a digital signal could have more than two signal levels. Binary digital signal levels could both be positive, one positive and one negative, or various such combinations, as long as only two levels are used. A switch on a flashlight is such a device.

3.2 DC CIRCUITS

3.2.1 Ohm's Law

Let us now turn our attention to electrical signals and their various characteristics. The strength of electrical signals is measured in volts.

During a given time span, a DC (Direct Current) voltage provides a constant voltage source, as seen in Figure 3.1(a). Here, regardless of the value of time, the voltage stays the same. What we see is a display of an oscilloscope after its leads are placed across a DC voltage source. The horizontal axis shows time and the vertical one shows voltage. See Figure 3.1(b). Batteries of flashlights and cars are examples of DC voltage sources.

On the other hand, Figure 3.1(c) shows an AC (Alternating Current) voltage supply. This voltage varies from +10V to –10V. For example, at t = 0.5s, the voltage is +10V, at t = 1.0s it is 0V, and at t = 1.5s it swings to –10V. The range of an AC source

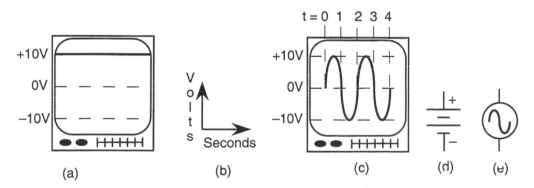

Figure 3.1 (a) DC voltage display. (b) Labels for an oscilloscope axes. (c) AC voltage display. (d) DC voltage symbol. (e) AC voltage symbol.

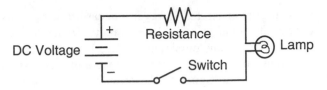

Figure 3.2 When the switch closes, current flows and the lamp lights.

goes between positive voltages and negative voltages. A household voltage source is an example of AC voltage and is rated at 120V. The schematic symbols for DC and AC sources are shown in Figures 3.1(d) and (e), respectively.

Figure 3.2 shows schematically an electrical circuit where a DC source is connected to a lamp. Resistance represents the amount of hindrance to the flow of current. Resistance can be introduced in the circuit intentionally. But the connecting wires, lamp, and even the battery also inherently provide some resistance to current. Resistance is measured in ohms.

If the switch is open, then no current will flow, and if it is closed, then it will. This is indicated by the lamp lighting when the switch is turned on and off. If the amount of resistance is increased, then less current will flow. The amount of current is determined by Ohm's law:

$$V = IR$$

where V is the voltage, I is the current, and R is the resistance. They are measured in volts, amperes (amps), and ohms, respectively. For example, if the source is 10V and R is 20 ohms, the current equals 0.5 amps.

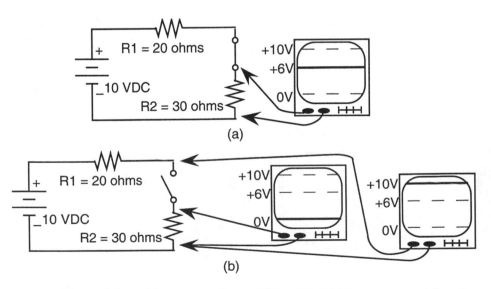

Figure 3.3 (a) When current flows, R2 has 6V. (b) When no current flows, R2 has 0V and the open has 10V.

Analog and Digital Signals

In Figure 3.3(a), we see that a 10 VDC source is applied across two resistors. If they are 20 and 30 ohms, then the total resistance the source experiences is 50 ohms. Using Ohm's law, we get a current of 0.2 amps, which must flow through all the components of this circuit. If we multiply this current by each of the resistors, then the voltage on the two resistors would equal 4V and 6V. The 6V across R2 measured with an oscilloscope is shown in the figure.

Now, if we open the switch as is done in Figure 3.3(b), no current will flow. Because the resistors need a current to have voltages applied across them, neither resistor would have a voltage. Note that across R2, the voltage reading is 0V. But the voltage across the open switch is 10V, because it actually measures the voltage across the source, even if no current is flowing.

3.2.2 Digital Signals

If we look at the oscilloscope the instant the switch is closed, the voltage on R2 will jump from 0V to 6V. This is shown in Figure 3.4(a). Similarly, the display will look like Figure 3.4(b) the instant the switch is turned off after being on. We will call the state when the switch is turned on (6V), a binary 1 level and the state when it is turned off (0V), a binary 0 level. Binary levels are also called logical levels and have only two states — 0 and 1.

A signal with only two voltage levels is an example of a digital signal while one with continuously varying values is called an analog signal. The signal shown back in Figure 3.1(c) is an example of an analog signal.

If we turned the switch on and off repeatedly, we would get the display as shown in Figure 3.4(c), and if we increase the rate at which the switch is changing states, then we get the display shown in Figure 3.4(d). The waveform of Figure 3.4(d) has a higher frequency than the one in Figure 3.4(c).

A clock on a computer is an example of a digital signal. A clock's rate of change is even or periodic, as shown in Figures 3.4(c) and (d). It provides no transfer of information, but only marks time in even increments, so as to keep all computer components in synchronization. Think of it as the computer's heartbeat.

Contrary to the clock, Figure 3.4(e) shows a digital signal where the intervals between the 1s and the 0s are not even or periodic. The uneven intervals can be used to encode information so that voice, data, video, images, etc., can be transmitted digitally.

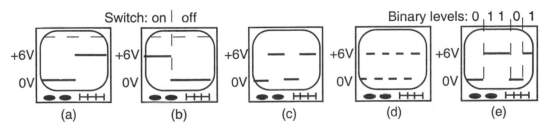

Figure 3.4 (a) Switch going on. (b) Switch going off. (c) A clock signal. (d) Increasing the clock frequency. (e) A digital signal.

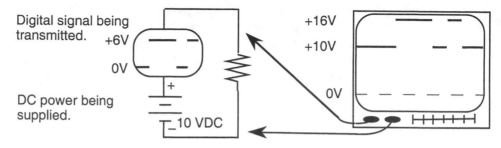

Figure 3.5 Phantoming power.

3.2.3 Phantoming Power

Many digital transmission lines need a device called a repeater. The purpose of a repeater is to "clean" a poor digital signal and retransmit a good one. To power such a device, which is usually installed in a remote location, one can send a voltage over the same line as the one being used to transmit the digital signal. This is called phantoming power.

Figure 3.5 shows such a circuit where the resistance represents the resistance of the transmission line. The voltage source is *added* to the digital signal that is being transmitted. From the oscilloscope display, we see that there is at least 10V available at all times to be used as a power source. Above this 10V, the digital signal which transfers the intended information is "riding". A repeater would separate the digital signal from the 10V. The 10V would be used for power and the digital signal would be repeated and retransmitted. Hence, such a transmission system allows the transfer of information while at the same time providing power to the in-line repeaters.

3.3 ANALOG SIGNALS

Figure 3.6(a) shows an analog signal and its three characteristics. The amplitude is the strength of the signal and is measured in volts. Figure 3.6(b) shows the strength of the signal being reduced. An example of this is when we turn down the volume on a radio.

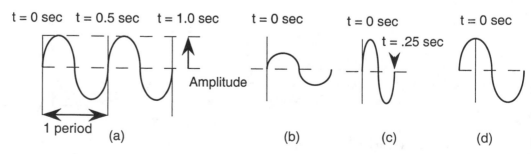

Figure 3.6 Varying the three characteristics of an analog signal.

Analog and Digital Signals

Period is another characteristic and is just the reciprocal of frequency. In Figure 3.6(a), the period is shown to be 0.5 seconds. It is measured over the time it takes a waveform to repeat itself. To find the frequency, we simply divide 0.5s into 1 and get 2 cycles per second. Figure 3.6(c) shows the period being cut in half to .25s and, hence, the frequency being doubled to 4 cycles per second. Hz (Hertz) is the unit used to measure the number of cycles per second. An example of doubling the frequency is when we play a note one octave higher than the last. Frequency determines the tone of a signal.

The timing of a signal is given by the phase. It is measured in degrees. The phase angle of a signal doesn't make any sense unless it is compared to a reference. Figure 3.6(d) shows the signal starting earlier than the one shown in Figure 3.6(a) and so has a positive angle phase shift.

3.3.1 Modulation

When a low-frequency information signal is encoded over a higher-frequency signal, it is called *modulation*. The encoding can be done by varying one or more of the characteristics we have just described. Notice the similarity of the word *modulation* to the word *modifying*. For instance, an audio signal (one that is audible to the human ear) can be used to modify an RF (Radio Frequency) carrier. When the amplitude of the radio frequency is varied in accordance to the changes in the amplitude of the audio signal, it is called AM (Amplitude Modulation), and when the frequency is varied, it is called FM (Frequency Modulation). See Figure 3.7(a). These are the methods used by the two kinds of broadcast stations.

In Figure 3.7(b) we are amplitude and frequency modulating a digital signal. Variations of these modulating methods are common with modems (MOdulator/DEModulator) that are used to transmit digital signals over an analog line. Here, the carrier frequency has to be audio, and not RF, to be able to send the digital signal over a voice-grade line.

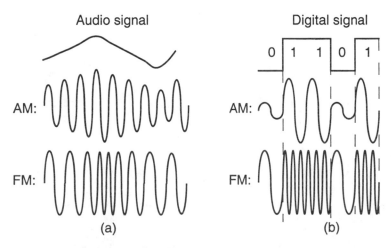

Figure 3.7 (a) Modulating an audio signal over RF carriers. (b) Modulating a digital signal over audio carriers.

3.3.2 Capacitors and Inductors

A capacitor is nothing more than two conductors that are near each other, but are not touching. It stores energy in an electric field and its effect is measured in farads. It passes AC signals but blocks DC signals.

Unwanted capacitance between two pairs of telephone wires can cause the conversation from one pair to be heard on the other pair. This is called *crosstalk*. It occurs because the wires are conductors separated from each other by an insulator introducing capacitance. Voice is an analog signal that the capacitance of the wires is able to pass, and so we have crosstalk.

To compensate for this capacitive effect, wires are twisted around themselves introducing what is called an *inductive effect*. Inductors, of course, also produce an inductive effect and inherently complement capacitors. Physically, inductors are made by coiling a wire and are increased in value by forming the coil around a magnet. Hence, they are also called coils. Their unit of measure is the henry, and they store energy in magnetic fields, block AC signals, and pass DC signals.

When a telephone wire pair becomes longer than 3 miles, it becomes necessary to add inductors to further compensate for the capacitive effect. These inductors are called *loading coils*. When digital signals are transmitted over such lines, these loading coils must be removed because digital signals don't like loading coils. The sharp rises and drops of voltages of a digital signal are actually composed of many high frequencies, according to Fourier analysis, which is studied in calculus. Electrical engineers tell us that loading coils are necessary for transmitting analog signals over long distances of telephone lines, but must be removed for transferring digital signals. Hence, usually when an analog line is converted to a digital line, the loading coils are replaced with digital repeaters.

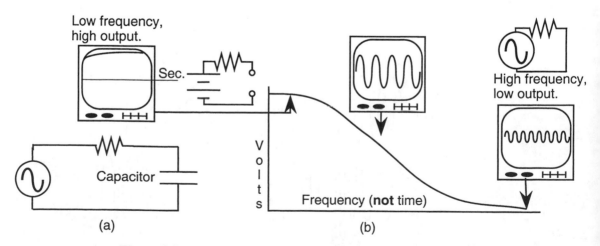

Figure 3.8 (a) A low-pass filter. (b) Its frequency response curve.
Oscilloscope displays are shown for several points along the curve.

3.3.3 Low-Pass Filter

In Figure 3.8(a) we have a circuit with a capacitor. Its frequency response curve is shown in Figure 3.8(b). How does such a curve differ from an oscilloscope display? The oscilloscope uses time or seconds for its horizontal axis, but the response curve uses frequency. The voltages on this curve are plotted by changing the frequency of the AC source. The oscilloscope measurements are shown at three points along the curve. Near the displays, the equivalent circuits are shown for low and high frequencies. The circuit in Figure 3.8(a) resembles these equivalent circuits at those extreme frequencies.

When the frequency is close to zero, the source appears as a DC source, since a DC source provides a constant voltage source. As seen by the low-frequency equivalent circuit, the capacitor blocks DC and opens the circuit, which makes it similar to Figure 3.3(b), and so all the voltage appears across the open.

When the frequency is high, the source appears more as an AC source and, as we said before, capacitors pass AC making the capacitor appear as a short. This is shown by the equivalent circuit for the high frequencies. Because the voltage across a short is zero, there is no voltage on the capacitor at the high frequencies.

We have seen why this circuit provides an output voltage for low frequencies and hardly any for high frequencies across the capacitor; thus it is called a low-pass filter. Such a filter passes low frequencies and shorts out the high ones.

3.3.4 Bandwidth

To Figure 3.8(a), we have added an inductor to give us Figure 3.9(a). This circuit is called a bandpass filter, since it passes a band of frequencies and blocks the rest. This is shown by its frequency response curve in Figure 3.9(b).

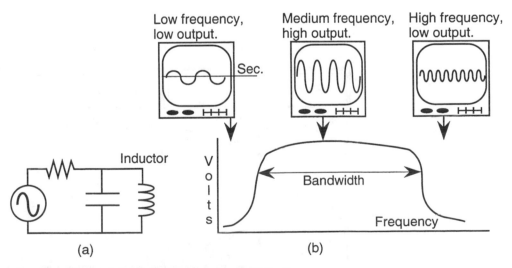

Figure 3.9 (a) A bandpass filter. (b) Its frequency response curve.

When engineers design an amplifier or a speaker, they attempt to make the response flat; that is, they try to let all frequencies for a range pass through uniformly, instead of amplifying one set of frequencies more than another. With an equalizer, a user also has the facility to do that.

The range of frequencies that a device or a transmission medium passes is called the bandwidth. The bandwidth for audio equipment is around 20 kHz while for a voice-grade transmission line it is only about 3 kHz. This difference in bandwidth is evident between the voice qualities of a disc jockey and a listener who calls into a radio station over a telephone line. The term bandwidth when used with digital transmissions refers to the number of bits per second or the amount of transmission capacity available.

It is easy to get mixed up when talking about the bandwidth of an analog signal and the bandwidth of a digital signal. The bandwidth of an analog signal is measured in Hz while that of a digital signal is measured in bps. For example, an ordinary telephone line has a bandwidth of 4 kHz for analog signals. The equipment to handle telephone lines process analog signals with this bandwidth. On the other hand, if we install a modem on this line and send digital signals, then this line has the capability of providing a bandwidth of 56 kbps. (Usually, lower case "b" stands for bits while upper case "B" stands for bytes. For instance, 56 kbps is 56 kilobits per second and 4 MB is 4 megabytes.) If we increase the bandwidth of an analog transmission channel, say by using a coaxial cable, then with its 6-MHz bandwidth per analog video channel we can increase the digital bandwidth from 10 Mbps to 40 Mbps depending on the encoding method. The amount of analog bandwidth determines how much digital bandwidth we can obtain from a transmission facility.

3.3.5 Metric Prefixes

This is as good a time as any to summarize metric prefixes. Table 3.1 shows the common metric prefixes. The first column shows the abbreviations for the prefixes and

Table 3.1 Metric Prefixes

Prefix	Meaning	Value (in powers of 10)
T	tera	+12
G	giga	+9
M	mega	+6
k	kilo	+3
–	–	0
m	milli	−3
μ	micro	−6
n	nano	−9
p	pico	−12

Analog and Digital Signals

the middle column shows their meanings. The last column shows which power of 10 each prefix represents. So if we had 700 kHz, then that would be the same as 700 (10^{+3}) Hz or 700,000 Hz. Just substitute the value of power of 10, or 10^{+3}, for the prefix (k). As another example, the value of 200 msec is 200 (10^{-3}) seconds or 0.2 seconds.

3.4 POWER

3.4.1 P = VI

Similar to Ohm's law (V = IR) is the power equation, which defines power as:

$$P = VI$$

where P is power in watts, while V and I are the familiar variables used in Ohm's law: voltage and current.

Back in Figure 3.3(a), we had obtained 0.2 amps of current through the circuit with 4V on R1 and 6V on R2. To calculate the power dissipated in R1, we simply multiply its voltage by the current, giving us 0.8 watts (4V times 0.2 amps). Similarly, we get 1.2 watts (6V times 0.2 amps) on R2. Because these two components are dissipating a total of 2.0 watts of power, the power source must be able to supply that amount.

Suppose there is a hair dryer rated at 1200 watts and the usual residential voltage it is plugged into is 120 VAC. The hair dryer must use 10 amps of current. This is found by substituting the known variables in the power equation and solving for I.

3.4.2 Decibels

Alexander Graham Bell, besides inventing the telephone, also worked to help those who had hearing disabilities. He noticed that the human ear detected changes in sound logarithmically. Consequently, using logarithms he defined a unit called the decibel. In telecommunications, this unit is used when working with power levels. Let us first review logarithms; then we will go on to decibels.

Logs: Logs (logarithms) complement powers of ten in a manner similar to how square roots complement squares. When we write:

$$10^X = 1000$$

we are saying, 10 must be multiplied by itself how many times to give us a 1000? The answer (or X) is 3. We can get this same answer by taking the log of both sides.

$$\log (10^X) = \log (1000)$$

And just as a square root reduces a square of a number to that number, so the log of 10 to the power of X reduces 10^X to simply X. You can think that the log of base 10 on the left-hand side of that equation cancels the 10, although a theoretician may not

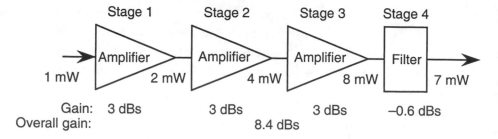

Figure 3.10 A 4-stage amplifier showing the various power levels.

like the usage of the term, "cancel." Our problem is now simplified to:

$$X = \log(1000)$$

Here, one can find using a calculator that the log of 1000 is indeed 3.

dBs: dBs (or decibels) specify the *difference* between two power levels. They do not specify the absolute power. A decibel is defined as:

$$dB = 10 \log (P2/P1)$$

where P1 and P2 are the power levels that are being compared in watts. Figure 3.10 shows a 4-stage device which consists of 3 amplifiers and one filter. The power at each point is also shown. By using a calculator to find the logs, let us find the gain for the first 3 stages.

Using the Formula: For stage 1, P1 is 1 mW (milliwatts) and P2 is 2 mW. Substituting these into the equation, we get:

$$dB = 10 \log (2/1) = 10 \log 2 = 10 (0.3) = 3 \text{ dB}$$

The gain of the first stage is 3 dB. For the second stage the gain is also 3 dB.

$$dB = 10 \log(4/2) = 10 \log 2 = 10 (0.3) = 3 \text{ dB}$$

From these two results, we see that as long as the power is doubled, the gain of the stage is 3 dBs. So the gain of the third stage must also be 3 dBs.

Adding dBs: Now, let us find the gains for several stages together. For instance, for stages 1 and 2 the gain is:

$$dB = 10 \log (4/1) = 10 \log (4) = 10 (.6) = 6 \text{ dBs}$$

where P2 is 4 mW taken at the output of stages 1 and 2 and P1 is 1 mW taken at the input of stages 1 and 2. These two stages are grouped together for this calculation. Similarly, the gain for the first three stages is:

Analog and Digital Signals

$$dB = 10 \log (8/1) = 10 \log 8 = 10 (.9) = 9 \text{ dBs}$$

From these calculations, it is evident that if we know the gains of the individual stages, we can add them up to find their composite gain.

Negative dBs: When the output power decreases as it does for stage 4, the gain in dB becomes negative. This can be confirmed by calculating the gain for stage 4.

$$dB = 10 \log (7/8) = 10 (-0.06) = -0.6 \text{ dB}$$

dBms: While the unit of dB specifies the ratio of powers, the unit of dBm specifies the actual or absolute power. This is done by referencing the input power to 1 mW, as shown below:

$$dBm = 10 \log (P2/1mW)$$

Hence, the power level for the input of stage 1 is:

$$dBm = 10 \log (1mW/1mW) - 10 \log (1) = 10 (0) = 0 \text{ dBm}$$

and for the output of stage 1 is:

$$dBm = 10 \log (2mW/1mW) = 10 \log (2) = 10 (.3) = 3 \text{ dBm}$$

3.5 SYNCHRONIZATION

Starting with this section, we will look at principles of digital signals in more detail. Synchronization is the primary issue when transmitting digital signals, especially now that the speeds are becoming faster each day. Once synchronization is achieved, the transfer of data becomes possible.

3.5.1 Three Kinds of Synchronization

When a device receives a data stream, it must determine precisely where each bit begins. This is called *bit synchronization*. Once it determines the precise time where each bit begins and ends, it must know how to group them into octets, or which bit is the first one out of a group of eight. This is called *character synchronization*. Once it determines the octets, it must be able to determine which octets form the address field, data field, and so on. This is called *logical synchronization* (or framing) and is usually handled by OSI's second layer, although it can also be established by hardware.

3.5.2 Asynchronous Communication

Bit and character synchronization can be established by either asynchronous or synchronous communication. Asynchronous communication is depicted in Figure 3.11(a). When no data is being sent, the line is idle and when a character is being sent, it is preceded by a start bit. The sudden change in voltage in the start bit signals the receiver that a character is being sent, and after the data bits are sent, a stop bit is sent.

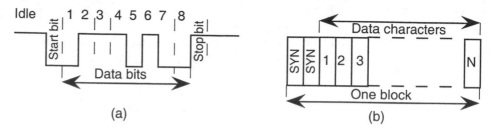

Figure 3.11 (a) Asynchronous communication. (b) Synchronous communication.

The receiver's internal clock uses the edge of the start bit to get itself in sync with the timing of the received signal.

Asynchronous transmission allows characters to be sent randomly and one at a time, since synchronizing information is carried with each character.

3.5.3 Synchronous Communication

Synchronous communication, as shown in Figure 3.11(b), is more efficient. Instead of transmitting one character at a time, it transmits one block of data at a time and places special SYN characters at the beginning of each block to provide synchronization. Since characters are sent in groups, larger buffers are needed than are needed with asynchronous transmission.

In synchronous transmission, the voltage level transitions which normally occur in the data are used to maintain the synchronization of the receiver clock. If too many consecutive bits have the same value (either all 0s or all 1s), then the clock might slip. Accommodations have to be made so that the clock stays in sync.

Asynchronous terminals typically operate from 300 bps to 19,200 bps, while synchronous terminals typically operate from 19.2 kbps to above 1 Mbps.

3.5.4 STM vs. ATM

Having nothing to do with synchronous and asynchronous transmissions as we have discussed so far, are the terms STM (Synchronous Transmission Mode) and ATM (Asynchronous Transmission Mode). With STM, each input channel is assigned a "slice" of time to transfer its data whether it needs to or not. Every channel takes its turn in order for sending data. If a channel has no data to send when its turn arrives, then that amount of time is wasted. With STM, the receiver knows that bits arrive at regular intervals. TDM (Time Division Multiplexing) is based on STM and will be covered in this chapter. With ATM, bits arrive as they are transferred through the network. With ATM a receiving terminal may get many bits of data contiguously and at another time, it may have to wait. ATM is covered in a later chapter.

Part of ATM's purpose is to accommodate *isochronous* traffic. Isochronous traffic means traffic that is sensitive to any latency or delay. If a response from a host to a terminal is slow in being received, one can live with that. It is data and is not isochronous. But if a voice conversation is being chopped into digital packets, then must arrive at the listener's end within a given amount of time, or else the conversation sounds unnatural. Voice and video are examples of isochronous traffic.

3.5.5 Clocking

As digital signals are transmitted at higher and higher rates, the problem of clocking becomes much more critical than it ever was with analog signals. *Jitter* is a problem associated with digital signals that can't stay in sync. There are four types of clocks which have been defined, based on their accuracies. A stratum level 4 clock is the least accurate type of clock and a stratum level 1 clock, which is based on atomic clocks, is the most accurate. Private networks can be synchronized by using their carrier's network clocks. But they can also be synchronized by using LORAN-C (LOng RAnge Navigation-C), Navstar GPS (Global Positioning System), or other independent clocking sources.

Many times a network is operated using two or more clocks. Even if they are stratum level 1 clocks, they can go out of sync after a while. A network that accommodates for such timing differences is said to be operating under plesiochronous operation. SONET (Chapter 20) allows traffic from one carrier to be transformed to another carrier at high speeds. It also makes allowances for plesiochronous operation, because different carriers use their own network clocks and may not be totally in sync with each other.

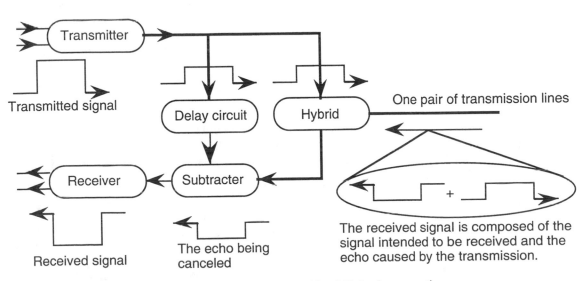

Figure 3.12 An echo canceling circuit provides full-duplex operation over one pair of wires.

3.6 ECHO CANCELLING

In various applications we need to transmit full-duplex over one pair of digital lines. The common method of achieving this is by using an echo cancelling at each end. Figure 3.12 shows a transmitter sending a positive pulse over the transmission line. Part of this positive pulse is fed back through the delay and hybrid circuits. The hybrid circuit transmits the pulse, but since the transmitting line is not perfect, some of the transmitted signal is reflected or echoed back.

While the transmitter is sending this positive pulse, it is also receiving a negative pulse from the other end. These two signals superimpose on each other on the same line. And assuming that the levels of these signals have the same magnitude and opposite polarities, they cancel each other and we see a straight line or 0 volts.

The hybrid circuit forwards this 0 V signal to the echo canceler, which subtracts the transmitted positive pulse from the delaying circuit, which enables the echo canceler to recover the negative pulse that was intended for this end. The amount of power that is echoed and the changes in the delays which occur in the echoed signal are automatically detected and compensated for or adapted by the echo canceler.

To summarize, echo cancelling allows a full-duplex transmission over a single-pair line by using an equalizing network. This is done by cancelling the effect of the transmission from the composite received signal to extract the intended received signal. Echo cancelling must be done on both ends of the digital line.

3.7 CODING AND ADDRESSING

Two lamps have a maximum of four possible combinations.

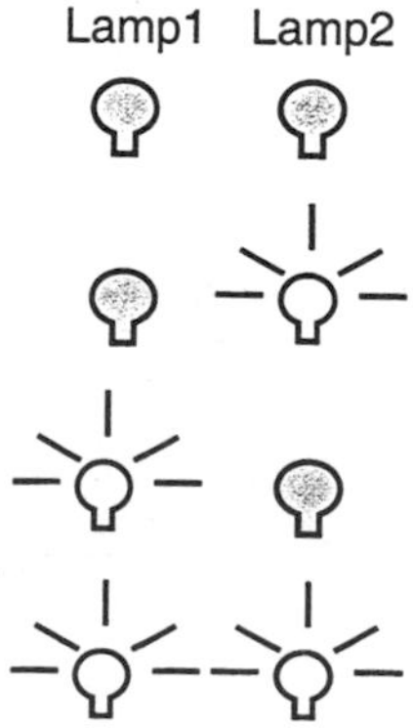

Lamp1   Lamp2

In digital systems, the smallest unit of information one can retrieve is a bit. Two bits are called a dibit, 4 are called a nibble, and 8 are called an octet. Generally, an octet is also called a byte, although, in some cases, a byte may not be 8 bits.

If only one bit of information is being sent, then only one piece out of a possible two pieces of information can be sent. For example, the two end points which are communicating may agree that if a binary 1 is being sent, that would represent that it is sunny and if a 0 is being sent that would mean that it is not sunny.

If the two end points would like to communicate with each other using more pieces of information, more bits are needed to encode those pieces of information. Using two bits allows one to communicate with

Pattern used to communicate	Communication protocol A	Communication protocol B
00	It is sunny.	I want to go home.
01	It is raining.	I am going home.
10	It is snowing.	I am almost home.
11	It is doing none of the above.	I am home.

Figure 3.13 The actual meaning of given bit patterns is predetermined by the communication protocol in use.

Analog and Digital Signals

000	100	0000	0100	1000	1100
001	101	0001	0101	1001	1101
010	110	0010	0110	1010	1110
011	111	0011	0111	1011	1111

(a) (b)

Figure 3.14 (a) The number of possible combinations using 3 bits. (b) The number of possible combinations using 4 bits.

four possible codes. This is shown in the side diagram where two lamps could have four possible combinations of states.

Figure 3.13 shows two examples of coding methods using two bits. Whatever method of coding is used by the transmitter, the same method of decoding must be used by the receiver. Encoding and decoding methods are part of the communications protocol that is used by all parties in the network.

If we increase the number of bits used to transmit information to 3, we have the possibility of encoding up to 8 different combinations. The number of combinations for 3 and 4 bits are shown in Figures 3.14(a) and (b). From these examples, we can see that, given the number of bits, one can calculate the number of possible codes available by this formula:

```
Number of possible combinations = 2 (The number of available bits)
```

Let us look at some examples of how to apply this formula. If a computer has only 128 octets of data, for the CPU to access any one of these octets, it must use 7 bits to address the proper octet, because with 7 bits, there are 128 (or 2^7) possible combinations, where each combination can be used to identify each of the 128 octets. However, each octet itself can store one out of a possible 256 (or 2^8) combinations of data. To access a specific location, we need digital signals on 7 wires, either 0s or 1s. On the other hand, to transfer data to that location in parallel, we need 8 wires.

Suppose a LAN has 30 computers and the transmitting computer must code the address of the receiving computer with every data frame which it sends. In this case,

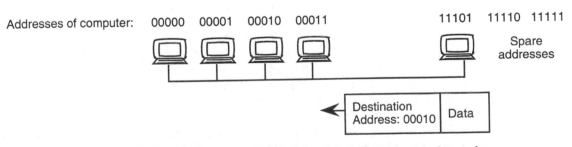

Figure 3.15 In this made-up situation, if we had 30 computers, then only 5 bits would be necessary for their addresses. Here, a data frame is on the LAN, with its destination address encoded in its header.

Analog and Digital Signals

how many bits must be used to encode the address? See Figure 3.15. If only 4 bits are used to encode the destination address, 2^4 or 16 computers can be accessed. If 5 bits are used, we have 32 combinations available out of which 30 can be used to assign addresses for existing computers, leaving us with 2 spare addresses for future additions.

That was a make-believe network exercise. We typically don't have the option to choose the number of bits of the address field, let alone assign the addresses to computers. In reality, Ethernet LAN cards have 48 bit addresses. Every LAN card has a unique physical address encoded in its ROM (Read-Only Memory) chip. The first 24 bits identify the vendor of the Ethernet card and the next 24 bits identify the serial number given by the vendor. There are 2^{24} vendor codes and manufacturers can assign up to 2^{24} serial numbers with each vendor code. There are a total of 2^{48} Ethernet cards possible.

On the Internet, each host must have a unique IP address. With IP version 4, there are only 32 bits allocated for each IP address because when TCP/IP was created, they didn't think the protocol family would last as long as it did. They thought some other set of protocols, like OSI, would become the accepted protocol. The number of possible hosts with version 4 is only 2^{32}, so with the new version of IP, version 6, the number of bits was increased to 128.

If the address field were increased from 32 to 33 bits, it would have doubled the available number of IP addresses. Adding 2 or 3 bits to the address field would have increased the number of addresses by a factor of 4 or 8, respectively. Therefore, increasing the number of bits from 32 to 128 is a drastic increase in the number of available IP addresses.

3.8 MULTIPLEXING

The process of sending several communication channels (or conversations) simultaneously over one link is called *multiplexing*. The process of separating them on the receiving end is called *demultiplexing*. Multiplexing and demultiplexing are done by a multiplexer, also referred to as a mux.

Multiplexing occurs in many forms. For example, when Sarah, my daughter, sends notes to all her friends in India, I simply place them in one envelope and mail them to her uncle in Mumbai. He then demultiplexes the envelope and sends the individual notes to their final destinations. It is cheaper for me to send the letters in one large envelope rather than send them as individual letters.

In Chapter 2 using Figure 2.7, we used the example of a card going to Chicago over an airplane route. There, many messages were multiplexed within the same bag or container. We also saw how many packets were multiplexed over the same link in a packet switched network in Figure 2.10(a). Multiplexing can occur at practically any layer of the OSI Reference Model. Figure 3.16 shows how multiplexing occurs at the physical layer or at the bit level.

In Figure 3.16(a), if no multiplexing is used between the users at the two sites shown, then separate communications lines would have to be paid for on a monthly basis. This is not only costly, but also becomes a management issue. With a multiplexer used at each site as shown in Figure 3.16(b), we would now need to pay for only one line and it would be easier to keep track of one line than several. There is an initial cost associated with the multiplexers, but after that cost is overcome, the savings occur every month in long-distance communications charges. Hence, the longer the distance between the two sites, the greater the savings. With a multiplexer, the hosts must communicate with each other in pairs. You cannot have the top host (or the host connected to port 1) from Site 1 communicate to the bottom host (or the host connected to port 3) from Site 2.

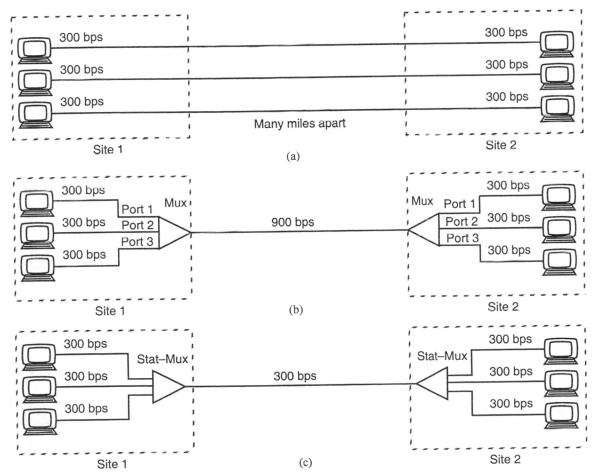

Figure 3.16 (a) Without multiplexers, the costs of separate communications links are high for each pair of hosts. (b) All the communications channels can be multiplexed over one link, bringing the communications cost down. (c) If the hosts are not continuously transmitting, then they can share one link running at low speed using a statistical multiplexer. If we wanted to be able to transmit to any host, then we would have to replace the stat-muxes with packet switches.

Also, notice that the sum of the input speeds of the multiplexers must not exceed the speed on the communications link. This is because each host takes its turn, in order, transmitting over the communications link. If one host is idle while another has a lot of data to send, then that is too bad. The busy host must wait to get its data through to the other side while the idle host wastes the time which is allotted to it.

This gives us a reason to use statistical multiplexers instead, as shown in Figure 3.16(c). Here, if the two ports are busy while one has a lot of data to send, the stat-mux will send all the traffic for the busy host contiguously. But now how does the receiving stat-mux know which host the data is meant for? This is done by sending data in a frame and having the frame header contain the address of the receiving port. A stat-mux must have more buffer or RAM than a regular mux to store and forward the frames it is receiving.

If the traffic over the link is low, that is, if the usage is low, then a low-speed link would be sufficient. This would lower the monthly cost of that link. Only corresponding ports of each stat-mux, however, must communicate with each other. If we needed any port from the mux of Site 1 to be able to communicate with any port from the mux on Site 2, then we would replace the stat-mux's with packet switches. The packet headers at each packet switch would direct the packet to the appropriate port. This would then create a two-node packet switched network. Consequently, all packet switches provide statistical multiplexing as well as switching. Let us next look at some common methods of multiplexing and briefly see how they work.

3.8.1 FDM

Figure 3.17 shows an FDM multiplexer. This mux is receiving 12 voice channels on its inputs and is combining them for transmission over one communication link.

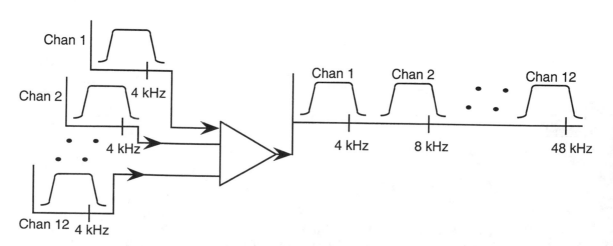

Figure 3.17 FDM (Frequency Division Multiplexing) transmits many analog channels over one link by allocating each channel a portion of the available bandwidth.

Analog and Digital Signals

Each channel uses a bandwidth of 3 kHz. To prevent adjacent channels from interfering with another, however, they are separated from each other using a guard band and are each allocated 4 kHz of bandwidth instead.

Each channel is offset on the output frequency spectrum so as to assign to each channel its share of the available bandwidth. This way many voice channels can be transmitted over the same link.

FDM is also used on analog cable TV. Each TV channel uses 6 MHz of bandwidth and a 100-channel cable TV system would require at least 600 MHz of capacity. To reduce interchannel interference, guard bands again are used, making the entire cable system operate at 750 MHz.

3.8.2 TDM

Instead of dividing the available frequencies among all the channels, one can divide the available time between them. This is called TDM (Time Division Multiplexing). Figure 3.18 shows two channels carrying digital signals into a TDM mux. Using its clock, the mux transmits the data from the first input over every odd time slot and transmits the data from the second input over every even one. This way, the data from both inputs are transmitted over one output. To be able to place the data bits for both input channels over the output, the output speed must be twice as fast as an input port.

For example, at t = 3 and t = 4, the first input is transmitting a binary 1 and the second one is transmitting a binary 0. The first input's binary 1 is transmitted at t = 3 and the second input's binary 0 is transmitted at t = 4. This way, the mux alternates between the inputs. Of course, on the receiver's side, the TDM mux must be synchronized so that it forwards the proper bits to each recipient.

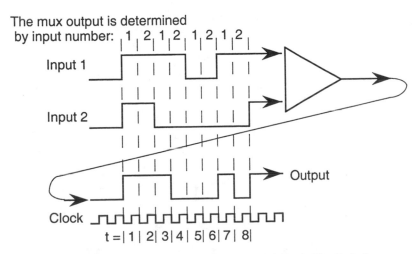

Figure 3.18 TDM (Time Division Multiplexing) transmits digital channels over one link by allocating to each channel a portion of the available time.

Figure 3.18 illustrates *bit interleaving*, since the mux changes the channel after every bit. On the other hand, if 8 bits from each channel are sent together, then the mux would be using what is called *byte interleaving* multiplexing.

One can easily see how TDM can be extended to more channels. But the link speed must be greater than the sum of the input speeds in the same way that the output bandwidth for a FDM mux must be greater than the sum of the input bandwidths. Yet, with TDM not much extra time is required for overhead, but with FDM, we had to separate the channels from each other forcing us to use more bandwidth than what was actually needed. Hence, FDM is said to be less efficient than TDM.

3.8.3 WDM

Similar to FDM is WDM (Wave Division Multiplexing). FDM is used with analog electrical signals while WDM is used with optical signals through optical fiber. FDM and WDM both use frequency division multiplexing. At optical frequencies, however, engineers more commonly characterize photons using their wavelengths instead of their frequencies. Therefore, at optical frequencies, the term WDM is used

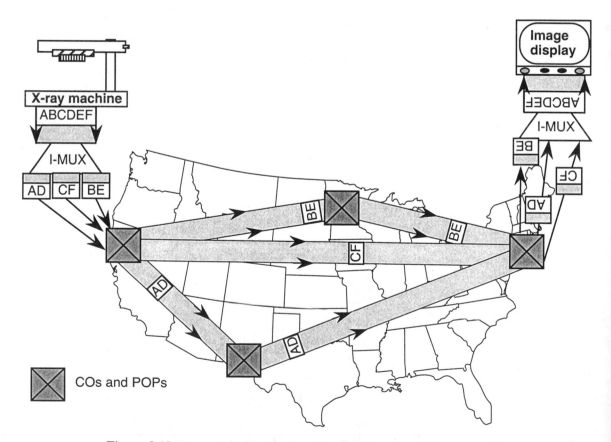

Figure 3.19 Large x-ray files can be transmitted in less time using several low-speed lines and inverse multiplexers at each end.

instead of FDM. Remember from section 3.3, the wavelength of a wave is simply the reciprocal of its frequency. Hence, if the wavelength goes up, the frequency goes down and vice versa. Each wavelength corresponds to a different color.

Without WDM, an optical fiber uses only one light source, going in one direction. This required old fiber installations to use two fibers, one for transmitting and one for receiving. Current deployment of fiber allows full-duplex transmission using WDM. This is like beams from two flashlights crossing each other without interference. The transmitters on each end of the fiber use light sources of different wavelengths (or frequencies).

Besides full-duplex transmission, WDM also allows many input electrical channels to be transmitted over different wavelengths of light over the same fiber. This drastically increases the capacity of the fiber, allowing it to transmit data at much greater bandwidths than previously has been possible. We will discuss fiber again in the next chapter.

3.8.4 Inverse Multiplexing

Multiplexing allows many slow-speed channels to be transmitted over one high-speed link. However, many times a high-speed link is not available, but instead, several low-speed links are more feasible for one reason or another. In such a case, devices called inverse multiplexers (imuxes) can be deployed in pairs, one at each end.

In Figure 3.19, we see that a location on the west coast is sending large x-ray files to a specialist on the east coast. Here, three low-speed links are used. They could be some type of inexpensive dial-up connections. By using imuxes at both ends, however, the large amount of data can be transported in a reasonable amount of time. The transmitting imux breaks up the data stream in such a way that the receiving imux can reconstruct it in the original order.

3.9 INFORMATION ENCODING

3.9.1 Methods of Transmitting Information

Information, as was discussed in section 3.7, is what the user wants to communicate. Examples of information are voice, data, video, fax, medical images, etc. Signaling determines how a connection is going to be made to the recipient so that he or she is ready to receive the information. Information can be transmitted using analog lines or digital lines. The type of line is determined not by looking at it physically, but by the type of equipment that is connected to it on the other side.

For example, COs place analog equipment on phone lines coming from residences. Hence a typical phone line is an analog line. If a CO were to attach digital equipment on that line, then it would be a digital line. ISDN (Integrated Services Digital Network) requires that the existing analog lines be converted to digital ones by having the COs and customers replace the end equipment. One should also remember that if there are any analog devices like loading coils in the transmission lines themselves, then they also must be removed or be replaced by digital devices.

Figure 3.20(a) shows that a simple telephone provides all the circuitry necessary to send voice over an analog line. It also shows that the device used to convert voice

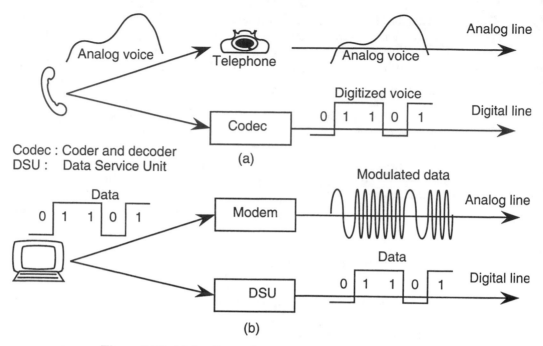

Codec : Coder and decoder
DSU : Data Service Unit

Figure 3.20 (a) Sending voice over analog and digital lines.
(b) Doing the same with data.

to a digital signal requires the introduction of a codec (COder and DECoder). A voice codec converts voice to digital, while a video codec converts a video signal to a digital one.

Today almost all voice is transmitted digitally. Hence, when voice arrives at a CO over a phone line, the line card at the central office converts the analog voice to the digital equivalent. Conversely, when the digital voice is sent to the customer over a phone line, the line card must first convert it back to the analog form. Most PBXs today also operate this way. So if you have a digital phoneset connected to a PBX, then the codec resides in your phoneset and the voice is transferred over the telephone line digitally. On the other hand, if you have an analog phoneset, then the codec is in the line card within the PBX.

To transmit data over an analog line, one needs a modem as seen in Figure 3.20(b). In section 3.3.2, we mentioned how digital signals are actually composed of very high frequencies which analog telephone lines are not capable of handling. Hence, we cannot place a digital signal directly on an analog line; it won't travel too far before it becomes indecipherable. We must use a modem to encode data, which is inherently a digital signal, into analog form so that it can be transmitted reliably over an analog line or facilities. Maybe it's best to think of a modem as being a "telephone" for computers. In order for a computer to "talk" into the PSTN, it must use a modem.

We can't think of modems as being simply analog to digital conversion devices or vice versa. For that matter codecs are too. Consider Figure 3.21. Here, data from a PC is being sent digitally to a modem, which in turn converts it to analog. This is done

Analog and Digital Signals

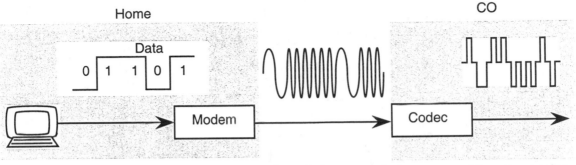

Figure 3.21 Data is sent over the telephone line and is converted to an analog signal. Then the CO converts it to digital using PCM.

to accommodate the analog equipment at the CO which is expecting signals in the voice frequency range. As soon as this analog signal arrives at the CO, it is converted to PCM (Pulse Code Modulations) as if it were a voice signal. This is a PCM signal which represents the analog signal which was modulated with data. At the receive side, these two conversions are done in reverse order so that the data arrives as it was transmitted.

To send data over a digital line, one needs a DSU (Data Service Unit, also called Digital Service Unit). A DSU provides the necessary interface for transmission of data over a digital line. A DSU makes sure that the signal levels are of the proper voltage. It maintains synchronization with end equipment. It also allows technicians to do loopback tests from the CO remotely. Actually, DSUs usually come with a CSU (Channel Service Unit) already built in, but we usually refer to the unit as a DSU. We will discuss DSUs more in the chapter on T1s.

It can get confusing to understand the difference between a modem and a codec. They both do analog-to-digital conversion and vice versa. However, keep in mind what kind of information each device processes. For instance, text may be encoded using a 7-bit ASCII code. This code is only decipherable to text displays or printers. A modem can convert such data into analog form. To retrieve this data from an analog signal, we need a modem and not a codec. A voice codec, on the other hand, can only decode digitized voice (which has nothing to do with ASCII) and turn it into voice which we can hear. In the same sense one doesn't send digitized voice to a printer, neither does one expect a modem to convert digitized voice into audio.

Some Review Questions
1. What does data naturally exist as?
2. What converts analog to digital?
3. What converts digital to analog?
4. What converts voice (air pressure) to analog?
5. What converts voice (which naturally exists as analog) to digital?
6. What interfaces data to a digital line?
7. What converts analog to data?

Answers
1. Digital 2. Modem and codec
3. Modem and codec 4. Phone
5. Codec 6. DSU 7. Modem

3.9.2 Advantages of Converting Voice to Digital

Let us discuss why most voice transmissions are being converted into a digital format. Many of the issues discussed here will also hold true for transmission of digital signals, in general, even if it is video.

Analog and Digital Signals

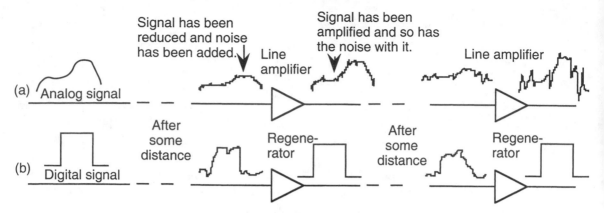

Figure 3.22 (a) The degradation of analog signals after being transmitted over a distance. (b) The regeneration of a digital signal after being transmitted over a distance.

Probably the most important reason for digitizing voice is that a digital signal is less affected by noise. In Figure 3.22(a), an analog signal is being transmitted over a transmission medium. When it arrives at the first line amplifier or repeater, the signal has become weak and has picked up noise and interference. To boost the weak signal, a line amplifier has been added. Unfortunately, it ends up amplifying the noise as well. If amplification is needed over several segments of a transmission path, the signal would become poor and not be suitable to be called "toll-quality".

If a digital signal on the other hand, as seen in Figure 3.22(b), is transmitted over the same medium, the regenerator at the other end can recreate the signal. Any "fuzziness" in the signal is eliminated, because the signal should be either a 1 or a 0 and nothing in between. The line amp cannot as easily eliminate the fuzziness in analog signals, because it can't distinguish noise from the signal as well. Although in the past engineers have spent a considerable amount of time and effort to design circuits to eliminate noise as much as possible, such circuitry is expensive.

Even as late as the 70s, one could tell when a call was being made across the continent or within the same town. Today, with digital transmissions, one has difficulty noticing any variations in voice quality. The maximum number of line amps for analog signals is limited to typically five, but the maximum number of repeaters for a digital signal is virtually limitless. Regenerators make digital signals insensitive to distance. The circuitry used for digital equipment is easy to design (if it hasn't been designed already to be used with computing devices). Because of this, digital equipment is inexpensive and reliable. FDM used with analog channels is inefficient and expensive. It uses guardbands to separate the signals between adjacent channels. This requires additional bandwidth that carries no information, but is necessary so that there is less interference between the channels. TDM used with digital channels is more efficient, uses less overhead, and is less expensive.

But because the bandwidth required for one voice channel (64 kbps) was significantly higher than the original data channel (300 bps), many ruled out the possibility of digitizing voice to ever become popular. Since then, more bandwidth has

Analog and Digital Signals

become available on network links, and the required bandwidth for a toll-quality voice channel is dropping as research and development continues in this field. For instance, in 1978, a video conference required 6 Mbps of bandwidth and employed sophisticated compression algorithm methods; in 1993 it required only 0.08 Mbps to provide the same quality signal.

Another advantage for digitizing voice that has become evident is that we can packetize digital voice. Once voice has been digitized using a codec, those bits can be placed as data in a packet going across a data network, like the Internet. If we did not have digitized voice, then we would not be able to use the Internet to transmit voice, or for that matter, music or video. The problem with packetizing voice is that data networks in general are built not to be sensitive to delay variations. It doesn't matter if data arrives slowly if we are waiting for text to appear on the screen, but if a packet carrying voice comes later than the previous packet, we would find the quality of the voice conversation to be unacceptable.

Transmission of digital signals depends on keeping synchronization within tolerance. If synchronization is not maintained, then we have an undesirable phenomena called *jitter*. Converting analog signals to digital signals also introduces *quantization noise,* which we will discuss in the following section on PCM.

3.9.3 PCM

A simple method of converting voice is shown in Figure 3.23(a). The voice signal is placed on an imaginary grid, where discrete voltage levels are assigned digital codes. Then the voice signal is sampled at an even rate and the voltage of the voice in digital form is transmitted. For example, at sample 1, the voice signal is close to a digital value of 01 and at sample 2, it is close to a level of 10, and so on. Then these bits are transmitted and the receiver constructs a signal from them. The difference between the actual voice signal and the reconstructed signal is called *quantization noise*, and it

Digitization of Voice
Advantages:
1. Noise immunity
2. Efficient multiplexing
3. Cheaper circuitry
4. Packetization
5. Reliable transmission
6. Distance-insensitive

Disadvantages:
1. Quantization noise
2. Synchronization critical
3. Delay-sensitive

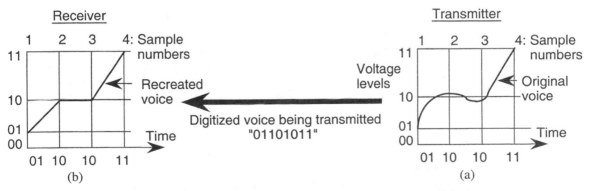

Figure 3.23 (a) A simple example of converting voice into a digital signal. (b) After the voice is reconstructed, the difference between its waveform and the original waveform is called quantization noise.

becomes an issue only if the voice is converted between analog and digital forms several times. Regenerators do not perform such conversions; only codecs do. It is best to carry digitized voice from end to end, although the encoding methods may differ from one country to another.

Figure 3.22(b) shows how the digitized voice is reconstructed using the decoder part of a codec. Because the voice signal is rounded off by the decoder circuitry, it is not possible to exactly recreate the original voice signal. This is because of quantization noise.

If we wanted to convert voice into digital form more accurately, we would need to increase the sampling rate as well as increase the number of levels. This would increase the number of rectangles and reduce their sizes on the grid. In order to accurately code voice into digital form, the sampling rate must be at least twice the highest frequency of the analog voice channel. This is called Nyquist's theorem.

Hence, the encoding method called PCM (Pulse Code Modulation) uses 8000 samples per second, corresponding to about two times the analog channel's bandwidth (or 2 times 4 kHz). It uses 8 bits to encode the levels for each sample providing a total of 2^8 or 256 levels. However, a level of 0 is not used because it would present too many 0s in a sequence (actually 8 zeros) for a clock to maintain synchronization.

Therefore, with 8000 samples per second and 8 bits per sample, the rate for one voice channel using PCM is 64 kbps. The method of performing PCM in North America and Japan is called the mu-law and the one used in Europe is called the A-law.

Another popular method of digitizing voice is called ADPCM (Adaptive Differential PCM). It uses 4 bits per sample, but only codes the differences between the extrapolated level and the actual level. So it doesn't need as many bits per sample as PCM does. Its bandwidth of 32 kbps provides a quality of voice that is indistinguishable from PCM.

To store the amount of voice generated by a conversation of 1 minute would require about 0.5 Mbytes of memory using PCM. This is because 1 minute equals 60 seconds and each second generates 64,000 bits. This amounts to 3,840,000 bits or, dividing by 8, yields 480,000 bytes. Of course, using voice compression techniques would greatly reduce this number.

CDs (Compact Discs) compared to PCM require much more bandwidth since they provide high-quality audio. An analog bandwidth of 20 kHz necessitates the sampling rate to be 44.1 kbps, which is about double the amount needed. Each sample is coded with 16 bits instead of the 8 bits which are used in PCM. Multiplying 44.1 kbps, 16, and 2 for each of the two stereo channels yields a rate of 1.4112 Mbps. This is considerably greater than PCM's 64-kbps rate; however, by the time error correction codes, synchronization bits, and other processing are added, the actual rate for a CD becomes 4.3218 Mbps.

3.9.4 Video Compression

Unlike an audio signal encoded on a CD, digitized video depends on complex compression algorithms. Notice that with CDs compression was not used. Without compression, a broadcast video signal would require 4.7 Mbps of bandwidth for color. HDTV (High Definition TV) would require 100 Mbps. But with compression, these rates can be reduced by as much as a factor of 100 with little apparent loss in quality. Medical images, such as X-rays, can be reduced by a factor of 3 but not much more than that without losing resolution.

There are two types of compression used with video—intraframe and interframe. Intraframe compression reduces the amount of data needed to send one frame. Interframe compression depends on the fact that two adjacent frames are usually similar to each other and only require the transmission of the differences between them. Both techniques make use of the characteristics of the human eye to make the picture appear good without having to transmit all of its details.

For example, since the human eye is more sensitive to brightness than it is to color, more bits per frame are used to encode the former than the latter. Also, the eye is less sensitive to abrupt changes than it is to gradual changes; hence, fewer bits are

Intraframe compression

Interframe compression

What is actually seen:

What is transmitted:

(b)   (c)

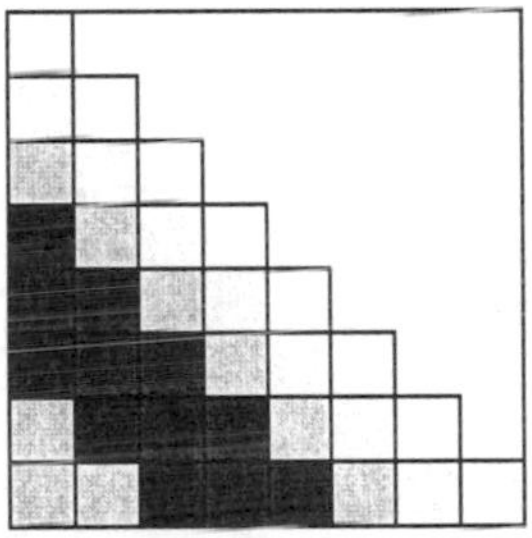

5	0	0	0	0	0	0	0
7	5	0	0	0	0	0	0
10	7	5	0	0	0	0	0
15	10	7	5	0	0	0	0
15	15	10	7	5	0	0	0
15	15	15	10	7	5	0	0
10	15	15	15	10	7	5	0
10	10	15	15	15	10	7	5

9	-5	2	1	0	0	0	0
-5	2	1	0	0	0	0	0
1	1	1	0	0	0	0	0
0	0	0	0	0	0	0	0
0	0	0	0	0	0	0	0
0	0	0	0	0	0	0	0
0	0	0	0	0	0	0	0
0	0	0	0	0	0	0	0

(a)

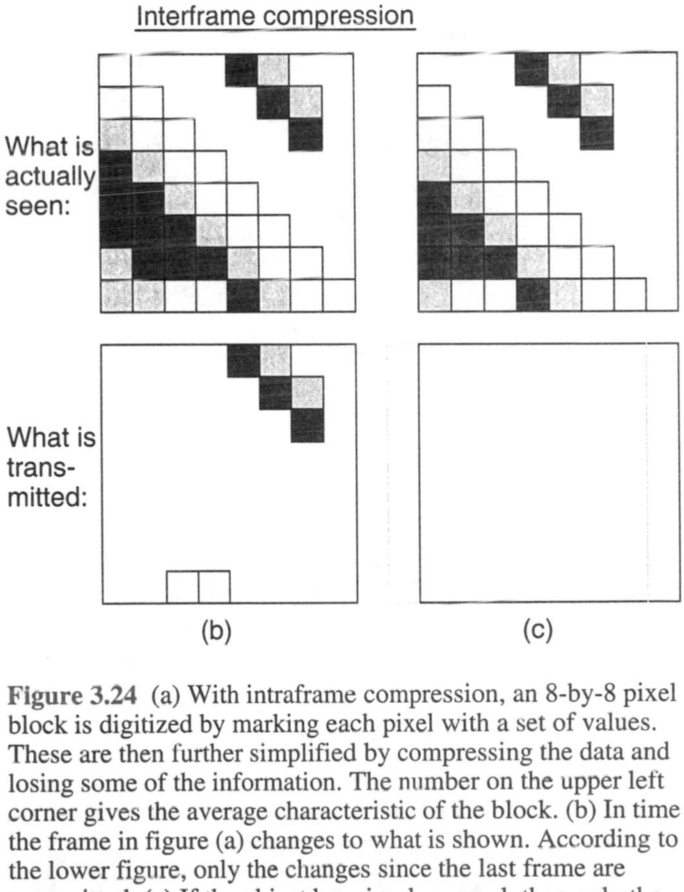

Figure 3.24 (a) With intraframe compression, an 8-by-8 pixel block is digitized by marking each pixel with a set of values. These are then further simplified by compressing the data and losing some of the information. The number on the upper left corner gives the average characteristic of the block. (b) In time the frame in figure (a) changes to what is shown. According to the lower figure, only the changes since the last frame are transmitted. (c) If the object has simply moved, then only the amount and direction of the shift is transmitted.

used to encode abrupt changes in signal than gradual ones. That is, less information is transmitted with small changes, because most current applications are for meetings ("talking heads") which have fewer changes than, say, a juggling act would have.

Briefly, video compression techniques typically divide a picture into blocks of 8 pixels by 8 pixels as shown in Figure 3.24. Depending on its color, brightness, and other characteristics, each pixel is assigned a value. See the middle grid of Figure 3.24(a). After this block is averaged and detailed information is removed, a much simpler grid is constructed as shown toward the bottom of the figure. This summarizes intraframe compression.

In Figure 3.24(b), a few changes are added to the frame. Instead of transmitting the entire frame, only the changes shown on the bottom of the figure are transmitted. Similarly, if the object in the block moves, then only the information concerning the shift is transmitted. See Figure 3.24(c).

EXERCISES

Section 3.1:

1. The voltage level of an analog signal can increase or decrease by how many levels?
   a. 1
   b. 2
   c. a continuous amount
   d. a discrete amount
2. A windshield wiper switch with four positions is an example of what kind of device?
   a. analog
   b. digital
   c. tertiary
   d. modal

Section 3.2:

3. When a DC voltage is added to a digital signal to transmit power, what is the process called?
   a. multiplexing
   b. filtering
   c. phantoming
   d. amplifying
4. What helps a circuit stay synchronized?
   a. clock
   b. an analog signal
   c. digitized voice
   d. phantom voltage
5. In a circuit, if 70 volts is applied to 35 ohms of resistance, how much current will flow?

Section 3.3:

6. In Figure 3.9, the high frequencies are being shorted by which device?
   a. battery
   b. resistor
   c. capacitor
   d. inductor
7. When converting an analog line to a digital one, which devices must be removed?
   a. batteries
   b. resistances
   c. capacitors
   d. loading coils
8. Besides the characteristics used to modify an analog signal as shown in Figure 3.7, what other signal characteristic could be modified as well?
9. How do capacitors and inductors differ?
10. Draw a high-pass filter circuit and explain its operation.
11. Draw an amplitude-modulated signal that modulates this data: 10010.
12. What is the wavelength of a 200 Hz signal? If the wavelength were to increase, what would happen to its frequency? How many kilohertz is 200 Hz?

Section 3.4:

13. If R2 in Figure 3.3 were 20 ohms, what would its voltage and power be?
14. In Figure 3.12, if the output of stage 3 were 12 mW, what would be its gain in dBs?
15. If the gain of an amplifier is 6 dBs, and its input is 2 mW, what is its output?
16. Find the gain of a filter whose input is 5 mW and output is 4 mW. You will need a calculator for this one.

Section 3.5:

17. Many times with asynchronous transmission, a parity bit is used with each character to allow for error correction. In that case, how many bits are needed to send each character?
18. Describe the difference between synchronous and asynchronous transmissions.
19. What do asynchronous transmission and ATM have in common?
20. How many stratum levels of clocking exist? Which one is the most accurate? What type of problem will become evident if synchronization is not maintained?

Section 3.6:

21. What type of transmission does echo cancelling provide?
    a. simplex   b. full-duplex
    c. half-duplex   d. tri-plex
22. How is echo cancelling achieved?

Section 3.7:

23. A 16-bit location in RAM can store how many whole numbers? If half of them are positive and half of them are negative (and one is zero) what is the largest positive number that is representable?
24. If 4096 colors need to be represented in a computer system, how many bits are needed to represent this many colors?
25. ASCII uses seven bits to represent characters. To be able to increase the number of characters by a factor of 8, how many more bits should be added to our code?

Section 3.8:

26. How many 300-baud terminals can be attached to a 2400-baud line using a TDM multiplexer?
27. Which type of multiplexing is used with digital signals? With analog signals? With optical signals?
28. Why is TDM said to be more efficient than WDM?
29. In a TDM multiplexer with two ports, if the input were 1101 and 1001, what would the output bits be? Assume that the first input is transmitted first.

Section 3.9:

30. Which device converts voice into digital form?
    a. modem   b. multiplexer
    c. codec   d. DSU
31. A voice digitizing method doesn't use compression. If it transmits at 16 kbps and has a sampling rate of 4000 samples per second, how many voltage levels can it encode?
32. What are the advantages of transmitting in digital form?
33. Describe, in your own words, how video is digitized and how it is similar to and different from digitizing voice using PCM?

34. To increase the quality of voice which is transmitted, what must be done to the rate at which the sampling is done and to the number of signal levels which are encoded?

Chapter 4

Transmission Systems

4.1 INTRODUCTION

When fiber was introduced in the late 1970s, many wondered if it would replace other transmissions media and become the dominant choice in the telecommunications industry. Although fiber is being deployed at a rapid rate on long-haul point-to-point runs, other technologies play a significant role in connecting many widely separated remote sites together, while yet others concentrate on cutting down costs. Even the inexpensive twisted pair has been developed so that it can now transmit at rates of up to 1 Gbps over limited distances.

Fiber, because of its initial cost, was once off-limits to desktops. But here again, prices have been dropping rapidly and fiber connector designs have been advancing, enabling installation of fiber to the computers on our desktops. Once fiber makes its way to desktops and into our homes, there is no telling how we will find ways of using all that bandwidth.

The first part of this chapter will present the transmission media that are used close to the ground, then will cover the ones that go over the earth, and then those that include space. The latter part will discuss systems that are generally associated with voice transmissions and PBXs. Discussion of cellular systems will be delayed until we get to that chapter.

4.2 TWISTED PAIR

4.2.1 Limitations of Twisted Pair Cabling

The telephone wires that commonly provided by the COs to residences use twisted pair wires. Since their bandwidth is rated at 3 kHz, they are also called voice-grade lines.

As seen in the last chapter, telephone wires inherently come with a capacitive effect. This creates crosstalk, the situation where the conversations from one pair interfere with the conversations of an adjacent one. To compensate for this, the pairs are twisted around themselves introducing a cancelling inductive effect. As more twists are added per foot, the cable becomes less susceptible to crosstalk. See Figure 4.1(a). On longer runs, loading coils are needed for the same purpose.

Although plain copper wire is inexpensive, there are many precautions one has to be aware of when installing it. As the distance of the cabling increases, its attenuation or its loss of signal increases. Data transmission rates have to be lowered. The cabling becomes more sensitive to EMI (Electromagnetic Interference) and RFI (Radio Frequency Interference). Effects from EMI can be reduced by installing the cable away from power lines, motors, elevator shafts, and photocopiers. If this can't be done, say, because the environment where the cable is laid is in an industrial setting, then cable with a metal shield around it can be used. This type of cabling is called STP (Shielded Twisted Pair). UTP (Unshielded Twisted Pair) is twisted pair cabling without an interference protective shield. Figure 4.1(b) shows an example of STP specified as Type 1. This type of cabling is more expensive, but it can be installed on longer runs than UTP.

Typically, the sizes of telephone lines range from 22 AWG (American Wire Gauge) to 26 AWG. The diameter of a 22 AWG wire is 0.025 inches and that of a 26 gauge wire is 0.016 inches. As the AWG number decreases, the wider the wire is and the lesser its resistance becomes, and its bandwidth rating increases.

When installing cabling, we must be aware that it is also rated for its *impedance*. Impedance is resistance to AC and it takes in account not only DC resistance but also resistance due to capacitive and inductive effects. When an electric load is placed at the end of a cable, its impedance should always be equal to the impedance of the cable or else the signal is not properly transferred to the load, but is reflected back into the cable. Again, this is what the electrical engineers tell us. They design circuits around those details; all we must remember is to install equipment that is proper for the cabling that is in place and to make sure that the impedance of the cabling and that of the equipment match.

4.2.2 Twisted Pair Standards

The EIA/TIA (Electronic Industries Association/Telecommunications Industries Association) has specified different types of cabling and how they should be installed in its 568 Commercial Building Wiring Standard. The EIA/TIA has defined five different kinds of UTP cabling from Category 1 to Category 5. Category 1 and 2 cabling are not suited for commercial building wiring. The other 3 categories of cabling are rated at 100 ohms of impedance. Their lengths should not exceed 90 meters from patch-panel to wall outlet and 100 meters between end-to-end equipment.

Category 3 cabling or voice-grade UTP (Unshielded Twisted Pair) is approved for data rates of up to 10 Mbps and analog signals of up to 16 MHz. It has at least 3 twists per foot and is meant primarily for voice transmissions. Category 4 UTP is designed primarily for data transmission. It is certified for rates of up to 16 Mbps and 20 MHz. The higher capacity is achieved by manufacturers ensuring that the cable has at least 10 twists per foot.

Category 5 cabling has become very popular since it was standardized in 1991. It has at least 36 twists per foot, and transmits data at 100 Mbps. Although STP can also be used for transmission at rates of 100 Mbps, it is almost half an inch thick, whereas Category 5 UTP is only 0.25 inches thick. This makes it easy to install around bends and inside ducts.

Category 5 UTP comes with 4 pairs. It is only slightly more expensive than Category 3 UTP. It typically uses the RJ-45 (Register Jack - 45) jack. The plug and the jack are shown in Figure 4.1(c) and (d). Don't confuse this jack with the RJ-48 used with T1s (T1s are covered in the next chapter). They look the same but use different pin layouts.

The RJ-45 modular jack is very easy to work with because it resembles the RJ-11 jack used in homes. The RJ-45 has 8 pins while the RJ-11 can have 6, or more commonly, 4 pins. The RJ-45 comes in two versions: the 568A and the 568B. The 568A calls pins 3 and 6 number 2 and pins 1 and 2 pair number 3, while the 568B reverses those pair numbers. Be careful not to mix the 568A and the 568B cabling schemes.

Because Cat-5 (as it is abbreviated) is a standard, companies don't have to worry about their supplier going out of business. There will be other suppliers available in that case. A standard also drives the prices down due to increased competition. There are other grades of UTP available, such as Cat-5E (enhanced). It has more attractive ratings. Also, Level 6 and Level 7 cabling are being marketed but they are not standards so one should stay away from them. However, fiber is becoming more attractive and any day it should bury these "emerging" UTP cabling schemes. IEEE has also standardized 1394, called FireWire. It is a multipurpose cabling scheme for PCs, TVs, and other consumer equipment.

The EIA/TIA also recognizes the IBM STPs which can run at lengths of up to 800 meters. These cables' impedance is rated at 150 ohms. Type 1 cable has four copper strands wrapped in a metallic foil or a shield. It can transfer digital signals at 16 Mbps and analog signals at 20 MHz. The Type 1A cable is rated at 155 Mbps and 300 MHz. This is defined in the EIA/TIA TSB-53 specifications.

These cabling types were originally designed for Token Ring Network LANs. They use bulky one-inch connectors. However, RJ-45 connectors can also be used with a UTP cable called Type 3 for distances of up to 45 meters.

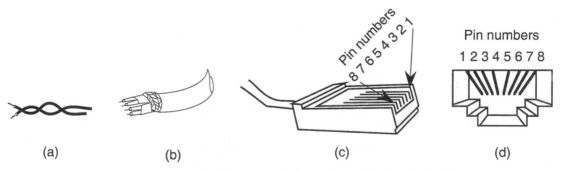

Figure 4.1 (a) Twisted copper wires. (b) Type 1 STP. (c) RJ-45 plug. (d) RJ-45 jack shown with the pin outs.

4.3 COAX

When many telephone transmissions were required to be placed on one medium, the twisted pair didn't provide the needed bandwidth. Coaxial cable (or just coax) was introduced which carried frequencies of up to 10 GHz. Coax has an inner conductor which is surrounded by a braided mesh, as seen in Figure 4.2(a). Both conductors share a common center axial, hence the term "coaxial." Coax comes in two types—baseband and broadband—and these types of coax are distinguished by how they are used.

4.3.1 Baseband Coax

Baseband coax was once widely used in Ethernet. It carries only one channel; that is, only one data transmission can exist on the cable at any time. The data is placed on the medium in digital form and rates of 10 Mbps are easily achieved. Data can travel in both directions. This cable has an impedance of 50 ohms.

4.3.2 Broadband Coax

Broadband coax with an impedance of 75 ohms is commonly used with cable TV. With CATV, it transmits analog signals in only one direction. To transmit in both directions, a dual cable system must be implemented. However, because of its large bandwidth of 300 MHz to 450 MHz, it can carry many channels simultaneously. Using FDM, one can send video, audio, and data. But since this is an analog system, modems are required for transmission of data.

For broadband coaxial systems, sophisticated devices such as amplifiers and splitters are necessary, as well as the services of skilled engineers to install and maintain them.

4.3.3 Waveguides

Waveguides are not a kind of coax. However, as transmitting frequencies are increased in a coax, they tend to travel in space, requiring no conductors. To guide such signals along a transmission path, they are placed in a hollow metal pipe called a waveguide. See Figure 4.2(b). Most waveguides in use are rectangular in cross section, with a two-to-one ratio for the two dimensions. They can transmit microwave signals with frequencies ranging over 100 GHz.

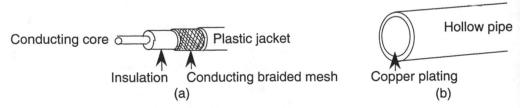

Figure 4.2 (a) Coaxial cable. (b) Waveguide.

Transmission Systems

4.4 FIBER

4.4.1 Overview

Fiber
  Advantages:
    1. Noise immunity
    2. Longer distances
    3. Low signal loss
    4. Better security
    5. Higher speeds
    6. Light weight
    7. Doesn't corrode
Disadvantages:
    1. Expensive
    2. Difficult installation

Just as microwaves are propagated and guided by confining them in a waveguide, optical signals or light can also be handled in a similar manner by sending them through an optical fiber. This is because as we increase the operating frequency of the microwave transmitters, we are approaching closer to the frequencies of light. Both radio waves and light are electromagnetic waves, although the frequencies of light are much greater than those of radio waves and microwaves.

Work with optical signals was done as far back as 1880 when Alexander Graham Bell received a patent for a photophone. This device transmitted voice using daylight rays for a distance of up to 200 meters.

But it was not until 1971 when Kapron, Keck, and Maurer at Corning Glass Works were able to send signals for a few hundred meters with losses of 20 dB per km. Only 21 years later, 5 Gbps optical signal was transmitted for over 5,000 miles without any repeaters or signal regenerators. Currently, the losses are less than 0.2 dB per km for a 1.55-micrometer wavelength infrared signal. Compare this with a 2.5 dB per km loss for a 1-MHz coaxial cable. Fiber is also very pure. A 3-mile thick piece of high-quality fiber would be as clear as a quarter-inch thick piece of glass used on ordinary windows.

Sending information by using light waves prevents interference from electrical sources, radio waves, lightning and so on. This enables error rates that are less than 10^{-9}. This number is equal to only one error in every billion bits. Fiber not only provides impressive low error rates, but also provides a very high data transfer rate.

Fiber is not susceptible to corrosion as is copper cabling. It is difficult to tap, providing excellent security. Also, it is immune to crosstalk. Lastly, fiber is not bulky but easy to handle. Because it is expensive and difficult to work with, however, other media still compete with it.

4.4.2 Construction

Fiber is mostly installed in pairs: a transmit fiber and a receive fiber. Many fibers are constructed similarly to what is shown in Figure 4.3. The core and cladding are constructed using glass. Light energy travels through these two sections. Surrounding them is a protective coating to prevent moisture from entering. The layer of Kevlar and other materials is added to give it its strength, so the fiber is not easily snapped. Finally, a polyurethane coating completes its construction. Since fiber can't carry electrical power to remote repeaters, such as the ones in transoceanic cables, copper cables must also be added if they are needed to deliver power.

The core and the cladding have different indices of refraction which force light rays at some angles to stay within the core while enabling others to escape. See Figure 4.4. When light enters the fiber, either from an LED (Light Emitting Diode) or an ILD (Injection Laser Diode), it travels through it due to total internal reflection.

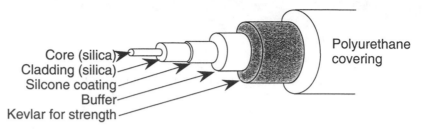

Figure 4.3 Typical fiber construction.

4.4.3 Types of Fiber

When the core diameter is large, there are more rays with varying angles of index which are accepted into the fiber than when the diameter is small. The mode of propagation of a light ray, which depends on its angle of incidence, is simply called a *mode*. So as the diameter of the core increases, the number of propagation modes increases, and the fiber is called a *multimode fiber*. In such a case, more rays arrive at the distant end out of phase from each other and can destructively interfere with each other. In a single-mode fiber, however, only one mode of propagation exists and there is no interference from other modes.

Based on the construction of the core and the cladding, there are primarily three types of fiber—multimode step index, multimode graded index, and single-mode step index. The typical diameters of their cores and claddings are shown in Figure 4.5. The index profiles show the index of refraction across the cross section of the fiber. Notice that there are only two values of index of refraction for the step index fibers. For these fibers the index of refraction doesn't change within the core or the cladding. In the graded index fiber, however, the core is made up of concentric layers of material which have a slightly different index of refraction.

The modes (or rays) in a multimode step index fiber can destructively interfere with each other. So its bandwidth is limited to around 10 MHz for distances of 1 km. Most of the power in a multimode fiber travels in the core, and so it is the easiest to manufacture.

In a graded index multimode fiber, because of the varying amounts of refractive indices of the core material, the modes do not sharply reflect, but are gradually

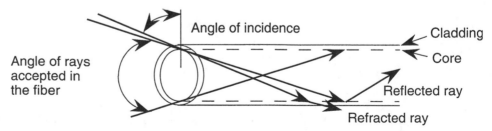

Figure 4.4 The angle of rays accepted in a fiber depends on the diameter of the core.

Transmission Systems

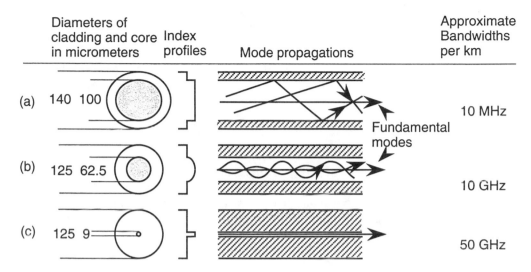

Diameters of cladding and core in micrometers	Index profiles	Mode propagations	Approximate Bandwidths per km
(a) 140 100		Fundamental modes	10 MHz
(b) 125 62.5			10 GHz
(c) 125 9			50 GHz

Figure 4.5 (a) Step index multimode fiber. (b) Graded index multimode fiber. (c) Step index single-mode fiber.

refracted into the core as seen in Figure 4.5(b). It provides a bandwidth of about 10 GHz.

Single-mode fiber propagates only one mode effectively. Up to 50 percent of the energy may be transferred through the cladding and the rest through the core. Since there is no intermodal interference, the bandwidth is in the order of 50 GHz. This type of fiber is typically used for long distances, but due to its small size, it is difficult to work with.

4.4.4 Harnessing More Bandwidth

Until the late 1980's electronic regenerators were used to regenerate optical signals along fiber. This required a three-step process: conversion of light into an electrical signal, regeneration of the electrical signal by retiming and reshaping of the waveform, and the conversion back to the optical signal using a semiconductor laser. Not only were such regenerators expensive, but they could regenerate only one frequency of light at a time. Additionally, the light signal had to be modulated using a single method.

Then in 1987, at the University of Southampton, England, a few researchers invented the erbium-doped all-fiber amplifier. These amplifiers do not require the conversion of light into an electrical signal, but amplify optical signals directly. Now light sources of different wavelengths can be transmitted through the same fiber and be amplified simultaneously through the same amplifier. Furthermore, these light signals could be of different bit rates and could be modulated using different methods. The erbium-doped amplifier amplifies them all together.

The erbium-doped amplifier is created by adding erbium ions to a few meters of silica fiber. A diode laser emits an infrared beam called a pump beam. This energy is

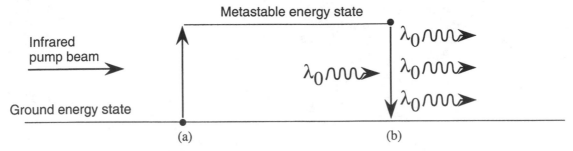

Figure 4.6 (a) An erbium ion is excited to a higher energy state by an infrared pump beam. (b) This ion, not being stable, is stimulated by an incoming signal photon to go back to its ground energy state. The shedding of energy generates new photons which are coherent with the incoming photon.

absorbed by the erbium ions. The ions are excited to a higher energy level or state. See Figure 4.6(a). The higher energy state is unstable and when the incoming signal photons arrive at the ions, they stimulate the ions to fall back to the ground state, emitting energy. This emitted energy is in the form of new photons that have the same wavelength and the same phase as those of the incoming signal. Hence, we have amplification.

Erbium ions emit light in the 1.53- to 1.56-micrometer wavelengths. This falls around the wavelength where silica fiber has the least amount of attenuation (or signal loss). These amplifiers have a gain that is greater than 30 dBs. Remember that every 3 dBs of gain represents a doubling of gain. Hence, 30 dBs of gain represents the signal strength doubled ten times. This is very substantial. The noise generated by such amplifiers is also very low, providing additional benefits.

Because of the many advantages of erbium-doped all-fiber amplifiers, WDM (Wave-Division Multiplexing) as covered in Chapter 3 becomes feasible. Other advances in optical technology include optical filters, optical switches, and routers.

4.4.5 Undersea Cabling

Today fiber is being laid out in the ocean continuously. It may cost around half a billion dollars to lay a trans-Atlantic cable. But before it is installed, all its capacity gets sold out. In two years, a company will recuperate all of its cost and thereafter, the profits are very high.

In such undersea plants, optical amplifiers are installed and not regenerators. Typically, they are 60 to 120 km apart. Regenerators recreate the signals as if they were coming from the original transmitter, while optical amplifiers simply amplify the signals including the noise and interference they carry with them. Careful design of an undersea plant is necessary so that transmitted signals can be interpreted at the other end of the ocean.

Regenerators are more expensive, more complex, more prone to failure, and are frequency-dependent. Optical amplifiers or erbium-doped optical amplifiers are sturdier. If more wavelengths need to be sent through an undersea plant using WDM, optical amplifiers don't have to be replaced as regenerators do. Optical amplifiers are not frequency-sensitive. They repeat whatever frequencies are provided at the input. Replacing an undersea amplifier or regenerator is an expensive task. The cable has to be brought out from the ocean floor on board a ship where it is replaced. Accurate maps and locating methods help maintenance crews to get hold of the fiber cable. Another interesting point about undersea cabling is that there is a power source on both ends of the ocean, feeding power to the optical amplifiers. Electric power running next to the optical signals in the fiber does not cause interference. This is one of the advantages of fiber.

4.4.6 Lowering the Cost

Traditionally, SC and ST connectors are used to terminate fiber cable. The older ST connectors are typically spliced, glued, and polished manually in the field which increases their cost. They have a bayonet locking system which is twisted in place when connecting. One such connector is needed for the transmit fiber and one for the receive fiber. Think of the ST connector which you must "Stick and Twist." The newer SC connector, or the "Stick and Click" connector, is shown in Figure 4.7(a). It has a push-pull locking system which allows it to be attached and used in pairs. Currently, SC connectors can be installed using a crimp lock mechanism, which reduces the installation time to 2 to 4 minutes. However, both of these connectors are twice as large as the familiar RJ-45 and are awkward to install.

About one-third of the fiber cabling cost for a building is dependent on the design of its connectors. In light of that, vendors have come up with fiber connectors which are twice as small as the ST and the SC connectors. They are as small as the RJ-45 connectors and fit into an RJ-45 wall plate. They provide the same click sound when inserted, assuring that the connection is secure. They don't need to be glued with epoxy or polished, but are simply snapped in place.

At the present time, there is no standard that is recognized by the TIA. However, one of these jacks, called the MT-RJ connector, is shown in Figure 4.7(b). The advantages of using such a fiber cabling system are many. LAN equipment, such as hubs, switches, and routers, which must have connectors, will become more cost

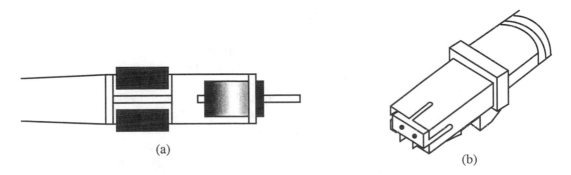

(a)

(b)

Figure 4.7 (a) The SC fiber connector. (b) The MT-RJ fiber connector.

effective as more fiber ports are installed in them. Because fiber can be installed for longer distances, fewer distribution frames are needed in a building. (Distribution frames will be covered at the end of this chapter.) These factors can bring the total cost of installing fiber below that of the installation of the newer variations of twisted pair cabling. This is especially true for larger installations. After reconsidering the advantages of fiber over twisted pairs of copper, one wonders how practical it will be to install even Cat-5 any more.

4.5 SHORT-HAUL SOLUTIONS

4.5.1 Microwave Radios

Laying of fiber over long distances is usually an expensive project. It requires obtaining rights of access where many times it is almost impossible to get them. Even after the fiber is finally laid, if some backhoe operator gets too excited, the cable can be cut, losing large amounts of communications. If a catalog sales outfit loses its incoming calls for too long, it can soon go into bankruptcy.

Instead, it is much easier to set up two towers and have a pair of microwave systems provide the needed communications link. These systems operate from 2 GHz to 23 GHz and provide a beam width between 1 to 5 degrees. They provide a line-of-sight solution that can span a distance of 60 miles. This limitation is determined by the heights of the towers and the curvature of the earth. Digital radios can provide a data rate of up to 44 Mbps.

These systems can be set up and made operational in a day. Their installation cost is much less than that for installing copper or fiber for the same distances. They have an expected lifetime of 20 years. Furthermore, one can initially buy a low-cost system and then increase its capacity as usage grows.

Many applications use microwave systems for backup. For instance, a site can use fiber going to one CO and have a standby microwave connected to an alternate CO, eliminating possible points of failures. Many times, these systems are also used to bypass the LEC (and its charges) to gain direct access to a POP.

The main disadvantage of microwave is obtaining an FCC license for its operation; although, in emergencies, temporary licenses can be obtained. Moreover, if a high-rise building is built obstructing the transmission path, alternate routes have to be investigated.

4.5.2 Infrared

Lasers and infrared beams are also used on a limited basis to obtain short-haul links. Infrared is a light signal, while microwave is a radio signal. Both, actually are electromagnetic waves that can be located on an electromagnetic spectrum. See Figure 4.8. Although weather conditions such as fog and rain attenuate (or reduce the strength of) microwave signals, they attenuate infrared signals even more. Infrared systems are usually limited to a range of only about a mile.

Infrared systems can also reach speeds of 44 Mbps and are as inexpensive and easy to install as microwave systems are. Their beam width is even narrower than that

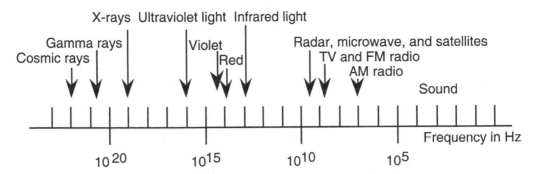

Figure 4.8 The electromagnetic spectrum. Visible light exists at around 10^{14} Hz. www.fcc.gov/oet/spectrum provides a complete table.

of microwaves. They can also be used to connect LAN stations in house. One of the biggest costs of setting up a LAN is its installation. LAN stations are difficult to move around once they are installed. Using infrared or other wireless means provide LANs with this flexibility. As with microwave, a line of sight is necessary, but an important advantage of infrared is that there is no licensing fee required.

4.6 SATELLITES

4.6.1 An Overview

While one-hop short-haul systems allow bypassing of the local telephone carrier, satellites allow one to bypass the entire PSTN. These "birds" are placed 22,300 miles above the equator so that they rotate at the same rate as the earth does (once a day). This is called a *geosynchronous* orbit. Satellites carry anywhere from 10 to 46 transponders. These transponders are microwave repeaters which receive uplink signals at one frequency, amplify them, and retransmit them at a different frequency. (LEOS or Low-Earth Orbit Satellites are relatively new.)

The area of the earth where the transmitted signal can be received is called the *footprint*. The delay for signals that take this round trip journey in space is about 300 milliseconds, which is substantially more than terrestrial transmission delays and therefore limits their usefulness for remote data entry.

Satellites are broadcast systems, where any station in the footprint of the downlink signal can receive the transmission at the same time as other receivers. For instance, a newspaper that is printed at various locations in America can get the transmission in less time than if the transmission were to occur over point-to-point links. Yet, the advantage of broadcasting also presents a problem of privacy. In order to protect privacy, the signal can be encrypted.

Table 4.1 shows three bands of frequencies where satellites can operate. The C band, referred to also as the 6/4 GHz band, is one of the oldest and the one most widely in use. Its capacity is being exhausted and the Ku band is now becoming widely used. The signals in the C band are weak and require larger earth stations compared to those

Table 4.1 Satellite Bands				
Band Names	Other Names	Uplink Frequencies	Downlink Frequencies	Available Bandwidths
C	6/4	5.925–6.425 GHz	3.700–4.200 GHz	500 MHz
Ku	14/12	14.00–14.50 GHz	11.70–12.20 GHz	500 MHz
Ka	30/20	27.50–30.00 GHz	17.70–20.20 GHz	2500 MHz

that use the Ku band. They are more susceptible to interference from microwave radios than the Ku band frequencies. However, the Ku band is more susceptible to interference from rain and other weather conditions than the C band is.

When satellites were first being deployed, they used a method called FDMA (Frequency Division Multiple Access) to divide up the satellite resources among the users. Currently, TDMA (Time Division Multiple Access) is more common. Figure 4.9 shows how three stations can use the same satellite simultaneously using either of these two methods.

With FDMA, all stations can transmit simultaneously but each one is allocated only a portion of the available bandwidth. With TDMA each station takes turns transmitting, but when its turn comes up it can use the entire bandwidth.

4.6.2 VSATs

Although geosynchronous satellites were launched in the late 1960s, they were cost effective only for large businesses. It was not until 1984, when the VSATs (Very Small Aperture Terminals) were first introduced, that satellites became more commonly used. These satellite systems are named after the small antenna dishes they use, which at one time were between 1.2 and 2.4 meters. Currently, their size is down to 18 inches. Although VSATs can operate in the C-band region, they are mostly used in the Ku-band region.

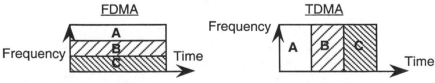

Figure 4.9 In FDMA, stations divide up the frequencies and transmit simultaneously. In TDMA, they divide up the time and wait their turns.

Transmission Systems

These systems are typically used for low-speed applications such as credit card authorization, inventory control, and production monitoring. So some of the biggest users of these systems are the automotive, retail, and financial industries. Until the end of the 1980s VSATs were deployed as a star network as depicted in Figure 4.10. Currently, they can be also be deployed in a mesh configuration.

In the star configuration one hub with a large antenna allows for the use of smaller antennas in many remote locations. Shell Oil uses more than 5,000 remote sites in its network. The large antenna at the hub is big enough to send strong signals which the smaller VSAT dishes can pick up. Also, the large hub is sensitive enough to pick up the weak signals sent by the VSATs. The channel from the hub to the remote site is called the *outbound channel* and the channel arriving at the hub is called the *inbound channel*. 20 Mbps for outbound channels and 1.7 Mbps for inbound channels are possible.

This arrangement, however, requires that all traffic use the central hub. So if two remote sites need to communicate with each other, the transmission must be relayed via the hub. Furthermore, since the cost of a hub can be high, it is commonly leased from a satellite service provider where it is shared between many users.

VSATs do provide several advantages. They are easily and quickly deployed in remote areas. Because of the easing of telecom regulations worldwide, VSATs face fewer obstacles in their installations. The VSAT service provider is a single point of contact when the network needs to be maintained, diagnosed for problems, or modified. This is also true for VSAT networks which span several countries. When crossing country borders and interfacing with different terrestrial networks, conflicts and delays

VSATs
Advantages:
 1. One service provider
 2. Smaller antennas
 3. Flexibility in management
 4. Dynamic bandwidth allocation
 5. Quick installation
 6. Asymmetric operation
    for Internet applications
 7. No dependence on terrestrial
    network infrastructure
Disadvantages:
 1. Hub: a single point of failure

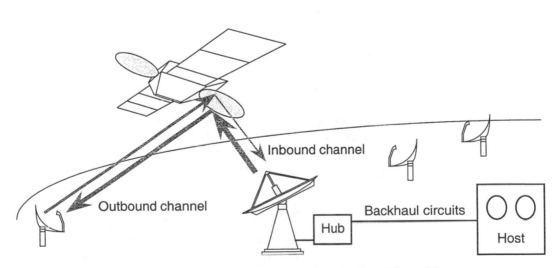

Figure 4.10 A star-configured VSAT network. The widths of the arrows indicate the relative strengths of the transmitted signals.

in setting up a new circuit can be minimized. An ISDN line in Europe may require 3 months of waiting before a carrier installs it. Contrast that to a day to have one technician to set up a VSAT site. A remote location, even in a country with no good terrestrial network to connect with, causes no problem in getting a site up and running. The smaller antennas now require only one technician instead of two, add less stress to roof structures, and are aesthetically less of an eyesore.

The cost is not primarily based on the distances between the stations, unlike with terrestrial transmission methods, but is based on the number of VSAT stations. Furthermore, if necessary, the stations can be easily moved to different locations, increasing the flexibility of the network map. They are also reliable, providing availability that is better than 99.5 percent. Their error rates are in the order of 10^{-7} compared to 10^{-5} for copper lines. The asymmetrical nature of VSAT communication makes it a good candidate for running Internet-based applications. Asymmetric means that the inbound and outbound channel speeds are different. This is typical of a web server transmitting a lot of data, as from a hub to a browser, while the browser has less data to send to the server. Finally, bandwidth can be added dynamically to a channel overnight without having to add more hardware.

4.6.3 Hubless VSATs

By increasing the size of the antennas to about 5 meters, transmissions can travel between the VSATs directly, without requiring the "double hop" via the hub. This places less demand on the satellite, and since it now requires no hub, this configuration is called a hubless or a mesh-configured network. With the elimination of the hub, a common point of failure, the network inherently becomes more reliable. With larger-sized VSATs, it is possible to get higher speeds.

This makes the network suitable to carry two-way video and LAN traffic. The network can be configured in real-time, allowing one to adjust bandwidths between sites or even add and delete sites as needed. This can be done without losing any data. However, unlike star-based networks which can accommodate hundreds of VSATs, these are more practical when used with less than 100 stations, partly because the bigger VSAT dishes are more expensive than those used with the star configurations.

4.7 PREMISES DISTRIBUTION

In this section we will see how transmission media is distributed in buildings. Building wiring planning, installation, maintenance, and documentation is an important segment of intrafacility networks. If all these elements are properly managed, the task of network specialists becomes easier and the wiring can provide good service for many years.

4.7.1 The Need for Distribution Frames

Getting a transmission media, whether twisted pair or fiber, from the telephone of a user's office to the PBX takes some planning. We cannot run a single Cat-5 cable from the telephone to the pin connections of the back of the PBX directly. What if we

Transmission Systems

want to change the phone? If the cabling is directly attached to the phone, we have to unsolder it and then solder it on a new phone. In order to have flexibility in the future, we run the cabling to a wallplate in the office: then changing over to a new phone is a snap. Similarly, we don't want to have to unsolder and then resolder all the connections coming to the pins of a PBX when we replace the PBX. Instead, we use what is called a *distribution frame* to connect with the PBX on one side and connect the cables coming from the offices and other locations from the building to the other side. Then using jumper cables at the distribution frame the two ends can be connected.

Figure 4.11 shows a telephone connected to the PBX using an RJ-45 jack and a distribution frame. All the lines coming from the PBX are connected to a group of punch-down blocks at the distribution frame. Similarly, the pairs from the users are terminated on another group of punch-down blocks. Then the pins from each set of these blocks are cross-connected with jumpers. Hence, distribution frames are also called *cross-connect systems*.

If a user, who has moved to another office, wants to keep his phone number the same, one way to accomplish that is to rewire the jumper so as to have the same PBX terminal number appear at a different jack in the building. Rewiring jumpers on a distribution frame is much easier and neater than working on the back panel of the PBX, which no one ever does. Troubleshooting a wire pair is also manageable using a distribution frame. Because of the flexibility and the ease of management provided by distribution frames, large buildings generally have several smaller distribution frames located in their various parts. The central distribution frame is called an MDF (Main Distribution Frame) and the smaller ones are called IDFs (Intermediate Distri-

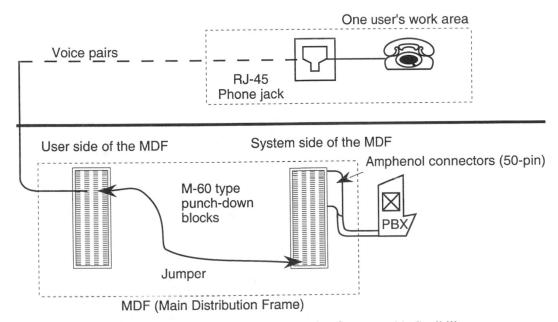

Figure 4.11 The wall jack and the distribution frame provide flexibility.

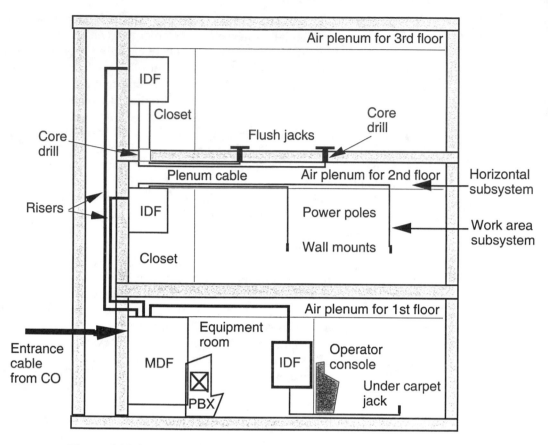

Figure 4.12 An example of the components of a premises distribution system. (Adapted from Robert Brunson.)

bution Frames). This provides a systematic and a hierarchical method of wiring a building. Figure 4.12 shows such a distribution system.

4.7.2 Five Areas of Building Cabling

Figure 4.12 shows the parts of a premises distribution. They are the work-area cabling, horizontal cabling, backbone cabling, the telecommunications closets, and the equipment room. The horizontal cabling runs from the work areas to the IDFs. The backbone cabling, which consists more and more of fiber, runs from the IDFs to the MDFs and also includes the cable entrance facilities from the COs. Cables from the IDFs to the MDF are also called riser cables because they are usually installed vertically. Care should be taken when planning the horizontal wiring, because not only is there more of it, but also rewiring it disrupts the workers in the offices.

Distribution of data cabling is done similarly. Most work areas are wired for both voice and data jacks. Cat-5 cabling is suited to carry data and voice, so the same wiring can be used for both. This makes installation simpler and cheaper, but the proper documentation and labeling should be done to distinguish them from each other.

4.7.3 DACS

Because most workers do not document what they have done when adding and removing jumpers on distribution frames, DACS (Digital Access Cross-connect Systems) can be used in place of distribution frames. If all the IDFs and the MDF are replaced by digital cross-connect switches, then all changes can be made from one management console which controls them. This can be done without having to send technicians to the various parts of the building where the IDFs are located. Moves, adds, and deletes can be done by one console operator without the use of jumpers. The connections are made electronically within the cross-connect systems. No need to worry if the jumper connections were done properly or not and whether they were electrically sound. If the person doing all the changes to the distribution frames leaves the company or gets sick, there is no need to rely on poorly kept documentation or one person's memory. The management console keeps accurate documentation and so there is less chance of errors. There is less chance of disconnecting the wrong person's phone when making changes in the digital cross-connect systems.

EXERCISES

Section 4.2:

1. Which of the following kinds of twisted pair wires is best suited to reduce external interference?
   a. STP
   b. Category 3
   c. Category 4
   d. Category 5
2. Doing which of the following will not reduce the reliability of twisted pair cabling?
   a. decreasing the AWG
   b. adding more adjacent pairs to the cable
   c. adding more twists per foot
   d. increasing the distance of the cabling
3. If the power placed in the cabling system is not being transferred but is being reflected back, what may be the cause of this problem?
4. What are the specifications for Category 3, Category 4, and Category 5 cabling?
5. Discuss some reasons why Category 5 UTP is a good choice for cabling.

Section 4.3:

6. Which of the following is not a characteristic of broadband coax?
   a. used with CATV
   b. transmits analog signals
   c. used with Ethernet LANs
   d. amplifiers and splitters are used with this coax.
7. What are some reasons why baseband coax has dominated broadband coax in the LAN arena?
8. Microwaves can be transferred from microwave transmitters to antennas using what kind of transmission media?

Section 4.4:

9. Which section of a fiber is nested inside all the others?
   a. core
   b. polyurethane coverings
   c. cladding
   d. kevlar

10. Which of the following is not an advantage of fiber?
    a. immune to noise   b. higher bandwidth
    c. easy to work with   d. can be used for long distances
11. Which types of rays stay within the fiber and which ones escape?
12. Name the three major types of fiber and discuss how they differ from each other.
13. Explain how erbium-doped fiber amplifiers work and their advantages.
14. Name some fiber connectors and describe how they are used and their characteristics.

Section 4.5:
15. Why is infrared more desirable than microwave transmission?
    a. no FCC approval is needed   b. it can be used for longer distances
    c. no concern for cable cuts   d. it is less effected by rain
16. Which of the following is not an advantage of microwave transmission over fiber?
    a. no rights of access are needed b. it can be installed in less time
    c. no concern for cable cuts   d. it provides a higher bandwidth
17. Which short-haul solution provides less attenuation due to weather conditions?

Section 4.6:
18. Which type of access method shares the available bandwidth among the various users in a satellite system?
    a. CDMA   b. DAMA
    c. FDMA   d. TDMA
19. Which of the following is an advantage of VSAT systems over fiber?
    a. it is quickly installed   b. higher bit rates
    c. it is less prone to error   d. better management capabilities
20. Transmission in which satellite band provides less interference from weather conditions and more interference from microwave signals?
21. When are star-based VSATs a better choice than mesh-based VSATS?
22. What type of orbit were older satellites placed in?

Section 4.7:
23. What is the advantage of distribution frames?
    a. less noise   b. it is easy to make changes
    c. more bandwidth   d. no documentation is needed
24. Which of the following is not a term for a distribution frame?
    a. IDF   b. MDF
    c. RDF   d. cross-connect system
25. What are some advantages of a digital access cross-connect system.
26. Discuss the five areas of a premises distribution system and explain their purpose.

Chapter 5

Business Network Services

In this chapter we will take a "quick tour" of the various telecommunications services that are available to business users. In the next chapter we will study the services available for the residential users. In the later parts of the text, entire chapters are devoted to some of these services and the technologies that support them. When studying the nuts and the bolts, or in our case, the bits and the formats of a technology, it becomes easy to lose focus on its purpose. We will use this chapter to find the purpose and features of each service and leave the details of how they are accomplished for the later chapters.

5.1 TYPES OF SERVICE

5.1.1 Switched Access

The most basic kind of network service with which we are all familiar from childhood is called POTS (Plain Old Telephone Service). Using a pair of twisted copper wires, a residential phone is connected to a CO from where a residential customer can dial out in the PSTN (Public Switched Telephone Network) or around the world. A POTS line coming into our home is an example of a *switched line*. This line, although dedicated from the CO to our homes, provides us with switched access into the telephone network.

Switched access provides us with connectivity to many points in the PSTN. We are not restricted to ringing only a single phone, but using a myriad of switches, such as the COs, POPs, MTSOs, etc., we can connect to anyone else who is connected to the PSTN. A set of switches allows us to make that connection. Hence, a POTS line provides us with switched access.

For such a line, we are generally charged for the duration and the distance of the call. After the call is disconnected, the same trunks and switch capacity can be reused for other calls. With switched access, the telecommunications facilities are *shared* among all the users. Hence, a dial-up line provides the user with *shared access*, providing better pricing for the user.

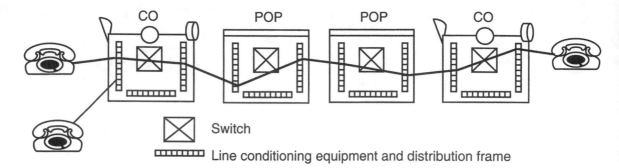

Switch

Line conditioning equipment and distribution frame

Figure 5.1 A switched access connection makes use of many switches and trunks only for the duration of the call.

In Figure 5.1, a connection is made between two end users or telephones. The switch capacities and the trunks are reserved for this call as long as the connection is up. The COs and POPs are connected with each other by the use of trunks. These trunks are terminated at the distribution frames from where they are connected to the switches.

If there is blockage somewhere along the path when making a call, the user may need to try again at a later time. But today alternate routes in the PSTN make it less likely for calls to get blocked. Accessing switches using analog lines degrades the quality of the connection and data speeds are normally restricted to low speeds. Furthermore, security becomes a concern with switched access because the facilities are shared among other users in the public telephone network. However, this problem can be overcome by having the called location call back to the caller to verify its address (or phone number), but then again, that takes more time and adds to the cost of the call.

5.1.2 Dedicated Access

In Figure 5.2, workers from the same company who work in two different cities need to call each other constantly throughout a business day. If the PBXs used switched access and the PSTN every time someone needed to make a call to the other city, the charges would add up substantially. When there is a large amount of traffic between two fixed end points as suggested in the figure, it becomes more cost effective to have a *private line* installed permanently between those two end points. Then only a fixed monthly charge has to be paid to the telecommunications carriers and no matter how much the private line is used, the charges stay fixed, unlike switched access where the charges are usage based. Other names for private lines are *tie lines* and *dedicated lines*, which provide dedicated access.

Notice in Figure 5.2 that the trunks from the PBXs are terminated at the distribution frames in the COs. To cross-connect these trunks to the trunks which are going to the POPs, physical jumpers must be installed to connect the proper pins between the two distribution frames. Technicians are needed in each CO and POP to install the jumpers correctly before the private line becomes available to the business

Business Network Services

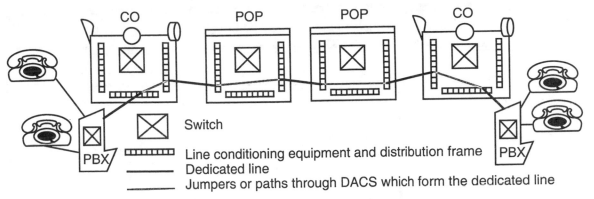

Switch

Line conditioning equipment and distribution frame

Dedicated line

Jumpers or paths through DACS which form the dedicated line

Figure 5.2 A dedicated line between two PBXs in different locations provides a permanent, non-switched connection between them.

customer. Actually, DACS (Digital Access Cross-connect Systems), as covered in Chapter 4, are used more today than physical jumper wires for interconnecting the distribution frames. In any case, installing a private line takes some time, say maybe a month, depending on through how many points it must be connected. This process is called *provisioning a tie line*.

If a private line is heavily used, that justifies its presence. If the line is not being used much, then it may be better to remove the private line and use switched access instead. Typically, with private lines, switched access lines are also used in case the private line is busy or has gone down. Careful traffic engineering studies have to be made on a regular basis to determine whether to add more private lines or to remove them.

Private lines are more secure than switched access lines. They can be fine-tuned using the line conditioning equipment at the distribution frames, which gives private lines more reliability for data transfers and higher bit rates than switched access lines. Table 5.1 summarizes the differences between these two types of accesses.

5.1.3 Private Networks

A collection of private lines connecting the various sites of an organization is called a *private line network*. A private network, or WAN, can connect PBXs together as shown in Figure 5.3. All the COs, POPs, and other intermediate points are shown simply as one PSTN cloud. To provide access to customers and points that are not in the private network, switched access lines are also needed from the PBXs to the PSTN. The switched access also provides alternate routes for the private line network traffic, that is, the traffic between the various PBXs.

This way, intracompany traffic mostly uses the private network, while traffic requiring connections to other locations uses the PSTN. Locations belonging to the organization of the private network, such as a traveling salesperson or a small remote office, can be connected to the private network using the PSTN. If LANs need to be interconnected over such a WAN, then routers may be used instead of PBXs.

	Switched Access	Dedicated Access
	Table 5.1 Comparison of Switched and Dedicated Accesses	
Other terms	Dial-up line Shared access	Leased, private, or tie lines
Examples	POTS , Sw64, ISDN	T1
Connection available	To many points	To one location
Billing	Usage based for call duration	Flat fee on a 24-hour basis
Security	Poor	Good
Quality of connection	Not that good	Good
Amount of bandwidth	Low	High, but costly as it increases
Redundant paths	Yes	Must be preplanned
Acessibility	A few seconds after dialing	Immediate, once installed
Method of connection	Signaling	Manually done on DACS
Time needed to connect	2–4 seconds	About 30 days for provisioning
Duration of connection	Typically 2–4 minutes	Months or years
Time needed to disconnect	1 second or so	A few days to order disconnection
Connecting to a new site	Matter of dialing, but dependent on network availability	Must wait for installation, but circuit is reserved for customer

5.1.4 Virtual Private Network

Having some locations of a private network use switched access and others use dedicated access lines makes the management of such a network complex. One must constantly monitor the traffic to decide how the network should be reconfigured to save

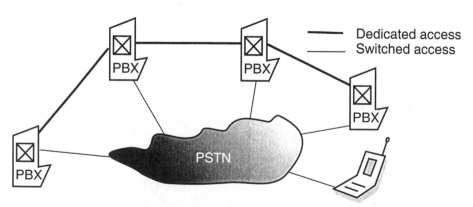

Figure 5.3 In this private network, many PBXs are interconnected using private lines. However, they can also connect to any point in the PSTN by using switched access lines.

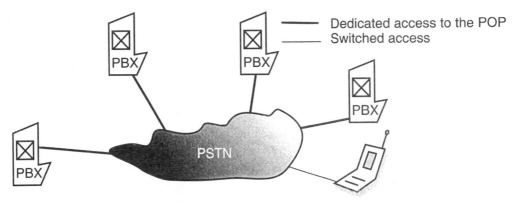

Figure 5.4 Since the PSTN cloud must be used for switched access anyway, why not use the PSTN to also carry private network traffic! Using a public network to create a private network is called a virtual private network.

costs. An alternate method of creating a private network is to have an IXC (like AT&T or Sprint) handle all the traffic, whether it is to a point on the private network (like a PBX) or a point on the public network (or the PSTN). Such private networks, which are configured using public network facilities, are called *virtual private networks* (VPNs) or virtual networks, for short. See Figure 5.4.

Instead of installing private lines between the PBXs, private lines are only installed from the PBXs to the switches of their respective POPs. Once the private traffic reaches the carrier's POP, then the traffic is routed using the carrier's public switches. Think of this as a star topology where the carrier's network is the one point or hub where all of the PBXs are connected. No traffic needs to go through the PBXs as with private tie-line networks. All the traffic is switched through the VPN (Virtual Private Network). Adding a new PBX to such a toplogy is simple. The PBXs don't need new physical ports added. No new long-distance tie lines have to be installed from the new PBX to the existing ones; only one short-distance access line has to be installed from the new PBX to the carrier's switch.

How does the carrier or the IXC figure out the configuration of the virtual network? The various points and databases belonging to the carrier's SS7 (Signaling System 7) network determine the configuration of the virtual network. SS7 also keeps track of the billing and how calls are handled. Managing such a network now becomes the problem of the carrier and not the customer or the organization using it. Plus, the customer is charged only for the carrier resources that are used. With a private network, extra bandwidth may be allocated to provide for the few times when the usage may increase. For most other times, however, this ample provisioning becomes a waste.

The Internet can also be used in this way. When an organization uses the Internet to transfer traffic between different sites, it is also called a VPN. Here again, a public network (this time the Internet instead of the PSTN) is used to create a private network. A VPN using the public Internet has more security concerns than the VPN we have just described. This is because traffic through the Internet is routed through many hands and organizations. There is no one carrier responsible for handling all the traffic like there is when an IXC's portion of the PSTN is used to create a VPN. With Internet VPN, each organization is responsible for monitoring the integrity and the security of its own VPN, but with voice-VPN that is not the case as much. An IXC has better control of the traffic which flows over the VPN it manages. The IXC owns the POPs and the SS7 network components, including its databases. But on the other hand, Internet VPNs are much less costly, which enables even small companies to install them. Internet VPNs is the topic of Chapter 27.

5.2 TRUNK TYPES

We have seen how PBXs are connected to each other and to POPs and COs using private lines. We have also mentioned that a PBX usually needs switched access lines to connect to the PSTN. In this section we will outline the specific types of connections that are usually available to PBXs.

The part of the distribution system where the customer's wiring and the telco's wiring interface is called the *demarcation* point or, simply, the demarc.

We have already discussed tie trunks, private lines, dedicated lines, and leased lines. They are all one and the same thing. A tie trunk is shown in Figure 5.5. Now let us look at some of the other types of connections.

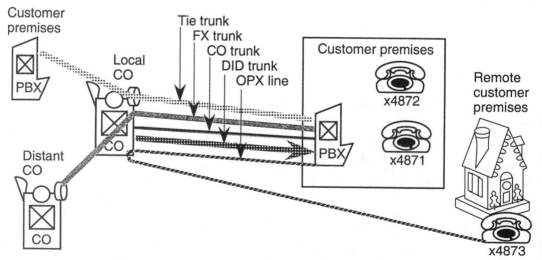

Figure 5.5 The various types of trunks used with a PBX.

Business Network Services

5.2.1 CO Trunks

Not every telephone connected to a PBX may simultaneously need to communicate with an outside line. Instead of having separate outside lines for each telephone, most installations have a much smaller number of trunks going to the local CO. By having the phones share these trunks, it cuts down on the cost while still providing access to the PSTN for every telephone.

A CO (Central Office) trunk, shown in Figure 5.5, is a popular trunk used between a CO and a PBX. It provides a PBX with switched access to the PSTN. A person in the public network can dial into the PBX over a CO trunk. Similarly, a private system phone can use the CO trunk to dial out. Hence it is a two-way trunk.

5.2.2 DID Trunks

A DID (Direct Inward Dialing) trunk is a one-way trunk used only to call into a private system. While a call coming into the PBX over a CO trunk generally requires an operator to transfer the call to the appropriate station, a DID trunk, working with the PBX, sends the incoming call to the appropriate station directly.

The customer is assigned a telephone number which may or may not be listed in the public telephone directory. This number does not require extra digits for an extension. When a person in the public network dials a DID number, the CO signals the PBX that a call is coming over a particular DID trunk. When the PBX is ready, the CO sends the last 4 or so digits so that the PBX can complete the connection. At another time, the same trunk can be used to connect a different PBX phone.

5.2.3 FX Trunks

Similar to the CO trunk is the FX (Foreign eXchange) trunk. It is used when a customer premise does a lot of calling to a distant location or even a distant state. If the call crosses LATA boundaries, then of course an IXC and its POPs are involved in providing the trunk. With the FX, the customer makes local calls at the distant location for a flat monthly rate for the trunk and for any local charges which may apply. Also, if the customer has many users who call in from that distant location into the PBX, they can make the calls as if they were local calls to them. In other words, after considering the flat monthly fee, you are making a distant area appear to be local for billing purposes.

5.2.4 OPX Lines

The last type of trunk is not really a trunk but a line, because it doesn't go to a switch but to a telephone. The OPX (Off-Premise eXtension) line typically connects a PBX to a remote customer site. If the main customer site and a remote customer site are, say, divided by a highway, then the customer is not allowed to string his own telephone line over the public area. The telco is allowed to do that for the customer by offering an OPX line.

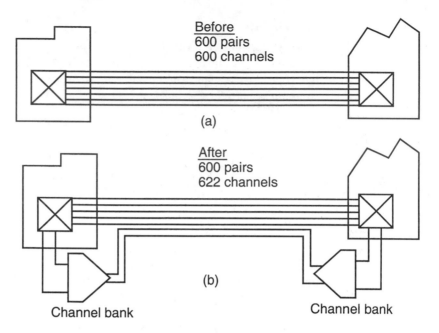

Before
600 pairs
600 channels

(a)

After
600 pairs
622 channels

(b)

Channel bank

Channel bank

Figure 5.6 (a) Before installing a T1 between two buildings in New York City, a 600-pair cable carried 600 voice channels. (b) After installing a pair of channel banks using two of the existing pairs, an additional 22 voice channels were made available.

5.3 TRANSMISSION CARRIER SERVICES

5.3.1 The T1 Carrier System

Many times digital signals are sent through copper wires over a limited distance. A common method of sending digital signals over a twisted pair of wires is called the T1 carrier system. T1 is sent over two twisted pairs of wires (or a total of four wires): one pair for transmit and the other for receive. T1 is a digital line, so a DSU is used on both sides of the tie line. The equipment on both sides of the line must be digital and if there are any loading coils placed in the transmission lines, they must be removed and usually be replaced by digital regenerators.

T1 was developed in 1963 by the Bell system. One of the first times T1 was deployed for other than a phone company's use was in 1977. Two buildings in New York City were connected with a 600-pair copper cable that had reached its maximum capacity. No additional pairs were available to accommodate new voice circuits. To lay another cable would mean digging up the streets and possibly disrupting all sorts of other cables and pipes that were buried. Instead, channel banks (or multiplexers with codecs) were installed on both sides of the cable. And using only 2 pairs of the existing cable, a total of 24 voice channels were made available, as illustrated in Figure 5.6.

This type of T1 multiplexing has been done by the phone companies since the 1960s and even before that using FDM (Frequency Division Multiplexing). However, the tariffs for T1s were deliberately overpriced, because the installation of T1s would result in savings for users and a loss of revenue for the phone companies. After divestiture, prices for T1s became realistic and there was a big rush to convert voice-grade tie lines to T1s.

A T1 carrier system can carry 24 voice channels that may be encoded using the PCM technique. (PCM was covered in Chapter 3. It uses 64 kbps to transmit one voice channel.) Some of the voice bits which are digitized are preempted to send signaling bits. So the 64 kbps used for one voice channel contain not only the voice bits but also signaling bits. Signaling is the information which sends off-hook conditions, dial tones, dialing digits, etc., and is covered in Chapter 8.

The 24 channels times the 64 kbps for PCM gives a rate of 1.536 Mbps. However, for synchronization purposes (also called framing), another 8 kbps is added to give a total rate of 1.544 Mbps. The term "T1" refers to twisted wire pairs used to send this signal. However, this signal in general is called a DS1 (Digital Signal level 1), which can be sent over any medium, including fiber. You can think of T1 as DS1 over twisted pair, although people misuse the term T1 when referring to DS1 over other media, such as microwave, satellite, coax, or fiber.

European countries and most countries outside of North America use a different system called the CEPT (Conférence Européenne des Postes et Télécommunications) system. It designates rates starting at the E1 (European-1) levels. An E1 level is derived by using PCM coding on 30 channels. However, this PCM coding doesn't include the signaling needed for the channels, as it does with T1s. E1 dedicates an entire 64 kbps channel just to carrying signaling for all the 30 channels and dedicates another 64 kbps channel for framing. Hence, together there are a total of 32 channels with a rate of 64 kbps. This provides a total rate of 2.048 Mbps. Other signal levels derived from T1s and E1s are shown in Table 5.2.

One should remember that international connections have to take in account that a T1 cannot be directly connected with a E1. Besides the differences in the number of

Table 5.2 Digital Hierarchies							
Used in Australia, Canada, Japan, and USA				Used in Europe and most other countries			
Signal Level	Carrier System	Rate in Mbps	No. of Channels	Signal Level	Carrier System	Rate in Mbps	No. of Channels
DS0	-	000.064	1	CEPT0	-	000.064	1
DS1	T1	001.544	24	CEPT1	E1	002.048	30
DS1C	T1C	003.152	48	CEPT2	E2	008.448	120
DS2	T2	006.312	96	CEPT3	E3	034.368	480
DS3	T3	044.736	672	CEPT4	E4	139.264	1920
DS4	T4	274.176	4032	CEPT5	E5	565.148	7680

channels and the methods of signaling, the method of converting voice to digital by codecs is different. As seen in Chapter 3, North America and Japan use the mu-law version of PCM and the rest of the world, pretty much, uses the A-Law.

Another commonly available service is T3 service. Again, T3 is a misnomer since DS3 never runs on twisted pair. In fact, coax can transport DS3 and that only for short distances. It runs at a 44.736-Mbps rate and can multiplex 672 voice channels. 28 DS1 signals can be multiplexed into a single DS3 using what is called an M-13 multiplexer. Those organizations who find T1 rates too high and a DS-0 channel (64 kbps) too low can install FT1s (Fractional T1s). FT1s provide rates that are incremental from DS0 up to DS1. Basically, FT1 allows the carriers to offer prices for customers who do not need the whole T1 service. Fractional T3 service is also available for those who need bandwidths of more than T1s and less than T3s.

A major problem with any of these T-carrier systems is that they stuff extra bits randomly into the bit stream to keep the transmission synchronized. This is covered in more detail in the chapter on T1s. Hence, for example, a T1's rate may not be exactly

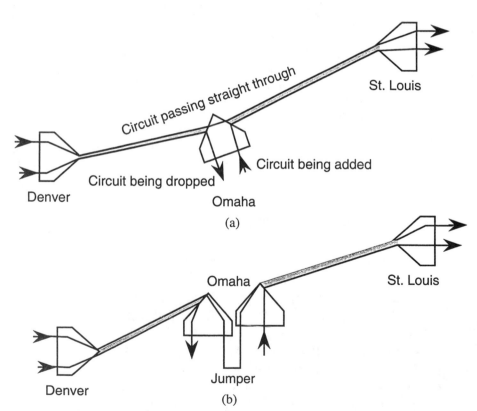

Figure 5.7 (a) Synchronous multiplexing allows circuits to be passed straight through without first being demultiplexed. (b) With asynchronous multiplexing, all circuits must be demultiplexed using two back-to-back multiplexers.

1.544 Mbps, but could vary by 75 bps, plus or minus. This ends up giving us *asynchronous multiplexing*. In asynchronous multiplexing, the equipment cannot access a single channel, drop it and use it, or add another one while other channels are transmitted straight through the equipment. In other words, while all the channels are being transmitted through a point, if one channel needs to be demultiplexed, then all of them must be demultiplexed and the channels continuing to the next point must be multiplexed again.

Let us look at an example to clarify this. In Figure 5.7(a), we see a site in Denver sending two channels using a multiplexer to Omaha. One channel's destination is Omaha and the other channel's destination is St. Louis. With synchronous multiplexing, the channel destined for St. Louis would go straight through the multiplexer in Omaha. A channel being dropped at Omaha frees up a channel on the T-carrier going to St. Louis. On that channel another circuit can be added, as shown in the figure. This configuration in Omaha is called an add-drop multiplexer or a drop-and-insert multiplexer since a circuit may be dropped from the carrier without affecting others while others can be inserted or added.

With T-carriers, however, this is not the case. See Figure 5.7(b). T-carriers use asynchronous multiplexing which requires all channels to be demultiplexed, and the channel which goes to St. Louis must then be multiplexed again using another multiplexer. This is because up to 75 bits can be added or removed per second, making it difficult for the multiplexers to pinpoint which bits belong to which channel. The configuration used in the site in Omaha is called "back-to-back multiplexers." This becomes inefficient, costly, and difficult to manage. SONET (Synchronous Optical NETwork), the next service discussed, overcomes this problem by using synchronous multiplexing.

To use a ludicrous analogy, imagine if commercial airplanes could carry small-sized "daughter airplanes" attached under their fuselages. Then an airplane going from Denver to St. Louis would not have to land in Omaha for those passengers who need to get off there. They could board the "daughter airplane" from the main aircraft and land in Omaha. They could be "dropped" there. Similarly, those passengers from Omaha who wanted to go to St. Louis would board a similar "daughter plane" to get "added" into the main aircraft. This kind of transport of passengers would be analogous to synchronous multiplexing, while the actual method that is used to transport passengers today is analogous to asynchronous multiplexing. Remember, multiplexing transmits many communication channels over the same link, which is similar to an airplane transporting many passengers on the same aircraft.

5.3.2 SONET

T1 was designed by the Bell Telephone Laboratories to transmit 24 voice channels digitally over metallic wires. T3 technology, which was an extension of T1, was then introduced to support transmission of 672 voice channels, over microwave systems. Since T1 and T3 were both based on the transmission of electrical signals, a new technology which was more appropriate for transmission of optical signals was needed. This technology needed to be designed so that the problems which were inherent with the T-carrier systems would be minimized, and thus be easier to network.

Table 5.3 SONET Interfaces				
Optical Carrier Designations	Synchronous Transport Signal	SDH Equivalent	Line Rates in Mbps	Payload Rates in Mbps
OC - 1	STS - 1	–	51.84	50.112
OC - 3	STS - 3	STM - 1	155.52	150.336
OC - 9	STS - 9	STM - 3	466.56	451.008
OC - 12	STS - 12	STM - 4	622.08	601.344
OC - 18	STS - 18	STM - 6	933.12	902.016
OC - 24	STS - 24	STM - 8	1244.16	1202.688
OC - 36	STS - 36	STM - 13	1866.24	1804.032
OC - 48	STS - 48	STM - 16	2488.32	2405.376
OC - 96	STS - 96	STM - 32	4976.64	4810.752
OC - 192	STS - 192	STM - 64	9953.28	9621.504

It was 1985 when Bellcore provided a solution for these issues in a specification called SONET (Synchronous Optical NETwork). Since then, SONET has become standardized by ANSI and as SDH (Synchronous Digital Hierarchy) by ITU-T. The term "optical" was dropped by ITU-T, because by that time SONET was being transported by other media, such as digital microwave.

SONET is a multiple-level protocol used to transport high speed signals using circuit-switched synchronous multiplexing. Using Figure 5.7(a), we have already seen one of the advantages of synchronous multiplexing. It is the only standard for high-speed fiber systems for WANs which has become the vehicle for making broadband services a reality. See Table 5.3 for the various optical carrier levels. Because it is a standard, terminal equipment made by different manufacturers are compatible. This capability is called Mid-Span Meet in SONET. SONET also provides management channels, which allows ease of management, troubleshooting, reconfiguring, and monitoring of the network.

International interconnections are much simpler than interconnecting T1s with E1s. From the table, we see that the signaling levels match, but SONET and SDH are also compatible in other respects. Most equipment comes with a simple switch which allows the user to select the termination from a SONET interface or an SDH interface.

5.3.3 ISDN

Purpose: Imagine that in our homes, all of our refrigerators, radios, toasters, etc., required different voltage sources, each had to have its own wiring, and the plugs for the appliances were all incompatible. Then we would not be able to move the appliances around the house as freely as we do today, because we would not be able to plug them into any AC outlet in the house. Although this sounds outlandish,

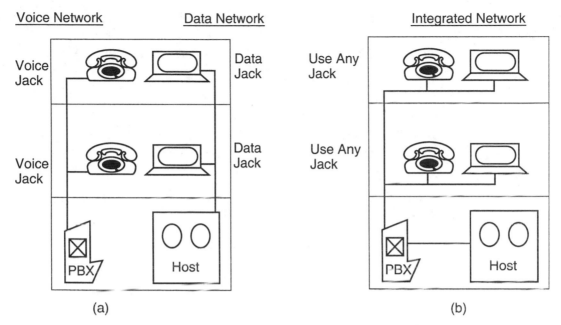

Figure 5.8 (a) Without ISDN, voice and data terminals need separate wiring. (b) With ISDN, the same wiring is shared by all terminals and all plug into the same jack.

currently we are doing just this sort of connecting with our telecommunications services. Customers are required to channel voice, switched digital data, packetized data, etc., on separate networks, because they all operate on different standards.

ISDN (Integrated Services Digital Network) brings integration of such services. One common outlet (RJ-45) can now provide integrated access to a variety of services, similar to the common AC jack. Currently, many buildings have separate networks wired for voice, video, data, security alarm systems, and so on. Each network type is independent from the others as shown in Figure 5.8(a). With ISDN, the same wire (and jack) can be used for any of these services, and as shown in Figure 5.8(b), they become integrated. In fact, each device doesn't need a separate wire as it did before, but multiple devices may share the same line. Consequently, ISDN provides flexibility, in that terminals are now portable, and provides efficiency, in that one line can be shared by multiple terminals.

ISDN is a natural evolution of the PSTN. The PSTN originally was designed to carry only voice over analog lines, but then in the 1950s, modems were introduced to carry data as well. However, due to the limitations of transmission rates and quality of modems, carriers had to create separate digital transmission networks to support data at higher speeds and with better quality. Something had to be done to eliminate incompatibilities in network services, and so ISDN was conceptualized.

Though presently the cost to convert to ISDN is rather high, over time, it may prove to be more economical than carrying voice and data over the present POTS services. Residences can continue using the same 2-wire pair for the local loop. Because the network will be entirely digital, the components will cost less and consume less power. Competition among equipment vendors will drive down the prices of ISDN devices, and because there is a limited set of standard interfaces, the production of these devices will become less costly.

However, the chances of ISDN replacing POTS for providing only one voice circuit to the home are quite small. Conceptually, the idea of ISDN was good: to make the local loop digital. No one really priced things out from the beginning. Converting to ISDN turned out to be an expense not only to the service user but also to the carriers. Yet, availability of ISDN is gradually increasing.

BRI Offering of ISDN: There are two versions or flavors of ISDN: BRI (Basic Rate Interface) and PRI (Primary Rate Interface). BRI is more suited for residential or SOHO (Small Office/Home Office) customers while PRI is more suited for business customers. An analog POTS line pair can be converted to a digital BRI pair, but a PRI service requires two digital pairs. Each of these two ISDN offerings defines a number of bearer channels called the B channels. Here is where information is sent, such as voice, video, etc. BRI and PRI also use what are called D channels where signaling is done.

Signaling is covered in more detail in Chapter 9. It provides line conditions, such as if the phone goes off-hook, or if the called party is busy, etc. Signaling is also the means by which a phone number is transferred to a switch so that it knows which phone or terminal device the person is trying to reach. On T1s, a few voice bits are discarded in order to use them for signaling. This is possible because the human ear cannot tell if a bit used for voice is missing or not. This is called *inband signaling* and it works fine if it is done only for voice channels but not for data channels. With data channels, if we lose a bit, that would be flagged as an errored frame and would require retransmission. However, with ISDN, all signaling is done in the D channels. This is called *out-of-band signaling* (the signaling is encoded outside of the voice band bits) or *clear channel signaling* (the voice band bits are clear and have no signaling bits in their place).

In the next section, when we discuss SW56 service, we will see that many times only 56 kbps is transmitted through a 64-kbps channel. That is because the equipment that was originally meant to carry voice considers certain bits to be signaling bits and not information bits. With data, we cannot afford to miss any bits, so the signaling bits (along with some other bits) are not used at all, making only the 56-kbps rate available. Hence, SW56 is used. If the carrier network is built using out-of-band signaling, then SW64 can be used instead and all available information bits can be sent over the entire 64-kbps channel.

In any case, the BRI version of ISDN provides two B channels at 64 kbps to be used for sending voice, data, etc. It also provides one D channel for signaling at 16 kbps. This yields a total rate of 144 kbps. Actually, the rate is higher (160 kbps) due to overhead bits needed for framing and other purposes. But BRI is available on a single pair of twisted wire. In other words, a POTS line can be converted easily to a BRI line: only the end equipment needs to be changed.

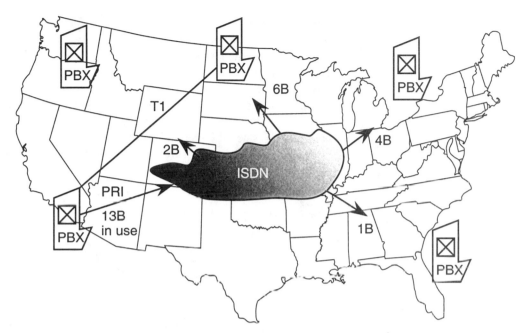

Figure 5.9 A T1 tie-line provides dedicated access to only one location, whereas ISDN access provides flexibility to configure the network dynamically using its D-channel signaling.

PRI Offering of ISDN: The PRI version of ISDN in North America and Japan provides 23B channels at 64 kbps and one D channel at 64 kbps. PRI can also be configured as a 24B access with no D channel if there is a D channel going to the carrier on one of the other PRI trunks. Including overhead, this adds up to be 1.544 Mbps, the same rate as that of a T1. In other parts of the world, PRI can be configured as 30B + D (64 kbps) or 31B. This adds up to be 2.048 Mbps, the same rate as E1. If PRI's rate matches T1's rate, then what does ISDN provide that T1 doesn't? At first glance, the answer to that question is the D channel.

Consider Figure 5.9. Here we have an organization with locations spread around the country. Between two of these locations there is a need for a lot of bandwidth, so a T1 circuit is dedicated for them. A varying amount of bandwidth, however, is needed between the other locations depending on the time of day. Hence, an ISDN connection with a total of 23 B channels is made available. As the need for new connections or an increase in bandwidth arises, the D channel modifies the network accordingly. With ISDN, one can connect to any other location with an ISDN access, whether it is part of the same company or not. In that case, it is just like a POTS service, except more flexible and digital in nature providing high-quality, reliable connections. Figure 5.9 shows that out of the 23 B channels that are available for the location shown, only 13 B channels are currently in use. Some of these channels may be used for videoconferencing, for voice calls, for transferring data, or whatever. At a later time, if it becomes necessary, an additional ten channels could be set up using the D channel. Hence, a T1 provides a point-to-point dedicated line, whereas ISDN provides switched connections. The D channel provides the signaling for the B channels and also allows them to be bonded providing multirate channels that are multiples of DS0s.

With a T1, however, the signaling for its channels can be sent inside each DS0 channel. Then with a T1 connected up to the POP, we can get switching on individual channels as shown with ISDN in Figure 5.9. On the other hand, using what is called *common channel signaling*, one DS0 channel can collectively send signaling for the other 23 channels, giving the same flexibility as ISDN but at a lower cost.

5.3.4 Digital Dial-up Bandwidth on Demand Services

SW56: Since voice is digitized for transmission, data (and video or other types of information for that matter) can also be digitized and made to go over the voice network. Whenever a voice call is made over a carrier's network, it is transmitted over a 64-kbps channel. Now the user can use that channel anyway he prefers. 64 kbps of data can be sent just as easily as 64 kbps of voice.

Furthermore, to increase the efficiency of transmission, manufacturers are selling CPE (Customer Premises Equipment) that takes several voice, data, and fax circuits and compresses them into one 64-kbps voice call. So for the price of one voice call, for example, an additional three voice circuits and one 9600-bps circuit can be obtained for free. This is done, of course, by using voice compression techniques that bring the bandwidth of one voice channel below 16 kbps. The equipment uses proprietary protocols, so only one vendor's product may be used at the end points of the network. For the price of one voice call, however, so many circuits can be compressed and switched that it provides an impressive cost savings in networking. Just hope that the vendor providing you with the proprietary gear doesn't go out of business. That is one reason why standards are better, but in this case, no standards-based solution exists.

In 1985, AT&T introduced switched 56-kbps data services and called it "Accunet Switched 56 kbps." It allowed a customer to dial a 56-kbps channel to whichever point it needed to be connected. This service was essentially used to back up dedicated lines.

Today all carriers provide this service and it is generally called SW56 (SWitched 56) service. On the other hand, since SW56 is not an international standard, this service is slowly becoming less popular than what it was at one time.

Digital Dial-up Services: A step above SW56 service is what is called digital dial-up bandwidth on demand service. It is very similar to switched digital services, except that the bandwidth on demand implies that the amount of bandwidth is adjustable as the customer's requirements change in real time. Just as one can call up anyone on an ordinary phone to have a voice conversation, digital dial-up services provide the same capabilities for digital transmissions; however, unlike a voice call where only one 4-kHz voice channel is provided between the end points, bandwidth on demand allows the user not only to set up a connection but also to specify its bandwidth. So the customer is billed according to the distance and duration as well as the bandwidth of a call.

Business Network Services

A user no longer has to fine-tune a digital tie-line with T1s or FT1s (Fractional T1s). When a T1 circuit lies idle or underutilized during the night or otherwise, the user is still paying for that line. However, with digital dial-up bandwidth on demand, a user creates a call only when there is data to transmit, and terminates it when done.

To give an example, once credit card companies used a large digital tie-line network to provide credit card authorization nationwide. It was critical that the network provide no blocking whatsoever. Therefore, the network was optimized for large-volume days such as the Monday after Thanksgiving, etc. For the few busiest days of the year, the network had the necessary capacity, but for the remainder of the year, the network was much underutilized.

After replacing the network with bandwidth on demand services, credit card companies paid only for the bandwidth that they needed. This provided no blocking of traffic even on busy days, which was a major concern, and yet the costs during other days were dramatically reduced. In conclusion, bandwidth on demand services provide maximum flexibility at minimum costs.

Videoconferencing among several locations is another popular application for such services. With a T1 network, one has to schedule a conference at a certain time. If an executive at one of the locations decides to postpone it because something else came up, then the bandwidth that was scheduled for the videoconference becomes unused. With on-demand services, the dialing for the videoconference can be done at the last minute, with no scheduling necessary. Also, the bandwidth can be selected at the time of the conference depending on what quality of video is desired.

Of course, there is a cut-off point, where changing to a tie-line network becomes more cost efficient. If the amount of traffic is consistently high, say for example over 5 hours per day, then using a T1 or an FT1 would be the better choice. One has to be current with the existing tariffs to make the proper decision between tie-lines and switched services. However, when tie-lines are converted to switched digital services over international boundaries, the savings become much more pronounced than the savings gained with domestic services.

Implementing Digital Dial-up Services: Initially, SW56 services were provided by an SW56 access line, and the two terms were used interchangeably. Now access to SW56 network services can be gained by an SW56 line, BRI, T1, or PRI. These services are provided by either the LEC or the IXC. If a T1 is used by the CPE to access the LEC, then up to 24 SW56 circuits can be set up through the carriers' networks. In this case, the customer only has to pay a fixed amount for the T1 between the CPE and the CO. However, he now has the flexibility to call up to 24 individual circuits, because he has the necessary access for that many circuits to the carriers' networks.

If a PRI is used for accessing the network, the customer has the greatest flexibility in that he can access SW56, SW64, SW384, SW1536, or multirate services. On the other extreme, SW56 access can't access SW64 or higher rate services.

Multirate services are a multiple of 64-kbps ISDN channels, such as 64 kbps, 128 kbps, 192 kbps, etc. The type of service that the customer is calling up is transmitted through the D channel of ISDN. The SW384 and SW1536 are called the H0 and the H11

ISDN circuits, respectively. The bandwidth of an H channel has to stay together within the network as one unit, and may only be subdivided at the CPE. Currently, SW56 service is the most widely available service, and with it, one can communicate between any access type, whether it be SW56, SW64, BRI, or PRI.

When bandwidth is requested to the carrier using ISDN H0, H11, or multirate channels, the network manages the allocation of bandwidth and the customer need only specify how much bandwidth is needed. This is called network-based bandwidth on-demand services. On the other hand, a customer's I-Mux (Inverse Multiplexer) can allow him to automatically dial as many circuits as are needed by the application (videoconferencing, file transfer, etc.). Here, the customer's equipment manages the allocation of bandwidth, and not the carriers' networks.

An I-Mux splits the customer's data over several individual circuits and sends it to the destination I-Mux. There the units of data arrive in different order, because of the diverse routing paths. So the remote I-Mux will adjust for delay, put these arriving units in their proper order, and present the data to the receiving application as if it were sent over one channel.

5.3.5 X.25

In Section 2.6, we discussed packet switched networks, and in the following section we contrasted their operation with the operation of datagram delivery networks. We mentioned that X.25 was a protocol used on packet switched networks and IP was a protocol used on datagram delivery networks. We also discussed at length how virtual circuits are created on X.25 networks and after the data was transferred how they are disconnected. We said that a VC (Virtual Circuit) was the collection of channel numbers and the links for the path through which the circuit was defined. We also said

Table 5.4 Comparison of PVCs and SVCs		
	PVCs (Permanent Virtual Circuits)	SVCs (Switched Virtual Circuits)
Resembles a . . .	Leased line	Phone line
Type of connectivity	Fixed, point-to-point	Varies, any-to-any
Traffic planning required?	Yes	No
Signaling required?	No	Yes
Address required?	No	Yes
Redundancy in network?	Yes	Yes
Relative flexibility	Poor	Good
Relative complexity	Low	High
Type of setup is done . . .	Manually, with a management console	On a call-by-call basis, on demand

that a PVC (Permanent Virtual Circuit) was a dedicated VC and an SVC (Switched Virtual Circuit) was created and dropped as needed. PVCs and SVCs are reviewed in Table 5.4.

X.25 was one of the first times where the concept of virtual circuits, instead of physical tie-lines, was used to create a network. Since then SS7, Frame Relay, and ATM have made improvements on the X.25 network, but they all use the concept of virtual circuits rather than dedicated circuits. The side diagram contrasts a tie-line network with an X.25 network. In a tie-line network, circuits have to be provisioned whose cost is based on distance. The longer the tie-line, the greater is the cost. Traffic engineering has to be performed on such networks on a continual basis, considering many factors such as, should more lines be ordered or less, should more capacity be planned or less, and so on.

With X.25 and other "virtual-type" networks, the cost of the circuit is simply the cost of one access line to the network "cloud." A connection to the network is distance insensitive. Since many customers can share the X.25 network, the service provider can oversubscribe the circuits. This is possible, because not all customers will be using the facilities of the X.25 network all the time. The headers in the packets will determine the destinations of the packets. These reasons make the X.25 network very inexpensive compared to a privately owned tie-line network.

Adding a new mux to . . .
a tie-line network,   an X.25 network

| M u x | M u x | M u x | M u x |
| M u x | The new mux | M u x | The new mux |

In the side figure, consider a tie-line network with three customer sites, while the fourth one is being added. For every site to have a direct connection to every other site, multiple hardware connections have to exist on the multiplexers. If a fully meshed network is not created, then traffic between two sites has to be tandemed through a third one. This loads down the intermediate site. When a new site is added, equipment has to be installed at each site to support its connections. Today, with hot-swappable equipment, however, it is not necessary to power down the equipment. In the figure, however, we see that more lines need to be provisioned with the tie-line network. With an X.25 network, adding a new site is very simple. No new ports have to be added; only the table entries have to be updated at the various sites. No physical changes have to occur at the older sites. Moving one site from one location to another and removing one site from the X.25 network are just as simple, even if the customer has a much bigger network. With a tie-line network, the complexity of any moves and changes increases as the network size increases.

Today the use of X.25 is significant in the USA and especially in developing countries. Its data rates usually max out at 64 kbps. The frame relay rates start at 64 kbps and go up to 45 Mbps, and ATM rates start at 1.5 Mbps and go up. It does error checking and correction in both the data link control layer and the network layer over every link of the virtual circuit.

5.3.6 Frame Relay

Advantages of Frame Relay over T1s: A network that is used to interconnect LANs must be able to handle very bursty traffic. This is because LAN traffic is usually sent at irregular intervals and runs at speeds from 4 Mbps to 100 Mbps. This is not suited for traditional T1 technology which was originally designed to carry voice, which is more predictable. Additionally, T1 networks are too difficult to reconfigure if certain applications require a sudden increase in bandwidth.

For instance, in Figure 5.10(a), we have three sites that are interconnected by a T1 network. The front-end processors provide communications for IBM main frame hosts, and there is also connectivity between low-speed PSNs (Packet Switched Networks).

If a router needs to be able to communicate with three other routers on the network, then we would need three connections between it and its mux. If the router is not local to the mux, the cost of these connections would increase. In any case, we would need three ports on the mux dedicated for the router.

The bandwidth allocated for each port of a mux would then be preset. If a router had a burst of traffic to fire into the network while the channels for the front ends and the PDNs were idle, it could not, since each port had its bandwidth already preallocated.

Figure 5.10(b) shows a private T1 network being converted into a private frame relay network. Here, the bandwidth can be reassigned instantaneously (or dynamically allocated) depending on which system demands it. Also, each device may communicate with any other, requiring only one port. This is because of statistical multiplexing, which is done using channel numbers on the frame relay network.

In Figure 5.10(c), we migrate to a public frame relay network. We would have to install FRADs (Frame Relay Assembler/Disassemblers), which are similar to PADs used in X.25 networks. They allow equipment that is not frame relay–compatible to be used in such networks. Now we don't have to lease the T1's. This lowers the operating costs.

Here, the added benefits are such that we don't have to pay for the dedicated T1 leased lines. We just pay for the service as we use it, as in virtual networks. And since the frame relay network is shared among many customers, the carrier can offer attractive pricing. Additionally, installing a new site with a T1 network requires that the network be redesigned, whereas with public frame relay networks, one simply needs to install a new access link. Furthermore, the prices for frame relay networks are not mileage-sensitive.

Advantages over X.25: Frame relay technology was originally developed through ITU-T's ISDN and X.25 standards. Although these standards were designed for 64-kbps circuits using SVC networks, a group of four equipment manufacturers (Cisco, DEC, NT, and StrataCom) increased the speed dial to DS-1 rates and simplified the protocol to handle only PVCs. This protocol was named LMI (Local Management Interface). Currently, frame relay is both an ANSI and an ITU-T standard.

Back in the days when X.25 was introduced, many analog lines had an error rate of 10^{-2} (1/100) or 1 error in every 100 bits that were transmitted. Then it was appropriate to check for errors at layers 2 and 3 on links between every node pair along the transmission path. It was better to detect and correct errors as soon as they occurred, rather than forward them to the next node.

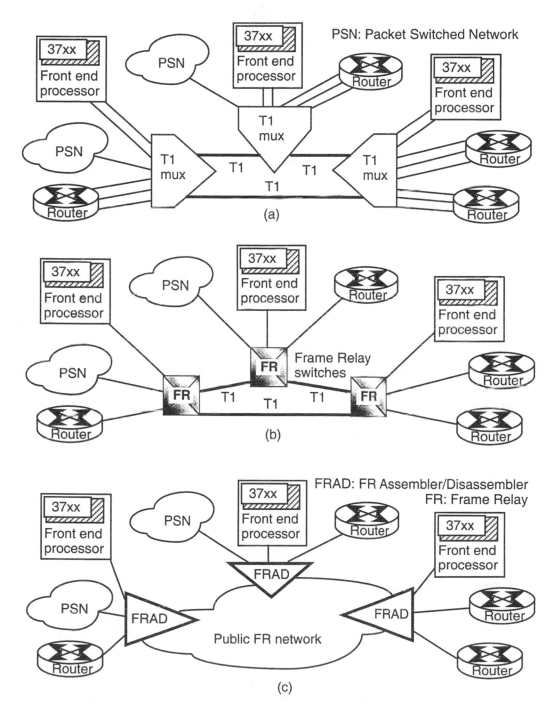

Figure 5.10 (a) A T1-based network. (b) Converting to a private FR network. (c) Converting to a public FR network.

Today, with more fiber being installed in our networks, this amount of error checking becomes an overkill, where error rates of 10^{-15} are achievable. Why check for errors every second when the possibility for one to occur is only once a week! There is no need to burden the network and make it less efficient by requiring it to check for nonexistent errors and correct them.

Frame relay, therefore, was conceived as a stripped down version of X.25, without its overhead. The network layer has been eliminated and error control is left up to the end nodes and not to this transmission protocol. Notice the similarity of frame relay with IP. In the Internet, IP doesn't do any error recovery; it leaves that up to the upper layers at the end points of the network. Frame relay also leaves error control to be done by the end points of the network. Actually, frame relay nodes do error checking. What if the destination of the frame is corrupted? The frame would be sent to the wrong destination, wasting network bandwidth. For that reason, error checking is done, but if an error has occurred, no retransmission is requested. Instead, the frame is simply dropped and discarded. It assumes that if the receiving-end user (or application) really misses that frame it will ask the transmitting application to retransmit.

The lack of error control in frame relay is what gives it its advantage—efficient and faster transmission. A frame relay switch is up to ten times as fast as a packet switch. This savings in time is multiplied by the number of switches along a path. Furthermore, a packet switch uses store-and-forward methods, which typically are configured with small frame-window sizes. This requires it not to send the next set of packets until the current ones are acknowledged. This type of bottleneck doesn't exist in frame relay, although, as we will see in a later chapter, it does introduce problems in controlling congestion.

In summary, let us list some advantages of public frame relay networks. Because only the second layer is used instead of all three layers, with even smaller headers than the second layer headers of X.25, the overhead of frame relay is very low. This makes it a fast protocol, even for transferring bursty traffic between LANs. Because of the redundant paths available in a public network, a public frame relay network is a reliable solution. It scales well. That means that more access points can easily be added or removed. It is a well established standard, making the price of the equipment low and the equipment readily available. When used with PVCs, it is best thought of as being an alternative to leased lines. However, when frame relay SVCs also become available by the carriers, frame relay solutions will increase their flexibility.

5.3.7 ATM

Why Yet Another Protocol? Let us now turn our attention to ATM (Asynchronous Transfer Mode). Originally, ATM was supposed to integrate all types of networks, whether they be LANs or WANs, whether they carry voice, data, or multimedia. Instead of having a different protocol and technology for each type of network, ATM was supposed to integrate them all. ATM has done that in the WANs, but high-speed LANs have kept ATM at bay. To see the beauty of ATM, let us first contrast it with existing technologies.

In Figure 5.11, let us suppose that we have a voice source and a data source contesting for a fixed amount of bandwidth on the transmission link. Remember that data traffic usually is bursty and comes in larger amounts than voice traffic, but can afford to wait a little while it is being delivered to its destination. This is in contrast with voice traffic which is packetized. It usually comes in smaller sizes, but cannot wait to be delivered to the listening ear.

At t = 0, or time frame 0, we have voice traffic that needs to be transmitted. This amount of traffic is labeled as V1, but at the same time, we have a burst of data coming in that is three times the amount as V1. Hence, these data units are labeled D1 through D3.

The height of these units represents the rate of transfer, say, in bits per second, and the width represents time. Hence, multiplying the rate times the time (or height times the length) represents the amount of data (bits) that has to be sent over the communication channel. This example shows voice being transmitted at t = 0, 2, and 5, while data is being transmitted at t = 0, 1, and 4. The amount of data sent at t = 4 is twice that sent by voice at t = 0, 2, or 5.

If we were using TDM (Time Division Multiplexing) technology to transmit this mix of traffic, as is done in T1 multiplexers, then each source would have to occupy its assigned time slot in the frames that are transmitted. In this example, the voice

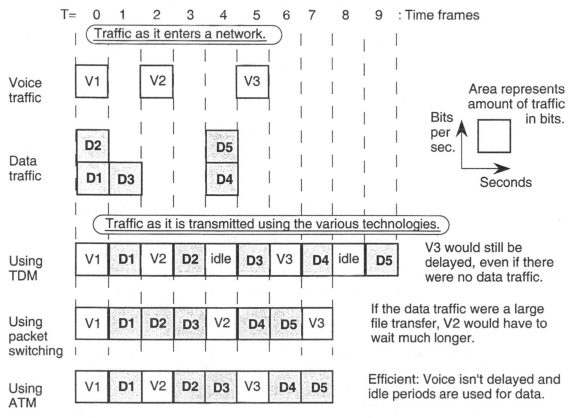

Figure 5.11 Comparing three technologies.

channel is assigned the even time slots and the data channel is assigned the odd time slots.

If we follow this example to t = 4, where we don't have voice traffic, but have data traffic, we cannot place the data traffic at that slot. That slot belongs to the voice channel and so the slot gets wasted. The receiver is synchronized to interpret all even time slots as belonging to the voice channel and the odd ones as belonging to the data channel, so we can't use a time slot for the wrong channel.

Now, when voice is being sent at t = 5, we cannot send it, because that channel belongs to data. Instead, that voice traffic has to be delayed to t = 6. For the rest of the time frames, we see that the data also has to be delayed to t = 9, even though there was bandwidth capacity at t = 8.

Here, there are two time frames wasted. If the voice channel were idle, then all five time frames for it would have been wasted. This is not only an inefficient use of bandwidth, but it delays the transmission of data, although delaying of data is not as crucial as delaying isochronous traffic.

Let us look at the advantages of packet switching over TDM. Here, instead of alternating between the two sources, we send each transmission as one unit rather than break them up into time frames. V1 is sent first, then D1 through D3 as one unit. Because of this data packet, V2 doesn't get out until t = 4. V3 is delayed two time frames for the same reason.

Packet switching technologies, such as X.25 and frame relay, make an efficient use of bandwidth. In the example, all data is transmitted 3 time frames earlier than it was with TDM. However, the voice traffic was delayed by 4 time frames (2 for V2 and 2 for V3), while with TDM, the voice was delayed by only 1 time frame. If the data transmission at t = 0 were a long file transfer, then V2 would have to wait a substantial amount of time. We can't afford to delay voice as we can data. Hence, TDM favors voice, and packet switching favors transmission of data.

With ATM, all traffic is broken into fixed, 53-octet cells; 5 for the header and 48 for information. At t = 2, although data has been waiting longer to be transmitted, this voice cell gets transmitted first. The same advantage of packet switching over TDM is achieved with ATM. It makes an efficient use of the bandwidth. They both finish transmitting before t = 8, with no wasted time frames. However, the advantage of ATM over packet switching is that the delay for voice is zero (versus 4 for packet switches). In fact, ATM proved to be even better than TDM here, because the delay for voice with TDM was one time frame. Notice that although ATM transmits data at a constant rate, it *adapts* to applications that are transmitting at varying rates.

With TDM, we know the destination of information by its time frame position. But with ATM, we need a header or label that gives the cell's destination. Hence, ATM is said to be a form of *label multiplexing*.

Study Table 5.5 to review the differences in the characteristics of voice and data transmissions. All phones produce the same type of traffic. This is not so with printers, LAN servers, web servers, mainframes, PCs, etc. Data produces traffic that comes in all shapes and sizes, so to speak. At one time, these differences required that the networks be designed for either voice or for data, but ATM unifies them into one seamless network.

Table 5.5 Differences Between Voice and Data Networks

	Voice	Data
Naturally is . . .	an analog signal	a digital signal
Rate at which information arrives	is constant	varies, bursty
Sizes of information blocks	small	small to huge
Sensitivity to delay?	yes	no, within reason
Sensitivity to bit errors?	no	yes

What is asynchronous about ATM? In Figure 5.11, the delay between D1 and D2 is one time frame, but between D2 and D3 there is no delay. The rate at which information is fed into the ATM network is not necessarily the same as the rate at which it comes out of the network. Hence it is called asynchronous. One cannot determine when the next data cell is going to arrive. Likewise, with start and stop bits used in asynchronous transmission, the receiver doesn't know when the next character, or rather, the next start bit is going to arrive.

Contrast this with TDM, which really should be thought of as STM (Synchronous Transmission Mode). There the interval between each transmission of data is known. It is fixed.

Terminology gets confusing though, when we think that STM is usually transmitted using asynchronous multiplexing and ATM is usually transmitted using synchronous multiplexing (or SONET). STM requires bit stuffing due to the input signals being timed from different sources. Each input channel is not synchronized to a common clock, while SONET requires all inputs to be synchronized to a common clock.

Other Benefits: Probably the most important benefit of ATM is that one network can serve all applications. As we have seen, isochronous traffic can be transmitted quickly and large file transfers can be made without wasting any bandwidth. But ATM goes beyond that. It can transmit channels at any rate effectively and not force the application to conform to the network's constraints.

For example, to transmit a 50-kbps channel over a T1 facility, one normally has to dedicate a full DS0 channel, wasting 14 kbps. Similarly, if one has to transmit at 10 Mbps, one has to play with inverse multiplexers and use 7 T1s and still have 0.7 Mbps of bandwidth left over. Additionally, these networks have to be provisioned beforehand.

On the other hand, ATM gives the amount of bandwidth that is required during connect time. ATM doesn't force the application to accept bandwidth in given increments. It doesn't force the application to conform to the network as previous technologies did. Instead, ATM conforms to the needs of the network applications.

Freedom to choose the amount of bandwidth is only part of the ATM advantage. It also provides the freedom to switch traffic between different end points as required, without requiring provisioning, such as with DACS switches. Additionally, the user pays only for what is used.

ATM also provides hardware-based switching. The fixed cell size enables switching to be performed by simple hardware circuitry, rather than through software. This permits switching to be performed at speeds of gigabits per second, and soon much faster. The hardware switching capability allows a smoother migration to optical switches as they become available. This almost-instantaneous switching capability allows ATM to remove the boundaries of LANs and WANs and make them appear seamless.

In summary, ATM adapts itself to the application, both in its transfer rate and the nature of its traffic. The fixed-length cells makes their processing and switching fast. Additionally, ATM is a connection-oriented protocol that provides both PVC and SVC connections.

5.4 VIRTUAL SERVICES

5.4.1 800-Type Services

In 1967, AT&T introduced 800 services which allow callers to call free to the 800 number. The owner of the 800 number pays for the incoming calls based on the volume of calls. Currently, 800 toll-free service is a high-profit business and it is often tied in with voice virtual networks. At the time of this writing, 888 and 877 are also included in this type of service.

Until 1993, when a CO received a dialed 800 number to connect, it would send the call to the proper IXC's POP by scanning the 3 digits following the 800 number. These three digits are called the NXX digits. AT&T had more NXXs allocated to them than the other carriers.

If a customer wanted to change carriers, he would have to change his 800 number as well, because the NXXs of the 800 numbers belonged to the carriers. Changing 800 numbers due to a change in carrier was something that businesses avoided, because to advertise the new number and make the public aware of the change would take time and effort. By using SS7 (Signaling System 7) networks, customers can change carriers and take their 800 number with them. This is called 800 number portability.

800 numbers allow stores to close their doors and do all their selling over the phone. More people are making purchases using these numbers. Companies have the ability to provide outstanding service by using an 800 number. Customers are more willing to buy products if they have an 800 number to call.

800 numbers also have their drawbacks. If an 800 service is out, it is difficult for a customer to detect it, especially if the activity on the 800 number is typically low anyway. Also, if someone calls a wrong 800 number, the company has to pay for that call. And what if one company advertises someone else's 800 number incorrectly? The company not at fault still has to pay for those calls and, worse yet, it loses business because of busy lines.

5.4.2 VPNs

In Section 5.1.4, we mentioned how VPNs (Virtual Private Networks) allow a business customer to use a public network to create his own private network. This allows the customer not to have to manage his network and still be able to cut costs more than if he had used private leased-line networks.

AT&T's VPN is called SDN (Software Defined Network). MCI's VPN is called Vnet and Sprint's VPN is simply called VPN. These networks are discussed later in the chapter on virtual networks.

Internet VPNs have recently really taken off and these are the subject of Chapter 27. The main issue there is security. Once the security issues are resolved, Internet VPNs will become much more acceptable. When the term VPN is used today, it is generally assumed to be an Internet VPN.

EXERCISES

Section 5.1:
1. When a physical connection between two COs or POPs is reserved for a particular customer, what kind of connection is it?
   a. dedicated
   b. switched
   c. virtual
   d. logical
2. A physical jumper can be used to tie one pin on a distribution frame to another. What can be used instead?
   a. MDF
   b. POP
   c. CO
   d. DACS
3. Which of the following is NOT a name for a dedicated line?
   a. private
   b. tie
   c. leased
   d. virtual
4. For each of the following, state whether it describes switched access or dedicated access.
   a. Connection can be made to any number of points.
   b. The cost is not usage-based.
   c. SVC, either of X.25 or of frame relay, is an example of this.
   d. You must dial the number using signaling methods.
5. In a private network, business locations are connected to each other by what kind of lines? To the PSTN, by what kind of lines?
6. Are dedicated lines connected through the PSTN? Are they connected through COs?
7. In general, define a virtual network.
8. List two types of virtual private networks and give an advantage of each over the other.

Section 5.2:
9. Which of the following trunk types connects a PBX to a distant CO?
   a. CO
   b. DID
   c. tie
   d. FX
10. Which of the following types of connections allows an outside number to dial directly through a PBX without an attendant?

a. OPX line   b. DID trunk
c. FX trunk   d. tie trunk

11. What type of connection allows a phone in a manager's home to be directly connected as an extension of the company PBX?
12. What are the pros and cons of using tie trunks over POTS lines?

Section 5.3.1 and 5.3.2:
13. How many pairs of twisted wire are needed to install a T1?
14. What is the rate of a T1 tie-line and how many voice channels does it typically multiplex?
15. How does T1 technology differ overseas?
16. Describe the operation of an ADM versus a pair of back-to-back multiplexers.
17. List some advantages of SONET over T1.

Section 5.3.3:
18. What kind of connector is used with ISDN?
    a. RJ-45   b. RJ-31
    c. RJ-11   d. DB-25
19. How many channels of each kind are used with BRI?
    a. 2–64 kbps and 1–16 kbps
    b. 1–64 kbps and 23–16 kbps
    c. 1–64 kbps and 1–16 kbps
    d. 24–64 kbps
20. Give some examples of signaling events.
21. When voice bits are preempted for signaling, what type of signaling is being used? Does ISDN use this type of signaling?
22. How do the D channels of PRI and BRI differ?
23. How does the D channel make PRI different from T1?

Section 5.3.4:
24. In a fully digital PSTN, what is the maximum bit rate that can be sent over one voice call?
25. What kind of service will suit a customer who finds the bit rate of DS0 to be too low and that of a DS1 to be too high?
26. Give an example of a network-based bandwidth-on-demand service.

Section 5.3.5:
27. For each of the following, list whether it better describes a PVC or an SVC:
    a. complex   b. signaling required
    c. can replace a lease line.   d. connection is set up manually
    e. flexible, can connect to many points

Section 5.3.6:
28. From which protocol was frame relay derived?
    a. T1   b. ATM
    c. X.25   d. Ethernet
29. Frame relay does error checking between which points?
    a. from hop to hop or over each link
    b. at each FRAD
    c. at the end points of the network
    d. frame relay doesn't do any error checking

30. List some advantages of frame relay over T1s.
31. List some advantages of frame relay over X.25.

Section 5.3.7:
32. What is the unit of transfer used in ATM?
    a. frame   b. cell
    c. packet   d. message
33. What is asynchronous about ATM?
34. What are some advantages of ATM?

Section 5.4:
35. How do carriers manage virtual networks that they market?
    a. voice switches   b. CO
    c. SS7   d. ATM
36. The ability to have your own 800 number and still be able to switch carriers is called what?
37. List the names of the VPNs marketed by AT&T, MCI Worldcom, and Sprint?

Chapter 6

Residential Network Services

Some of the services considered in this chapter are actually services targeted for businesses; but since their technologies are related to the residential offerings, they are included here.

6.1 56k MODEMS

The PSTN runs at 2400 baud. A baud is equal to one analog cycle. Modem designers have been able to encode several bits of information on each baud. Hence, if four bits are encoded on a single baud, that would give the modem a rate of 9600 bps. The theoretical limit for the speed of a modem is about 34 kbps, but then again, at one time that limit was said to be around 14.4 kbps. When a modem first connects with another one, it performs handshaking. This is the process used to check which protocol is to be used. A higher-level protocol can communicate with all the lower-level protocols.

In the side figure, different modem protocols are listed. Handshaking is the process that determines the lowest level protocol with which both ends can communicate. After handshaking is done, training is done. This is the process that determines at which bit rate the modems can operate safely over the connection, that is, with minimum error. Just because your car can go 100 mph, doesn't mean that you can get to your destination without any collisions at that speed. By the same token, during handshaking, if the modems have agreed to operate at V.34, for instance, then during training they might agree that operating at 24 kbps provides the least amount of error hits. Training between modems is performed to determine the highest speed of operation given a particular modem protocol. In this analogy then, handshaking determines which car to use and training determines at which speed to drive it.

International Modem Standards

V.32	9.6 kbps
V.32bis	14.4 kbps
V.34	28.8/33.6 kbps
V.90	56 kbps

At the time of this writing, the 56-kbps modems are popular. They overcome many problems associated with the previous generation modems, which we will refer

126

to as voice-band modems. Voice-band modems were designed to operate only in the voice band of 3.1 kHz. Although previously we have said that each voice channel occupies 4 khz of bandwidth, the more precise figure is between 300 to 3400 Hz, which is a bandwidth of 3.1 kHz. Let us first look at a voice-band modem to better appreciate how the 56k modem works. (It is easier to say "56k modem" than to say "56 kbps modem.")

In Figure 6.1, we see a home computer being connected to an ISP (Internet Service Provider). In this setup, the Internet server of the ISP must first convert the data into an analog signal so that it can be transmitted over the analog line. A modem does this task. Because of the advantages of digital signals, today all communication in the PSTN is done using digital signals. Voice signals are converted into PCM (Pulse Code Modulation) using codecs placed right into the line cards of the COs (Central Offices). Hence, the modulated data over the analog signal is converted into PCM, that is, a digital signal which is passed through the PSTN. Finally, all these signal conversions are done in reverse order at the other end.

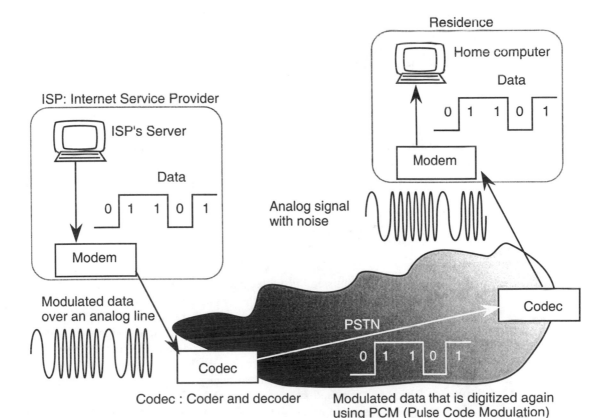

Figure 6.1 Voice-band modems require conversions between analog and digital signals in many points in the telephone network, the PSTN. This introduces analog line noise, quantizing noise, and voice-band filter limitations.

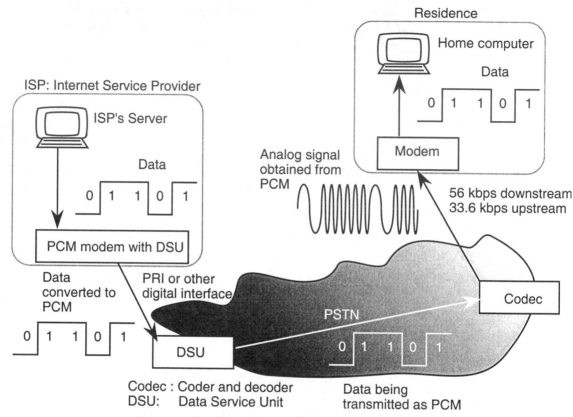

Figure 6.2 A 56-kbps modem relies on the transmitting ISP to convert the data directly into PCM. The ISP must be connnected via ISDN-PRI or some other digital interface with the telephone network. A DSU-like device provides the interface for the digital line. The receiving end, from the codec to the home computer, is the only place in the network where the signal is affected by analog line noise.

This type of transmission provides many hindrances to the maximum rate that can be obtained with the modems. First, there is noise from the transmission of analog signals over the analog lines at both ends of the transmission. Digital signals are immune to such line noise. Second, once the modulated analog signal is converted to PCM at the codec in the CO, quantizing noise is introduced. Remember that quantizing noise is caused by the differences between the original signal voltages and the transmitted bits representing the signal voltages. Last, the amount of bandwidth is limited to 3.1 kHz by the bandpass filter circuits located with the codecs. On the other hand, the 56k modems can utilize the entire 4-kHz analog bandwidth without being constrained by these filters.

When a 56k modem is used, as shown in Figure 6.2, the transmitting end, in this case an ISP, must be connected to the CO using a digital interface. Usually this would be a PRI interface of ISDN. DSUs (Data Service Units) or similar devices at each end of the line properly terminate the digital line. The ISP server uses a special modem. We call it a PCM modem. This modem doesn't convert data into analog signals, but converts the data into a digital signal as if it were converted from analog to digital at the ISP and then to PCM at the codec. These conversions are done in the same circuit card, which eliminates the analog noise of the line, the quantizing noise, and the bandpass filter of the codec. Directly from the ISP's location to the codec in the last CO, the signal is unaltered but simply transmitted. This enables the designers of 56k modems to achieve this data rate. This rate is only from the ISP or the server to the residence. From the residence up to the ISP, the rate is only 33.6 kbps. Of course, if the line cannot handle these high rates for some reason, then the rate is adjusted to lower levels automatically. Reasons why the bit rate may need to be dropped include analog and digital conversions or the PCM signal being compressed somewhere in the network.

Being able to drop the transmission rate because of poor transmission conditions in the network is a major advantage of these modems. It should also be noted that 56k modems operate as *asymmetric* devices. This means that the rate of transmission is different in each direction. Asymmetric services usually operate at a higher rate for downstream transmissions than for upstream transmissions. This is because information from the World Wide Web comes in larger amounts to the clients than the clicking of the mouse or keyboard-entered data that is sent up from the clients to the web servers.

6.2 CATV AND CABLE MODEMS

CATV (CAble TV) systems have been operating in the US for quite some time. This system uses broadband coaxial cable to provide a large number of TV programs with good quality to homes. This is usually a RG-59 (Radio Grade 59) cable providing 75 ohms of impedance and transmission for RF (Radio Frequencies). The conventional CATV system is analog in nature. Considering that the bandwidth of a POTS line is around 4 kHz, the bandwidths of cable plants of 350, 750, and 1000 MHz are quite attractive. However, the cable bandwidth is shared among all the users, whereas 4 kHz of bandwidth is dedicated for each POTS customer. The higher the bandwidth of the cable, the greater is its channel capacity. Each TV channel takes up 6 MHz of bandwidth, so a 750-MHz cable can provide 100 such channels.

The newer CATV systems are installing the 1-GHz cable and may soon develop a digital standard. We will limit our discussion to the analog system, which is the most prevelant at the time of this writing.

Figure 6.3 shows a general CATV system reconfigured to provide Internet access. All transmission for the CATV is done at the headend office. Usually each city would have one headend office operated by one cable company (unless there is no company with enough money to dominate the market in the city). Typically, broadcast programs are received at the headend office from satellite dishes. Programs may also be obtained from local TV stations and from video playback units. Using FDM (Frequency Division Multiplexing), these channels are multiplexed and transmitted over the cable plant. *Splitters* are used to branch out the signal for distribution. Amplifiers are used to increase the range of the cable plant. Microwave and fiber links

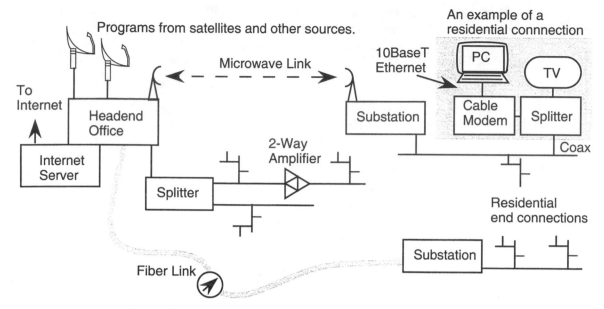

Figure 6.3 CATV networks start at the headend office and, by means of splitters and amplifiers, signals are distributed within a city.

are also used to bring the signal to a neighborhood that is located far from the headend office. Substations provide the necessary terminations for these links and the distribution of the signal in that geographic region.

CATV is basically a one-way broadcast system. Pay-per-view programs use the PSTN or the telephone to get information from the customer. This is called a *telco return path*. At one time, the FCC had mandated that the 5 MHz to 42 MHz spectrum should not be used for downstream transmission, in case in the future this capacity was needed for upstream transmission for interactive video. CATVs never ended up using this part of the spectrum, so all amplifiers were one-way, downstream amplifiers.

Now that the cable infrastructure is being converted to provide Internet access, this low end of the spectrum is used to provide transmission upstream. This required that the amplifiers be converted to two-way amplifiers. These amplifiers are called *bandsplit amplifiers* because they amplify the downstream frequencies one way and amplify the upstream frequencies the other way. Unfortunately, the 5- to 42-MHz bandwidth is more susceptible to interference from refrigerators, garage door openers, gas stove igniters, etc.

Typically, a cable company provides Internet access as well. They are, in many cases, the ISP for the cable customer. The cable customer uses a cable modem to access the Internet and the program channels. Because filters are used to separate the different signals, a customer can watch a program while someone else in the house is connected to the Internet. When the cable modem is installed, the installer selects which cable channel the customer will use to receive the downstream signals. This downstream 6-MHz channel can provide up to 30 to 40 Mbps for the customer. This channel is shared among all the customers, however, so if there are many cable users on the Internet, the

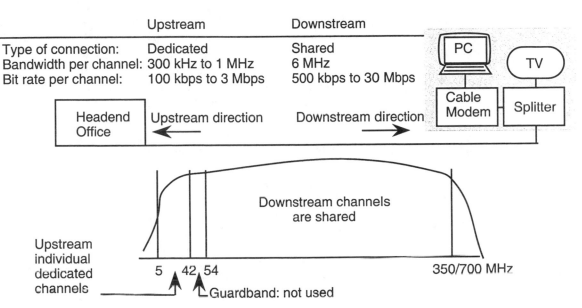

Figure 6.4 The lower part of the available bandwidth is used for upstream cable modem transmissions and the upper part is used for the downstream transmission of program channels and Internet access.

effective rate is much lower. Sharing also raises the issue of security. Once a channel becomes too congested, the cable company can preempt a program channel and use it for additional Internet access.

The industry has chosen the inexpensive Ethernet card, normally used in the PCs of a LAN, to be used in a PC connected to a cable modem. As we will see in the next chapter, Ethernet LANs can handle rates of 10 Mbps and above. The connection to the Internet is always on. One doesn't have to dial a number or wait for the connection to be set up. Starting up a browser like Netscape is as fast as starting up an application like WordPerfect.

Figure 6.4 summarizes how the available bandwidth is utilized in the cable plant. The downstream 6-MHz channel used for Internet access is shared among other cable users using the same facilities and can provide rates in the order of 30 to 40 Mbps if no one else is on the cable at the same time. Because the bandwidth is being shared, once other users get on the cable, the bit rate will drop down. On the other hand, going upstream, each cable user gets his own dedicated channel, which can be configured to provide data rates from 100 kbps to 3 Mbps.

6.3 xDSLs

6.3.1 The Potential of xDSL (Digital Subscriber Lines)

A typical local loop line that provides POTS service uses a UTP cable. This is an unshielded twisted pair of wires of gauges 24 and 26 AWG (American Wire Gauge). Although only about 4 kHz of bandwidth is passed over this local loop to provide basic telephone service, it is possible to operate it at up to 1 MHz of bandwidth. The wire pairs installed in our homes have always had the capacity of passing up to 1 MHz of bandwidth; however, the basic voice service always needed only 4 kHz of bandwidth out of it. Hence, all electronics relating to POTS was designed with the 4-kHz constraint. If we replace this equipment, then we can tap the higher frequencies to send data at much higher rates. This data could then be sent at the same time as voice. The design and the implementation, however, are not as easy as it sounds.

This would mean that we would have to change the equipment in the line cards at the CO and in the homes to get this bandwidth. But once we do that, we could drastically increase the rate of transmission over this twisted pair. One of the proposed DSL technologies promises to deliver up to 52 Mbps over 1000 feet of twisted pair and is called VDSL (Very high Digital Subscriber Line). The reason people want this high data rate for their homes is because of the increase in usage of the World Wide Web. When fiber is installed to the curb, VDSL will deliver that high speed from the fiber terminal into the home over a twisted pair of wires. However, once xDSL becomes popular, it will be only a matter of time before video-on-demand becomes available.

But then again, if the average user started to access information at higher rates, then it would become necessary to increase the bit rates of the backbone trunks in the Internet. However, local access (or the "last mile" as it has been called) has traditionally been a bottleneck in most networks, and the industry has made it a priority to overcome this limitation. The LECs (Local Exchange Carriers) are busy providing a solution; otherwise other companies, such as cable, wireless, satellites, or CLECs (Competitive LECs) will do it. Furthermore, the Telecommunications Act of 1996 has triggered all the carriers to compete in the residential broadband access market.

There are many variations of DSLs and they are collectively called xDSLs. The lower case x signifies that it is a letter holder and could be substituted by some other letter. The primary problem with the various versions of DSLs being deployed is the fact that long ago, when the telephone company installed the local loops, no attention was given to the possibility that any frequencies above 4 kHz would ever be used over them. That is, the local loops were installed just to pass voice. Let us now at over the obstacles that have been overcome in providing xDSL to the masses.

6.3.2 Challenges Facing xDSLs

One of the basic problems in operating a local loop at high frequencies is that the *distance* over which the wire pair is used becomes limited. With coaxial cable, the transmission bit rates aren't limited by distance as they are with twisted pairs. With copper wire, the higher the frequencies of operation, the more power is lost in the wires. That problem can be diminished if the operating frequencies are lowered, but then the available bit rate would also become less. Hence, there is a tradeoff. If longer distances are required, then the bit rate has to be lowered, and if higher bit rates are required, then the range of the distances must be lowered.

The local loops, if greater than 18,000 feet (3.4 miles) in length, would normally have *loading coils* on them, which would have to be removed. Loading coils or inductors block the passage of high frequencies, unlike capacitors. Loading coils are placed to compensate for the capacitive effect of the transmission lines. When loading coils are removed, the capacitive effect increases *crosstalk* between adjacent wire pairs. Crosstalk causes coupling of the signal from one pair to adjacent pairs. This is common because many wire pairs are installed together over telephone poles or underground. (Remember that these lines are not shielded by any metallic mesh, but are separated from each other only by insulation.) Furthermore, crosstalk is more severe for higher frequencies. That is why during test runs, when one line was converted to a particular type of DSL, any additional lines which were converted would not work.

Years ago party lines were popular. These lines allowed several homes to share the same phone line and take turns using the phone. At that time, *bridge taps* were installed in the local loop pair. These taps were placed in case another customer wanted to share the same line. They were not properly terminated because they did not affect the low frequencies used on POTS lines. Currently, when a line has to be converted to a DSL, these bridge taps have to be removed or properly terminated.

Many times a group of homes can be located far from a CO. Instead of running individual POTS lines from each home to the CO, they can be multiplexed at that distant location using T1 technology. By using fewer wire pairs, those circuits can be brought to the CO digitally, where they are demultiplexed into individual lines again. Of course, the transmission is both ways for a POTS line, so the multiplexing and demultiplexing is done at both ends. Such a system is called a DLC (Digital Loop Carrier) system. DLC systems can combine 24 POTS lines on only two pairs, the same as a typical T1 circuit. Fiber can also be used for DLC systems.

DLC: Digital Loop Carrier

Analog lines to customers at a distant location

CO

The digital multiplexers convert only 4 kHz of analog signals properly. Now if an attempt is made to pass DSL signals using high frequencies through the serving area concept, then frequencies above 4 kHz will not be passed and higher bit rates would not be achievable. Hence, to get around these multiplexers, xDSL equipment, which would normally be at the CO, can be placed in the neighborhood. Then, the neighborhood box can be connected to the CO using fiber. It is said that about a quarter of all POTS customers are on such a digital carrier loop system.

Other challenges which xDSL had to face were as follows: The differences in wire guages along a cable run and splices made from connecting pairs from two different rolls of wire were not conducive for passing high frequencies. Copper is also susceptible to corrosion, especially if it is buried underground. Poor connections from old wires make it difficult for high frequencies to be transmitted. Let us now turn our attention to several of the possible DSL solutions. Only a few are selected, although others exist. Unlike 56k modems and cable modems, HDSL and IDSL are symmetric (same rate in both directions) technologies, while ADSL is asymmetric.

6.3.3 HDSL (High-speed Digital Subscriber Line)

HDSL, mentioned in the first edition of this text, was the first DSL to be implemented. Actually, before that, ISDN was the first technology that converted a POTS line to a digital subscriber loop. Over two twisted pairs, HDSL can transmit in both directions at 1.544 Mbps, the same as a T1. However, HDSL is much easier and cheaper to install because it uses no repeaters. Hence, the line is easier to maintain. The interface used to connect to an HDSL line is the same as that used to connect to a T1.

Typically, T1s require repeaters every mile or so. HDSL can transmit without repeaters for 12,300 feet (or 2.3 miles). Using range extenders, equipment vendors have been able to even double that distance limitation. Another way the distance can be extended is by using thicker wire. If 19 AWG wire is used, the transmission range can reach 22,800 feet without repeaters. We will shortly see how HDSL provides repeaterless operation for long distances while T1s can't.

T1s were designed in the 1960s while HDSL was designed in 1990. Hence, the coding methods used for T1s and HDSLs are different. The method used for T1s is called AMI (Alternate Mark Inversion) and that for HDSL is called 2B1Q (2 Binary, 1 Quarternary). They are presented in detail in the chapters on T1s and ISDN, respectively. 2B1Q is less susceptible to crosstalk interference and codes four voltage levels instead of two. The second enabling factor for the HDSL advantage over T1 is echo cancelling, which was covered in Chapter 3. See Figure 6.5.

The main reason that HDSL signals can be transmitted for longer distances than T1s is because the operating (analog) frequency for HDSL is one-fourth that of a T1. T1s operate at 772 kHz while HDSLs operate at 196 kHz. To figure out how the same bit rates can be obtained from 772 kHz and 196 kHz bandwidths, we will need to do some simple calculations.

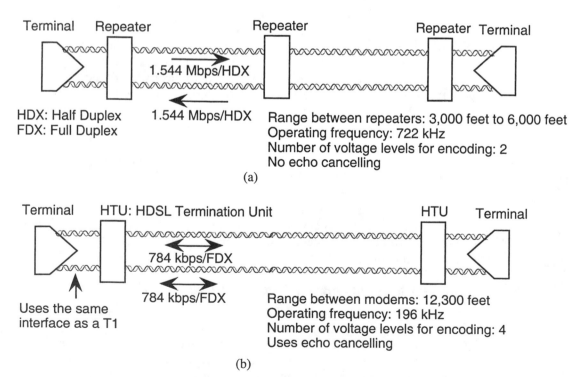

Figure 6.5 (a) A T1 span which requires 3 to 4 repeaters. (b) Over the same distance, HDSL would require none.

Residential Network Services

If we double the 772-kHz bandwidth, we get a bit rate of 1.544 Mbps. This means that by using AMI, each analog cycle of a T1 can encode two bits. By using 2B1Q, HDSL encodes 4 bits per cycle, so its 196-kHz bandwidth yields 784 kbps. However, using echo cancelling, 784 kbps is transmitted in full-duplex on both lines, giving a total rate of 1.544 Mbps in each direction.

It should be noted that HDSL does not provide analog voice service on the same transmission facility, as some of the other DSLs provide. On the other hand, HDSL is well established in the industry. The HDSL/2 version of HDSL uses the CAP-QAM (Carrierless Amplitude/Phase and Quadrature Amplitude Modulation) technique to achieve the DS1 rate of 1.544 Mbps in both directions on a single pair.

If only one pair of HDSL is used, then 784 kbps is available in both directions. Out of this rate, 768 kbps is available for user traffic. The rest is used for framing and overhead. This version of HDSL is called SDSL (Single pair DSL).

6.3.4 IDSL (ISDN Digital Subscriber Line)

Another symmetric DSL service is called IDSL. On one pair of wires, it can transmit up to 144 or 160 kbps full-duplex. Basically, it uses the BRI interface of ISDN. Since it does not need the D channel to provide switched access, it can be used to send information along with the B channels. IDSL, however, can be used to provide a dedicated line for a switched service. For instance, IDSL can provide a connection to a frame relay switch, which is a type of switched service. An advantage of IDSL is that it can reuse circuitry which was developed for ISDN in many cases, making it more affordable. Also, you may recall that one of the challenges facing DSLs in general was the DLC system, which multiplexes many POTS lines over a digital link. IDSL is one DSL that is not hampered by these carrier loop systems because it uses low speeds of ISDN, which was originally designed for the 4-kHz voice band.

6.3.5 ADSL (Asymmetric Digital Subscriber Line)

Back in Figure 6.3, we saw how a cable system was configured to piggyback Internet traffic over cable TV. Here in Figure 6.6, we see how POTS service can be modified to piggyback Internet traffic over voice. ADSL operates at a bandwidth of 1 MHz, whereas a voice-band modem operates at only 4 kHz. That is why ADSL can provide data rates of up to 8 Mbps downstream and 1 Mbps upstream.

We have the same twisted pair coming in the home as with POTS line. However, a frequency splitter separates the frequencies up to 4 kHz for the old telephone and/or fax lines, while the higher frequencies are diverted to the ADSL modem. The range of frequencies between 4 kHz to 25 kHz is a guardband that reduces interference between the voice channel and the ADSL channel. See Figure 6.7(a). Similar to cable modem, an Ethernet interface connects the PC to the ADSL modem. This allows someone on the phone to be talking while someone else is using the PC at the same time. ADSL, like cable modems, is always on and doesn't need to dial into the ISP to be connected.

On the CO side, frequencies are separated by using a splitter. The lower frequencies up to 4 kHz are directed to the PSTN or the voice switch, while other frequencies are sent to what is called a DSLAM (Digital Subscriber Line Access Module). This is a collection of ADSL modems, one modem for each customer. Of

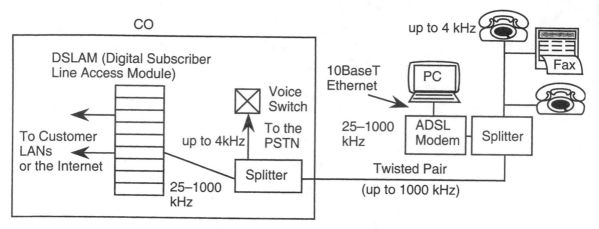

Figure 6.6 High-speed ADSL data is sent over one twisted pair of wires using frequencies from 25 kHz to 1 MHz asymmetrically, while the voice service is unaffected.

course, every customer has to own a separate splitter and a separate connector on the DSLAM. The ADSL modem at the customer's site is also called an ATU-R (ADSL Terminal Unit - Remote) and at the CO is called ATU-C (ADSL Terminal Unit - CO). ADSL is an analog technique, that is, it modulates the data over analog signals and also carries voice in analog form. On the other hand, HDSL and IDSL are digital technologies which transmit information in digital form.

The advantages of the splitters are two-fold. On the customer side, it allows the same wiring to serve the telephones as before. The rest of the house from the splitter doesn't have to be rewired. On the CO side of the service, the voice switch can serve only voice as before, and the Internet traffic can be routed to equipment designed just for it. Internet connections are on for long durations compared to voice connections and Internet traffic loads the voice switch considerably. More capacity has to be planned for voice switches to handle data connections. Diverting data traffic away from the voice switches and over Internet routers provides a more appropriate usage of available resources. Another reason why the phone companies like ADSL is that it provides a means by which they can compete with the cable carriers.

Originally, the concept of ADSL was envisioned by Bellcore to provide video dial tone. It would allow residential customers to dial and request that a video be played back to them over the facility. The video-on-demand would provide a downstream rate of 1.544 Mpbs with an upstream 64-kbps channel over 18,000 feet of copper wire. However, there is currently more interest for it to provide Internet service. All ADSL lines are rate adaptive; they adjust themselves to the highest rate possible in each circumstance. When the modems come up, they test to see how fast they can transfer data and if someone turns on an electric ignitor for a gas stove or introduces some other kind of interference while the data is being transmitted, the data rate will be automatically adjusted. Once the interference is removed, the data rate will again be increased to what it was before.

Residential Network Services

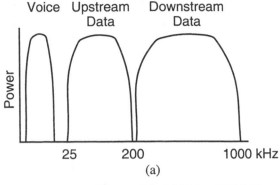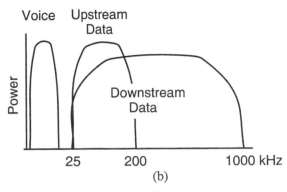

Figure 6.7 (a) Using FDM (Frequency Division Multiplexing), the upstream and the downstream bandwidths are separated. (b) Using echo cancelling, they overlap.

To install ADSL, the phone company has to send a technician to install a frequency splitter. The phone companies would like to avoid having to do a "truck roll" for each customer throughout the country. Hence, a simpler version of ADSL called UDSL (Universal aDSL) was created. Other names for it are G.Lite and "splitterless" ADSL. G.Lite prevents the telco from having to install a splitter in the home although splitters still have to be installed at the COs. However, the data rate is lower than that of ADSL. With G.Lite, the phones and PCs are connected to the same wire pair. This brings the high frequencies from the data channel into the voice circuit and the information on the voice circuit comes to the data channel. Nonetheless, since the data rate is lowered, the interference between the voice and data channels becomes negligible.

Figure 6.7(a) shows how voice is sent in the lower part of the frequency spectrum using FDM (Frequency Division Multiplexing). Upstream data is modulated over carriers in the 25 to 200 kHz range and the downstream data uses the bandwidth from 200 kHz to 1 MHz. The bandwidth for downstream data can be increased by using echo cancellation, as shown in Figure 6.7(b). FDM keeps the bandwidths of upstream and downstream signals separate, while with echo cancelling they overlap. This is actually how ADSL operates.

6.3.6 Modulation Techniques Used on ADSL

Originally, AT&T's CAP (Carrierless Amplitude/Phase modulation) technique of modulating data over a single analog carrier was used. This was the old standard method of modulation used with modems, so all the engineers were familiar with it. It was a tried and true method.

ANSI then decided on a modulating scheme called DMT (Discrete Multitone Transmission). This is an ingenious approach which uses 256 different carriers instead of just one, each having a bandwidth of 4 kHz. In a normal transmission line, abnormalities exist at certain frequencies in the transmission spectrum, making operation at those frequencies impossible. This is due to wire line impairments which we

	Per channel	For voice band	For upstream band	For downstream band
Channel numbers	-	1 – 6	7 – 32	7 – 256
Number of channels	-	6	26	250
Bandwidth in kHz	4.3125	25.875	138	1104
Bit rate in kbps	32	-	832	8000

Figure 6.8 Some approximate figures for DMT (Discrete Multitone Transmission).

listed at the beginning of this section, such as, mismatched wire gauges, unterminated bridge taps, and so on. DMT, with its 256 carriers, will automatically turn off certain carriers which are inoperable, and keep the other carriers on which can operate at their highest potential. Furthermore, DMT uses echo cancellation, which further increases the bit rate.

Theoretically, each of these 256 carriers is capable of delivering from 0 to 60 kbps. Together, that amounts to about 15 Mbps. In practice, however, only 32 kbps is transmitted on each carrier, giving a total rate of about 8 Mbps downstream and 832 kbps upstream. If you are following the calculations, remember that we are using echo cancelling, which actually gives us 250 downstream carriers and 26 upstream carriers. Figure 6.8 provides some calculations done for the DMT carriers.

EXERCISES

Sections 6.1 to 6.3:
For the next four questions, choose from these answers:

  a. 56k modem　　　　　　　　b. cable modem
  c. ADSL　　　　　　　　　　　d. IDSL

  1. Which of these services are asymmetric?
  2. Which of these services are always on?
  3. Which one provides another connection with a data connection simultaneously?
  4. Which one uses an Ethernet card in its implementation?

Section 6.1:

  5. For a 56k modem, which part of the transmission path is analog?
     a. from the ISP to the PSTN　　　b. within the PSTN
     c. from the PSTN to the customer　d. within the customer's PC
  6. The process of deciding which protocol to use when modems first get connected is called what?
     a. focusing　　　　　　　　b. handshaking
     c. training　　　　　　　　d. learning
  7. What is the maximum speed of a 56k modem in each direction?
  8. Explain the difference between handshaking and training.
  9. Is the equipment on both ends of a 56k modem connection identical? If not, what are some of the differences?
  10. List some ways in which a 56k modem achieves its speed.

Residential Network Services

Section 6.2:

11. In order to support uplink transmission, what did the cable companies have to do?
    - a. install fiber
    - b. install different kind of amplifiers
    - c. install a two-way cable.
    - d. install phone lines at the customer's site.
12. Which direction of a cable modem connection is shared among other users in the neighborhood and which direction provides dedicated channels for the users?
    - a. only uplink is shared
    - b. only downlink is shared
    - c. uplink and downlinks are shared
    - d. uplink and downlinks are both dedicated
13. What part of a cable modem uses Ethernet LAN technology?
14. To divide the cable signal to different locations in a neighborhood, what equipment is used?
15. To boost the cable signal strength, what equipment is used by cable companies?
16. How many headends does a cable company usually have in each city?
17. Describe the frequency spectrum used in a 750-MHz cable plant and the assignment of the channels.

Section 6.3:

18. Which of the following is NOT an obstacle in providing digital service over a local loop?
    - a. weather conditions
    - b. unterminated bridge taps
    - c. unmatched wire guages
    - d. loading coils
19. Which type of DSL provides repeaterless T1 operation?
    - a. HDSL
    - b. IDSL
    - c. VDSL
    - d. ADSL
20. For the previous question, give two ways in which this is achieved.
21. Describe a DLC and its purpose.
22. DLCs are obstacles to which type of DSL?
23. What are some other names by which ADSL modems and DSLAMs are known?
24. What type of ADSL provides splitterless operation? Why is a splitter viewed as a disadvantage?
25. What are some reasons why phone companies were anxious to roll out ADSL?
26. Which ADSL modulation technique uses only one carrier?

## Chapter 7

LANs:
Basic Concepts

7.1 INTRODUCTION

7.1.1 The Beginning of LANs

In the early 1980s, when PCs (Personal Computers) began to proliferate in businesses, office workers were relieved that they were becoming less dependent on a central host. Many of the tasks were done right on the PCs that were sitting on their desks. They were able to accomplish tasks themselves, rather than having to wait for the data processing department to get around to doing them.

However, it soon became evident that these processors would have to be networked, since workers typically have to work with each other. Initially, "sneaker-netting" (hand-carrying files on diskettes from PCs to PCs) proved sufficient, but soon, as the volume of such data transfers increased, networking became essential.

A LAN is a private network that allows computer-related devices to communicate with each other within a range of a few miles, typically within the boundary of a building. It connects computers and their peripherals with each other under decentralized control.

Basically, LANs allow sharing of resources. These resources could be information, such as data files, multimedia files, electronic mail, voice mail, or software. They could be peripherals, such as special-purpose printers, plotters, scanners, or storage devices. LANs also provide workstations to share each other's processing capabilities or to access a central host. Of course, with these advantages LANs also bear some disadvantages, concern for security of files and accounts being a major one.

7.1.2 Comparing LANs with Phone Networks

The components which are present in a telephone network, such as a local PBX network within a building, are also present in LANs. Even though PBX networks were originally designed to carry voice and LANs were designed to carry data, they both have components which provide similar functions.

	Phone Networks	LANs
Table 7.1 Comparison of Phone Networks and LANs		
Terminal Device	Telephone	NIC (Network Interface Card)
Media	Twisted pair of wires	UTP, fiber
Topology	Star	Star and ring
Access method	Dialing a phone number	CSMA/CD and token passing
Communication method	Spanish, English, etc.	NetWare, TCP/IP

As seen in Table 7.1, both of these types of networks have to have a terminal device, a point where the network ends or the point from where information originates. A NIC (Network Interface Card) or a network adapter is inserted in the node (PC, printer, router, etc.) of a LAN. Any device which is attached to a LAN must have the appropriate type of NIC inserted in it from where the node can access the network. Each NIC has a unique physical address encoded in it so that when it is powered up, it knows its physical address. A telephone has no such address. A telephone's number is determined by the jack into which it is plugged. However, with a NIC, no matter which device you insert it in, the physical address is the same. This address is hard coded into its ROM (Read Only Memory). Other names for this address, as we will see, are MAC addresses, hardware addresses, and NIC addresses.

A telephone network uses a phone wire installed in a star topology. Similarly, a LAN must also use a transmission media installed using a selected topology. However, with LANs, there is a wider selections of media and topologies available.

A telephone can access another telephone by dialing. Similarly, there are access methods (which we will cover shortly) that allow one NIC to access another. But once a person accesses another phone the two parties can't communicate with each other if they can't speak the same language. In the same manner, an operating system which gains access to another operating system through the NIC can't communicate if they don't use the same communication protocol, such as NetWare or TCP/IP.

Hence, for a LAN to operate properly we need to decide on one access protocol, which is determined by the type of LAN that is chosen. But we also need to determine which communication protocol to use. That is determined by what application we need and whether or not the operating system can support it. Also, notice that on a PBX network a single access protocol (dialing) is used, while more than one communication protocol can exist simultaneously (Spanish and English). In the same manner, on a given LAN, one access protocol is used, but two or more different communication protocols may exist simultaneously. In other words, on a given LAN one computer could be "talking" NetWare while another one may be "talking" TCP/IP. In fact, by opening two different windows, your PC could be communicating in TCP/IP using Netscape in one window, while in the other window it could be communicating in NetWare with a local Novell server, simultaneously.

Now that we have identified the five major components of LANs, the NIC, the media, the topology, and the access and communication protocols, we can study each of them further. In Chapter 4, we have already looked at the various kinds of transmission media. In the following two sections of this chapter we will consider topologies and access methods and in the following chapter we will look at TCP/IP, the most widely used communications protocol. The access protocols function at the lower two layers of the OSI model and the communication protocols function at the layers above those.

7.2 TOPOLOGIES

Before a LAN is installed, careful planning must be done on how to wire up or physically lay out the network. Once the network is installed, it becomes very difficult and expensive to alter the layout, or the *topology* as it is called. Hence, LANs connected using wireless technologies are gaining acceptance. Let us now look at three basic types of topologies and their derivatives.

7.2.1 Star

The star topology [Figure 7.1(a)] may be implemented when using existing telephone wiring to set up a LAN, since that is how in-house wiring is installed. In such a case, the installation of a LAN is simple, especially if there are wire pairs that are not used.

The star topology has a central node or hub to which the workstations are separately connected. Even though the reliability of the network depends on the reliability of the central node, monitoring, controlling, and troubleshooting of the LAN becomes easy because of it. Every station requires two interfaces, one at the station and one at the central node; a separate circuit or line from the hub is also required.

When a star network is cascaded, as shown in Figure 7.1(b), it is called a tree. Because of its exceptional managing characteristics, many LANs are physically wired using the star configuration.

7.2.2 Bus

The most popular topology at one time was the bus topology. See Figure 7.1(c). Network components are connected to one common wire, called the bus, over which they communicate. They can listen to all the traffic on the bus, which is broadcast by the transmitting device; however, only the device to which the traffic is addressed receives this data.

Sometimes, the main cable (the bus) is connected to the NIC using a drop wire and sometimes it is connected directly to the NIC. If the main cable is "cut" and the two cables are separately connected to two connectors on the NIC as shown in Figure 7.1(d), the topology is called a "daisy chain." There is no common bus over which communication occurs, but instead signals are received and retransmitted as they travel through intermediate nodes.

LANs: Basic Concepts

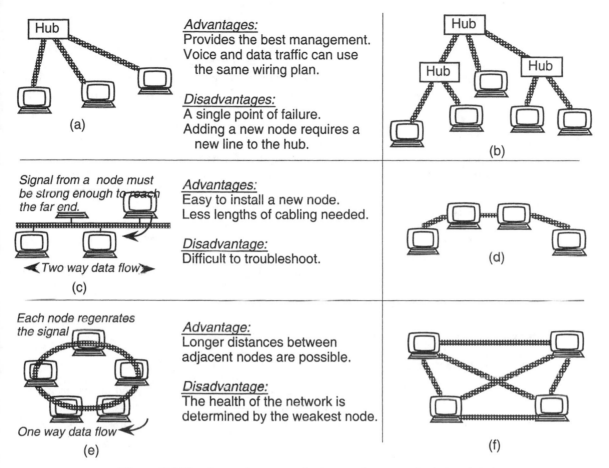

Figure 7.1 The three primary topologies are shown on the left and their derivatives are on the right. (a) star, (b) tree, (c) bus, (d) daisy chain, (e) ring, (f) mesh.

The bus provides a simple topology that is fairly easy to install. Separate connections for each station from a central hub are not required as in the star topology. Even though the bus doesn't have a hub that is a common point of failure, bus topologies are more susceptible to failure. It is difficult to isolate a failure when determining a fault. If one of the NICs on the bus has a poor connection, it brings down the entire network. Trying to find which NIC is the culprit then becomes difficult. The bus topology also has strict constraints on the placing of the stations as well as their number.

However, one reason why the bus was popular at one time is because its NICs are typically passive devices (don't repeat signals), allowing the network to stay up even when one station fails. Because the NICs are passive, their costs are low.

7.2.3 Ring

The ring topology is like the daisy chain topology, but with all nodes connected in a circle. See Figure 7.1(e). When additional paths are placed between the nodes of a ring, as shown in Figure 7.1(f), the network becomes much more resilient to failure. This topology is called a mesh and it commonly appears in WANs. The figure shows a fully connected mesh network.

The ring connects each node with a point-to-point link until all the nodes are connected in a circle. This makes the ring more suitable for fiber-based LANs, since fiber-link transmission requires a transmitter and a receiver. Traffic travels in only one direction. All node interfaces are active; they retransmit the received signal. This makes the NICs more costly, but allows the distances between adjacent nodes to be longer than those used with a bus.

Theoretically, the ring provides a relatively simple design with circuit costs lower than those for the star. The ratio of throughput to the rate of the transmitted signal speed is higher than that for the bus. However, since the ring nodes are active, providing store-and-forward switching, they are more vulnerable to failure. Furthermore, if one node is slow or error-prone in relaying the ring signals, then the performance of the entire network is degraded.

7.3 ACCESS METHODS

7.3.1 CSMA/CD

Once the LAN is laid out with the chosen topology, we need an access method so that one node can get the attention of another, and so that data can be transferred. The first and most popular access method is called CSMA/CD (Carrier Sense Multiple Access with Collision Detection).

The rules of this protocol are relatively simple. In fact, CSMA/CD is the protocol which polite people use when having conversations in a room. Suppose that there are a few people in a room and someone wants to talk. If no one is talking, then that person may start saying his sentence. Assuming that all the other people in the room are polite, no one else will start saying what they want to say until the person is finished with his "transmission." When it becomes quiet, two people, thinking it is all right to say something, may start their conversations simultaneously, but then they would back off because there was a "collision" of their two sentences. Both messages would be garbled. Then they would each try again.

Now let us see how CSMA/CD is used in LANs. The station that wants to use the transmission media for sending data must first listen to the media to hear if any other NIC is transmitting. If not, then the station may transmit immediately. While the transmission is taking place, the transmitter must also listen to hear if anyone else has begun transmitting on the line or not. If there is someone else transmitting, then the station must abort the transmission and, after waiting a random amount of time, may start the process over. This process continues until all the data has been transmitted without being destroyed by another transmission.

Let's consider an example. In Figure 7.2, three network nodes are shown on a bus topology, with nodes X and Y being close to each other while node Z is a distance away

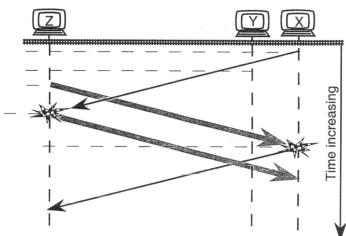

No one is on the line, so X transmits.

Y can't transmit, because it hears X.
Z can't hear X yet, so it transmits.

Z detects a collision and it stops transmitting.

Now, X detects a collision and it stops.

X and Z wait a random amount of time before attempting to transmit again.

Figure 7.2 A CSMA/CD access method scenario.

from them. First, node X listens to the line to make sure that no one else is using it. Then it begins its transmission. After a short time, node Y is prevented from transmission, because X's signal has had time to reach Y. Node Z, however, which is much further away from X than Y, hasn't heard X's signal on the line yet, and so has begun its transmission.

Eventually, node Z hears X's signal and stops its transmission, and likewise, X hears Z's transmission and also stops. They then both wait an arbitrary amount of time and attempt again to transmit their data.

Notice that once a collision is detected, the data that was sent up to that time can't be used, and the entire block of data must be retransmitted. In other words, the throughput of the data is always less than the bandwidth of the medium. For this reason, in Ethernet, which uses CSMA/CD, the throughput may be as low as 30% of the total bandwidth available on the media. Of course, this figure depends on how the network is configured and used. For large networks with a lot of network traffic, CSMA/CD simply doesn't work because of its "transmit if you can" method.

Nonetheless, the performance of this access method is good for low to medium traffic loads and only becomes poor when there are many stations attempting to transmit simultaneously, at which time one has to install bridges and routers to divide up the network into several LANs.

In the chapter on ISDN, we will introduce CSMA/CR (CSMA with Collision Resolution). This protocol, as we will see, provides better throughput than CSMA/CD. With CSMA/CR, no data has to be retransmitted, even after a collision occurs on the line. However, in CSMA/CD, the entire block of data has to be retransmitted after a collision.

7.3.2 Token Passing

CSMA/CD is a contention or nondeterministic type of access method. This means that several nodes may try to access the entire bandwidth of the media all at the

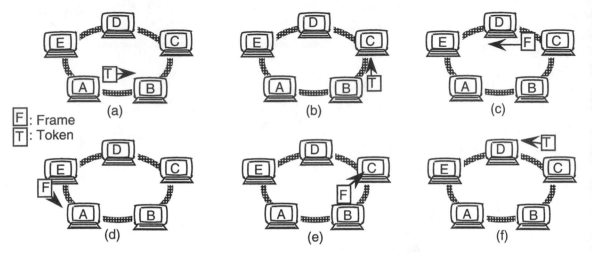

F: Frame
T: Token

(a) (b) (c)

(d) (e) (f)

Figure 7.3 (a) A token passes through B, since it has nothing to send. (b) C has data to send, so it removes the token. (c) C sends a frame of data for E. (d) Data is received by E and it sets the copy bit, acknowledging it. (e) C gets the acknowledgment. (f) C places the token back on the ring to give others a chance to transmit.

same time. It is also said to be a probabilistic access method, because how long a node has to wait to gain access to the network depends on the amount of traffic at that time.

Contrary to CSMA/CD, token passing is a non-contention-based access method, where every network node is guaranteed some amount of the available bandwidth. Also, instead of being probabilistic, it is considered to be deterministic, because the access to the network is predictable.

Token passing is used primarily on ring and bus networks, where all nodes are logically placed in order. Data signals are passed from node to node until they come back to the transmitting node. While the data is circulating, the receiving node copies the data into its buffers. If a node wants to transmit, it must wait to receive a certain bit pattern called the *token*. Once the token is received, instead of placing it back on the ring, data is sent in a frame by the transmitting node. Then when the receiver identifies its own address in the frame, it receives the frame and checks for errors.

If the frame is received error-free, a copy bit is set at the end of the frame by the receiving node and the frame arrives back at the sender. Here, the sender can check the copy bit to see if the frame was received or not. If it was, then the token can be sent to the next station down the ring, or else the frame can be retransmitted. Figure 7.3 illustrates such a sequence of events as node C sends data to node E. In (a), node A has sent a token to B, which doesn't have any data to transmit. So node B passes the token down to C, which does have data to send (b).

In (c), node C removes the token from the ring and sends a data frame to node E. Node D, realizing that the frame is for someone else, simply passes the frame down the ring. In (d), the frame is read by node E without any errors, and the frame is sent back to node C with the copy bit set. This is shown in (e). Finally, in (f), node C,

	Ethernet	Token Ring Networks	FDDI
Table 7.2 Types of First Generation LANs			
Media Topology Access method Speeds Typical frame sizes Standards	Coax and UTP Bus and star CSMA/CD 10 Mbps and up 1526 bytes Ethernet II and IEEE 802.3	STP Star-wired ring Token passing 4 and 16 Mbps and up 4500 bytes IEEE 802.5	Fiber Ring Token passing 100 Mbps 4500 bytes ANSI X3T9.5

realizing from the copy bit that the frame was received, removes the frame and places the token back on the ring to give someone else a chance to transmit.

7.4 TYPES OF LANS

Table 7.2 shows the three primary types of LANs which exist today. They are Ethernet, token ring, and FDDI (Fiber Distributed Data Interface). We will concentrate on Ethernet and its variations in this chapter. Token ring, FDDI, and higher-speed Ethernets will be covered in more detail in a later chapter on LANs.

Ethernet: There are many variations of Ethernet, but they all mostly use CSMA/CD for the access protocol. They all use the same frame structure and have a maximum frame size of 1526 bytes. Logically, they all use the bus topology, but physically the newer ones use the star topology. The transmission media can vary from coax and UTP (Unshielded Twisted Pair) to fiber, and the operating speeds are 10 Mbps, 100 Mbps, and 1 Gbps. Because they use CSMA/CD, however, their throughput is typically only 30 to 50%. Hence, a 10-Mbps Ethernet can transmit only about 3 Mbps of data successfully. The rest of the bandwidth is wasted due to collisions and the overhead required for the frame headers. IEEE has standardized Ethernet as the 802.3 specifications.

Token Ring Networks: These use NICs which are active, that is, they repeat the signal which they retransmit to the next node down the ring. That is why the distances between adjacent NICs can be as far as 300 meters. This is typically longer than for Ethernet. Also, token ring networks have a frame size that is larger than that for Ethernet.

Figure 7.4 shows how a concentrator called an MAU (Multistation Access Unit) connects the nodes of a token ring network. Notice that physically the topology is a star, because all the nodes are connected to a MAU, but logically the topology is a ring. The path of the transmission signal goes in order from one NIC to the next until it

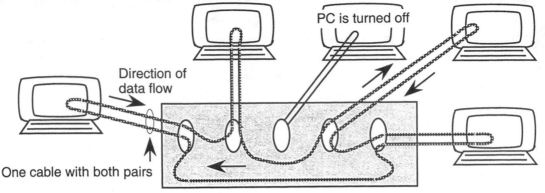

PC is turned off

Direction of data flow

One cable with both pairs

MAU (Multistation Access Unit) or Concentrator

Figure 7.4 A token ring network uses a star-wired ring topology. Logically, the data flows in a ring. Physically, the nodes of the LAN are connected in a star. The MAU serves as the hub of the star. If a PC is turned off or the NIC is not working, the MAU will isolate that branch from the rest of the network.

comes back where it was originated. It is best to think of a token ring network as a star-wired ring.

Initially, these networks used STP (Shielded Twisted Pair), but today you may see UTP as well as fiber being used. Originally, token ring networks ran at either 4 Mbps or 16 Mbps. Even if only one NIC was rated at 4 Mbps, the entire network had to operate at that rate level. Because of the token passing access protocol used with them, one can get about 95% throughput. The rest of the bandwidth is used for framing overhead, headers, and spacing needed between frames. The IEEE standard for it is designated as 802.5.

Token ring as well as FDDI can be configured using dual rings. Figure 7.5(a) shows such a configuration. One ring, called the primary ring, is used to transfer data when the LAN is working normally. The secondary ring is a backup ring. If one node

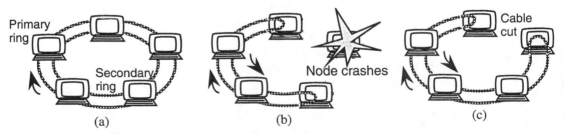

Primary ring

Secondary ring

Node crashes

Cable cut

(a)　　　　　　　　　　(b)　　　　　　　　　　(c)

Figure 7.5 (a) A dual-ring configuration where the primary ring transfers data. (b) If a node becomes disabled, the rings can wrap themselves around, and use the secondary ring. (c) If the cable is cut inadvertently, the ring can again heal itself.

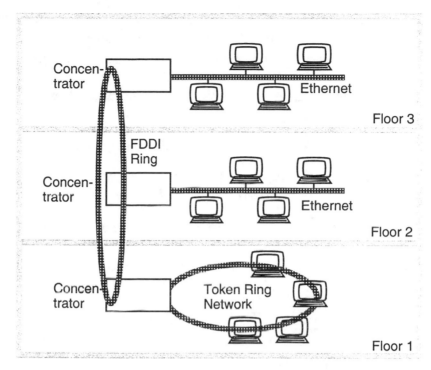

Figure 7.6 FDDI can be used to interconnect LANs on different floors of a building or in different buildings in a campus environment.

crashes (shown in Figure 7.5(b)) or if the cable between two nodes is cut by mistake (shown in Figure 7.5(c)), then the NICs in the adjacent nodes detect this. Then they loop themselves around. By using the secondary ring, the transfer path is completed. If another problem occurs, then the LAN is segmented into two parts. Hence, it is advisable to correct the problem as soon as possible and not to continue to operate in the "wrap-around" mode.

FDDI: Figure 7.6 shows a simplified diagram of an FDDI network. FDDI runs at 100 Mbps and uses fiber. It was standardized by ANSI under the X3T9.5 specification. It is typically used for backbone networks to carry data for longer distances such as in a high-rise building or several buildings in a campus environment. Hence, it is usually installed as a ring. Because it carries a large amount of data between LANs, it is made resilient to failure by installing dual rings.

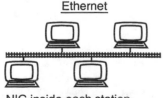

Ethernet

NIC inside each station.
One terminator at each end.

7.5 BASIC ETHERNET LAYOUTS

Table 7.3 shows the three basic Ethernet layouts. They are called 10Base5, 10Base2, and 10BaseT. They all use the same frame format, which we will look at later, and they all use the CSMA/CD access method. There are many more types of Ethernets, but they all can be

LANs: Basic Concepts

Table 7.3 Types of 10-Mbps Ethernets			
	10Base5	10Base2	10BaseT
Year standardized	1983	1988	1990
IEEE standard	802.3	802.3a	802.3i
Media	Thick coax	Thin coax	Cat 3, 4, or 5
Topology	Bus	Bus	Star-wired bus
Access method	CSMA/CD	CSMA/CD	CSMA/CD
Segment length	500 meters	185 meters	100 meters
Nodes per segment	100	30	Depends on hubs

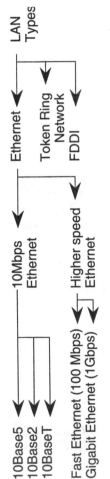

thought of as connected to each other using a bus topology as shown in the side figure. Physically, they are connected differently, but logically they all share the same channel. That is, only one NIC can transfer data successfully at any time. Starting with this side figure as our reference, let us see how the different types of Ethernets are wired.

7.5.1 10Base5

10Base5 is the oldest type of Ethernet and yet you might find it being used as a backbone network. A backbone network is a network used to interconnect other networks. Unless fiber is used, this type of Ethernet provides the longest range of all Ethernets, but its thick coax cabling is expensive and bulky to work with.

In Figure 7.7, we see that the "bus" part of the LAN may actually be installed in the ceiling or behind the walls. One terminator is required at both ends of this cable because of electrical engineering reasons. If the bus is improperly terminated, then the entire network will not work. A transceiver which is connected on this cable performs the CSMA/CD functions for the NIC. The NIC is installed inside the PC and is connected to the transceiver using a 15-wire drop cable. A DB15 connector is used on both ends of this cable.

7.5.2 10Base2

A simpler version of Ethernet is called 10Base2. It uses a coax that is thinner than 10Base5, but unlike 10Base5, its NIC includes the transceiver. Again, a terminator at both ends of the cable is necessary. Instead of the cable being out of reach from the end users, the cable is actually installed at the PC. If a user wants to move his PC, he may remove the cable from its back by mistake. This would improperly terminate the coax cable and bring the entire LAN down. Furthermore, it would not be obvious who removed the cable. You would have to go to different offices and check all the connections. If only the connector is loose instead, then it would be even more troublesome to locate the fault.

LANs: Basic Concepts

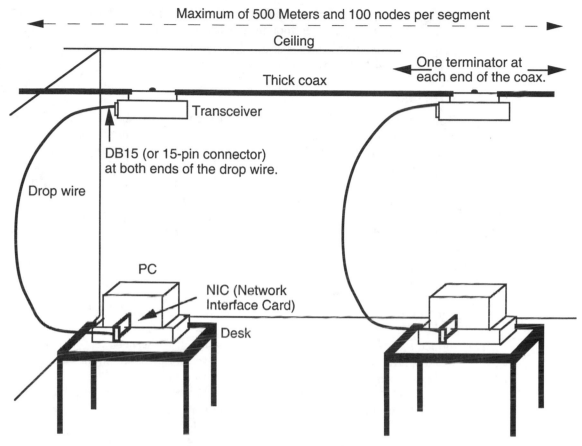

Figure 7.7 A common layout for 10Base5.

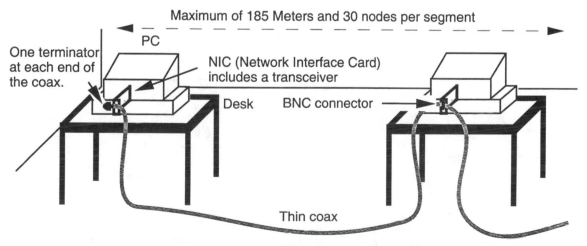

Figure 7.8 A 10Base2 layout combines the transceiver with the NIC and uses a thin coax.

LANs: Basic Concepts

In any case, this is a pure bus topology. Only one communication channel exists, which all NICs must share. Even though it is less expensive than 10Base5, it has a smaller range than 10Base5. Furthermore, fewer nodes can exist on each LAN segment. For the actual numbers, refer to Table 7.3.

7.5.3 10BaseT

Topologically, the 10BaseT layout is a different kind of "animal" altogether. In Figure 7.9(a) the basic Ethernet layout is shown. Logically, 10BaseT conforms to this schematic. In more detail, it can be drawn as shown in Figure 7.9(b). Instead of the bus extending for lengths of meters, it is basically located inside the hub. The hub may be a small box sitting on someone's desk or it may be mounted on a rack that may be 19 or 23 inches wide. In any case, the bus is inside the hub.

Hubs are powered by AC. This is because they repeat any signal that arrives from one port to all the other ports. Figure 7.9(b) shows an 8-port hub. Each port is accessed through a RJ-45 jack. The UTP cable is usually a Cat-5 cable and uses one pair of wires to transmit and one pair of wires to receive. Although Cat-5 is sold as a 4-pair cable, only two pairs are used with 10BaseT. The cable with an RJ-45 plug on both ends connects the hub to the NICs in a star configuration. Because the bus is inside the hub, however, this topology is actually called a star-wired bus. Physically, it looks like a star and logically, it operates as a bus. 10BaseT networks are used in more localized environments since they don't have the range of the older Ethernets. The distance from the hub to the NIC must not exceed 100 meters, so for a large installation, we may need more hubs and racks to mount them than if fiber runs are used.

In Figure 7.9, we see that the NIC on the far left side has sensed no carrier on the bus, so it has sent a data frame to the hub. The hub is an OSI physical layer device and so it simply repeats the signals (or the data frame) to all other ports. It doesn't know to which NIC the frame is addressed and so it repeats it on all the other ports. If a NIC is defective or is sending "garbage," the hub can isolate that link and keep the rest of

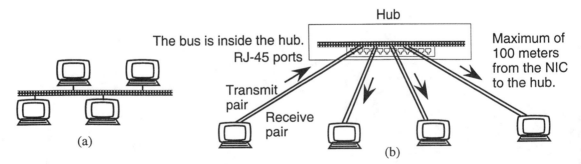

Figure 7.9 (a) The original Ethernet configuration. (b) The 10BaseT configuration. Here, the bus does not extend for meters, but resides in the hub. The NIC in the far left side has found the bus to be silent so it has transmitted a data frame to the hub, which in turn repeats the signal to all other active nodes.

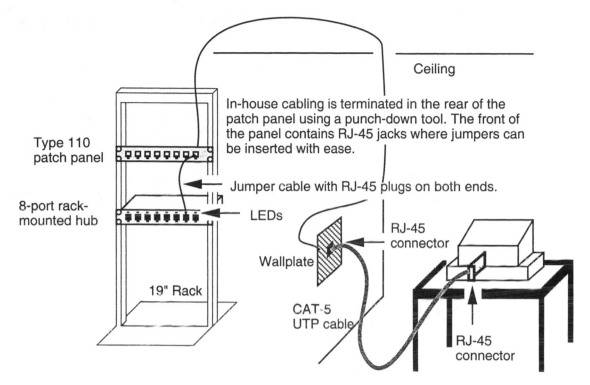

In-house cabling is terminated in the rear of the patch panel using a punch-down tool. The front of the panel contains RJ-45 jacks where jumpers can be inserted with ease.

Ceiling

Type 110 patch panel

8-port rack-mounted hub

Jumper cable with RJ-45 plugs on both ends.

LEDs

RJ-45 connector

Wallplate

19" Rack

CAT-5 UTP cable

RJ-45 connector

Figure 7.10 The physical layout of a 10BaseT station. All cabling is usually Cat-5 and uses RJ-45 plugs and jacks. Other PCs or stations are connected in the same manner and also terminate at the hub.

the LAN in good working order. Whenever the problem is corrected, the hub will bring up that link without requiring any human intervention. LEDs (Light Emitting Diodes) on the hub indicate which links are active, inactive, or defective. Traffic management data can also be gathered by the hub to find out which nodes need more bandwidth capacity.

We will be depicting 10BaseT networks as shown in Figure 7.9(b). However, it won't hurt to get an idea how this layout is physically installed. Figure 7.10 shows that it doesn't look any thing like the schematic. Notice that all the parts of Figure 7.9(b) are present in Figure 7.10. However, the path from the NIC to the hub can get a little confusing. Incidentally, all of it typically uses Cat-5 wiring.

Starting at the NIC, we see a cable connecting the NIC to the wallplate in the office. From the wallplate to the closet where a rack is installed, another cable is installed. This cable run is pretty much fixed since it runs behind the walls and through the ceilings. This cable is connected at a patch panel in the rack. Usually, it is a type 110 or EIA/TIA 568 patch panel. Because this cable run is usually not replaced, it is punched down on the rear side of the patch panel.

From the patch panel to the hub, a jumper cable is attached. The hub is mounted in the same rack or could be mounted on a different rack for that matter. RJ-45 modular

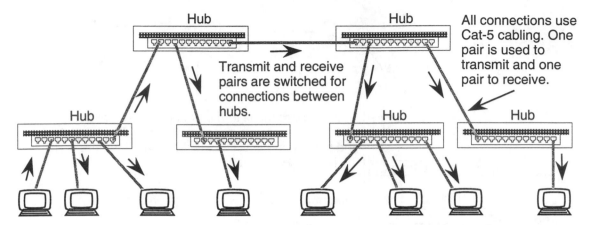

All connections use Cat-5 cabling. One pair is used to transmit and one pair to receive.

Transmit and receive pairs are switched for connections between hubs.

Figure 7.11 The data frame which is sent by the node on the far left side is repeated by all the hubs. However, between any two pairs of nodes, only a maximum of 4 repeaters may exist. Remember, during this transmission, no other NIC can transmit successfully.

plugs at both ends of the jumper cable and the office wire make them easy to replace and move. If the NIC shown in the figure needs to be connected to a different hub, it is only a matter of finding the correct jumper and moving it to the proper hub. Because this figure is large and shows many of the midpoints in the actual cabling, we will resort back to the simplified diagrams such as the one shown in Figure 7.9.

Once all the ports of a hub are populated, we may need to add more capacity. This can be accomplished by adding more hubs or replacing an existing hub with more ports. In Figure 7.11, notice that all the hubs are connected together using the ports on the front. Whenever hubs are connected in this fashion, you are not supposed to connect more than four hubs per transmission path. This is because Ethernet originally specified that no more than four repeaters may be used between any two nodes. Because hubs act as repeaters, they must be installed using the same rule. Although six hubs are shown in the figure, there are not more than four hubs in any transmission path. For instance, the node on the far left-hand side is sending a data frame. That frame is repeated by the hub to which it is connected. From this hub all the nodes to which it is connected get the frame as well as the hub above it to which it is connected. By the time all the nodes get the data frame, there are not more than 4 hubs through which the signal goes. By the way, only the NIC whose address matches the address in the data frame reads the frame in its buffer and all the other NICs ignore that frame.

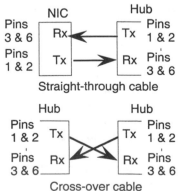

When a port of a hub is connected to a NIC, a straight-through cable is used. This cable orders the pins or the wires in the cable so that the hub's transmit pair lines up with the NIC's receive pair. In the side figure the transmit pins are denoted by a "Tx" and the receive pins by a "Rx." However, when two hubs are connected using their ports, a cross-over cable should be used which joins the pairs so that the

154   LANs: Basic Concepts

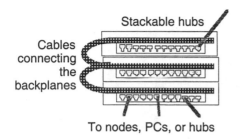

Stackable hubs

Cables
connecting
the
backplanes

To nodes, PCs, or hubs

transmit and receive pairs match properly. This is because we don't want both ends to transmit on the same wire or to receive on the same wire. Some ports have a MDI/MDI-X button that will cross over the pins using a straight-through cable. Other hubs have autosensing ports which will do that for you automatically. In any case, the pairs need to be switched when interconnecting two hubs using their ports. For the same reason, when connecting two NICs directly without a hub, a cross-over cable must be used.

Now a 10BaseT network can have a large number of nodes connected. However, even more hubs can be added by using what are called stackable hubs. See the side figure. If hubs are stacked, then there is a special cable called the stacking cable which connects their busses or backplanes together. This cable is connected in the back or the sides of the hubs, and not from the front using the ports. Now the stackable hubs can count as one hub when applying the 4-repeater rule. Also, they don't use any ports, so you end up gaining additional ports by stacking them rather than connecting them from the front. See Photos 7.1 to 7.8 for more details on the physical layouts of 10BaseT networks.

7.6 ETHERNET FRAMES

NIC Addresses: In Chapter 3 we have already mentioned that all Ethernet NICs have a 48-bit hardware address coded in them. Usually, this address is burned inside a ROM chip so when power is turned on for the node, that NIC knows its own address. The first 24 bits of this address are called the vendor code and the last 24 bits are the serial number. From the first 24 bits, one can know which vendor manufactured that NIC. There are other names for the NIC address. They include hardware address, physical address, and MAC (Media Access Control) address.

Vendor Codes for
Ethernet Addresses
Given in hex.
Leading digits are 0s.

3Com	6010 to 6040
3Com	608c
AT&T	3d, 55
Cisco	00000c
HP	80009
Intel	00aa00
Motorola	8700 to 8710
Sun	80005

The Basic Ethernet Frame: When data is sent over Ethernet, using any of the above layouts, all the bits are enclosed in what is called a data frame. Just as a letter must be enclosed in an envelope when being mailed, so data bits must be placed properly according to the Ethernet protocol. The format in which data is placed in an Ethernet frame is shown in Figure 7.12(a). At the beginning of the frame, bits are altered between 1s and 0s so as to get the sending NIC properly synchronized with the transmitting NIC. This field is called the preamble and is not shown in the figure. Soon after the preamble, the address of the NIC to which the frame is being sent is placed by the transmitting NIC. Then comes the NIC address of the transmitting NIC. These addresses are the 48-bit addresses or 6-byte addresses, as we have just seen. Then comes the type field, which specifies in which protocol the data is encoded. If the type field is 0800 (in hex) then that means that the frame is carrying IP information. If the type field is 8136 or 8137, then the information field is carrying NetWare traffic. This way, one LAN can carry many different protocols and they don't get confused.

RJ-45 jack for 10BaseT

DB-15 connector
for 10Base5

BNC connector
for 10Base2

Photo 7.1 An Ethernet "combo card" NIC.

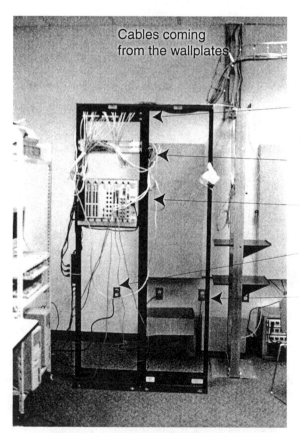

Cables coming
from the wallplates

Patch
panel

10BaseT
hubs

Unused
concentrator

Power for
the hubs

19" rack

Photo 7.2 An example of a 10BaseT
wiring distribution center.

Front view of
patch panels

Jumpers

10BaseT hubs

LEDs

Photo 7.3 A closer view of the patch panels
and the two hubs.

Cables punched down on the patch panels.

Jumpers

Hub

Photo 7.4 The rear view of the patch panels.

Photo 7.5 A front view of the patch panel.

One cross-over cable, connecting the two hubs from the front.

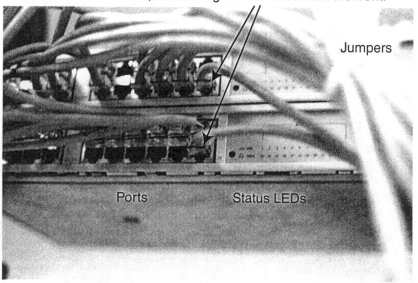

Photo 7.6 Two 24-port hubs seen from the front.

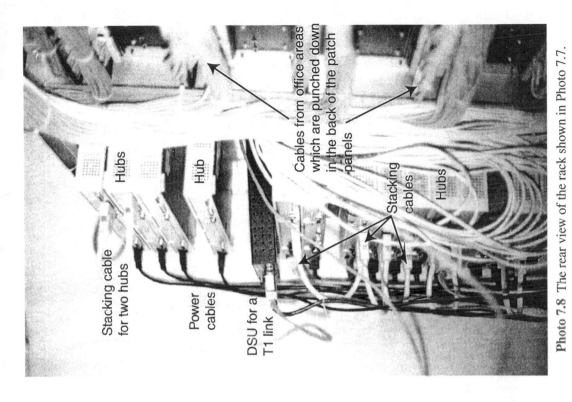

Stacking cable
for two hubs

Power
cables

DSU for a
T1 link

Hubs

Hub

Cables from office areas
which are punched down
in the back of the patch
panels

Stacking
cables

Hubs

Photo 7.8 The rear view of the rack shown in Photo 7.7.

Cat-5 cables coming from
the ceiling and walls

Patch panels

Patch panels
and hubs

Hubs

Photo 7.7 Another example of a 10BaseT
wiring center. Notice all the jumper cables.

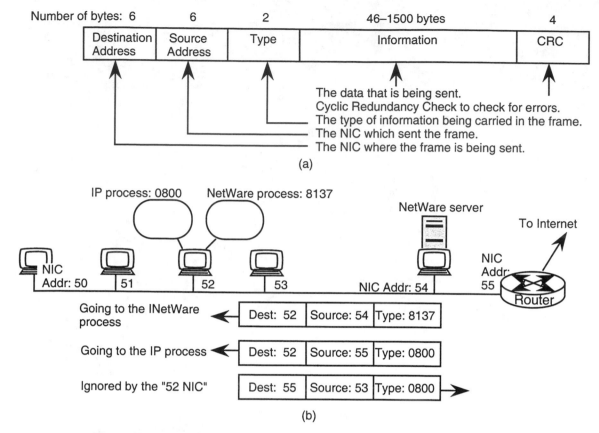

Figure 7.12 (a) Basic format of the Ethernet frame. (b) NIC addresses are shown to be simplified. The NIC whose address is 52 will accept the first two frames since they are addressed to it. The first one has a type field that matches the NetWare process and is forwarded to it. The second one is forwarded to the IP process and the last one is ignored by that NIC.

The information field is where the data is placed, and the CRC (Cyclic Redundancy Check) field is where a code is placed by the transmitting NIC that allows the receiving NIC to see whether or not the frame was received without errors. If the frame is received with errors, then the receiving NIC will discard that frame. Now you may wonder what happens to the processes that are waiting for some response. How are these processes going to operate properly if frames are discarded by the NICs due to errors? Why aren't the NICs requesting for retransmissions? Well, if the processes that are waiting for the NIC to deliver the frames have to wait too long, they themselves will request the retransmission. You can imagine the NIC saying to itself while discarding a frame, "If my process really wants that frame, it will ask for the retransmission itself."

The Type Field: Now let us look at an example of how the addresses and the type fields function using Figure 7.12(b). NIC addresses are shown for the items on the LAN from 50 to 55. Of course, NIC addresses are 6 bytes long, but I have simplified them here. On this LAN, there are two protocols running. There is a NetWare server communicating with the local machines using the NetWare protocols. Also, there is a router which provides access to the Internet for the LAN. This router is communicating with the LAN clients using the IP protocol.

The PC with the NIC address of 52 has two windows open. One window is running an application which is communicating with the NetWare server. The other window at this PC, let's say, is running Netscape and is using IP packets to communicate through the router to the Internet. Three Ethernet frames are shown arriving at NIC 52. Only the three fields are shown for simplicity. The information and the CRC fields are also there but are not shown. The first one is coming from NIC 54 and its type field is 8137, which corresponds to the NetWare protocols. Because the destination address of 52 matches its own hardware address, NIC 52 copies the frame into its buffer. It does an error check and if there is an error, it simply ignores the frame. Let us say that the frame came in without errors and so now the PC looks at the type field and sends the information or the data portion of the frame to the NetWare process. That process then further figures out what to do with the data which it has received.

The second frame is also destined for NIC 52 and so NIC 52 copies the frame into its buffer, does an error check, and sends the frame to the IP process that is running NetScape. The last frame is not even addressed to NIC 52, so this NIC ignores the frame altogether. This way, there can be many different protocols running on one LAN. We could have Macintoshes connected on the same LAN with PCs and the type field will identify which frame belongs to which process and so on. If collisions occur, then the NICs will retransmit the frames which were unsuccessfully sent.

7.7 EXTENDING THE RANGE OF LANS

OSI Layers		Device	Transfers
3.	Network	Routers	Packets
2.	Data Link	Bridgoo	Fiames
1.	Physical	Repeaters	Bits

Standard Ethernet has a range of 500 meters and 10Base2 has a range of only 185 meters. What are the different methods of interconnecting Ethernet or LAN segments to each other? The various methods are outlined in the side figure. Repeaters are the simplest solution which operates at the physical layer of the OSI Reference Model. This means that a repeater only processes bits. It doesn't care how those bits are placed into a frame or a packet. Whatever bit it reads on one side of the repeater is the bit it will place on its other side.

A bridge is more sophisticated, but not as much as a router. A bridge operates at the second layer. It reads the bits that arrive at its port and organizes them into bytes and fields. It combines these fields to identify entire frames. Then it reads the NIC or MAC addresses that are in the frames to determine what should be done with each frame. A router needs to know the network layer address. Typically, this is the IP address. Decisions made by a router are determined by the IP address.

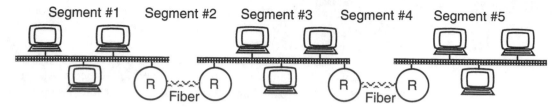

Figure 7.13 The 5-4-3 Rule. Five segments can be interconnected using 4 repeaters, out of which only 3 segments may have nodes attached. The fiber-based segments are used for long distances.

7.7.1 Repeaters

The simplest solution is to add more Ethernet segments and connect them using repeaters. Then with more segments existing in the network, more nodes can be added. Figure 7.13 shows five segments interconnected using four repeaters. According to standards specifications, we are not allowed to add more than four repeaters using the 5-4-3 rule. This rule states that you can have up to 5 segments using 4 repeaters, 3 of which may be node-bearing segments. That leaves us with two segments which cannot have any nodes. They are used to interconnect LAN segments which may be in different buildings or on different floors. This is a general rule, but it is possible to successfully place more repeaters and more segments in the LAN.

Being able to add segments by using repeaters allows us to extend the range of the LAN. For example, if all five segments in Figure 7.13 were 10Base5 segments, each of which can have a maximum range of 500 meters, then the total range obtained by this configuration would be 2500 meters. This not only allows us to extend the range of the LAN from 500 meters to 2500 meters, but also allows us to add more nodes on the entire LAN. Each segment has a maximum number of nodes which can be attached to them. For 10Base5 the maximum number is 100 nodes per segment, so this setup will enable us to serve a total of 300 nodes. Two segments, according to the 5-4-3 rule, are not allowed to have any nodes.

Now we can serve more nodes by interconnecting segments using repeaters. But all those nodes must share one communications channel among them. If most nodes are idle most of the time or are not communicating with other nodes in the network, but are only doing local processing on their PCs, then adding more nodes may prove to be an acceptable solution. We are assuming that the nodes on the LAN are sending data packets to each other only occasionally, so that sharing one communications channel among all of them is not a performance issue.

However, if there is a lot of internodal traffic on a LAN, whether there is one segment or five, then there is a continuous problem with collisions. With more traffic present, there is a greater probability of collisions. And as the number of collisions increases, the performance of the LAN degrades. All the nodes on the five segments shown in Figure 7.13 are on the same *collision domain*. A collision domain is the collection of LAN segments over which all nodes must share the same communications channel. For example, while one node in the figure is transmitting, no other node may transmit successfully. Otherwise, another collision occurs.

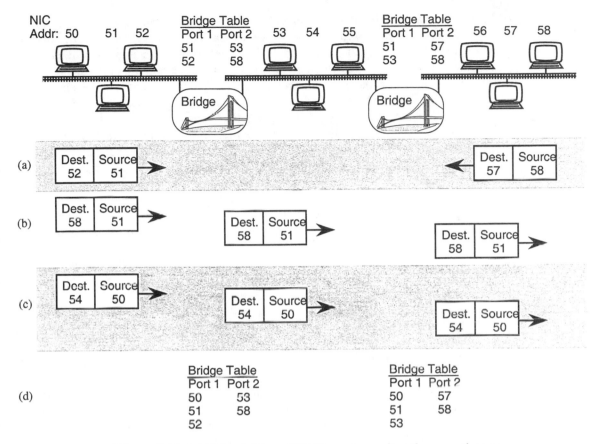

Figure 7.14 (a) Using bridges, NIC 51 can transmit at the same time as NIC 58. The bridges know from their tables that they are on separate segments. The bridges filter the frames from going to other segments. (b) NIC 51 can also transmit to a node on a different segment, if necessary. (c) Using source addresses, the bridges update the tables. (d) The updated tables.

In summary, repeaters are a good solution to increase the size of a LAN and to add a number of nodes. They are easy to install and don't require any skill. They are simple devices, operate at the physical layer of the OSI model, and repeat whatever electrical signal is present on either side. Hence, they are fast and inexpensive.

7.7.2 Bridges

In Figure 7.14 we have replaced the repeaters with bridges. Bridges operate at the data link layer of the OSI model, so they don't simply repeat the bits from one port to another but based on the MAC address determine whether or not the frame should be forwarded to the other port. Bridges actually read the NIC or MAC addresses in the data link layer frames before making this decision. Therefore, repeaters repeat bits while bridges forward frames. If a bridge decides to pass a frame from one segment to another one, that is called *forwarding*. If the bridge decides not to pass a frame to the adjacent segment, then that is called *filtering*. Because bridges are more intelligent than repeaters, there can be many communications channels available at the same time in a LAN. In this figure, there are three possible communications channels. Each communications channel in a LAN environment is also called a *collision domain* because over each communications channel, a different collision can exist.

For instance, in Figure 7.14(a) we see that on the far left side, the NIC whose MAC address is 51 is transmitting to the NIC whose MAC address is 52, which is on the segment. Now, this transmission can exist at the same time that NIC 58 is transmitting to NIC 57, which is on a separate segment. Two communications channels over two different segments exist in this example, each corresponding to a different collision domain. How do the bridges know to filter these data frames so that they don't get forwarded on to each other's LAN segments and end up colliding and making the transmissions unsuccessful?

Each bridge maintains a *forwarding table* indicating which NIC addresses are on which ports. The left bridge, for instance, knows that NIC 52 exists on its port1. Hence when that frame comes into the bridge, it knows there is no need to forward that frame to port2 onto the middle segment, so it filters that frame. Similarly, the bridge on the right-hand side knows from its table that NIC 57 is on its port2 side, so there is no need to forward that frame either.

However, in Figure (b), when NIC 51 transmits a data frame to NIC 58, the left bridge knows from its table that NIC 58 is on its port2. Hence this bridge forwards that frame. All that this bridge knows is that NIC 58 is somewhere on its right-hand side and not necessarily attached directly to that segment. In fact, NIC 58 isn't directly attached to the middle segment and so when the right-hand-side bridge gets the frame destined for NIC 58, it also forwards it to its right-hand-side segment. Again, the bridge determines this from its forwarding table. No one else can transmit successfully at this time because the frame traversed over all three segments.

How do the bridges build these forwarding tables which allow them to determine which frames to forward and which ones to filter? These tables are built using the *source NIC addresses* in the frames which are transmitted on each segment. For example, in Figure (c), we see that NIC 50 is transmitting a frame to NIC 54. Each bridge, as it gets the frame, cannot find 54 in its forwarding table. Hence, each bridge forwards the frame to the next segment, hoping that somewhere along the line NIC 54 will receive the frame. Notice, the right-hand bridge doesn't realize that it doesn't need to forward the frame to the far right-hand segment, so it does it anyway. This is called *flooding*. Flooding is the process when a frame traverses many segments because the bridges don't know where the destination is. During this transmission, the two bridges did not find out where NIC 54 is located, but they did find out where NIC 50 is from the source address field in the frame.

Hence, in Figure (d), we see that the two bridges have updated their forwarding tables to include NIC 50 on Port1. Now when NIC 54 provides a reply to NIC 50 (or any other NIC, for that matter) the bridges will add an entry for NIC 54 at the appropriate ports. That is, NIC 54 will be added to Port2 by the left bridge and to Port1 by the right bridge.

164

Table 7.4 Comparing Repeaters and Bridges

	Repeaters	Bridges
Operates at which layer of the OSI model?	Physical	Data link
Transfers what?	bits	frames
Which frames does it forward to the other segment?	All	Necessary ones
Does it forward broadcast frames?	Yes	Yes
Does it forward frames with errors?	Yes	No
Can it connect dissimilar LANs, including FDDI?	No	Yes
Can it connect at dissimilar speeds, including 100 Mbps?	No	Yes
Does it creates more channels and collision domains?	No	Yes
Which one is faster?	This one	-
Which one is easier to connect and configure?	This one	-
Which one can be installed in loops, providing redundancy?	-	This one

Table entries that are not referenced for a certain amount of time are deleted automatically. For instance, if no one sends any frames to NIC 52 or if this NIC doesn't send any frames, then its entry in the left bridge will be deleted. If necessary, it will be added again later as outlined above. Keeping the number of table entries to a minimum uses less RAM in the bridges and makes the lookup process more efficient.

In summary, bridges operate at the data link layer of the OSI model. This means that they process frames instead of individual bits. Bridges allow LANs to localize traffic. Suppose that each segment in Figure 7.14 represented a different department, where there is a lot of traffic within each department, but interdepartmental traffic is minimal, say about 20% of the entire traffic; then using bridges provides a better solution. Connecting segments using bridges creates additional collision domains and more transmissions can occur simultaneously—one on each segment. However, bridges do more processing than repeaters, so they are slower and more expensive. They still don't require much skill to install and to maintain. See Table 7.4 for a comparison between repeaters and bridges.

7.7.3 Routers

Do the people in the post office in New York City know or care where the streets are located in San Francisco? No, they only care about how the streets are laid out in their own city. When they get a letter to be delivered to a particular street in San Francisco, they forward that letter to the people in the San Francisco post office. The San Francisco folks know where the streets and people are located there. If the world were made up of only a few people who all lived in one city, then we would not need the complex postal system which we have today.

In the same manner, when a LAN begins to grow in size, bridges are not sufficient. If bridges were all that LANs had, then that would be analogous to the New

York post office knowing where all the streets in San Francisco are located. Instead of all the post offices requiring to know where all the streets in the world are located, it is more manageable if this knowledge is distributed among all the post offices.

This is where routers become necessary in LANs. Back in Figure 7.14(c), when a frame was sent to NIC 50 and the bridges weren't aware of its location, that frame was flooded through the entire LAN and all its segments. If the LAN is small in size, then such flooding does not place much of a demand on the network. When the LAN becomes large, however, we need a way to localize such traffic. Routers help us do that. Broadcasting is another phenomenon that we will look at in the next chapter that requires all the NICs in a LAN to read a frame and possibly respond to it. Bridges also do not localize broadcast messages, but routers do.

Each node on the network has a NIC address. MAC address, hardware address, physical address, and Ethernet address are also names used for NIC addresses. Besides the NIC address, a node can also be assigned an IP address, which is saved in some configuration file in the node. When the node is booted up, that file is read and the node knows itself as having the IP address stored in that file. A NIC or MAC address, on the other hand, is stored in the NIC itself and can be changed only by replacing the NIC. Table 7.5 summarizes the differences between these two types of addresses. We'll have more to say about them in the next chapter.

Figure 7.15(a) shows how an IP packet is placed inside an Ethernet frame when it needs to be transported across a LAN. The IP packet contains the final destination of the packet, while the NIC address, placed inside the frame header, gives the destination address of the next hop.

Figure 7.15(b) shows three routers. Think of each router as a post office belonging to a particular city. Each router only knows the layouts of the LANs connected to it. For example, the NIC addresses of the nodes for LAN1 and LAN2 are

Table 7.5 Comparing MAC and IP addresses		
	MAC	IP
Relates to which OSI layer?	Second	Third
What type of address is this?	Physical	Logical
Where are the addresses used?	In bridging	In routing
How many bits are used?	48	32
How are the address bits abbreviated?	Hexadecimal	Dotted decimal
Give an example of its address.	00:aa:00:52:3f:e4	129.117.202.178
How are the addresses structured?	Nonhierarchical	Hierarchical
With whom are the addresses associated?	NIC vendor	Organization
Does the address change if the NIC is replaced?	Yes	No
Where is the address stored?	ROM in the NIC	Configuration file

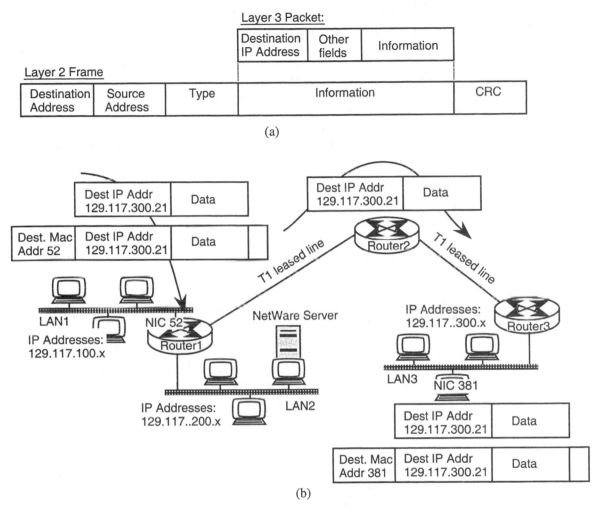

Figure 7.15 (a) A packet from the third layer of the OSI model is placed in a frame of the second layer. (b) The path that a packet takes from a node on LAN1 to a node on LAN3.

known only by Router1, or they can be found out only by Router1. Similarly, the NIC addresses for LAN3 are known only by Router3. Router2 is a router for other routers and doesn't have any LANs connected to it.

When a PC on LAN1 sends an IP packet to 129.117.300.21, that PC realizes that all the PCs whose IP addresses begin with 129.117.100 are connected directly to it on LAN1 and that this address which begins with 129.117.300 is somewhere else. Therefore, to send this packet is the job of its default router, Router1. In other words, this packet is "going out of town." Hence, the PC first places the packet inside an Ethernet frame and directs it to Router1's NIC address (NIC 52). Notice that this NIC doesn't know the NIC address of the final PC which is on LAN3.

Router1 looks at its routing tables and decides to send this packet over a T1 link to Router2. The packet is placed inside T1 frames (not shown) and sent to Router2, which sends it to Router3. Router2 knows that all the addresses beginning with 129.117.300 are in Router3's jurisdiction. Hence, Router3 uses another Ethernet frame to place this same packet and directs it to NIC 381. Out of the three routers, only Router3 needs to know that IP address 129.117.100.21 is assigned to the PC with NIC 381. In this fashion, routers efficiently route packets among themselves without having to maintain an exhaustive amount of information about all the individual nodes. For example, Router2 doesn't bother with any NIC addresses. Its primary function is to process packets between other routers.

Notice from Figure 7.15(b) that MAC addresses are physical addresses that have no geographical identity. A NIC with a MAC address of 52 could be on LAN1, while a NIC with a MAC address of 53 could be on LAN3 or somewhere else. IP addresses are logical addresses, however, while MAC addresses are physical. If you replace the PC with NIC 381 with another PC and another NIC, it could be assigned the same IP address, but its MAC address would be different. IP addresses are hierarchical, which makes routing between such addresses possible.

Routers are much more complex devices than bridges. Routers can choose between alternate routes. Alternate routes can be based on a number of matrixes, such as reliability of the link, security of the link, its cost, or speed. Routers can provide firewall functionality. They can decide which packets are allowed on the LAN segments that are connected to them and which packets can leave. This is also based on a number of different parameters. Today, routers can prioritize traffic and guarantee QoS (Quality of Service). This is necessary in order to transmit voice over routed networks. As far as such capabilities, bridges don't even come close. See Table 7.6 for a summary of routers and bridges.

Table 7.6 Comparing Routers and Bridges		
	Routers	Bridges
Decisions are made at which OSI layer?	Third	Second
Decisions are made using which addresses?	Typically IP	MAC
Typically used in what size networks?	Large	Small
What is the relative cost?	High	Low
What is the relative processing speed?	Slow	High
What amount of skill is needed for its configuration?	High	Minimal
How much choice exists in selecting routes?	A lot	Little to none
How much overhead traffic exists?	Low	High
How well can security be controlled?	Good	Poor

LANs: Basic Concepts

7.7.4 Switches

The Motivation: Routers have their disadvantages. Among them is that it is expensive to purchase them and to employ the skilled personnel to maintain them. For an Ethernet LAN in which all nodes must share the available bandwidth, the demand on the network increases drastically as its utilization starts to go up. For example, a 15-node Ethernet segment will have an average bandwidth of about only 0.3 Mbps per node. That is a drastic drop from the 10 Mbps which is available on Ethernet. This figure is approximated using the following assumptions: Due to the CSMA/CD access method used on Ethernet or the amount of collisions, the efficiency is assumed to be 45%. This brings the effective rate down to 4.5 Mbps. With 15 nodes sharing this bandwidth, that makes the average bandwidth per node only 0.3 Mbps or 300 kbps. As more nodes are added to the network, not only do we have to divide the 4.5-Mbps rate by a larger divisor, but also the 4.5-Mbps rate becomes smaller due to more collisions.

The first thing that a network manager could try before installing a router between these nodes is to install what is called a layer 2 switch. This will alleviate the poor network performance issue without requiring much effort and little cost. Figure 7.16 shows such a network. Here, one switch with six ports is installed and, depending on the bandwidth requirements of each node and with which other nodes they typically communicate, will determine how the LAN is segmented. For example, the top two nodes require the largest amount of bandwidth, so they are each placed on a switch port by themselves. They each get a full 10 Mbps bandwidth.

Now, instead of having only one communication channel existing we have a maximum of six channels existing at any given time. Six channels are possible when the nodes are communicating with other nodes that are on the same segment or on the same port connection. The two nodes at the top of the diagram can also communicate to the switch, which can hold a limited number of frames in its buffers.

The total bandwidth is increased from 10 Mbps to 60 Mbps. Furthermore, since fewer nodes are contesting for the bandwidth of the segment on which they are located, there are fewer collisions. This increases the total network efficiency. If we assume that the network efficiency goes up to 75%, then the total bandwidth becomes 45 Mbps,

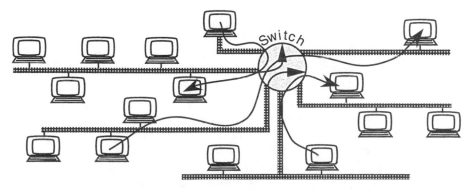

Figure 7.16 A Layer 2 switch is shown here transmitting to three different nodes or NICs simultaneously.

giving each node an average bandwidth of 3 Mbps. This is ten times the amount we had before the switch was installed. No wonder switches became popular overnight to reduce network traffic!

Think about the old days when residential customers used party lines for telephone circuits. This type of service costs less than the dedicated service which we enjoy today. With party lines, if you wanted to make a call, you would first see if any of your neighbors were using the line. If they were, then you would have to hang up and try later. When dedicated phone line rates became reasonable each residential customer enjoyed his own private line and calls could be made without waiting. The same is true with installing a switch in an Ethernet network. Nodes can be placed directly on a switch port, allocating them a full 10 Mbps of bandwidth with no collisions.

Operation of Switches: In Figure 7.16 there are three nodes transmitting *at the same time* to nodes on three other segments. The switching fabric, or the electronics of how the switching is accomplished, allows several simultaneous paths for frames in the switch. The amount of bandwidth internal to the switch is called the *backplane speed*. This speed determines how many frames can be switched simultaneously and the amount of blocking encountered by frames arriving at the switch at any time.

Of course, frames from two segments addressed to nodes on a third segment cannot be delivered by the switch at the same time. If two frames are contesting for the same output port on a switch, either one frame gets blocked (or dropped) or gets stored in a buffer temporarily until that port becomes free. In any case, at least one out of these two frames will get forwarded to the correct segment.

When a frame arrives at a port, the switch will look at its destination MAC address and forward it to the port on which that MAC address resides. All other ports will not receive that frame, unless, of course, the switch hasn't yet learned that MAC address and doesn't have it in its forwarding table. In that case, the frame will have to be flooded to all ports hoping that the destination address is on one of those ports.

Doesn't this sound just like a bridge? Yes, it does. In essence, a switch is nothing more than a modern, up-to-date bridge. Switches can do the same thing that bridges can do and more. However, vendors have simply added more features and upgraded bridges and called them layer 2 switches! It is a marketing ploy. Hence, yesterday's bridges have grown up to be today's layer 2 switches. Let us look at the basic differences between these two types of devices as outlined in Table 7.7.

Bridges are basically driven by software programs. They require a processor, such as a RISC processor, to execute their commands. By the time switches were created, they were placing all the software functionality into ASIC (Application Specific Integrated Circuits) chips. See Chapter 1 for a more in-depth discussion of ASIC technology. Instead of the forwarding decisions being made by software, they were being performed by the logic circuitry "hard-wired" in the ASIC chips. Not only did this prove to be much faster than software-based decision making, but also proved to be less expensive, and the unit required less space. The disadvantage of hardware-based switching is that new software upgrades are not possible. Hence, vendors have placed most of the logic in hardware and some of the logic, which is not as permanent, into software.

Table 7.7 Comparing Bridges with Layer 2 Switches

	Bridges	Switches
Forwarding and filtering decisions are made in . . .	Software	Hardware
Device used in making decisions	RISC CPU	ASIC
Typical number of ports available	2	Many
Relative cost per port	High	Low
Relative speed	Slow	Fast
Number of frames that can be forwarded at a time	1	Many
Can the store-and-forward method be used for forwarding?	Yes	Yes
Can the cut-through method be used for forwarding?	No	Yes

Another reason that switches perform faster than bridges is that they can forward several frames simultaneously. For example, if the switch in Figure 7.16 were replaced by a bridge, then the three frames shown would have to take turns being forwarded.

Switches, as well as bridges, need buffers on each port to temporarily save the frames that are to be forwarded until the port on which they are to be sent becomes free or available. Bridges use the store-and-forward method of forwarding frames. Switches can use both this method and the cut-through method. Both methods are shown in Figure 7.17. In the store-and-forward method, the device receives the entire frame, including the FCS (Frame Check Sequence) code at the end of the frame. Using this field, the device can do an error check on the frame and forward it to the appropriate port only if it is error free. Another advantage of this method is that it doesn't require all the ports to be running at the same rate, whether they be all 10 Mbps or all 100 Mbps.

With the cut-through method, the frame is forwarded as soon as the destination MAC address is read by the switch. Hence, while the frame is being received, its earlier portion is being forwarded to the correct port, that is, if there were no errors in the MAC address; and that can't be verified until the entire frame is received by the buffer. This method has its tradeoffs. If the network is error-prone, then the store-and-forward method would be appropriate. Otherwise, and if all ports are running at the same rate, the cut-through method would prove to be faster.

Replacing a 10BaseT hub with a switch has added advantages. With a hub, if one node is putting out too many frames with errors, all the nodes will experience a performance drop. A switch, on the other hand, using the store-and-forward method of forwarding frames, can eliminate such garbage frames from the network. Also, a switch provides better security than a 10BaseT hub by forwarding frames to only the appropriate port, while a hub will repeat the frames to all ports.

There are basically four characteristics of a switch that determine its performance and these should be considered when buying a switch. These characteristics are the speeds handled by the switch ports, the capacity of the backplane, the frame forwarding method, and the amount of memory, both for the forwarding tables and for

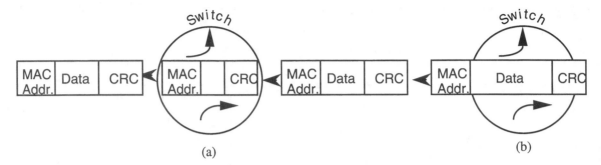

Figure 7.17 (a) The store-and-forward method. (b) The cut-through method.

the port buffers. A 10BaseT switch with a 40-Mbps backplane can switch only 4 ports at any time. However, all 10 Mbps and 100 Mbps switches are fully nonblocking. If the amount of RAM is not enough for the forwarding table, entries will get deleted more often and more address learning will have to be performed by the switch. When a switch has both 10-Mbps and 100-Mbps ports, then more buffer is needed because data will be arriving from the 100-Mbps ports at a faster rate than what the 10-Mbps ports can receive.

What Comes after Switches? The two nodes on the top of Figure 7.16 have a switch port dedicated just for them because they generate more traffic than the rest of the nodes. If they are servers, however, and need to communicate with the other nodes constantly, then their 10-Mbps link becomes a bottleneck. That is, if several nodes are hitting the server simultaneously at 10 Mbps and the switch can only transmit to the server at the same rate, the buffers of the switch will soon become full. There are protocols which allow switches to provide flow control and prevent the stations from overflowing the buffers. It would be better, however, if the "pipe" going to the server was at a higher speed than the speeds at which the other segments operate.

Hence, in the side figure, we have a server operating at 100 Mbps while the other nodes are operating at 10 Mbps. Now the tenfold capacity of the server segment should prove sufficient to handle the traffic from the other segments. Ethernet running at 100 Mbps is called Fast Ethernet (FE). Ethernet can also run at 1 Gbps. This is called Gigabit Ethernet (GE).

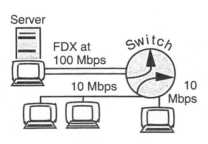

We can further alleviate the congestion problem over the server link by making that link full-duplex. This will allow the server to receive and transmit at the same time. From the switch to the server we have a full-duplex connection. That means that the CSMA/CD protocol is not used here and that there are no collisions. Transmission is done on one pair of wires and the receiving is done on another pair. This gives us an effective data rate of 200 Mbps. Before closing this section, it should be noted that so far we have discussed only layer 2 switches. Hardware- or ASIC-based routers are called layer 3 switches. More will be said about these advances in Chapter 23.

172   LANs: Basic Concepts

EXERCISES

Section 7.1:
1. A crude method of networking is achieved by using simple 3-1/2" diskettes. What is a term used for that?
   - a. snickering
   - b. sancking
   - c. sneaker-netting
   - d. sneaking
2. What type of access method is used with telephone networks?
   - a. CSMA/CD
   - b. polling
   - c. token passing
   - d. dialing
3. What are some advantages of LANs?
4. What are some disadvantages of LANs?
5. What is the difference between an access protocol and a communications protocol? How do they relate to the OSI model?

Section 7.2:
6. Which type of topology is primarily used in WANs?
   - a. star
   - b. ring
   - c. mesh
   - d. bus
7. Which advantage is not generally associated with the star topoplogy?
   - a. doesn't have a single point of failure
   - b. easy to troubleshoot
   - c. easy to manage
   - d. easy to get traffic statistics
8. Which topology provides longer distances between adjacent nodes?
9. Which topology is the most difficult to troubleshoot?
10. Which topology can use the same wiring as the in-house, telephone wiring?

Section 7.3:
11. If in a room we passed a stick around and agreed that the only person who could talk is the one who has the stick, which protocol would this resemble?
    - a. CSMA/CD
    - b. Demand Priority
    - c. polling
    - d. token passing
12. In CSMA/CD, what is the condition when two NICs transmit simultaneously called?
    - a. polling
    - b. collision
    - c. carrier sensing
    - d. multiple access
13. Which of the following is NOT a rule used in CSMA/CD?
    - a. Listen before you transmit.
    - b. Listen after you transmit.
    - c. Listen while you transmit.
    - d. If someone is on the line, do not transmit.
14. When two NICs transmit simultaneously using CSMA/CD, which NIC stops its transmission first: the one which started transmitting first or the one which started transmitting second?
15. Which access method is usually used on a bus and which one on a ring?
16. In token passing, which bit is set by the receiver indicating that it copied the data in its buffer?

Section 7.4:
17. What is the concentrator for a token ring network called?
    - a. MAU
    - b. hub
    - c. root
    - d. centralizer
18. What is the standard for token ring networks?
    - a. IEEE 802.3
    - b. IEEE 802.5
    - c. IEEE 802.6
    - d. ANSI X3T9.5

LANs: Basic Concepts

19. Which types of LANs use a token passing protocol?
20. Which type of LAN is good to be used to interconnect buildings in a campus?
21. If a token ring network has 10 NICs rated at 16 Mbps and 20 NICs rated at 4 Mbps, at what speed will the LAN operate?
22. What type of topology allows FDDI to be more resilient to failure?

Section 7.5:
For the next five questions, use this set of choices:

a. 10Base5   b. 10Base2
c. 10BaseT   d. all of the above

23. Which type of Ethernet uses a transceiver that is separate from the NIC?
24. Which type of Ethernet provides for the longest length segments?
25. Which type of Ethernet provides the best level of management?
26. Which type of Ethernet uses a pure bus topology with no drop cables?
27. Which type of Ethernet uses CSMA/CD?
28. What are the advantages gained by migrating from 10Base5 to 10Base2? What are the disadvantages?
29. What are the advantages gained by migrating from 10Base2 to 10BaseT? What are the disadvantages?
30. What are the purposes of straight-through, cross-over, and stacking cables?

Section 7.6:
31. An Ethernet NIC uses how many bits for its address?

a. 10   b. 24
c. 32   d. 48

32. When a frame arrives at a NIC, how does that NIC determine that the frame is for itself?

a. MAC address   b. Type field
c. data field   d. CRC field

33. For the question above, explain the purpose of the other fields in the Ethernet frame.
34. Can one Ethernet LAN run NetWare and WindowsNT network software simultaneously?

Section 7.7:
For the next six questions, use this set of choices:

a. repeater   b. bridge
c. switch   d. router

35. A 10BaseT hub acts like what?
36. Which device operates at the network layer of the OSI model?
37. This device may not check for frames with errors, but just passes them to the next segment.
38. When LANs become large in size, this device becomes necessary.
39. This device is a modern version of a bridge.
40. This device processes packets.
41. In Figure 7.14, after the tables are updated, NIC 54 sends a reply frame to NIC 50. Which bridge will forward the packet and which will filter it? How do they decide?
42. When a frame is broadcast to all segments of a LAN with bridges, what is that process called?

43. What are some advantages of repeaters over bridges?
44. What are the advantages of switches over bridges?
45. What are the advantages and disadvantages of routers compared to bridges?

Chapter 8

TCP/IP:
Basic Concepts

We have referred to the Internet and its set of protocols (TCP/IP) in Chapters 1, 2, and 3. We have already mentioned how TCP/IP is required for a host to be directly connected to the Internet, without which the World Wide Web would not be possible. In this chapter we mostly concentrate on IP but also look at how IP fits in the entire picture of other related protocols. TCP/IP is so important for today's networks that Chapter 26 is devoted to a treatment of these protocols in more depth. However, you will notice that no information is repeated here from the earlier chapters nor will any information be repeated later.

At the time of the first edition of this text, there were other protocols which were contesting to be dominant. Fortunately, all those protocols are converging to TCP/IP, which makes life a little easier for those who are new to the field. Hence, in this edition we take the time to go into TCP/IP in more depth.

8.1 NUMBER SYSTEMS

In this chapter we will work with different numbering systems. If you know how to do that, you may skip this section without losing continuity.

We like to work with the decimal numbering system, since we have ten fingers on our hands. Computers, as you know, work in the binary numbering system. The circuitry to process numbers in the binary system is easier, faster, and cheaper to design and manufacture. Hence, we need to know how to convert between these two numbering systems. However, binary numbers with their strings of 1's and 0's get pretty long, so we use the hexadecimal numbering system to abbreviate binary numbers. We will go over the types of number conversions that we will need throughout this chapter.

Decimal, binary, and hex use ten, two, and sixteen symbols, respectively, to represent numbers. The bases of these numbering systems are 10, 2, and 16, respectively. In Figure 8.1(a), we see that the sum of 1 and 1 in binary is 10 since the digit 2 doesn't exist, and in Figure 8.1(b), we see that, in binary, adding 10 to 1 gives 11 (or

3 in decimal). Also, adding 1 to 11 gives 100 in binary (or 4 in decimal), again, because binary has only two symbols: 1 and 0.

The hexadecimal numbering system, on the other hand, needs 16 symbols, so after going past the symbol 9, we borrow the first 6 letters of the alphabet. We could have used any other six symbols for that matter, but the convention here is to use the letters. Figure 8.1(b) shows how counting is done in these three numbering systems and also how conversion between them is done.

Figure 8.1(c) shows how a larger decimal number is evaluated. This is done by adding up the number of 1's, the number of 10's, the number of 100's, and so on. When converting a binary number, we do the same thing, but the base is 2 instead of 10. See Figure 8.1(d). Hence, we add up the number of 1's, the number of 2's, the number of

```
    1
  + 1
  -----
  1 0    in binary
     (a)
```

5 3 7 in decimal

$7 (10^0) = 7 (1) = 7$
$3 (10^1) = 3 (10) = 30$
$5 (10^2) = 5 (100) = 500$

537

(c)

1 0 1 in binary

$1 (2^0) = 1 (1) = 1$
$0 (2^1) = 0 (2) = 0$
$1 (2^2) = 1 (4) = 4$

5

(d)

Decimal	Binary	Hexadecimal
0	0	0
1	1	1
2	10	2
3	11	3
4	100	4
5	101	5
6	110	6
7	111	7
8	1000	8
9	1001	9
10	1010	A
11	1011	B
12	1100	C
13	1101	D
14	1110	E
15	1111	F
16	10000	10
17	10001	11

(b)

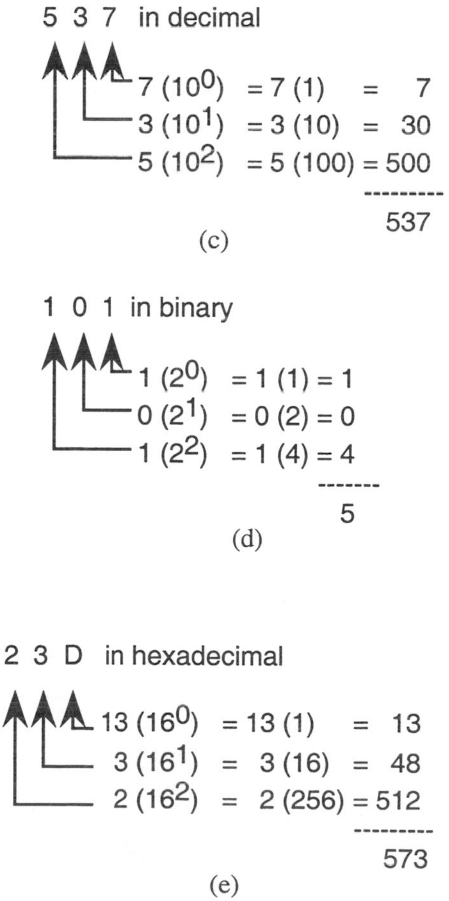

2 3 D in hexadecimal

$13 (16^0) = 13 (1) = 13$
$3 (16^1) = 3 (16) = 48$
$2 (16^2) = 2 (256) = 512$

573

(e)

Figure 8.1 (a) In binary, adding 1 and 1 gives 10. (b) The conversion chart between the three numbering systems. (c–e) The methods of converting numbers in all three numbering systems are similar. Only the bases are different.

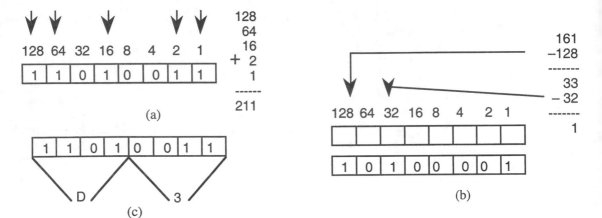

Figure 8.2 (a) When converting "11010011" from binary to decimal, simply add the powers of 2 in whose place a 1 appears. (b) When converting 161 to binary, start with the highest power of 2 and subtract the powers as they fit. (c) Converting from binary to hex, always group the bits by four.

4's, and so on. Because binary numbers can only be either a 1 or a 0, another simpler method of doing this conversion (than the one shown in the figure) will be shown shortly. Finally, in Figure 8.1(e) we see the method of converting a hex number to decimal. Here we add up the number of 1's, 16's, 256's, and so on. Notice that the number D in hex corresponds to 13 in decimal. This is obtained from the chart shown in Figure 8.1(b).

Number Conversions: Let us look at an easier method of converting a binary number into decimal. In Figure 8.2(a), 11010011 in binary is being converted. First, place the powers of two above each bit as shown. Then add the powers under which a 1 appears. In our case, these are 128, 64, 16, 2, and 1. Hence, 11010011 in binary is equivalent to 211 in decimal.

In Figure 8.2(b), 161 in decimal is converted to binary. When converting from decimal to binary, first find the largest power of 2 which can be subtracted from it. For 161, it is 128. After subtracting it, find the next largest power of 2 that can be subtracted. Keep doing this until a 0 remains. Then insert a 1 in the places where the power was subtracted and a 0 in the others. In our example, after subtracting 128 from 161, we are left with 33. 64 cannot be subtracted from it, so a 32 is subtracted. Hence, our number begins with "101." Last, a 1 remains, and that makes 161 in decimal equivalent to 10100001 in binary.

When converting a binary number to hex, convert bits in groups of four starting from the right-hand side. In our example, we have eight bits, so it doesn't matter from where you group bits into fours; but when that is not the case, make sure you group the bits starting from the lowest order bit (or from the right-hand side).

In Figure 8.2(c), 11010011 in binary is converted by substituting each four-bit binary number with its equivalent hex digit. The hex digit equivalents are found from the chart shown in Figure 8.1(b). For example, 0011 in binary is the same as a 3 in hex and 1101 in binary is a D in hex. Each group of four bits can be written simply as one hex digit, so hex numbers are used to simplify the representation of binary numbers. Conversion from hex to binary is simply done in reverse order, allocating four bits for each hex digit. Hence, A0F is not "1010 1111," but is "1010 0000 1111." (The spaces are placed between each group of four bits only for readability.)

If you are allowed to use a calculator on tests, then using a calculator is much easier. It must have the functions to convert between the three numbering systems. On a TI-30 (Texas Instruments) calculator, for instance, to convert a binary number, first press the [3rd] key, then the [bin] key. Then the display should read "bin." The [3rd] key activates the third set of functions available on this calculator, which include the number systems. Now enter the binary number. To see its equivalent number in hex, press the [3rd] and then the [hex] key. To see it in decimal, press the [3rd] and then the [dec] key. Other conversions are done in a similar manner.

8.2 ARP

8.2.1 An Office Analogy

Let us start with a simple protocol called ARP (Address Resolution Protocol). Imagine that I am in my old office where there are many workers in cubicles which are located in a large room. We all get phone calls from the outside and never know when we might have to transfer a call to one of the other workers. In order to be able to transfer calls, I have a lookup sheet on my bulletin board giving the extensions of many of the workers who are located in our large office. Figure 8.3(a) shows this sheet as it appears when I come to work one morning.

Sure enough, I get a phone call but it is really for Magan. So I look them up on this sheet and transfer the call to Magan with no problems. But then later, I get a call for Serena. I look for her on my sheet, but don't find her name there. Now I have to tell the caller to wait while I find out her extension. I stand up at my cubicle and yell out (broadcast), "Serena are you here? and if so, what is your extension?" At this time every other worker stops what he is doing and listens to my request, but when they find out that the message is not for them, they disregard the message. Only Serena answers me, giving me (unicast) her extension, which I add to my list is seen in Figure 8.3(b). (For this analogy to be more accurate, Serena would also update her table, adding my

Melissa	802	Melissa	802		
Jon	895	Jon	895		
Varsha	844	Varsha	844	Melissa	802
Magan	858	Magan	858	Varsha	844
Kristen	861	Kristen	861	Magan	858
		Serena	879	Serena	879
(a)		(b)		(c)	

Figure 8.3 (a) List of phone extension numbers. (b) Serena's extension is added. (c) Since Jon and Kristen were not referred to in the last two days, they are omitted from the list.

name and extension if necessary.) Then I transfer the call and the phone rings on Serena's table. Now the next time I get a call for her, I don't have to yell out again, but just look up on my list and transfer the call. Of course, if Serena is not in the office space, I can't transfer the call and the caller has to try again later.

I don't have any memory, so every time I have to transfer a call, I have to do a table lookup and possibly get up and yell for an extension. Additionally, every time I look up someone on my sheet, I write next to it the time that that person's extension was searched. Searching takes time, so when I find out an extension that has not been searched within the last two days, I remove that entry. If necessary, I can look up that extension again by using "YP (the Yelling Protocol)." In Figure 8.3(c), I have shortened my lookup list by removing two entries that have not been used within the last two days. This will make future lookups faster.

8.2.2 ARP Over Ethernet

ARP works exactly the same way. With ARP, however, IP addresses are matched up with MAC addresses as worker names are matched up with phone extensions. Just as no phone call can be transferred without knowing the destination extension, so no communication on Ethernet can take place without knowing the destination MAC address. All communication on Ethernet is done using Ethernet frames and all Ethernet frames require a MAC address in their DA (Destination Address) field. An IP datagram cannot be placed directly on the LAN. It must be placed inside an Ethernet frame first. In this chapter and Chapter 25, we'll be referring to the IP PDU (Protocol Data Unit) as a datagram instead of a packet, although the term "packet" is more commonly used.

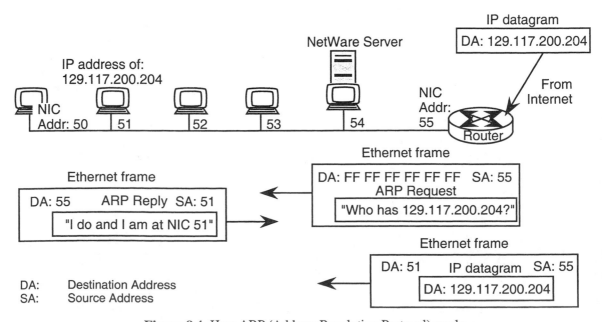

Figure 8.4 How ARP (Address Resolution Protocol) works.

In Figure 8.4 we see a LAN connected to the Internet. From the Internet, an IP datagram arrives at the router. The router looks at the IP address and verifies that this address is on its LAN. Then it looks to see if that IP address is in its ARP table. It needs the MAC address of the node with that IP address in order to send it over the Ethernet. If that IP address isn't in the ARP table, then the router will broadcast an ARP Request packet inside an Ethernet frame, asking everyone who is connected to the LAN if they have the IP address of 129.117.200.204. All nodes will read that frame, but only the one who has that particular IP address will respond. Notice that the Ethernet frame, which carries the ARP Request packet, has as its broadcast address all binary 1's, which converts to F's in hexadecimal notation.

Here, the node with a MAC address of 51 responds. (Here, we have simplified the 48-bit or the 12-hex-digit MAC address simply as 51.) This is seen in the second Ethernet frame being transmitted. Node 51 finds the address of the node that is doing an ARP Request by its SA (Source Address) field. Node 51 determines that Node 55 is requesting its MAC address. Hence, it sends an ARP Reply only to Node 55, giving its own MAC address of 51. At the same time Node 51 updates its ARP table to include Node 55's MAC and IP addresses. Once Node 55 (the router) obtains Node 51's MAC address, it can send the IP datagram which was waiting to reach its destination. At this time, the router can update its ARP table for future reference.

8.3 IP ADDRESSES

8.3.1 Dotted Decimal Notation

We have already mentioned that IP version 4 uses 32-bit-long addresses in Chapter 3. The next version of IP, called IP version 6 (IPv6), uses 128-bit-long addresses. We will primarily be using version 4 in this text. At this time it will be well worth your time to review Section 3.7 on Coding and Addressing.

Figure 8.5 shows how the 32 bits of IP addresses are converted to a form called dotted decimal notation. These bits are first grouped into four groups of 8 bits. Then each of these groups is converted into a decimal number. The four decimal numbers are then separated by a decimal point. Notice that the highest number that is possible for each of these four numbers is 255. That occurs when there are eight binary 1s.

Contrast this form of abbreviation of binary numbers with the form used to abbreviate MAC addresses. To abbreviate the 48 bits used in MAC addresses, hexadecimal digits are used instead. That gives us 12 hex digits with each hex digit

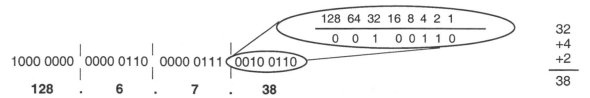

Figure 8.5 The IP address in binary being converted to the dotted-decimal format. In groups of eight, add up the positional weights for each bit that is a "1."

abbreviating 4 bits. The convention used with IP addresses is the dotted decimal notation.

8.3.2 Assignment of IP Addresses

You may recall from Chapter 3, when we were studying the concept of powers of 2, how MAC addresses for Ethernet NICs are assigned. The 48 bits are divided into two groups: 24 bits to code the manufacturer of the card and the last 24 bits to code the serial number of the card. The central authority, currently IEEE, simply manages which vendors are assigned which vendor codes, officially called OUIs (Organizational Unique Identifiers). Then each vendor can manufacture up to 2^{24} NICs, giving each a unique serial number. That is, each vendor is given a block of MAC addresses where the particular block is identified by its vendor code.

The problem with this scheme is that large manufacturers need several vendor codes, while small manufacturers never end up using all of the 2^{24} serial numbers that are available to them. The scheme of assigning blocks of IP addresses is different from this. It takes into account that large organizations need a large block of addresses and small organizations need a small block of addresses. There are also blocks of addresses for moderately sized networks.

In Figure 8.6, we see how these blocks are categorized by three classes: class A, B, or C. A large organization, like GE, needs a large block of addresses, and so they are given a class A network. (Shortly, we'll see how these classes are identified from IP addresses.) GE, for example, is given all the IP addresses from 3.0.0.0 to 3.255.255.255, that is, a total of 2^{24} addresses. Rutgers University, although it has other blocks of addresses, has a class B network with IP addresses ranging from 128.6.0.0 to 128.6.255.255. In this block they only get 2^{16} addresses. Similarly, smaller networks get smaller chunks of addresses. These blocks of addresses are called class C networks.

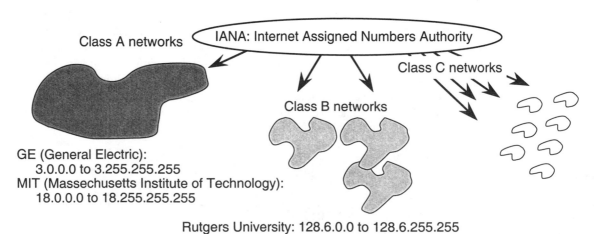

Figure 8.6 IP addresses are assigned in blocks of large, medium, and small sized networks. Examples shown were obtained from www.arin.net/whois.

There are only a few class A networks, each with many hosts, and there are many class C networks, each with only a few hosts. The network shown for GE is identified simply as 3.0.0.0, or just 3. The network shown for Rutgers is identified by 128.6.0.0 or just 128.6. I looked up these numbers from www.arin.net/whois. You can look up who has which addresses, which addresses are assigned to whom, as well as other interesting information from this web site. IANA (Internet Assigned Numbers Authority) through ARIN (American Registry for Internet Numbers) manages the assigning of IP addresses. Other continents have other registries. Other sites that you may find interesting are www.iana.net and www.internic.net.

Use of classes simplifies the management of address assignments. However, it also makes routing of packets more efficient. When an IP datagram needs to be delivered, a router doesn't need to know the precise location of the destination host. It only needs to know to which network to route the datagram. For example, if a router in Rutgers gets an IP datagram with a destination address of 3.121.7.203, it will first look at the first dotted decimal number, 3. Without examining the rest of the bits, it can send that datagram to a router in the GE network. The routers in the GE network will then examine the other bits and proceed to route the datagram until it reaches its final destination.

The assigning of IP addresses is hierarchical like many other things on the Internet. Just as the central authority assigns blocks of addresses to organizations, by the same token, an organization can delegate the administration of smaller blocks of its addresses to other managers. In the side diagram, we see that Rutgers University is responsible for all the addresses from 128.6.0.0 to 128.6.255.255. Instead of one Network administrator keeping track of which node has which address, he can assign groups of addresses to LAN managers of different buildings and/or campuses. Notice that all the addresses that are derived from 128.6.3.0 are managed by the manager at Douglass College while the addresses that are derived from 128.6.1.0 are managed by the manager at Busch Campus, and so on. This makes the management of addresses distributed. That is, the IANA keeps tabs on who has which network and each of those network administrators keeps tabs on who has which subnetwork.

Let us now turn our attention to how to identify classes.

8.3.3 Address Classes

If we enumerate all the binary numbers of the first 8 bits of an IP address, we'll end up with a list, which is summarized on the left side of Figure 8.7. This list will extend from "0000 0000" to "1111 1111." What has been done is to block this set of addresses (a total of 2^{32}) into five address classes. Addresses for the last two classes are not assignable.

If the first bit of the first octet of the IP address is a 0, then the address is classified as a class A address. From the figure, we see that a class A address' first decimal number must fall in the range from 0 to 127. Similarly, as we go down the list, we see

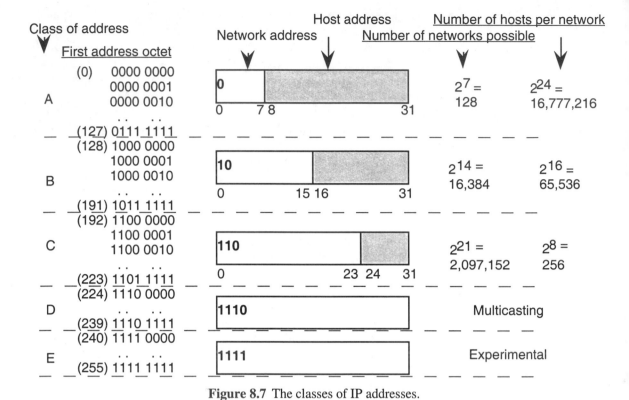

Figure 8.7 The classes of IP addresses.

that class B addresses begin with a binary "10" and are in the range from 128 to 191. Class C addresses begin with a "110" and fall in the range of 192 to 223. Likewise, class D and class E addresses are shown, which are used for multicasting and experimental purposes only.

Class A, B, and C addresses are further broken down into two parts. One part provides the network address and the second part provides the host on that network. As seen in the figure, a class A address has only 7 bits allocated to specify the network number and 24 bits allocated to specify the host number. This means that there are 2^7 or only 128 networks that have a class A address, but each of those networks may have up to 2^{24} or 16,777,216 hosts on them.

As seen in the figure, class B address uses 14 bits to specify the network number and 16 bits to specify the host number. Likewise, class C uses 21 bits for the network ID and 8 bits for the host ID.

Many of Rutgers' hosts and networks use a class B address, because they start with a 128. Notice that there are 256 class B networks that start with a decimal 128, but only one class A network that starts with a decimal 26. This is because a class B network is specified by the first 16 bits (or two dotted-decimal places) and a class A network is specified by only the first 8 bits. Hence, the addresses for Rutgers' hosts begin with the same two dotted decimal numbers; namely, 128.6.

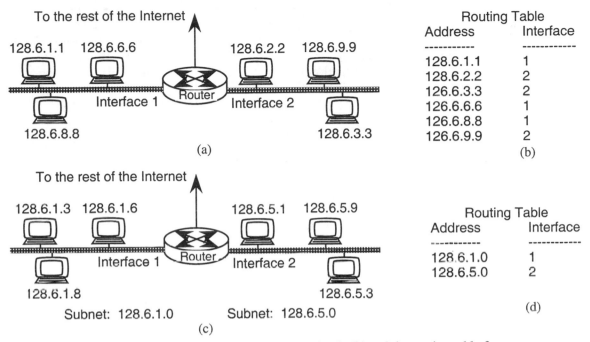

Figure 8.8 (a) Assigning addresses randomly (b) and the routing table for these addresses. (c) Using subnets (d) and its effect on the routing table.

8.4 SUBNETTING

8.4.1 Motivation for Subnetting

Suppose that we are the administrators for Rutgers and that we are assigned the class B network of 128.6.0.0. Then we have at our disposal 2^{16} IP addresses, which we can assign to our hosts in any order that we please. Our first shot at assigning these addresses is shown in Figure 8.8(a). To start with, we have only two LANs or networks located in two different physical locations. We assign the addresses with no plan in mind. They are just assigned in the order in which the hosts are connected. Our main router to the Internet has two local interfaces as shown. Each interface connects to a local network.

Now imagine what our router has to do. First, it will have to keep a table that has everyone's IP address and the interface to which it is connected. See Figure 8.8(b). As nodes are added, the table becomes larger. Furthermore, routers share their routing tables with others to let them know what is connected to them. The large table places more demand on the network as it is periodically transmitted. Looking up entries is also time consuming, not to mention the administrative nightmare of keeping track of the locations of all these IP addresses.

Recall that creating classes identified on which network a particular IP address is located. Routing our datagram to the GE network was simple since we didn't have to examine all 32 bits. Similarly, we can divide our network, 128.6.0.0, into subnets as

		Network address	Host number		
Class B addressing without subnetting		Network address		Host number	

		Network address		Subnet address	Host number
Class B addressing with subnetting on the octet boundary		Network address		Subnet address	Host number
IP address	(128.6.7.38)	1000 0000	0000 0110	0000 0111	0010 0110
Subnet mask	(255.255.255.0)	1111 1111	1111 1111	1111 1111	0000 0000
Address of the subnet	(128.6.7.0)	1000 0000	0000 0110	0000 0111	0000 0000
Host number within this subnet	38	0000 0000	0000 0000	0000 0000	0010 0110
Broadcast address for this subnet	(128.6.7.255)	1000 0000	0000 0110	0000 0111	1111 1111

Figure 8.9 ANDing the IP address and the mask bits yields the subnet address. The IP address bits for which the mask bits are 0 yield the host number and the IP address with the host bits set to 1 yields the broadcast address.

shown in Figure 8.8(c). What happens here is that the router knows all the hosts starting with 128.6 are on its network. Now it also knows that all the addresses starting with 128.6.1 are connected to its local interface 1 and all the ones starting with 128.6.5 are available on its second interface. Grouping the address assignments by using geographic locations makes the routing table much simpler. The tables become easier to do lookups and to share them with other routers. The management of IP addresses is a lot simpler. These advantages are much more apparent as more hosts and routers are added.

Another reason to create subnets is to establish security between different workgroups. Creating subnets isolates workgroups from each other and traffic doesn't go into an area of the network where it doesn't belong. When two networks are geographically separated from each other, or use two different MAC protocols, or are separated by a router, then subnetting becomes necessary.

8.4.2 How to Subnet

Let us now do an example of how to identify subnets. We will start with the 128.6.0.0 address space. According to Figure 8.7, a class B address allocates 16 bits for the host address. These host address bits can be further subdivided into a subnetwork address and a host address. At Rutgers, as with many other locations, this division is done on an octet boundary. Although this doesn't have to be the case, it makes interpretation of numeric addresses easier. Exactly how subnetting is used, if it's used at all, is a local issue and doesn't involve the rest of the Internet.

TCP/IP: Basic Concepts

In order to facilitate routing, a bit mask called a subnet mask is defined to quickly separate the subnet address and the host number from an IP address. This subnet mask allows a router to know which bits are used to identify the subnet and which bits are used to identify the host. At the top of Figure 8.9, a class B addressing scheme is redrawn and under it is our class B address scheme using one octet for subnetting. Here, the third octet is used to represent the subnet address and the fourth octet is used to represent the host number. In this case, the subnet mask of 255.255.255.0 is used.

Using an IP address and the subnet mask, let us see how the subnet and host addresses are derived. The IP address of 128.6.7.38 gives a subnet address of 128.6.7.0. This is found by ANDing the mask and address bits. The result of ANDing is a logical 1 only if the ANDed bits are both 1s; otherwise, the result is a logical 0. The host number, on the other hand, is found by masking out the IP address using only the 0 bits of the mask. From the illustrated mask, the IP address of 128.6.7.38 identifies host 38 on the subnet 128.6.7.0.

A broadcast address for a subnet is specified by setting all host bits to 1 on a subnet address. So, for our example, if the host, pilot, wants to broadcast a message to all the nodes on its subnet, it will set the address as 128.6.7.255. Let us now do some more examples of subnetting since many are asked about it in job interviews.

8.4.3 Subnetting: Example 1

Explain all the information that you can obtain from the 5 host bits on the following IP address: 1101 0110 1001 0010 1110 0111 0100 **1101**. The host bits are shown in bold throughout these examples.

	Subnet bits	Host bits
Mask	1	0
Subnet address	IP bits	0
Host number	(none)	IP bits
B'cast address	IP bits	1

Solution: Since the first bit is not 0, it isn't a class A address and since the following bit is also not zero, it isn't a class B address either. This is a class C address. In decimal, this address is 214.146.231.77. The side figure gives a good chart to help you calculate the various addresses. We have five host bits. That means that we have 27 subnet bits. According to the chart, the subnet bits are set to 1 and the host bits are set to 0 for the subnet mask. Hence, the subnet mask is 1111 1111 1111 1111 1111 1111 111**0 0000**. Converting to dotted decimal now gives a mask of 255.255.255.224. Notice, when finding the addresses in binary (or the mask), you don't need to be concerned about the four 8-bit boundaries needed to convert them into decimal form. Only worry about which are the host bits and which are the subnet bits.

Also, once you have the address in binary form and convert it to the dotted decimal form, don't concern yourself with which are the host bits, but concern yourself with the 8-bit boundaries instead. Let's do the subnet address next.

According to the side chart, here the subnet bits are the same as the IP address bits and the host bits are set to 0. This makes the subnet address to be 1101 0110 1001 0010 1110 0111 010**0 0000**. This makes the subnet address to be 214.146.231.64. Using the chart again, the host bits give the number of the host on the network. Hence, **01101** has a host id of 13. In other words, the IP address of 214.146.231.77 is host number 13 on the subnet 214.146.231.64.

IP Address	1101 0110	1001 0010	1110 0111	0100 1101	214.146.231.77
Subnet Mask	1111 1111	1111 1111	1111 1111	1110 0000	255.255.255.224
Subnet Address	1101 0110	1001 0010	1110 0111	0100 0000	214.146.231.64
Host Number				0 1101	13
Broadcast Addr.	1101 0110	1001 0010	1110 0111	0101 1111	214.146.231.95

Figure 8.10 Summary of the calculations for Example 1.

As for the broadcast address, we use the last entry on our side chart. This indicates to use the IP address for the subnet bits and to set the host bits to 1. After doing that, we get a broadcast address of 214.146.231.95. The last decimal number turned out to be 0101 1111 in binary. The last 5 bits shown in bold again are the host bits while the first three bits in this group came from the subnet bits. Figure 8.10 summarizes these calculations.

The mask indicates the number of host bits and the number of network bits. An IP address and its subnet mask can be given succinctly using the address/prefix length notation. The prefix length gives the number of 1s in the subnet mask. Hence, the IP address of this example and its mask can be written down simply as 214.146.231.77/ 27, since there are 27 1's in the subnet mask.

8.4.4 Loss of Addresses

Let us continue with the numbers we obtained for that last example. We said that the IP address, or 214.146.231.77, was host number of subnet number 13 on the subnet address of 214.146.231.64. The questions that now come to mind are how many hosts are possible on this subnet and how many subnets are possible using this mask for the entire network.

There are 5 bits to encode the host ID. That gives us 2^5 or 32 hosts possible on this particular subnet. Out of these addresses, 0 0000 is used to identify the subnet. This is seen in the subnet address of 214.146.231.64. Also, all 1's or 1 1111 is the address used for broadcasting datagrams to all nodes on the subnet. That leaves us with only 30 available addresses which we can assign to hosts. Usually, the router needs an address for its interface to the subnet as well. In any case, there are only 30 addresses that are assignable. In fact, there are always 2 addresses less than the number combinations possible mathematically because all 0's is used by the subnet address and all 1's is used by the broadcast address.

Now let us look at how many subnets are possible on the 214.146.231.0/27 network. With 3 bits left for the subnet part of the address, we get a total of 2^3 or 8 possible combinations. Again, we lose two of these addresses. 000 is used to address the network and 111 is used to address all subnets. That leaves us with a total of only 6 subnets. Two subnets are always lost for this reason. If there were 4 bits used for the subnet part of the address, then out of the 16 possible subnet addresses, only 14 would be actually available.

Figure 8.11 shows that we have 6 available subnets and each subnet can accommodate up to 30 addresses. That gives us a total of 180 assignable addresses. If we had not subnetted, then we would have had a total of 254 addresses. However, the advantages mentioned before in subnetting far outweigh this disadvantage.

6 subnet	times	30 addresses each				equals 180 addresses

~~000~~					
001		~~00000~~	01000	10000	11000
010		00001	01001	10001	11001
011		00010	01010	10010	11010
100		00011	01011	10011	11011
101		00100	01100	10100	11100
110		00101	01101	10101	11101
~~111~~		00110	01110	10110	11110
		00111	01111	10111	~~11111~~

Figure 8.11 Subnetting reduces the number of available addresses.

What if we move the subnet and host bit boundary one bit to the right? What would happen to the number of hosts per subnet and to the number of subnets? If we reduce the number of host bits, we would reduce the number of hosts, but we would also increase the number of subnets. What would happen to the number of available IP addresses?

If we use 4 host bits, that would give us 14 addresses per subnet. Then we would also have 4 subnet bits, which would also give us 14 subnet addresses. Multiplying these two numbers gives us a total of 196 addresses. If we move the host and subnet bit boundary to the right by another bit, that would give us 30 subnets with 6 hosts each. Therefore, if you want to have a maximum number of available IP addresses, always make the number of host bits and the number of subnet bits equal. If you have a class B network and you want to utilize the maximum number of addresses, use 8 bits for the subnet part and 8 bits for the host part, although that may not necessarily be the right decision to make in all circumstances.

8.4.5 Subnetting: Example 2

Let us look at one last example of assigning subnets and addresses. In Figure 8.12, we have an organization that is assigned the network 200.200.200.0. This is a class C network, so only 254 addresses are available. After much study and questioning, it is determined that at the home office we'll have a maximum of 50 interfaces. The term interface is more accurate than host because a host may have several interfaces. We have three branch offices that would require only 20 interfaces, ever. We are assuming that we will never add another branch, at least in this example. A leased line connects the routers at each branch to the router at the home office. These lines would also need IP addresses, one at each end. Each line should be on its own subnet.

From the table in the figure, we add up the number of addresses and subnets. We get 116 interfaces and 7 subnets. Suppose that we use 4 subnet bits and 4 host bits to divide up our network: That would give us a maximum of 14 addresses on 14 subnets. This would not work since the home LAN and the branch LANs require 50 and 20, respectively. If we use 3 subnet bits, that would only give us a total of 6 subnets. That won't work either. If we use 3 host bits, then again we don't have enough addresses for four of our subnets. The solution to this problem is to use what is called *variable-length subnetting*. With variable-length subnetting, we can alter our subnet bits or mask depending on the subnet, however, you have to make sure either all routers know the

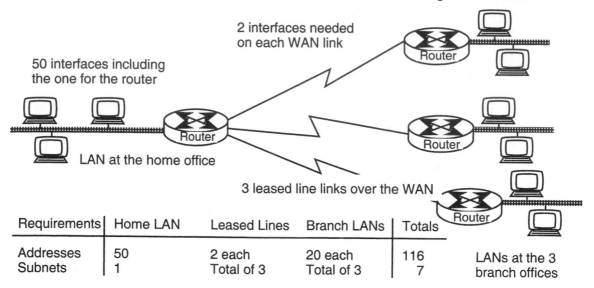

20 interfaces at each branch
including the ones for the routers

2 interfaces needed
on each WAN link

50 interfaces including
the one for the router

LAN at the home office

3 leased line links over the WAN

Requirements	Home LAN	Leased Lines	Branch LANs	Totals	
Addresses	50	2 each	20 each	116	LANs at the 3
Subnets	1	Total of 3	Total of 3	7	branch offices

Figure 8.12 An example of creating subnets.

masks of each network or you use routing protocols, such as OSPF and RIP-2, which advertise the masks with their routing tables.

Solution: The best way to start the solution is to accommodate the subnet with the largest number of hosts. The home office LAN requires 50 addresses and the smallest subnet that will provide that many addresses is a subnet with 2 bits. If we use 2 subnet bits, that would give us 6 host bits, which would provide up to 60 hosts. This is sufficient for the home office.

In the side figure, we enumerate all the combinations of the two subnet bits. The first pair and the last pair cannot be used since they represent network and broadcast addresses. Let us use the 10 subnet and leave the 01 subnet addresses for the other interfaces which need addresses. The 10 subnet gives us addresses from 1000 0000 to 1011 1111, that is from 128/26 to 191/26. The interface on the LAN side can be assigned the address 200.200.200.129 and the other hosts in the home office can be assigned addresses from 130 to 190. Remember that 200.200.200.128 is the subnet address and 200.200.200.191 is its broadcast address.

0 0 ← Cannot use
0 1 ← For other hosts
1 0 ← Use this subnet
1 1 ← Cannot use

Let us next assign addresses for the branch locations since they are the next largest subnets. Here, the smallest sized subnet that can accommodate 20 hosts each is a subnet with 3 subnet bits. That will give us 30 hosts on each subnet. In the side figure, I have enumerated all the combinations using 3 subnet bits. As always, 000 and 111 cannot be used since they are subnet and broadcast addresses. Addresses beginning with 100 and 101 have already been

0 0 0 Cannot use
0 0 1 For Branch 1
0 1 0 For Branch 2
0 1 1 For Branch 3
1 0 0 Used by home
1 0 1 Used by home
1 1 0 Not used
1 1 1 Cannot use

TCP/IP: Basic Concepts

(00) 0	These addresses fall in the	32 to 63	Branch 1
(01) 1	range of the subnet address		
(10) 2	for the 6-bit mask.	64 to 95	Branch 2
(11) 3			
		96 to 127	Branch 3
4 to 7	Link 1		
8 to 11	Link 2	128 to 191	Home Office
12 to 15	Link 3		

Figure 8.13 All addresses begin with 200.200.200. Each address range includes the first address as the subnet address and the last address as the broadcast address. For example, 200.200.200.4 is the subnet address and 200.200.200.7 is the broadcast address for Link 1, with 5 and 6 being assignable.

assigned to the home LAN. We cannot reassign these addresses. That leaves us with addresses that begin with 001, 010, 011, and 110. We choose to pick the contiguous blocks of addresses and use the first three.

Branch 1 uses the addresses from 0010 0000 to 0011 1111 or from 200.200.200.32 to 200.200.200.63. The address of 32 is its subnet address and the address of 63 is its broadcast address. Branch 2 gets the addresses from 0100 0000 to 0101 1111, that is, from 64 to 95. This time I left off the 200's. Branch 3 gets the addresses from 0110 0000 to 0111 1111, that is, from 96 to 127.

Finally, we are left with the leased line links. Since each end requires one address, only two interfaces are required on each of the three subnets. The smallest subnets which can provide two interfaces are ones with 6 subnet bits. With 2 host bits, that gives us 2 addresses per subnet. 00 and 11 cannot be used. We decide to pick addresses that begin with 0000. When assigning addresses for the home LAN, we did not use addresses in this range because the address beginning with 00 was its subnet address. All the addresses for the branches did not begin with 000. Hence, we are safe to pick these addresses.

0000 00	Cannot use
0000 01	For Link 1
0000 10	For Link 2
0000 11	For Link 3
0001 00	Unused
etc.	

For Link 1, we pick 0000 0100 as the subnet address or 4. Its broadcast address is 0000 0111 or 7. Assignable addresses are then 0000 0101 (5) and 0000 0110 (6). For Link 2, we pick 0000 1001 (9) and 0000 1010 (10). Finally, for Link 3 we pick 0000 1101 (13) and 0000 1110 (14). We summarize these addresses in Figure 8.13 to make sure no addresses overlap.

8.5 DECODING PACKETS AND FRAMES

8.5.1 Introduction

Now let us see how an Ethernet frame can be viewed on a network. We'll see how an IP datagram is encapsulated into an Ethernet frame and what other PDUs (Protocol Data Units) are encapsulated in there. In Chapter 2, we explained how OSI encapsulates the PDUs from each layer as it transmits data over a network. Each layer adds its own header as seen in the side figure. We also saw how, on the receiving side, these PDUs are extracted from each other, while the headers are stripped off by the module in each layer. In this section, we will see how that is done by looking at a frame that

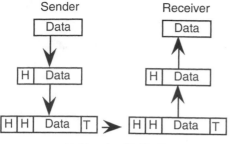

Sender   Receiver

H: Header, T: Trailer

was captured on a LAN. After this, we will be in a position to describe the layers which make up the TCP/IP Protocol Suite.

8.5.2 A Protocol Analyzer

In Figure 8.14, we have captured an Ethernet frame using the Ethereal Network Analyzer for Unix. This is free software which runs on Linux. In this figure, there are three windows whose sizes are adjustable. The window at the top is labeled (a) and highlights the frame whose details are shown in the bottom two windows. There are scroll bars on the right-hand side of these windows, which allows you to select one of the many frames that are captured in the buffer of the analyzer.

In the last and third window, labeled (e), is the actual data that makes up this frame. Each byte of data is shown as a pair of two hex digits. Remember that each hex

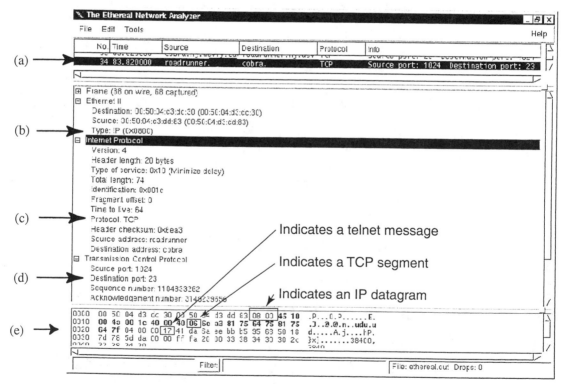

Figure 8.14 (a) The frame being examined. (b) 0800 in hex, in the Ethernet frame Type field, indicates that this is an IP datagram. (c) The protocol number in the datagram header indicates that there is a TCP segment in the datagram. (d) The destination port field, in the TCP header, indicates that this segment is carrying a telnet message. (e) The raw data seen in the frame.

digit abbreviates 4 bits. The far left column of numbers (or going vertically) shows 0000, 0010, 0020, and so on. These are simply the position numbers for each byte. These positions are labeled in hex. Hence, data is shown in groups of 16 bytes, each taking one row (or going across horizontally). The data, which is shown in hex, is also translated into ASCII characters to its right. Usually this looks like garbage unless we are looking at actual text that is being transmitted in the frame.

To help us interpret the data as it appears in the frame, the middle window shows the parts that make up this frame. The items labeled (b), (c), and (d) show the values of the various fields existing. There are many fields shown here, but we will concentrate on only a handful. The purpose here is not to understand the makeup of each protocol shown, but rather how the layering process is accomplished.

Notice that in the middle window "Internet Protocol" is highlighted. This highlights the data of the IP layer's header in the bottom window. These bytes are shown in bold by the analyzer. Toward the end of the first row, starting at "45" to the beginning of the third row at "7F," all these bytes of data belong to the IP header and are shown in bold. That makes this IP header 20 bytes long. What are the bytes before the IP header? They belong to the Ethernet header. What are the bytes that come after it? They belong to the headers of the upper-layer protocols and possibly data from the application. Let's "peel off" the headers of this frame as one peels off layers of an onion. First, in Figure 8.15(a), try counting in hex to better understand the positions of each byte of data. Some bytes are already marked off for you.

8.5.3 Decoding the Protocols in the Layer

Ethernet Layer: When the NIC gets this frame, it checks the error code at the end of the frame, which is not seen in our packet capture. If there is an error, it will discard the frame. It will check to make sure the frame's destination address matches its own. When the Ethernet driver gets this frame, it is interested in only the first 14 bytes. (Other kinds of Ethernet frames and their differences will be covered in Chapter 23.) The first 6 bytes tell the host that this frame belongs to it. This is labeled as MAC DA (Media Access Control – Destination Address). The SA (Source Address) is the MAC address from where this frame arrived. The Type field of 0x0800 determines that the data portion of the Ethernet frame is an IP datagram. "0x" in front of a number is used to signal that the number is represented in hexadecimal form. The Ethernet driver (the MAC layer) only cares about its own header, so the rest of the data is shown as grayed out. Because this is an IP datagram, the MAC software forwards the rest of the frame to the IP process. There are other values of the Type field and they are shown in the side figure. The Type field will always occur at locations 0xC and 0xD.

Type	Protocol
0800	IP
0805	X.25
0806	ARP
8035	RARP
809B	Appletalk
80D5	SNA
8137	Novell
8138	Novell

IP Protocol: Now that the MAC layer has forwarded the rest of the frame to the IP layer, the IP layer proceeds to process its header. Usually, its header is 20 bytes long and so it counts that many bytes and examines only these bytes. One of the things that it does is check from where the datagram came. This is encoded in bytes 0x1A, 1B, 1C, and 1D. In Figure (c), these bytes are circled as 81 75 64 75. This is the source IP address in hex. The following four bytes, 81 75 64 7F, are the destination IP address.

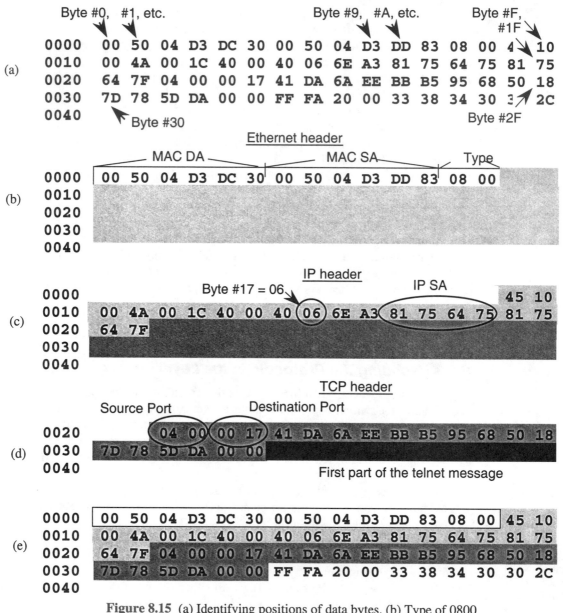

Figure 8.15 (a) Identifying positions of data bytes. (b) Type of 0800 determines that this frame is carrying an IP datagram (c) Protocol of 06 determines that the packet is carrying a TCP segment. (d) Destination port of 17 determines that this segment is carrying a telnet message. (e) Locations of all three headers are shown.

Protocol Field	Process
0x01	ICMP
0x02	IGMP
0x06	TCP
0x08	EGP
0x11	UDP

After performing other tasks relating to the header, the IP layer needs to know to which process to forward the rest of the frame. This part is shaded in darker gray and is ignored by the IP process. Byte number 0x17 indicates to the IP process that this

194   TCP/IP: Basic Concepts

part is to be forwarded to the TCP protocol. 0x06, which is the same as 06 in decimal, is called the protocol number and in this case it is the code for TCP. Other protocol numbers are shown in the side figure on the previous page.

TCP Protocol: Now the TCP process gets what's left. This is shown in Figure (d). Typically, TCP counts off 20 bytes as well to locate its header and ignores the rest which is shaded in darker gray. The header and what's after it is called a TCP *segment*. In other words, the PDU for TCP is a segment. Among many other things, TCP finds out to which application to forward the rest of the data. This information is coded in a field called the *port* number. From the middle window of Figure 8.14, we see that there is a source port number as well as a destination port number. The one that we are interested here is the smaller port number of 0x0017 or 23 in decimal. This is the destination port. This number signals the TCP process that a telnet message is enclosed in this TCP segment. Now the TCP process forwards the data portion of its segment to the telnet process. Telnet is the protocol used in the application layer in this example. Other well known port numbers are given in the side figure.

UDP/TCP	Port	Application
TCP	0x14 = 20	FTP (data)
TCP	0x15 = 21	FTP (control)
TCP	0x17 = 23	telnet
TCP	0x19 = 25	SMTP
UDP&TCP	0x35 = 53	DNS
UDP	0x43 = 67	Bootp server
UDP	0x44 = 68	Bootp client
UDP	0x45 = 69	TFTP
UDP&TCP	0x50 = 80	http (WWW)
UDP&TCP	0x89 = 137	NetBIOS

Application Layer Protocol: However, there may be many users logged into our server remotely. (Any other host than the one in question is called a remote host.) Each user invokes its own copy of the telnet process. How does the TCP process know to which copy of the telnet process the data should be forwarded? This is given in the source port number. The source port number allows TCP to identify to which connection the data belongs. Notice that this number is large, 1024 in decimal or 400 in hex, compared with the destination port number of 23. When the user shown in this frame established a telnet session, the server assigned him the port of 1024. The next user who logs into this server will be assigned a different port, possibly 1025. See the side diagram. After the user's telnet client gets a port number during the establishment of the session, it must continue to use that port number as long as the connection is up. This way, TCP can multiplex telnet messages from many sources and not get the messages mixed up. Notice, when a telnet packet goes the other way, i.e., from the server to the client, the source and destination port numbers will be switched. The smallest numbered port is always the well known port or the application and the larger port number identifies the connection.

Destination port: 23
Telnet server
Source port: 1024
Source port: 1025
Internet

For incoming packets, the source ports allow a server to differentiate between the connections.

8.5.4 Examples

There are many other values for the fields, which we have listed in the side figure. We will use these numbers to try to decode the frames shown in Figure 8.16. Here are the answers:

```
        0000    00 50 04 D3 DC 30 00 50 04 D3 DD 83 08 00 45 10
        0010    00 4A 00 1C 40 00 40 11 6E A3 81 75 64 75 81 75
(a)     0020    64 7F 04 00 00 50 41 DA 6A EE BB B5 95 68 50 18
        0030    7D 78 5D DA 00 00 FF FA 20 00 33 38 34 30 30 2C
        0040

        0000    00 50 04 D3 DC 30 00 50 04 D3 DD 83 08 22 45 10
        0010    00 4A 00 1C 40 00 40 06 6E A3 81 75 64 75 81 75
(b)     0020    64 7F 04 00 00 17 41 DA 6A EE BB B5 95 68 50 18
        0030    7D 78 5D DA 00 00 FF FA 20 00 33 38 34 30 30 2C
        0040

        0000    00 50 04 D3 DC 30 00 50 04 D3 DD 83 08 00 45 10
        0010    00 4A 00 1C 40 00 40 06 6E A3 81 75 64 75 81 75
(c)     0020    64 7F 00 15 04 00 41 DA 6A EE BB B5 95 68 50 18
        0030    7D 78 5D DA 00 00 FF FA 20 00 33 38 34 30 30 2C
        0040
```

Figure 8.16 Three examples for decoding Ethernet frames.

In Figure 8.16(a), we find 0x0800 in the location of the Type field. That makes this an IP datagram encapsulated inside an Ethernet frame. Now we look down to location 0x17 and find 0x11 there. From one of the previous side charts, this is a UDP datagram. Fortunately, the source and destination ports appear in the same location in the UDP header as they do in the TCP header. Hence, we see a 0x0050 at location 0x25 and interpret this as an http application.

In Figure 8.16(b), the Type field is not 0x0800, so it's not an IP datagram. It is not 0x0806 either, so it is not an ARP packet. Neither is it a Novell packet. Therefore, the second layer protocol is some other protocol and we cannot identify any more information about this frame from what we know so far.

Figure 8.16(c) shows that this is an IP datagram which is carrying a TCP segment. Positions 0x22 and 0x23 shows a 0x0015 so this must be an FTP application.

8.6 TCP/IP LAYERS

8.6.1 An Overview

From the analysis of our Ethernet frame capture, we observed the four layers shown in Figure 8.17. The first layer is called the network access layer. Ethernet was the protocol that we used in this layer. The other layers in order are called the internet, transport, and application layers. As far as mapping these layers with OSI, the network access layer usually corresponds to the first and second layers. The internet layer corresponds to the third or the network layer. The transport and the application layers of both models match up rather nicely. However, the TCP/IP architecture has left out the session and the presentation layers to simplify the architecture.

TCP/IP: Basic Concepts

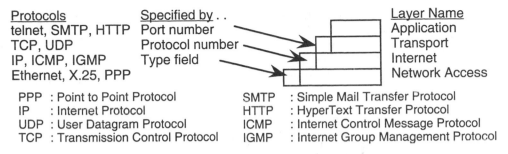

Protocols	Specified by . .	Layer Name
telnet, SMTP, HTTP	Port number	Application
TCP, UDP	Protocol number	Transport
IP, ICMP, IGMP	Type field	Internet
Ethernet, X.25, PPP		Network Access

PPP	: Point to Point Protocol	SMTP	: Simple Mail Transfer Protocol
IP	: Internet Protocol	HTTP	: HyperText Transfer Protocol
UDP	: User Datagram Protocol	ICMP	: Internet Control Message Protocol
TCP	: Transmission Control Protocol	IGMP	: Internet Group Management Protocol

Figure 8.17 The TCP/IP network architecture.

As you can see, there are many protocols included in the TCP/IP protocol suite. We will introduce some of them in this chapter and leave the remainder of them for Chapter 25.

Figure 8.18 shows the layering process of TCP/IP in a little more detail. The protocols used in the various layers are shown. IP must be used in the internet layer. ICMP (Internet Control Message Protocol) and IGMP (Internet Group Management Protocol) can also be used in this layer. However, they too must be encapsulated in an IP datagram. At the transport layer, there is a choice of only two protocols: TCP and UDP (User Data Protocol). The applications above this layer decide which of these two protocols it will invoke.

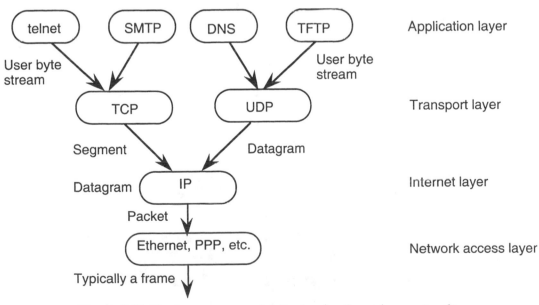

Figure 8.18 The Internet protocol suite showing the various protocols and the units of transfers between them. A packet is either a datagram or a fragment of one.

An application using TCP sends a stream of bytes, which the TCP process groups into units of exchange called *segments*. These applications do not worry about the number of bytes which are transmitted. TCP manages their correct order.

Applications that use UDP must be aware of the size of data that they send because UDP doesn't group the bytes into smaller chunks. Whatever chunk of data it receives from the application is forwarded to the IP process as a datagram. If the size of the datagram is too large to be allowed on the network access layer, then IP must fragment a large datagram into smaller-sized packets.

For example, the largest amount of data allowed on Ethernet is 1500 bytes, plus the additional Ethernet overhead. IP, if necessary, will divide a datagram into fragments of 1500 bytes. The largest-sized data that is allowed on a physical network is called the MTU (Maximum Transfer Unit). The type of physical network the data is transferred on determines the value of MTU, which is measured in bytes. If packets are transferred over several physical networks, then the smallest MTU of these networks becomes the MTU for the entire path since the network with the smallest MTU becomes the constraining factor in determining the largest size.

In section 2.6 we introduced the concept of how IP datagrams are delivered over the Internet and in section 2.7 we discussed the differences between connection-oriented and connectionless deliveries. We also discussed tunneling and encapsulation. You may want to review those sections now before going further.

8.6.2 The Network Access Layer

The Internet is an interconnection of many networks. In fact, that is why the DoD (Department of Defense) funded the development of TCP/IP. Instead of mandating that all research universities and government agencies buy all new computers and networks running the same operating system on the same hardware, and so on, TCP/IP enabled all existing networks and hosts to be interconnected. As long as the hosts implemented this set of protocols it didn't matter what kind of host, operating system, connection (slow speed or high speed), etc., it had. Every type of host and network was able to attach to the Internet. Today, this still holds true.

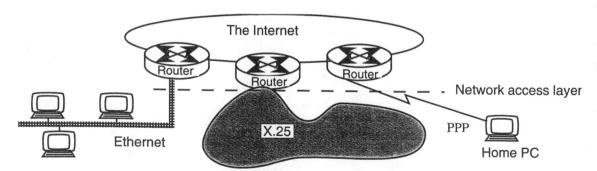

Figure 8.19 The Internet is an interconnection of networks. These networks could be LANs, WANs, or dedicated access lines. The network access layer provides the means of connecting them.

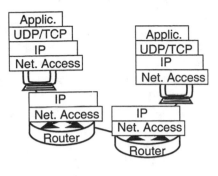

Technically, this layer is not really defined in the Internet Suite of Protocols. Nonetheless, this layer allows any type of connection to the Internet. As seen in Figure 8.19, a LAN, a WAN, and a dedicated access connection are shown being connected to the Internet using this layer.

As with a LAN or PPP (Point-to-Point Protocol), the Network Access Layer can be composed of two layers. As with an X.25 network, it can be composed of three layers. See Figure 2.13(c). If an SNA network is attached to the Internet, then this layer provides the services of all seven layers of the OSI model. This layer provides connectivity to the Internet no matter what is connected to it.

8.6.3 The Internet Protocol

We will use Table 8.1 to describe and compare the three protocols: IP, UDP, and TCP. As seen in the table, typically the size of the IP header is 20 bytes. IP is said to be a protocol that is used by all hosts along the path of a datagram. UDP and TCP are said to be end-to-end protocols. These are protocols which are handled only by the end hosts, the transmitting and receiving hosts. See the side figure.

As discussed in sections 2.6 and 2.7, IP is connectionless. That is, to send data no connection has to be established. Data can be fired into the network as soon as it becomes available. This is one of the reasons why processing IP datagrams is fast. Routers in the Internet must use IP to forward packets. All packets belonging to the same datagram or message travel independently from each other since each packet's header contains the destination IP address.

Table 8.1 Comparison of IP, UDP, and TCP Protocols			
	IP	UDP	TCP
Typical size of the header in bytes	20	8	20
Name of the PDU (Protocol Data Unit)	Datagram	Datagram	Segment
Is this only an end-to-end protocol?	No	Yes	Yes
Is it connection-oriented?	No	No	Yes
Processing-wise, is it fast or slow?	Fast	Fast	Slow
Does it provide a reliable transfer of data?	No	No	Yes
Does the checksum include the header?	Yes	Yes	Yes
Does the checksum include the data?	No	Yes	Yes
Is using the checksum mandatory?	Yes	No	Yes
When an error is found, is retransmission requested? Or is the PDU silently discarded?	No No	No Yes	No Yes

TCP/IP: Basic Concepts

However, there is no reliable transfer of data. Reliability means that there is no acknowledgment of data, either positive or negative. Packets may come out of sequence, they may be duplicated, or they may become lost. No retransmission of data packets are requested. If packets arrive at an intermediate router too fast, it can simply drop or discard them, but it will try its best to route it. For this reason, IP is said to provide a *best effort* service. There is no guarantee that the packet will get to its destination. When packets are dropped, IP will try to send a ICMP error message back to the sender stating that the packet was dropped. TCP, on the other hand, provides reliability, if necessary.

The IP header contains a field called the header checksum. This field helps a host check for errors only in the header. No errors are checked in the data portion of a datagram. Hence, when a packet arrives, chances are that it arrived at its proper destination, but its data may be corrupted. If, on the other hand, the headers were not checked for errors, then packets may end up at the wrong locations, unnecessarily using up network bandwidth. Routers on a path of a packet only have to check for errors in the headers, and not the data as well. That is another reason why IP processes are fast. Furthermore, header lengths are fixed usually at 20 bytes and this also helps in keeping processing overhead low.

In all three protocols mentioned in Table 8.1, notice that if any error is found with its PDU, the PDU is discarded. However, when an IP module finds an error in its header, it will not silently discard it. It will try to send an ICMP Parameter Problem message back to the sender along with the header of the datagram which had the error. Also, the first 64 bytes of the datagram, which may include headers from other layers, are also sent in this message.

UDP, TCP, ICMP, and IGMP all check for data errors and they all use IP to transport their PDUs. Hence, it would be redundant if IP checked for data errors as well, so IP doesn't.

8.6.4 UDP

As seen in Table 8.1, UDP has a small header of only 8 bytes. It also is connectionless. These are two reasons why UDP works fast. Like IP, reliability is not an issue with UDP. No positive or negative acknowledgments of transmitted datagrams are received. If an application requires reliability, it must use TCP instead of UDP. However UDP can check for errors in both the header and its data field. If an error is found, it is silently discarded without generating any retransmission requests or error messages. A checksum is optional with UDP but should always be used.

If UDP doesn't provide reliability or acknowledgment of data, and provides no connection, why would an application want to use UDP in the first place? The primary purpose for using UDP is it provides a means to code the port numbers of the applications. Maybe the application doesn't need a connection or maintains its own. Additionally, reliability may not be an issue for an application. For example, RIP (Routing Information Protocol), which uses UDP, sends out its routing tables at regular intervals. If one transmission gets lost, well there are more that are coming. Furthermore, why set up a connection for a transmission that is made up of only a few bytes? The overhead of establishing a connection in such instances is higher than sending the actual data. It is for these reasons that using UDP over TCP makes more sense for an application. The advantages UDP provides over IP is it provides data integrity and port addressing, while over TCP, it provides processing speed.

8.6.5 TCP

If speed is all that is required by an application, then UDP suffices. However, over UDP, TCP provides connection-oriented data transfers and reliability. Data streams arrive at their destination applications in order. Errors are removed and corrected. Duplicate data is dropped. If one or more of these services are necessary for an application, then TCP becomes mandatory. These facilities which are provided by TCP require more time than UDP. Additionally TCP's header is larger than UDP's.

From Table 8.1, we see that when TCP detects an error using its checksum field, the segment is silently dropped and no error message is generated. No negative acknowledgment is sent. Then how does TCP provide reliability? With TCP, only positive acknowledgments are sent. When the transmitting TCP module sends out a segment, it starts a timer and if within a certain time period if it doesn't receive an acknowledgment, it will retransmit that segment.

Retransmissions can cause duplicate segments to arrive at the destination TCP module. It is TCP's responsibility to delete duplicates. Also, TCP segments are delivered over IP datagrams which may not arrive in the order in which they were sent. It is TCP's responsibility to sequence them back in order.

TCP establishes a connection with the destination before data is transmitted, after which it drops the connection. During the connection establishment and the data transfer phases, the TCP protocol sends out how much buffer space it has available. This signals the transmitting TCP module how much data to send without receiving any acknowledgments. If the TCP module sent all the data that the receiving module can accept, then the transmitting module has to wait until its timer expires. Then if it still did not receive any acknowledgments, it can start retransmitting. This is the mechanism TCP uses to provide data flow control.

In summary, TCP drops duplicate segments. It sequences them and recovers lost ones. It checks for errors and, if none are found, provides acknowledgments. A lack of acknowledgments signals that the segments must be retransmitted. TCP also provides flow control. In other words, TCP provides a connection-oriented service and a reliable transfer of data.

8.6.6 ICMP

The unit of transfer used by ICMP (Internet Control Message Protocol) is called a message. It has a fixed-size header of 4 bytes. The length of its data portion may vary. The primary purpose of this protocol is for two IP modules to communicate with each other, although applications can also access its services directly without using either TCP or UDP. Because IP has no mechanism of sending error messages, ICMP is used for that purpose by IP. Additionally, no errors are generated by another ICMP error message. Otherwise, errors could generate more errors. To further restrict the number of error messages generated, only one ICMP error message is sent if a fragment that is a part of a group of other fragments fails. The implementation of ICMP is mandatory in all hosts (that includes routers as well) where IP is used.

Error Messages: ICMP typically generates error messages for IP. As was said previously in the IP section, an ICMP error message contains the header and the first 64 bytes of the datagram that caused the error. Receiving this information helps the source host to locate the cause of the error. Only error reporting is done, and no mechanism exists for correcting errors. When a source host receives an ICMP error message from a datagram which it sent, it must communicate with the application that generated that datagram to correct the problem. ICMP itself cannot correct the problem. Typically, it is the source host that causes errors in the IP datagrams and not the intermediate routers. Also, when an error is detected, only the source IP address is available in the datagram. For these reasons, ICMP error messages are usually sent to the source host rather than an intermediate router.

There are only five types or categories of error messages. These are: Destination Unreachable (network, protocol, port, etc., are unknown), Source Quench (to slow down the source), Time Exceeded (packet may be stuck in a loop), Parameter Problem (problem with the IP header), and Redirect (informing a source host of a better route).

Query Messages: Besides error reporting, ICMP also uses query messages. Typically, query messages fall into two types: query request and query response. Ping is an application that uses ICMP query messages called Echo Request and Echo Reply. Ping allows one to see if there is a physical connection to a host and to see if it is up or not. Usually, if doing a ping to a host does not work, then nothing else (for example, telnet, ftp, DNS, or any other application) will work with that host. On the other hand, if any one of these applications works on a host, then ping has to work. This is because ping does a minimum check to see if there is a connection and that the host is up. Hence, if an application works with a remote host, then a ping to it should work.

The way ping is implemented, however, causes a security hole on servers, so ping may be disabled by that host's administrator. If that is the case, then if ping doesn't work, an application may still work, and if an application works, then there is no assurance that ping will too.

EXERCISES

Section 8.1:
1. What numbering system is used mostly to abbreviate long binary numbers?
   a. hex   b. octal (base 8)
   c. decimal   d. base e
2. Using the answer for Question 1 above, how many binary digits (bits) are abbreviated by one digit of this numbering system?
   a. 2   b. 4
   c. 10   d. 16
3. The number 101101 appears in which of the following number systems?
   a. binary   b. hex
   c. decimal   d. all of the above

4. Convert c0.a0.d3.49 from hex to decimal. Then convert it to a binary number.
5. Convert 1011010111 from binary to hex and then to decimal. Also, convert A09 from hex to binary and then to decimal.
6. How many numbers exist from 1 to 100 in hex? In hex, which numbers come after 19, 99, af, 3f, 39, and ff? Which numbers come precede 40, c0, dd, and 500?

Section 8.2:

7. A MAC address is to be found for an IP address. In which situation will an ARP Request packet NOT be sent?
8. Which type of ARP packet is a unicast packet?
9. Is an ARP Request sent over the Internet through routers? Why or why not?
10. Explain how and when ARP tables increase and decrease in size.
11. What is the purpose of the ARP protocol?

Section 8.3:

12. Which of the following classes of addresses do NOT use a host address field?
    a. class A   b. class B
    c. class C   d. class D
13. Convert 120.243.118.3 to binary and then to hex.
14. What is the largest dotted decimal number that is possible? For example, which of the following numbers are invalid? 1024.893.0.260
15. Suppose class B addresses began with the bits "10," and following the $10_{(decimal)}$ bits were the network address. If the total length of the IP address is $32_{(decimal)}$ bits, how many class B networks would be possible and how many hosts would each network have?
16. Go to www.arin.net/whois and find out who has the network 129.117? What class address is this? What is the range of host addresses this network has?
17. What is the difference between how Ethernet MAC addresses are assigned by its central authority and the way IP addresses are assigned by its central authority?
18. What are two advantages of creating classes? Can you think of a disadvantage?

Section 8.4:

19. For the address of 1101 0010 0110 1110 0001 1101 1001 0110, give its address class, the subnet address, the broadcast address and the host address, if subnetting is done using the last 4 bits for the host. Give your answers in both binary and decimal forms. How many hosts does this subnet have? What is the class of this network? How many subnets does this network have? In total how many assignable IP addresses are available using this subnetting scheme? If no subnetting were done, how many assignable IP addresses would have been available?
20. In what situations would you want to increase the number of host bits and reduce the number of subnet bits? In what situations would you want to do the reverse? In what situations would you want to not have any host bits, i.e., not want to subnet at all?
21. Why is subnetting done?
22. Suppose that we have at our disposal the range of addresses starting from 198.8.234.0 to 198.8.234.255. How would you create the subnets if we need a maximum of 20 subnets with 5 hosts each? For the first three subnets and the last one that are possible using this scheme, list all their subnet addresses, their masks, and their broadcast addresses. For the first subnet and the last one, also list all their possible IP addresses.

23. For this problem use a variable-length mask. Suppose we have been assigned the network of 203.45.3.0. We have a corporate office that needs 58 hosts on its LAN. There are three remote branch offices, connected by WAN links: they will need 10, 20, and 24 hosts on their LANs respectively. Give the subnetting scheme and explain how different interfaces will be assigned addresses. Make the home office LAN subnet to be 203.45.3.64 so it would be easier for you to compare each other's addresses.

24. Continuing from the above question, suppose that we had 5 remote locations. How many IP addresses would be available at each location? Explain how the addresses would be assigned to the remote locations and the WAN links.

Section 8.5:

25. Which field in the datagram header specifies whether the data portion of the datagram goes to TCP or UDP?
    a. type of service   b. destination port
    c. protocol   d. destination address

26. On the Ethereal Protocol Analyzer shown in Figure 8.14, what does the middle show?
    a. the number of the packet selected.   b. the purpose of the packet
    c. the actual data   d. the interpretation of the data fields

27. Starting with the Ethernet packet, what are the fields that are examined by the various protocols to forward its data portion to the upper layer?

(a)
```
0000    FF FF FF FF FF FF 00 00 C0 D3 DD 83 08 06 00 01
0010    08 00 06 04 00 00 00 00 C0 D3 DD 83 C0 75 B9 64
0020    FF FF FF FF FF FF 41 DA 6A EE BB B5 95 68 50 18
0030    7D 78 5D DA 00 00 FF FA 20 00 33 38 34 30 30 2C
```

(b)
```
0000    00 00 0C D3 DD 83 00 00 0C D3 DD 53 08 00 45 00
0010  · 00 2C 00 01 00 00 40 06 8B 3A C0 99 B8 2C C0 99
0020    B8 21 04 2B 00 19 41 DA 6A EE BB B5 95 68 50 18
0030    7D 78 5D DA 00 00 FF FA 20 00 33 38 34 30 30 2C
0040
```

(c)
```
0000    00 50 04 D3 DC 30 00 50 04 D3 DD 83 08 00 45 00
0010    00 38 30 BC 00 00 80 01 A8 03 C0 99 B7 64 C0 99
0020    B7 02 05 00 04 47 C0 99 B7 32 45 00 00 68 50 18
0030    7D 78 5D DA 00 00 FF FA 20 00 33 38 34 30 30 2C
0040
```

(d)
```
0000    00 50 04 D3 DC 30 00 50 04 D3 DD 83 08 00 45 00
0010    00 38 30 BC 00 00 80 11 A8 03 C0 99 B7 64 C0 99
0020    B7 02 00 89 04 47 C0 99 B7 32 45 00 00 68 50 18
0030    7D 78 5D DA 00 00 FF FA 20 00 33 38 34 30 30 2C
```

Figure 8.20 Four Ethernet frames to be decoded for Exercise 28.

28. Decode each of the packets shown in Figure 8.20. Use the information that was covered in this chapter. Use only the values that are given in the side figures. If a value is not listed, then label the protocol at that layer to be unknown.

Section 8.6:
29. Which of the following is NOT a layer defined in the TCP/IP protocol architecture?
    a. data link   b. application
    c. internet   d. transport
30. If the TCP layer in a host receives an error in a segment, what does it do?
    a. It sends a NAK.
    b. It requests the transmitting process to reduce the window size.
    c. It discards the segment and simply waits until the segment is resent.
    d. It sets the ACK flag to 0.
31. All data being processed through TCP/IP protocols must be processed by which layer?
32. Name the transport layer protocol that is unreliable.
33. What are some differences between the OSI reference model and the TCP/IP architecture?
34. Which application level command uses ICMP messages?
35. Name the five types of ICMP error messages.
36. What are the similarities and differences between IP and UDP protocols?
37. What are the advantages of UDP over TCP?
38. What are the advantages of TCP over UDP?

Chapter 9

Signaling

9.1 WHAT IS SIGNALING?

Imagine if we were made with all of the parts of the body, but didn't have our nervous system. Then we would not be able to tell our legs to walk or to perform even the simplest actions. We would be paralyzed. Similarly, in a much simpler sense, a telephone network with sophisticated digital switches all interconnected would be useless if there were no method of communication defined among them. Therefore, signaling is said to be the nervous system of a network. It is the exchange of control information between two points in a network that establishes, maintains, or removes a connection.

9.2 STEPS TAKEN IN PLACING A CALL

9.2.1 Call Origination

We will use Figure 9.1 to outline the steps taken to complete an interoffice call. Here office means the CO (Central Office). In the telephone industry, the term EO (End Office) is used to refer to the switching equipment connected to a telephone which processes calls. I'll refer to it simply as the CO.

First, the calling party takes his or her phone off the hook, which completes an electrical circuit through the pair of wires. Current starts to flow and the equipment at the CO notices this current. Then the CO connects a register to the line to store the subscriber's dialed digits, and then it provides a dial tone, signaling him that the dialing can begin.

When a phone is on-hook, it draws no current from the CO and is said to be in the idle state. Conversely, when it is off-hook, it draws current and is said to be in the active state or to seize the line.

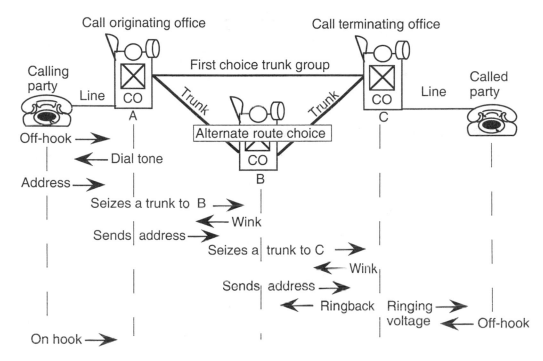

Figure 9.1 Exchange of signals over interoffice trunks.

9.2.2 Call Routing

The switch at CO-A searches its routing guide, and finds that the calling party is located at CO-C. The guide indicates that the direct trunk to CO-C is the first choice in routing the call. However, since all of the trunks to C are active, CO-A consults the routing guide again and finds an alternate route choice as the trunk group to CO-B.

CO-A finds and seizes an idle trunk connected to CO-B. CO-B connects a register to the circuit and sends a "wink," which is an off-hook condition followed by an on-hook condition. Sensing that CO-B is ready, CO-A sends the digits of the calling party.

Noticing from the received digits that the called party is not directly connected to it, CO-B obtains a connection to CO-C in the same manner that CO-A obtained one to CO-B. CO-C then realizes that the called party is connected to it and not to another CO, so it provides a ringing voltage to the phone, provided that the phone is idle. A ringback, which is also called an audible ringing tone, is transmitted by CO-C back to the calling party's phone.

9.2.3 Answer Supervision

When the called party picks up the phone, the ringing voltage and the ringback tone are removed by CO-C. An off-hook signal, which is called an answer supervision signal, is transmitted to CO-A, and CO-A now knows that the called party has answered the phone. If necessary, a record for billing can begin and the call is connected.

9.2.4 Disconnect and Call Clean-up

Figure 9.1 shows that the calling party has hung up first. However, the called party may hang up first instead. This is called the disconnect phase. The call clean-up phase restores all the trunks to their idle conditions, and CO-A will stop the billing recording at this time.

9.3 TYPES OF SIGNALING FORMATS

Signaling which has only two states, such as on-hook or off-hook, presence of current or no current, application of a frequency or the absence of it, is said to provide a supervisory function.

Address signaling function is provided where a phone number is present in the signaling.

Information signaling is provided by tones and recorded announcements such as ". . . this number has been disconnected."

A dial tone is a combination of 350 Hz and 440 Hz signals. A ringback tone consists of 440 Hz and 480 Hz. A busyback signal or line busy tone uses combinations of 480 Hz and 620 Hz tones interrupted every second. A reorder tone or all trunks busy tone is the same as a busy tone but is pulsed twice as fast as a busy tone.

An alerting function is provided by the ringing, flashing, and receiver off-hook tones. The ringing voltage of 90 VAC at 20 Hz activates the ringer on a phone. It typically is on for 2 seconds and off for 4 seconds.

Flashing is done by the subscriber after being connected. The subscriber momentarily goes on-hook and immediately goes off-hook again. Since the on-hook condition is for a short duration, the switch doesn't mistake it for a disconnect. Flashing allows an operator to get back on the line to signal a PBX that a special function code is to follow or to place a call on hold.

9.4 SIGNALING DELAYS AND INTEROFFICE SIGNALING

There are three types of delays present when processing a call over a network: dialing delay, answer delay, and post dialing delay. Dialing delay is the amount of time taken from getting a dial tone until the last digit of the phone number is dialed. The use of tone dialing over rotary pulse dialing has helped to reduce this kind of signaling delay. Answer delay is the time taken for the called party to pick up the phone from the time the first ring was heard.

Lastly, post dialing or ringing delay is the time between these two delays. It is the time taken between when the caller dials the last digit and the time when the phone starts ringing at the distant end.

9.4.1 Per-trunk Signaling

Notice back in Figure 9.1 that if a direct trunk were available from CO-A to CO-C, this delay would have been shorter. Conversely, if a call had to go through many switches, then this delay would increase. This is because all of the switches which lie in the path of the call would do their switch processing one at a time. For example, in Figure 9.1, CO-C could not start its switching process until CO-B received the phone address from CO-A.

The signaling described in Figure 9.1 is an example of per-trunk signaling, also known as CAS (Channel Associated Signaling). This means that all of the signaling (supervisory, addressing, information, and alerting type) is sent over the same physical path as the voice.

9.4.2 Common Channel Interoffice Signaling

Today telephone carriers use CCIS (Common Channel Interoffice Signaling), which is quite different in nature from per-trunk signaling. The idea behind CCIS is to avoid using expensive voice grade trunks to send signaling. Instead it separates the signaling from the voice path, and uses an entirely different network just for signaling. Furthermore, since signaling information is basically data, that is on-hook, off-hook conditions, addressing, etc., it makes the signaling network a packet data network.

Figure 9.2 shows how three switches are connected to each other using CCIS. Here, the voice paths are separated from the signaling paths. STPs (Signaling Transfer Points) are used in the signaling network to properly route packets of signaling. So when CO-A finds no trunks available to CO-C to make a call, it notices free trunks to CO-B. Then CO-A sends the address of the destination phone it wishes to connect to, to an STP. After the STP network has found out that the destination phone is idle and available to take a call, all involved switches are directed and simultaneously notified to complete the voice path to CO-C. After making a continuity check of the path, the ringing is activated.

Since the STPs are critical for network operations, they are deployed in pairs, so if one fails, the other one can take all of the signaling traffic. SS7 (Signaling System 7), which is the current implementation of CCIS, is the topic of Chapter 18. SS7 is a type of packet switching network, so it is left for discussion later in the text.

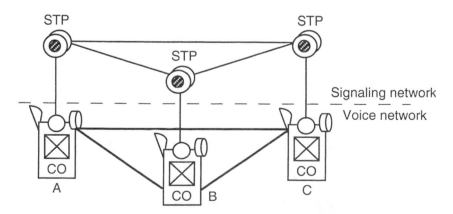

Figure 9.2 CCIS uses a data packet network that is separated from the voice network. STPs (Signaling Transfer Points) are the packet switches that comprise the signaling network.

9.4.3 The Advantages of CCIS

The advantages of CCIS are many. First, the post dialing delay is reduced drastically. Within a LATA, a connection is made as soon as the last digit is dialed. For a coast-to-coast call the typical delay is 4 seconds as compared to 20 seconds experienced with per-trunk signaling.

Furthermore, not as many voice trunks are as necessary as before, because the voice trunks only handle voice, and each call uses the voice trunks for less time. With per-trunk signaling, the called switch provides the busyback signal over the voice trunk. With CCIS, in such a case, the voice trunks are not used at all. Information that the distant phone is busy is relayed to the calling switch over the signaling network, and the calling switch provides the busyback signal to the phone.

One of the early reasons why CCIS was introduced was to provide 800 number service. Since then CCIS has become the vehicle to provide calling card, virtual network, ISDN, and many other new sophisticated services.

The signaling network, a packet switched network, is very efficient in transporting data. The signaling for all of the circuits is handled over a common link from the switch to the STP, and every voice circuit doesn't need its own separate link.

This is the reason why it is called common channel signaling. The signaling for all of the calls is sent over this common channel. With per-trunk signaling, the signaling for each call between a pair of switches travels on a separate channel, which is unlike CCIS.

9.5 KINDS OF ADDRESS SIGNALING

9.5.1 Dial Pulsing

Rotary dial pulses have been the traditional method of signaling an address (or a phone number). Once a phone goes off-hook and it receives a dial tone, it can start sending the first digit. In Figure 9.3, the digits being sent are 4 and 2. The number of times the line is made to go on-hook determines the digit that is being dialed. Since the duration of the break is relatively small, about 60 milliseconds, the switch does not inadvertently disconnect the phone. The percent break of dial pulsing is defined to be the ratio of break duration to the pulse period. This is usually kept at 60%.

Although the waveform of dial pulsing looks digital, it is slow and the dialing delay depends on the digits dialed. A zero requires 10 pulses and since each pulse period is 100 milliseconds long, it takes one second just to dial the number zero.

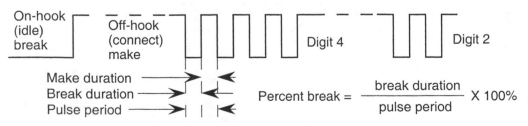

Figure 9.3 Typical train of rotary dial pulses.

9.5.2 DTMF Signaling

With tone signaling or DTMF (Dual-Tone MultiFrequency) signaling, all digits are transmitted with the same small delay, around 120 milliseconds. The digits are placed in a matrix, as shown in Figure 9.4. Here dialing a number activates two different signal generators: one determined by the row the digit is in and the other determined by its column. For instance, when a "1" is dialed, a 1209 Hz and 697 Hz tone are superimposed and transmitted.

DTMF provides "*" and "#," characters not found on rotary dials. However, the letters "q" and "z" are still missing. The four positions available from the right column are not currently used, but could be used for special purposes.

It seems as if the assignment of these frequencies was made randomly. But in fact, these frequencies were chosen to minimize false signaling due to harmonic interference and the human voice. False signaling is the misinterpretation of control signals due to unintended causes.

DTMF reduces dialing delay, especially if a prerecorded number is dialed. It uses solid-state equipment, which reduces the equipment needed at the switches. It is also compatible with modern electronic switches and provides end-to-end signaling.

End-to-end signaling allows a phone to interact with a computer on the dialed end of the circuit. Voice processing applications, covered in Chapter 9, would not be as advanced as they are today without DTMF. In essence, DTMF allows an ordinary telephone to have the functionality of a computer terminal.

9.5.3 MF Signaling

DTMF signaling is used for subscriber lines and MF (MultiFrequency) signaling is used between switches or for interoffice trunks. MF signaling, which came before DTMF and is now being phased out by SS7, uses combinations of two frequencies out of a possible six. See Table 9.1 for how these frequencies are used. In MF signaling, the human voice could possibly simulate one of these control signals (false signaling), so the duration of the tones was increased. Also, before the digits were transmitted a

	ABC	DEF		
1	2	3	11	697 Hz
GHI	JKL	MNO		
4	5	6	12	770 Hz
PRS	TUV	WXY		
7	8	9	13	852 Hz
	OPER			
*	0	#	14	941 Hz
1209	1336	1477	1633 Hz	

Figure 9.4 DTMF uses a grid made out of row frequencies and column frequencies to assign frequency pairs to the digits. 11 through 14 are currently not used.

Table 9.1 MF Frequency Pair Assignments			
Frequencies (in Hz)	Digit	Frequencies (in Hz)	Purpose
900 + 700	1	1700 + 700*	Ringback from coin control
1100 + 700	2	1700 + 900*	Delay operator
1100 + 900	3	1700 + 1100*	Start of address
1300 + 700	4	1700 + 1300	Transit code
1300 + 900	5	1700 + 1500	End of address
1300 + 1100	6		
1500 + 700	7		* These frequency
1500 + 900	8		combinations have other
1500 + 1100	9		functions as well
1500 + 1300	0 or 10		

start-of-address frequency pair was sent and afterwards the end-of-address frequency was sent.

9.6 SIGNALING TYPES PROVIDING SUPERVISION

9.6.1 SF Signaling

Unlike the addressing signaling methods which were just described, SF signaling is used to exchange on and off conditions or to provide supervisory signaling. With SF (Single Frequency), when a customer line is idle a continuous tone is transmitted, and when the tone goes off, the CO knows that the customer is seizing the line. See Table 9.2. If the CO provides a tone, that is interpreted as a ringing condition, and if the tone is absent, it is interpreted as an idle condition. SF can also provide addressing, if the tone is turned on and off as with dial pulsing.

DTMF, MF, and SF signaling are considered as facility-independent signaling formats. This means that these tones can be sent over twisted pair, coax, microwave, fiber, or any other transmission facility. Dial pulsing is an example of facility-dependent signaling, in that it can only be used on a twisted pair with a –48 VDC power source. Dial pulsing is also categorized as DC signaling, in that it requires DC voltage and current to operate. The signaling types which are being described next, loop start and ground start, are also types of DC signaling.

9.6.2 Loop Start Signaling

In analyzing circuits with DC loop currents, keep in mind that AC signals can ride on top of DC voltages. Dial tones, DTMF signals, and voice are examples of such AC signals. If a path is open for DC current, using a capacitor, it can short AC signals.

Table 9.2 SF (Single Frequency) Operation		
	From customer line to CO	From CO to customer line
Tone ON Tone OFF	idle seizure	ringing idle and busy

The purpose of these descriptions is to study DC loop currents and not the AC voltages that are also typically present.

Loop start signaling is commonly used on residential or subscriber loops, and it requires only one pair of wires. One lead of the pair is called the tip and the other is called the ring.

Figure 9.5(a) shows a phone on-hook. Notice that the contact is open in the phone at that time, allowing no current to flow in any direction. No current yields 0 volts across all three resistors. That is, since voltage is equal to current times resistance, and current is zero, voltages across all the resistances are zero. Furthermore, the voltage on the tip side of the pair is 0V, and from the ring it is −48 VDC.

Figure 9.5(b) shows that when the phone goes off-hook the contact is closed, the circuit is completed, and current may flow through the loop. At the CO about 20 volts is dropped both on the tip lead and on the ring lead, leaving only 8 VDC across the telephone. The presence of DC current is detected at the CO, which then attaches a dial tone generator and a digit receiver to the circuit. All AC signals ride on top of the DC voltage.

When a call comes in, and an incoming 90 VAC ringing voltage arrives, it rides on the DC voltage and activates the ringer.

9.6.3 Advantages of Ground Start Signaling

Ground start signaling uses DC loop currents and one twisted pair as does loop start signaling. However, ground start signaling is used primarily with PBXs and not on subscriber loops. Using loop start signaling with PBXs introduces several of the following problems which are not present in ground start signaling. First, let me clarify a definition. A ground start line between a CO and a PBX is referred to as a trunk on the PBX side and is referred to as a line on the end office side.

Suppose a PBX which is not equipped to detect dial tones sends an off-hook condition over a loop start line. Then it must wait a prespecified amount of time before sending out its dialing digits, expecting that enough time has passed to receive the dial tone. By chance if the CO hasn't sent the dial tone yet and isn't ready to receive the digits at that time, then the dialing digits will get lost. With ground start this problem is eliminated.

If, on a line, a ring is received that begins with the 4-second quiet period instead of the 2-second ringing period, and at the same time, the PBX seizes that line to make

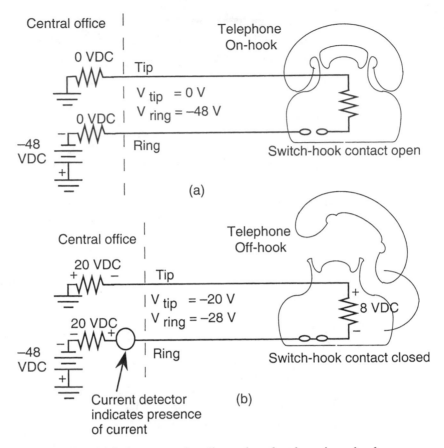

Figure 9.5 (a) In loop start signaling, when the phone is on-hook, no current is present and the voltage across the ring is −48 volts. (b) When the phone goes off-hook, current flows and this voltage becomes −28 volts. The current detected in the loop is noticed by the CO and it connects a digit receiving register and sends a dial tone.

a call, then the two calling parties are surprisingly connected. This is called glare and is more common on home phones which use loop start signaling. In a business environment, however, this phenomena is undesirable. With ground start, the CO provides a positive trunk seizure.

The last advantage ground start signaling has over loop start is that the former provides answer supervision. This means that if the distant end hangs up while the PBX has that party on hold, then the CO can signal the PBX that the trunk has become free and is available to initiate other calls.

9.6.4 Operation of Ground Start Signaling

In Figure 9.6, (a) shows the idle condition for ground start signaling, (b) and (c) show how an outgoing call is made, and (d) and (e) show how an incoming call is received. Notice that in loop start, one two-position switch is used, and here two three-position switches are used.

In the idle condition, neither batteries draw current, since both switches are in the open condition. In Figure 9.6(b), the PBX is initiating a call by grounding its ring lead. This causes current to flow in the ring lead, which is detected by the CO. The CO realizes that the PBX has gone "off-hook," and it attaches a digit receiver, sends a dial tone, and grounds its tip. The current in the tip lead is now detected by the PBX and

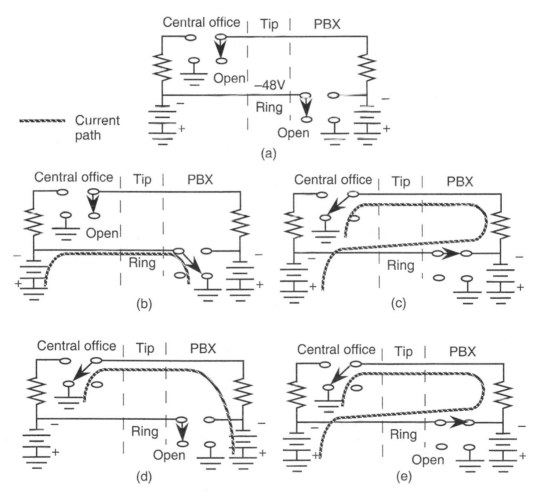

Figure 9.6 Ground start operation. (a) When the line is idle, the tip is open at the CO and the ring is open at the customer end. (b) In an outgoing call, the customer grounds the ring. (c) The CO notices this and grounds the tip, then the customer completes the loop. (d) In an incoming call, the CO grounds the tip first. (e) Then the customer completes the loop.

it knows that the CO is ready to receive digits. It does this by first closing the loop on the ring lead. Now a loop is established and dialing can commence.

Let us now look at how an incoming call is received by the PBX after the line has been idle, as in Figure 9.6(a). Figure 9.6(d) shows that the CO will ground its tip lead to signal the PBX that it has an incoming call.

The PBX notices the current in the tip lead and restricts that trunk from being used for outgoing calls. After the PBX detects the ringing voltage, the PBX places a loop closure across the tip and ring leads as seen in Figure 9.6(e).

The CO detects the loop closure, terminates the ringing, and provides a voice path to the PBX. If the distant party hangs up first, the CO will open the tip lead, which the PBX detects, and the PBX will open the ring lead.

On the other hand, the PBX can terminate the call by opening the ring, causing the loop current to stop. This is noticed by the CO which, in turn, opens up the tip lead, returning the line to the idle state as shown in Figure 9.6(a).

9.7 DIGITAL CARRIER SYSTEMS

Signaling is inherently data and so it is natural to encode it using bits. We have seen how a presence of current or frequency can carry one meaning and the absence of current or frequency the opposite. Similarly, in digital carriers, such as the common T1, any of the signaling functions can be implemented by setting certain bits as either a one or a zero. The bits which carry such information are called signaling bits, and the collection of them for one voice channel is called a signaling channel.

9.7.1 Robbed Bit vs. Clear Channel Signaling

As seen in the next to last entry of Table 9.3, there exists no separate signaling channel for the T1, while one does exist for the European E1 system. This is because with a T1, the signaling bits preempt or take possession of one voice bit out of every 48 voice bits, on any given voice channel. The loss of these occasional voice bits is not detected by the human ear. So the T1's 64-kbps voice channel not only includes the voice bits, but also the signaling bits. This is called robbed bit signaling, because the signaling bits in effect have "robbed" some of the voice bits.

On the other hand notice that, with the E1 transmission format, there is a separate channel just for signaling. This is because E1 does not rob voice bits to place signaling bits on instead, but transmits only voice on the 64-kbps voice channels.

The signaling for all of the 30 voice channels is combined into a separate 64-kbps signaling channel. The fact that no signaling appears in a voice channel is said to make the channel clear and so E1 provides clear channel signaling. Both domestically and internationally, ISDN calls for clear channel signaling.

9.7.2 Common Channel Signaling

Common channel signaling has two meanings. Common channel interoffice signaling, as depicted in Figure 9.2, provides a signaling network that is separate from the voice network. A link from a switch to the corresponding STP pair is a common link to carry signaling for all of the voice circuits associated with the given switch.

Table 9.3 Comparison of T1 and E1 Formats		
(BW = Bandwidth in bits per second)	T1	E1
BW of one voice channel	64 k	64 k
Total number of voice channels	24	30
BW taken by all voice channels	1536 k	1920 k
BW taken for framing	8 k	64 k
BW taken for a separate signaling channel	—	64 k
Total BW of the carrier system	1544 k	2048 k

Here, in the E1 system, we have seen what may be called common channel digital signaling. The 30 signaling channels that were separated from their respective voice channels are combined into one common signaling channel. As we'll see in Chapter 10, another T1 formatting scheme called the M44 format also uses clear channel and common channel digital signaling techniques.

9.7.3 In-band vs. Out-of-band Signaling Method

Robbed bit signaling is also said to be in-band signaling, because the bits used for signaling occupy the same (in-band) bits that were originally intended for voice. Likewise, if the signaling bits don't use the voice bits for transmission, the signaling bits are said to be "out-of-band" from the voice bits. So out-of-band signaling is the same as clear channel signaling.

Sometimes a digital network management channel is sent along with the voice channels, to get error statistics and so forth. In this case, the management channel is also said to be in-band, contrary to having a management channel that is sent over a different facility than the voice channels. There will be more on this in Chapter 10.

What I have just described here is in-band and out-of-band digital signaling method. These should not be confused with in-band and out-of-band analog signaling methods.

In a typical voice-grade line, 300 Hz to 3300 Hz of bandwidth is available to transmit voice. Any signaling which uses frequencies within this range is called in-band (analog) signaling. MF, DTMF, and SF signaling use frequencies within this range, and so they are considered to be in-band analog signaling methods. The outdated N1 carrier system used a 3700 Hz signal which fell out of the voice bandwidth, and is an example of out-of-band analog signaling.

9.8 SIGNALING INTERFACES

As we have seen so far, signaling information can be sent over a variety of transmission facilities. On the local loop a metallic or a copper wire is used for sending

DC loop currents. On the other hand, MF signaling has been widely used between offices, and if microwave or fiber is connected between them, one can't send DC currents, but only analog or digital signals.

In order to convert one signaling system to another kind, one needs to use an interface between them. In other words, an interface is a piece of equipment which uses a technique to interconnect two dissimilar transmission facilities or signaling methods.

9.8.1 4-wire Termination Set

At the CO, 2-wire subscriber lines are interfaced with 4-wire metallic facilities using 4WTSs (4-Wire Termination Sets). See Figure 9.7. The 2-wire circuit for the local loop is economical and is used over short distances. 4-wire circuits require two pairs of wire, one for transmit (the T and R leads) and one to receive (the T1 and R1 leads). 4-wires provide a better quality of transmission and are used for longer distances. Unlike on the local loop, the direction of transmission is separated on long-distance facilities, so 4WTSs are used for interfacing at this point. The 4WTS is also called a hybrid circuit and it simply interfaces a 2-wire circuit to a 4-wire circuit.

9.8.2 E&M Signaling Interface

A very common interface used between metallic facilities and analog facilities is called the E&M interface. This interface is used for conversion between DC loop currents and in-band analog signaling. It is used on tie trunks between PBXs. The "e" lead stands for the "e" in rEceive (or Ear) and the "m" lead stands for the "m" in transMit (or Mouth). Also, SB and SG stand for Signal Battery and Signal Ground, respectively.

Figure 9.8 shows a 4-wire tie trunk between two PBXs. The tie trunk is considered as an analog facility in this case. Typically, there is an E&M interface at each PBX. This interface consists of an MFT (Metallic Facility Terminal) and an AFT (Analog Facility Terminal). The figure shows the condition of the interfaces during the idle condition. No current flows in any of the leads and there is no SF tone placed over the tie trunk.

If the calling PBX has to initiate a call for one of its users and has stored the dialed digits in a register, it requires a tie trunk to place a call. The seizure of the trunk is accomplished in the following manner, and is explained using the step numbers shown in the diagram.

Figure 9.7 A 4WTS or a hybrid circuit converts a 1-pair line to a 2-pair one. On the 1-pair line, the receive and the transmit share the same pair, but on the 2-pair side of the hybrid the transmit and receive signals are kept separate.

In step 1, the 2-wire to 4-wire conversion is done, and in step 2 the MFT provides a loop closure across its M and SB leads. The presence of current in this loop is detected at the AFT, which in turn applies an SF signal over the tie trunk. Remember that DC currents can't travel very well over long distances, so the SF signal is used over this analog facility. This is step 3.

Step 4 requires the called PBX's AFT to notice an SF tone, and so in step 5 it closes the loop on its E and SG leads. The presence of current here is noticed by the MFT and causes the PBX to connect a register to receive the dialed digits. When it is ready, it then closes the M and SB leads. This is step 6.

The AFT notices the current, and sends an SF tone in step 7. The SF tone is noticed by the calling PBX's AFT and closes the E lead loop, causing current to flow here. Finally, in step 8, when the MFT notices the current, the calling PBX transmits the dialed digits stored in the register over its T and R leads. The digits are received on the called end over the T1 and R1 leads.

Once the connection is made by the distant PBX to the appropriate phone, conversation can take place over the T, R, T1, and R1 leads, and the connection phase of the signaling is complete.

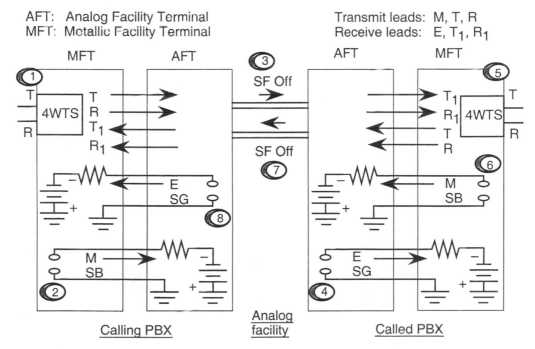

Figure 9.8 Conditions of E&M signaling interfaces used with an idle 4-wire tie line. (1) PBX finds a free trunk to make a call. (2) M lead is closed, current flows. (3) SF signal goes on. (4) E lead is closed for current to flow. (5) Called PBX is ready for the call. (6) It closes the M lead. (7) SF signal is turned on by the AFT. (8) The E lead is closed, and now the tie line is seized to pass the dialing digits.

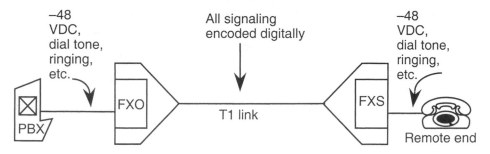

Figure 9.9 One circuit is shown here on a digital carrier such as a T1, where all analog signaling is converted to specific patterns of 1s and 0s.

9.8.3 Digital Signaling Interfaces

Figure 9.9 shows an example of how conventional analog signaling interfaces with digital signaling of a T1. Here, a T1 private line connects the PBX to a remote location making the phones at the remote end look as if they are part of the PBX system. The channel bank on the PBX side receives up to 24 voice channels from the PBX and multiplexes them over the digital T1 carrier, and the channel bank at the remote end reverses this process.

FXO (Foreign eXchange, Office) forms the analog-to-digital interface at the PBX side, while FXS (Foreign eXchange, Subscriber) is the interface at the remote end.

When the phone is idle, the line card at the PBX provides –48 VDC to its channel bank, and the FXO converts that to 1s and 0s for that voice channel over the T1. At the remote end, the FXS, recognizing this pattern in the received 1s and 0s, provides –48 VDC for the remote phone. This way the PBX thinks it has a phone attached to it, while the phone thinks it has a PBX line card attached to it, even though the signaling is converted to digital form between them over the T1.

So now, if the remote phone goes off-hook, the FXS interface notices it and transmits a certain pattern of 1s and 0s over the T1 for that circuit. This pattern, interpreted by the FXO, simulates a loop closure for the PBX just as if the phone had done so directly. The PBX now provides a dial tone, which the FXO converts to a different digital pattern, which the FXS then, in turn, converts back to an audible dial tone that is heard on the phone.

In this fashion, the FXO and FXS interfaces perform conversions between analog signaling for the end points and digital signaling for the T1 carrier which exists between them. In the E&M interface discussed earlier, one can easily see how a digital transmission medium can substitute a digital 1 for an SF tone and a digital 0 for the absence of the SF tone. Thus digital signaling interfaces are easily incorporated in place of many types of analog signaling forms.

EXERCISES

1. When a calling phone goes off-hook, it is said to
   - a. provide answer supervision
   - b. seize the line
   - c. go in a post dialing mode
   - d. initiate call routing
2. An off-hook condition immediately followed by an on-hook condition is called what?
   - a. a digit
   - b. a disconnect
   - c. supervision
   - d. a wink
3. Which of the following signaling functions were NOT covered in the text?
   - a. supervision
   - b. information
   - c. testing
   - d. alerting
4. Which of the following is a facility-independent signaling format?
   - a. loop start
   - b. DTMF
   - c. E&M signaling
   - d. ground start
5. What device is used to convert 2-wire to 4-wire signaling?
   - a. E lead of E&M signaling
   - b. M lead of E&M signaling
   - c. a plain telephone
   - d. 4WTS
6. When the CO lets the PBX connected to it know that the distance party has hung up, what is that called?
7. A loud pulsing tone heard on a phone when it stays off-hook too long is an example of what kind of signaling function?
8. The time between the dialing delay and the answer delay is called what?
9. How is the time between the dialing and the answer delays reduced by the carriers?
10. What is the total number of frequency pairs possible with MF signaling? How many of them are used?
11. Give two names for the type of signaling which makes signaling bits use some voice bits for transmission.
12. Explain how an interoffice call would take place if a trunk between CO-A and CO-C were available.
13. What are the different types of signaling functions, and what do they mean?
14. Explain the benefits of CCIS over per-trunk signaling.
15. If you were given the choice to pick four characters for the last column of frequency pairs available in Figure 9.4, which would you choose and why?
16. What are some reasons why ground start signaling is better than loop start signaling?

Chapter 10

Switching

10.1 BASIC SWITCHING

10.1.1 Why Switch?

If four homes needed access to each other without switching, they would have to be connected as shown in Figure 10.1(a). Every location would need a separate phone for each of the other three locations, as well as separate lines for them. Imagine an entire city being wired this way. Every time a home needed to call a new location, the telco would have to install another line between them and connect another pair of phones. It would be a big task just to label each phone, specifying where each one is connected.

Without switches, each location needs n–1 phones and the network needs n(n–1)/2 phone lines to gain full access to the network. Here, n is the number of locations in the network. So a town with only 1000 customers would require the installation of half a million lines.

Fortunately, our telephone networks are connected using switches housed in COs. See Figure 10.1(b). In this case, each location needs only one phone and one line. However, now the entire network depends on the reliability of the CO. So, the COs are built so that they are not as affected by floods, earthquakes, or other calamities.

Another disadvantage of introducing switches is that we need a method of communication between the switches and the end users. This is necessary for a caller to be properly connected to his destination. As seen from the last chapter, this is called signaling. Signaling (also spelled signalling) transfers information between a user and a switch or between two switches.

As the number of COs that need to be interconnected increases, the problem of requiring more and more cross links reoccurs, but this time between the COs. To alleviate this problem, tandem switches are installed. See Figure 10.1(c). A tandem switch is a switch for switches, and serves the same basic purpose that the switch in Figure 10.1(a) does for telephones.

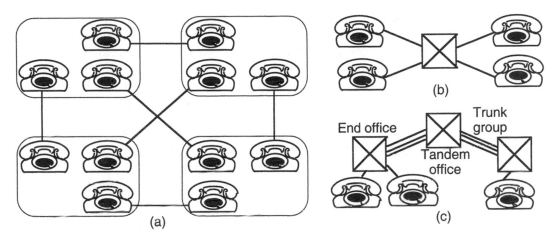

Figure 10.1 (a) Connecting four locations without a switch. (b) Here, with a switch. (c) A tandem switch connects switches.

10.1.2 Parts of a Switch

A switch is made up of two basic parts: the switching fabric or the switching network and its control. The fabric is where the individual lines or trunks are connected to complete the communications paths, and the control mechanism signals the elements in the fabric when and how to make the connections.

Even the earliest type of switch, the switchboard and its operator, exhibits these two properties. The operator himself or herself is the controlling mechanism that determines which patch cord should be connected to which jack. The physical switch board with its plugs, cords, jacks, and lamps is the switching fabric where the communication path is completed.

10.1.3 Space vs. Time Division Switching

Two approaches to building a switch are called space division and time division switching. Figure 10.2 shows examples of each. In each case, the inputs A, B, and C are connected to outputs E, F, and D, respectively. In these diagrams only the switching fabrics are shown; the control mechanisms needed to determine the overall states of the switches are not shown.

In Figure 10.2(a), the three switches on the left are performing what is called concentration, since each one reduces many inputs to one path. They select one of the input terminals. The switches on the right are performing expansion, since they select the proper outputs for the connections.

Here, the switches are set and don't change for the duration of the call. Also, two simultaneous connections can be established over different physical paths. Since the physical paths are separated within the space occupied by the switch, this approach is called space division switching.

Contrast this with time division switching, depicted in Figure 10.2(b). Here, one switch is shown at three different times. During the first time interval the connection for A is made, during the second interval the connection for B is made, and so on. This process is repeated and the information between the input and output terminals is passed, each connection taking its turn. Since the three connections must share the one physical path, they have to take turns sharing that path in a round robin fashion.

Notice that the connections don't divide up the physical space taken by the switch between themselves, but divide up the available time instead. Hence, this approach is called time division switching. It is very similar to time division multiplexing, as depicted in Figure 3.11. The only difference between them is with TDM. The connections between input terminals and output terminals are pretty much fixed. That is, input 1 connects to output 1, input 2 connects to output 2, etc., whereas, with time division switching, a given input can connect to any of the other outputs determined by the control mechanism in real time.

Figure 10.2(c) shows a matrix or a coordinate switch. Does this use space division or time division switching? Notice that it has three inputs on the left and three outputs on top. To provide a full set of connections between them, there is a total of 9 switches. Since each connection uses a different physical path, the switch is considered to use space division switching, although it has more switches than the one in Figure 10.2(a). It uses only 2-position switches, while the one in Figure 10.2(a) uses 3-position switches. Currently, switching in a matrix fabric is accomplished by using semiconductor technology such as VLSI (Very Large Scale Integration) which condenses many transistors on one chip.

10.1.4 Blocking Factors

The two space division switches in Figures 10.2(a) and (c) are considered to be fully nonblocking. That is, all inputs can be provided with a connection to the outputs which are idle. A blocking switch is one that is designed with the idea that not all

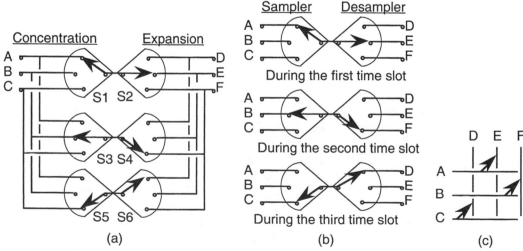

Figure 10.2 (a) Space division switch. (b) Time division switch. (c) Matrix switch. Each example connects A to E, B to F, and C to D.

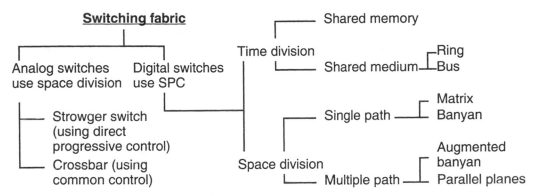

Figure 10.3 Categories of switching fabrics.

terminals will require simultaneous connections, so why build larger and expensive switching fabrics?

A blocking switch can be visioned by eliminating switches S5 and S6 in Figure 10.2(a). In that case, any two of the three inputs can get a connection, but if the third input requires one, it will get a busy signal. This would then be classified as a 33% blocking or a 67% nonblocking switch, since a third of the inputs are blocked, or two-thirds are not blocked when the switch reaches its full capacity.

10.1.5 Further Categorizing of Switches

Besides space division and time division switching, switches can be further categorized as shown in Figure 10.3. The first switch was manual, i.e., the cordboard. The generation of switches that followed were primarily electromechanical, meaning that they used relays that were activated by electrical currents. These switches typically employ space division techniques and will be covered in the next section.

After the electromechanical switches came the digital switches which may use either time division or space division switching. Each of these switching categories is controlled by a technique that is unique to them. The Strowger switch uses a controlling technique called direct progressive control. The crossbar uses a method called common control, and most of the digital switches use a method called SPC (Stored Program Control). First, let us discuss these controlling techniques. Then we will outline the operation of the other switch types shown in Figure 10.3.

10.2 METHODS OF CONTROL

10.2.1 Direct Progressive Control

In 1892, the Strowger or the step-by-step switching system was invented by Almon B. Strowger and was first installed in independent telco COs. Interestingly, the Bell system didn't install these automated systems until about 25 years later. The step-by-step switch uses the direct progressive control mechanism to determine the switch states and provide the connections. The dialed pulses from the user's telephone directly select and control the switch position, from one switch to the next. The path selected by the dialed pulses is the same path through which the voice travels.

Figure 10.4 shows how an interoffice call is made using step-by-step switches. Here, the telephone on the left is calling the one on the right by dialing 427-5587. The three stages of these switches are line finders, selectors, and connectors. When the user on the left picks up the phone to make a call, the line finder connects that phone line to the first selector.

This selector provides the dial tone. After receiving the first dialed digit, 4 in this case, it selects the 4th bank or position on the switch. Then it looks for an idle line to the next selector. Similarly, selectors 2 and 3 switch in accordance with the 2nd and 3rd dialed digits. In this example, these three digits designate an exchange that is located in a different CO. So these are hard wired using trunks to the 427 exchange. The calling phone continues to control the switches in this exchange as well, until the connector switch completes the connection using the last two digits.

10.2.2 Common Control

Another method of controlling the switching fabric is called common control. This type of controlling mechanism has typically been found with the crossbar switch. The crossbar switch was invented by L. M. Ericsson in Sweden only ten years after the step-by-step switch was invented. It played a dominant role until digital switches became widely available.

A basic block diagram of a crossbar switch is shown in Figure 10.5. The line link frame is a matrix switch as is the trunk link frame. The former connects lines while the latter connects trunks to the switch. Wires called junctors are used to tie these two switching frames together.

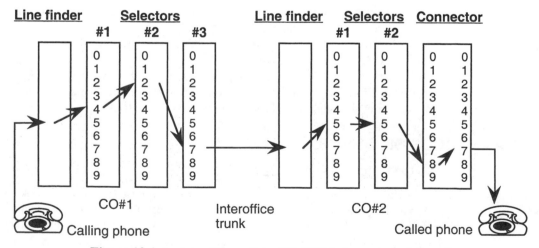

Figure 10.4 An interoffice call to 427-5587 being switched through step-by-step switches.

When a telephone goes off line, a register supplies a dial tone and stores its dialed address. Using this stored number, a logic circuit called a marker reserves an idle trunk and sends individual commands to the switches to connect the path. Translators aid the marker in converting the dialed number into specific switch settings.

After the connection is made, which takes less than a second, the services of the marker and other common control devices are not needed and can be used to establish another call while the previously connected one is still in progress. Since its equipment is shared among many calls, it is called a common control switch. A major advantage of this type of switch, besides not needing as much equipment, is alternate routing. That is, if one path through the switch is occupied by another call, then another path can be investigated. This was not possible with the step-by-step switch.

10.2.3 Stored Program Control

Both of the previous generation switches were hard-wired and inflexible. If a new telephone service (such as call waiting, call conference, etc.) was to be made available, the switches had to be redesigned and then had to be individually rewired. With SPC (Stored Program Control), the switch operates under the direction of a CPU (Central Processing Unit) and the software running it. If a new service is required, then generally only the software has to be rewritten and tested. Then simply by distributing and installing the copies of the software upgrades on each switch, the new service becomes available. Also, there is less expertise required at each switch. AT&T's 4ESS (Electronic Switching System), for instance, although introduced in 1976, is still AT&T's primary switch because the software running them has been upgraded many times since.

Figure 10.6 outlines the functions of an SPC system. At the heart of this switch is a special-purpose CPU. It is designed for real-time processing of logic and input and output operations, rather than for arithmetic processing. It has access to two types of memory: one where the software program is loaded and a database of customer configurations are kept, and the other where information on call progress is kept. The

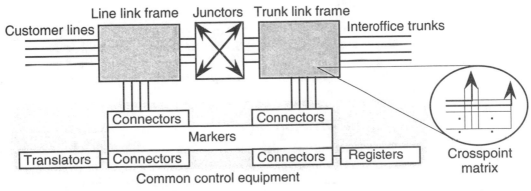

Figure 10.5 A functional block diagram of a typical common control switch.

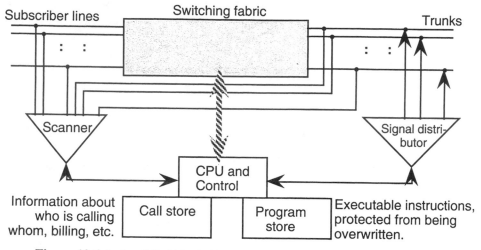

Figure 10.6 A simplified block diagram of a stored program control switch.

memory where the program is stored is protected from being inadvertently written over and doesn't change until a new release of the generic software is installed or an end user subscribes to a new service or alters it.

The call store memory is used to keep the digits of the calling party as they are received, the status of the lines and trunks, etc. The lines and trunks are constantly scanned at a high rate by the scanner to see which have changed their states. For example, if a line has gone off-hook, then the CPU will provide a dial tone, and while the subscriber is dialing the first digit, it will scan and serve other lines. When an incoming call from a trunk is received, the scanner detects it. The program instructs the control circuitry as to what to do in each situation. It specifies how paths are to be set up for calls in the switching fabric, when to provide a ringing signal or a busy signal, and so on. The distributor circuitry sends signals over the trunks to the next CO when attempting an interoffice call.

10.3 DIGITAL SWITCHING

So far we have considered switches that were initially used to handle voice switching in analog form. The 4ESS is a digital switch, but the trunks connecting to it were originally analog and were then converted to digital. Now, let us consider digital switches which are used to perform switching of voice, data, fax, etc., in signals that are in digital form.

10.3.1 Time Division Ring

To understand the operation of a time division ring, let us first consider an analogy of a train shown in Figure 10.7. This train has 4 cars (which represent 4 time slots) and it is used to switch calls for up to 8 telephones. These telephones bring their voice bits (or digitized voice) to their respective platforms, labeled A through H, at a rate of 64 kbps. Since the data from the telephones arrives at a rate of 64 kbps, the train itself must rotate at 64,000 rotations per second. Additionally, since the train has 4 time slots (or cars), there are a total of 256,000 time slots rotating per second.

Let us say that the engineer of this train is the control mechanism of the switch. As phone G requests a connection to phone A from the engineer, the engineer notifies both A and G that the car W has been assigned for this connection. So as G sees the train passing by, it dumps the next bit in car W, which A then removes.

Similarly, if A needs to communicate back to G, the engineer may assign another car, say car Z, to do that transfer of voice bits. So, for a connection, 2 cars or 2 time slots are used—one for each direction. For this example, what is the nonblocking factor? How can the nonblocking factor be increased?

Since there are 8 telephones and only 4 time slots, the nonblocking factor is 50%. Since only 4 telephones can be active at any time. The nonblocking factor can be increased to 75% by adding two more cars (or time slots) and the switch can be made fully nonblocking by making it an 8-car train. To handle conversations (or 8 digital transfers) the speed of the ring must be 8 times 64,000 rotations per second or, simply, 512 kbps. As can be seen, this analogy fits the actual operation of the time division ring very gracefully.

10.3.2 Time Division Bus

Basically, if the time division ring is pulled at opposite points and straightened, then we have what is called a time division bus. Here again, 2 time slots need to be assigned for each conversation. Sometimes time division busses are referred to as time slot interchanges or loops.

As an example, let us calculate the minimum speed it takes a time division bus to be able to provide nonblocking switching capacity to 200 voice terminals.

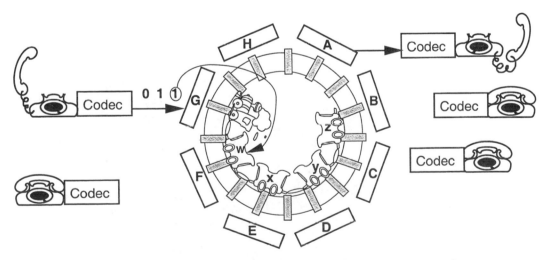

Figure 10.7 This time division ring-based switch can support up to 4 conversations or 8 phones with no blocking.

200 voice terminals translate into 100 conversations and require 200 time slots. Assuming PCM-coded voice at 64 kbps, we need a bus speed of 12.8 Mbps or 200 times 64 kbps.

10.3.3 Time-space-time Switching

Time-space-time is a common technique used in PBXs and telco switches. It allows many time division switched busses to be interconnected with no blocking. In Figure 10.8, there are 4 such busses shown in devices called modules A through D. These busses are connected to each other via a matrix switch providing a fully nonblocking capacity.

An intramodule call, or a call between two phones which are connected to the same module, doesn't get switched through the matrix. An intermodule call must be first switched in the time domain on the caller's module, then be switched in the space domain in the matrix, and finally be switched again in the time domain in the called party's module. Hence, the term "time-space-time" is used for this type of switch.

Figure 10.8 shows two bits on the bus in module A which are to be switched to the B and C modules. First, the connection is made for B and then the one for C. This way, the bits are properly routed to their destination. The clock speed of the matrix switch must be four times that of the clocks of the time busses, so that it can accommodate the switching required for all four modules within a bus's one time frame. Bits for an intramodule call are simply redirected to the originating module. It is evident that the control elements for such a switch are quite complex, because they must be able to direct the various components of the switch in strict synchronization.

As an example, let us say that each of the modules provides a nonblocking capacity of 256 calls at 64 kbps. Each call requires 2 time slots, so we need 512 time slots at 64 kbps. This results in a bus speed of 32.768 Mbps (or 64 kbps times 512). Suppose that the maximum number of such modules which can be connected to the space switch is 10: then the switching speed of the matrix must be 327.68 Mbps.

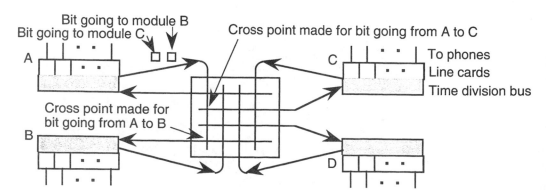

Figure 10.8 A time-space-time switch. Two bits are shown coming from module A going to B and C. Between the times that these two bits are switched, the matrix switches a bit for each of the other modules.

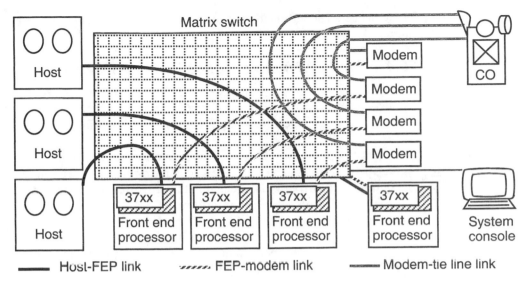

Figure 10.9 A device called a matrix switch (this term doesn't refer to the matrix switching fabric) provides excellent network management.

10.3.4 Matrix Switches

When a data center has many hosts communicating to many locations via tie lines, the interconnections of in-house equipment can be difficult to manage. If a modem fails, for instance, the network operations personnel are under pressure to switch to the spare modem quickly. Being in a hurry may result in bringing a working circuit down, perhaps because a good modem on a working line was replaced by a defective one by mixing up the cables and patch cords.

By using a matrix switch, managers can plan for reliable recovery and provide correct switching between devices. The term "matrix switch" here does not refer to the type of switching fabric as has been described up to this point, but to the type of device.

Figure 10.9 shows hosts, FEPs, modems, and tie lines connected via a matrix switch. Spare equipment and a system console are also connected to it. Now, a working modem can be swapped with a failed one, by simply clicking on an icon on the system console. Through the system console, the switch can be programmed so the cutover is done automatically. It can also provide monitoring and line statistics of all the interconnections.

10.4 ADVANCED SWITCHING CONCEPTS

ATM (Asynchronous Transmission Mode) was covered in Chapter 5. Here we will only look at switching techniques that are commonly used with ATM. Since the topics are complex and changing, only a survey of these concepts will be presented. The switches discussed in this section assume that information is parcelled into fixed-sized bundles called cells. Cells are 53 bytes long and contain 48 bytes of data and a

5-byte header. The information in the header is used to switch the cell to the correct output.

10.4.1 Time Division vs. Space Division Revisited

Flipping back to Figure 10.3, we recall the two types of switches used with digital signals—time division and space division. We also have seen the operation of the ring, bus, and matrix switches. Now, let us consider the operation of the remaining ones.

Time Division Switching: A shared memory time division switch can be seen in Figure 10.10. As the samples are received in the switch, they are entered in the buffer. The output from the buffer is selected in the order that the switching is to take place.

Time division switching fabrics are efficient for multicasting (transmissions from one source to many destinations) or broadcasting (transmissions from one source to all destinations). This is because the transmitted bits are going past all the outputs. Instead of only one port being signaled to copy the bits, more than one port can be signaled to copy them. This is analogous to ports other than A reading the bits from car W in Figure 10.7. In addition, with time division switching, instead of having all the ports operate at the same speed, bandwidth on demand can be accessed dynamically by having the ports allow for variable input rates.

Space Division Switching: While in time division one transmission path is shared by all ports, in space division, many transmission paths are available at any given time. Hence, for one-to-many transmissions, such as broadcasts, time division is preferred, and for many-to-many transmissions space division is suitable. The capacity of a space division switch is determined by multiplying the port speeds by the average number of concurrent paths that are available in the switch.

In Figure 10.3, space division switching is divided into single path and multiple path categories. This means that with the former, there is only one physical path for a given input-output port pair, whereas with multipath space division switching, data arriving from a specific input port to a specific output port may travel different paths each time. In either case, multiple transmissions may occur simultaneously in the switching fabric.

Typically, cells of data use a routing tag in the header which enables the switching elements in the fabric to provide fast switching, by inspecting the tag. This is called self-routing. In other cases, label-routing schemes are used that rely on table lookup. Label routing provides efficient multicast switching, but requires maintenance of these tables.

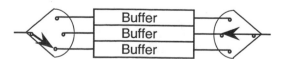

Figure 10.10 A shared memory switch.

10.4.2 Single Path Fabrics

One of the disadvantages of a matrix switch, shown in Figure 10.2(c), is that the number of crosspoint switches required for it is the product of the number of input and output ports. So if there are 8 inputs and 8 outputs, the fabric requires 64 switches.

In a Banyan switching fabric, shown in Figure 10.11, switching between 8 inputs and 8 outputs is provided using only 24 switching elements. Although the switches are twice as complex as the ones used in a matrix, the saving is still substantial. Additionally, much of the control is distributed in the fabric itself.

The Banyan switch is made up of binary switching elements that switch the call to one of two paths determined by one of the address bits. In Figure 10.11, the 8 inputs are connected to the left column of 4 switches. Any of these cells arriving at these 8 inputs can be switched very quickly to any of the 8 outputs shown on the right. As a cell arrives at any of the binary switching elements, the switch routes it to either the binary 0 or 1 output.

As an example, a path is shown for a cell arriving at input number 4 with a destination address of output 011 in its header. The MSB (Most Significant Bit) of the address, which is 0, routes the cell to the 0 output of the first switching element. The lower middle switching element switches the cell to its binary output 1 and so does the last switch.

Since all cells arriving at input destined for 011 follow this path, this fabric is considered to have a single path. However, other transmissions are possible at the same time, such as a cell headed from input 1 to output 000.

If two cells are contending for the same output, only one can be switched at that point. So unlike the matrix switch, the Banyan switch is a blocking switch.

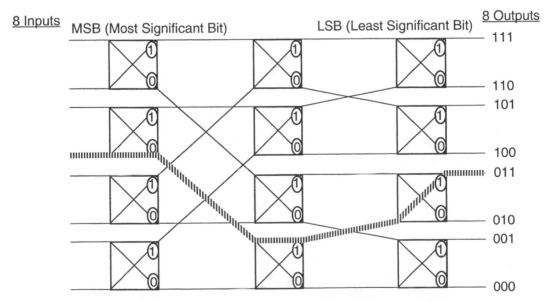

Figure 10.11 A Banyan switch fabric with a path to output 011.

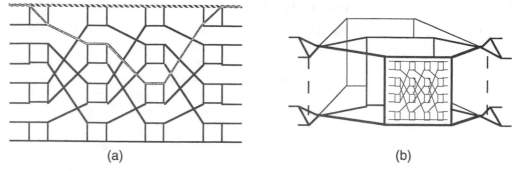

(a)　　　　　　　　　　　　　　　　　　　(b)

Figure 10.12 Two multipath fabrics: (a) Augmented Banyan. Here two paths between a port pair are highlighted. (b) Parallel planes.

When the switching elements of a Banyan switch are converted to, say, 4 inputs and 4 outputs (instead of 2 inputs and 2 outputs), then we have what is called a delta network. The delta fabric switches cells on 2 or more address bits rather on just 1 bit as is done in Banyan switches.

10.4.3 Multipath Fabrics

Figure 10.12(a) has added another column of switches to the basic Banyan switch, making it what is called an augmented Banyan switch. It provides more than one path between a set of input-output ports, as can be seen from the two paths shown in the figure. Hence, this is called a multipath fabric. For every column of switches that is added, (or stage of switches that is added), the number of available paths doubles.

Another example of a multipath fabric is shown in Figure 10.12(b). It is called switching planes in parallel. It provides better reliability and performance, because the failure of one plane still maintains switching capacity.

10.4.4 Buffering and Contention Resolution

Regardless of the type of switch fabric that is used, there may be a need to do buffering. In a switching element, two cells may contend for the same output. If buffering is used external to the fabric, whether at the input or output ports, then a mechanism is required for contention resolution inside the fabric.

One mechanism that is used is to simply discard one cell. Another one is to deflect the cell in the wrong direction within the fabric. If enough stages are left within the fabric, a path to the correct output is possible. Otherwise, the cell may have to be recirculated back to the input ports. Cells may also be routed, based on their priority. Another method that is possible is reservation of output ports by the input ports. Much research and development in such switching architectures is well under way.

EXERCISES

1. Which of the following is NOT a space division switch?
   a. step-by-step   b. crossbar
   c. shared memory   d. matrix

2. Which of the following parts is NOT part of the crossbar switch?
   a. markers
   b. registers
   c. connectors
   d. selectors
3. A method of switching that requires the switching elements to route cells based on the information in their headers is called what?
   a. label routing
   b. self routing
   c. direct routing
   d. header routing
4. Which of the following is an advantage of time division switching?
   a. multicasting
   b. multipath switching
   c. a smaller number of cross points is needed
   d. less maintenance on switching tables is required
5. Which part of a stored program control switch first notices when a line goes off-hook?
   a. distributor
   b. CPU
   c. fabric
   d. scanner
6. If another stage of switching elements is added to Figure 10.12(a), the augmented Banyan switch, how many paths will be available between every input-output pair?
   a. 2
   b. 3
   c. 4
   d. 6
7. Find the bus speed of a recently announced ATM-based LAN switch that supports up to sixteen 155-Mbps ports.
8. What are the maximum and minimum number of concurrent paths possible in Figure 10.11?
9. What type of switch interconnects other switches?
10. What kind of switch preceded the step-by-step switch?
11. In Figure 10.2(a) if the three switches on the left connected 5 inputs and the three switches on the right connected 5 outputs, what would be the nonblocking factor?
12. Suppose the modules in Figure 10.8 each connect 512 telephones. They are all using ADPCM or digitized voice at 32 kbps. If each module has a nonblocking factor of 40%, what is the bus speed for the modules?
13. Explain the two parts of a switch.
14. How can one tell if a switch is a time division switch or a space division switch? Can you design a switch that is based on frequency division?
15. List the three types of control methods and explain them. Give the advantages of the latter two over the first one.
16. How are analog switches differentiated from digital ones?
17. Try to draw a Banyan switch which has four inputs and four outputs.
18. With high-capacity switching systems, what advantage does space division have?

Chapter 11

PSTN

In this chapter the development of the PSTN (Public Switched Telephone Network) will be explored. This is also referred to as the DDD (Direct Distance Dialing) cloud. The PSTN originally was built to carry telephone traffic, but today it is evolving into an information network that carries more than just voice. For this reason, it may now be more appropriate to refer to it as the Public Switched Information Network.

11.1 BACKGROUND

Until the early 1980's, calls were routed in the PSTN using a method known as hierarchical routing. This is illustrated in Figure 11.1. All switching centers in the country were categorized as regional, sectional, primary, toll, or end offices. When a lower-level office could not complete a call directly to the distant office, it required the services of the upper-level offices.

Each lower-class office was directly subject to upper-class offices and the trunk group between such offices were called a final trunk group. For offices in two different areas that had a heavy usage between them, a high-usage trunk was installed. So when a call could be completed using this type of a trunk, the upper final trunk groups and their offices were avoided, and the call was completed using a smaller number of nodes.

Consider Figure 11.1. Whenever phone 1 called phone 2, only the local office which connects the two phones handled the call completely. If phone 1 made a local call to phone 3, the call would go through the tandem switch, but if a direct trunk were available between the two end offices then that would be used instead. If calls were made across a wider geographical region, as when phone 1 called phone 4, the call would have to go through the two respective toll offices.

In such a case, if a high-usage trunk existed between the two toll centers, it would be used; otherwise, free trunks to upper-class offices would be searched in order to complete the call. In extreme cases, a call would have to be switched through all the upper-class offices and all the final trunk groups before it found a path to its destination.

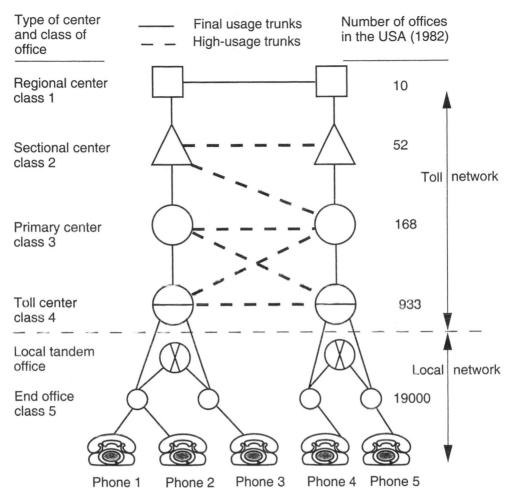

Figure 11.1 Outdated hierarchical routing.

Using many switches added noise, interference, and connection delay time to the voice call.

Completing a coast-to-coast call in this manner may have taken up to 20 seconds, with noise and interference added by the many switches. Today, IXCs complete calls using digitized voice in six seconds and use only two or three switches. This is because today's networks are not hierarchical (where each switch has a primary path to only one other switch up the ladder), but each switch has direct links to all other switches. This architecture is called a flat network. The remainder of the chapter will cover the operation of flat networks.

11.2 THE LOCAL TELEPHONE NETWORK

11.2.1 The Distribution Plant

In Figure 11.2, the wiring for the POTS (Plain Old Telephone Service) connection is shown from a residence to the central office.

The wiring inside the residence is called IW (Inside Wiring), and since divestiture, time and material for this inside wiring have to be paid for and maintained by the subscriber. He/she may have the telco provide this service or may do it him/herself. This wiring is connected to the NID (Network Interface Device), at which point the telco's responsibility begins. The NID is the demarc for the home and is nonexistent for older lines. It is equipped with a termination block and protection against power surges.

A SNID (Smart NID) is also sometimes used, which provides remote loopback from the CO. This allows the telco to test the continuity of the wire pair directly from the CO without having to send a technician to the house. This is accomplished by the CO sending a special signal to the SNID, which then places itself in the loopback mode.

From the NID, a connection is made to the telephone pole using a drop wire. In some developments, if the cable is buried, then the connection is made to a pedestal. The distribution of the subscriber lines from the SAC (Serving Area interface Concept) to the home is called the wire feeding plant or simply the distribution plant.

The SAC is a distribution frame safely placed on a lot away from hazards. This marks the boundary between the feeder and the distribution plants. Just as an IDF (Intermediate Distribution Frame) typically serves one floor or an area within a building, so does the SAC distribute the wiring to one serving area or distribution area for the telco.

From the SAC there are two ways to get to the CO via the feeder plant. One method simply sends the analog voice over a cable consisting of many wire pairs. Another method involves using a T1 multiplexer which is commonly called the SLC-

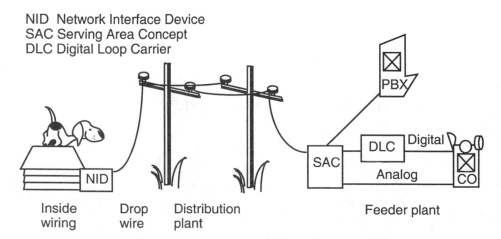

NID Network Interface Device
SAC Serving Area Concept
DLC Digital Loop Carrier

Inside wiring Drop wire Distribution plant Feeder plant

Figure 11.2 Local facilities network from the home to the CO.

96 (Subscriber Loop Carrier), pronounced "slick 96." (This is an AT&T trademark: its generic name is DLC (Digital Loop Carrier).) This multiplexer allows four groups of 24 voice circuits to be multiplexed onto 10 pairs of wire. With T1, one pair is used to transmit, and one is used to receive. Hence, 8 pairs are needed for four groups of T1s, and an extra two pairs are used to automatically back up an active pair, in case it fails. Fiber can also be used here instead of copper. The DLC system is more economical, serves more customers with far fewer wire pairs, is easy to maintain, and is more compatible with interoffice digital trunks.

11.2.2 Inside the CO

For the central office to activate a phone for a subscriber, it must have its TN (telephone number), CP (Cable Pair number), and OE (Office Equipment designation).

TN is the phone number assigned as it appears in the phone book. CP indicates the pair number at the CO which is connected to the NID at the customer's home. Finally, the OE specifies the actual line circuit that is dedicated on the CO's switch. When a phone number is changed, CP and OE designations remain the same; however, in electronic switching systems, the TN for the existing OE is changed through software, that is, through a terminal.

The cables from all the exchange areas that are served by the CO enter the cable vault or the cable entrance facility, which is usually located in the CO's basement. This can amount up to 200,000 pairs of wire. From here the cable pairs are cut down on termination blocks on the VMDF (Vertical side of the Main Distribution Frame). The heat coils and carbon blocks are located here for protection purposes. See Figure 11.3.

From the VMDF all pairs are cross connected over to the HMDF and from there the dial-up circuits are sent to the switches and the tie lines are sent to the toll equipment. In other words, the lines from the street come to the VMDF whereas the connections for switch and toll equipment come to the HMDF and the jumpers between these two sides of the MDF cross connect the lines to the appropriate equipment.

The lines from the switching equipment are connected to the HMDF (Horizontal MDF). Depending on which subscriber, specified by its CP, needs to be connected to which OE, a cross connect jumper is punched down between these two points.

Lines also come to the HMDF from the toll equipment. Toll equipment allows the CO to condition leased lines so that the signal levels are correct going out of the CO. In Figure 11.3, pair numbers 1001 through 1004 go to the switch and pair 1005 comes to the toll equipment, gets conditioned, and goes back out on pair 1006 to a different destination than from where it came.

There are basically four types of trunks leaving a CO. Interoffice trunks going to other COs are one kind; others are trunks going to PBXs, IXC trunks going to POPs, and trunks to cellular MTSOs (Mobile Telephone Switching Offices).

11.2.3 Interoffice Signaling Using SS7

The network in the North New Jersey LATA will now be used as an example in explaining interoffice signaling. This will allow us to refer to real names and a real network. Remember that an SS7 (Signaling System 7) network is a packet switched network, and that all information is passed on this network using data packets.

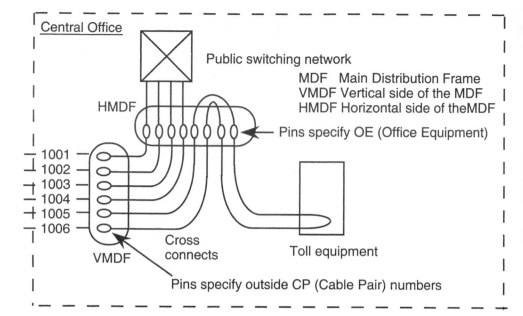

Figure 11.3 Dial-up lines coming into the CO go to the switching network, while dedicated lines get conditioned in the toll equipment and are routed out to other locations.

New Jersey Bell has approximately 130 COs in this area. There are 4 local tandems and 2 equal access tandems. A local tandem, shown in Figure 11.1, is used when no direct trunk is found between two COs. A maximum of two local tandems may be needed to complete a call within this area. Local tandems, in New Jersey, are also called sector tandems. Equal access tandems, on the other hand, allow IXCs to gain access to the local network.

The North New Jersey LATA, illustrated in Figure 11.4, has one STP (Signal Transfer Point) pair, one STP in Newark and one in New Brunswick about 30 miles away. The STPs are of type #2A and are made by Lucent Technologies. All the COs which are part of the SS7 network have direct 56-kbps signaling channels to both STPs. The STPs share their workload and continuously monitor each other's performance. If one STP fails, the other will force all the signaling traffic on itself and send out alarms indicating that the other STP has malfunctioned.

It is acceptable for an LEC to place an STP pair in two different LATAs, as long as only the signaling crosses the LATA boundaries and not the traffic itself. The STPs shown in the figure also have links to the STPs in the adjacent LATAs, so that privileged calls can be made near the LATA boundaries. Privileged calls are local calls that are handled by an LEC near and across a LATA border.

The STP's rack has a circuit pack for each CO, where a DSU (Digital Service Unit) exists for each signaling channel. A DSU simply interfaces equipment with a digital line. The circuit packs for each CO communicate signaling data with each other using a CNI (Common Network Interface) ring. The CNI ring uses the same mechanism used in token ring networks.

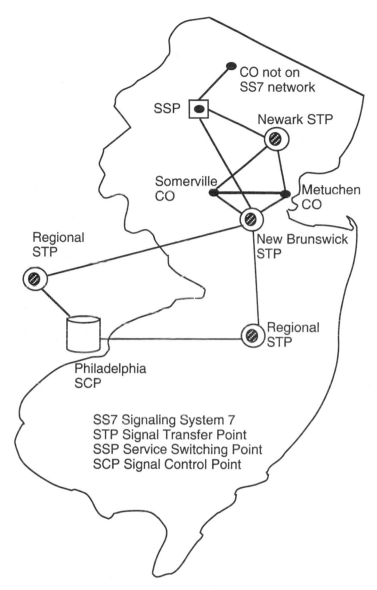

Figure 11.4 Bell Atlantic's North New Jersey SS7 network. For the sake of clarity, the links from the regional STPs to the Newark STP are not shown.

The COs that don't have direct access to the STP pair can become part of the intelligent network by connecting to an SSP (Signal Service Point). MF signaling is used between such a CO and the SSP. The SSP then converts the older MF signaling to SS7 signaling over the links to the STP pair.

Let us now consider how a call is connected over the local network. Suppose a caller in Somerville dials 555-6789 in Metuchen. The CO in Somerville will realize that the exchange 555 is not in Somerville, and will request the STP in New Brunswick over the signaling network that it wants to place the call to 555-6789. If the 555 exchange was located in Somerville, then the STPs would not be utilized, and the Somerville CO would complete the call itself.

The New Brunswick STP realizes that 555 is a Metuchen exchange and asks the Metuchen CO if circuit 6789 is idle. If phone 555-6789 is idle, then the STP is notified, and the STP sends packets to both the Somerville and the New Brunswick COs, giving instructions to connect the call on the trunk. Then the two COs make a continuity check over that trunk, which is reserved for that call, and the phone rings in Metuchen. The ringback signal for the caller in Somerville is provided by the Somerville CO.

Conversely, if 555-6789 were busy, then the Metuchen CO would notify the STP which in turn would notify the Somerville CO. Now the busyback signal is provided by the Somerville office to the caller in Somerville. Notice that a trunk between the COs is not used to provide this busyback signal as it would have been used in older signaling methods.

Finally, if anyone wants to make a call using a Bell Atlantic credit card, then authorization is obtained from a database called the SCP (Signal Control Point), located in Philadelphia. The SCP is also used when an STP needs to convert a Bell Atlantic 800 number to a POTS number. All 800 numbers have to be converted to their POTS equivalent before the call can be routed to its destination. Access to an SCP is provided via a regional STP over the SS7 network.

11.3 THE AT&T NETWORK

11.3.1 Overview

Let us now turn our attention to inter-LATA communication networks. AT&T is an example of an IXC (Inter eXchange Carrier) that provides communications services between LATAs and to foreign countries. On a typical day 230 million calls are processed, up from 140 million in 1993. In 1996, a record number of 68 billion calls were processed out of which 99.99% of the calls were completed on the first attempt.

For management purposes, AT&T divides its network into four components: transmission facilities, the international network, the North American network, and network services. The network control center is located in Bedminster, N.J., and the regional control centers are in Atlanta and Denver.

The total network transmission facilities are over 3 billion circuit miles (up from 2 billion in 1993), about 12,000 times around the world if it were wrapped continuously. AT&T belongs to a consortium of owners of TAT8, TAT9, and TPC cables. These are trans-Atlantic and trans-Pacific fiber cables, each of which can support up to 40,000 to 80,000 conversations. FASTAR is a completely automated network restoration system. If a cable is accidently cut anywhere, this management system can reroute 95% of the circuits well within 2 minutes.

The fastest growing component of the AT&T network, and for that matter many other networks, is the international network. IDDD (International Direct Distance Dialing) can be done to more than 200 nations. This means that without the caller needing operator assistance, AT&T can deliver the call to those countries. The network

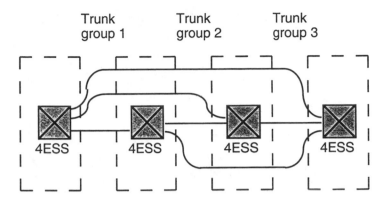

Figure 11.5 Switches in four cities located in a straight line can be fully connected using only three trunk groups by multiplexing the links.

can reach a total of 270 countries with only a handful that cannot be reached due to political restrictions.

11.3.2 North American Network

Domestically, AT&T has 135 4ESSs (Electronic Switching Systems), out of which 7 are used for international gateways. The 4ESS is a toll and tandem switch, that is, no telephone lines can be connected to it, only trunks from other switches. It can process 700,000 calls in an hour compared to the 5ESS, which can handle 200,000 calls per hour. In regions where demand is low, 5ESSs are used, but the backbone of the American network consists of the 4ESSs.

The first 4ESS was installed in Chicago in 1976. The last one was installed in Atlanta in 1999. AT&T is planning to move to smaller switches like the 5ESSs from Lucent and the smaller DMSs from Nortel. This way, it can provide direct connections to more customers of smaller size. An ATM-based network in the core will eventually provide convergence of technologies. One ATM network will be used to provide all types of services, including voice, data, video, IP, etc.

The 4ESSs are configured in a virtually fully connected mesh network. There is a direct trunk from every 4ESS to virtually every other 4ESS. These trunks may go through intermediate 4ESS sites but they are not switched there. As shown in Figure 11.5 most switches have direct links to each other, but these links are shared or multiplexed over a common physical media.

The trunks between the 4ESSs carry only voice, data, or image traffic; signaling is transported over a separate network called the signaling network. Physically, the signaling network may share the transmission facilities of the 4ESS network, but logically these two networks are kept separate.

The signaling network consists of 12 mated pairs of STPs, which are connected in a fully meshed network. That is, every STP pair has a direct link to every other pair. For reliability purposes, a given STP pair may be hundreds of miles apart and the workload shared between them. Each STP handles 50% of the traffic and, if necessary,

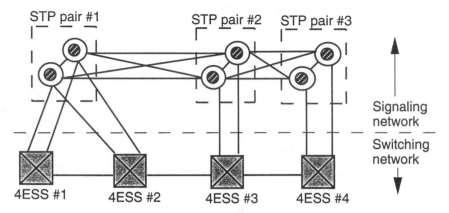

Figure 11.6 A segment of AT&T's SS7 network. Not all links between the STP pairs and between the 4ESSs are shown.

is capable of handling all of the calls of the pair. All signaling links run at 56 kbps and each 4ESS is "homed" or linked to only one STP pair, as shown in Figure 11.6.

11.3.3 Call Processing Over the Signaling Network

In Figure 11.6 if a call originates at 4ESS#1 and it needs a channel to 4ESS#2, then it will send a packet to STP pair #1 asking for the channel. STP pair #1 will interrogate 4ESS#2, providing the called party's phone number, if a path exists to the destination where the call is going. If 4ESS#2 can't complete the call, it will tell the STPs and the STPs will notify 4ESS#1. The 4ESS#1 will then provide the busyback signal to the caller and no trunks between the 4ESSs will be utilized.

However, if 4ESS#2 can complete the call to its destination, the STPs will give the go-ahead to the switches to switch simultaneously to the trunk specified by 4ESS#1's original request. Then a continuity and quality check is made on that trunk and the call is completed. Now the services of the STPs are not required.

If a call is to be completed between two 4ESSs not homed to the same STP pair, such as a call between 4ESS#1 and 4ESS#3, the same procedure is followed, but now the two pairs of STPs must communicate with each other in deciding which trunks to use.

If no free trunks are available between two switches, a third intermediate switch must be used to route the call. And if all three switches are homed to three different pairs of STPs all three pairs of STPs are required to process the call. For example, if in Figure 11.6 4ESS#1 needs to make a call to 4ESS#3 and no free capacity is available on the direct link between the two switches, the call may be routed via 4ESS#4. In such a case the three switches are connected to three different STP pairs and all of those STPs must then send packets to complete the call.

11.3.4 RTNR (Real Time Network Routing)

In no case are two intermediate 4ESS switches used for call completion, but only one intermediate switch is ever needed to complete the call. However, since most

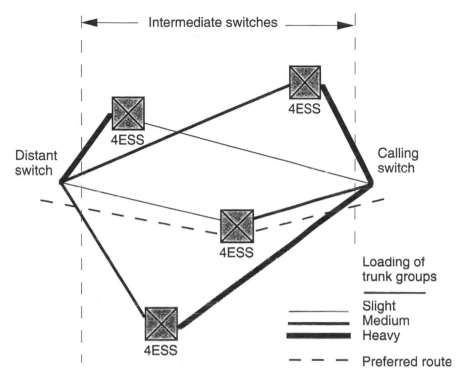

Figure 11.7 RTNR dynamically decides the best intermediate switch to complete a call by assessing the various trunk group usages.

switches are all fully connected to each other and there are over 120 of those, there are that many alternate routes possible.

RTNR dynamically calculates more than 134 possible routes to complete the call using one other 4ESS. By restricting itself to only one additional switch, RTNR keeps the signal quality high and calls can be completed in 4 to 6 seconds compared with over 20 seconds using the older hierarchical routing.

Prior to RTNR, AT&T used DNHR (Dynamic Non-Hierarchical Routing), which was not really a dynamic method of routing. It allowed for 14 alternate routes for every call between every 4ESS pair. These routes were preprogrammed in the 4ESSs for ten different time blocks during the day.

RTNR allows a 4ESS to calculate the most efficient route on a call-by-call basis. If a direct trunk is unavailable to the distant 4ESS, it will interrogate it via the signaling network for the status and capacity of the trunks connected to it. Then by comparing the traffic of the trunks connected to itself and the trunks connected to the distant 4ESS, the calling 4ESS will decide which other 4ESS to use as an intermediate switch. Then the appropriate connections are made through the signaling network. In Figure 11.7, the calling 4ESS has received the traffic loads of the distant 4ESS to 120 other switches. From this data, the calling switch decides to use the intermediate switch with the lightest load on both trunk groups.

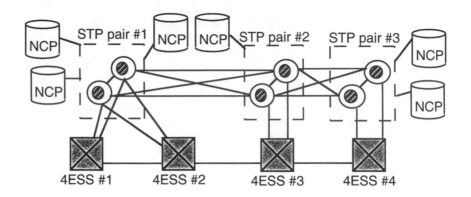

Figure 11.8 NCPs (Network Control Point) connected to the STPs provide advanced network services.

11.3.5 NCPs (Network Control Points)

The last component of the AT&T communications network is network services. These services include SDN (Software Defined Network), its virtual network, 800 and 900 services, and calling cards. They are provided by many databases called NCPs which are part of the signaling network and are connected to STPs, as shown in Figure 11.8. These are AT&T's equivalent of NJ Bell's SCPs described in the local telephone network section of this chapter. The NCPs form a distributed database, storing data pertaining to 800 numbers, SDN customers, and so on.

For example, when an STP has to route an 800 number, it knows which NCP has the POTS (Plain Old Telephone Service) number conversion for it. Through the NCP the 800 number is translated into a POTS number and the STP can then complete the call. For instance, 1-800-544-3498 may be converted to 408-345-3277 in San Jose. Advanced 800 numbers provide geographic or time-of-day routing, which means that the call is directed to a different POTS number depending on the caller's area or on the time of day the call is made,

Authorization for a calling card is done through the NCPs. Also, SDN customers' virtual network databases are stored here. All data in the NCPs is duplicated in at least one other site, and the STPs know which NCP has the data for the given customer or the number being called.

11.4 THE MCI NETWORK

Figure 11.9 shows the network architecture of MCI. It is divided into three layers: the administrative, logical, and physical layers. Let us first discuss the physical layer.

11.4.1 The Physical Layer

In this layer, the transmission network is 100% digital, although the media types are not all alike. This network is tied to a software-controlled distribution frame called a DACS (Digital Access and Cross connect System). This adds flexibility to the transmission network by being able to be reconfigured using a console. Customers can reconfigure their networks easily using the interfaces shown at the administrative layer.

A signal travels from the transmission network through the DACS to the switch. MCI has approximately 90 switches, some of which are Nortel's DMS-250s and others of which are DSC's DEX6000Es. Each switch has an AP (Adjunct Processor) to relieve it of its non-switching processing load. This allows the switches to function more swiftly and efficiently. APs provide CDR (Call Detail Recording) for each call to help expedite billing and provide up-front fraud detection to prevent unauthorized users from gaining access to private networks. It also provides protocol conversions between the MCI switches and other computer systems in the MCI network.

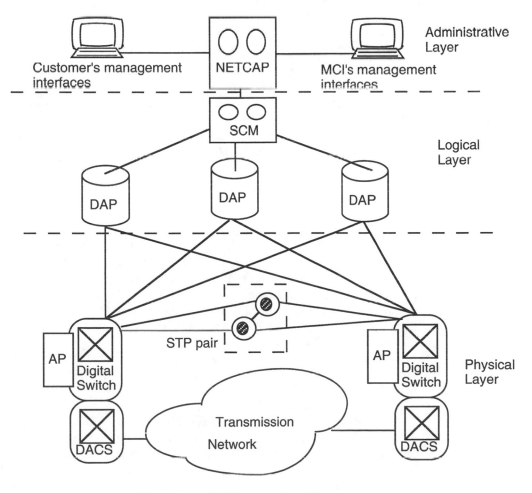

Figure 11.9 MCI's network architecture.

Each switch is homed to only one of five pairs of STPs. The STP network utilizes ANSI's version of SS7 called TR-TSY-950. As in the AT&T network, an ordinary POTS type of phone call uses only the physical network resources.

11.4.2 The Logical Layer

800 number conversions, credit card authorization, and virtual networks use the DAPs (Data Access Points), similar to the NCPs that are used in the AT&T network. A major difference here is that the DAPs are connected directly to the switches. The DAPs are VAX 8700 minicomputers made by DEC. All 90 switches have a direct link to each of the three DAPs. So even if two links fail, a third DAP link exists. The X.25 protocol is used over these links.

The data in all three DAPs is kept synchronized, meaning that the data is kept the same. This is done by the SCM (Service Control Manager). The SCM is an IBM 3090 mainframe which continuously downloads data from the NETCAP (NETwork CAPabilities manager).

11.4.3 The Administrative Layer

The NETCAP is also a mainframe and it provides an interface between the management systems and the rest of the network. When a customer or MCI configures or reconfigures a customer-specific network, the NETCAP provides the necessary security checking. It then screens the customer's inquiries and commands to make sure that they are of the proper format and prevents the customer from inadvertently misconfiguring his network. NETCAP then notifies the network elements and the appropriate billing computers.

11.5 THE SPRINT NETWORK

The backbone of Sprint's network consists of more than 50 DMS-250 switches made by Nortel. It has three DMS-300 switches which act as international gateways. It is also a fully connected mesh network where every switch has direct access to every other. The trunk between two switches is called an IMT (Inter-Machine Trunk). The entire network uses 26,000 miles of single mode fiber and has 321 POPs, at least one in every LATA. The bandwidth of the fiber varies from 565 Mbps to 100 Gbps depending on the traffic requirement on the IMTs. Using DWDM, this capacity is constantly being increased.

Like AT&T, Sprint uses a flat, nonhierarchical network architecture. It uses fewer switching points to reduce noise and possibility of failure. The routing mechanism is called DCR (Dynamic Controlled Routing). DCR uses time zones and peak time load differences to optimize its routing.

In 1993, the fiber network consisted of 23 loops. Today, it has SONET 228 rings which add survivability to the network in the event of failure. RDPS (Reverse Direction Protection Switching) allows switched traffic to be rerouted automatically in case there is a failure in the transmission path. Figure 11.10 shows how a fiber is terminated at a switch. First, the optical signal is converted into an electrical signal and demultiplexed into a number of DS-3 signal levels using an FOT (Fiber Optic Termi-

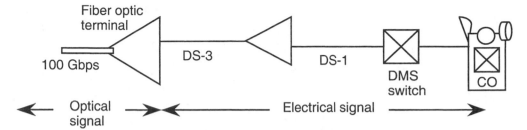

Figure 11.10 The optical signal coming off the fiber is demultiplexed into DS-3 levels, which are further demultiplexed into DS-1 levels. DS-1 is the signal level that is received by the Sprint switch.

nal). Then a bank of M13 multiplexers separates the DS-3 channels into DS-1 channels and the switch will separate the DS-1 channels into DS-0 channels as necessary.

Sprint uses 4F-BLSR architecture for its SONET rings. Its operation is discussed later in Chapter 20. The fiber backbone network is the physical network that is used to carry traffic from seven logically separate networks. Instead of installing a physically different fiber network for each type of network, the traffic from all these networks is aggregated over a single fiber network. These logical networks are as follows:

(1) The circuit switching network is used for dialing a call. (2) The SS7 network carries the signaling for the switches. (3) Private leased lines are for businesses that need fixed amounts of bandwidth from point to point. (4) SprintNet, formerly Telenet, is the world's largest X.25 network, and (5) frame relay. All these logical networks share the bandwidth on the fiber network. Also, (6) Sprint's ISDN and (7) their intranet backbone are on this network. The intranet backbone which is completely separate from the public Internet provides a safe means of transmitting information using TCP/IP.

Sprint made a change to SS7 in December of 1988. Figure 11.11 shows that the DMS switches have SPs (Signaling Points) associated with them. These SPs help the STPs and the DMS switches to perform call processing more efficiently.

The STPs are connected to SCPs (Service Control Points). The SCPs act like the NCPs in the AT&T network. That is, they provide the "database dips" needed for 800 number conversions, credit card handling, and virtual network routing.

Like AT&T's distributed NCP network, Sprint has also moved from a centrally located SCP management system to a distributed one. Sprint's intelligent network system is called DINA (Distributed Intelligent Network Architecture).

Sprint's network is managed and controlled from its NOCC (Network Operations Control Center) in Kansas City. The NOCC is supported by two RCCs (Regional Control Centers), one in Sacramento and one in Atlanta. An OSSC (Operational Support Systems Center) provides more redundancy. All centers interact with each other and the network is constantly under observation by teams and software at all locations. This drastically reduces any possibility for human error of any kind. Every 15 minutes all international and domestic switches report their current status to the NOCC. This helps the centers in deciding how traffic should be rerouted during normal operation and also for possible disasters.

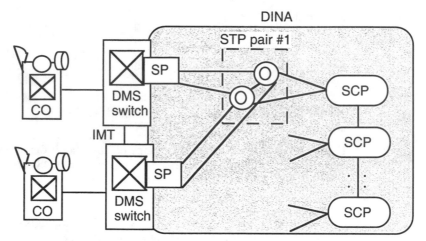

SP   : Signaling Point   SCP : Service Control Point
DINA : Distributed Intelligent Network Architecture   IMT : InterMachine Trunk

Figure 11.11 Sprint's network architecture.

11.6 INTRODUCTION TO SS7-BASED VIRTUAL NETWORKS

In section 5.1.4, we introduced virtual private networks. Virtual networks use public networks to create a private network. Although a customer uses public network facilities, it appears to him as though he has his own private network. The public network could be an IXC's portion of the PSTN which is controlled through its SS7 network or it could be the public Internet. In 1993, the SS7-based virtual networks became very popular, and those types of virtual networks are covered here. The Internet-based virtual networks are called VPNs (Virtual Private Networks) and they are the topic of Chapter 27. Although the SS7-based virtual networks are not as much publicized today as they once were, they are still quite common and available. AT&T calls its virtual network offering SDN (Software Defined Network), MCI calls its network Vnet, and Sprint calls its network VPN (Virtual Private Network).

11.6.1 Purpose of VNs (Virtual Networks)

There are many problems associated with designing and maintaining a private network based on tie-lines. The private network designer must decide whether and how a call should hop off the private network to gain access to the public network. Users have to constantly monitor the traffic patterns in deciding whether to add more trunks on some links or to remove trunks on others. Cost analysis has to be done at regular intervals to see how the network can be optimized. Also, pricing plans from the various carriers serving the different sites have to be constantly evaluated. Sorting out data from stacks of bills each month from the carriers can also be very tedious. Furthermore, as more sites are added to a private network, the problems of managing it become overwhelming.

Virtual networks, first introduced in 1984 by ISACOMM (which later became part of Sprint), take away the burden of managing a private network by having the carrier's signaling network take care of it. Because much of the traffic originating on a private network is sent over public facilities anyway, such as WATS and DDD service, why divide up the traffic so that some of it goes over tie lines and the rest of it goes over the PSTN? Let the PSTN carry all of the traffic over its switched facilities and end up providing the customer with savings and advanced networking features.

In Figure 11.12(a), a private network is shown. Remote offices don't carry enough traffic to warrant a tie-line, so to reach them from the corporate private network, one must dial a 10-digit public number. This gives the remote office a sense of not belonging to the company. Yet in Figure 11.12(b), using a virtual network, all of the sites are part of the private virtual network. This does not require that the sites

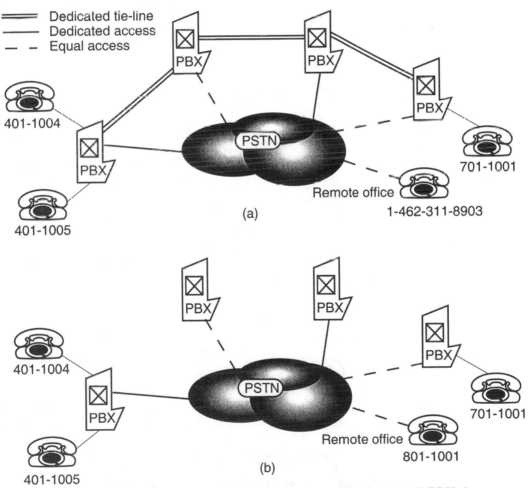

Figure 11.12 (a) Shows a private tie-line network where all PBX sites are part of a 7-digit uniform dialing plan. The remote office is accessed via the 10-digit public numbering plan. (b) A virtual network equivalent, where all sites are part of a 7-digit private numbering plan. Notice the absence of point-to-point tie-lines.

meet a minimum size requirement or generate a certain amount of traffic. People who are on the move, whether at home, or at a public phone, or even using a cellular telephone can be part of the private virtual network. All of the traffic generated flows through the PSTN. In other words, a virtual network provides the desirable features of a private network while its calls traverse public switched network facilities.

The manner in which the calls are processed and routed is specified by the customer who provides parameters to the carrier's intelligent signaling network. Think of virtual networks as being similar to long distance centrex services. With centrex the local carrier does the switching for one location. Similarly, with a virtual network, the IXC does the switching for a private network. (However, BOCs also provide virtual network services.)

Many corporations use a private tie-line network in combination with a virtual network. A combination of both types of networks is called a hybrid network. It is used when traffic between two or more nodes is so heavy that use of interconnecting tie-lines between those nodes produces significant cost savings over use of the PSTN.

11.6.2 Operation of Virtual Networks

When a call originates from a phone, it enters the carrier's POP through one of the VN (Virtual Network) access methods (to be described shortly). The carrier's switch will detect which VN customer is calling and forward the customer number, the calling party's number, and the called party's number to the SCP (Signal Control Point) through the STP (Signal Transfer Point). Recall that the SCP is a general name for AT&T's NCP and MCI's DAP. Sprint calls it an SCP. The SCP provides the translation of the 7-digit private phone number to the corresponding 10-digit public phone number or the POTS number. The entire call can be completed within 4 to 6 seconds.

Virtual networking is not a new technology, but a new form of packaging advanced technology. To the user it is just another form of low-cost bulk long distance service. The advanced technology that VNs rely on is in the carrier's SS7 network. The intelligence of the signaling networks makes virtual networking powerful. Unlike older signaling techniques, SS7 is software controlled, and to add a new feature to a VN offering, the carrier needs only to modify the software and update the change to all the installations.

VN service can be thought of as having four elements. One element is the method of accessing the POP from each customer location. The second is the transport and switching mechanism of the carrier's network. Third is the customer's VN description stored in the carrier's signaling databases. And last is the network management component which performs network monitoring, reconfiguration, and traffic analysis.

11.7 ADVANTAGES OF VIRTUAL NETWORKS

11.7.1 Ease of Management

Probably the greatest advantage of VNs as already mentioned is not having to constantly optimize the network as in the case of a private tie-line network. Since all the traffic goes through the PSTN, managing the network becomes easy. Expensive tie-lines are replaced by low-cost access lines to the associated POPs.

11.7.2 Corporate-wide Dialing Plan

Typically, the traditional tie-line networks of Figure 11.12(a) use a private 7-digit dialing plan to call any phone in the private network, and use the 10-digit public dialing plan to call anywhere in the public domain of phone numbers. So a user who is on the private network would dial a 7-digit number to dial another user on the private network or a 10-digit number to dial a user off the private network. An off-net user would have to dial 10 digits to call anyone, regardless of whether the destination is on or off the network.

When a VN is installed, the dialing plans for any of these phones can stay the same as before. Users don't have to be made aware of the VN installation; it is transparent to them. 7-digit dialers can continue dialing the same 7 digit numbers, and 10-digit dialers can continue dialing the same 10 digit numbers. Users don't have to be retrained in dialing on or off the network. The PSTN does the necessary number conversions. 7-digit private network plans and 10-digit public network plans can co-exist all on the same VN. If the customer chooses, he/she can instead use a 7-digit dialing plan for all locations.

11.7.3 Better Cost-to-performance Ratio

Provisioning is the process by which a VN is installed and made to work. It involves more than just the installation of lines and software. When a new node is installed in a VN by a carrier, this change is transparent to the existing users. Getting such a service started is called provisioning the network.

At one time, it took 10 to 45 days to provision virtual network changes. Now virtual networks are more adaptable to satisfying new networking needs quickly, and providing maximum performance for a network. Customers can do some of the provisioning themselves.

There is no capital investment necessary. When VNs were first introduced, only large companies could afford to pay for their high initial setup charges, but due to promotions that waive tariff charges, it now is possible to avoid these charges. In some instances, companies have saved over a million dollars annually by converting to the use of VNs. In short, VN users have all the benefits of private networks without having to bear their problems and costs.

There is no need to have trained personnel at all sites to maintain the network. In a traditional private tie-line network, if reliability was a concern between two cities, then a redundant tie-line was usually installed between them, adding to the cost of the network. With a VN, however, the carrier's network itself inherently has redundant paths between many locations, making failure of an entire VN unlikely. In fact, VNs boast of providing 99.8% or better availability; that is, the failure can be less than two hours annually!

11.7.4 Other Advantages

Other advantages of virtual networks include the concepts of virtual offices and virtual companies. Now a worker's office doesn't have to be located physically in a given place. The office may be wherever the worker happens to be: at home, in a car, or at a public place.

Many times different companies depend on each other to provide a seamless service to their customers, such as the businesses used by an advertising agency. A virtual company is created by interconnecting the networks of such physically different but related organizations into one virtual network. This creates a sense of community among them and helps them to work better to yield better overall services.

Yet other advantages include the flexibility that is gained by being able to change the network as demands change. There is a single point of contact when problems arise. The rates are reduced as the usage increases. This saves the customer from having to do extensive traffic studies each month. Finally, virtual network calls can be given priority over regular switched calls. Emergency calls have a higher priority. This is advantageous especially if there is a catastrophe in one part of the country, such as an earthquake, when everyone is trying to call their friends to see if they are fine.

There is no need to have PBXs from the same manufacturer at each node, as is the case in a private network. One doesn't have to replace the PBXs when a VN is installed. Furthermore, you can give calling card users the cost benefits of a VN, even though calls originate from off-net sites. With a private network, only one call can traverse a trunk at a time. So if the traffic demands more calls between two points, then more trunks are needed. With VNs, however, the user isn't concerned about having enough trunks—the PSTN supports the long-haul traffic.

11.8 TYPES OF ACCESS

Another advantage of VNs over private tie-line networks is the number of access methods VNs provide their customers besides the traditional dedicated access line. Customers use their local trunks to provide switched access into the VN, and then as traffic volume increases, more local trunks may be added or may even be replaced with dedicated access facilities. The access methods outlined here apply not only to VNs but also to other long distance services.

11.8.1 Switched Access

In Figure 11.13, the PBX has a switched access to a POP through a CO. A call from the PBX to the POP can go by either of the two paths shown. If the direct path is busy, the call is switched over the alternate path. Similarly, residential phones calling long distance through a POP also employ switched access to the POP.

When the trunk between the CO and the POP is shared by many users, a customer's line to that CO trunk, although used only by that customer, is called a switched access line.

There are four categories of obtaining switched access to a POP and they are called "feature groups." Figure 11.14 illustrates these four types of feature groups. On the left, the PBX has a local trunk to the nearest CO or the end office. This CO can then provide switched access to an AT&T POP using feature group C, or to the other IXCs' POPs using feature groups A, B, or D via other COs. Let us now discuss these feature groups.

Feature group A type of switched access was made available after divestiture to reach a non-AT&T POP. One had to use DTMF signaling and not rotary dial telephone

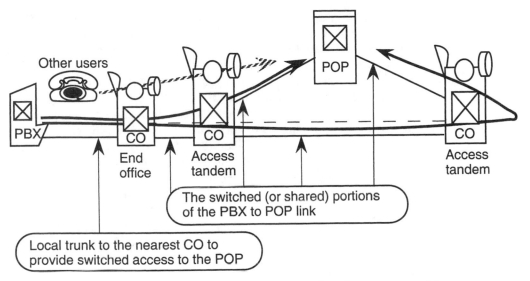

Figure 11.13 Switched access to an IXC's point of presence provides no predetermined path to it. Also the path is shared with other users, and it can go through either of the tandem switches.

to reach the "alternate carriers." So to call long distance using a non-AT&T carrier, one had to dial a local phone number, after which the caller heard a second dial tone from the POP.

The connection to the POP was provided over the "line" side rather than the "trunk" side of the telco's switch. Although this was a low-cost connection, it used only one pair of wires for both transmit and receive voice paths. Trunk side connections of a switch, on the other hand, use 4-wire connections to keep the transmit and receive paths separate in order to provide high-quality voice transmission.

Feature group A makes the POP look like an ordinary phone number, and this type of access is not necessarily routed through a tandem. So this type of access is becoming less and less common.

Feature group B is a predivestiture local access method. This type of access is obtained by dialing toll-free 950-0xxx or 950-1xxx. As an example, to obtain access to MCI, one must dial 950-1022 and for Sprint, 950-1033. This is a common nation-wide number.

After hearing a tone or an announcement, the user must dial the extra digits. This type of access is provided by two pairs of wires and has better transmission quality on the trunk side of a telco switch. This switch could reside in either an end office or an access tandem office. A tandem office switch must be upgraded to an electronic switching system for it to provide feature group B access. Because an authorization code still has to be entered in order to use this type of access, feature group B is also becoming less common in accessing IXCs.

Recently, however, large nationwide companies such as pizza chains are using this access as an inexpensive way to obtain 800 number capabilities. Instead of dialing the 11 digits typically associated with 800 number dialing, pizza customers can dial one 950 number anywhere in the country, and be connected to a pizza chain's nationwide network. In this case, the POP at feature group B in Figure 11.14 would then represent the pizza chain's network node switch. This switch would be in the same LATA as the serving CO. With the 950-1xxx designation for this type of access, only 1,000 numbers are possible, but the NANPA (North American Numbering Plan Administration) is working with the BOCs (Bell Operating Companies) to add another 9,000. Not only does this access provide a high quality 4-wire connection, but it also provides ANI (Automatic Number Identification) and answer supervision. Using feature group B instead of an 800 number requires that the user have its own network in place to interconnect private nodes between LATAs. Because of this overhead associated with 950 access, most companies find 800 service more suitable.

Feature group C access can only be provided by AT&T. A user need only dial a 1 to access the AT&T POP. This access offers 4-wire connections and automatic number identification. This type of access provides a very short call setup time because, due to predivestiture conditions, these lines are sent directly to the AT&T POP. See Figure 11.14.

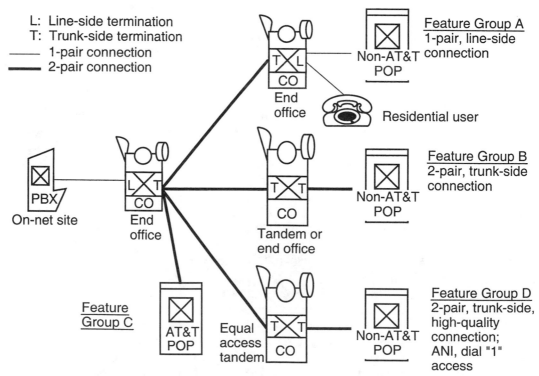

Figure 11.14 The four groups of switched access, where feature group D provides the highest quality connection to non-AT&T POPs. However, switched access to AT&T is faster than access to the other carriers due to the existence of predivestiture connections.

Feature group D circuits are also 4-wire trunk side connections, and provide an even higher level of quality than feature groups A and B. This high quality is maintained by the federal courts, with a requirement of a maximum of one tandem office for these circuits and the tandems have to be fully electronic. Instead of dialing a 7-digit number to access the POP, one needs only to dial 1.

According to MFJ, accessing any IXC should be just as easy as accessing AT&T; hence these are also called equal access circuits. Since the LEC provides the POP with ANI (Automatic Number Identification) with the call, rotary pulse dialing telephones can also be used.

A customer can access a POP two ways using equal access. Presubscription or primary access requires the customer to simply dial a 1, the area code, and then the 7 digits, whereas non-presubscription or secondary access requires the customer to dial 10xxx, the area code, and then the 7 digits. These are also known as "casual callers."

Accessing a VN using any of these switched access feature groups is simply called switched access. A location that uses a switched access to access a VN is called an on-net location, since the location presubscribes to the IXC and all calls are connected to the POP. This type of access is ideal for small locations that don't have the traffic volume to necessitate a dedicated line.

11.8.2 Dedicated Access

DAL (Dedicated Access Line) or special access line is used to provide dedicated access to the VN. The line is strictly for the use of one user and it is not shared. Instead of paying on a per-call basis, the user pays one flat monthly charge. The circuit doesn't go through a switch at the CO, but is hardwired there to be routed to the POP. Of course, only high-volume customers find it economical to install a DAL. These are usually T1s today.

A DAL differs from a WAL (WATS Access Line) in that a DAL provides a dedicated linkup to the POP whereas the WAL provides a dedicated link only up to the equal access point. From there it is switched, as seen in Figure 11.15. Also, a WAL cannot be used for placing local calls or for receiving any calls.

A DAL could be a single-channel analog line or it could be carried over a high-capacity digital line, such as a T1 or a T3. Often, as few as six single-line DALs might equal the cost of a T1 dedicated access line, in which case the customer gains 18 channels (24 minus 6) for little or no additional cost. Whether the break-even point is as few as 6 or as high as 14 DALs is simply a financial question and is determined by costs of the single-line DALs as opposed to the cost of the T1. These costs are determined by the distance between the user's site and the POP and by the tariff rate for each.

11.8.3 Remote Access

A person can use an 800 number to access the VN while he/she is traveling and has no access to a company phone. This is called remote or 800 number access and is considered an off-net call. There are various forms of remote access.

Basically, the user dials an 800 number, possibly an authorization code, and the called number. He/she thereby has access to any VN location (on-net location) or any

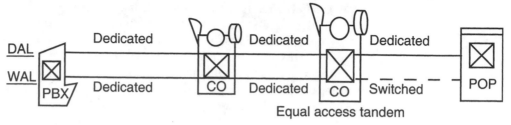

Figure 11.15 The top link shows a DAL (Dedicated Access Link) providing a dedicated channel up to the POP. And the bottom link shows a WAL (WATS Access Link) which provides a dedicated channel up to the equal access tandem. WALs cannot be used for placing local calls or for receiving calls.

DDD call (off-net location). As with private tie-line networks, however, the caller may be restricted from calling certain areas.

AT&T's version of remote access is called NRA (Network Remote Access). Soon the BOCs will be providing 800 number portability, and a customer will be able to keep the same 800 number and still be able to switch its IXC.

Lastly, an on-net location is any location that is defined in the customer's VN description, which resides in the carrier's database. The location could be served by switched or dedicated access. It could even be an employer's residence, as long as it is defined in the database. Conversely, any location not defined in the customer's database is referred to as an off-net location.

Compared to private networks, VNs offer a broad range of accessing methods which bring the advantages of a private network to the smallest customer sites and even to the customer's transient employees.

EXERCISES

Section 11.1:

1. In 1982, the telephone network was divided into how many sections? See Figure 11.1.
   - a. 10
   - b. 40
   - c. 52
   - d. 100
2. Give reasons why the old hierarchical routing of telephone calls took longer than the current methods?
3. What type of office connects two COs together in the local network?

Section 11.2:

4. What device interfaces a residential home wiring with the local telephone network?
   - a. SAC
   - b. NID
   - c. SLC
   - d. IW
5. When a person moves from one house to another house within the same area, and wishes to keep the same phone number, what must be changed for that customer?
   - a. TN
   - b. OE
   - c. CP
   - d. HMDF

6. What type of signal is sent over the voice path between two COs in an SS7 environment?
   - a. busyback
   - b. ringback
   - c. dial tone
   - d. DTMF tones
7. Which device multiplexes 96 subscriber lines to the CO using 10 pairs of wire?
8. Name the SS7 type of office which allows a CO not on the SS7 network to be part of that network?
9. Explain how switched lines and dedicated lines are routed in a CO using Figure 11.2.
10. Using Figure 11.4, describe the steps of how a call from Metuchen to a Bell Atlantic 800 number located in Somerville occurs.

Section 11.3:

11. If AT&T had 117 4ESS switches, how many alternate routes would be possible between two switches that use one other intermediate switch?
   - a. 100
   - b. 115
   - c. 116
   - d. 117
12. Which AT&T routing technique utilizes the instantaneous loading capacities of the intermachine trunks?
13. Describe how an AT&T credit card call is made.
14. What are the future plans that AT&T has to expand its network?

Section 11.4:

15. Which of the following is not a layer in the MCI network?
   - a. application
   - b. logical
   - c. administration
   - d. physical
16. What is the name of the processor that helps each MCI switch with its non-switching related tasks?
17. What types of switches are used by MCI? Are they made by only one manufacturer? What are the advantages if this is so, or what are the advantages if this is not so?

Section 11.5:

18. What are the names of the SCPs as referred to by AT&T, MCI, and Sprint?
19. What is the name of the routing method used by Sprint?
20. How many miles of transmission lines does Sprint have compared with AT&T's? What are the advantages and disadvantages of having more miles of transmission facilities compared to having fewer miles?
21. Sprint is converting its fiber rings to what type of SONET rings?
22. What is Sprint doing to increase the capacity of its existing fiber?

Section 11.6:

23. Which of the following is NOT an advantage of virtual networks?
   - a. They require a substantial amount of capital investment in networking products, which can be regained if the products are resold on the secondary market.
   - b. They drastically reduce the amount of traffic engineering that has to be done on a private network.
   - c. Network configuration changes can be done within a reasonable amount of time.
   - d. They provide better reliability over traditional tie-line networks.

24. MCI calls its virtual network by which name?
    a. VPN   b. SBS
    c. Vnet   d. SDN
25. Where is the customer's data stored in a virtual network? What do the three major carriers call this database?
26. Name the four elements of a virtual network.

Section 11.7:
27. A private network dialing plan usually has how many dialing digits?
28. Discuss the virtual network advantages that are management related.
29. Discuss the virtual network advantages that pertain to a uniform dialing plan.

Section 11.8:
30. Which type of feature group is the least commonly used in virtual networks?
    a. Feature group A   b. Feature group B
    c. Feature group C   d. Feature group D
31. Which type of call can be made with WALs?
    a. inbound local calls   b. inbound inter-LATA calls
    c. outbound local calls   d. outbound inter-LATA calls
32. Which type of feature group is used for providing high-quality access to non-AT&T POPs? Choose from the choices in exercise 2.
33. Which feature groups use trunk-side terminations for the POPs?
34. Typically, what type of access allows a person in transit to use a virtual network?
35. Discuss equal access, its characteristics, and the two methods of acquiring it.

Wireless Communication and CDMA

12.1 AMPS

We will start this chapter by giving a thorough description of AMPS (Advanced Mobile Phone Service). This is the analog system that is still widely used in the United States. Then we will be in position to understand the components and issues relating to modern digital systems. Modern digital systems are considered to be second-generation solutions. In the last part of the chapter we will go over CDMA, which is a widely used wireless access method that forms the basis of many proposals for third-generation wireless standards.

12.1.1 Overview

The formal name for the modern cellular phone system is AMPS. EAMPS (Extended AMPS) is used to refer to the newer set of frequencies allocated to cellular service that provides a total of 832 channels instead of the 666 allocated for AMPS.

The basic concept behind AMPS (or EAMPS) is simple, but the design and implementation are complex. A geographical region is divided into circular areas, called cells, that are between 2 to 12 miles in radius. For design purposes, they are shown as hexagonal areas. In Figure 12.1, each cell is served by a cell site which has a transmitter, a receiver, antenna, and related equipment. Cell sites are directly tied to an MTSO (Mobile Telephone Switching Office), which is tied to a tandem or to the class 5 offices (or COs) in the local telephone network. The local telephone company is also referred to as the wire-line company, which may be a BOC (Bell Operating Company). The MTSO is like the CO for the cellular system. In a given region, half of the available cellular service is provided by the resident wire-line company and half by the competition.

All calls originating from the local telephone network are switched to the proper cell site where the mobile phone has the best reception. And likewise, all calls originating from the mobile phones are sent to the MTSO by the cell site with the best signal. The MTSO then forwards the call to the CO.

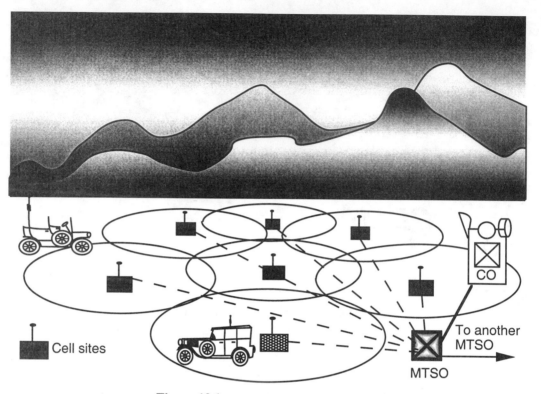

Figure 12.1 A cellular telephone system layout.

Depending on which cell site has the best signal level, a mobile unit latches on to that cell site at any given time, and all communication occurs with that one cell site. As the vehicle travels out of one area and into another, the cell site, noticing the drop in signal level, hands off the communication to the other cell site with the MTSO's assistance. This is called handoff.

12.1.2 Advantages of AMPS

Actually, before AMPS and IMTS (Improved Mobile Telephone Service), we had LMR (Land Mobile Radio) systems. These are also called two-way radios and are still widely used in emergency vehicles, taxis, etc. Before a mobile radio is installed in a vehicle, its frequency is set by a technician and that frequency channel is dedicated for that specific radio. No one else can use that channel in the given region, even if it is idle. For police cars and trucking outfits, this is not a waste of frequency bands because they are constantly using the channels. But for personal use where the mobile phone is not used around the clock, such systems did not prove to be efficient.

When IMTS, which preceded AMPS, was introduced it provided a wireless system where channels were assigned as they were needed. When a person disconnected his call, his channel then became free to be assigned to another caller. This way,

Wireless Communication and CDMA

IMTS was able to provide mobile telephone service for more customers than the number of available call channels. This was possible because everyone who needed wireless service did not need it 24 hours a day.

IMTS used large coverage areas, typically 20 miles in radius. This required that transmitters have an output power of up to 250 watts. Also, the same radio frequency could not be used in two areas that were closer than 75 miles; otherwise there would be interference in a channel also used by the other station.

This limited the number of channels available for mobile phones. In the mid-1970s for instance, New York City had only 12 channels serving about 550 customers with almost 4,000 customers on a waiting list. There was no way of expanding the service dynamically if the demand in the region increased.

AMPS, developed by AT&T, on the other hand, used many cells in a serving area. But the cells were smaller than before, the transmitted output was reduced to 100 watts for a cell transmitter, 3 watts for a mobile transmitter, and 0.6 watts for a portable unit. And since the output power was low, two cells could be as close as two miles (one cell apart) and still use the same set of frequencies. Interference from nearby cells using the same channels is called co-channel interference. As long as the C/I (Carrier-to-Interference) ratio is at least 17 dBs, co-channel interference is negligible. This means that two cells using the same set of channels will not cause interference if the selected cell's signal strength is at least 17 dBs greater than the interfering cell's signal strength.

All this provided more channels per given amount of bandwidth. And if demand for service grew in one area, then cells could be split into smaller cells yet, where cells would reduce their effective output power. The net effect of this was to increase the number of channels available in a given area. Of course, the design and planning of splitting cells became a complex procedure, but now at least it was feasible.

The technique of sectoring cells also improves the utilization of the frequency spectrum, or the available bandwidth. Sectoring involves dividing the cell into usually three pie-piece-shape sectors. Now instead of transmitting all available channels in a cell in all directions (using an omnidirectional antenna), three directional antennas are used to transmit one-third of the available channels in each of the three sectors. Sectoring allows placing cells closer together by facing the sectors which use the same channels in opposite directions. This increases the channel capacity of the system.

12.1.3 Reasons for Irregular Cell Shapes

Usually, cells are depicted as having hexagonal shapes for designing purposes, but realistically, antennas send off signals in circular patterns. However, circular radiation patterns are also not what is eventually achieved, as shown in Figure 12.2.

The initial deployment of the cellular system simply placed cells in regions where there was a high concentration of population and vehicular traffic, instead of placing them in a honeycomb-like grid. Also, if the center of a cell happened to fall in a river or off to a spot where a convenient tower or building stood, then the area covered by the cell would be moved somewhat. Sometimes a directional antenna was used to avoid interference with other systems. Some communities didn't allow a tower, so again a directional antenna tilting downwards would be placed outside the town. In general, the terrain of the area covered by a cell, such as tall buildings, mountains,

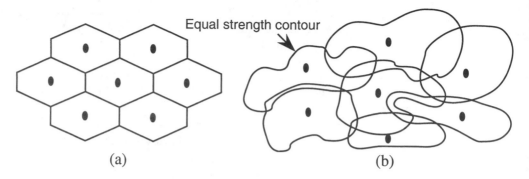

Figure 12.2 (a) Hexagonal shapes used in designing cellular networks. (b) The actual shape of the cells is seldom uniform.

valleys, etc., changes the desired shape of the area covered by the cell. All of these factors change the desired symmetric cells to cells that are irregular in shape.

12.1.4 Distribution of Cell Channels

The FCC (Federal Communications Commission) has allocated 824 to 851 MHz and 869 to 896 MHz for cellular service as shown in Table 12.1. This makes 25 MHz of bandwidth available for transmitting and 25 MHz for receiving. Because each one-way channel requires 0.03 MHz, dividing .03 MHz into the available 25 MHz provides a total of 832 channels for the cellular system.

832 channels are divided into two equal groups of 416 channels called block A and block B. Channels in one block are for use by the wire-line company and channels in the other block are for use by the non-wire-line company. In any case, each mobile's receive channel frequency is 45 MHz above its transmit channel frequency. For instance, channel number 333 transmits at 835 MHz and receives at 880 MHz from the mobile.

Table 12.1 Allocation of Channels		
	Mobile Transmit	Mobile Receive
Bandwidth per channel	.03 MHz	.03 MHz
Frequency range for blocks A & B	824–849 MHz	869–894 MHz
Total spectrum allocated including unused portion	824–851 MHz	869–896 MHz
Number of channels for block A	416	416
Number of channels for block B	416	416
Total number of channels	832	832

Wireless Communication and CDMA

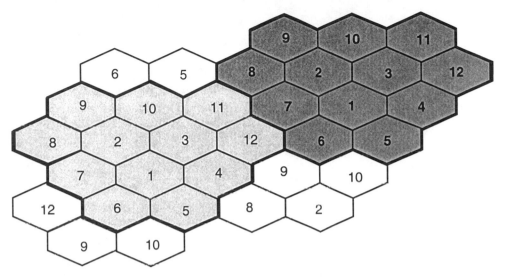

Figure 12.3 Frequency reuse pattern with $k = 12$.

12.1.5 Frequency Reuse

Considering only one block, or one cellular company's bandwidth allocation in a region, there are 416 available channels, 21 of which are used for signaling. This leaves 395 channels for voice traffic. Each cell site requires only one signaling channel to communicate signaling information with all of the mobiles in its area. So every twenty-first cell in a cell pattern uses the same signaling channel.

If every cell communicated using all of the available 395 channels, then channels from adjacent cells would interfere with each other. Hence, to reduce the amount of co-channel interference, cells are grouped together so that the channels allocated to one cell are unique in that group of cells . The number of cells in such a group is called the frequency reuse pattern or simply k. That is, the 395 channels are partitioned into k number of channel groups. This way, two cells that use the same set of channels are not adjacent to each other but are separated.

For example, consider the cellular system shown in Figure 12.3 where k is 12. Here approximately 32 (or 395/12) voice channels are available to each cell. Two cells labeled with the same number use the same group of 32 channels. However, the co-channel interference, that is, the interference between two such cells, is negligible because they are sufficiently far apart. The value of k is typically 7 but may range from 4 to 21. As k is decreased, more channels become available per cell, but the chance of co-channel interference increases. To further reduce the amount of co-channel interference, cells are typically divided into 3 sectors where the available channels are further divided into three groups, each group supporting communications in one-third of the cell area. In Figure 12.3, this would mean that each sector would have 10 or 11 (32/3) channels per sector.

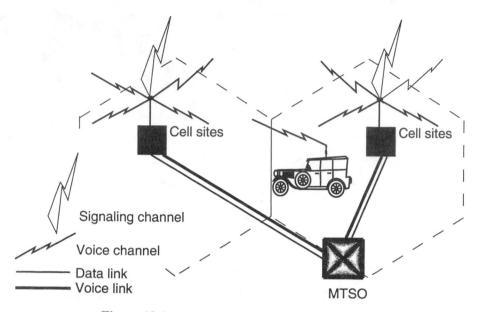

Figure 12.4 Operation of system between two cells.

12.1.6 Operation

When a mobile unit is turned on and no calls are being made or received, it is said to be in the idle condition. In the idle condition the unit scans all 21 signaling channels and latches on to the cell site which has the strongest signal; usually that means the closest cell site. Now the mobile unit is capable of receiving and making calls since it has a radio link established with a cell site. See Figure 12.4. This is called self-location. The cell isn't aware of which mobile units are listening to it. After about a minute or so, the mobile unit rescans the 21 channels and may lock (or monitor the signaling channel) to different cell sites each time.

In some cellular systems, a mobile will notify the cell site when it locks on to it. This is called registration. This information is helpful for the MTSO when it needs to know its location to complete a call made to it.

When the mobile unit wants to place a call, it transmits the called digits over the signaling channel to the selected cell site. The cell site forwards the phone number to the MTSO, which then connects the cell to the wire-line CO. At the same time, the MTSO assigns a free full-duplex voice channel from the selected cell site to the mobile unit. The cell site tells the mobile unit which channel has been assigned for this call over the signaling channel, and it will then tune its transmitter and receiver to that voice channel. Finally, when the phone rings at the destination, it will be heard over the cellular phone.

When a call originates from the wire-line network, the CO detects that the phone number falls in the range of numbers assigned to a particular cellular company. The CO then forwards the phone number to the corresponding cellular company's MTSO. Because the MTSO doesn't know where the mobile unit is (unless registration is used), it sends the phone number to all the cell sites and to other MTSOs and their respective cell sites. Then all cell sites page the phone number on their respective signaling channels, hoping the mobile unit is on and is in the vicinity of one of the cell sites. When the mobile phone detects its own phone number being paged, it will answer the cell by retransmitting its own phone number and the ESN (Electronic Serial Number) of its mobile unit over the signaling channel to the cell site. ESN confirms the proper identity of the mobile unit so that the correct party is charged for the phone call. (The ESN is also transmitted when a mobile is making a call.) The MTSO checks the ESN and the phone number for a match, and will assign a full-duplex voice channel between the cell site and the mobile unit, and the call processing is complete.

Regardless of who initiated the call, once the mobile unit turns off the transmitter, a special signal is sent over the signaling channel and the MTSO frees the voice channel for another call.

12.1.7 Handoff

A mobile unit which is communicating via a cell site may eventually travel into another cell. The original cell site then notices that the signal strength from that unit is decreasing. It will then request the MTSO that another cell site be assigned to communicate with that unit. The MTSO then asks the other cells nearby to check the signal strength on the voice channel that is being used. The cell site that has the best reception with that mobile unit is told to communicate with the mobile unit, but this time, it would be on a different channel, a new voice channel that is free and is one of the channels allocated for that cell site. The handoff process disrupts communication for up to 200 milliseconds, which doesn't affect voice calls as much as it does data transmissions.

12.1.8 Cell Splitting

One of the advantages of cellular telecommunications systems is that if the traffic increases for a given cell so that it reaches its load capacity, the cell can be split into several cells, thereby increasing the number of channels in the area.

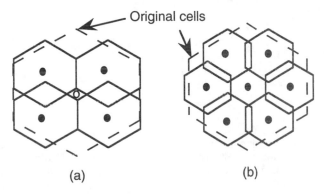

Figure 12.5 Two methods of splitting a cell: (a) The original cell is eliminated. (b) The original cell reduces its effective coverage.

Two ways in which a cell can be split are shown in Figure 12.5. The first method doesn't use the original cell site but divides the cell into four parts, creating 4 new cells. The other method, which is more common, shows that the original cell size decreases, but surrounding it, six new cells are created.

If we suppose that the original cell site had 70 channels, and is split into 6 new ones, then the total of 7 cell sites will each initially use 10 channels. However, each of these cells could eventually increase their capacity to 70 channels, which would increase the available channels in the region. This is all easier said than done. Engineers have to be very careful when splitting cells so that the rest of the system works without interference or interruption.

12.2 INTRODUCTION TO MODERN WIRELESS SYSTEMS

12.2.1 Wireless Systems Model

AMPS was the first major cellular system. Today with research being done on many different fronts of digital systems, many protocols are surfacing. To identify components of the various methods used in second- and third-generation systems, the model shown in Figure 12.6 is typically used.

These parts can be placed into five categories: radios, switches, databases, processors, and external networks. The radios shown in Figure 12.6 are the cell phone

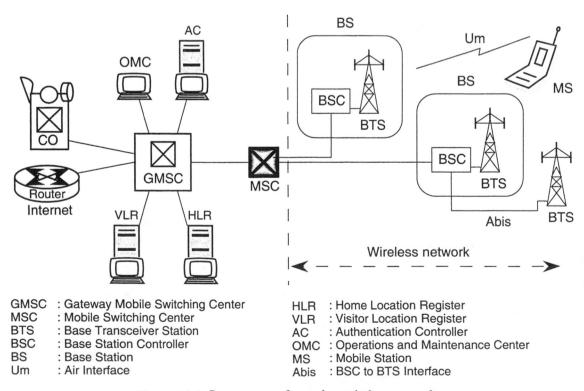

GMSC	: Gateway Mobile Switching Center	HLR	: Home Location Register
MSC	: Mobile Switching Center	VLR	: Visitor Location Register
BTS	: Base Transceiver Station	AC	: Authentication Controller
BSC	: Base Station Controller	OMC	: Operations and Maintenance Center
BS	: Base Station	MS	: Mobile Station
Um	: Air Interface	Abis	: BSC to BTS Interface

Figure 12.6 Components of a modern wireless network.

and the base stations. The BSs (Base Stations) include the BSC (Base Station Controller) and the BTS (Base Transceiver Station). A BSC can control several BTSs and the interface between these components are called A$_{bis}$ (BSC-BTS Interface). The Um (Air Interface) defines the interface of how communication takes place between the MS (Mobile Station) and the BS.

The switches shown are MSC (Mobile Switching Center) and GMSC (Gateway Mobile Switching Controller). Traditionally, these replace what was called the MTSO in the AMPS system. The GMSC, as its name implies, connects external networks to the mobile network. These networks include the PSTN (shown by the CO in the figure), the Internet, ATM, and other types of networks including the SS7 network.

The databases and the processors are connected to the switching centers. The databases are called HLR (Home Location Register) and VLR (Visitor Location Register). The HLR permanently stores subscriber data relating to network intelligence and the VLR temporarily stores subscriber data for customers who are being served by the network in the region in question. An AC (Authentication Center) provides authentication of mobile subscribers' identities. ACs and other components which provide voice messaging and announcements are examples of processors.

12.2.2 Basic Wireless Principles

Access Methods: There are basically three methods by which a transmitter accesses the air interface to transmit to the given receiver. FDMA (Frequency Division Multiple Access) uses different frequencies to do that. We have seen how FDMA is used in AMPS already. Transmitters using different frequencies can transmit at the same time.

Transmitters using TDMA (Time Division Multiple Access) transmit at the same frequency but take turns at transmitting. CDMA (Code Division Multiple Access) is different than the other two. Transmitters using CDMA transmit at all of the frequencies at all times. However, a transmission to a particular receiver is identified by a particular digital code that is overlayed on the transmission. The receiver decodes his message by applying his code to the composite transmitted signal. After he correlates his code with the transmitted signal, his message is decoded clearly. For someone who doesn't have a message coded for him in the composite received signal, the signal appears as simply noise. Let us look at an analogy.

Suppose you came into an airport where people were talking in Mandarin, Portuguese, Spanish, and Arabic. If you only understood English, you would only hear noise. On the other hand, if you only spoke Arabic, you only hear Arabic. If you only spoke Spanish, you would hear Spanish and a little Portuguese since these two languages are similar. A CDMA engineer would refer to these two languages as not orthogonal while he would refer to Mandarin, English, Spanish, and Arabic as being orthogonal.

CDMA has to also address the issue of what is called power control. If you only understood Arabic, and the people speaking Arabic were at a different corner of the airport than you were, you would only hear noise. Also, even if you were close to them, but a Mandarin speaking person was making an announcement using a loud speaker system, you would still hear noise. With CDMA, power control becomes a critical issue. More on that later.

Vocoders: PCM (Pulse Code Modulation) used in the PSTN requires that each channel have 64 kbps of bandwidth. Where fiber is becoming more and more common today in the phone network, 64 kbps per channel is no big deal. With wireless systems, however, the capacities of the allocated frequency bands are fixed. There is a greater need to reduce the bit rate of the voice channels here.

Codecs used with PCM actually digitize audio signals and then decode them. Instead of digitizing the audio, vocoders (a specialized types of codecs) encode *parameters* describing the audio signal. This reduces the bit rate of the audio signal down to 8 to 13 kbps, a drastic reduction from 64 kbps. By reducing this bit rate, more subscribers can be allowed on the air at any given time. This rate can be instantaneously reduced further because people in typical conversations don't transmit audio continuously but are often listening or taking pauses.

A codec using PCM is like taking a recording of a person playing the piano, and then replaying the recording at a different time. A vocoder is like writing down on staff paper the musical notation of a person playing the piano and then having someone else replay it. The actual recording would take a lot more bits to store than the musical notation would take. Just like the transcriber writes down the parameters of the notes played, vocoders also transmit only the parameters of the voice. This enables vocoders to operate at a much lower rate than PCM-based codecs.

12.2.3 The Wireless Spectrum

Figure 12.7 shows the various wireless systems and where they appear in the electromagnetic spectrum. All frequency bands for mobile transmit channels appear

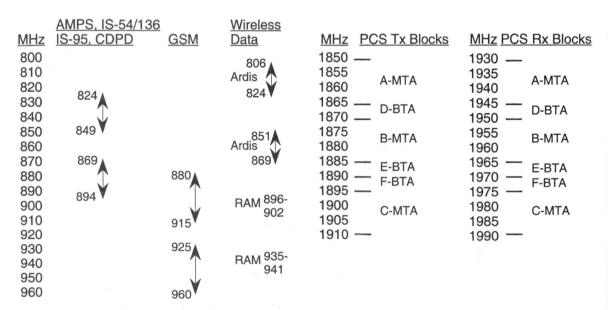

Figure 12.7 Frequency allocation of major wireless services. All mobile receive (Rx) channels in existence are higher in frequency than the mobile transmit (Tx) channels.

before the mobile receive channels. The frequency bands for AMPS are from 824 MHz to 849 MHz and 869 MHz to 894 MHz, as we have seen. These are the same bands where second-generation digital systems exist. They are IS-54, IS-136, and IS-95, which will be covered later on. IS-95 is now called TIA/EIA-95.

Ardis (Advanced Radio Data and Information Server) from Motorola and RAM Mobile Data from RAM Broadcasting and BellSouth provide up to 19.2 kbps of data services. Ardis provides special-purpose terminals called "bricks" to subscribers while RAM provides a modem that works with any laptop.

A more standardized approach for sending wireless data is called CDPD (Cellular Digital Packet Data). It can be overlayed in the same frequency range as existing cellular networks. It uses digital transmission even if used in the cellular region. It uses a technique called "channel hopping" which allows it to switch channels instantaneously during a transmission. Furthermore, it is designed to carry data at a rate of 19.2 kbps. However, rates of 9.6 kbps are more common. GSM, used primarily in Europe, is also covered later on and exists from 880 MHz to 960 MHz.

PCS (Personal Communications Services or Systems) exist near the 2-GHz range as shown in Figure 12.7. There are six blocks of frequencies. The three blocks called A, B, and C are used by MTAs (Major Trading Areas) and blocks D, E, and F are used by the BTAs (Basic Trading Areas). Each MTA band is 30 MHz with 15 MHz to transmit and 15 MHz to receive. The BTA bands are each only 10 MHz. The protocols used in this frequency range include TIA/EIA-95, IS-136, GSM, and others including third-generation systems.

12.2.4 Fixed Wireless Systems

After this range of frequencies, we get above 2 GHz. Here there are several ISM (Industrial, Scientific, and Medical) bands that are defined. See Figure 12.8. These are unlicensed bands, which makes equipment operating in these bands faster to deploy. Broadband wireless access is also available in these bands. Equipment used in the ISM bands mostly uses DSSS (Direct Sequence Spread Spectrum) technology, which is similar to CDMA. There is potential for interference with other equipment operating in these regions, and so different companies are expected to use different coding methods to minimize interference.

2.150–2.162	MMDS			27.500–28.350	LMDS
2.400–2.4835	IEEE 802.11b Unlicensed ISM			29.100–29.250	LMDS
2.596–2.644	MMDS			31.000–31.075	LMDS
2.650–2.656	MMDS			31.075–31.225	LMDS
2.662–2.668	MMDS	5.725–5.875	Unlicensed UNNI	31.225–31.300	LMDS
2.674–2.680	MMDS	24.000–24.250	Unlicensed ISM		

MMDS : Multipoint Multichannel Distribution Services   ISM : Industrial, Scientific, and Medical
LMDS : Local Multipoint Distribution Serves)   UNNI : Unlicensed National Information Infrastructure

Figure 12.8 Fixed wireless frequency spectrum. All frequencies are in GHz.

IEEE has defined the 802.11b standard in this band, which provides wireless LAN connectivity. This standard promises to provide data rates of up to 11 Mbps. Special collision avoidance techniques are used since collisions are difficult to determine in a wireless environment. It cannot be easily determined using spread spectrum techniques whether received noise is caused by a collision or is normal noise. Hence, the access method is called CSMA/CA (CSMA with Collision Avoidance). A sophisticated coding method called CCK (Complementary Code Keying) is used to transmit several bits of data with each code. This enabled the IEEE 802.11b protocol to increase its transmission rate from 2 Mbps to 11 Mbps.

The next set of frequency bands we see in Figure 12.8 is called MMDS (Multipoint Multichannel Distribution Services). Here "multipoint" and "multichannel" words are also switched. These channels have been around since 1990. However, they were allocated to provide television programs over the air. Therefore, this band is also called wireless cable. In 1999, both Sprint and MCI Worldcom bought up operating companies in these bands and this market is expected to take off, given that the FCC will allow two-way communications to support Internet access.

Above the MMDS bands, LMDS (Local Multipoint Distribution Service) bands exist. With MMDS, blocks of 200 MHz are allocated, while with LMDS, blocks of 1 GHz are allocated. However, LMDS equipment has a higher cost and shorter range of coverage, and is more susceptible to atmospheric conditions.

12.2.5 PCS

Conventionally, we communicate over the PSTN by dialing a location. With a PCS (Personal Communications System), we'll be able to dial a person regardless of his location. It will be the concern of the signaling system to locate the called person and provide the connection. No longer will people need to provide a home number, work number, a mobile phone number, and their daily schedule. We will only need to know that individual's number to reach them on the phone.

An individual needs to carry only one low-power pocket phone and if he is in his home then this phone acts like a cordless phone, communicating with the home's base station. If he is in a car, it acts like a cellular system. If he is in a shopping center, it communicates with a microcell base, and if he is in his work place it communicates over his wireless PBX system. Each time, the least expensive method of wireless communication is selected. Also, by using the closest base station, whether it be a PBX or cordless base station, you are getting the best available reception.

This is the ultimate objective of PCS. PCS today is offering more features and services than cellular service provides. Furthermore, all service in the PCS bands must be digital. Typically, PCS cell sizes are smaller than the cellular cells.

12.3 DIGITAL WIRELESS SYSTEMS

12.3.1 Europe's GSM

In 1982, a digital cellular standard that was uniform throughout Europe was established. This was unlike the non-uniform dialing plans in the PSTNs and the

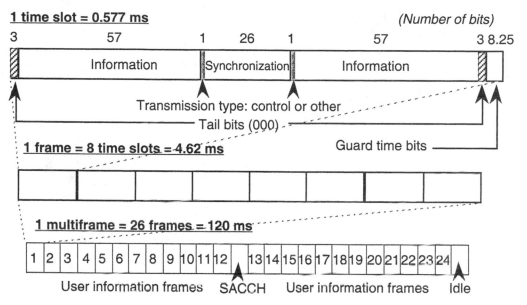

Figure 12.9 Slot and frame formatting used in GSM.

incompatible analog mobile cellular systems which existed at that time. It came to be known as GSM (Global System for Mobile communication).

GSM uses TDMA (Time Division Multiple Access), as well as FDMA, to provide cellular access to its users. Voice is digitized at a rate of 13 kbps using a technique called LPC-RPE (Linear Predictive enCoding with Regular Pulse Excitation). The basic "building block" for GSM is called a time slot which has a duration of 0.577 milliseconds. One time slot transmits 156.25 bits as seen in Figure 12.9. A time slot begins and ends with 3 tail bits which are always 0s. During the guard time, which occupies 8.25 bits, no transmission occurs to accommodate for RF (Radio Frequency) rise and fall delays.

Two groups of 57 bits are used to transmit user information. The single bit adjacent to a group of information bits is used to designate whether control information is being sent, interrupting a speech or data channel. Lastly, 26 bits are used to keep the digital transmission in sync. Each mobile terminal is assigned its own time slot.

8 of these time slots comprise a frame and 26 frames comprise a multiframe. Out of these 26 frames, two frames are used for other purposes. One is called the SACCH (Slow Associated Control CHannel) and is used for sending low-bandwidth control information; the other is left idle.

12.3.2 North America's IS-54/136

Unlike Europe, which at one time had 5 different analog cellular standards, Canada and the USA have only one—AMPS. However, Europe was allocated a new frequency block for its GSM system, whereas North America was restricted to evolve

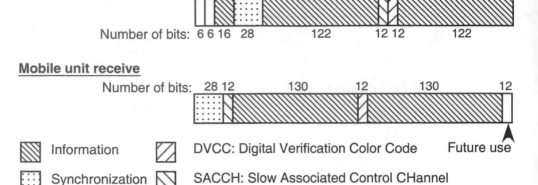

Mobile unit transmit

Guard time Ramp time

Number of bits: 6 6 16 28   122   12 12   122

Mobile unit receive

Number of bits: 28 12   130   12   130   12

⬚ Information   ⬚ DVCC: Digital Verification Color Code   Future use

⬚ Synchronization   ⬚ SACCH: Slow Associated Control CHannel

Figure 12.10 IS-54/136's time slots. 6 time slots make up a frame.

a digital system out of its existing analog frequency band. Hence, this system is called a dual-mode system. It is called EIA's IS-54 (Electronics Industry Association's Interim Standard 54).

IS-54 digitizes speech at a rate of 13 kbps using a technique called VSELP (Vector Sum Excited Linear Prediction). The structure of its time slot is different depending on whether the mobile is transmitting or receiving. See Figure 12.10. A frame consists of 1,944 bits and takes 40 milliseconds to transmit. A frame is divided into 6 time slots. A time interval of 6 bits in the mobile unit transmit frame is used to turn off the transmission and the same amount of time is used to bring the power back up to the operating level. These are called the guard and ramp times, respectively. A total of 260 bits is used for either transmitting or receiving. The 28-bit pattern used for synchronization is determined by the position of the slot in the frame.

The DVCC (Digital Verification Color Code) prevents a mobile phone from communicating with an interfering digital cell site. Replacing the "blank and burst" signaling used in AMPS, the SACCH (Slow Associated Control CHannel) provides transfer of messages between the cell site and the mobile set. By interrupting user data fields, a FACCH (Fast Associated Control CHannel) is also available to send messages which are urgent.

IS-136 is an upgrade of IS-54. It provides compatibility with the AMPS system and dual-mode phones are able to switch between the IS-136 and the AMPS systems. IS-136 brings with it more advanced features than those that the IS-54 standard provided, namely, over-the-air programming, longer battery life, caller ID, and other intelligent network features.

12.3.3 Europe's DECT

DECT (Digital European Cordless Telecommunications) is a European standard much different from GSM or IS-54. It uses microcells that are overlayed with GSM cells. Since DECT is a low-power system, it can't hand over calls when an automobile is traveling at highway speeds. However, via GSM interworking, it can be used as a cellular phone and in a business environment, and it can communicate with a wireless PBX fixed port. It can be used as a residential cordless phone, to replace the local loop to the CO, to provide wireless LANs, to function with a telepoint, and to support other applications. Telepoint is a wireless public pay telephone.

Some applications such as cordless PBXs and wireless LANs are closed environments. That is, only one vendor may supply all equipment for the system. Standards for such systems are not fully specified, freeing the manufacturer to design their systems the way they want to, as long as their system can co-exist with other DECT systems. However, other applications are required to conform to a set of specifications called the PAP (Public Access Profile), which ensure that one manufacturer's base station can operate with other manufacturers' mobile sets.

Table 12.2 Summary of TDMA Cellular Systems			
	GSM	**IS-54/136**	**DECT**
Mobile transmit frequency in MHz	890 – 915	824 – 849	1880 – 1900
Mobile receive frequency in MHz	935 – 960	869 – 894	1880 – 1900
Spectrum used by system in MHz	50	50	20
Bandwidth occupied per carrier in MHz	0.200	0.030	1.728
Number of frequency channels	125	832	10
Number of users supported per carrier	8	3	12
Total number of user channels	1000	2496	120
Modulation data rate of channel in kbps	271	48.6	1152
Rate of digitized voice in kbps	13	8	32
Rate of voice including error control (kbps)	22.8	13	32
Method of speech encoding	LPC-RPE	VSELP	ADPCM
Type of modulation used	GMSK	DQPSK	GFSK
Name of one of the control channels	SACCH	SACCH	C
Mobile output power in milliwatts	3.7 – 20,000	2.2 – 6,000	250

ADPCM: Adaptive Differential PCM
C: Control information channel
DECT: Digital European Cordless Telecommmunication
DQPSK: Differential Quadrature Phase Shift Keying
GMSK: Gaussian Minimum Shift Keying

GSM: Global System for Mobile Communication
IS-54/136: Interim Standard-54/136
LPC-RPE: Linear Predictive enCoding with Regular Pulse Excitation
SACCH: Slow Associated Control Channel
VSELP: Vector Sum Excited Linear Prediction

Briefly, DECT uses 10 RF carriers which are each 1.728 MHz wide. Each carrier supports a frame that has 12 full duplex channels using 24 time slots. A frame is a 10-milliseconds-long time slot and a time slot consists of 480 bits. 16 bits are used for a preamble, 16 for synchronization, 64 for a control channel, 320 for user information, and 64 bits for guard time. Other characteristics of DECT, as well as GSM and IS-54, are summarized in Table 12.2.

12.4 QUALCOMM'S CDMA (TIA/EIA-95)

12.4.1 Spread Spectrum Communication

Spread spectrum technology has been used by the military since WWII to prevent the enemy from jamming communication signals. During the 1980s most of the engineering community believed that this technology would not work with digital cellular systems because it was too complex and would be prohibitively expensive. Fortunately, a few "Einsteins" of our day at a company called Qualcomm proved otherwise and developed CDMA.

With spread spectrum communication, everyone is given a unique code from which they can interpret their transmission. It causes little interference to other users. In a military operation, jamming of a signal is possible once the enemy detects activity in a given frequency band. The presence of spread spectrum signals is difficult to detect. These transmissions do not occur over a narrow band but over a very large bandwidth so that the transmitted power is distributed over the bandwidth of the signal. The effect of this is that an enemy "hears" only noise. Furthermore, these signals can easily be made secure using encryption algorithms.

Basically, there are two types of spread spectrum signals: direct sequence and frequency hopping. CDMA uses the direct sequence type where each transmission is given its own code. Frequency hopping has to do with changing the frequency of the carrier periodically. In both cases, synchronization is a very important requirement in order for the receiver to interpret the intended signal correctly. The remainder of the chapter will cover the details of the TIA/EIA-95 standard for CDMA.

12.4.2 Basic CDMA

CDMA uses what are called 64-chip Walsh codes. Walsh codes enable a cell to operate with 61 conversational channels, three being used by the system itself. These channels are said to be orthogonal to each other. That is, the communication of any given channel goes undetected by the others. In geometry the x, y, and z axes are said to be orthogonal, since each axis can be varied independently from the others.

Figure 12.11 illustrates how CDMA works. Here, user 1 is given a Walsh code of "+ + − −" and whenever user 1 transmits a binary 1, it transmits "+ + − −" and whenever it transmits a binary 0 it transmits 0. Similarly, user 2 is assigned a code of "+ − + −" so that when it sends a binary 1 it sends that sequence, and for a binary 0 it sends just a 0. These are symbols and they are made up of chips, 4 in this example. User 3's code is "+ − − +."

Now as Figure 12.11 shows, let us see what happens as user 1 transmits a bit sequence of "110," user 2 transmits "101," and user 3 transmits "010." Each of these

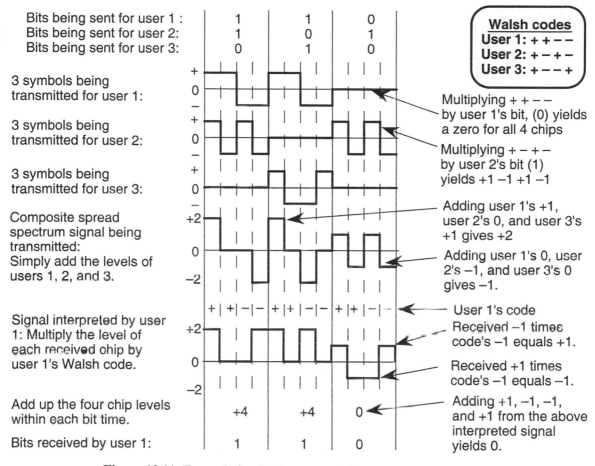

Bits being sent for user 1 :   1   1   0
Bits being sent for user 2:   1   0   1
Bits being sent for user 3:   0   1   0

Walsh codes
User 1: + + – –
User 2: + – + –
User 3: + – – +

3 symbols being transmitted for user 1:

Multiplying + + – – by user 1's bit, (0) yields a zero for all 4 chips

3 symbols being transmitted for user 2:

Multiplying + – + – by user 2's bit (1) yields +1 –1 +1 –1

3 symbols being transmitted for user 3:

Composite spread spectrum signal being transmitted:
Simply add the levels of users 1, 2, and 3.

Adding user 1's +1, user 2's 0, and user 3's +1 gives +2

Adding user 1's 0, user 2's –1, and user 3's 0 gives –1.

Signal interpreted by user 1: Multiply the level of each received chip by user 1's Walsh code.

User 1's code

Received –1 times code's –1 equals +1.

Received +1 times code's –1 equals –1.

Add up the four chip levels within each bit time.   +4   +4   0

Adding +1, –1, –1, and +1 from the above interpreted signal yields 0.

Bits received by user 1:   1   1   0

Figure 12.11 Transmission for three users being sent over one carrier and how user 1 interprets its transmission to be "110." The codes for each user are shown in the inset.

bits is converted into 4 chips using the above encoding method. So user 1 transmits "+ + – – + + – – 0 0 0 0," user 2 transmits "+ – + – 0 0 0 0 + – + –," and user 3 transmits "0 0 0 0 + – – + 0 0 0 0." Now if we add the corresponding chips vertically, for each user, we end up with " 2 0 0 –2 2 0 –2 0 +1 –1 +1 –1." For example, for the very first chip, user 1's +1, user 2's +1, and user 3's 0 gives a +2 and so on.

Now, all users receive the same sequence of 0, +1, –1, +2, and –2. How do they interpret the bits intended for them? Let us consider only user 1. User 1 will multiply each chip that it receives with the chip of its code, that is, "+ + – –." So for the first chip, +1 times +2 yields +2. For the second chip, +1 times 0 yields 0, and so on. So the first four chips equal "2 0 0 2." Then these values are added, giving 4. Following the figure, user 1 gets 4 for the next four chip-times and gets a 0 for the next four chip-times. If the 4 is interpreted as a binary 1 and 0 is interpreted as a binary 0, user 1 will receive its intended "110" bits from the composite signal. Using the same decoding method for users 2 and 3, we can arrive at "101" bits intended for user 2 and "010" intended for user 3.

The reason why this works is because the codes for the users are orthogonal. Notice if the corresponding chips for user 1's code $(+ + - -)$ are multiplied by user 2's code $(+ - + -)$, we get "$+ - - +$." If we add these, we get a 0. Similarly, if user 1's code is multiplied by user 3's code, the sum of the chip-products becomes a 0. However, if we do the same operation on a user's code with itself, such as "$+ + - -$" times "$+ + - -$," the sum of the chip-products is 4. Hence, these codes are said to be orthogonal.

12.5 ERROR HANDLING

12.5.1 CRC

For every 22 bits of voice that are coded, a 6-bit CRC (Cyclic Redundancy Check) field is added. If the receiver detects that as an error, instead of decoding those 22 bits, a momentary silence is heard on the receiver's earpiece. The idea is that it is better to hear nothing for an instant than to hear a sound that doesn't belong at that time. The human ear cannot detect that 22 bits were missing in the received signal, anyway.

Data, on the other hand, cannot be dropped. It has to be corrected. One approach that is used to correct errors is to send a CRC code with every data frame and, if the receiver detects an error, retransmit that frame. In wireless systems where frequency capacity is at a premium, we don't have the luxury to retransmit errored frames. Also, retransmission takes time. One way to minimize errors is to increase the output power of the transmitters, but that would mean that fewer customers could be served at any given time. Another method is to send each bit twice, that is, a 1 is sent as 11 and a 0 is sent as 00. But then if a transmitted 1 is received as a 10, the receiver would not be able to tell whether a 1 was transmitted as 10 or a 0 was transmitted as a 10. The error could not corrected. We could transmit each bit more than two times, but there is a better method called FEC (Forward Error Correction) using convolutional coding.

12.5.2 The Convolutional Coder

TIA/EIA-95 and all CDMAs use the continuous codes method instead of the block codes method of FEC. Specifically, TIA/EIA-95 uses the convolutional coding method type of continuous codes. This method takes up less time than other methods, is easy to design and implement, and does a very good job of correcting errors. We will now go through a complete example of how convolutional coding provides forward error correction, but bear with me because this will take some time.

The circuit that creates the convolutional codes is shown in Figure 12.12. It is based on the logical circuit called the exclusive-or circuit. The table for it is also shown in Figure 12.12. If both inputs to this circuit are 0 or both are 1, then the output is 0; otherwise, the output is 1. This circuit can also have three inputs. In that case, you exclusive-or any two bits, take that result, and exclusive-or it with the third bit. The complete chart for three input bits is shown in the side diagram.

Coming back to Figure 12.12, there are two such circuits in the convolutional coder: One with two inputs is on top and one with three inputs is on the bottom. The

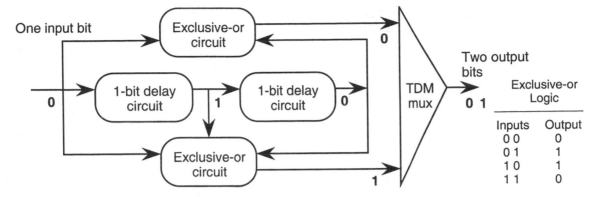

One input bit

0

Exclusive-or circuit

1-bit delay circuit   1-bit delay circuit

1   0

Exclusive-or circuit

0

TDM mux   0 1

Two output bits

Exclusive-or Logic

Inputs	Output
0 0	0
0 1	1
1 0	1
1 1	0

Figure 12.12 The convolutional coder is based on the exclusive-or logic. At the current time, a 0 is at the input, a 1 is here from the clock cycle before, and a 0 is in the circuit from 2 cycles ago. The input to the mux becomes 1 and a 0 which appear at its output.

Exclusive-or Logic

Inputs	Output
0 0 0	0
0 0 1	1
0 1 0	1
0 1 1	0
1 0 0	1
1 0 1	0
1 1 0	0
1 1 1	1

coder also has 1-bit delay circuits which temporarily store the last two bits which had arrived in the coder. The input is shown on the left. The outputs of the exclusive-or circuits are fed to a TDM (Time Division Multiplexer), which outputs these bits one at a time.

The circuit currently has a 0 at its input. The bit that had arrived before this one was a 1 which is shown after the 1-bit delay circuit. The bit that had arrived before that one was a 0 which is shown after the two 1-bit delay circuits. Using these bits, we can evaluate the outputs of the two exclusive-or circuits. The output of the top circuit is 0 since its inputs are both 0 and the output of the bottom circuit is 1 since its inputs are 0, 1, and 0. Using these two outputs, the multiplexer outputs a 01. Let us look at some more examples.

In Figure 12.13(a), we have been feeding 0s to the circuit, which ends up outputting pairs of 0s. For every input bit there are two output bits per clock cycle. In Figure 12.13(b), we input a 1 to this circuit, which pushes the two left 0s to the right and the rightmost 0 disappears from the circuit. The pushing of the bits to the right are done by the 1-bit delay circuits. At this time, there is an odd number of 1s at both of the exclusive-or circuits, which yields 11 from the output of the multiplexer.

Now in Figure 12.13(c), another 1 arrives. This pushes the leftmost two bits to the right. Here, there are two 1s on the bottom exclusive-or circuit, which outputs a 0 and there is a single 1 to the top circuit, which outputs a 1. Figure 12.13(d) shows the coder after another 1 arrives at the input.

Figure 12.14(a) shows the same sequence of bits in a table under the column marked as "Current input bit." We have taken the same input bits from Figure 12.13 and added a few more input bits. These inputs are 0, 0, 1, 1, 1, 0, 1, 0, 0. The output of each clock cycle is shown in the last column as a pair of bits. The middle two columns show the output for both of the 1-bit delay circuits.

We can take any two of these columns to define the state or the condition that the coder is in. We might as well take the first two columns. That gives us the four states shown in Figure 12.14(b). Using Figure 12.14(b), let us trace the path that our coder

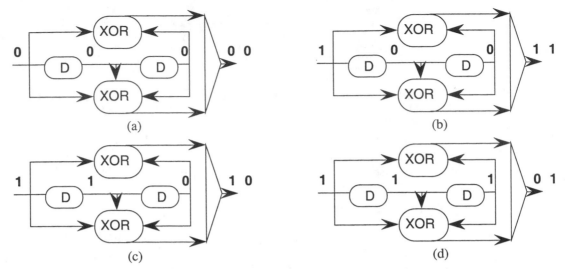

Figure 12.13 (a) Initially, all the coder is cleared. (b) An input of 1, provides an output of 11. (c) Then another 1 arrives, giving an output of 10. (d) After 1 arrives again, the output becomes 01.

takes using the input bits shown in Figure (a). Initially, we are in state 00. At the clock time of 1, we get a 0, which places the coder back at state 00. The code outputs 00, which is not shown in Figure (b). At the clock time of 2, a 1 arrives and this places the coder in state 10, which outputs a 11. With each input bit, we can either stay in the same

Clock time	Current input bit	Last input	Previous to last input	Output at this time
	0	0	0	
1	0	0	0	0 0
2	1	0	0	1 1
3	1	1	0	1 0
4	1	1	1	0 1
5	0	1	1	1 0
6	1	0	1	0 0
7	0	1	0	0 1
8	0	0	1	1 1

We will use the values
of these two bits to
define the state in
which the circuit is.

(a)

(b)

Figure 12.14 (a) The given input data stream yields the output shown in the last column. (b) Tracing the input bits in the state diagram gives the path shown.

Wireless Communication and CDMA

state or go to another state. The figure then traces the path the coder takes for all 8 clock cycles.

After studying this coder, we come up with a more general state diagram. See Figure 12.15. This diagram shows the four possible states that the coder can be in. It also shows the transitions of the states. A solid arrow shows the transition when a 0 is received at the input and a shaded arrow shows the transition when a 1 is received. The bit pairs shown in boxes are the outputs of the convolutional coder for those given transitions.

For example, suppose that we are in state 10, seen at the leftmost corner of the diagram. Here, if we get a 1 at the input, then we go to the 11 state and we output a 10. On the other hand, if get a 0 at the input (shown by the solid line), then we go the 01 state and output a 01. Since the values of the states can be confused with the values of the output, they are all labeled. Notice, from state 10 we cannot go to state 00 or stay in state 10. This feature will enable us to correct errors.

12.5.3 The Viterbi Decoder

Now it's time to study the Viterbi decoder which is named after one of the engineers at Qualcomm. Let us take the outputs as shown in the output column of Figure 12.14(a) and string them along the top of Figure 12.16. The output bits were 00, 11, 10, 01, 10, 00, 01, 11. Let us also assume that the second bit of the next-to-the-last pair was received incorrectly and hope that our Viterbi decoder can correct it. It will turn out that most of the errors will be corrected. However, errors which occur next to each other are not as easily corrected, as we will see in this example. Because the last pair (11) is being received correctly, the decoder will be able to interpret the 00 as 01. You will need to reference Figure 12.15 as we discuss this.

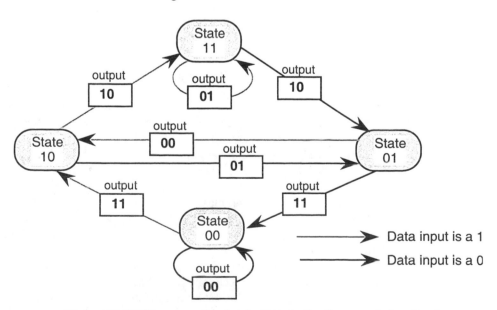

Figure 12.15 The generalized state diagram for the convolutional coder.

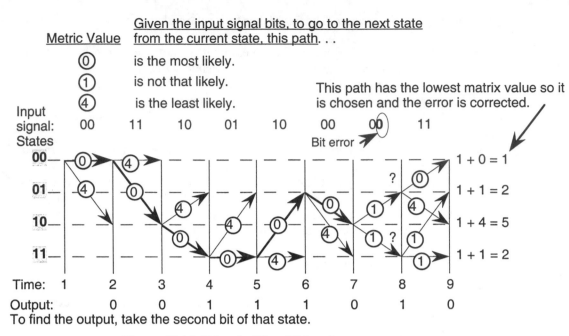

Figure 12.16 Using the Virterbi decoder, we can correct errors.

Before we can decode our input signal stream, we will need to evaluate metric values. Metrics are placed for each of the two possible state transitions, taking in account the current state of the decoder and the pair of bits at the input. Cumulative path metrics will enable the decoder to correct errors.

From Figure 12.15, we see that if we are in state 00 and the output is 00 then the chance that we stay in state 00 is the most likely. To the state transitions which are most likely we assign a metric of 0, meaning that both bits arrived error free. This is seen as the horizontal arrow from Time 1 to Time 2 in Figure 12.16. Also, the output values of Figure 12.15 are now the input values for Figure 12.16. To state transitions where one bit arrived error free, we assign a metric of 1. To state transitions where both bits arrived error-free, we assign a metric of 4. These numbers (0, 1, and 4) are calculated using vector algebra, which we don't need to cover. Actually, precise analog voltage values are normally used to calculate the metrics, which provide better error correction than logical values.

Initially, the decoder is cleared with all 0s. This places us in the 00 state as shown at Time 1. Our input is 00 as given above the diagram. If our state is 00 and the input is 00, then our metric to stay in that state is 0 since no bits would have to be changed. However, from state 00 we could also go to state 10 according to Figure 12.15. In that case, our input would have to be 11. However, since the received input is 00, meaning both bits would have had to change, we assign that transition a metric of 4. Out of the two metrics, we pick the lowest one and stay in state 00. This is shown by the bold arrow. The output for this clock cycle will be a 0 which will be available after another clock cycle. The output is the second bit of the new state. Our new state is 00 whose second bit is 0. Hence, 0 is the output. This is seen at Time = 2.

Let us do one more example. Consider the decoder at Time = 3. The current state is 10. From here, according to the state diagram, we can either go to the state of 01 or to the state of 11. Our input signal is 10 which is what we would need to go to the state 11. Hence, that path has a metric of 0 which is the most likely case. To go to the state 01 our input would have had to be 01 according to the state diagram. However, our input is 10, that is, if the transmitted value was actually 01, then both of the bits would have had to flip for our received value to be a 10. Therefore, the metric value to go to the state 01 is 4, which is the least likely value. We take the path with the value of 0 which places us in the state 11. The output then becomes the second bit of this state, which is 1.

Notice, the output as shown under the time line is the same as the input as shown in the first column of Figure 12.14. However, as we decode we find trouble at Time =7. The state at that time is 10 and the input is 00. There is no way of knowing which bit was flipped due to error. Hence, we calculate the metric for each of the possible two transitions. If we were to go from state 10 to state 01, the second bit was flipped, so we assign that transition a metric of 1. On the other hand, if we were to go from state 10 to state 11 the first bit was flipped, so we assign that transition also a metric of 1. This forces us to see what happens at the next cycle.

At Time = 8, we calculate four metrics, two starting from the state of 01 and two starting from a state of 11. They as shown in the figure are 0, 4, 1, and 1. Then we accumulate the total values for each of the four branches and arrive with 1, 2, 5, and 2. We pick the least value of 1. Now we are at a better position to tell what happened at Time = 8. We output a 1 for that time and a 0 for Time = 9. This matches what was transmitted and the received error was corrected.

Our convolutional coder has an R factor of 1/2. This means that twice as many symbols are generated as the number of bits which arrive. It is also called a half-rate coder. One-third rate coders provide better error correction and they are also used in CDMA. The number of delay circuits plus one is given by the K factor. We have here a coder with K = 3. CDMA uses coders with a value of K = 9 which also improve the correction method.

12.5.4 Block Interleaving

As stated before, analog voltage values are used, which provide better error correction. Also, if the input bit pair arrived with an error at Time = 8, then it would have been less likely that the error would be corrected. Typically, in a wireless network, say when a car is making a turn around a high rise building, the power level drops or picks up suddenly and momentarily. There is a high chance that errors are induced on bits which are close to each other. To disperse the positions where errors occur so that they aren't received successively, a technique called block interleaving is used. This also helps to reduce the amount of uncorrected errors.

For example, in Figure 12.17 the transmitter is sending 12 bits. If the bits were sent in sequence and errors occurred due to some signal fading, and bits 5, 6, and 7 became corrupt, then these errors would not be as readily corrected because these

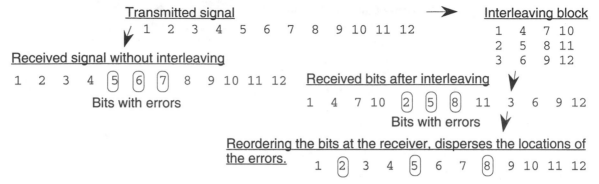

Figure 12.17 Block interleaving disperses the errors to make it easier for the Viterbi Decoder to correct them.

errors would appear next to each other. Interleaving these twelve bits as shown on the right-hand side of the figure would end up sending the bits out of order. Now, if the errors occur in sequence, as would usually occur, when the receiver places them in the proper order, the errors become separated from each other. Now error correction will work better.

The disadvantage of this method is that a delay is added due to the blocking of the bits before they are sent. Also, a delay is added at the receiver to unblock the data. In TIA/EIA-95, on the downlink traffic channels, a matrix of 16 columns and 24 rows gives a block of 384 symbols which gives a delay of 20 ms. On the uplink channels an interleaving block of 18 by 32 is used, giving a total of 576 data symbols.

12.6 CDMA vs. SSMA

12.6.1 Some Terminology

Actually, implementation of CDMA (Code Division Multiple Access) also uses SSMA (Spread Spectrum Multiple Access). CDMA itself uses Walsh codes and SSMA uses what is called PN (Pseudorandom Noise) codes. Each type of code has its own function, and using both types of codes in a standard allows access to more MSs (Mobile Stations) and more BSs (Base Stations) within a geographic area than if only one type of code were used. Using two methods of coding gives us a way to identify more transmitting sources and more receiving stations than if only one method were used. The term *code layering* is used to indicate that a data stream can be first coded with one code, then another. For the rest of this section, let us use the term CDMA to mean the modulation of a signal by Walsh codes and SSMA to mean modulation by PN codes.

Before we go into the differences of CDMA (or Walsh codes) and SSMA (or PN codes), let us discuss a few terms. One term that we will need to understand is *spreading*. There are two types of spreading. One is called orthogonal spreading, which occurs due to Walsh codes, and the other is called spectral spreading, which occurs due to PN codes. In Section 12.4.2, every bit was converted into four chips. The ratio of number of chips to the number of bits is called the orthogonal spreading factor. There it was 4.

Spectral spreading occurs when a channel is transmitted across a wide range of frequencies instead of being transmitted in a narrow frequency band. The complete name for this as used with CDMA is DSSS (Direct Sequence Spread Spectrum).

Correlation is another important term. It means a systematic connection to something. In our case, it means how well we can decipher the signal that is intended for us. In section 12.4.2, we saw how Walsh codes provided excellent separation of transmitted channels. A CDMA receiver, to which a particular Walsh code was assigned, was able to pick out the data signal that was intended for it. This is called auto-correlation. The receiver was also able to reject signals which were not intended for it. This is called cross-correlation.

In the analogy that was used in section 12.2.2, if you spoke Arabic your auto-correlation was very good with the group of passengers who spoke Arabic and you had poor cross-correlation with those spoke Mandarin, for example. In order to provide excellent separation of channels, this is what we want. It would be ideal to have auto-correlation at 100% and have cross-correlation at 0%.

12.6.2 Walsh Codes

Walsh codes are also called orthogonal codes because the data transmitted on one channel doesn't add interference to the data streams of other channels. The x, y, and z coordinates used in solid geometry are said to be orthogonal because varying one component, say x, doesn't affect the others. In our analogy, the Mandarin language is orthogonal to the other languages.

Walsh codes, compared with PN codes, provide excellent separation of channels. Their percentage of auto-correlation is very high compared with the percentage of cross-correlation. However, Walsh codes require very precise synchronization among all the transmitted channels. Hence, they are used by the BS (Base Station) since a given BS has easier control of synchronization of its transmitted channels. On the other hand, Walsh codes are not used by the transmitters of the MSs (Mobile Stations). To maintain synchronization of each among several MSs' transmitted signals would be almost impossible.

TIA/EIA-95 uses Walsh codes of length 64. This gives it an orthogonal spreading factor of 64. Figure 12.18 shows how these codes are generated. At the top of the figure we start with 1. If we want two of these codes, then we come down to the second level of the tree; if we want four codes we come down to the third level, and so on. Every time you come down a level you get two new codes which are twice as long as the parent code. The first half of each pair of new codes has the same bit pattern as the parent. The second half of *one* sibling also repeats the same pattern while the second half of the *other* sibling repeats the same pattern, but with those bits reversed.

For example, consider the second level where the Walsh codes are 11 and 10. To find the third level codes of 1111, 1100, 1010, and 1001, generate two codes from 11 and two codes from 10. Let us look at the branch where 10 is the parent and 1010 and 1001 are the children. Here, we take the 10 for the left-half side of these two codes, then add 10 to one and the inverse of that, 01, to the other.

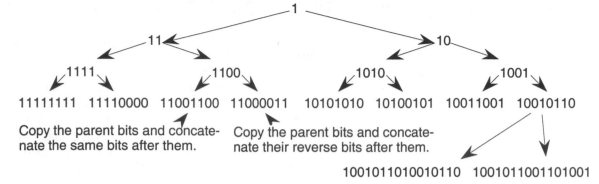

Figure 12.18 Generating Walsh codes.

Notice, the length of the code is also the number of codes that are available at that level. TIA/EIA-95 uses 64-bit length codes so there are 64 such codes. This means that 64 different signals can be transmitted at the same time, each using a different code. Due to engineering and design problems, however, only about 20 channels are generally feasible with about 7 channels used by the system. If the length of the code were increased, more channels could be supported by the CDMA system. The data rate for each channel, however, would then decrease.

OVSF (Orthogonal Variable Spreading Factor) codes is another coding method that is related to Walsh codes in that it allows channels to transmit at different rates. Going back to Figure 12.18, we could assign codes for two channels from the third level, namely, 1111 and 1100, and we could assign codes for four channels from the fourth level, namely, 10101010, 10100101, 10011001, and 10010110. What we have now done, as its name implies, is to vary the spreading factor for the channels. The two channels will now be able to operate at twice the data rate as the channels for which codes are assigned from the fourth level. This makes the wireless system more flexible. Those who need an instantaneous increase in bandwidth can be assigned smaller codes at the time they need it and when their demand decreases, their code lengths can be increased again.

12.6.3 PN Codes

Layering or adding PN (Pseudorandom Noise) codes over the transmitted signal introduces the access method called SSMA (Spread Spectrum Multiple Access). Just as Walsh codes spread the signal by multiplying the bit rate by 64, PN codes also add another layer of spreading. Unlike Walsh codes, each PN code has an equal number of 1s and 0s. The PN code is so named because, although to the other users the transmission appears as random noise, it is interpreted as a clear channel by the receiver. PN codes are long codes, which allows SSMA to assign over 4 trillion codes to provide each person privacy.

Figure 12.19 shows two MSs (Mobile Stations) transmitting on two different channels by using two different PN codes. Remember that while CDMA increases the

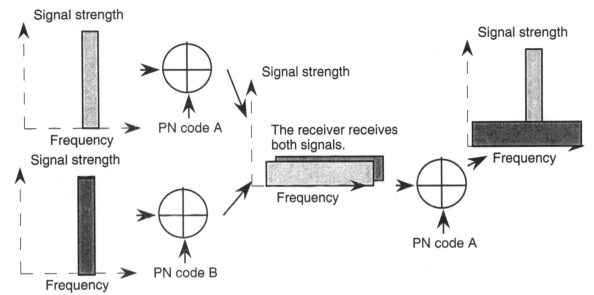

Figure 12.19 Two channels from two MSs are spread using two PN codes. The composite carrier shows both signals as being combined in air. The receiver is shown to correlate this composite signal with its own PN code, namely, A. When this is done, the signal for A is recovered while the signal for B appears as low-level interference.

number of bits per second to a greater number of chips per second, SSMA spreads that signal from over a narrow channel to a wider bandwidth. Hence, the term, "spread spectrum." We are in effect "spreading the spectrum."

The frequency spectrum occupied by each channel is now much larger and they are combined together at the receiver. The receiver, to decode the signal from A, will apply the PN code for A. After this is done, the original signal from A is recovered while the signal from channel B appears as low-level interference. As more channels occupy the frequency spectrum, the level of interference will start creeping up, making it difficult for the receiver to separate the signal from each channel.

Since all channels occupy the same bandwidth, which for TIA/EIA-95 is 1.23 MHz, it makes it easy for engineers to design the wireless system in the field. With other systems, frequency planning becomes tricky and co-channel interference becomes a big concern. With SSMA, adjacent cells can use the same frequency range. It is the PN code that provides separation between the transmitters. Frequency reuse can be 1 instead of 7 or 12, as shown previously in Figure 12.3. Hence, design is done by code planning, not frequency planning.

There are two types of PN codes. The short PN codes are specified by a 15-bit mask, which gives a code of 32,768 chips or 2^{15}. The long PN codes use a 42-bit mask. These lengths are for TIA/EIA-95 while third-generation standards use longer codes. The purpose of both types of PN codes is different. The short PN code identifies the BS signal, while the long PN code identifies the MS signal.

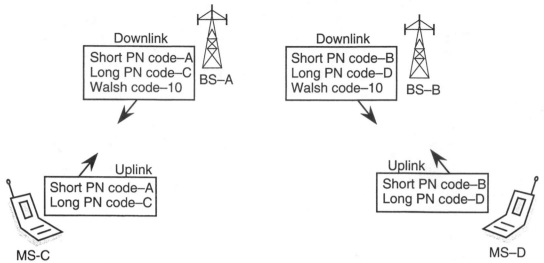

Figure 12.20 Walsh codes identify the forward channels, the phases of the short PN codes identify the BSs, and the long PN codes identify the MSs.

12.6.4 PN and Walsh Code Layering

PN codes provide a *good* level of channel separation, which depends on the ratio of chip rate to data stream bit rate. However, Walsh codes provide an *excellent* level of separation. On the other hand, Walsh codes requires that the transmitting channels be perfectly synchronized while PN codes don't require that.

Therefore, Walsh codes are used in the downlink signals so that the MSs can differentiate between data channels arriving from one BS. One BS can maintain strict synchronization among all its transmitted channels, so it uses Walsh codes to identify its transmitting channels.

The short PN codes identify BSs while the long PN codes identify the MSs. The long PN codes are based on the ESN (Electronic Serial Number) of the MSs. All uplink transmissions are done using only the PN codes.

Short PN Codes: To make this a little clearer, consider Figure 12.20. Here, there are two BSs (Base Stations) called A and B and two MSs (Mobile Stations) called C and D. The BSs transmit with a short PN code. It turns out that all BSs use the same short PN code but differ from each other only by their phase angles. This makes it easier for the MS to look for just one short PN code but over different phase offsets. The BSs also transmit using the short PN codes to make it easier for the BSs to lock onto the signal that is intended for them.

Long PN Codes: The BSs also transmit by spreading the long PN code over its transmitted channels. One of two types of long codes may be used. One is called the public code, which is determined by knowing the ESN of the MS. The other is called the private code. It is used for security and is determined by the authentication and encryption process. The MSs also use these codes for their uplink channels. It takes about 42 days for the long codes to repeat themselves, making it virtually impossible for an intruder to detect the code. On the downlink signal, the long PN code is used for encryption while on the uplink, it is used for channel separation or identification.

Walsh Codes: The third type of code that is used, as we have already seen, is the Walsh codes. They are used only by the BSs, since it is easier for them to keep these codes in exact synchronization. Each Walsh code identifies the channel that is being used. In the figure, the two BSs are transmitting using the same Walsh code of 10.

12.7 CDMA TRAFFIC CHANNELS

Let us look at the basic CDMA system by now looking at the traffic channels. There are two kinds of downlink channels and two kinds of uplink channels. The downlink channel types are traffic and broadcast channels. The uplink channels are traffic and access channels. The downlink channels are separated using the Walsh codes. The broadcast channels are the pilot, sync, and paging channels. The pilot channel provides initial synchronization, the sync channel provides BS identification, and the paging channels connect incoming calls to the correct MSs. The access channels allow MSs to make outgoing calls. Let us look only at the traffic channels in detail to get an idea of how signals are processed, in general.

Figure 12.21 shows the block diagram of the circuit for downlink traffic channels. The input to the vocoder is a 64-kbps PCM signal. The name of the vocoder is QCELP (Qualcomm Code Excited Linear Prediction). There are two kinds of such vocoders and they are identified by their rate set numbers. A rate set 1 vocoder will reduce the voice rate down to 1.2 kbps, 2.4 kbps, 4.8 kbps, and 9.6 kbps. A rate set 2 vocoder provides a higher quality signal at 1.8 kbps, 3.6 kbps, 7.2 kbps, and 14.4 kbps. All systems must be able to handle rate set 1 coding. Whenever the voice activity goes low, a lower rate coding is used.

This signal is then fed to the CRC coder. The CRC allows the receiver to detect errored frames and also determine the rate of the voice signal. It is then fed to a half-rate convolutional coder which doubles the number of bits.

Then we see the symbol repeater. This unit increases the rate of the low-rate signals to the appropriate rate. Out of this unit, all rate 1 signals are adjusted to 19.2 ksps (kilosymbols per second) and all rate 2 signals are adjusted to 28.8 ksps. If rate increase is necessary, then the symbols are repeated. However, the composite power of all repeated symbols is kept the same as those which are not repeated.

Next comes puncturing. This is done only if rate set 2 vocoders are being used. In order to use the same block interleaver, 2 bits out of every 6 bits are removed. This will bring the symbol rate from 28.8 ksps to 19.2 ksps. Forward error correction will correct any errors at the receiver.

After puncturing comes the block interleaver which we discussed before. Then come the long code, Walsh code, and the short code spreading of this signal. There is also a power control generator placed in here. It sends a single bit 800 times per second pre-empting the data stream bits. Again, errors are corrected by the receiver. Depending on the value of this bit, the receiver will either reduce or increase its transmitted

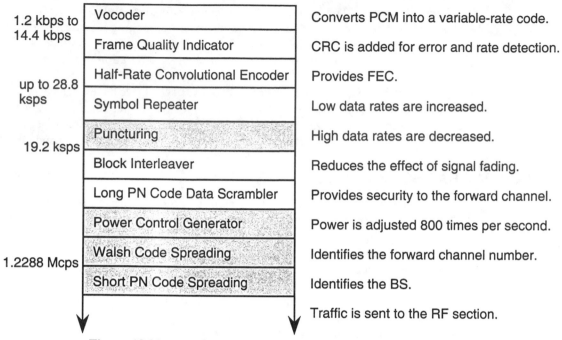

1.2 kbps to 14.4 kbps	Vocoder	Converts PCM into a variable-rate code.
	Frame Quality Indicator	CRC is added for error and rate detection.
up to 28.8 ksps	Half-Rate Convolutional Encoder	Provides FEC.
	Symbol Repeater	Low data rates are increased.
19.2 ksps	Puncturing	High data rates are decreased.
	Block Interleaver	Reduces the effect of signal fading.
	Long PN Code Data Scrambler	Provides security to the forward channel.
	Power Control Generator	Power is adjusted 800 times per second.
1.2288 Mcps	Walsh Code Spreading	Identifies the forward channel number.
	Short PN Code Spreading	Identifies the BS.
		Traffic is sent to the RF section.

Figure 12.21 The functional diagram of the forward, downlink traffic channel. Shaded blocks are not present in the uplink channel.

power by 1 dB. The BS is continuously requesting the MS to either increase or decrease its output power by 1 dB. Remember from our analogy, that the person speaking Mandarin using a loud speaker made it difficult for the person who understood Arabic to hear those who were speaking Arabic. We need to keep the transmission power of the MSs arriving at the BSs uniform. This is basically how the downlink traffic channel is engineered.

Figure 12.22 shows the basic operation of the uplink traffic channel. Many parts are the same as those for the downlink traffic channel. A 1/2-rate convolutional coder is used for rate set 2 vocoders and a 1/3-rate coder is used for rate set 1 vocoders. The rate set 2 vocoders provide better voice-quality signal and hence are not hampered by the lower-quality, 1/2-rate convolutional coders.

The Walsh coder does not provide any spreading as we have seen it does with CDMA. It does not provide any separation of channels or any such identifications. It substitutes every 6 symbols with a corresponding 64-bit Walsh code. A one-to-one matching of codes is done. Here, all 64 Walsh codes appear in the bit stream. See the side figure. The purpose of this processing is to add more forward error correction. With 64 bits there are 2^{64} possible combinations. Due to error in the air interface, all these combinations may occur. However, only 64 of those codes are valid combinations. This provides another level of forward error correction.

6 bits	64 bits
000000	1st Walsh code
000001	2nd Walsh code
000010	3rd Walsh code
000011	4th Walsh code
⋮	⋮
111111	64th Walsh code

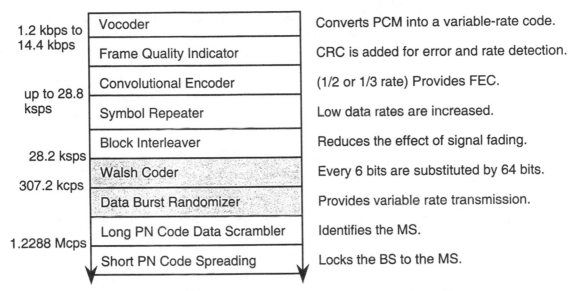

	Vocoder	Converts PCM into a variable-rate code.
1.2 kbps to 14.4 kbps	Frame Quality Indicator	CRC is added for error and rate detection.
up to 28.8 ksps	Convolutional Encoder	(1/2 or 1/3 rate) Provides FEC.
	Symbol Repeater	Low data rates are increased.
28.2 ksps	Block Interleaver	Reduces the effect of signal fading.
307.2 kcps	Walsh Coder	Every 6 bits are substituted by 64 bits.
	Data Burst Randomizer	Provides variable rate transmission.
1.2288 Mcps	Long PN Code Data Scrambler	Identifies the MS.
	Short PN Code Spreading	Locks the BS to the MS.

Figure 12.22 The functional diagram of the reverse, uplink traffic channel. Shaded blocks are not present in the downlink channel.

The data burst randomizer compensates for variable-rate transmissions. When voice activity is low and few bits need to be transmitted, the transmitter will turn off momentarily, conserving power. The randomizer will transmit the voice frames at different intervals in a time period rather than at the same period at all times. Last we have the long and short PN code spreading, which we have discussed already.

12.8 SUMMARY OF CDMA

Not only does CDMA provide greater capacity, but since k is 1, the network planning and placement of cells are greatly simplified. During the handoff process, the cell site from which the mobile unit is leaving, as well as the site to which the unit is entering, maintain contact with the unit. There is no sudden switchover between the cell sites, as is the case with AMPS. This is called a soft handoff between the cells and it works well, especially when transmitting data. Hard handoff occurs only when a unit changes its operating frequency from one 1.25-MHz band to another.

AMPS and TDMA are susceptible to interference caused by multipath fading. This occurs when a transmitted signal bounces off mountains or buildings interfering with the primary received signal. CDMA turns the multipath signals into an advantage. By using a rake receiver, up to three different signals that have traveled different paths are combined into one strong coherent signal, making the reception clear even in typically difficult places.

One of the obstacles that CDMA had to resolve was the near-far problem. This occurs when a mobile unit close to the base station is received with more effective power than a unit further away. Power is controlled using various means. Open loop power control adjusts the transmit power based on the level of receive power. A base station controls the amount of power from the mobile units so that the power from a nearby unit doesn't drown out the power from a unit far away. This is called closed loop power control. Outer loop power control maintains a specified error rate from each of the mobile units. The overall effect is that the mobile units require minimum power to operate.

When there is a traffic jam in an area, many people use their mobile phones, loading down the system. CDMA provides a sophisticated method of load balancing, where the capacity of a geographical region is temporarily increased by distributing the increase in traffic to adjacent cells.

EXERCISES

Section 12.1:

1. If the bandwidth per channel for cellular systems were .025 MHz instead of .03 MHz, how many channels would be available in each block?

   a. 500   b. 832

   c. 1000   d. 1200

2. Which of the following systems were NOT designed digital wireless?

   a. IMTS   b. LMR

   c. TDMA   d. EAMPS

3. When $k = 12$, how many simultaneous conversations are possible per cell?

   a. 12   b. 18

   c. 26   d. 32

4. When a cellular radio locks on to the strongest signaling channel while idle, what is this condition called?

5. When a mobile radio leaves the territory of one cell and goes into another cell, what operation is performed by the cell sites?

6. Draw a frequency reuse pattern for $k = 4$.

7. Describe how a "wire-line" phone completes a call to a mobile phone.

Section 12.2:

8. Which of the following is a new designation for MTSO?

   a. BTS   b. MS

   c. MHC   d. HLR

9. Which of the above is an example of a database system used in wireless systems?

10. If we have two pairs of two kinds of animals that communicate and hear at two different ranges, can each pair communicate simultaneously? If so what type of access method will they be using?

11. If we have two pairs of the same kind of animal, can both pairs communicate simultaneously? Which access method will they need to use to do so?

12. Which types of wireless standards can be used in the AMPS cellular band?

13. What are the advantages of MMDS over LMDS?

14. What are the characteristics of a cellular system versus a PCS system?

Section 12.3:

15. Name some second-generation wireless standards which use TDMA.

16. What are some differences between GSM and IS-136?

17. What are some similarities between GSM and IS-136?

18. Why is DECT used in a location where GSM is also available?

Section 12.4:
19. Name two types of spread spectrum access methods.
20. Suppose that in Figure 12.11, you were receiving the composite signal as shown in the fourth signal trace. If you were user number 4 and your Walsh code were ++++, what would be the signal that you would extract?
21. Extract your signal showing the same intermediate traces if you were user 3 and your Walsh code were as shown in Figure 12.11.
22. Using Figure 12.11 again, draw the same signal traces if the inputs for user 1 were + − +, for user 2 were + + −, and for user 3 were − + −.
22. The Walsh codes used in a region are supposed to have a certain relation with each other. What is that relation called?

Section 12.5:
23. In Figure 12.13, at Time = 5, the convolutional coder goes from which state to which one?
24. For the above question, draw the circuit, showing all the bits at each position as is done in Figure 12.13.
25. Re-create Figure 12.14, but this time use this input bit stream: 0, 0, 1, 0, 1, 1, 1, 0, 0. Draw both the table and the path that is traced through the state diagram.
26. Now draw the trellis diagram or the equivalent of Figure 12.16 for the output you got in the above question. Show your output.
27. For Figure 12.16, show your output if the input started as 00, 10, 11, and 01. Is the error corrected?
28. Redo Question 26, and this time add a single bit error at the 10th bit and do the calculations to show whether the error is corrected.

Section 12.6:
29. When two types of coding methods are superimposed on a transmitted signal, what is that called?
30. The ratio of output chips to the number of input bits is called what?
31. When a receiver rejects a signal which is not meant for it, that is called what?
32. Describe the differences between SSMA and CDMA.
33. What are the different kinds of codes used in SSMA and CDMA and for what purpose are they used?

Sections 12.7 and 12.8:
34. What are the different types of downlink channels and what are they used for?
35. What are the different types of uplink channels and what are they used for?
36. What is the difference between a 1/2-rate and a 1/3-rate convolutional coder? Which is better and why?
37. How many rate sets are used for CDMA vocoders? Which type is required?
38. What type of handoff is used in CDMA? Why is it better than traditional handoffs?
39. What are the two types of power control that are used in CDMA?

Chapter 13

Private Switched Networks

13.1 BACKGROUND

This chapter will primarily discuss PBX concepts, and it can be thought of as a chapter on voice-based LANs. When PBXs are mentioned, modern, sophisticated equipment comes to mind. However, it is interesting to note that PBXs existed even in the early 1900s. These were called manual PBXs and they consisted of a switchboard with an operator making connections using cords and jacks. Then in the 1920s, automatic PBXs utilizing step-by-step switching equipment were introduced. And in the 1950s, PBXs were sporting the crossbar switches.

Today PBXs and associated equipment can perform a wide variety of functions, many of which will be covered in Chapter 14. These devices/switches allow both voice and data communications.

Yet PBXs in this country, at one time, were owned by the telephone companies and were leased to their business customers. In 1968, the FCC ruled in the Carterfone Decision that customer-provided equipment may be directly connected to the public telephone network as long as a carrier-provided protective coupling device was used. This was the birth of the interconnect industry and it prompted manufacturers, many from Japan and Europe, to sell voice-based products. All the excitement in competition stimulated the further development of new products.

13.2 CENTREX

13.2.1 What is Centrex?

Centrex, which is a contraction of the words central and exchange, began in 1965. Centrex involves leasing a "PBX" at the central office, instead of owning one on the customer premises. Since all the voice switching is done at the CO, all the telephones must have their own pairs of wire going to the CO. Leasing these pairs to the CO becomes one of the most costly items when considering the feasibility of making the Centrex decision.

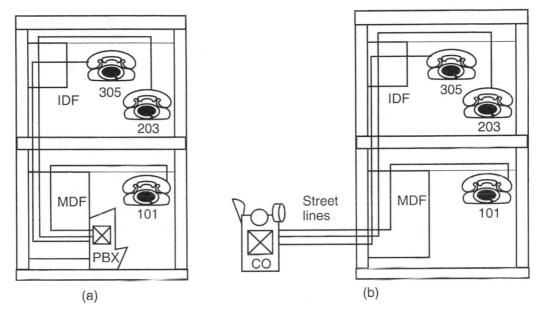

Figure 13.1 (a) PBX does the on-premise switching. (b) Centrex service does on-premise switching at the CO over leased lines.

Consider Figure 13.1 where both a simplified diagram of a PBX and Centrex installation is shown. Notice that in the PBX system, phone 101 could ring phone 203 and only the inside wiring would be used because the switching would be done locally. However, in the Centrex system, when the same call is placed, the connection is made at the CO on their Centrex switch. Here two "street" pairs to the CO are utilized to make a connection between two phones within a building.

Nortel's S/DMS supernode, DMS-100, and Lucent's 5ESS are examples of common Centrex switches.

13.2.2 Centrex Advantages

Even though the requirement of many lines from the customer's premises to the CO typically makes Centrex more costly than acquiring one's own PBX, there are a number of reasons why Centrex is more attractive than PBX to many telecommunication managers.

Centrex service rates are constantly being restructured, and depending on what the telcos are allowed to offer by the regulatory agencies, the tariffs for Centrex are in many places more attractive than the cost of using a PBX. And if the customer's premises are in the vicinity of the local CO, the mileage charges for the Centrex lines are inherently lower.

To preserve a company's cash flow, Centrex is an attractive alternative. The incentive to purchase a PBX for tax advantages varies from year to year, and it should be investigated. If a company is unsure of how or if it is growing or decreasing in size, no commitment has to be made on the capacity of the voice switching system. In fact, some PBXs have a limit to their capacity, while Centrex has no such limit.

Installing a city-wide network using a PBX requires lines and trunks from many locations to all be brought to a PBX via the CO. Because the lines may have to come through the CO anyway, it's more natural to switch them there, rather than bringing them to another location to be switched and then routing them through the CO again to their destination. See Figure 13.2.

Centrex allows a network to expand to the outer reaches of a city by adding remote modules at the remote locations. This is called on-premise Centrex and is also shown in Figure 13.2(b). This eliminates much of the street wiring.

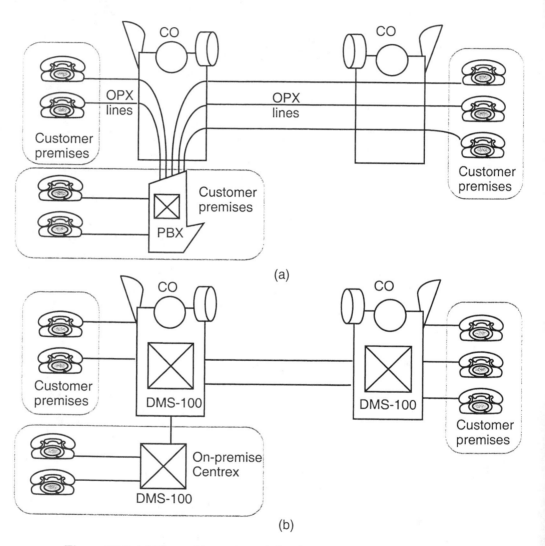

Figure 13.2 (a) Networking scattered sites in a metropolitan area requires leasing of many lines. (b) Centrex networking is a more natural solution for a metropolitan area network.

Private Switched Networks

Centrex also allows a uniform dialing plan for an organization. If people move from one location in a city to another one outside the city, they can keep the same phone number if the two locations are part of one Centrex plan. Also, in such an arrangement, only one operator is needed to handle calls. Every site doesn't need its own operator.

Furthermore, with Centrex no maintenance is required on the user's part. All repairs on the switch are done by the telco. SMDR (Station Message Detail Recording), which gives exhaustive data reports on who called whom, for how long, and at what cost, etc., used to be mailed by the CO on a magnetic tape every month. Now a Centrex customer can retrieve these reports as often as needed from a terminal by using a modem.

Similarly, it used to be the case that when one person moved from one location to another and wanted to keep the same phone number, the "move" had to be done by the Centrex technician. Now customers have their own terminal from which they can not only do moves but also change phone station features, add new phones, and so on. This type of activity is called performing MACs (Moves-Adds-and-Changes) to software translations.

Probably the most important reason to choose Centrex over PBX is that Centrex is generally more reliable than PBX systems, although PBXs can be made just as reliable. Centrex, when located at the CO, is well protected against earthquakes, fires, and sabotage. Technicians trained on the equipment are at the location 24 hours a day. No time is lost in transporting technicians and parts to PBX sites. Of course, many large PBXs have a trained technician on site during business hours, but with Centrex, even small customers can have fast service around the clock.

Other advantages are that no PBX room is needed that has to be kept cooled; no insurance is needed on the equipment; and not as much staff is required to administer Centrex. However, Centrex is more closely regulated by the FCC and the state agencies. Its services are not homogeneous through all the LATAs and the SMDR information available may have some limitations.

13.2.3 CO-LANs

In 1985, Bell Atlantic offered the CO-LAN service for the first time. CO-LANs allow customers to send and switch data over their voice network, which is a form of voice/data integration. The first method of accomplishing this was using DOV modems (Data Over Voice). This device is required at both the CO and the customer premises, as shown in Figure 13.3(a). The DOV modem allows the transmission of both voice and data (up to 9600 bps) over a single pair of wires. So with the same wiring as for voice networks, customers receive data networking with only a nominal increase in charges.

The transmission of simultaneous data over the voice pair is done by modulating the data into an analog signal at around 100 kHz. This analog signal which carries the data information is then frequency multiplexed into the output. Since the voice is being carried at around 3 kHz and the modulated data at 100 kHz, it is easy to separate the data signal from the voice signal using filters at the CO. See Figure 13.3(b)

The problem is that typically on a voice line, loading coils are needed every 3 miles, and these coils prevent transmission in the low end and the high end of the 4-kHz voice band. DOV modems multiplex the modulated data in this area of the

IVDT: Integrated Voice/Data Terminal   FDM: Frequency Division Multiplexer
IVDM: Integrated Voice/Data Multiplexer TDM: Time Division Multiplexer
DOV: Data Over Voice

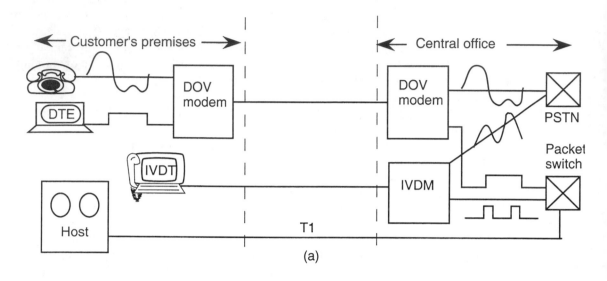

(a)

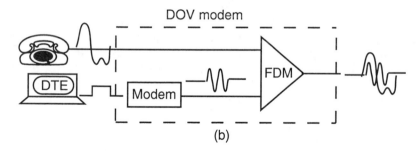

(b)

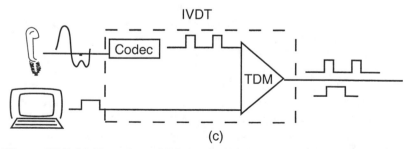

(c)

Figure 13.3 (a) Operation of CO-LAN showing the analog version using a DOV modem and the digital version using an IVDT. (b) A DOV modem combines voice and data into analog form. (c) An IVDT combines voice and data into digital form.

bandwidth, so loading coils can't be used with them. Therefore, this limits the range of CO-LANs using DOV modems to 3 miles.

DOV modems at the CO do the same thing but in reverse. The demultiplexed voice goes to the voice switch and the data is directed to a packet switch. The voice and the data can be switched back to the customer's premises or can be routed to distant locations over the PSTN and packet networks. As shown in the diagram, data can also be switched back to the customer's site using a T1 link, typically to a host.

With the introduction of ISDN, a more sophisticated and expensive alternative exists using IVDTs (Integrated Voice/Data Terminals). This is also depicted in Figure 13.3(c). It allows for transmission of data at speeds up to 64 kbps. Signalwise, it is just the reciprocal of a DOV modem. Instead of modulating the data, it digitizes the voice and instead of frequency division multiplexing the analog signals, it time division multiplexes the digital ones. However, to the end user, the effect of either method is practically the same.

13.3 KEY SYSTEMS

13.3.1 The 1A2 System

Key systems were first introduced in 1953 when Bell Telephone came out with the 1A1 system. Ten years later, the 1A2 which followed it was a very popular product for a long time. Key systems allow a small business having 50 telephones or less to subscribe to fewer lines than the number of keysets (or phones) it has. This is possible because the outside lines are shared among the keysets.

In Figure 13.4, a simple 1A2 system with a 3 by 5 configuration is shown. The 3 stands for the number of lines coming from the CO and the 5 is the number of keysets which are connected. These phone lines are being subscribed from the CO and the phone numbers, using any combination, can be terminated at any of the keyphones during installation. When the number 238-1001 is called from the outside, all the stations with that number on it will ring and any of them can pick up that line. When someone does pick up a line, that number will light up at the other phones indicating that it is in use. For calling out, the keysets would get their dial tone from the CO.

The 1A2 key system was called a "fat cable" key system, because no matter how many phone numbers were assigned to a keyphone (the maximum being five in most sets), a 25-pair cable had to be snaked to the set. This was because each of the 5 possible phone numbers needed 3 pairs. Installing this fat cable around facilities was very costly and bulky.

The 1A2 keyset was more complex as compared to a PBX phone set which used "skinny" wire. The emphasis on calling with the 1A2 was with the outside world whereas with a PBX one must first dial an access code, typically a "9," to get to an outside line. In a PBX system, usually an attendant, a person or an automated system handled the incoming calls, but with the 1A2, incoming calls were handled by anyone who had the number terminating at their keyset. Another difference between the 1A2 and the PBX is that the 1A2 simply passed the CO's dial tone, whereas the PBX provides its own. The 1A2 was also limited in that no SMDR (Station Message Detail Recording) was available. No tie trunks or DID (Direct Inward Dialing) trunks were

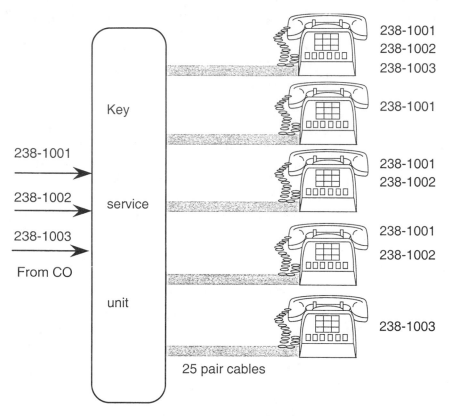

Figure 13.4 An atypical, 3 by 5 configuration of a 1A2 key system. Typically, the three incoming numbers would terminate at all of the keysets.

supported by these key systems. It did not contain any switching intelligence. The collection of the users selecting the various buttons on the keyphones was the switching intelligence of the system.

13.3.2 EKS (Electronic Key Systems)

In 1983, twenty years after the introduction of the 1A2, a number of vendors started coming out with EKSs. Unlike the 1A2 sets, the sets of these systems use only a two- or three-pair wire, so these key systems are called "skinny-wire" systems. The KSUs are much smaller than before; they use microchips instead of electromechanical parts and are much easier to install. They can have tie-lines and DID trunks, and the incoming calls can be taken by a receptionist, similar to the PBX. In fact, today almost all of the features available on PBXs are available on EKSs, and this makes it hard to distinguish EKSs from small PBXs.

Nortel's Norstar is one example of an EKS. It has an open architecture interface which allows third-party vendors to write special-purpose software for it. The Norstar can be programmed from a PC, and this stimulates writing of applications for the system by creative minds other than the NT engineers. Traditionally, this was unheard

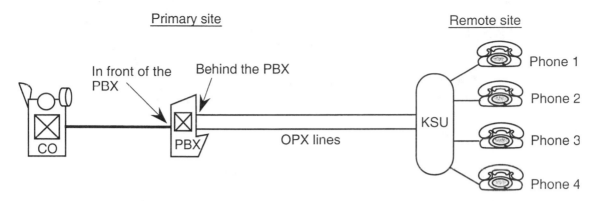

Figure 13.5 Key system connected behind a PBX or Centrex can maximize its utilization.

of in the PBX marketplace; PBX makers did not share their system software internals with others, so only they could enhance the feature set of their PBXs.

This makes EKSs in some ways superior to PBXs. For instance with a PBX, if a person changes his office location and wants to keep the same phone number, a technician must code this change on the PBX. With the Norstar, however, a person only needs to take the phone along to the new office and plug it in there and the KSU will detect the move. No one has to program the change. This is done by a physical address hard coded in the keyphone sets at the factory. Such benefits are not yet widely available on PBXs.

Key systems can also be also used behind a PBX or Centrex. The term "behind" means on the customer's side of the switch, and "in front" means on the public network side of the switch. In Figure 13.5, a KSU is shown to be connected behind the PBX using OPX lines. Although OPX lines would typically go through one or more COs, logically they make the key system appear to be part of the CO.

Without the key system, four telephones at a remote site would normally require leasing four OPX (Off Premise Extensions) lines from the telco. With the EKS located at the remote site, however, only two OPX lines may prove to be sufficient. In this configuration, if two remote phones are using the OPX lines to call out, then a third remote phone could not call anyone outside of its own facility.

Incidentally, in this example, if a caller from the PBX gets transferred by a remote site keyphone to a third person at the PBX, it is possible for the keyphone to signal the PBX and not the KSU to do the transfer. If the transfer were done through the KSU, then both OPX lines would be tied up unnecessarily.

13.4 OTHER SMALL VOICE SYSTEMS

13.4.1 Hybrid Systems

A hybrid system is similar to a key system, except that on a key system a caller chooses the line to make a call, but on a hybrid system the caller simply picks up the phone and the KSU-like device chooses a line that is free to make the call. So the hybrid system has a pool of lines to pick from to make a call, while on a key system if all the lines designated for a set are busy, then that set can't make an outside call even though there may be other lines available. The tariffs for key system lines are less than those for hybrid lines. Companies who want less blocking of calls don't mind paying more for the hybrid system lines. The difference between these two systems from a given vendor many times is just in the software that comes with the unit.

13.4.2 KSU-less Systems

Lastly, the KSU-less system is ideal for telephone systems that have less than ten phones. They are less expensive than a key system, don't require a KSU, and are very easy to install.

13.5 EXAMPLES OF PBX FEATURES

The remainder of this chapter is devoted to PBXs. Features for PBXs are usually categorized into three groups: features for the stations (phones), features for the attendant console (traditionally thought of as the switchboard), and features for the system in general. A sample of a few features will be presented here, just so the capabilities of the PBX can be illustrated. Most PBXs can be acquired with over a hundred features.

13.5.1 Station Features

Two common station features are call-transfer and call-forward. Call-transfer allows the called party to hand over the call to a third party, so that the third party and the original calling party may communicate.

Call-forward on the other hand, allows a person to go for lunch or to be absent and have someone else answer their calls for them from their own phone.

Call-park is another station feature. It is more commonly used in hospitals. For example, if an outside caller dials the hospital for a specific doctor, the attendant would tell the caller to stay on hold. The attendant would park the call on a phantom number, that is, an extension that doesn't have a phone connected to it, and would page over the loudspeaker for that doctor, asking her to call that extension. Then that doctor can call from any phone in the hospital, dial an access code, and that extension would be connected to the caller. No ringback tone would be heard by the caller.

13.5.2 Attendant Features

An example of a PBX attendant feature is called intercept. This feature prevents the attendant (operator) having to say, "Not a valid phone number, please consult your directory." Also, this prevents the phone system from being congested with ring-no-answer conditions.

Automatic recall allows a party in a conversation to get the attendant back on the line.

A PC can also be used instead of an attendant console. Using a Windows-based environment, an attendant can easily keep track of several calls and enter special notes for calls as needed. This makes the job of an attendant easier and at the same time provides a professional atmosphere for outside callers. Having wordprocessing and spreadsheet applications available between calls on the same machine makes it easy to stay productive.

13.5.3 System Features

Classes of service is an important system feature. This is a priority rating given to voice terminals (telephones). 64 different priorities can be assigned. A priority of 1 is given to the most important phone sets and 64 is usually assigned to the least important phone, such as in the cafeteria. Usually only 8 different classes of service are assigned for simplicity. A telephone with a high class of service will have more station features activated on it, will be allowed to make toll calls, and will be given other privileges. The services associated with each class are programmed by the telecom manager.

SMDR (Station Message Detail Recording), already referred to in the section on Centrex, provides reports of which extensions were called by whom, at what time, for how long, and at what cost. This type of information helps to manage telecommunications costs, bill departments on their utilization, and control phone abuse. CDR (Call Detail Recording) is another name used for it.

13.6 LUCENT TECHNOLOGIES' DEFINITY

As an example of a PBX system, Lucent Technologies' DEFINITY ECS (Enterprise Communications Server) is introduced. Explaining a specific PBX will be more beneficial than studying PBXs in general. All major manufacturers are constantly improving their products due to competition in the market.

13.6.1 Telephone Instruments

As with other PBXs, the DEFINITY supports 2500-type sets. These are the analog-type desk or wall phones commonly used in homes. They come with two pairs of wire, out of which only one pair is used. These are analog-type phones because the spoken voice is sent out of the phone over one pair in analog form and the line card of the switch, where the pair terminates, has the codec to convert the voice to digital form.

Lucent's 8400, 9400, and 6400 series telephones are examples of digital phones. A digital phone converts voice into digital form before it is sent out on the wire pair. The line card in the PBX then doesn't have to digitize the voice. The digitizing takes place in the handset. These phones are also examples of feature phones. With an ordinary 2500 set, station features can be accessed by inputting dial access codes to activate and deactivate features. A feature phone, however, allows the user to activate a feature simply by pressing a preprogrammed button instead of the keys of the keypad. This is also an example of a vendor-specific phone; that is, it will work only with one vendor's equipment.

At one time, vendor-specific phones were connected mostly by two pairs of wires. With one pair of wires, however, twice as many phones can be connected to a line card at the PBX. The DEFINITY telephones mentioned can be connected using either one or two pairs of wires, including ISDN BRI connections.

Integrated voice/data workstations include a digital telephone and a PC running PC/ISDN Platform software. An interface card plugs into an eight-bit expansion slot in the PC which is connected to a voice terminal (phone) using a standard phone jack. With the workstation connected to the DEFINITY system, a person can communicate to a host or other PCs, while talking to a person in another location. The PC/ISDN Platform provides an open software interface for which customers and independent developers can create their own applications. Currently applications are available for advance message centers, terminal emulations, attendant workstations, etc.

In the DEFINITY line of products, a Quorum A-28 Conference Bridge and SoundStation are available. The bridge allows up to 28 phones to be connected to a conference call. This bridge can be connected so that either all parties may talk or, if used in a lecture mode, only one party may talk. The SoundStation picks up conversations of many people talking normally in a room and provides a conference environment over a call.

13.6.2 Station Links

The connection from the voice terminal to the DEFINITY at one time was done using four pairs of wire. One pair carried the digitized voice at 64 kbps, another carried data at 64 kbps, a third carried signaling and framing at 32 kbps, and the fourth carried DC power from the wiring closet to the workstation. The two 64-kbps channels, called information channels, together with 8 kbps of signaling and 24 kbps of control and framing bits form Lucent's proprietary DCP (Data Communications Protocol), running at 160 kbps. Today the trend is to use fewer pairs of wires to reduce the cost of installation and line cards. Using multiplexing techniques and phantoming of DC power, the number of pairs was reduced to two. Currently, DEFINITY station links using only one pair are available. Phantoming means transmitting both the digital signal and the DC voltage over the same line. The 9400 and the 6400 telephone set, for instance, use only one pair while the 8400 set can use either one or two pairs.

13.6.3 DEFINITY Block Diagram Overview

In Figure 13.6, a simplified overview of the DEFINITY ECS is shown. The DEFINITY can support up to 250,000 calls per hour depending on its configuration.

Computers of various kinds can be connected to the DEFINITY providing non-switching types of applications, such as word processing, terminal emulation, message center processing, call detail recording, call management systems for ACD environments, and UNIX and local area networking. Audix is Lucent's voice mail system. The DEFINITY can also support TCP/IP and provide routing if connected using IP trunks.

The PPN (Processor Port Network) is the master controller for the DEFINITY system, and may have up to 800 terminals connected to it directly. As more terminals are required, EPNs (Expansion Port Networks) are attached to the PPN until the limit is reached for adding terminals and EPNs, at which time other DEFINITY systems can be networked by adding more PPNs and starting the expansion process over again. In Figure 13.6, two DEFINITYs are shown as being networked.

The EPNs may be located with their respective PPN or may be placed up to 5 miles away using a fiber connection. EPNs may be placed even up to 100 miles away

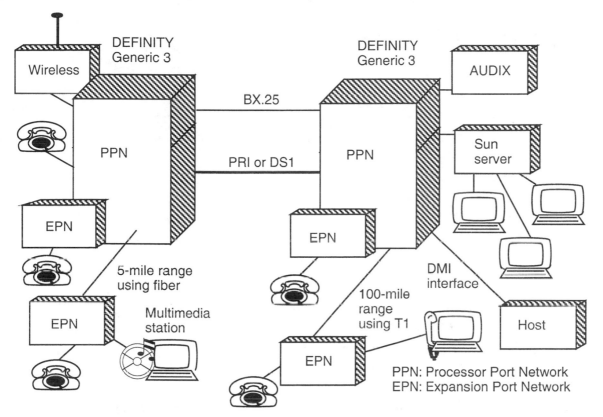

Figure 13.6 An overview of a DEFINITY ECS (Enterprise Communications Server).

by using a T1 link. Each T1 provides up to 24 terminals, and with a maximum of four T1s, 94 information channels can be supported. Two channels out of the 96 channels are required by the system. Terminals connected to any of these EPNs using fiber or T1/ISDN links appear as being part of the same DEFINITY system.

The DEFINITY can be connected to up to 126 base stations providing wireless service to up to 500 telephones. The wireless system can be designed to accommodate up to 4 million square feet of coverage. It uses the PWT (Personal Wireless Telecommunications) technology and provides support to all DEFINITY features for the wireless handsets.

Multimedia calls can be established only with voice or video. Once the call is initiated, data channels can be added. MMCH (Multimedia Call Handling) allows you to control voice, data, and video features using the telephone set. Sharing of PC applications is also possible using the multimedia option.

13.6.4 Configurations

Figure 13.7(a) shows that only one PPN is sufficient to have a complete PBX system with 800 ports or less. As more lines and trunks need to be added, up to two

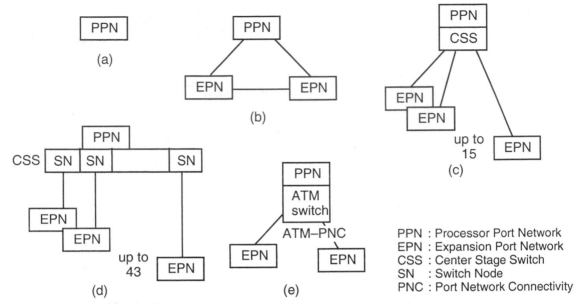

Figure 13.7 (a) For under 800 stations, one PPN is sufficient. (b) For under 2000 stations, 1 PPN and 2 EPNs can be configured. (c) For more ports, a PPN, a CSS, and up to 15 EPNs can be utilized. (d) A CSS with SNs can allow up to 43 EPNs. (e) A CSS can also be replaced by an ATM switch.

EPNs can be interconnected as shown in Figure 13.7(b). When a third EPN has to be added then one must migrate to a more sophisticated configuration, which can accommodate up to 15 EPNs as shown in Figure 13.7(c). In this configuration, one must add extra carriers or circuitry called the CSS (Center-Stage Switch) in either the PPN cabinet or the EPN cabinets.

If additional EPNs are required, then SNs (Switch Nodes) must be added in the CSS. This will accommodate up to 43 EPNs. See Figure 13.7(d). By replacing the CSS with an ATM switch, as shown in Figure 13.7(e), a more standards-based configuration can be implemented. An interface called the ATM-PNC (Asynchronous Transfer Mode – Port Network Connectivity) is used in this case. With this interface, the DEFINITY system can be made ready for expansion solutions that are nonproprietary. ATM-PNC can also be used with the PPN directly.

13.6.5 DEFINITY Architecture

Figure 13.8 shows a block diagram of the DEFINITY. This is comprised of the PPN, EPN, and the CSS blocks. At the heart of the PPN is a RISC (Reduced Instruction Set Computer). RISC architecture allows computer instructions to run faster because the CPU has to look through a smaller table of instructions.

The PPN also contains RAM. Call-processing, system programs, and administrative procedures are handled through here. Mass storage systems provide connectivity with SCSI-based tape and disk storage devices. System access and maintenance provide an interface to the DEFINITY management terminal. This terminal allows one to monitor line conditions, and to manage the entire system from one central location.

The DEFINITY uses a packet bus, which provides efficient communication for the system among the various modules. The packet bus is extended through the EPNs. Along with the packet bus, a TDM bus that carries actual information runs in parallel with it. The final module shown in the PPN is the expansion interface. It provides a uniform method of interconnecting the various modules: PPNs, EPNs, and CSSs with each other. Typically, these modules are connected with each other using fiber links.

The CSS provides a fully non-blocking connection between all the port networks. This is accomplished through the space-division switch which has fan-out, fan-in, and multiplexer circuits that provide the necessary cross-point connections between the time-slots of the port network busses. Therefore, when the CSS is used in a system, the PBX is said to be "switched connected," or else it is said to be "directly connected."

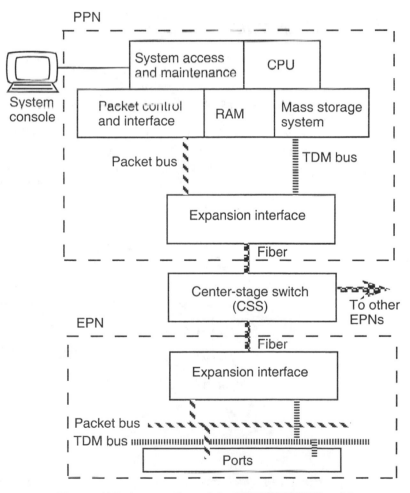

Figure 13.8 An overview of the DEFINITY ECS architecture.

Each EPN contains an Intel processor, a time slot interchanger, a TDM (Time Division Multiplexed) bus, a packet bus, and the port circuits. The processor in the EPN communicates with the CPU in the PPN over the packet bus. It scans the ports and provides a dial tone to anyone who is off-hook. It does intramodule switching as well as other real-time intensive processing.

The EPN processor takes off the TDM bus the information (voice, data, etc.) bits which need to communicate with other EPNs and places them appropriately on the time-multiplexed channel to the CSS. The CSS then switches these bits to their respective EPNs. So the EPN basically transfers the bits between the local TDM bus and the fiber optic channel connecting the CSS. An intramodule call is handled by one EPN and doesn't require the CSS, but intermodule calls first are switched over the TDM bus on the calling EPN, then are space-division switched through the CSS, and finally time-division switched on the called EPN. This is called time-space-time architecture and is commonly used in all PBXs.

13.7 TANDEM TIE-LINE NETWORKS

In Figure 13.9 an example of a PBX network of the 1960's using immediate start tie-lines is shown. Here if phone 1 wants to call phone 2, it would simply get its PBX's dial tone and dial phone 2's extension, because they are both part of one PBX system. However, if phone 1 in Miami wanted to call phone 4 in Houston, then phone 1 would first listen to the Miami PBX's dial tone and would dial trunk group access code 3. Then it would listen to the Atlanta PBX's dial tone and would dial 5 to get the Houston PBX's dial tone. Now phone 1 can dial phone 4's extension to make the connection.

Notice that in this network the caller does all the switching between the nodes manually. If the trunk group from Atlanta to Houston were busy, the caller would have

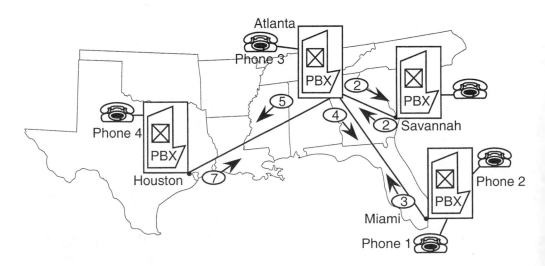

Figure 13.9 A tandem tie-line network, showing the necessary codes to gain access for the specified PBX.

to try again until all the links to the destination are available. The caller would have to know the trunk group access codes and how the network was configured in order to make a network call. Also, the extension numbers for two phones could be the same, and so to uniquely identify a phone in the network by the phone number was not sufficient, because one had to know its location. If the caller had lost track of which PBX's dial tone was being heard, then the caller would be lost in the network and would have to start again.

13.8 PRIVATE NETWORKS

Nortel calls its PBX network scheme ESN (Electronic Switched Network) and Lucent calls its PBX network schemes ETN (Electronic Tandem Network) and DCS (Distributed Communication System), and others call theirs by yet other names. We will call all such networks, regardless of the vendor, private networks. One key difference between ESN and ETN is that ESN uses a central management center called the CMC (Communications Management Center), which has data links to all the switches. All network operations are performed and monitored from this central point. The advantages of private networks become apparent after having considered tandem tie-line networks in the last section.

13.8.1 Private Network Features

Private networks perform a number of networking features which earlier networks didn't provide. One such feature is the uniform dialing plan. This permits each terminal set to have its own unique identity (phone number) in a corporate-wide network. Typically, each PBX would have a unique 3-digit code similar to a CO's exchange, and each terminal would have a 4-digit extension number. This is called a 7-digit private dialing plan. Now the phone in Miami simply has to listen for one dial tone and dial the 7-digit number of phone 4 in Houston. Then the PBX in Miami, detecting the first 3 digits, forwards the call to the Atlanta PBX, and it does the same by forwarding the call to the Houston PBX.

Then the Houston PBX recognizes its own first 3 digits and completes the call using the last 4 digits. Here the switching between the PBXs is done automatically and not by the caller. Furthermore, regardless of from where the call is made, the dialed digits are the same. This allows one directory for all locations. With the tandem tie-line network, the set of access codes to reach phone 4 depends on where the caller is located.

CAS (Centralized Attendant Service) allows one location to handle attendant (or switch-board operator) services for all PBX locations. So there is no need to staff an attendant at every location, as there is if the PBXs are not networked.

Feature transparency provides the same features and PBX resemblance to all users, regardless of their location. To the user it looks like one large PBX rather than a network of PBXs.

DISA (Direct Inward System Access) is a nightmare for some companies. It allows an authorized employee of the corporation to dial into a PBX, provide an authorization code, and then have access to any of the PBX network resources. This allows the user to dial anywhere else on the private network or dial off onto the public network without using an attendant. Some DISA numbers with authorization codes have been sold on the black market allowing people to make international calls to their friends at the expense of the private network owners. Security measures should be taken within the PBX if DISA is to be utilized.

There are two methods of completing a call if alternate paths to the destination exist. One method is called AAR (Automatic Alternate Routing), which provides the best path to route a call over the dedicated tie-line network. The other method uses the PSTN to complete a call and it is called ARS (Automatic Route Selection).

13.9 ARS (AUTOMATIC ROUTE SELECTION)

13.9.1 The Decision-making Process of ARS

ARS software determines the most inexpensive way to complete a toll call over the public network. LCR (Least Cost Routing) is similar to ARS except that it decides the best route to take based on the time-of-day discounts. Many times the two terms are used interchangeably.

ARS is a table-driven option that can be obtained with the purchase of a PBX. It can block 900 numbers, dial-the-weather, and other unnecessary calls based on the area code, exchange, or even the terminal phone number.

When a long distance call is made, say from Atlanta to Houston as in Figure 13.9, ARS will monitor the tie trunk available to Houston and try using it to complete the call. From Houston, DDD service can then be used.

If the tie trunks are busy, a WATS line can be used to reach Houston directly. If neither a tie trunk nor a WATS line is available, the PBX will wait typically for 10 seconds to see if one of them becomes free. If not, it will then give a 5-second warning tone providing a chance for the caller to hang up and try later. Finally, if the caller wants to try immediately and doesn't hang up, the PBX will dial over the DDD network to Houston.

This is an example of the decision process that must be done by the PBX to complete a call using ARS. Typically, it's good to have at least 50% of the calls use tie trunks to control long distance costs. The cost per call-minute is lowest for them. Usually 35% of the calls go over WATS lines and approximately 15% use DDD services.

13.9.2 A Case Problem

A Kansas City firm has extensive calling requirements to San Francisco, which has an area code of 415. Therefore, it has an FX trunk going there. Also the company has a WATS service area 3 to call customers on the west coast. See Figure 13.10.

Workers in group A need to call only numbers in 415 that have an exchange of 247, that is 415-247-xxxx numbers. They must use the FX trunk group as a primary choice and the WATS service as a secondary choice. They are restricted from using DDD services.

Workers in group B are required to call all numbers in area code 415 regardless of the exchange. Group C workers are allowed to call any west coast state. Both group

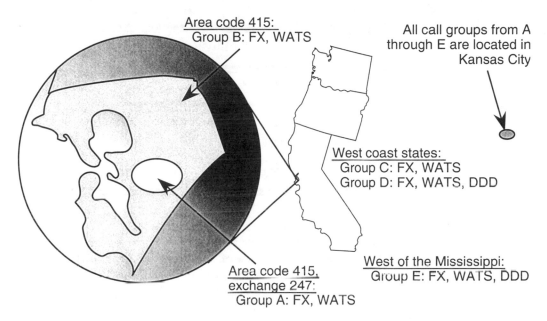

Figure 13.10 ARS restrictions placed on various groups of workers located in Kansas City in the case problem.

B and C workers are to use FX and WATS services only. Group D workers are also allowed to call any west coast state, but they may utilize DDD services as well.

Finally, group E workers are allowed to call anywhere west of the Mississippi River, and if necessary to use DDD services. Of course, when group E calls Nebraska, the FX trunk and WATS service are not usable. Describe the calling patterns and FRL (Facilities Restriction Levels) is needed to program the PBX. Each trunk group to a geographical region is assigned a number, called an FRL. If a trunk's FRL is high, then that trunk group has more calling restrictions, etc. When a caller calls over a trunk group, the PBX checks to see if the FRL allowed for the caller is greater than the FRL assigned to that trunk group before letting the call go through.

Solution: First define the routing patterns that are required. The first pattern, called pattern 02, provides calls only to 415-247-xxxx. Pattern 03 provides calls to 415 except for the 247 exchange. Pattern 04 includes all California, Oregon, and Washington area codes, except 415. Lastly, pattern 05 includes all area codes west of the Mississippi except for the west coast area codes. These are the areas the PBX is allowed to call. Notice that routing patterns don't overlap one another.

Next, we must find the FRLs (Facility Restriction Level) that are needed. We start with the group that has the most calling restrictions (group A) and proceed with the groups which are given increasing calling privileges. Group A may call via FX or WATS trunks only to routing pattern 02. So they get the lowest FRL of 1. See Table 13.1. Then for the next group that has fewer restrictions, we give a FRL of 2. 2 is then

Table 13.1 Facility Restriction Levels			
Patterns	FX	WATS	DDD
02	1	1	4
03	2	2	4
04	3	3	4
05	5	5	5

filled in the boxes corresponding to pattern 03 with FX and WATS as the transmission facilities. When a call is to be made by a phone which has an FRL of 2 to 415-247-xxxx (pattern 02), it falls in the first row of Table 13.1. Since 1 from the table is less than the 2 of the FRL of the caller, the call is allowed to connect, first by using FX and then by using WATS trunks. In general, if the FRL is equal to or greater than the FRL of the trunk group, then the call will be allowed to be carried by that trunk group.

Similarly, because workers of group C require added privileges, we have to create a new FRL that is greater than the previous ones, which is 3. Now group C workers with FRL of 3 may call patterns 02, 03, and 04 without being able to utilize DDD services since a higher-numbered FRL has authorization to use lower-numbered FRLs. Then group D workers need added privileges to use DDD services; an FRL of 4 is assigned to them. Lastly, since group E workers may call more areas, they are given an FRL of 5.

In summary, when an outside call is made, first the pattern is selected (rows in the table), then the facilities are checked (columns in the table) from left to right to see which one is available to use. If the number in the cell, specified by the row and the column, is less than or equal to the FRL of the caller, the call is allowed to go through. Otherwise, a busy signal is sent. If trunk queuing is available on the system, the caller will be called back when a trunk is available with his/her FRL.

13.10 NETWORK ROUTING

Suppose our corporation has just acquired a western firm and it interconnects two networks using high-capacity trunks between Atlanta and Las Vegas. See Figure 13.11. These two primary sites are called nodes and they would require a special software upgrade to handle network routing as it is being described.

Let us suppose Miami's phone 1 is calling a phone in San Diego. The preferred path of course is through the Las Vegas node, the LA PBX, and then to San Diego. If the trunk from Las Vegas to LA is busy, then the node at Las Vegas has two options in order to complete the call.

One, it can convert the private 7-digit phone number to the public 10-digit phone number, and maybe to a number of even more digits, if an extension is also needed. Then it can dial the terminal in San Diego over the public network. This is called TEHO (Tail-End Hop-Off).

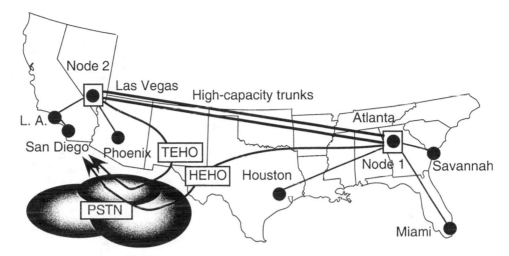

Figure 13.11 Two methods of hopping off a private tie-line network over the public network.

The alternative is to backhaul the traffic to Atlanta, let Atlanta do the phone number conversion, and have Atlanta use the DDD network to reach San Diego. This is called HEHO (Head-End Hop-Off).

It becomes tricky deciding where to hop off the private network into the public domain. As in Figure 13.12(a), if node 2 is close to the destination, it may be better to hopoff there and to incur less DDD charges than doing a hop-off from node 1. However, this uses a circuit between the nodes and if it is the last available one, the next call from node 1 to node 2 would also have to use the DDD network.

It might have been better, as shown in Figure 13.12(b), to have a HEHO for call 1 and let call 2 go over the private network, rather than have both calls be routed over the public network.

Doing cost estimates, traffic engineering studies, trunk usage analysis, and various such tasks on private networks can be very tedious. Virtual networks are

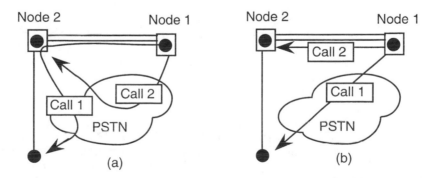

Figure 13.12 The tradeoffs of using two types of hop-offs.

quickly replacing these private tie-line networks. Virtual networks eliminate the tie trunks, use the DDD network for all of the calls, and allow the intelligence in the carrier's network to decide how to route the call. This is the topic of chapter 11.

EXERCISES

Section 13.2:
1. What is one of the advantages of owning a PBX over having Centrex?
   a. reliability　　　　　　　　　　　b. fast service
   c. high data rates　　　　　　　　　d. easy to expand
2. What device is used to provide LANs in a Centrex setting?
   a. modem　　　　　　　　　　　　　b. DOV modem
   c. EKS　　　　　　　　　　　　　　d. ISDN
3. What type of voice switching system uses the CO to do the on-premise switching?
4. Does an IVDT convert voice to digital or data to analog? What type of multiplexing does it incorporate?
5. Describe the pros and cons of using Centrex over owning a PBX.
6. How does a DOV modem work and how is it used?

Sections 13.3 and 13.4:
7. Which of the following is NOT a characteristic of the 1A2 key system?
   a. It uses 2-pair wires to the voice terminals.
   b. Typically, one doesn't have to dial an access code to get an outside line.
   c. It does not allow tie trunks to be connected to it.
   d. Incoming calls are generally not handled by attendants.
8. Which type of voice system uses a "pool" of outside lines, rather than outside lines assigned to specific stations?
   a. KSU-less system　　　　　　　　b. EKS
   c. 1A2 system　　　　　　　　　　　d. hybrid system
9. A set of OPX lines from a PBX to a remote location can be reduced by using what device behind the PBX?
10. Give the reasons for owning a PBX over owning an EKS system.
11. What are some differences between a key system and a hybrid system?

Section 13.5:
12. Which PBX feature allows an operator to connect an incoming call to a person who is not by their phone set?
    a. call-transfer　　　　　　　　　b. call-park
    c. call-intercept　　　　　　　　　d. class of service
13. What are some advantages of having a PC being operated as an attendant console?
14. For a higher class of service, does the phone terminal have more or fewer privileges?
15. What is another name for SMDR?

Section 13.6:
16. Lucent's DCP uses what speed for voice, data, and signaling?
17. How does the switching in a CSS differ from the switching done in an EPN?
18. Explain the difference between the packet bus and the TDM bus.
19. What is the nomenclature of an ordinary residential phone set?

20. Explain the functions of the various blocks shown in Figure 13.6.
21. What are the two methods of extending the range of an EPN?
22. What is the difference between a PPN and EPN?

Sections 13.7 and 13.8:
23. Which type of network requires the caller to know the trunk access codes to various locations when making a call?
    a. tandem tie-line
    c. Electronic Switched Network
    b. Distributed Communications System
    d. Electronic Tandem Network
24. Name the advantages of private networks over tandem tie-line networks which provide features resembling the features of a PBX.
25. What type of networks are preferred over private tie-line networks?
26. When each PBX of a private network has its own three-digit code, for example, and each of its attached phones has a four-digit number, which feature is being utilized?

Sections 13.9 and 13.10:
27. When backhauling is done, what type of hop-off is performed?
28. Explain the reasons for using TEHO versus the reasons for using HEHO.
29. Describe the patterns and facilities restriction levels required for the following ARS problem. Draw a table.

A Boston firm has an FX trunk to New York and one to Detroit. Group A workers can call anywhere in the states using DDD service. (All international calls are blocked automatically.) Group B workers can call to New York using FX first, then WATS, and then DDD, but they can call Detroit using FX only. Group C workers have just the opposite privileges of Group B workers: They can call Detroit using any of the three transmission services, but can call New York using FX only.

Chapter 14

Voice Processing, ACDs, and CTI

14.1 INTRODUCTION

A voice processing system attempts to complete incoming and outgoing calls automatically, without requiring any personnel to handle the calls. It processes telephone-based transactions automatically. The incoming calls may require a connection to a specific extension, access to some information, a facility to store a voice message in the event the called party is not available, or a combination of such services. Traditionally, these services were provided by an operator or a secretary of some sort. The current technological advances are automating many of these tasks, which are mundane and routine for human beings. If designed and implemented with care, these systems can save considerable amounts of money and provide better services for callers. Computers interfacing with phone calls can't get tired, can't lose their temper, can't resign from their jobs, don't need to be trained, can work without needing breaks, can handle many calls simultaneously, and can work around the clock.

The first part of this chapter covers the many kinds of voice processing systems; then it continues with ACD (Automatic Call Distribution) and IVR (Interactive Voice Response) systems. An ACD is a voice switch similar to a PBX, but it is designed to be used with a group of agents, any of whom can answer incoming calls or make outgoing calls. For instance, when an airplane reservation is to be made, the caller can be served by any agent and chances are that such a call goes through an ACD. The ACD places calls in a "queue" to route them to agents in some order. More on that later. Let us now consider the various kinds of voice processing systems.

Most of these voice processing systems can come as stand-alone units or they can be integrated with a PC, a host, or a PBX. The PC-based products can serve a dual purpose of serving as a PC station and as a voice processing system. PC-based products offer open architecture with a choice of many components to provide a wide range of technologies. They have the flexibility to be networked in a LAN configuration or to be integrated in a large scale system design.

All the technologies which this chapter explores are finally culminated with CTI (Computer Telephony Integration). CTI provides a standards-based method of allowing the data servers to communicate with the ACDs. This is done so that customers who are calling into a call center are served promptly and efficiently. All the previous technologies tried to reduce the dependence on hiring more personnel to serve customers. CTI recognizes the importance of the personal touch of an agent with a customer, but uses the integration of the voice switch and the data server to make their interaction pleasurable. CTI today is also used to serve customers from the World Wide Web more effectively.

14.2 METHODS OF PROVIDING SPEECH

14.2.1 Recorded Speech

The first voice processing system was introduced in 1931 by the Audichron Company in Atlanta. This system located in a CO was provided by Coca-Cola. Callers would call this number and, before hearing a short advertisement, would get the current time and temperature played back on two 78 rpm records. This is an example of audiotext, a kind of voice processing system.

The information that audiotext or a voice processing system provides is generally prerecorded from someone talking into a microphone, as shown in Figure 14.1(a) Today this can be done using digitized speech. The natural analog voice is converted into digital form using techniques similar to PCM (Pulse Code Modulation), but compression techniques are also used to better utilize the memory space available. Remember from Chapter 3, one minute of voice takes 0.48 Mbytes of storage space using PCM. However, ADPCM and other more efficient voice encoding methods are commonly used, since they take less space.

The voice data in PCM form is not intended for printing. Voice is meant to be heard on a speaker and not seen on a terminal. Similarly, text typed on a keyboard is meant to be seen on a screen and not be heard on a telephone. So protocols such as PCM are used for telephones to communicate with each other, and protocols such as ASCII are used between terminals.

14.2.2 Text-to-speech Conversion

At one time, voice processing systems stored only digitized speech. Currently, however, TTS (Text-To-Speech) or *synthetic speech* technology is available from many vendors. Here a new announcement can be recorded without having someone talk into a microphone, but by simply typing the message on a keyboard, as in Figure 14.1(b). The benefit of a message stored in text is that it takes much less memory than a similar message stored by speech digitization. It is also easy to compose and edit. TTS is now starting to be implemented in applications that require playback of information stored on a database in large amounts and with information that is subject to frequent change.

TTS technology is tricky to design using the English language. A word ending with "ough" may have any one of its seven pronunciations, such as in "dough," "rough," "through," "cough," etc. Also, there are about a hundred words that are pronounced differently depending on their context. For example "... did you read what I read about the present which was presented ..." Another example is the simple word

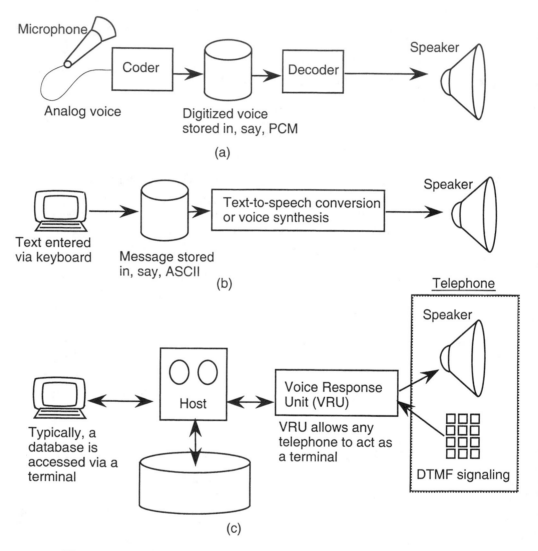

Figure 14.1 (a) Audiotext or digital announcers store messages that are accessed by anyone calling in. Messages are simply played back either from digitized speech or through voice synthesis. (b) A TTS (Text-To-Speech) system "reads off" stored text. (c) A VRU allows information that is generally private to be accessible via a telephone. Here the data may be updated as well through the use of DTMF.

Voice Processing, ACDs, and CTI

"the" which can be pronounced as "thee" or "thuh" depending on its usage. Many such rules of language make text-to-speech technology difficult to engineer.

14.3 AUDIOTEXT INFORMATION SYSTEMS/PROGRAMS

Audiotext systems, also called information center mailboxes and voice bulletin boards, are more sophisticated than the original audichron system and provide the caller with the option to choose the information he or she desires. They can be used to access stock quotes, theater performance times, train schedules, store locations, and so on. The information is provided by the caller choosing selections from audio menus. For example, "If you want the sports score of today's game, enter 1, or if you want the sports score of yesterday's game, enter 2."

Digital announcers, also called passive intercept devices, are similar to bulletin boards, but they usually provide a single canned announcement, such as a change in the phone number, hours of operation, skiing conditions, and so forth.

Fax is used to augment many types of voice processing systems. The kinds of fax processing applications are fax-on-demand, fax mail, and fax broadcasting. Facsimile-on-demand is also similar to voice bulletin boards, but instead of a message being played back to the listener, information is faxed back to the caller. Fax mail digitally stores the fax at the receiving end, and is printed when the recipient is ready for it. Fax broadcasting transmits an image to a number of destinations, where the destinations are predefined in a distribution list.

Systems like the one shown in Figure 14.1(c) have a lot of data and must store it in a computerized database. Here, the data is generally entered from a terminal keyboard and not through a microphone. To convert this type of data into spoken words TTS (Text-To-Speech) may be used or the information can be faxed out, for example, in a bank-by-phone application. The system that provides the capability of transferring electronic data into spoken language and DTMF (or touch tone) signals into data is called an IVR (Interactive Voice Response) system. The term IVR is very broad in its context and is used synonymously with voice processing systems. Unlike with the other systems mentioned above, IVR not only plays back information, but also allows callers to "interact" with the system, through a telephone's DTMF input, to enter or change data in a database.

Another difference between these systems is that the systems in Figure 14.1(a) and (b) generally provide information that is meant for the public, while an IVR can perform security checks before providing information that is personal to the caller. More on IVRs later.

14.4 VOICE RECOGNITION

DTMF signaling was developed in 1958 by AT&T, and although we take it for granted these days, it was crucial in facilitating the advance of voice processing technologies. In some cases, the spoken voice is the only method of accessing and controlling a voice processing device. Instead of pressing keys on a keypad, the user commands the system by giving commands audibly. The user may just have to answer "yes" or "no" or provide a number from "0" to "9" to the questions, and the system will decipher what was said in the mouthpiece. Some systems can recognize a much larger vocabulary.

VR (Voice Recognition) is also referred to as speech recognition or ASR (Automated Speech Recognition) and it has two forms. One is SIVR (Speech-Independent VR) which detects certain words that are being spoken regardless of the speaker. *Speaker verification* is another form where the speaker who is talking is identified by his or her voice.

Basically, SIVR devices perform the "recognition" from the utterance of spoken English instead of identifying DTMF signals. This is done using the following four steps as depicted in Figure 14.2. The first step involves extracting special features of the voice from the input waveforms in order to reduce the amount of data that needs to be processed. This is done using DSP (Digital Signal Processing) chips. The second step matches the features of the given word with a possible correct model. Speech models, also called word patterns or templates, are stored in a collection beforehand. The third step, called DTW (Dynamic Time Warping) adjusts the chosen vocabulary template with the rate at which the word is being spoken by the individual, since every person voices their words at varying speeds. Lastly, an event detector circuit, many times using HMM (Hidden Markov Modeling), decides whether the word being spoken is close enough to the template or it should tag the word as not being in the vocabulary. HMM has proven to be accurate for speaker-independent and continuous speech, where no pauses are required between the spoken words. Artificial intelligence plays a significant role in the development of this technology.

Speaker-dependent voice recognition allows one to identify the caller. Sprint has introduced a "voice" credit card, where instead of dialing the credit card number to place calls, the callers identify themselves by their voices. This is more secure than a password, which can be stolen. Furthermore, a caller needs only to say "CALL HUSBAND" to dial the user's husband at work. There's a lot of potential in applying this type of technology in the future.

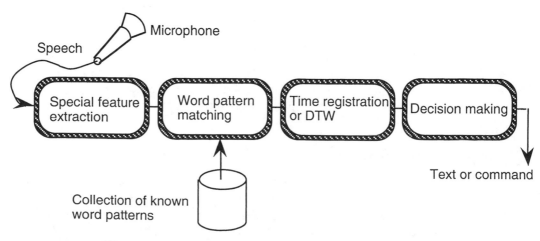

Figure 14.2 Four steps in matching an utterance to "recognize" speech as command input.

A point often underemphasized is that voice recognition also allows a more natural interface to a computer. One doesn't have to drag a keyboard around in a warehouse for instance; a portable phone that interfaces with a voice recognition system is sufficient. It also allows a person to enter data at a speed of 200 words per minute instead of the typical 30 wpm for typed-in data. Voice recognition is a more accurate form of data entry than typed-in data. In a working environment where hands are busy and eyes are busy, voice recognition provides a means to enter data at the same time.

14.5 VOICE MAIL

In 1979, Gordon Matthews of VMX Inc. received a patent and installed the first voice mail system. VM (Voice Mail) allows a caller to leave a message after hearing a prerecorded greeting if the called party is unavailable or busy. VM, also called voice messaging, is an integrated system for all users or extensions, and it has many more features than an answering machine. It also allows users to retrieve their messages from any location and not necessarily only from their own phone.

14.5.1 Why Voice Mail?

Sometimes missing an incoming call can mean a loss of a sale, service, or more importantly, one's own credibility. If customers can't reach you, because you are not by your phone, they're going to go elsewhere. Conversely, you can't stay by your phone continuously, because there are other responsibilities you may have to attend to. Secretaries may use the pink "While you were out" slips to let you know who called, but even those can be lost in the shuffle of a busy desktop. The slips are also prone to human error. Important information, because it is mistakenly felt as trivial by the secretary, may be left out completely.

A message center can be used instead, where a human interface is necessary for projecting a caring and personal image. Here the message center operator types in the name, number, and message of the caller for the person who is unavailable. When that person calls in the message center, the operator reads off any messages waiting for him. But again, with a message center it is hard to emphasize certain points and to leave a more personal message to the caller with all the inflections commonly heard in normal conversations. Messages from the message center are available only when someone is attending it. VM messages can be retrieved even at night.

To take down a message either on a slip or on a terminal requires an extra person. Even if a human touch is desired for important incoming calls, a tired or aggravated operator will not sound as nice as a pleasantly recorded VM greeting.

Preventing "telephone tag" is another reason for using VM. This occurs when two parties call each other at a time when the called party is not available to pick up his/her phone. With VM, the called party can leave a thorough and detailed message, such as, "I tried the "modify routine" command that you recommended and I got error number 000512; what should I do next?" This may not be as efficient as talking to the person directly, but at least some progress has been made in reaching a solution. In this example, the service technician would have time to look up solutions or to ask the co-workers for assistance before calling back.

Now that corporations and even small companies are competing in the international arena, telephone tag becomes more common when the caller is at work and the called party is at home sleeping. VM becomes attractive when workers are in different time zones.

With VM, people don't chitchat as much as they do in a real live conversation, so usually only business matters are discussed. It also offers more confidentiality and privacy than a message taken by a person. If a manager needs to call a department meeting, she may have to type a memo, make copies, and distribute it to her department members and hope they get it. With VM, a message is recorded once and the system, already knowing the people in the department, sends a copy of the message to each person's voice mail box. Not only that, but VM can tell the sender who listened to the message and at what time. VM is also useful for service technicians to keep in touch with their managers and to find out what customer to service next.

14.5.2 Size of the VM System

A VM port provides access to the VM system from the PBX, one user at a time. So if we want up to 10 users to simultaneously access the VM system, then we must have 10 ports available. The proposed VM unit should have one voice port for every 40 users. However, once data becomes available after the system is in place, the number of ports can be adjusted. 40 users per port is a quite conservative ratio. For light users 100 users per port will suffice. At any given time, one port allows only one user to access the VM.

A rule of thumb for the amount of memory is to have 6 minutes of storage space per user. Again, this number can be drastically different depending on how the users utilize the system. So for example, a system for 1000 users should have at least 1000/40 or 25 ports and have a storage capacity of 1000 times 6 minutes or 100 hours.

14.6 AUTOMATED ATTENDANTS (AAs)

Dytel Corp. in 1984 introduced the first automated attendant system. AAs attempt to replace attendant console operators, formerly thought of as switchboard operators. When a caller dials into an office a recording is heard, such as, ". . . if you have a touch tone phone and know your party's extension, you may dial it now; if you need a sales representative, you may dial 1 now, etc. . ." Typically, such systems use AAs, which many times are integrated with voice mail systems and other voice processing devices.

14.6.1 The Case for AAs

With a typical private voice switching system, such as with a PBX, centrex, or key system, there are many trunks coming in from the CO (central office) and many lines going to the phones or the extensions. This method of answering incoming calls creates the well known "hourglass" effect, as shown in Figure 14.3. Many trunks are coming into the operator and many lines are going out from the operator. Just like all the sand must pass through a narrow hole in an hourglass, so all incoming calls must pass through the operator. Using DID (Direct Inward Dialing) trunks and DISA (Direct

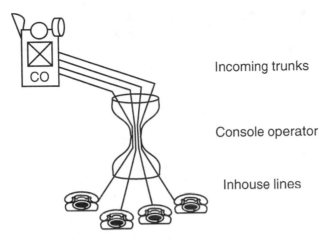

Incoming trunks

Console operator

Inhouse lines

Figure 14.3 The "hourglass effect" occurring due to a single console operator.

Inward System Access) features is an attempt to correct this bottlenecking problem, but that isn't sufficient.

In fact, one study shows that only 25% of all calls are successful on the first try. For this reason, the console operator has to handle call attempts a number of times in order to successfully complete a call. The amount of frustration, on the operator's part, increases even more during the busy hours, which typically occur during 10 AM – 11 AM and 2 PM – 3 PM.

One solution is to add another attendant console, but that requires hiring an extra person. Another solution is to add more DID trunks, but not only are their costs going up, but also, they are useless for callers who need to get an extension number first.

14.6.2 Advantages of AA

A console operator can handle only one call at a time, but an AA can handle 10, 20, or 50 calls at one time. The console operator is forced to let incoming calls keep ringing, because a single operator can't handle multiple calls simultaneously. If an overworked operator does answer an incoming call before the caller hangs up, the operator isn't necessarily going to sound pleasant. The operator's job is boring and tedious. With an AA, the incoming calls are answered in one ring, and the voice announcement they hear is courteous and cheerful, because the AA doesn't get tired.

So even if a live operator is preferred by upper management, the operator can also be a reason for losing sales. An operator is also more prone to human errors, directing the incoming calls to the wrong destination, and so frustrating the caller.

If an outside caller needs to relay some information to a person in-house after hours and after the operator has gone off duty, the outsider cannot call in, but the insider must call out instead. AA allows outsiders to directly call into a facility, without an operator. And outsiders can dial directly to an extension, even if DID trunks are not available. It also allows one to access VM from outside after hours.

Table 14.1 Advantages of Automated Attendants
1. Handles multiple calls simultaneously.
2. Isn't irritated by incoming calls.
3. Caller can control his/her call routing.
4. Available 24 hours/day.
5. Fast response time.
6. Provides call management data.
7. Less expensive than hiring operators.

With AA, outside callers have quick access to workers inside a facility. The connections are made quickly, especially if the callers know what extension they want. AA does a routine job at a low price. A reasonable PC-based AA can cost around $10,000. That is much less than one has to pay an operator; besides, the AA works 24 hours a day.

How calls are being handled, how many callers drop off and for what reason, should more trunks be added or should their number be reduced: The answers to all such questions would normally come from interviewing the console operators. Now the AA can obtain statistics to provide call management data. This data is accurate, it doesn't depend on anyone's memory, and can be used to streamline the operation.

Lastly, a small company's manager may have to work as an operator while doing other tasks. Now, AA allows both big and small companies to project a professional image to outside callers. Table 14.1 summarizes the advantages of AAs.

14.6.3 AA Features

Operator Anywhere: This feature prevents dead-end calls. No matter which voice menu the caller is in, the caller can reach a live operator simply by dialing "0."

Call Sequencing: If many callers are on hold, this feature will put them on a queue as they call in so that the first to go on hold will be the first who gets answered.

Call Screening: The caller is prompted for his or her name, which is recorded. Then the system calls the intended extension and plays back the name saying "Mr/Ms. So N. So is on the line." If the called party wants to be connected, one key on the keypad is pressed, otherwise, a different key is pressed. In that case, the called party may hear something like this "Mr. No Not Yet is unavailable right now, but if you care to speak to his backup assistant, Mr. Back Jack, please press 1 now..." etc. This feature should be used with great care, since people are more used to being screened by a live secretary than by a machine. The machine can't be diplomatic about it.

Screened Transfer: Suppose, in the previous example, "Mr/Ms. So N. So" pressed "1" and was transferred to Mr. Back Jack. If this were a screened transfer, the system, already having the caller's name, would ask Mr. Back Jack if he cared to talk

Voice Processing, ACDs, and CTI

to him or her, before giving her a choice of being transferred to yet another party, to the VM box, or to a live operator.

Monitored Transfer: Suppose "Mr/Ms. So N. So" had pressed 1 as before, but now the AA will make sure that the call is completed and Mr. Back Jack did answer the phone before dropping off. This prevents the caller from getting a busy or a ringback tone and being "jailed" in the call path.

Directory Assistance: VM also supports this feature. AA can provide the caller with the extension just by having the caller provide the first few letters of the last name.

14.7 INTRODUCTION TO CALL DISTRIBUTION SYSTEMS

14.7.1 How Are ACDs Used

"Please stay on hold, all of our agents are currently busy, one will be with you shortly . . ." We are all too familiar with this line which is an example of how ACDs are used. Catalog sales, nationwide hotel chains, car rental agencies, and a host of other applications use ACDs to distribute their incoming calls to agents. In an ACD environment, all agents are equally capable of handling the calls. When a caller simply wants someone to take an order, to make a reservation, or to provide a service, and isn't interested in getting through to a particular person, then chances are the call is being routed through an ACD.

ACDs can be bought as stand-alone units or PBXs can be configured to function as ACDs with the proper software. The stand-alone units have a higher traffic volume capacity and provide better reporting capabilities than their PBX counterparts. Currently, there is a big push by the BOCs to provide CO-based ACD service. It is very attractive for call centers to hire well qualified agents who may be handicapped or who, for some other reason, prefer to work from home. Since this service is leased, no initial capital investment is needed. Basically, most advantages outlined for Centrex in Chapter 13 also apply to CO-based ACD service.

14.7.2 Comparisons of UCDs and ACDs

UCDs (Uniform Call Distributors), which are not capable of handling a high volume of traffic, provide an alternative to ACDs. They always route the incoming calls to the same set of agents. In Figure 14.4, the ACD will typically send the first call to the first agent, the second call to the second agent, and so on in rotation, even if in the meantime agent 1 becomes free. So the next incoming call is automatically routed to the agent who has been idle the longest.

However, if the ACD unit in the figure was configured as a UCD, then four incoming calls would be routed in sequence to agent 1, agent 2, agent 3, and back to agent 1 if agent 1 has become idle. This way, agent 6 would have to take a call only if the other five agents were busy. The distribution of calls is done in the same manner as it is done in a hunt group with a PBX system. With the UCD, order is present, but with an ACD the workload is distributed evenly among the agents. The UCD system

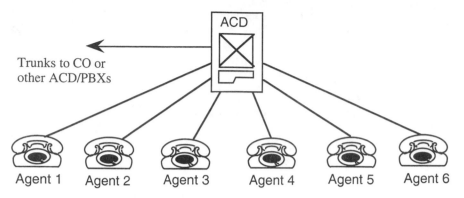

Figure 14.4 An ACD distributes workload for inbound or outbound calls evenly.

works well in a smaller office where a few workers are dedicated to handling incoming calls. When the call volume is low, the rest of the workers can concentrate on other work, but during peak hours they are available to relieve some of the traffic load.

14.7.3 Call Sequencers

A simpler device than a UCD is what's called a call sequencer or an ACS (Automatic Call Sequencer). Using a call sequencer, there are lamps and buttons for every line that is connected to an agent's station. When a caller goes on hold, the lamp for that line flashes and as the caller continues to stay on hold, the rate at which its lamp flashes increases. When an agent becomes free to answer a call, he/she will select the line for which the lamp is flashing the fastest. The line for which the lamp is flashing the fastest signals the call that has been on hold the longest.

Here, the switching intelligence collectively is the group of agents deciding on which button to press or whose call to answer next, whereas with an ACD (or a UCD), the device provides the switching intelligence.

14.7.4 Call Centers

ACDs are only part of a bigger picture called call centers. In a call center, there are trunks coming from the CO into the ACD, which distributes the calls to the agents. Similarly, access to the data in a host is provided by a terminal for each agent. See Figure 14.5. Also, the call center managers can oversee the entire operation and provide assistance as needed. ACDs are used for inbound (incoming) calls or outbound (outgoing) calls. Telemarketing is an example of ACDs used as outbound devices.

ACDs were first introduced by Collins Radio in 1973, when Continental Airline's reservation office in New York City needed a high-capacity, special-purpose switch to handle a high volume of incoming calls. Later, Collins was bought out by Rockwell International and today Rockwell owns almost 50% of the stand-alone ACD market. Its Galaxy model GVS-3000 is capable of supporting 1200 agents.

Voice Processing, ACDs, and CTI

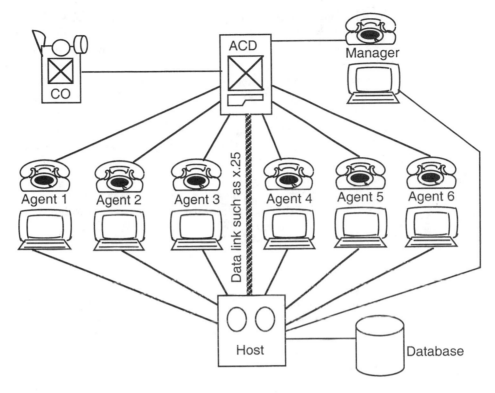

Figure 14.5 An ACD is only part of a bigger picture called a call center.

14.8 OUTBOUND TELEMARKETING

ACDs not only provide a means of distributing incoming calls to available agents, but also provide outbound calling which is used in telemarketing today. Telemarketing is a type of business where agents call customers to try to sell a product or service over the telephone.

Speed dialing is the most rudimentary type of telemarketing. When an agent is done with a call the "next-call" key is pressed. Then the autodialer dials the next phone number from a database and the agent hears the call progress tones until someone answers or until the agent hangs up.

The next step up from speed dialing in sophistication is power dialing. A power dialer contains a database of names and numbers, and the rate at which to dial these numbers automatically is preset. Because typically, out of every four dialed numbers, only one number is contacted, power dialers dial many more calls than there are agents, and calls are directed to the next available agent only if the call is answered on the receive end. The rate of dialing is preset and fixed. So if more contacts are being made than expected, calls would have to be abandoned by the system. Furthermore, in these situations, more switch and trunking capacity is dedicated than what the agents can accommodate.

In contrast to these methods, predictive dialing uses sophisticated mathematical algorithms as well as real-time statistics to adjust the rate at which calls are being dialed. Here also, a computer with a database of names and numbers is connected to the ACD via a data link. A pacing algorithm residing in the host instructs the ACD when to dial the next number. It decides how fast to send the numbers to the ACD for dialing out by comparing the agent statistics sent to it by the ACD.

The ACD can detect the differences between ringing, no answer, busy, and a live person answering at the distant end. The ringing, no answer, and busy conditions are sent back to the host for further action on its part. These phone numbers are stored and are automatically rescheduled for calling back. However, a live person answering the call causes the ACD to connect the call to an agent and supply this information to the host. The host can then update the agent's screen with the called person's data. In effect, predictive dialing systems use fewer resources to help a business make more sales than with the other systems.

14.9 WHY ACDs?

Unlike PBXs, ACDs are money-making devices and are indispensable for companies that use them. Many stores have closed their doors and are using a call center and an 800 number to conduct their business. ACDs play such an important role in call centers, that they have stringent reliability requirements and users don't mind paying up to 15 million dollars for one of these devices.

Usually, to get new customers for a product or service, a business has to create, promote, and pay for an advertisement giving a phone number to call. 95% of the cost to win a new customer goes into such efforts while only 5% of this cost goes into the call center itself including trunks, staff, and equipment. The cost of the ACD is typically less than 1 percent of the total cost, and to mismanage the call center and to have an inadequate ACD system is foolish. The call center can either take advantage of all the previous advertisement efforts or nullify them.

The call center provides the first impression of the company to prospective customers, and because it is more costly to gain new customers through advertising than to keep the current ones, businesses are providing excellent service with 800 numbers to keep the current customer base satisfied. Typically, this is done through the use of ACDs.

The purpose of an ACD is to give better service to customers by handling their calls faster with shorter call-holding times. As the time to answer calls decreases, less of an opportunity is given to customers to take their business elsewhere. Also, reports provided by the ACD are invaluable to management in achieving this objective.

14.10 GATES

Many times, agents are divided into functional groups called gates or splits, and incoming calls are routed to the appropriate gate. Functional groups are categories such as sales agents, support agents, etc. As calls are received by the ACD, they are put in a queue or a waiting list. The calls are placed in this queue in the order they are received, just as customers in a bank lobby may form a line (or a queue) as they wait for a teller to serve them. The call waiting the longest in a queue is the first one to be connected to the next available agent.

Each gate in an ACD has its own queue of calls and if a queue in one gate gets too large or callers have to wait too long to be served, calls may overflow to other gates with shorter queues. Sometimes, calls from certain trunk groups may have a higher priority than the other calls, in which case, these calls may "cut in line" ahead of the calls already in queue. This is especially the case where overflow calls are redirected to other gates, since they have already waited on queue at the original gate. To handle overflow calls from other gates, agents should be trained to serve customers from gates other than their own.

This is analogous to a bridge which has separate lanes for cars and trucks. If there are too many trucks and only a few cars on the bridge, the lanes with the trucks become congested even though the car lanes are half empty. However, if cars and trucks are all allowed to share the lanes together, then chances of traffic congestion become less. Likewise, cross-training agents to handle calls from different gates prevents callers from having to wait on "eternity hold."

Overflowing of calls to other gates can be done manually by the call center manager or it can be done automatically. Automatic overflow is accomplished by programming the overflow threshold in two ways. One is based on the length of time a call is on hold, while the other is based on the number of calls that are on hold. Overflowing of calls from the primary gate to other gates within one ACD is called intrasystem overflow. Overflowing calls from one ACD to other ACDs is called intersystem overflow. Queue lengths can also be reduced by providing the caller with an option to leave a voice message, ask for a fax, etc.

14.11 THE TIME LINE

14.11.1 Network Setup

Figure 14.6 shows a timeline for an incoming call. Depending on the type of trunk being terminated at the ACD, time is required for setting up a connection.

Call centers may use WATS trunks to receive incoming calls, for which billing begins as soon as the ACD answers the call. If there are callers in the queue it is not necessary for the ACD to answer the call on the first ring, because the caller will be

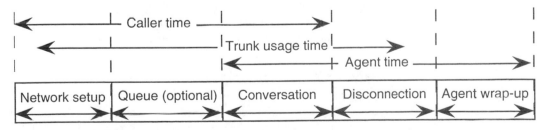

Figure 14.6 The time line of an incoming call showing the components of the call process.

placed on hold anyway. By allowing the phone to ring a few times before placing it on hold, trunk costs can be reduced.

14.11.2 Queuing

Queue time is an important part of the timeline. For every caller who hangs up because of being placed on hold too long, less revenue is received by the company. Most people will wait on hold for 40 seconds without music and 60 seconds with music. Typically, systems are configured so that callers wouldn't have to wait for over 20 seconds on hold.

Of course, as more agents are added (more trunks also have to be added) the smaller the queue length becomes and fewer calls are on hold. This is desirable during the busy hours; however, for most of the day when the call center is not busy, more agents and trunks will be idle. Therefore, the call center manager must juggle these items so that calls are not lost due to inadequate resources (trunks and agents), and expenses are not wasted due to insufficient call volume. Queuing helps to make efficient use of agents and trunks, and ACD reports provide the data for management to adjust these numbers.

Many call centers keep historical data for months and years to help predict the number of agents required for special times when business may be heavy.

If the ACD is integrated with the host, and ANI (Automatic Number Identification) is available, the ANI service provides a means for the host to know the complete phone number of the caller, regardless of where the caller is located in the country. The host then can look up the phone number in its database and identify the caller and search for the caller's record, if the caller is a previous customer. So while the customer is in queue and on hold, the host is actually doing work and getting the record.

Now when the call is forwarded to an agent, the data record from the host is also forwarded to the agent's screen. This simplifies the agent's work, gives faster service to the customer, and frees up the trunk sooner. This is an example of switch-to-host integration. If ANI is not available, a VRU can prompt the caller to enter his/her identification number while on hold to provide the same record look-up service.

14.11.3 Conversation

If the average call duration is two minutes, which is typical, then the trunk to agent ratio should be about 1.2 : 1. For applications where the call duration is only .5 seconds, such as credit card verification, this ratio can be as high as 3.0 : 1. That is, for every agent that is present, there are 3 trunks that are available.

14.11.4 Disconnection and Wrap-up Time

After the conversation is over, the ACD can signal the CO to disconnect the call as soon as the agent hangs up instead of waiting for the caller to hang up. This frees up the trunk sooner for a new call. The agent can press a special key to make himself or herself unavailable for calls while finishing up the paperwork associated with the previous call.

14.12 ACD FEATURES

Out of more than 130 features available on ACDs, only a very small sampling is listed here; first some call handling features are given, then some management information features are given.

14.12.1 Call Handling Features

Direct Outward Dialing: Without the assistance of an operator, agents can make outside calls.

Incoming Call Identification: A message either in the headset or on the agent console or terminal identifies the caller's city or the trunk group. This helps the agent to know some information about the caller before the conversation begins.

Prioritization of Trunk Groups: This enables preferred customers or certain trunk groups to have shorter holding times than other callers.

Call Forcing: This allows the ACD to route the next incoming call to an agent as soon as he or she hangs up. Without this, after an agent completes a call, a button is pressed to signal the ACD that he is ready for the next call.

14.12.2 Management Information Features

Management Information Reports: These are just as important to call centers as call processing features. There are all types of reporting available with ACDs: ones that are standard and ones that are customer specific; ones that are generated at any time interval (from real-time data and hourly reports to annual reports) to those that are generated by every split, every trunk, every agent, or every system.

Agent-level Reports: These provide the number of calls handled, average conversation length, average time spent in wrapping up calls, amount of breaks taken, and any such imaginable items. Although an agent who handles more calls doesn't necessarily make more sales, he or she may provide better, personalized service to the customers.

Queued Call Reports: These specify the number of calls on hold per gate in increments of say 5 minutes. These reports also provide the average time a caller waits before the call is answered or before the caller abandons the call (hangs up).

Trunk Activity Reports: These indicate when all trunks in a trunk group are busy, how many trunks were out and at what times, and so on.

14.13 ACD NETWORKING

Figure 14.7 shows a network of ACDs linked together with tie-lines. A network control center that Rockwell calls an RMC (Resource Management Center) is a minicomputer where the activities of the ACDs are monitored and controlled by the

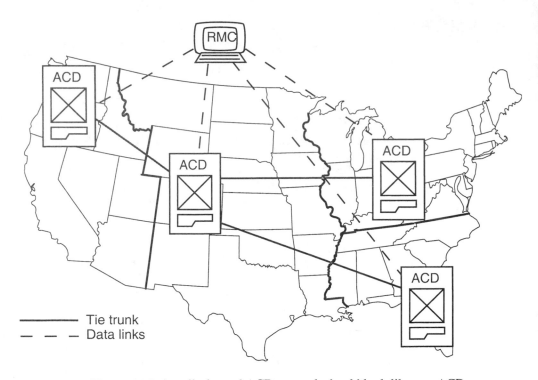

Figure 14.7 A well-planned ACD network should look like one ACD rather than separate ones.

network manager. The RMC is connected to all of the ACDs with X.25-type data links. These networks can comprise from 2 to about 20 linked ACDs, and usually, each switch serves one area of the country.

14.13.1 Advantages

The foremost reason for networking ACDs is the ability to generate one comprehensive report to include the activities of all of the switches. ACDs that are isolated from each other would generate a number of separate reports, making it necessary for someone to sort out the data manually. This could take days or weeks. Having one single report to present to upper management is much more desirable. This provides the network managers with up-to-the-minute reports and enables them to make wise decisions that will impact the health of the entire call center system.

Overflow and diversion are the next important reasons to network ACDs. Overflow means that if one call center is swamped with calls, perhaps because of some product promotion in that area, calls can automatically be directed to other centers with a lighter load. Managers can set up service level thresholds. A 100% service level indicates that all of the calls are being answered and none are being abandoned. Typically, a service load of 85% is chosen. In this case, when the service level approaches this amount, calls are switched automatically to other centers. Diversion means that all calls to a gate or an ACD are directed to another ACD.

As the analogy of sharing lanes by trucks and cars was applied to overflowing calls from one split to another, so can it be applied here where calls can be overflowed from one system to another. If there are 500 agents on each of the 10 isolated ACDs, then each ACD has a maximum of 500 agents available, even if agents on other ACDs are idle. By networking the ten ACDs, however, resources are shared and we have one large system with 5000 agents available.

Networking allows workload to be distributed between call centers. If one area has a number of agents absent due to a flu of some kind, other centers can relieve such a center. Networking also adds reliability to the system in that if one center is down, calls from that center can be diverted to other locations.

Another advantage is that it is easier to staff the centers to provide 24-hour service to callers. With isolated ACDs, every center must be manned 24 hours a day to provide round the clock service. However, when networking, as in Figure 14.5, agents on the east coast can start going home at 5 PM because on the west coast it is only 2 PM, and agents are available there to handle the east coast calls. Similarly, as the east coast agents are available at 9 AM, they can handle the 6 AM west coast calls. Although international ACD networks are a rarity, they could provide much easier round-the-clock service than domestic networks.

14.13.2 ACD Network Links

About half of all ACD networks use T1 tie-lines for interswitch links, although they are costly and not as flexible as DDD service. ACDs provide direct T1 interfaces and analog trunks are not as desirable to provide access to ACDs, because they are subject to electrical noise and excessive signal level loss.

Other ACD networks use DDD services to distribute the calls among the various ACD sites. This is done via a terminal such as AT&T's Routing Control Service terminal. If one ACD center is flooded with calls while the others are not, the terminal allows the network manager to redirect 800 number calls from one ACD to another within five minutes from when the change was made. The change actually affects the SCP (Signal Control Point) of the IXC where the customer's networking data is stored.

At one time, different areas of the country had their corresponding 800 numbers to dial and if an ACD needed the capacity to accept calls from other areas it would need a separate trunk group for every such area. DNIS (Dialed Number Identification Service) avoids having to use separate trunk groups for every 800 number, because each 800 number can have its own 4-digit DNIS number. Now only one trunk group is necessary as the carrier transmits the four DNIS digits to the ACD before each incoming call.

DNIS typically consists of four digits, but the public network is capable of sending up to seven. It can also be used to identify the area code or groups of area codes that a call originated from. Now when a call comes into an ACD, the DNIS signals the ACD where the call is coming from and this information can be provided to the agent's headset or on his or her data terminal. Knowing where the call is coming from allows the agent to be properly oriented and to serve the customer better. This information is also collected by the ACD MIS system or the host database and is used for market research.

14.14 INTERACTIVE VOICE RESPONSE (IVR) SYSTEMS

As seen in the last section, call centers employ agents who take calls through an ACD and fulfill the requests or transactions through a host. This section introduces the technology that sets forth to automate this process of interfacing callers to hosts, without requiring any call center agents.

So back in Figure 14.5, think of the six agents and their related equipment being replaced by one IVR unit. With a call center, the agents act as the translator between the voice of the caller and the data residing in a database, while the agents communicate with the computer using a data terminal. An IVR system inserted between the voice trunks and the host allows the callers to interact directly with the database. An IVR allows the caller's touch tone phone to be used as a data terminal and the IVR does the translation between the voice (which includes the DTMF pulses) of the caller and the data of a host. With a call center, the agents interact with a host and interpret what they see on their monitors. An IVR using synthesized voice can "read off" what would normally be seen on an agent's screen. If the caller doesn't have a DTMF phone, the IVR can use voice recognition to interpret the caller's audible response. Pulse-to-tone converters can also be used to convert the dial pulsing to digits on a limited basis.

Many more people have access to a telephone than to a data terminal. IVR benefits both those who call and those who are called. It provides better and faster service to customers (less time on hold), and greater savings to companies who incorporate it.

But an IVR is capable of providing more functions than being a substitute to a call center. It can incorporate all of the voice processing technologies covered earlier in this chapter into one unit. It can be programmed using the C programming language, which can be time consuming, or it can be programmed using an application generation package. An application generation package uses prewritten macros (units of programming code) and menus to help the user create a set of instructions for the IVR, so that when a customer calls in, he or she is properly served. These instructions can be commands for a host, doing credit card verification, updating a database, or other such activities.

IVR makes a telephone appear as a data terminal to a host, and a host to appear as an agent to the caller. Some IVR systems provide simultaneous access to two different types of hosts, which is required for certain applications

IVR is interactive, which means that the user and the host "act upon each other." So as well as retrieving information through a host, IVR allows the user to command the host in return and is able to transfer money, to make payments to preauthorized vendors, or to place orders and perform other transactions. IVR systems allow college applicants to track their entrance applications or allow customers to get a status of an order or shipment.

14.15 CTI (COMPUTER TELEPHONY INTEGRATION)

14.15.1 What is CTI?

While IVR substitutes call center agents with technology, CTI realizes the importance of a personal touch and uses technology to aid agents and the calling customers. CTI (Computer Telephony Integration) makes the job of the agent more efficient, which enables the customer's calling experience to be more pleasurable. Efficiency of the call center is improved by integrating the voice switches, such as PBXs and ACDs, with database servers using a standard.

When a customer gives his address and personal information to an agent and that agent ends up transferring the call to a more specialized agent who is better suited for the call, we don't want to have the customer repeat his personal information for the new agent. When a customer calls into a call center and is placed on hold, from ANI (Automatic Number Identification) we can retrieve his records from a database server and have this information displayed on the agent's screen as soon as an agent becomes available. In CTI, these functions are called "screen pops." When a customer visits the company's web server and requires an immediate response to his question, CTI enables a seamless interface with the call center.

CTI provides automation to a call center by providing functional and physical integration. This automation is standardized so that not only can the large companies afford CTI, but smaller ones as well. When a switch needs to instruct a data server or when a server needs to respond to a switch with some piece of information, we need to define an API (Application Programming Interface). An API enables a voice switch and a data server to communicate with each other. Let us look at some standard APIs which are defined in the industry.

14.15.2 Standard APIs

When an operator receives a call at a PBX console, he can transfer the call or handle the call in a number of ways. When the call is connected to the correct party, the operator removes himself from the call. In this case the operator is called the *third* party.

On the other hand when an employee on an ordinary phone line transfers a call to another extension, the employee is thought of as a *first* party. A third party handling a call has more functions available than a first party does. This is because a third party has direct control of the entire PBX while an ordinary extension can control only the functions which are provided on its telephone line.

Two major CTI solutions are categorized in the same fashion: the first-party and the third-party approaches. The third-party approach is called TSAPI (Telephony Services API) and was formalized in 1992 by AT&T (now Lucent Technologies) and Novell. Lucent provided a CTI interface on their Definity switch while Novell provided the LAN software. Later other PBX manufacturers incorporated TSAPI. Prior to this, IBM had created CSA (CallPath Services Architecture) and also DEC which provided interfaces to various types of switches.

Figure 14.8(a) shows the TSAPI approach to CTI. The call center agent's phone and the PC are not directly connected. Voice and data paths are kept separate through individual networks. A special server called the CTI server connects the LAN to the voice switch through the TSAPI interface. Now, for instance, when an inbound call comes in, the switch can communicate with the database server to retrieve the customer record through the CTI server using ANI.

In 1993, Intel designed TAPI (Telephony Application Programming Interface) and Microsoft and other companies soon joined this approach to CTI. TAPI provides a first-party call control model and is shown in Figure 14.8(b). Notice the absence of a CTI server here. Also notice that the communication between the database server and the voice switch is done through the telephone line and no special physical interface is required on the voice switch. Voice and data signals are transported over the same phone line. Windows programmers can access the switch through the DLL (Dynamic Link Library). Applications that are written for TAPI only work under Windows.

TMAP (Tapi-to-tsapi MAPping) translates TAPI to TSAPI to some degree, but does not provide full CTI control in itself. An API that does not compete with any of these APIs is called JTAPI (Java Telephony API). This API exists on top of TSAPI and TAPI and provides multivendor telephony applets that work on practically all platforms. Sun, Lucent, Dialogic (now part of Intel), Intel, IBM, and Nortel were the first developers of JTAPI.

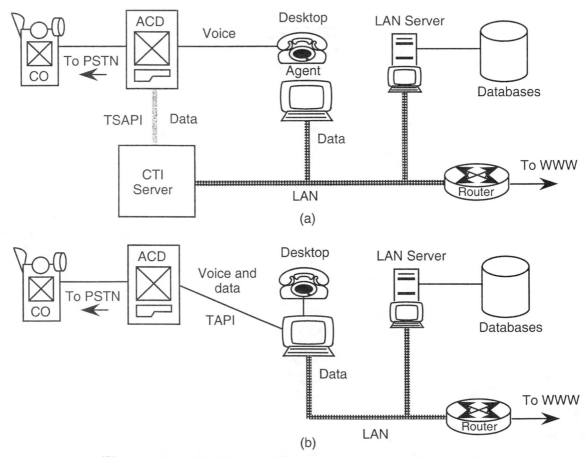

Figure 14.8 (a) TSAPI uses a CTI server that controls both the switch and the data server. (b) TAPI uses the telephone line to directly connect the CTI application on the PC to the switch.

Other developments in CTI include the formation of ECTF (Enterprise Computer Telephony Forum) in 1995. The S.100 and H.100 are two important specifications that have been standardized by ECTF. JAIN (Java Api for Integrated Networks) is based on a JavaBeans component architecture that integrates AIN (Advanced Intelligent Networks), traditional wireline and wireless networks, and Internet-based networks.

14.15.3 CTI and the Web

Traditionally a customer called into the call center using the PSTN, maybe by calling an 800-type number. Now customers can gain access to the call center through the enterprise web server. There might be a "Call Me" icon on the web page which requests a calling agent to call the customer on his telephone line while he is connected to the web page over his data line. Text and other information can be shared very easily between the calling agent and the customer when they are looking at the same "screen." This feature is called Web Callback.

Instead of the agent calling back on a phone line, a customer may request that a chat session be set up. In that case, the two can chat and the agent can help answer the customer's questions while referring to the same page in a catalog. When a customer does not have separate voice and data lines (or channels) a chat session is appropriate.

A Web Callthrough may also be possible. This feature uses the H.323 standard of sending voice over the Internet connection, or VoIP (Voice over IP). This way, the customer can stay connected to the web server while talking with a call agent.

EXERCISES

For questions 1 through 4, match the description with the correct voice processing system.

a. voice mail   b. automated attendant
c. audiotext   d. voice response unit
e. interactive voice response unit   f. transaction processing
g. voice recognition

1. By use of a keypad, certain stocks owned by a user are sold.
2. By dialing, the user hears a prerecorded weather forecast for the day.
3. By use of the keypad, data is selected and retrieved from a database.
4. Messages of the caller are stored here if the called party is unavailable.
5. What is call processing?
   a. It is NOT the same as voice processing.
   b. It is the same as call accounting where statistics are kept of who called whom, at what time, and for how long.
   c. It is a type of automated system, which completes calls coming in without human assistance.
   d. It is the technology which processes voice in analog form into digital form.
6. What type of call distribution system always forwards the incoming calls to a certain set of agents?
   a. ACD   b. UCD
   c. call sequencer   d. IVR

7. Which of the following phases of the ACD time line does not include the agent's time?
   a. disconnection
   b. wrap-up
   c. queue
   d. conversation
8. Which of the following ACD features describes the maximum time a caller was placed on hold during the day?
   a. incoming call identification
   b. queued call reports
   c. trunk activity reports
   d. agent-level reports
9. Functionally, what is the opposite of speech synthesis?
10. Give two examples of information providers.
11. What is the name of the effect caused by many incoming calls being switched by a few attendants?
12. For 400 users, how many hours of memory and how many ports are typically needed?
13. Which automated attendant feature will record the name of the caller and ask the called party if he or she wants to answer the call?
14. ACDs were first used in which industry?
15. One reason to network ACDs is to direct calls to other centers when the primary center is being flooded with calls. What is this feature called?
16. What type of telemarketing system simply dials more numbers than there are agents available, without relying on the current activity of the center?
17. Why are voice messages stored on DASDs (Direct Access Storage Devices) ?
18. Give reasons to network VM.
19. Give reasons for networking ACDs.
20. Explain the differences and similarities between ANI and DNIS.
21. What is gating? How does that improve the operation of a call center?
22. Why do you think IVR systems are on the rise, while VM systems have plateaued out?
23. What is the difference between ACDs, UCDs, and ACSs?
24. What does CTI provide that IVR doesn't?
25. Which CTI solution provides third-party call control? Why is this called third-party?
26. List some CTI standards.
27. Are you aware of any web-based call center functions that have emerged but are not mentioned in this chapter? If so, what are they?

Chapter 15

T1 Networking

15.1 ADVANTAGES

15.1.1 Savings in Operating Costs

Savings in operating costs is only one reason why companies have converted to T1s. T1 multiplexers and bandwidth managers can cost up to $100,000 per location; still, within one year the savings in phone bills can pay for this investment.

15.1.2 Simplification

T1 circuits allow networks to be simplified. In Figure 15.1, Seattle and Minneapolis locations are linked together using separate lines. The two PBXs require 12 voice circuits, the four CAD (Computer Aided Design) circuits run at 56 kbps, some synchronous terminals need a number of 9600 bps lines, and a group IV fax circuit requires another 56 kbps line.

Figure 15.2 shows how the same applications can be integrated by using only one T1. This one circuit is much more easily managed, monitored, and controlled than many discrete circuits. In this example, the 12 voice-grade circuits occupy 12 DS-0 (Digital Signal level 0) channels, the five 56-kbps channels occupy 5 DS-0s, and the three 9.6-kbps channels can be subrate multiplexed into one DS-0 channel. This makes a total of 18 (12 + 5 + 1) DS-0 channels. Multiplexing these on one T1 link, which provides 24 DS-0s, provides 6 spare DS-0 channels for future expansion. This assumes standard T1 formatting. If proprietary formatting is used, even more capacity can be gained in one T1 circuit.

Here we have simplified only a two-point network. Imagine the simplification achieved by converting a 15- or even a 100-node network to all T1s. This advantage, gained by simplifying the network, introduces yet other T1 advantages.

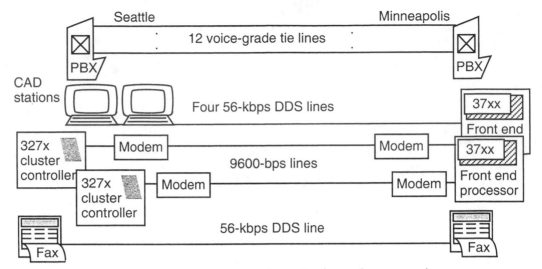

Figure 15.1 Discrete lines for each application make a two-point network difficult to manage.

15.1.3 Reliability

Managers all agree that reliability is far more important than cost savings for most networks. When a network goes down, it reflects upon the manager's competence. Revenue is lost every minute the network is down, and can very easily exceed the savings achieved by converting to T1s.

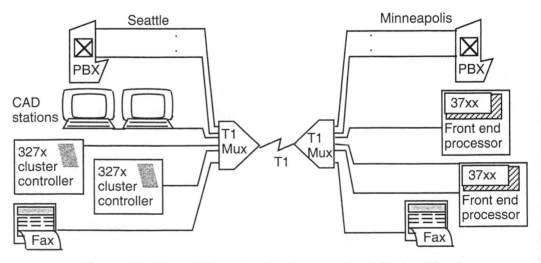

Figure 15.2 Consolidating all applications on a single T1 simplifies the network substantially.

T1 Networking

One may think that a loss of one circuit in Figure 15.1 is not as serious as the loss of the T1 in Figure 15.2. However, to introduce redundancy in Figure 15.1, all circuits would need redundant circuits, whereas with a T1, only one redundant circuit is needed. In a T1 network, there are several routes available between any two nodes, so that if the primary route fails, an alternate route can be selected automatically.

IXCs provide inherent redundancy when purchasing a T1. Now if the IXC's portion of the T1 link fails, the link is automatically rerouted within a second. Normally, the access portion of a link is the weakest, and spare circuits should be leased or alternate routes should be explored through the use of CAPs (Competitive Access Providers) or other methods. Remember, if a cable is cut that houses both the active and the spare pair, then probably both will get cut. Similarly, if both the LEC's and the CAP's cables go over the same bridge or area, then at that point a catastrophe may knock out both access networks. In other words, ordering extra lines even from different carriers doesn't necessarily prevent a failure.

In Figure 15.3, if the link from A to D fails, then the T1 multiplexers can be programmed to route traffic through points B and C automatically. If not enough capacity is available on the alternate path, then less important circuits can be "bumped off" the network to make room for the important A to D circuits. Priorities of the circuits, of course, have to be determined and preprogrammed.

The control cards, data switching components, power supplies, and all critical components of the T1 muxes should be duplicated. Port cards are not duplicated unless the equipment they are connected to is also protected from failure or if they support many channels. Components which are duplicated, if not continuously tested, may fail when needed.

15.1.4 Network Control

T1 networks are not engraved in stone. They are flexible and can be changed as necessary. This gives the network user more control over the network. Certain circuits can be temporarily disconnected to create bandwidth for a videoconference channel.

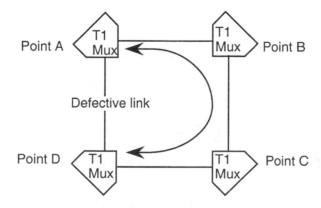

Figure 15.3 With alternate paths available in a network, traffic between two points can be automatically rerouted when a link fails. Here traffic between points A and D is routed through points B and C.

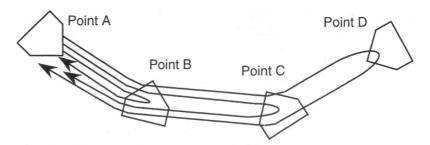

Figure 15.4 Remote loopback tests initiated from point A can help to isolate a faulty link. A loopback test usually sees if the transmitted signal pattern is received on the receive side. In this example, if the loopbacks are good to points B and C, but not to D, then a fault lies in the link between C and D.

Once the conference is over, normal traffic can be restored on the network. Similarly, at night during a certain time frame, a large chunk of the bandwidth can be automatically allocated for backing up a data center. To see if productivity at branch centers can be increased by increasing the terminal data transfer rates, then it can be easily tried. If no improvement is noticed, then the transfer rates can be configured back to what they were.

A major advantage in controlling a T1 network is achieved by having a control management center. No longer are network operators depending on personnel at remote sites to physically place a jumper on the right pins to provide a loopback test on a circuit or to physically rewire a circuit to reroute it on a different leg of the network. Instead, the operator using a management console at the central site can signal the T1 equipment to provide loopbacks, reroute channels, obtain line quality statistics, and so on.

Figure 15.4 shows how remote loopback tests can be performed from point A to points B, C, and D. By knowing the loop-codes for the T1 devices in the path, devices can be forced into a loopback mode one at a time, and tested to see if a transmitted test pattern matches the received one. If the tests are good to B and C but not to D, the problem is determined to be between C and D. Proper parties can be notified without much dispute between the vendors and the carriers.

Back in the setup of Figure 15.2, there is more than 6 DS-0s' worth of bandwidth available. So if new circuits are to be installed, the capacity is already there and one doesn't have to wait for the carriers to get around to installing the circuits.

15.2 T1 SIGNAL TRANSMISSION

15.2.1 DS-1 over Various Media

Originally, T1 circuits used two pairs of copper wire to send 1.544 Mbps in each direction. This was done by removing loading coils and inserting repeaters every mile, which is the typical distance between manholes in city streets. These DS-1 signal rates can be sent over other mediums as well. Coaxial cable repeaters are needed every 40 miles. Fiber repeaters are used every 30 to 100 miles. DS-1s can also be transmitted using microwave or satellites. However, transmission of DS-1 rates over any of these mediums is currently called T1.

15.2.2 The Bipolar Format

The maximum distance that T1s could be transmitted over copper was doubled to 1 mile by sending the signals in a bipolar format, as shown in Figure 15.5(a). This was due to improved synchronization. The bipolar method alternates the voltage for every mark between +3V and −3V. It is also called AMI (Alternate Mark Inversion). This provides a built-in error detection scheme. If a bit is lost due to an error, that is, if a 1 is misinterpreted as a 0 or vice versa, then two consecutive pulses of the same polarity is detected and it is flagged as an error. This event is called a bipolar violation (BPV), since it violates the rule of alternating the polarity of marks.

For example, in Figure 15.5(a), if the first −3V pulse is lost, then a bipolar violation occurs at the second +3V pulse, as shown in Figure 15.5(b). Also, if the third 0 is lost and becomes a 1 then a bipolar violation is detected at the fourth +3V pulse.

From Figure 15.5(b), notice that every mark provides one transition between plus or minus 3V and 0V. These transitions aid the receiver to keep its clock synchronized with that of the transmitter. So T1s use a rule that is called the "ones density rule" to ensure that the receiver stays synchronized. This rule requires that on the average, at least 1 out of every 8 bits, or a minimum of 12.5% of the bits should be marks.

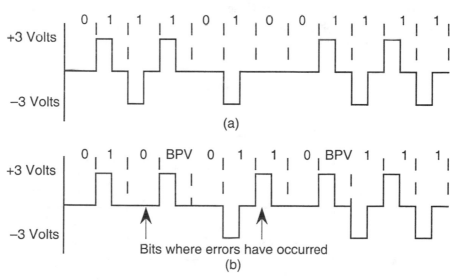

Figure 15.5 (a) The bipolar format of a T1 signal enforces the polarity of every logical 1 to be opposite that of the previous logical 1. A logical 0 is always represented by 0 volts. (b) Due to errors on the line, if the second 1 in (a) is misinterpreted as an 0 or if the third 0 in (a) is misinterpreted as a 1, then in either case the bipolar rule is violated. This is called a bipolar violation or a BPV for short.

15.2.3 The B8ZS Technique

Figure 15.6(a) shows that nine consecutive zeros are to be transmitted in the data stream. They will provide no voltage level transitions. With so many zeros, the receiving clock may drift and interpret them as being either 8 or 10 zeros instead. What the signal needs here is some marks to keep the receiver synchronized so as to maintain the ones density rule.

Digitized voice, according to the encoding scheme, doesn't allow 8 successive zeros. With data, however, a long string of zeros is quite possible. As we'll see later, 56-kbps DDS (Digital Data Service) channels use only 7 bits out of every 8 possible bits to send data so that a mark can be forced at every 8th position to accommodate the ones density rule.

Another method of enforcing the ones rule is shown in Figure 15.6(b). With this method, the transmitter, when noticing 8 successive zeros, will induce BPVs at the 4th and 7th zeros and AMI compatible marks at the 5th and the 8th zeros. This is a code that signals the receiver that the BPVs are not really data errors but that this pattern replaces a string of zeros in the data instead. So the receiver will convert this pattern back to 8 zeros before forwarding the data to the terminal device. See Figure 15.6(d). This technique is called B8ZS (Binary 8 Zero Substitution) and it enables T1 to transmit consecutive zeros while still keeping the T1 equipment synchronized.

15.3 FRAMING TYPES

As covered in Chapters 2 and 3 and as outlined in Figure 15.7, a T1 channel bank receives 24 voice channels. Each channel is sampled 8000 times a second and 8 bits are used to encode the voltage level at each sample yielding a 64-kbps rate per channel,

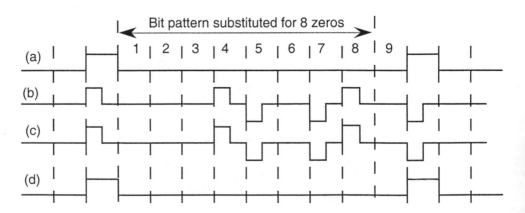

Figure 15.6 (a) Data with 8 or more consecutive zeros being sent to a T1 mux. (b) Signal being sent over the T1 span, where BPVs are inserted at the 4th and the 7th zeros to signal a stream of zeros. (c) The transmitted signal being received at the distant mux. (d) It determines the BPVs at the 4th and 7th positions as a signal for consecutive zeros and provides the original data stream to the terminal equipment.

using PCM. The 24 voice circuits with 64 kbps each require a total of 1.544 Mbps of bandwidth. This rate is obtained by multiplying 64 kbps by 24 and adding 8 kbps for framing purposes. Framing allows the receiving equipment to know which bits belong to which channel, and so on. Let us now look at how these bits are organized or framed.

15.3.1 The D4 Frame

Figure 15.7 shows how one D4 frame is constructed. It combines one sample or 8 bits from each of the 24 channels, yielding a total of 192 bits. One bit is used for framing so that the receiver knows where a frame starts and ends. So one D4 frame occupies a total of 193 bits. A time slot is considered to be one sample or 8 bits.

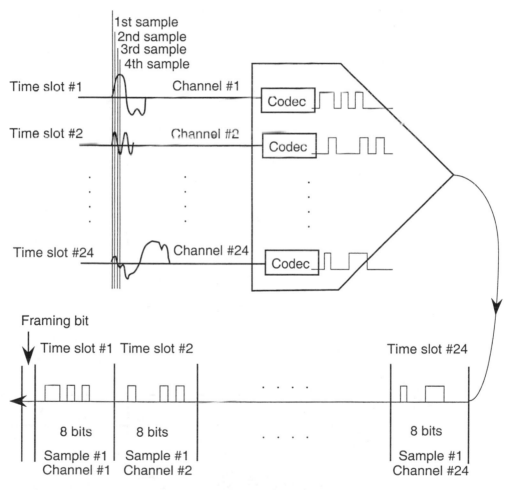

Figure 15.7 The codecs in the I/O ports of a T1 mux digitize up to 24 voice channels. In D4 framing, the corresponding 8-bit samples from each of the 24 channels are multiplexed using byte interleaving. Together with one framing bit, the D4 frame requires 193 bits.

Notice also that the data stream is byte interleaved and not bit interleaved. This means that the first byte from channel 1 is placed first, then the first byte from channel 2, and so on. A frame that is bit interleaved places all the first bits from the 24 channels first, then all the second bits, and so on.

15.3.2 The Superframe (SF)

An SF (SuperFrame), shown in Figure 15.8, is composed of twelve of these D4 frames. So a superframe consists of 12 voice samples from each of the 24 voice channels. With 12 framing bits, this makes an SF 2,316 bits long. The framing bits, which are always "100011011100," allow the receiver to know where the frame starts and where it ends. Notice that the 1s and 0s come in groups of 1s, 2s, and 3s. The framing bits allow the receiver to block off frames and maintain logical synchronization.

	F	Channel #1 1 2 3 4 5 6 7 8	Channel #2 1 2 3 4 5 6 7 8	. . . . .	Channel #24 1 2 3 4 5 6 7 8
D4 frame #1	1				
D4 frame #2	0				
D4 frame #3	0				
D4 frame #4	0				
D4 frame #5	1				
D4 frame #6	1	A	A	. . . . . .	A
D4 frame #7	0				
D4 frame #8	1				
D4 frame #9	1				
D4 frame #10	1				
D4 frame #11	0				
D4 frame #12	0	B	B	. . . . . .	B

Figure 15.8 An SF (Super Frame) combines 12 D4 frames as depicted in Figure 15.7. An SF contains 12 voice samples from each of the 24 voice channels with framing bits as shown. Also, the 8th voice bit in every 6th sample is preempted to place a signaling bit instead. This is called robbed-bit signaling.

The least significant bit of every 6th D4 frame is used for signaling that channel. This one bit that originally came from a voice sample is lost and signaling information is placed here instead. As mentioned in Chapter 5, this is called robbed-bit signaling.

With voice (or video), if a bit is lost in every 6th byte, the ear (or the eye) cannot notice it; however, when data is integrated with voice in a T1 multiplexer, one cannot afford to lose any data bits, because an error in data can mean the wrong character is displayed on a monitor, a check is drawn on the wrong amount, or any other such abnormalities.

So in order to send data through a T1 link, only the first 7 bits of each time slot are used and the 8th bit is forced to a 1. This prevents data from using the signaling bits. Therefore, the highest data rate through one DS-0 channel is not 64 kbps but 7/8th of that, which is 56 kbps. This restriction applies only to signals being processed by classical channel banks and not by proprietary T1 muxes.

15.3.3 Extended SuperFrame (ESF)

Figure 15.9 shows an extended superframe (ESF), which is twice as large as an SF. Here, instead of 2 signaling bits per frame per channel, there are four, labeled A through D. Also, there are 24 framing bits instead of the 12 with SF.

Out of these 24 bits, only 6 are used for logical synchronization, whereas the SF used all of its 12 bits. This provides 18 bits per frame for other purposes. This includes 6 bits for error checking using the CRC (Cyclic Redundancy Check) method.

The remaining 12 bits are used to implement a T1 management channel called FDL (Facilities Data Link). Depending how the bits are set on this channel, line quality statistics can be obtained while live traffic is being sent over the T1. By means of a loop-up code sent over the FDL, distant equipment can be signaled into a loopback mode. Similarly, sending a loop-down code over the FDL can signal it back into normal service. These features make the ESF format a preferred method of transmitting T1s.

15.3.4 Other Framing Formats

When the DS-0s of a T1 circuit are switched in the public network, it is necessary that it conform to D4, SF, ESF framing. If it is a dedicated T1 link, however, then any format can be implemented by the user to gain more bandwidth efficiency. This is as long as the end equipment is compatible and the T1 is framed. For the end equipment to be compatible it is usually provided by the same vendor. A *framed* T1 means that every 193rd bit is a framing bit; how the data is organized in the other 192 bits is left up to the user. A *formatted* T1, also called channelized T1 or DS-1, means that the T1 is bundled into 24 DS-0s and is used mostly for voice. A framed T1, however, can be used to send signals of any rate, such as 256 kbps or 768 kbps, as long as they fit in a DS-1. Because of fewer restrictions, a framed T1 can be easily used for many applications, including CAD or video.

A common interoffice voice formatting technique is the M44 format. This format, intended for voice, compresses 44 voice clear channels on one T1. See Figure 15.10. There is also an M48 format which uses robbed-bit signaling to place 48 voice channels on one T1.

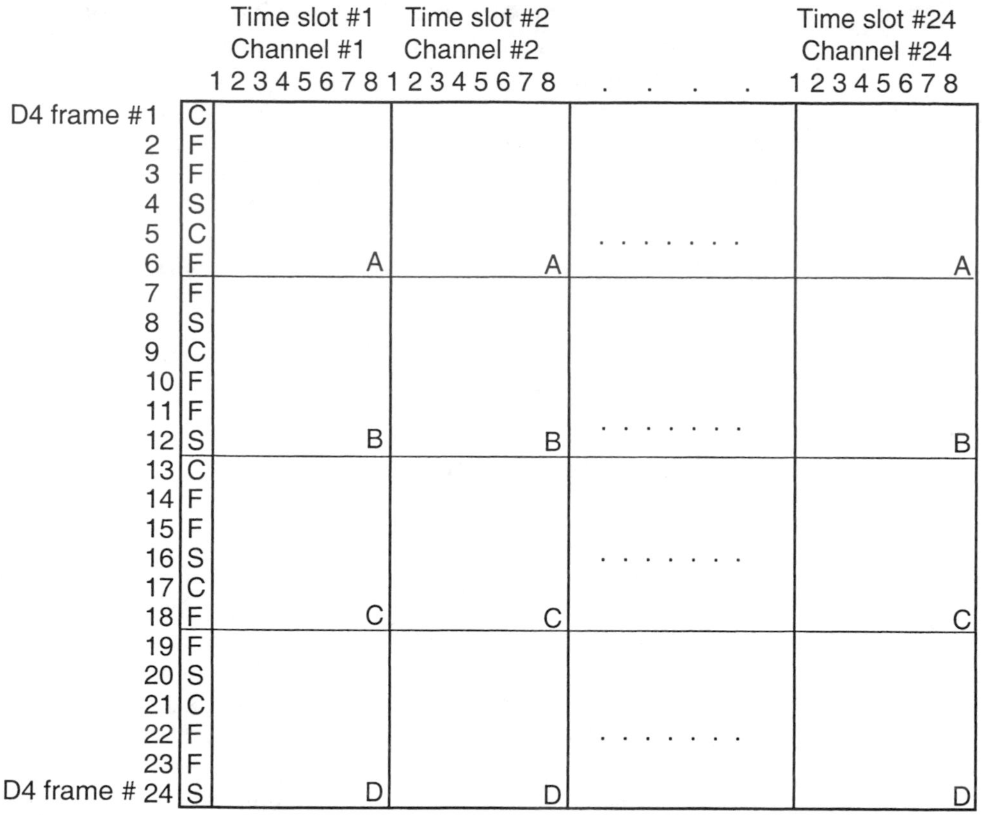

Time slot #1 Time slot #2   Time slot #24
Channel #1   Channel #2   Channel #24
1 2 3 4 5 6 7 8   1 2 3 4 5 6 7 8   . . . .   1 2 3 4 5 6 7 8

```
D4 frame #1   C
          2   F
          3   F
          4   S
          5   C
          6   F        A          A      . . . . . . . .        A
          7   F
          8   S
          9   C
         10   F
         11   F
         12   S        B          B      . . . . . . . .        B
         13   C
         14   F
         15   F
         16   S
         17   C
         18   F        C          C      . . . . . .            C
         19   F
         20   S
         21   C
         22   F
         23   F
D4 frame #24  S        D          D      . . . . . . . .        D
```

Figure 15.9 ESF uses only six "S" bits for synchronization and they are "001011." The "C" bits are used for error detection and the "F" bits are used for the FDL (Facilities Data Link) channel.

The M44 format divides T1's 24 DS-0 (64 kbps) channels in half, creating 48 32-kbps channels. These 48 channels are grouped in 4 bundles of 12 channels. Each bundle contains 11 voice channels using 32-kbps ADPCM coding, and one 32-kbps channel which contains the signaling for the other 11 channels. Since the voice bits are not robbed for signaling purposes, the voice channels are said to be clear. To send a 56-kbps data channel, one needs two of these 32-kbps channels.

The M44 format uses common channel signaling, which means that one common channel carries the signaling for the 11 voice channels in the bundle. Because the signaling is separated from the voice, channels cannot be switched at DS-0 levels. With M44, an entire bundle must be kept together while switching. If switching has to be done at DS-0 levels, the M44 format is changed to other formats, which include signaling with the voice.

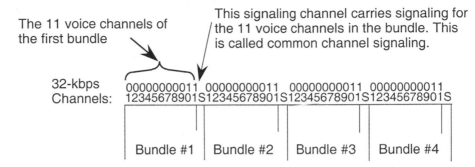

Figure 15.10 In the M44 format using ADPCM, each voice channel requires only 32 kbps of bandwidth. In one T1, there can be 48 of these channels, each running at 32 kbps. These 48 channels are divided into four bundles of 12 channels each. And in each bundle, there are 11 voice channels and one signaling channel.

15.4 NETWORK INTERFACING

15.4.1 At the Customer's End

The primary network interfacing device at the customer's end of a T1 span is the CSU/DSU (Channel Service Unit/Data Service Unit). This is a combination of a CSU and a DSU in one box. The CSU provides a means to obtain a network loopback, while the DSU provides a means for obtaining a local loopback to test the CPE. The CSU also helps to protect the network from sending undesirable conditions and regenerates the incoming signal. The DSU converts between unipolar and bipolar formats.

Figure 15.11 shows how a T1 line is brought to a customer's premises from the CO. At one time, the demarcation point was between the DSU and the CSU. Then the CO would send power over the T1 line to power up the CSU. This allowed the CO to perform a loopback test even if there was a power failure at the customer's site. Since then the FCC has allowed the customer to own both the DSU and the CSU, as long as it meets FCC specifications. Therefore, today the demarcation point (or demarc, for short) has moved to the network side of the CSU.

Now that the customer is powering the CSU, some telcos are installing a NIU (Network Interface Unit) or a smart jack at the customer's side to enable them to perform loopback tests even if the customer is without power.

One of the functions of the CSU is to keep the T1 "alive" in the event of a CPE failure. The keep alive signal tells the CO that the CPE has failed, and it isn't the telco's concern. A keep alive signal could be a loopback noticed by the CO, or it could be a continuous stream of ones either framed or unframed.

The CSU is also usually responsible for enforcing the ones density rule, either by the B8ZS method or some other method. It is also the last place where the incoming signal is regenerated and alarm conditions are indicated.

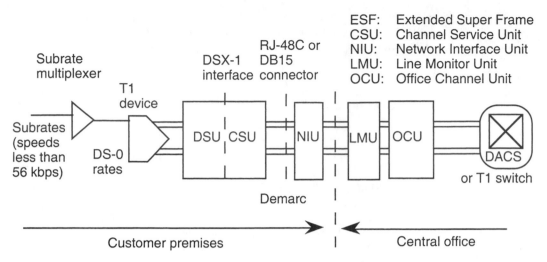

Figure 15.11 A T1 circuit requires only 2 pairs of copper wire, one to transmit and one to receive. Here, all of the T1 signal processing units are shown, both in the customer's premises and in the CO.

15.4.2 At the Telco's End

OCU (Office Channel Unit) is similar to a CSU, except it is located at the CO. Using a LMU (Line Monitor Unit), the CO can do a loopback test between the CSU and OSU. Of course, the T1 link has to come down for this test, if it isn't down already. While the line is active, the LMU can command the CSU using the FDL channel of the ESF to provide line quality statistics as needed.

15.5 T1 SWITCHING

15.5.1 Channel Banks, Muxes, and Switches

Initially, devices that combined 24 analog voice channels into a DS-1 rate were called channel banks. Channel banks were not able to multiplex data, because they were primarily a device for voice circuits. T1 multiplexers, on the other hand, generally accepted voice or data circuits. They also performed subrate multiplexing, i.e., multiplexed a number of data channels at slow speeds (2.4 kbps, 4.8 kbps, etc.) onto one DS-0 channel. One standard for this is called SRDM (SubRate Data Multiplexing). T1 multiplexers can be managed and controlled via a terminal where a channel bank, used for more stable networks, is controlled by setting DIP switches. Today, the distinction between channel banks and T1 multiplexers is becoming more blurred. Typically, a channel bank is inexpensive and a mux is more sophisticated. Bandwidth manager is a term used for high-end T1 multiplexers.

The "common" T1 multiplexers are also called M24 multiplexers for the number of voice channels they multiplex. The difference between a mux and a switch is that a mux will separate the incoming T1 into 24 DS-0 channels where each channel communicates with the corresponding channel on the far end. A T1 switch, on the other hand, is able to divert the channels with a rate less than or equal to 64 kbps in any order so that any channel on the transmitting end can connect with any channel on the receiving end.

15.5.2 Intermediate Node Switching

If two T1 circuits are connecting Denver, Omaha, and St. Louis as shown in Figure 15.12, we call the site at Omaha the intermediate node. Denver has some channels which terminate at Omaha, such as channel A, and some which continue on to St. Louis, such as channel B. Similarly, St. Louis has channels going to the other two destinations. The node at Omaha is then responsible for sorting out channels from both ends and either "dropping" them off at Omaha or passing them through over the "other" link.

15.5.3 D/I (Drop and Insert) Using Single-link Muxes

Figure 15.12 shows the "drop-and-insert" method of routing circuits using two single-link muxes. At Omaha only four channels are shown per T1 in the inset for

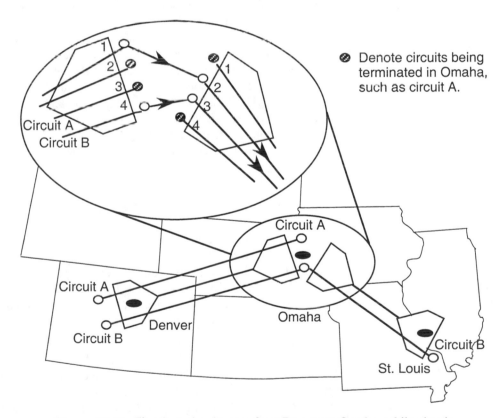

Denote circuits being terminated in Omaha, such as circuit A.

Figure 15.12 Circuit A simply goes from Denver to Omaha, while circuit B is first "dropped" in Omaha on channel 4 and then "inserted" in the link to St. Louis on channel 3.

convenience. In this arrangement, all circuits are demultiplexed down to the baseband level, which is the DS-0 level for channel banks and subrate channel level for muxes. These channels can be directed to their proper destinations from the I/O (Input/Output) ports on the muxes. The circuits that terminate in Omaha can simply be dropped there and the ones that need to continue over the next hop must be first dropped and then inserted. As an example, the B circuit in the diagram is dropped at channel 4 and then inserted in the second mux in channel 3.

This is the simplest switching method possible at an intermediate node, and it has some drawbacks. Namely, the cost of I/O ports for all of the channels becomes expensive, but more important is the "spaghetti tangle" created by the cables interconnecting the two multiplexers. It is also mandatory that all T1s be maintained in common synchronization, as well as use bit buffers.

Managing the circuits at this node can be difficult, especially if there are more than two T1 links to maintain. If one I/O port fails, someone may have to physically pull out the right cord and reinsert it in the proper jack. The job could have been easy and could have been done remotely from one central site, if the patch cords between the muxes were software controllable.

Another problem with this configuration is the introduction of quantizing noise in the voice channels. When voice is digitized, there is a slight amount of error introduced at each sample, and as the number of voice-to-digital conversions increases, this quantizing noise becomes significant. Our voice circuit B from Figure 15.12 will go through two voice-to-digital conversions (once at Denver and once at Omaha) and go through two digital-to-voice conversions (once at Omaha and once at St. Louis). This is also called D/A/D (Digital to Analog to Digital) conversion. Usually, a voice channel can go through three to five of these drop-and-insert nodes without experiencing any degradation. This is assuming that PCM is used. As the data rate of the voice channels is decreased below 64 kbps, the degradation becomes more acute.

15.5.4 Add and Drop

An add-and-drop device is also called a D/I multiplexer and it is shown in Figure 15.13 at Omaha. This configuration is logically similar to that of Figure 15.12, except that instead of having two multiplexers back to back, each with a single T1 link, here there is a single multiplexer with two T1 links.

Our single channel B from Denver goes through this equipment without being demultiplexed and multiplexed again in Omaha. Therefore, no I/O ports are needed for channels that are passed. Furthermore, since data bits are transmitted as they enter the node, no quantizing noise is introduced.

15.5.5 DACS (Digital Access and Cross-connect System)

With traditional private leased-line circuits, the end points are fixed. Figure 15.14 shows such a voice-grade tie-line from Denver to St. Louis going through distribution frames at the COs and POPs at the three cities. If that circuit had to be rerouted so that it goes from St. Louis to Minneapolis instead, the technicians at the necessary POPs and the COs would have to change jumper wires through their distribution frames to install the new path. This can take days to complete.

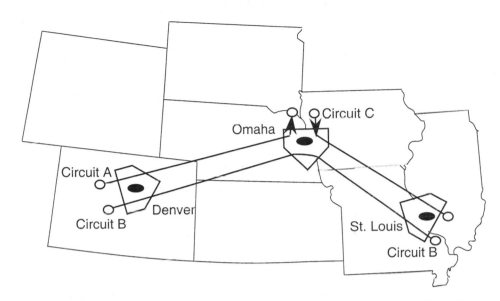

Figure 15.13 Omaha now has an add-and-drop type of multiplexer. Circuit B which originates at Denver is simply passed through to St. Louis without being demultiplexed. Circuit A is dropped in Omaha while circuit C is added there. (These are really two-way circuits.)

With T1s, the distribution frames and the "jungle of jumpers" at the COs and POPs are replaced with software-controlled distribution frames called DACS (also abbreviated as DCS). Now, as long as the Minneapolis site has access to its CO, carrier operators using a terminal can almost instantaneously signal the DACS in Omaha to switch the T1 to go from St. Louis to Minneapolis. Users truly appreciate the flexibility gained in private T1 networks by the use of these "electronic patch panels." Also, planning for disaster recovery is easily done through the use of DACS, since band-width-on-demand is available through DACS.

DACS switches circuits not only at DS-1 levels, but also at DS-0 levels. So if a user has many remote locations within a LATA, each with one DS-0 channel requirement, then without a DACS one would have to bring all these DS-0 channels to a customer premise, where they would be multiplexed and would then transmit the group of these channels to their destination as seen in Figure 15.15(a). However, with a DACS, the DS-0 channels can come directly to the POP where all the channels can be concentrated and then transmitted without the customer having to buy T1 gear. See Figure 15.15(b).

Because of DACS, private networks, instead of being "pinned up" for long periods of time, can now evolve into a "cloud" or into switched networks.

15.5.6 Proprietary Switching vs. DACS

However, DACS do have a few disadvantages. In-band signaling over the FDL channel cannot control the DACS. In fact, the DACS destroys the FDL bits for its own use making it useless for the end user. A separate signaling network to the DACS

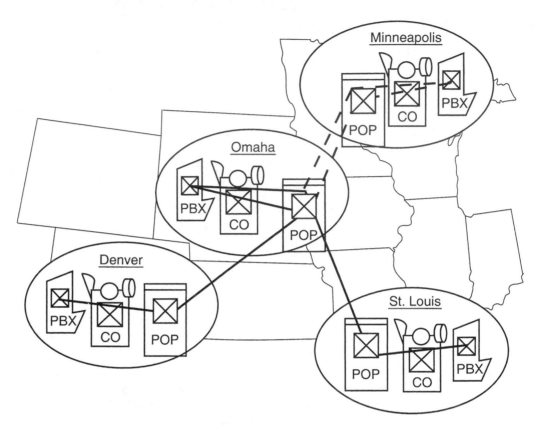

Figure 15.14 The solid line shows that installing a voice-grade tie-line from Denver to St. Louis via Omaha would have to utilize the distribution frames at all the POPs, COs, and customer locations. If this circuit had to be routed to Minneapolis instead of St. Louis, then the dotted line shows that jumpers at distribution frames would have to be installed at the POP in Omaha and at all three places in Minneapolis.

controller is needed so that the centralized management system can monitor and control it. When network maps are entered or changed they must be entered or changed by a technician through the use of a DACS controlling system. Unlike the way in which an in-band signaling channel can direct a T1 mux to change its configuration, the DACS needs separate links to control it by the end user.

DACS also cannot switch at rates below 64 kbps. So if one M44 T1 with 32-kbps voice channels must pass through a DACS, that T1 must be converted into two 24-channel T1s. Of course, only a total of 44 channels can be distributed between the two T1s. This type of conversion is done by BCMs (Bit Compression Multiplexers).

Switching through a DACS can be done either by a transparent connection or on a channel-by-channel basis. In a transparent connection, the D4 frames in one superframe don't necessarily stay in order, but the superframes are reassembled using a different order of D4 frames. This keeps the delay through the DACS to two byte-times. The

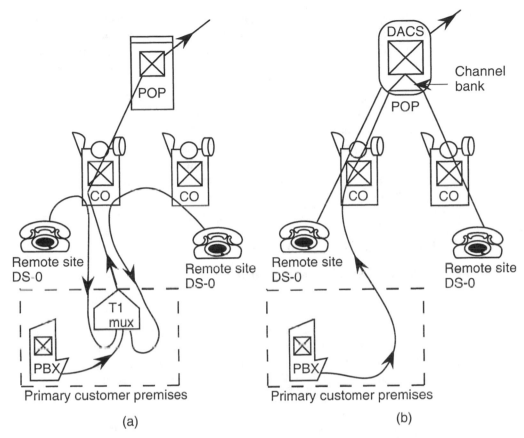

Figure 15.15 (a) Without a DACS, all remote site circuits have to be brought to the customer's premises in order to multiplex them on a T1 circuit. (b) With a DACS and a channel bank located at a POP, this isn't necessary.

channel-by-channel DACS connection preserves the content of each superframe, but that forces the delay through the DACS to be up to 48 byte-times.

DACS are primarily used by carriers and most of the limitations associated with them are not present in private networks, which use proprietary channel switching muxes. For instance, Timeplex's Link100 can switch channels at 400-bps granularity. This means that, while a DACS can switch channels in 64-kbps increments, the Link100 can switch them at 0.4-kbps increments. And while the DACS doesn't allow in-band signaling, proprietary muxes provide such capabilities.

15.5.7 CCR

AT&T has a computer located in Freehold, NJ, which controls all of its DACS nationwide. Other carriers also have similar setups. Using several levels of security, users can either dial up or have a direct access into this computer to change their own networks. The customer using a terminal located at his or her own premises can reconfigure the network as needed without having to wait for the carrier to do it. AT&T calls this service CCR (Customer Controlled Reconfiguration). MCI calls it Digital Reconfiguration Service.

A more sophisticated and expensive service by AT&T is called BMS-E (Bandwidth Management Service-Extended). It reconfigures even faster than CCR and also provides AAR (Automatic Alternate Routing), performance monitoring, traffic measurements, and self-initiated testing for the customer.

All carriers are developing management systems that allow customers to gain greater access to their facilities. Although these systems provide added control for private networks, they create a concern over the security and stability of the public network infrastructure.

15.6 NETWORK DESIGN CASE STUDY

15.6.1 Stating the Problem

Let us look now at a simple case study involving the design of a T1 backbone network.

Figure 15.16 shows the corporate office and the main data center in Kansas City for a certain retail store chain. Besides Kansas City there are 6 remote locations. There are four other regional distribution centers around the country with the corresponding number of stores or remote locations as shown. Atlanta, besides being a regional center, is also a backup data center where data is backed up from the main data center, in case Kansas City experiences failure.

The traffic engineering department has done extensive traffic analysis and has given us the requirements shown in Tables 15.1 and 15.2. The first row in Table 15.1 shows that we need seven 56-kbps channels from Kansas City to Atlanta, 3 to Seattle, 3 to Dallas, and 3 to New York. From Kansas City to Atlanta no 9.6-kbps channels are needed, but to Seattle, Dallas, and New York we need five 9.6-kbps channels each. Similarly, on the links from Atlanta to Seattle, Atlanta to Dallas, and Atlanta to New York we need three 56-kbps and five 9.6-kbps lines each.

The data requirements are for every store to have the following 9.6-kbps lines: two to Kansas City, two to Atlanta's data center, and five to its own regional distribution center. This information is not given in a table, but all these data requirements are summarized graphically in Figure 15.17.

Table 15.2 shows the voice channel requirements. From Atlanta to Kansas City there are 40 needed. From New York to Kansas City and Atlanta there are 20 and 25 required respectively, and so on. There are no entries in half of the table because these numbers are already provided in the other cells of the table. The remote stores don't have any voice tie-line requirements.

15.6.2 The Analysis

Table 15.3 shows the 9.6 kbps data requirements from each of the New York stores to its regional center and to Atlanta and Kansas City using the requirements

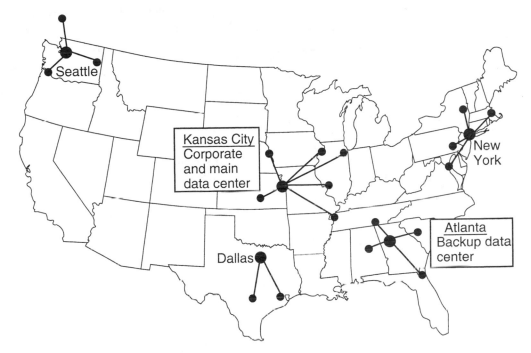

Figure 15.16 Traffic from the outlying locations is concentrated at the four regional centers and at one corporate center in Kansas City. The data center is located in Kansas City and its backup is located in Atlanta. We are about to create a T1 backbone network to support these access networks.

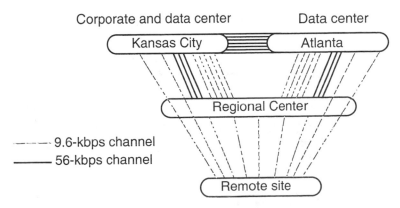

Figure 15.17 This summarizes the requirements for the case problem. From each remote site, there are two 9.6-kbps lines to each of the two data centers and five 9.6-kbps lines to the corresponding regional center. From each of the 3 regional centers, there are five 9.6-kbps and three 56-kbps lines to the two data centers.

Table 15.1 Regional's Data Requirements

From/To	AT	SE	DA	NY
KC 56k	7	3	3	3
KC 9.6k	0	5	5	5
ATL 56k	0	3	3	3
ATL 9.6k	0	5	5	5

Table 15.2 Regional's Voice Requirements

From/To	KC	AT	NY	SE
Atlanta	402	-	-	-
New York	0	25	-	-
Seattle	5	3	2	-
Dallas	11	9	7	1

Table 15.3 New York's 9.6k Requirements

From/To	AT	KC	NY
NY 1	2	2	5
NY 2	2	2	5
NY 3	2	2	5
NY 4	2	2	5

Table 15.4 Seattle's 9.6k Requirements

From/To	AT	KC	SE
SE 1	2	2	5
SE 2	2	2	5
SE 3	2	2	5

Table 15.5 Dallas' 9.6k Requirements

From/To	AT	KC	DAL
DAL 1	2	2	5
DAL 2	2	2	5

Table 15.6 Atlanta's 9.6ks

From/To	AT	KC
AT 1	7	2
AT 2	7	2
AT 3	7	2
AT 4	7	2

Table 15.7 KC's 9.6ks

From/To	AT	KC
KC 1	2	7
KC 2	2	7
KC 3	2	7
KC 4	2	7
KC 5	2	7
KC 6	2	7

given above. For example, from each of the 4 stores for New York (labeled NY1 through NY4), there are 5 lines going to the New York regional center and 2 each going to Atlanta and Kansas City. Refer to Figure 15.17.

Table 15.4 shows 3 rows for Seattle stores, because there are 3 stores in that region. Similarly, Table 15.5 for Dallas has 2 rows because only 2 stores are located in the Dallas region.

Notice that Table 15.6 for Atlanta, although it has 4 rows for each of the 4 stores, has only 2 columns: one for Atlanta regional and one to Kansas City corporate offices. From each store in the Atlanta region, we need five 9.6-kbps lines for the regional center and two 9.6-kbps lines for the backup center. Because the regional and the backup centers are the same for Atlanta, a total of 7 of these lines are needed.

For the same reason, the stores in Kansas City, as shown in Table 15.7, also only have 2 columns: one for lines to Atlanta and one for Kansas City.

Now let us reduce all traffic requirements in multiples of DS-0 levels, in order to design the backbone network. To do this, we'll assume PCM coding, which will require 64 kbps for each voice channel. For 56-kbps channels, we also need to dedicate an entire DS-0. Lastly, since a DS0 typically carries a maximum of 56 kbps of data, it can't support six 9.6 channels, which require 57.6 kbps (9.6 kbps times 6). So each DS-0 can carry only five 9.6-kbps channels.

Table 15.8 summarizes the total data requirements in terms of DS-0s between the cities. First let us look at how this requirement is 11 between Kansas City and Atlanta. From Table 15.1, there are seven 56-kbps channels required. Also, from Table 15.6, we need eight 9.6-kbps lines from each of the stores in Atlanta to Kansas City and from Table 15.7, we need twelve 9.6-kbps lines from each of the stores in Kansas City to Atlanta. The total number of 9.6-kbps lines between these cities is 20, which reduces the requirements to 4 DS-0s, given that each DS-0 supports only five 9.6 kbps-channels. So the 7 DS-0s due to the seven 56-kbps lines and the 4 DS-0s due to the twenty 9.6-kbps lines require a total of 11 DS-0s between the two cities.

Let us consider the requirement between New York and Atlanta, which is 6, in Table 15.8. From rows 3 and 4 of Table 15.1, we need three 56-kbps lines and five 9.6-kbps lines. This gives a total of 4 DS-0s for the New York regional center requirements.

Looking at Table 15.3, there are eight 9.6-kbps lines going from the stores to Atlanta, which is an additional 2 DS-0s; together with the first 4 DS-0s from Table 15.1, the total requirement is 6 DS-0s, as seen in Table 15.8.

Other numbers in Table 15.8 are calculated similarly. Notice that between New York, Seattle, and Dallas no requirements are given, so there are no DS-0s. Also, notice that the last column in Table 15.3, which is a column of 5s, does not get included in Table 15.8. This last column of 5s is the amount of bandwidth needed going to the New York center and does not go over the backbone network to the other cities, whereas the first two columns of 2s do go over the backbone network and get included.

Finally, Table 15.9 shows the total voice and data DS-0 requirements. This is obtained by adding the corresponding cells between Table 15.2 (the total voice requirements) and Table 15.8 (the total data requirements). For example, between Atlanta and Kansas City we need 40 DS-0s for voice from Table 15.2 and 11 DS-0s from Table 15.8 for data needed, giving a total of 51 DS-0s.

15.6.3 Design

The next phase of this case problem is to design the map of the network, realizing there are 24 DS-0s in each T1. Table 15.9 is used for this entire process. First we'll start off by placing a T1 link for the larger numbers in the table. So between Atlanta and Kansas City we need 2 T1s to start to accommodate the 51 DS-0s. There are 3 DS-0s (51 − (24 times 2 links)) that still need to be routed, so let's place a 3 with this link. See the Kansas City-Atlanta connection in Figure 15.18(a). Similarly, satisfying the large number requirements first, the rest of the links are introduced in Figure 15.18(a), where a positive number over a link is the additional number of DS-0s that still have to be routed and a negative number over a link specifies the number of spare DS-0s available.

For example, when placing T1 between Kansas City and Dallas for its 16 DS-0s, 8 spare DS-0s are still available so a −8 is placed over that link. Rates to Seattle may be higher than to other cities, so we want to limit the number of links there.

After satisfying the links shown in Figure 15.18(a), the entries, 9, 2, 7, and 1 of Table 15.9 remain to be accounted for in our network. The next largest number that needs to be taken care of is the 9 DS-0s between Atlanta and Seattle.

Let us place a third T1 link as shown in Figure 15.18(b) between Kansas City and Atlanta. Now the 3 between them shown in Figure 15.18(a) and the additional 9 going to Seattle take up 12 of the DS-0s over this new third T1 link. This leaves another 12 spare. For the Kansas City to Seattle link, the 9 channels from Atlanta need to be forwarded to Seattle. So now the number of spares from Kansas City to Seattle reduces to 4 from 13.

Figure 15.18(c) shows that the addition of 7 DS-0s between New York and Dallas is satisfied by adding another link from New York to Atlanta and then routing the 7 to Dallas from there. This reduces the number of spare DS-0s to 3 between Dallas and Atlanta. Furthermore, adding the 7 between New York and Atlanta that still needed routing in Figure 15.18(b) with the 7 going to Dallas takes up 14 DS-0s on the new T1 link, leaving 10 spares. This is shown in Figure 15.18(c).

Table 15.8 DS-0 Data Requirements				
From/To	KC	AT	NY	SE
Atlanta	11	-	-	-
New York	6	6	-	-
Seattle	6	6	0	-
Dallas	5	5	0	0

Table 15.9 Total DS-0 Requirements				
From/To	KC	AT	NY	SE
Atlanta	51	-	-	-
New York	26	31	-	-
Seattle	11	9	2	-
Dallas	16	14	7	1

T1 Networking

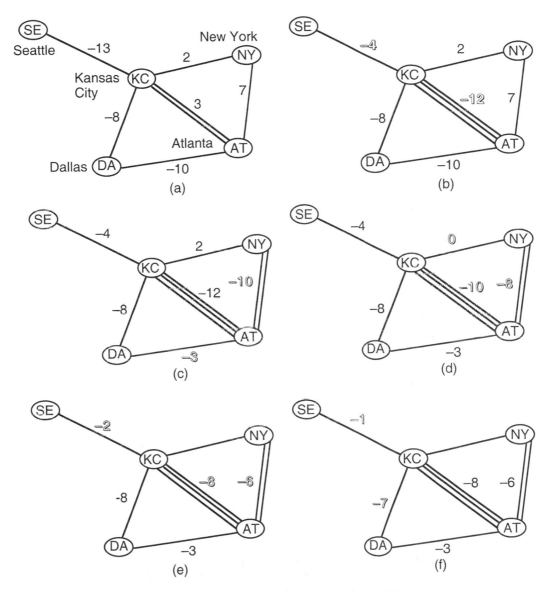

Figure 15.18 Positive numbers on the link show the additional number of DS-0s that still need to be satisfied, and the negative numbers show the spare number of DS-0s. The new values from the previous figure on each link are shown in bold. (a) The initial setup. (b) Add 9 channels from Seattle to Atlanta. Notice another T1 is added. (c) Add 7 channels from Dallas to New York by adding another T1. (d) Reroute the 2 channels needed between New York and Kansas City. (e) Add 2 from New York to Seattle. (f) Finally, add 1 from Seattle to Dallas.

Figure 15.18(d) shows the number of spares left after routing the 2 DS-0s from Figure 15.18(c) between New York and Kansas City via Atlanta. Figure 15.18(e) shows the map after adding 2 DS-0s required according to Table 15.9 from New York to Seattle via Atlanta and Kansas City. Finally, Figure 15.18(f) shows the network after adding the one DS-0 from Table 15.9 from Dallas to Seattle via Kansas City.

15.6.4 Additional Design Issues

The final network achieved here is not necessarily the best solution. There are other solutions that may be better; after experience one can approach optimizing the solution. However, there are a few important concepts that should be emphasized here. One is that no T1 tariffs were taken into account. These would have to be obtained before designing such a network. The link between New York and Kansas City is packed, while there is ample capacity via Atlanta. Traffic should be balanced across links and a couple of DS-0s should be routed via Atlanta for this purpose.

If ADPCM or some other voice compression technique is used instead of PCM, the entire design would have to be redone and would yield considerable savings. We have also assumed that the T1s were formatted or channelized. If they were simply framed, then we would not have to design the network in bundles of DS-0s, such as requiring five 9.6-kbps channels per DS-0.

Lastly, installing fractional T1s connecting more city pairs than shown in our final network of Figure 15.18(f) would give a network that is reliable and resilient to failure. This is because the network would have more paths to route channels and the loss of an FT1 would be less catastrophic than the loss of a full T1.

EXERCISES

1. How many pairs of twisted copper are used to pass T1 signals?
   - a. 1
   - b. 2
   - c. 4
   - d. none; ordinary wire cannot be used for T1s.
2. "Only one circuit is needed rather than many different kinds" refers to which of the following advantages:
   - a. lower costs
   - b. simplification
   - c. reliability
   - d. network control
3. What is the bipolar format?
   - a. Two voltage levels are used: +3V and 0V.
   - b. Every mark is encoded with the opposite voltage polarity (+3V or −3V) as the previous mark.
   - c. All spaces are encoded with a −3V and all marks are encoded with +3V.
   - d. All spaces are encoded with 0V and all marks are encoded with +3V.
4. A D4 frame contains how many 8-bit voice samples per channel? For how many voice channels?
   - a. It contains 24 samples for one voice channel.
   - b. It contains 1 sample for one voice channel.
   - c. It contains 12 samples for each of the 12 voice channels.
   - d. It contains 1 sample for each of the 24 voice channels.
5. Which T1 interfacing device does unipolar to bipolar conversion?
   - a. NIU
   - b. DSU
   - c. CSU
   - d. LMU

6. What is a multilink multiplexer?
   a. a multiplexer with many outputs
   b. a multiplexer with many ports
   c. a multiplexer used with many DACS
   d. a DACS with many multiplexers connected to it
7. What device converts a 44-channel T1 into two 22-channel T1s?
   a. DACS   b. BCM
   c. inverse multiplexer   d. CCR
8. Which of the following is NOT a disadvantage of DACS?
   a. Transparent switching requires the T1 signal to be delayed by 48 bytes.
   b. Customers cannot control it using in-band digital signaling.
   c. It cannot switch at rates below 64 kbps.
   d. One cannot keep the order of the D4 frames the same and still maintain a minimum delay.
9. Being able to change the bandwidth of a T1 by dropping a few channels for a videoconference temporarily explains which T1 advantage?
10. Which segment of a typical T1 has the weakest link as far as reliability is concerned?
11. If data to be sent is "1100010000000000000100111," where the first "1" is +3V, what are the voltages of the bits as they are converted to output the signal? (There is a string of 12 zeros in there.)
12. What percent of an SF frame carries frame synchronizing bits? Answer the same question for an ESF frame.
13. What unit is being used by the telcos to gain loopback tests in case the customer's power fails?
14. What type of mux will pass voice channels from one link to another link without doing D/A/D conversions?
15. What device is useful to combine DS-0 channels from many remote locations at a POP?
16. In Table 15.8, explain how 5 was calculated to be the number of DS-0s between Kansas City and Dallas.
17. Out of the advantages listed for T1, which do you consider to be the most important? Why?
18. What is the purpose of the bipolar format? How is that achieved?
19. Explain the purpose of the FDL channel? Where is it found? What are some functions not discussed in the text that you would like to see supported on this channel?
20. In Figure 15.11, explain the purpose of the various interfaces.
21. List the disadvantages of using the drop-and-insert method with single-link muxes over the other options.
22. List the advantages of DACS and CCR.
23. What are the functions provided by a CSU?
24. Design the following T1 network using the techniques discussed in the text:

    Los Angeles is the corporate office in this exercise, and Portland, Salt Lake City, and Denver are district offices. Denver and Los Angeles are the two data centers. All four cities each have three sales offices or remote sites, making a total of 12 sales offices.

    The data requirements are as follows: From each sales office to the LA office are two 9.6-kbps lines. From every district office to LA there are ten 9.6-kbps lines.

From every district office to both data centers there is one 56-kbps line. Between data centers there are four 56-kbps lines.

The voice requirements are as follows: From Denver to LA there are 23 voice channels. From Portland to LA and Denver there are 7 and 3 voice channels, respectively. From Salt Lake City to LA, Denver, and Portland there are 15, 6, and 2 voice channels, respectively.

Draw the traffic matrixes and design the network as shown in the example. Draw the final map with the amount of spare DS-0s on each link. Correct solutions may not necessarily be identical.

## Chapter 16

SNA

16.1 THE SNA ENVIRONMENT

SNA was introduced in 1974 by IBM as a proprietary solution to eliminate the chaos of the many types of networking protocols which existed in that era. Today it is the most dominant network architecture with well over 40,000 networks installed worldwide. The number of stations attached to these networks, of course, far exceeds that number. Before detailing the SNA architecture, protocols, and how it is implemented, let us take a simplistic view of SNA and its purpose.

16.1.1 How SNA Was Initially Used

Figure 16.1 shows a number of terminals that are geographically dispersed and are connected via the network to a host, which in IBM's terminology is a mainframe. The mainframe is located at the corporate data center and for the sake of an example, let us say it is used to provide database access for agents of an airliner.

A database is a sophisticated collection of data records that are organized so that access to those records is done efficiently. Two popular database management systems by IBM are called IMS (Information Management System) and DB2 (DataBase/2). IMS, a traditional approach, uses a hierarchical method of organizing data. This method uses parent-to-children or inverted tree structures. Alternatively, DB2 uses a relational database structure where data is logically organized in tables.

As an example, on the remote terminals might be travel agents who have authorization to access the database. The agents issue requests, called transactions, for the database. These requests may be asking for availability of seats for a particular flight on a given date, or may be asking to cancel a reservation, or any number of such queries. These requests, which are made to the database by the many travel agents nationwide, are processed by programs called transaction applications. After accessing the database these applications send responses back to the agents, stating whether the requests were satisfied or not. The applications, which interact with the agents, as well as the agents themselves are users of the SNA network and are hence called end users.

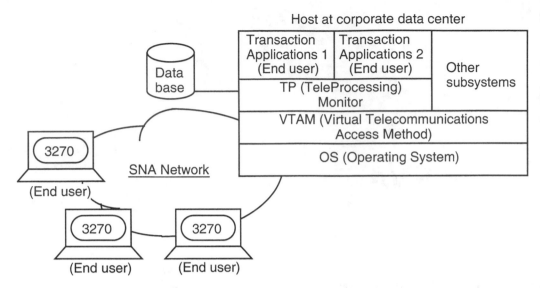

Figure 16.1 A high-level view of the SNA Network, with the end users of the network highlighted.

Although this scenario of how SNA was originally implemented is quite trivial, today SNA has evolved into a more mature networking architecture. It can support sophisticated services such as file transfers, distributed processing, distributed databases, electronic mail, and so forth.

16.1.2 Teleprocessing at the Host

Now let us briefly describe the major software components of the host, which are needed to process these transaction applications from remote sites. As shown in Figure 16.1, they are called the operating system, VTAM (Virtual Telecommunications Access Method), and TP (TeleProcessing) monitor.

The host itself is managed and controlled by the operating system. It schedules all jobs and manages all resources. MVS (Multiple Virtual Systems) is an example of a popular operating system that is used on IBM mainframes. Unlike AT&T's UNIX, MVS was not designed to handle communications over a network. This was partly due to its complexity and size. Hence, MVS needs VTAM to perform communications-related tasks. VTAM then interfaces with a TP monitor under whose control the transactions are processed. Now each type of TP monitor doesn't have to deal with communications procedures, because they are provided in this module—VTAM.

Two common types of TP monitors are CICS (Customer Information Control System) and IMS/TM (Information Management System/Transaction Manager), which was formerly called IMS/DC. If the applications ran under the supervision of the operating system directly instead of the TP monitor, then each application would require a single memory partition or region of address. This would load down the operating system. However, a TP monitor relieves the operating system of much of the burden by managing all transactions in one partition. This makes the host run efficiently and also streamlines the development of software applications.

Just as the operating system controls the operation of the entire host and its resources, the TP monitor controls the transaction applications which process the transactions. The TP monitor does this by running several applications in one memory partition so that the operating system thinks it is running one job. Yet in fact, the TP monitor is actually running many processes simultaneously. From the applications' perspective, the TP monitor is the operating system, and from VTAM's or the operating system's perspective, the TP monitor is the application so VTAM must first connect itself to the remote user and then the user may establish a connection with the TP monitor of its choice.

TP monitors are examples of subsystems; other examples of subsystems include TSO (Time Sharing Option) and JES (Job Entry Subsystem). TSO and JES are subsystems that don't run under TP monitors, but must run under telecommunications access methods, such as VTAM.

Currently, the term "TP monitor" is also being used for Unix-based OLTP (On-Line Transaction Processing) systems. These TP monitors are integrated with client/server systems, which originally provided relational databases for a small number of client workstations. In contrast with the traditional TP monitors, such as CICS, these systems provide a better price to performance ratio and a GUI (Graphical User Interface). When compared against client/server-based database systems, TP monitors support a large number of concurrent transactions, access to traditional data, and better security.

16.2 SNA HARDWARE

So far we've been primarily discussing the host, and have said very little about the SNA network cloud that connects the terminals to the host. Traditionally, SNA has had just that orientation, a hierarchical network where devices are controlled by other devices which in turn are ultimately subject to the host.

Today SNA is becoming what is called a "flat" network, where terminals are becoming less dependent on the host. This new rapidly changing architecture is called APPN (Advanced Peer to Peer Networking). Nonetheless, we'll present SNA here as a hierarchical network and discuss these current trends towards the end of the chapter. Let us now "open up" the SNA cloud of Figure 16.1 and look at the many hardware components, as shown in Figure 16.2, which are typically used with SNA.

16.2.1 The Host and Its I/O Channel

At the top-left corner of Figure 16.2, a mainframe, or a host in SNA terms, is shown. In a purely distributed environment, any intelligent workstation is also called a host. The family of hosts based on system 370 are the 30xx, 43xx, and 93xx series. The letter "x" is used in product nomenclature to indicate that there are other related models with numbers substituted in place of the "x"s. So for example, the 30xx designation encompasses models 3090, 3080, and 3030.

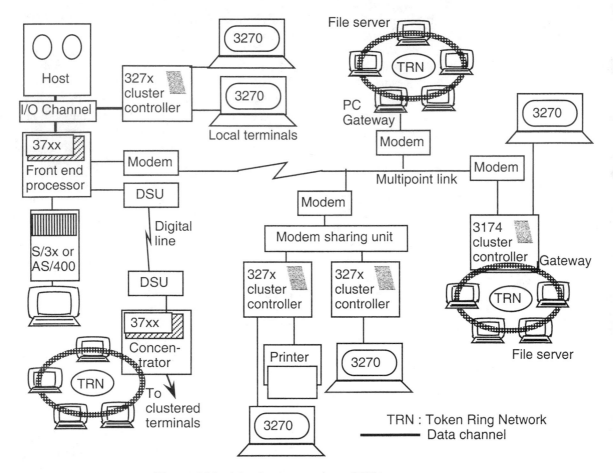

Figure 16.2 A hardware overview of SNA components.

Connected to the host is a processor responsible for all input and output operations of the host. It is called the I/O (Input/Output) channel and it exchanges information between the host and other devices connected to it locally, such as disk and tape drives, cluster controllers, communications controllers, etc.

16.2.2 The FEP

The communications controller can be used either as an FEP (Front End Processor) connected to a host or as a concentrator remotely located from a host. We will simply refer to it as an FEP. All network transmission lines are connected to the FEP, which is a communications processor to assist the host. Among other tasks, it does error detection and recovery, assembly and disassembling of packets, buffering of data from low-speed lines to the high-speed data channel for the host, etc. SNA's designations for it are 3705, 3720, 3725, and 3745.

If many transmission lines exist from one geographical area to the FEP, then the cost of these lines could become prohibitive. In such a case, a communications controller could be located in the area where these lines originate. This communications controller would then collect the data from these points and send it over just one high-speed link. Here the communications controller would be called a concentrator. Figure 16.2 shows one using a digital link.

16.2.3 The Cluster Controller

Attached to the FEP, traditionally, has been the cluster controller. It comes in models 3174, 3274, and 3276. In Figure 16.2, three of them are shown to be sharing a multipoint link and one is shown to be channel attached. Typically, it communicates with the FEP using the SDLC (Synchronous Data Link Control) protocol and with the terminals using BSC (Binary Synchronous Communication). SDLC is defined by SNA, but BSC predates it. The FEP polls the cluster controller and the cluster controller polls its terminals.

The 327x terminals, usually connected to the cluster controller, are called dumb devices. This is because they are unable to do any local processing. It is the most widely used synchronous terminal and it operates on the BSC protocol using a coax cable. However, PCs networked in LANs are quickly replacing the 3270 family of products.

The 3172 deserves an extra word here. Introduced in 1989 to connect various kinds of LANs to SNA, it has become a low-cost box for all purposes. It supports not only SNA protocol, but also TCP/IP (Transmission Control Protocol/Internet Protocol), APPN (Advanced Peer to Peer Networking), and OSI protocol stacks. It reduces the number of instruction cycles required by the host by off-loading the TCP/IP stack. It can not only attach LANs but also interconnect hosts and their peripherals using channel-to-channel connections with T1s. It can also perform many of the 3745 FEP routing functions.

16.2.4 Connecting LANs

Practically any kind of LAN can be used in SNA, although we've only shown TRNs (Token Ring Networks) in the figure. An intermediate router, sometimes called a gateway, is used to connect a LAN to the SNA network. Typically, in a LAN, the file server and the gateway would be two different stations, so that the workload would be distributed between them.

The word "gateway" has many meanings. In OSI terminology, a gateway can be the most sophisticated kind of device, performing protocol translations for all seven layers. On the other hand, IP (Internet Protocol) routers are also called gateways. Here protocol conversion is done only for the lower three layers of the OSI model. They are called gateways because the network addresses are different on both sides. Finally, the same term in SNA marketing literature refers to a device which does protocol conversion for only the lower two layers. In this chapter, we'll refer to gateway as meaning an SNA gateway.

The functions of a gateway in an SNA network can be provided by a PC, 3745, 3174 cluster controller, and a few other devices. Figure 16.2 shows three of these methods. A gateway is connected to the SNA network with an SDLC interface and to the LAN with a NIC (LAN Network Interface Card) or a TIC (TRN Interface Card).

The gateway, upon receiving an SDLC frame from the SNA network, strips off the SDLC header and the trailer, then appends the MAC (Media Access Control) header, the LLC (Logical Link Control) header, and the MAC trailer to the data portion of the frame, before sending the frame to its proper destination on the LAN. When stations on the LAN send data to the host, this process is reversed. In other words, only the headers and trailers of the second layer are replaced, while the headers and data from the upper layers are kept intact.

The PCs on the LAN would be emulating the 3270 terminal so that the host thinks it is talking to 3270 terminals. Also, the FEP would normally be polling the 3174 or the PC gateway on behalf of the stations on the ring. (This is called group polling.) Otherwise, the FEP would have to poll each individual station on the rings.

16.2.5 The AS/400 and Local and Remote Devices

The AS/400 (Application System/400) is a minicomputer, which is also called a midrange computer or a distributed processor. Running the OS/400 operating system, it provides intense multiuser processing for business environments. Predecessors to the AS/400 were Systems 36 and 38.

Lastly, any device that is attached to the I/O channel is considered a local device, whereas devices connected to an FEP are called remote devices. For instance, in Figure 16.2, even if the AS/400 were physically close to the FEP, it would be thought of as being remote, since it is connected to the FEP.

16.3 NAUs AND SESSIONS

16.3.1 NAU Defined

Back in Figure 16.1, an end user was said to be an application or the person using the program via a terminal. Either of these end users create and transmit data using RUs (Request/response Units). In order to deliver the RUs to their proper destinations, SNA defines NAUs (Network Addressable Units). NAUs are logical communication ports to the SNA network through which end users and SNA devices can gain access to the network. Terminals, cluster controllers, applications, VTAM, and TP monitors are all examples of NAUs. Any device or application that must transmit and receive data in the network must have an NAU. LU (Logical Unit), PU (Physical Unit), and SSCP (System Services Control Point) are the three types of NAUs.

16.3.2 LUs

LU is an NAU type that is required by the end users to gain access to the network. Figure 16.3 shows where LUs may be found in an SNA network, and their types. The LU itself is defined in the software supporting the particular device. This software provides a wide range of functions and intelligence which are categorized as LU types.

LU type 0 supports pre-SNA protocols such as the BSC 3270 terminal. LU type 1 is used for terminals using batch transfers of data while LU type 3 is used for printers.

LU type 2 is used by an application program communicating with an interactive device, such as the 3270, using the SNA data stream. Initially, the LU function for the 3270 was actually located in the software running at the cluster controller. However, on a PC, this software may be in the PC itself.

LU type 6.2 is a general-purpose program-to-program LU that enables two terminals to communicate with each other using minimum resources from the host. This is a deviation from the traditional hierarchical networking concept. Another name for it is APPC (Advanced Program to Program Communication) and it is covered later on. The CICS TP monitor can act as any of these LU types simultaneously depending on which LU type it is communicating with. Therefore, an LU type is an NAU that is determined by the capabilities of both partners of a session.

16.3.3 PUs

A PU is not a physical device but rather a set of functions and routines provided in the device's software which require network access. It is a resource manager for SNA devices providing configuration services, requesting software downloads, generating diagnostic information, and so on. PUs manage and control LUs that are connected to them.

As with LUs, PUs are divided into categories called PU types. PU types are also called SNA node types. Currently, the important node types are 2, 2.1, 4, and 5. These are illustrated in Figure 16.4. PU type 5 is implemented in VTAM, while type 4 is implemented in NCP (Network Control Program) running in the FEP. PU type 2 is associated with cluster controllers, and PU type 2.1 is needed to support APPN and is the most advanced type of all PUs. It can communicate directly with peer or adjacent PU2.1s without requiring the facilities of the host.

In Figure 16.4, the functions of a PU are shown to be provided either in the gateway or in the PCs of the TRN. If the PU functions are provided in the PCs then the gateway only has to do MAC/LLC to SDLC conversions. However, the host then has to maintain tables and manage sessions with the individual PCs.

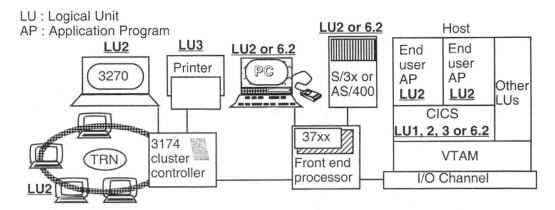

Figure 16.3 Examples of where various types of LUs may be found.

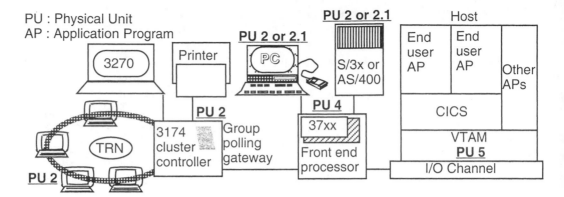

PU : Physical Unit
AP : Application Program

Figure 16.4 Examples of where various types of PUs may be found.

On the other hand, placing a single PU definition in the gateway and providing only the LU definitions in the workstations can lighten the load on the host processor and also reduce the memory requirements for the workstations.

16.3.4 SSCP, Domains, and Addressing

Just as a PU controls and manages all LUs attached to it, the SSCP controls and manages all PUs and LUs logically attached to it, except in APPN. SSCP is a subset of VTAM and hence exists only in the host. It is responsible for initializing the network and deactivating it. All devices that are under the control of the SSCP are said to be in its domain. The PUs help the SSCP to manage the resources of the network. For example, the SSCP or VTAM must activate the PUs in the NCP and the cluster controller before it can activate the LUs for the end user at the terminal.

Figure 16.5 shows a multidomain network. This is a network with more than one domain. A domain consists of one type 5 node (host) and its associated network, including the type 4 nodes (FEPs). Each domain is further divided into subareas, where a subarea consists of one type 4 or type 5 node and its associated network. The host and the FEP themselves are called subarea nodes. Any SNA node that is not a subarea node is called a peripheral node.

In a multidomain network, all subareas are assigned unique identifiers called subarea numbers. Figure 16.5 shows four subareas. Furthermore, within each subarea, every NAU is assigned an element number. So to identify an NAU, one must provide the subarea number as well as the element number. Peripheral nodes do not use these subarea-element number pairs in addressing the devices connected to them. Instead they use local forms of addressing which are called local addresses and link station addresses. For the sake of simplicity, we'll abbreviate them as LOA and LSA, respectively.

These LSA and LOA pairs are unique within each subarea. For instance, in Figure 16.5 an LSA of 4 and LOA of 4 addresses the 3270 terminal in subarea 3. The LSA identifies the controller and the LOA identifies the terminal. This LSA and LOA pair may not be assigned to any other device in this subarea, although it may appear in other subareas.

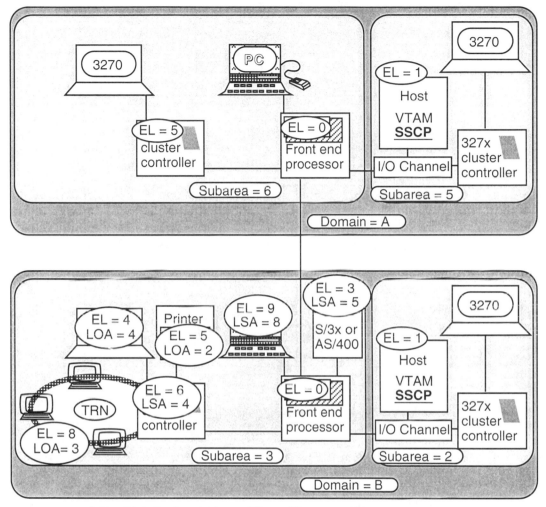

LSA : Link Station Address   EL   : ELement address
LOA : LOcal Address   SSCP : System Services Control Point

Figure 16.5 Traffic within a subarea uses the LOA-LSA form of addressing and between subareas uses the subarea-element form of addressing.

Now, when the application in the host sends a message to the 3270, it knows and uses only the subarea and element address pair. This address pair is then translated into the local identifiers by the NCP, residing in the FEP, before being sent to its destination.

Consequently, the FEP is also called a boundary function node, because it does this type of address conversion. A host may also serve as a boundary function node for the peripherals attached to it via the I/O channel. In conclusion, the subarea-element pair is used to address devices residing in subareas, while the local addressing form is used by the subarea node to address the peripheral nodes from the boundary function out.

16.3.5 Sessions

Two end users can communicate with each other when their NAUs have established a session. In other words, an SNA session between two NAUs is necessary for an orderly flow of traffic between them. When a session is being initialized, the NAUs determine if protocols used between them are compatible. If not, then the session cannot be initiated. There are four types of sessions, three involving SSCP and one that is set up between two LUs. Specifically, the session types are called SSCP-SSCP (used in a multidomain network), SSCP-PU, SSCP-LU, and LU-LU.

SSCP sessions are typically set up when the network is brought up. These sessions provide network control between the various network resources that are available, while the LU-LU sessions provide communication capabilities between applications. An LU-LU session cannot be established until all the NAUs in the path have established the necessary SSCP-type sessions.

Figure 16.6 illustrates the steps involved in setting up sessions in a single-domain network, in order that a network terminal may access CICS. Here the host LU is called

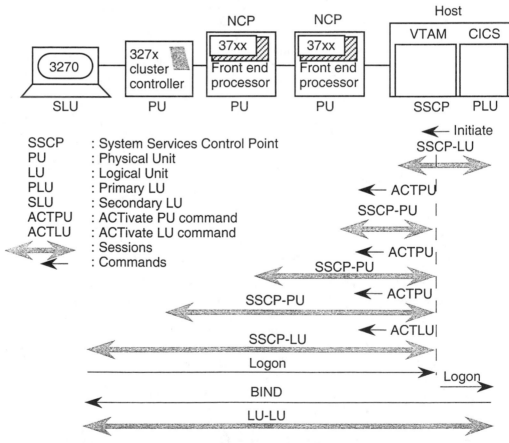

Figure 16.6 The order in which sessions are established while bringing up a network.

the PLU (Primary LU) while the network LU is called the SLU (Secondary LU). PLUs may participate in many LU-LU sessions, but SLUs may only participate in one. This basically applies for dependent LUs but not for the independent LU 6.2. CICS first initiates a session with VTAM to establish a SSCP-LU session, making itself available for other LUs to log on to itself. Then, VTAM (or SSCP) initiates sessions with all the PUs in the order that they are physically connected to the LU. This is done by issuing ACTPU commands: first to the first FEP, then to the next, then to the cluster controller. Lastly, it initiates a session with the LU associated with the 3270 terminal.

So now the user logs onto CICS, the host LU. SSCP sends the log on message to the host LU, providing a profile of the SLU. Using this information, the host LU can determine whether or not it can support a session with that network LU. If it can, it will issue a BIND command and the LU-LU session will be established. This process of establishing an LU-LU session is called binding.

16.4 SNA ARCHITECTURE

16.4.1 SNA Layers

Figure 16.7 shows the seven layers of SNA. Layer 1 or the physical layer may be implemented by a modem or a DSU using the RS-232 protocol as usual. The second layer is typically implemented by the SDLC (Synchronous Data Link Control) protocol. Both of these layers parallel the functions of the first two layers of the OSI reference model. SDLC is part of the SNA definition, but RS-232 is not.

As OSI's network layer (X.25) performs routing and congestion control over the transport network, so does the path control layer, layer 3, in SNA. However, unlike X.25, SNA doesn't have permanent and switched virtual circuits. The path control layer also provides segmentation, which divides large messages into smaller segments.

A connection-oriented service sends all message units along one physical path for a session, and this path is determined before traffic is transmitted. SNA provides such a connection-oriented service. The transmission control layer, layer 4, checks for session sequence numbers, pacing, and encryption. Pacing prevents one NAU from sending data at a rate that is faster than what the receiving one can accept. This feature is called data flow control and, interestingly, it is provided by other layers but not the data flow control layer.

The data flow control layer, layer number 5, provides chaining, session responses, assignment of session sequence numbers, etc. Layer 6 is called the NAU services layer and its functions approximately correspond to OSI's presentation control layer. The NAU services layer includes the transaction and presentation services sublayers. The presentation services provide programming interfacing and data formatting and transaction services, and are covered in Section 16.8.3. The last layer, the applications or transaction services layer is the user at the terminal or the application running at the host.

16.4.2 SNA Units of Exchange

As data is sent by the application layer, the sixth layer adds an FMH (Function Management Header), and the resulting combination is called an RU (Request/re-

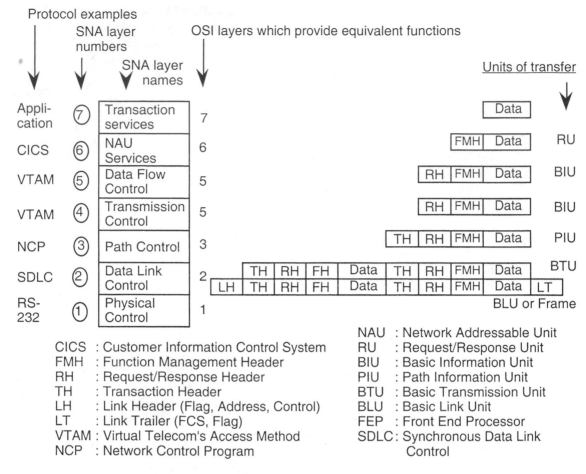

Figure 16.7 SNA Architecture. Typically, a host supports all layers, whereas an FEP supports layers 1 through 3.

sponse Unit). An RU could be a request RU, a response RU, or a control RU, which is also a request and is used for network management. The fifth layer adds an RH (Request/response Header) to the RU, which then becomes a BIU (Basic Information Unit).

The path control layer adds a TH (Transmission Header), which specifies the routing information and whether the BIU associated with it is a complete message or one of several segments which make up a larger message. Depending on how much data the second layer is able to buffer, it may then combine multiple PIUs into a BTU (Basic Transmission Unit) for the SDLC protocol to process. SDLC processes frames or BLUs (Basic Link Units). Let us next look at the second, third, and upper-layer protocols in more detail.

SNA

16.4.3 LU Profiles

The presentation services (part of NAU services), data flow control, and transmission control layers all support a range of possible protocols. For each of these three layers, SNA selects sets of protocols and categorizes them into profiles so that a specific PS (Presentation Services) profile represents a given set of protocols supported by the PS layer. Depending on what set of functions is needed, the appropriate profile number is selected when setting up a session. Similarly, the sets of protocols supported by the data flow control and transmission control layers are called FM (Function Management) and TS (Transmission Services) profiles, respectively.

These profile numbers are then used to identify LUs and their capabilities so that each LU is defined in terms of the profile number for each of these three layers. For example, LU type 2 uses a PS profile of 2, a FM profile of 3, and a TS profile of 3; LU type 6.2 uses a PS profile of 6.2, a FM profile of 7, and a TS profile of 19.

16.5 SDLC

SNA supports a number of data link control protocols, out of which we'll discuss one, SDLC. SDLC is used to build upon topics in Chapters 17 through 20.

Figure 16.8 shows the format of three types of BLUs used in SDLC. They are called information, supervisory, and unnumbered frames. This figure should be continuously referenced while studying this section. Unlike BSC (Binary Synchronous Communication), SDLC is a bit-oriented and full-duplex protocol. Hence, SDLC makes more efficient use of the transmission facilities than BSC. Additionally, it can combine data, acknowledgments, and poll all in one frame.

16.5.1 The Flag and the Address Fields

An SDLC frame always begins and ends with a flag with a fixed bit pattern of "01111110." The same flag can be used to end the previous frame as well as begin a new one. In order that this pattern may not appear anywhere else in the frame, a technique called "bit stuffing" is used. This requires that the sending station transmit an extra 0 after every 5 consecutive 1s and that the receiver remove one 0 after every 5 consecutive 1s. If the receiver doesn't detect a zero after 5 consecutive 1s, but a zero after 6 consecutive 1s, it assumes that it is the terminating flag. See the graphical explanation given in Figure 16.9 on page 379.

After the flag, the next field is an 8-bit address providing the LSA (Link Station Address) or typically the cluster controller ID. This is an example of an individual address. An example of a group address is when a 3174, used as a gateway, polls all PCs on a TRN. The FCS is a 16-bit CRC character that is used for error detection on the preceding fields.

16.5.2 The Control Field

The control field has a number of purposes. If its last bit is zero, it identifies the frame as carrying information. The information field encapsulates information that is passed down from the upper frames. The other two types of frames, supervisory and unnumbered, don't carry information from the upper layers. The length of this field is a multiple of 8 bits, except for the stuffed bits.

The Ns is a 3-bit field, and it identifies the frame number of the frame being transmitted. This is also called a frame sequence number. With 3 bits allocated for Ns, frame numbers can range from 0 (binary 000) to 7 (binary 111) or it can have 8 possible values. The Nr specifies the next frame number that the transmitter is expecting from the distant end. If station A transmits a frame with its Ns equal to 2, then when station B transmits its frame, it will set its Nr to 3, indicating that 3 is the next frame it is expecting from A.

Because there are only 3 bits allocated for Ns and Nr, the maximum number of frames that can be transmitted without requiring a response from the receiving end is 7. This figure is called the window size. Imagine, if a transmitter did send 8 frames in a row from Ns = 0 to Ns = 7 and then waited for an acknowledgment from the opposite end. Now if the opposite end responds with an Nr of 0, the transmitter wouldn't know whether it is asking to retransmit the first frame number 0 or if it is acknowledging the seventh frame and is requesting the transmission of a new frame numbered 0. To avoid this ambiguity, the window size is kept to 7 for SDLC frames. SDLC also has facilities to provide window sizes of 127, where the Ns and Nr fields are extended.

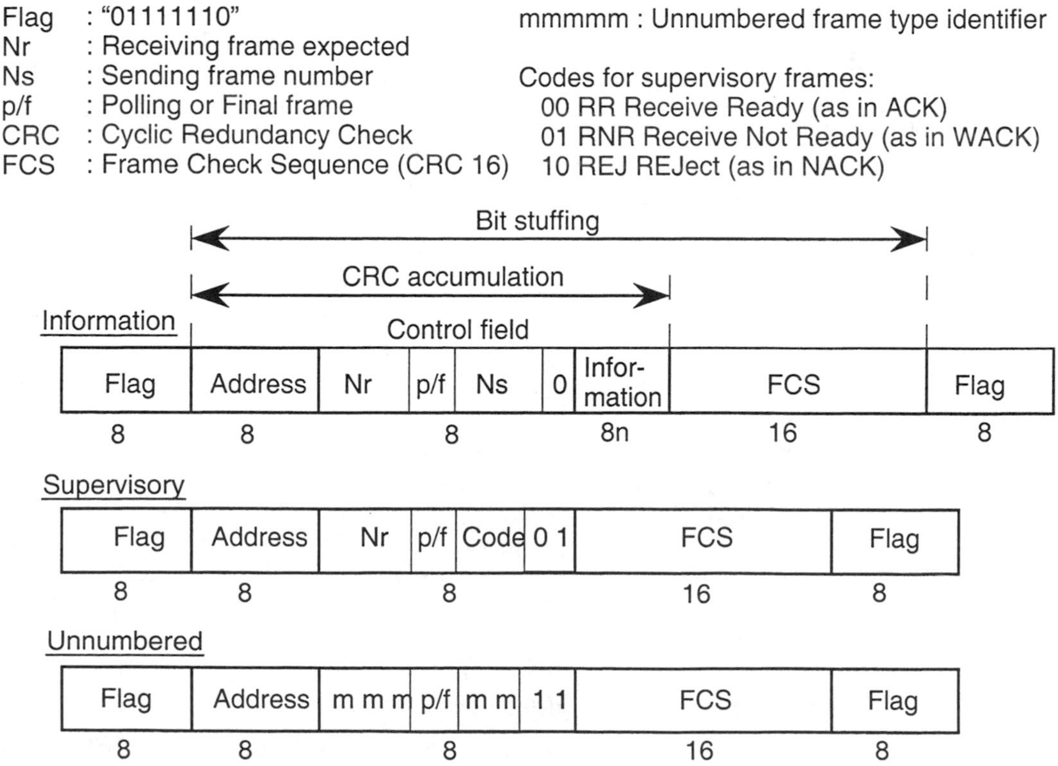

Flag : "01111110"
Nr : Receiving frame expected
Ns : Sending frame number
p/f : Polling or Final frame
CRC : Cyclic Redundancy Check
FCS : Frame Check Sequence (CRC 16)
mmmmm : Unnumbered frame type identifier
Codes for supervisory frames:
00 RR Receive Ready (as in ACK)
01 RNR Receive Not Ready (as in WACK)
10 REJ REJect (as in NACK)
Bit stuffing
CRC accumulation
Information
Control field
Flag
Address
Nr
p/f
Ns
0
Infor-mation
FCS
Flag
8
8
8
8n
16
8
Supervisory
Flag
Address
Nr
p/f
Code
0 1
FCS
Flag
8
8
8
16
8
Unnumbered
Flag
Address
m m m
p/f
m m
1 1
FCS
Flag
8
8
8
16
8

Figure 16.8 The three SDLC frame type formats. Fields which don't exist in all types are shaded, and the number of bits in each field is shown.

Data to be transmitted.

₀₀₀01111100111111110011 10...

Data actually transmitted after stuffing a zero after every 5 consecutive 1s.

$\bigvee$ $\bigvee$

₀₀₀011111000111110111001110...

Data received is the same.

₀₀₀011111000111110111001110...

Data interpreted after removing one zero after every 5 consecutive 1s.

₀₀₀01111100111111110011 10...

Figure 16.9 Bit stuffing prevents the flag (01111110) from appearing anywhere inside a frame.

The poll/final bit may be used over master-slave connections. In these types of connections, the primary device controls a secondary one. For example, an FEP acts as the primary device to a cluster controller and a cluster controller acts as the primary device to an end terminal. The poll/final bit is used as a poll bit for frames originating at the primary and is used as a final bit for frames originating at a secondary. That is, it is set to 1 by the primary if it is polling a secondary; otherwise it is set to 0. For frames originating at a secondary, this bit is set to 0 if it is not the last frame in a sequence of frames; otherwise it is set to 1.

Figure 16.10 summarizes the purposes of the control and address fields by showing an exchange of two frames sent by the FEP and one frame as it is sent by the controller. First the controller sends its frame number 0 then its frame number 1. This is shown in the Ns field. The first frame has the P/F field set to 0, because it is not the last frame, and the second frame has this field set to 1, signaling the controller that this is a poll. Then the controller sends its frame number 0 and acknowledges the FEP's frame number 1 by setting its Nr to 2.

Now let us turn our attention to the other two types of frames as shown in Figure 16.8. If the last bit in the control field is a 1, then no information is being sent. In other words, it is either a supervisory or an unnumbered frame. The control field of the supervisory frame ends with a "01" and the control field of the unnumbered frame ends with a "11."

In BSC terminology, supervisory frames are used to send ACKs, NACKs, and WACKs. The supervisory code for an acknowledgment is RR (Receive Ready), for a negative acknowledgment it is REJ (REJect), and for a wait with an acknowledgment it is RNR (Receive Not Ready). An RNR indicates to the sending station to temporarily stop the transmission because the receiver's buffer is full.

Finally, SDLC has 14 types of unnumbered frames used for initializing a connection, removing a connection, and other functions. These types of frames also appear in X.25 and ISDN, and their discussion will be left for Chapters 17 and 20.

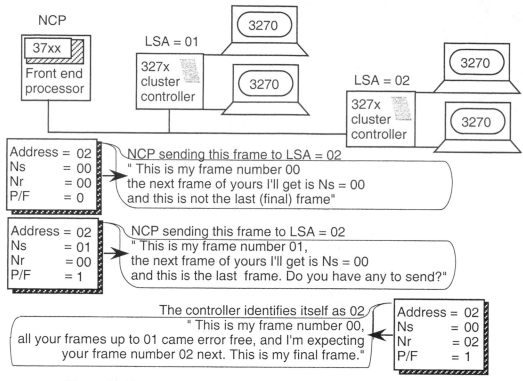

Figure 16.10 An example of frame exchanges on a multipoint line.

16.5.3 An Example of an SDLC Transmission Exchange

Figure 16.11 shows an FEP (Front End Processor) being connected to two cluster controllers via modems and a CO, which is providing a multipoint link. Here, the FEP and the cluster controller serve as examples of primary and secondary stations, respectively. There is a protocol analyzer inserted between the FEP and its modem to monitor the traffic on the link. The left side of the display shows the frames sent by the FEP and the right side shows the frames as they are sent by the cluster controllers. The address field specifies to which cluster controller frames are being sent or from which one they are being received.

To begin with, the FEP sends a supervisory frame to the cluster controller C2 with a code of RR, because the FEP has no errors unresolved. The P/F bit is 1, and since it is the FEP setting it, this bit indicates that C2 is being polled. Supervisory frames have no Ns field, but do have an Nr field. The 0 bit for Nr indicates to C2 that the FEP is expecting its frame number 0 next. The good CRC indicates that the frame has no errors at this point.

In the figure, C2 sends the next frame, because it has just been polled. It has an option to send information frames, but apparently, it doesn't have any information, so it also sends an RR type of supervisory frame. It is expecting frame number 1 from the

FEP next; hence the Nr is 1. Also, there are no more frames that will follow this one, so the P/F is 1, and the frame is good coming through the analyzer.

Next, the FEP polls the C3. It is expecting frame number 5 from C3 next. Unlike C2, C3 does have data to send, so it sends information frames starting at frame number (or Ns of) 5. It sends four frames, and because the Ns field is only 3 bits long, the Ns rolls back to zero after frame number 7. All frames have been received without error, and all of their P/F bits are set to 0 except for the final one. When the cluster controller sets the P/F bit, it takes on the meaning of whether or not it is the final frame. Polling is only done by the primary (the FEP in this case).

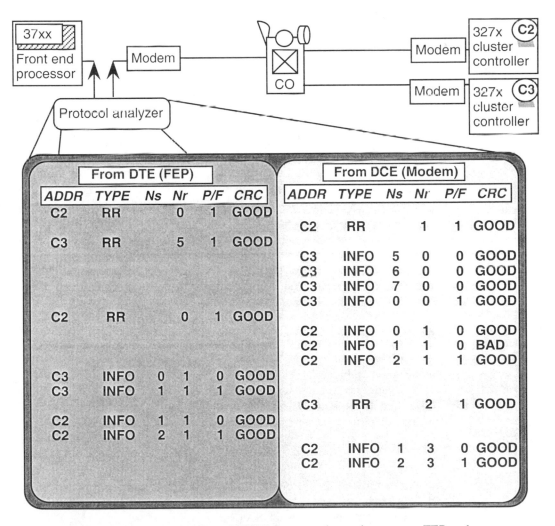

Figure 16.11 A snapshot of SDLC frame exchange between an FEP and its two cluster controllers, as seen on the screen of a protocol analyzer.

After this, the FEP polls C2 again to see if it now has any data to send. This time C2 does have data. It sends frame numbers 0, 1, and 2. Notice that frame number 1 has an error, but before the FEP notifies C2 about this error, it first sends information to C3 and polls it. Notice that the FEP has acknowledged C3's four frames (5, 6, 7, and 0) by sending an Nr of 1, since C3's frame number 1 is what the FEP is expecting next.

C3 has no information, so it sends an RR frame; however, it acknowledges the FEP's frames 0 and 1 by setting the Nr to 2.

Now, the FEP gets back to C2. It signals that it received frame number 1 with an error, by setting the Nr to 1. While the FEP notifies C2 about this error, it sends two information frames. Then C2 retransmits all the frames starting with the problem frame, which was frame number 1, and at the same time it acknowledges the FEP's frames 1 and 2 by setting the Nr to 3. The exchange then continues.

16.6 THE PATH CONTROL LAYER

Moving up the SNA architecture stack from the data link control layer, we come up to the path control layer. It routes traffic between the various nodes within the SNA network. These nodes include the peripheral nodes as well as the subarea nodes. Based on the path of a session, subarea nodes are further categorized into boundary function nodes and intermediate nodes. A boundary function node is the subarea node that is closest to the end node of a session that is in progress, whereas intermediate nodes are the subarea nodes that lie in the path of a boundary function node and the host. For example, in Figure 16.12, if CICS is in session with LUa via SA7 (Sub-Area node 7), then SA6 is the boundary function node while SA4 and SA7 are the intermediate nodes.

In this section, let us first consider the terms and the issues dealing with the routing between subareas and then do the same by extending the discussion to include the routing within the subareas. Typically, FID 4 (Format ID 4) is the TH (Transmission Header) used between subarea nodes and carries subarea-element forms of addressing, and FID 2 is the TH used between a subarea node and its peripherals. FID 2 TH carries the local form of addressing.

16.6.1 Routing between Subareas

Virtual Routes: A TG (Transmission Group) is a collection of parallel links between two subarea nodes. For added reliability or to provide different classes of service, multiple TGs can be placed between them. Various TGs are shown in Figure 16.12. As PIUs (Path Information Units) travel over TGs, they are assigned TG sequence numbers, which appear in the TH field.

As a PIU travels from one subarea node to another, its TH carries the address of the destination subarea or boundary function node, which helps the intermediate node properly route the PIU. So for instance, in the figure, SA3 knows that all PIUs going to SA6 should be directed to go to SA4 and it doesn't know where SA4 will direct those PIUs. All that SA3 cares about is that the next node is SA4. In SNA, this complete end-to-end path determined by each SA (Subarea Node) forwarding the PIU to the next SA node is called a virtual route. This differs from X.25's virtual circuit, as we'll see in Chapter 17.

In Figure 16.12 notice that there are three virtual routes available for traffic between CICS and LUa. These are VR1: SA3-SA4-SA6; VR2: SA3-SA4-(over TG1)-SA7-SA6; and VR3: SA3-SA4-(over TG2)-SA7-SA6. These virtual route paths are then defined in the routing tables of all pertinent SA nodes. Also, the entire virtual routes are not defined in any one of the SA nodes, but each SA node only has the forwarding address for the virtual routes which pass through it.

During session setup, one virtual route will be defined as the primary route and the others as alternate routes. All traffic in both directions for the session will follow the selected virtual route. If the virtual route in use fails during a session, the session fails and while the session is being reestablished, another virtual route will be selected.

Virtual routes are two-way routes and they are comprised of two one-way routes called explicit routes. In other words, a virtual route is defined in terms of an outbound explicit route and an inbound explicit route. These routes are defined in what are called path tables, which reside in VTAM and NCP.

Class of Service: To provide prioritization of traffic, SNA nodes also contain COS (Class Of Service) tables. These tables specify the priority of traffic originating or terminating at nodes in the network. So in Figure 16.12, if LUa is to be given a higher priority than LUb, then the primary route for LUa could be VR1 (Virtual Route 1) and the alternate routes could be VR2 and VR3. Likewise, the primary route for LUb could be VR2 and the alternate routes could be VR1 and VR3.

Now if VR1 failed, perhaps due to a break in TG1 between SA6 and SA4, then the traffic for LUa would be routed over VR2, or if necessary over VR3. But in either case, it would have a higher priority than the traffic for LUb. This type of "bumping" of traffic, or who can bump whom, is spelled out in the COS tables. Each COS is given a COS name, which is selected during log-on procedures.

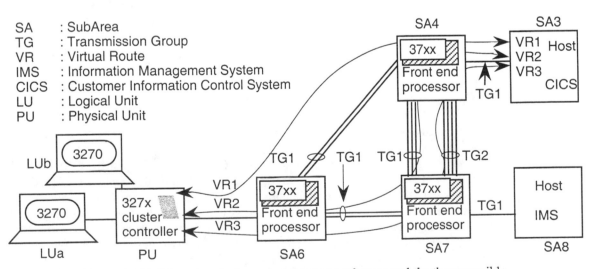

Figure 16.12 The transmission groups between subareas and the three possible virtual routes between SA3 and the PU are shown.

Virtual Route Pacing: When a subarea node temporarily cannot accept more data because its buffer is getting full, it can stop the transmitter from sending more PIUs by not sending pacing responses. When the buffer is getting empty and it can receive more data, it can then send a pacing response. This signals the subarea node to send another group of PIUs.

What has just been described is called path control pacing or virtual route pacing. This technique allows subarea nodes to signal transmitting nodes whether to send more PIUs. The number of PIUs which can be sent by a transmitting node without requiring a response from the receiver is called the window size. This can be increased or decreased depending on the amount of congestion and activity occurring at the receiving node.

Virtual route pacing affects the data flow for the PIUs of all sessions between two adjacent subareas. Likewise, SNA also has what is called session pacing (covered in Section 16.7), which controls the data flow between two end users and only affects the particular session between them. It is necessary to provide both types of pacing. Virtual route pacing is required when all affected sessions are running fine, but the resources to support them are being strained. Session pacing allows the shutting down of a specific session if that application is in trouble.

16.6.2 End-to-end Path Control Routing

So far we've been considering the issues of routing traffic between SAs. Now we will see how traffic is routed from the boundary function nodes to their peripheral nodes, but first let us review SNA address types.

The subarea-element form of addressing is only used between SAs that are provided in the TH of the FID4 type of PIU. The peripheral nodes do not use this type of addressing. Instead, they understand LSA (Link Station Address) and LOA (LOcal Address) forms of addressing. The subarea nodes do not use this local form of addressing, but the boundary function nodes provide the conversion between these two forms of addressing.

Consider Figure 16.13. Here IMS is sending a message to LUa. VTAM doesn't know the local address pair (LSA and LOA) of LUa, but it does know its subarea-element pair (SA = 6, EL = 2), which it provides in the FID 4 TH. The data link protocol between the host and the FEP is not shown in the figure.

The NCP at SA7 notices that the destination subarea address of the PIU is 6 and not its own. After searching its tables, it adds an SDLC address of 4, since SA6 is on the other end of this link.

SA6's NCP notices its own address of 6 in the TH and it strips off the SDLC header, trailer, and the FID 4 transmission header. Then it adds a new TH of type FID 2, with an LOA of 2, which corresponds to subarea 6 and element 2. It also adds a new SDLC header and trailer, giving the address (LSA) of 2. Notice that this boundary function node has done an address type conversion and, in so doing, has also done a TH type conversion, although there are other differences, besides the address forms, that are present in the two types of THs.

The controller at LSA of 2 then detects this frame as being its own and using the LOA of 2, given in the TH, directs the information to LUa.

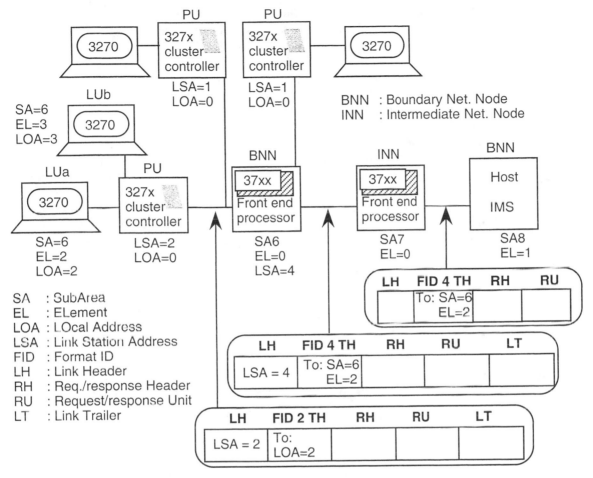

Figure 16.13 The conversion of the subarea-element form of addressing to the local forms of addressing as it is done in the transmission header by the front end.

16.7 CHAINING, PACING, AND SEGMENTING

This section concentrates on the functions that are provided by the upper layers of SNA, namely NAU services, data flow control, and transmission control.

16.7.1 Chaining

In many transaction processing systems, it becomes necessary to identify a number of requests as one unit of work so as to maintain the integrity of the database (or databases). If all of the requests are successful then the database can be committed, or else, using the saved records of all changes, it can be rolled back to its initial state. The mechanism used to treat such logical data or RUs as one entity is called chaining. The PIUs belonging to a chain are called elements.

When an LU-LU session is first established, the PLU (Primary LU) finds out the buffer size of the SLU (Secondary LU). The PLU determines in what amounts to divide a message or in what sizes to send the PIUs, so that the SLU's buffer may not overflow.

In Figure 16.14, an application has a 4800-byte message to send to the SLU. Because its buffer size is only 1600 bytes, during session activation, the PLU or CICS has agreed to send elements that are not greater than 1600 bytes. This will allow the SLU to receive the message in three parts, each of which can fit in its buffer. (The figure also shows how each element may be divided into four segments to accommodate the cluster controller's buffer size, but we'll get to that later.) Each of the three elements of the chain is given a sequence number in the TH. This number is called the SNF (Segment Number Field) and the chain elements are labeled as SNF = 1 through SNF = 3. In the RH, there are two fields which are called BC (Begin Chain) and EC (End Chain) which let the SLU know which elements are the first, last, and the intermediate elements. The BC bit is 1 for the first element, the EC bit is 1 for the last element, and the rest of the bits for all elements are set to 0.

16.7.2 Session Pacing

Sometimes the transmitted PIU size is made smaller than the receiver's buffer size. In such cases, the PLU may send several PIUs consecutively, without requiring a response from the SLU, as long as the SLU has room for that many units in its buffer. After the SLU has completed processing these PIUs, it would then send a response to the PLU to transmit the next set of PIUs. This procedure enables the SLU to control the rate at which the PIUs are sent and is called session pacing, contrary to the virtual route pacing described in Section 16.6.1. The number of PIUs that are sent consecutively is called the size of the pacing window. Furthermore, it is important to note that SNA uses a pacing mechanism that permits smooth flow of traffic when no congestion exists between the end points.

Therefore, chaining divides up messages into smaller units, so that these units may fit in the SLU's buffer, while session pacing allows the receiver enough time to process the data that is in its buffer before another load of data is transferred to it.

16.7.3 Segmentation

As the chain is being sent to the SLU, the elements are sent through the boundary function node (or FEP2 in Figure 16.14) to the PU. At the FEP2, the PIUs or the chain elements may have to be divided further, because of the PU's small buffer size. The dividing up of PIUs into smaller PIUs by a boundary function node is called segmentation. However, bits for segmentation are coded in all FID types, so it is possible that segmentation can occur anywhere in the network. With APPN, it may occur between hosts.

In our example, the PU's buffer is only 400 bytes, while the PIUs arriving at FEP2 are 1600 bytes long. So FEP2 has to divide each PIU into 4 segments or a total of 12 segments to send the entire 4800-byte message. In the figure, the first chain element is shown to be segmented into four smaller size PIUs.

The RH, being the same as the chain element's RH, is transmitted only in the first segment and not in the rest of them. However, the TH appears in all of the segments.

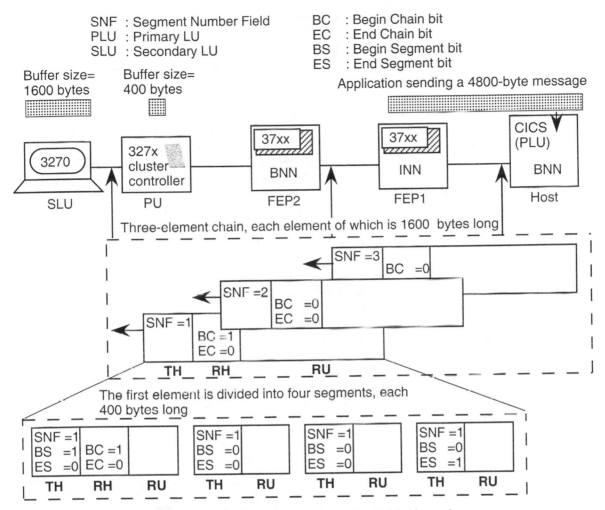

Figure 16.14 A 4800-byte-long message has to be divided into a 3-element chain, because the buffer of the SLU is only 1600 bytes. Likewise, FEP2 has to divide each of these PIUs into 4 segments, since the PU's buffer size is only 400 bytes.

Here, the SNF portion is copied in every segment, identifying all these segments as belonging to the same chain element. Furthermore, the BS (Begin Segment bit) and ES (End Segment bit) fields of the TH are set, similar to the BC and EC fields of the RH field, identifying the first, last, and the intermediate segments.

16.8 APPC OR LU 6.2

16.8.1 Introduction

Since its inception in 1974, SNA has been a host-driven network. All resources and users were totally dependent on the host, and if the host ever failed, the network came to a grinding halt. In 1984, IBM introduced APPC (Advanced Program to Program Communications), which was the beginning of turning SNA into a network that was not totally oriented to a host. In SNA terminology, this means a mainframe. In 1991, APPN (Advanced Peer to Peer Networking) was introduced, which didn't require an SNA network to have a host at all. In this section, we will outline APPC and in the next section outline APPN.

To facilitate APPC, a new LU type called LU 6.2 was introduced. These two terms are now interchangeable. Also, about the same time, LEN (Low Entry Networking) was introduced so that two peripheral LUs could communicate with each other and establish a session between them. This was a drastic deviation from the established SNA environment where all LU-LU sessions required a host LU. See Figure 16.15. However, LEN required a creation of a new PU type called PU 2.1. Without LEN, each peripheral LU could maintain only one session at a time with a host LU and would have to be the SLU in such a session. With the advent of LEN, network LUs could maintain several sessions at a time and also act as PLUs.

APPC allows for distributed transaction processing in real time. This means that when a request is initiated by a terminal operator with a transaction application running on a host, that transaction may initiate another transaction to yet another host. Upon receiving its response, the original host may either satisfy the operator's request, fail the request, or perhaps follow through with another transaction before providing the response to the operator. Here the term host is used to mean mainframes, minis, or micros.

Let us revert to the example of the travel agent that was introduced at the beginning of this chapter. Let us say that the agent's customer has a reservation with Airline-A from Miami to Rio de Janeiro on a particular date. Because of a change of

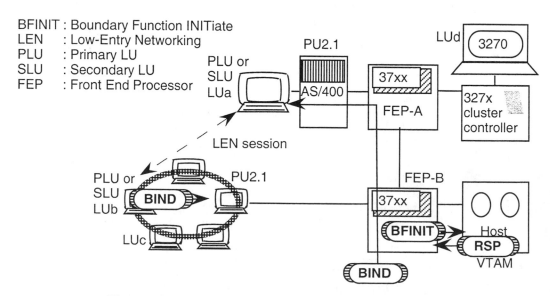

Figure 16.15 The steps taken in setting up an LEN session.

plans, the customer wants to fly to Brasilia and then to reach Rio de Janeiro using a domestic carrier called Airline-B. However, the agent cannot determine if the connection is good between these two airlines without interrogating both airlines' databases. Airline-C also flies from Miami to Brasilia and the reservations should be changed to this airline if it provides a better connection. The agent initiates a distributed transaction which interfaces with the databases of all three airlines, canceling and making reservations as they become necessary.

APPC allows the travel agent to provide these types of real-time services to her customers, regardless of the hardware and their vendors, the programs, or the operating systems that are running at the various nodes, as long as they are LU 6.2 nodes. In other words, APPC provides an open architecture interface which is less vendor-dependent.

16.8.2 LEN

At first, LEN was provided only between directly connected nodes, such as LUb and LUc as shown in Figure 16.15. However, starting with NCP version 5.2 and VTAM version 3.2, the host and FEP began supporting LEN. These new releases of the subarea node software allow LUa and LUb to communicate with each other, even though they are not directly connected. The LEN session between them is shown with a dashed line.

In order to establish a LEN session that crosses subarea boundaries, VTAM has to know or find out where these LUs are located, and provide this information to the NCP that needs it to create a session.

When creating a LEN session, first VTAM must establish SSCP-PU sessions with each of the pertinent FEPs. The type 2.0 boxes need VTAM to set up a LEN session, while the 2.1 boxes don't require the services of VTAM at all.

Using this addressing information, VTAM establishes an SSCP-PU and an SSCP-LU session with the controller and its terminal. However, it only adds the independent LUs' names and addresses to its Resource Definition table, and doesn't establish sessions with the type 2.1 nodes or their associated LUs.

Now, if LUb wants to establish a session with LUa, it sends a BIND request to FEP-B. FEP-B will then send a BFINIT (Boundary Function INITiate) message to VTAM, expecting LUa's network address from it. VTAM responds with this address and then the BIND is forwarded to LUa by FEP-B. This establishes a LEN session between LUa and LUb, and VTAM is then no longer needed even to terminate the session. Notice that VTAM only provided the mapping of addresses.

APPC allows us to have an intelligent entity on both sides of a session. Without it, an LU 2.0, typically a 3270 terminal, could participate in only one session at a time, but LU 6.2 allows participation in multiple sessions simultaneously. When an LU 6.2 has multiple sessions with another remote LU 6.2, these sessions are said to be in parallel.

16.8.3 APPC Architecture

If the network shown in Figure 16.15 didn't provide LEN, then only connectivity would have existed between LUa and LUb. By introducing LEN, however, these LUs were able to communicate. APPC takes networking between these nodes a level higher by allowing the transaction application programs at these nodes to communicate using LEN sessions. The communication between two LUs is called an LU-LU session, and the communication between two TPs (Transaction Programs) is called a conversation. Because of this concept of a conversation, the term "program-to-program communication" is used.

To allocate a conversation, a session is first automatically established, if one is not already available. A conversation must use a session and a session may only support one conversation at a time. A conversation may also be called a thread, and if a TP requires several conversations with other TPs, the TP is called a multithreading TP.

Figure 16.16 illustrates many APPC concepts. Let us for now notice that there are two sites communicating with each other using all 7 layers of SNA. At the top of the stack, TPs are shown as ATPs (Application TPs), which participate in conversations with each other. Also, to support these conversations, two parallel sessions are made available by the LUs.

The session establishes a path for a conversation between the peer presentation services layers. The NAU services layer (layer 6) is subdivided into two layers called the transaction services and the presentation services layers.

The presentation services provide the interface between the transaction program and LU 6.2. This is called the LU 6.2 API (Application Program Interface). This layer makes sure that the calls made by the TP are of the proper format and are converted to the proper data streams.

The transaction services provide management of sessions between LU 6.2s and the services of STP (Service Transaction Program). STPs are similar to TPs; however, they are written as part of the LU 6.2 package to provide it with enhancements. When a service is needed by many TPs, it is prepackaged as one unit as an added feature to APPC. This allows writing of TPs to be done easily, since the bulk of the coding is implemented in the STPs. The interface between an ATP and an STP is called an STP-defined API.

Some examples of STPs are DIA (Document Interchange Architecture), SNADS (SNA Distributed Services), and CNOS (Change Number Of Services). DIA provides a centralized library of documents and the services necessary to manage and distribute them in an office environment. However, it doesn't actually use LU 6.2 protocols. SNADS is a distribution service between DIA sites, and the user doesn't have to log on to SNADS as he/she must log on to DIA services. CNOS allows one to increase or decrease the number of parallel sessions between LUs.

Figure 16.16 also shows that there are two kinds of conversations. If the conversation uses STPs, it is called a basic conversation, whereas if it interfaces directly to an ATP, it is called a mapped conversation. STPs use basic conversations. Basic conversations are more flexible and powerful because they use harder-to-program low-level programming calls. Mapped conversations, on the other hand, are easier to use, but are not as efficient. TPs which are commonly used have already been designed so that they are compatible and are made available. Before LU 6.2, application design teams had to write TPs that could not communicate with TPs written by other design teams. With APPC, much of the work is already done for the programmer. All that he/she needs to know is the names of the remote LU and the remote TP.

Without getting into the details of the data streams between the various interfaces, let us only identify them as depicted in Figure 16.16. At the lowest level for both mapped and basic conversation, the data stream is called the GDS (for Generalized Data Stream). It contains a GDS header and data. Several GDSs can be combined into one RU.

Mapped conversations use what is called data records, which are converted into MCR (Mapped Conversation Record) before being transformed into a GDS. TPs with basic conversations use the data stream called logical records.

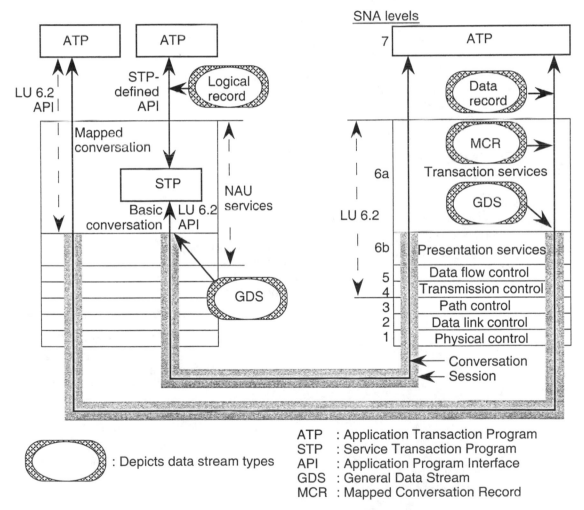

ATP : Application Transaction Program
STP : Service Transaction Program
API : Application Program Interface
GDS : General Data Stream
MCR : Mapped Conversation Record

Figure 16.16 Conversation types and their data stream types at key points.

16.8.4 An APPC Conversation Example

Let us now look at an example of how data is transferred over an APPC conversation. In Figure 16.17, the TP at site A has a file that needs to be transferred to the TP at site B. TPa requires a confirmation from TPb after every 8 records.

To initiate a conversation, TPa sends an ALLOCATE verb or a command to its LU, giving the names of the destination LU and the destination TP as parameters for this verb. To do this, the TP must first be in the reset state, after which it enters the send state. To create a conversation, a session must be available between the two LUs. If not, LUa will create a session. Then TPa sends its 8 data records to its LU by sending them with 8 SEND_DATA verbs. Because it wants a confirmation after 8 records, TPa sends a CONFIRM verb to its LU and waits.

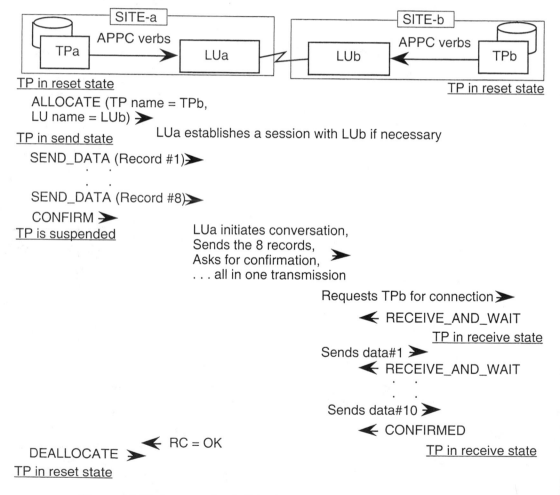

Figure 16.17 An example of allocating and deallocating an APPC conversation with transmission of data.

All this time, no information from TPa is sent to TPb but is buffered by LUa. The RU can be sent automatically when it becomes full or it can be explicitly sent by the user. LUa now flushes its buffer and transfers this information to LUb. LUb then starts up TPb. Upon receiving the conversation allocation request, TPb sends a RECEIVE_AND_WAIT verb to its LU and changes its state from reset to receive.

LUb then deblocks the data in sizes that fit the TPb's buffer. Notice that here the TP's buffer size is smaller than the record size so more units of data (10 in our example) are transferred to TPb than the original number of records (which was 8). After each unit of data, TPb sends a RECEIVE_AND_WAIT and goes into the receive state by sending a CONFIRMED verb.

This CONFIRMED verb is translated into a RC (Return Code) of "OK" by LUa to indicate that all the data was received correctly by TPb. At this point, TPa may send another 8 records by sending SEND_DATA verbs until the data is confirmed by the remote TP, or else TPa may terminate the conversation by sending a DEALLOCATE verb to LUa. After this, both TPs will enter the reset state.

Notice that in the sending state a TP may only send data, ask for a confirmation, send error messages, or deallocate a conversation. Likewise, a TP may only receive data when it is in the receive state. Conversations are half-duplex transfers that conform with most business-related transactions, which are inherently half-duplex as well.

16.9 APPN

APPN (Advanced Peer to Peer Networking) introduces distributed processing in SNA networks, which orients network devices away from a central host completely. This architecture is more compatible with the LAN and router environment that is spawning most businesses today. Hence, APPN is also called the new SNA architecture. It doesn't use architectural concepts such as PUs, SSCPs, or subareas. Old SNA architecture, especially relating to type 4 and 5 nodes, was implemented on specific devices, making SNA appear device-dependent. APPN, on the contrary, doesn't bind itself to specific devices per se, but makes itself open to be implemented over any intelligent devices. APPN is the next logical derivation of SNA from APPC. APPC still required VTAM to store and provide routing information between subareas while setting up a session, while APPN allows the absence of VTAM altogether.

APPN may be implemented using only PCs and AS/400s, without using any expensive hosts or front ends. (However, typically users would have an old SNA network that they would want to migrate to a LAN-based transport.) This will give them added reliability, better utilization of links, and less demand for FEP ports. This allows users to expand their networks without replacing their existing equipment. Figure 16.18 outlines such an integration of an old SNA network with APPN.

APPN defines two types of nodes. The EN (End Node) resides at the end points of the network and requires a connection to an NN (Network Node) to gain full access to the network. An NN and all the ENs connected to it is called a domain. The NN acts as a network server for the ENs in its domain.

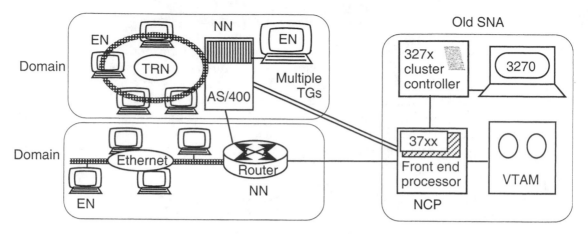

Figure 16.18 An example of integrating new SNA with the old SNA.

When an EN requires the address of a remote LU, it can obtain it from the NN dynamically and store it in its own network address directory for future use. There are several types of devices which can act as NNs or ENs or both.

The figure shows an AS/400 and a router acting as NNs while the PCs are shown as ENs. One physical link between two NNs is called a transmission group, and several transmission groups may exist between them.

Every APPN node contains two kinds of NAUs. LU 6.2 is one type and the other is called a CP (Control Point). A CP roughly replaces the PU and only one CP exists per node. This introduction of a new NAU type brings with it a new session type called the CP-CP session, or simply the CP session. CP sessions are full-duplex and require the use of two parallel LU 6.2 sessions, each of which is half-duplex. CP sessions are necessary for nodes to pass addressing and routing information.

An NN maintains two types of directories. One is called the local directory, which contains information about the ENs and LUs in its domain, and the other is called the distributed directory, which contains information about other domains and their respective LUs. An NN can also determine the best route between two nodes in the APPN.

The integration of an old and new SNA is shown in Figure 16.18. Both NNs may act as SNA gateways to VTAM and its resources. An EN may communicate with a host LU using this gateway feature and a 3270 terminal emulation, or else it may communicate with another EN using the NN as a network server. No one can predict how this evolution of multivendor SNA into a LAN and router-based network will lead into many viable alternatives.

EXERCISES

1. What is an end user?
   a. only a host application
   b. only a person using a terminal that accesses the SNA
   c. only a terminal
   d. a host application and a person using the SNA

SNA

2. What is a remotely connected device?
   a. a device that is connected to the I/O channel
   b. a device that is connected to an FEP
   c. a device that is at least 1 mile from the host
   d. a device that is at least 10 miles from the host
3. Which of the following is a communications controller?
   a. an FEP   b. a modem
   c. a DSU   d. a cluster controller
4. What is the logical network address that is required to access SNA called?
   a. LU   b. PU
   c. NAU   d. SSCP
5. What type of session is created when binding occurs?
   a. SSCP-SSCP   b. SSCP-PU
   c. SSCP-LU   d. LU-LU
6. Specific characteristics of LU types are given by what item?
   a. session sequence numbers   b. virtual routes
   c. explicit routes   d. profiles
7. In SDLC, which field determines what type of frame it is?
   a. address   b. information
   c. control   d. code
8. Which of the following is NOT a path control layer function?
   a. segmentation
   b. virtual route pacing
   c. conversion between FID 4 TH and FID 2 TH
   d. class of service
9. Which software component aids the host's operating system, such as MVS, to communicate with remote terminals?
10. What is the nomenclature of the most flexible kind of cluster controller?
11. What is a network that has more than one host running called?
12. What is a collection of parallel links between two subarea nodes called?
13. A virtual route is defined using which two other types of routes?
14. APPC introduced what new type of session?
15. APPN introduced what new type of session?
16. How many conversations are possible between two TPs using one session?
17. Discuss the various methods of using an FEP.
18. What are some basic differences between LUs and PUs?
19. What are some basic similarities between PUs and SSCPs?
20. How is a domain defined both in the old SNA and in the new SNA?
21. What is a virtual route and how is it defined?
22. Discuss the steps for how an LEN session is initiated.
23. Explain the items in Figure 16.16 in your own words.
24. Compare and contrast segmenting versus chaining. Which are based on LU's buffer size? Which are based on PU's buffer size? Which is done by PU? By LU? Which one determines SNF numbers? Pacing window?

Chapter 17

X.25

17.1 DEVELOPMENT

17.1.1 Origins

In the early 1960s, Paul Baran of the Rand Corporation first conceptualized a packet switched network. Afterwards, the DoD (Department of Defense) worked with Rand Corp. to develop this type of network for the transmission of both voice and data. The security of transmission and the fault tolerance of the network were very attractive to the DoD.

The network consisted of many switches or nodes that were connected with each other over a wide area by leased lines. Packet switched networks can be placed in two broad categories, each of which will be introduced here.

17.1.2 The Datagram Concept

Originally, Paul Baran used the datagram concept (as covered in Chapter 2) of delivery in packet switched networks. DTE, or the Data Terminal Equipment, was the terminal device, such as a remote terminal or a computer. When the DTE sent a message to another DTE connected to the network, it would break up the message into small parts called datagrams. As shown in Figure 17.1, these datagrams had a header added to the front of them, providing the destination address, source address, datagram number, and other such information. The datagrams would be sent into the network using various links. The nodes, by looking at the header and their own routing tables, could determine which link to forward the datagrams to or keep them, depending on the destination addresses.

Security was enhanced in this type of network, because if anyone tapped onto a line, they would only get fragments of the transmission. The network also didn't have a single point of failure, because if one link or node failed or was sabotaged, traffic could be routed using alternate paths. The control for this network was distributed with many nodes, and this was in sharp contrast with the hierarchical networks that were

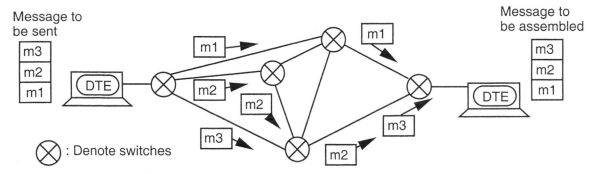

Figure 17.1 The datagram approach to packet switched networking.

used in the AT&T PSTN (Public Switched Telephone Network) as well as the forthcoming SNA data network of IBM. In the SNA network, if the host failed, the entire network crashed, but the packet networks were less susceptible to failure.

In 1967, DoD started ARPANET (Advanced Research Projects Agency NETwork), connecting many universities and government agencies across the country. This was the first test bed for packet switched networks. It used the datagram type of protocol. It was fast and performed as well as it did in theory. The value of such networks was realized, and soon many research projects sprang up to improve on this basic concept.

17.1.3 Packetization Concept

Many protocols were introduced to connect a DTE with a packet switched network. ITU standardized this interface in 1974 and called it X.25. ISO (International Standards Organization) also adopted X.25 to be the protocol used in the first three layers of their OSI (Open System Interconnect) reference model.

X.25 differs from Paul Baran's original concept of datagrams in many ways. Datagrams are still used in the TCP/IP protocol suite, but even ARPANET now runs on X.25. X.25 uses packets instead, which utilize a call connect phase to establish a link with the distant DTE. During the call connect phase, on most X.25 implementations, a path is selected through the nodes and links, and all the data during the data transfer phase travels on this given route. The fixed route is called a virtual circuit. Unlike X.25, datagrams formed out of one message use different routes depending on which links are available. Of course, since all packets use one route, it does not provide the best possible security. However, the billing for a connection is more like what customers expect from PSTN, since the path and the duration of the call are known. As you may remember, we discussed the differences between X.25 and datagram networks as used in the Internet in sections 2.5 and 2.6. In the rest of this chapter, we will use the terms X.25, packet switched networks, and packet networks interchangeably.

17.2 PURPOSE

Ever since 1880, the PSTN (public switched telephone network) has been developing into a network with low cost, high reliability, fast connection time, and good quality. Packet switched networks have the same basic objectives, but instead of providing a network designed to pass voice and make phone calls, it is designed to pass data and make interactive data connections. Packet switched networks also provide high quality, reliability, low-cost connection, and fast connect time.

The PSTN was originally designed to handle only voice, but in the 1950s people started using this infrastructure to transmit data as well by using modems. However, the transmission of data was limited by the analog equipment of the phone system, and so packet networks were introduced specifically for networking data terminals and hosts. These data terminals and hosts are called DTEs or data terminal equipments.

The telephone network and the packet network both use a mesh topology, which provides a terminal, with access to any other terminal, whether it be a phone or a DTE. The mesh type of topology also provides high reliability in the network, in that if one link or point fails, then the traffic can be rerouted easily using alternate links and points.

In the PSTN, once the connection is made, any protocol can be used during the conversation. It could be spoken English or another language, or it could be modulated data using ASCII, EBCDIC, or any other protocol. Similarly, a packet network also provides connectivity, and two end points using the same protocol can have a dialogue. Sometimes, a packet network is misunderstood and is thought to do a protocol conversion, such as an IBM host talking to a DEC host, but all that a packet network provides is connectivity. Services such as protocol conversions are provided by the upper layers of the OSI model.

Let us now switch our attention to the differences between PSTN and packet switched networks. The telephone network is inherently a circuit switched network. This means that once a connection is made between the end points, there is one circuit dedicated to carry their conversation, and no other conversation can be transmitted on that same circuit. In a packet network, the link between two end points is shared by other connections. Data is typically transferred in packets of 128 bytes, and these packets are statistically multiplexed on each link that a connection is made across, while over the PSTN, digitized voice is time division multiplexed on the intermachine trunks. Statistical multiplexing was covered in section 3.8 and will be reviewed shortly. The units of information that are conveyed over the X.25 network are octets or bytes, while the PSTN primarily supports 4 kHz voice. Another main difference between the PSTN and packet networks is that it may take around ten seconds to make a long distance connection and in a packet network it usually takes less than one second.

17.3 DIAL-UP LINES, LEASED LINES, AND PACKET NETWORKS

Dial-up lines, which use the telephone network, are easily available, and they provide access to many points readily. See Figure 17.2. The user is charged only for the time that the connection is made. However, accessing the switches using analog lines degrades the quality of the connection and data speeds are normally restricted to 9.6 kbps. They also have problems with security that can be overcome by the host calling back to the caller to verify its address (or phone number). However, that takes time and is costly.

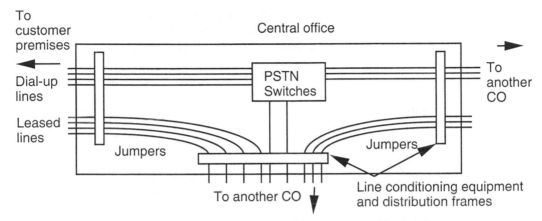

To customer premises

Central office

Dial-up lines

Leased lines

PSTN Switches

To another CO

Jumpers

Jumpers

To another CO

Line conditioning equipment and distribution frames

Figure 17.2 The difference between installing dial-up and leased lines inside a CO. The jumpers could be replaced by DACS (Digital Access Cross Connect Systems).

Leased lines, on the other hand, provide better security and data speeds can be up to 19.2 kbps for voice-grade lines. They don't go through switches. Payment is on a 24-hour basis, so these lines are used for high volumes of traffic. However, they are expensive and time-consuming to install, and don't come with redundant paths for added reliability. You may remember these differences from Section 5.1.

Packet switched networks, as depicted in Figure 17.3, try to capitalize on the strengths of both the dial-up network and the leased lines. Packet networks are said to have a reliability of better than 99.9%. That is just a few hours of outage during a year. If a node or a link within the network dies, the network is automatically "healed" by alternate routing. This is done without any loss of data and without the end users being aware of the failure. They provide data speeds of up to 64 kbps with an error rate of 10^{-9}. This means that there is one error in one billion bits! This makes a typical packet network a highly accurate network.

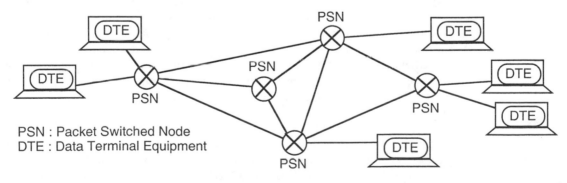

PSN : Packet Switched Node
DTE : Data Terminal Equipment

Figure 17.3 A packet switched network allows terminals at various locations to communicate with each other.

Many users can share the same link. If one user has stopped transmitting momentarily, data packets belonging to other dialogues can be sent on the same link. Of course, the protocols used by the various users on the same link don't have to be the same.

Packet networks also provide speed conversions through the buffers that are available in the nodes. This means that a host running at 64 kbps can be talking to a terminal running at 1200 bps.

17.4 PUBLIC DATA NETWORKS (PDNs)

There are basically two varieties of packet switched networks. A private packet switched network belongs to a private company which leases lines connecting the various nodes to each other. The private network, as the name implies, is accessed and used by one company, whereas a PDN or public data network is generally made available to any company or individual, just as the PSTN is made available to the public for voice calls.

In either case, these are considered to be either MANs (Metropolitan Area Network) or WANs (Wide Area Networks). A MAN has all its network access points restricted to one metropolitan area, whereas a WAN may span many cities, states, or nations. For example, Infopath is owned by NY Telephone and is available to all users in the New York city area. Also SprintNet, formerly Telenet, is owned by Sprint and is available to users and subscribers in the US. Infopath is regarded as a MAN where SprintNet is considered to be a WAN.

PDNs are referred to many times as VANs or Value Added Networks, because PDNs not only provide connectivity between many sites, but also may provide computing or database services.

The two most widely used PDNs in the United States are BT Tymnet by British Telecom and SprintNet. There are many others, and they all provide X.25 connectivity. Transpac is famous for going into most homes that have a phone in France. It provides a small data terminal that can be used to get on-line directory service, which eliminates the problem of printing and distributing telephone directories, discarding old ones, and keeping the data up to date. Transpac is also used for educational purposes. Networks, such as First Data Resource, provide a means of clearing credit card charges. With a dedicated line going to one of their packet network points, companies can get a credit card charge authorized using their clearing house in 5 to 6 seconds.

Many countries have at least one PDN. In Europe, the PDNs are owned by the PTTs (Post Telephone and Telegraph), a government agency similar to our US Postal Service. TELPAC in Mexico and EASTNET in the Philippines are other examples of PDNs.

PDNs are not used for transferring large volumes of data, but are cost effective for low- and medium-volume traffic. They don't charge by the distance of the call but by the amount of traffic that is sent and also according to the connect time. PDNs have all the advantages of a typical packet switched network, and many times they are used in conjunction with a private network in case the private network fails or carries too much traffic that needs to be diverted elsewhere.

Basically, there are two ways to access a PDN and the method chosen depends on how much usage the PDN gets. If the PDN is used a lot a leased line is installed to a dedicated port of the PDN. If the usage is occasional, a dial-up line is used to access the PDN. Dial-up ports of a PDN must have enough modems to accommodate the number of callers that may be calling in, or else callers will be blocked.

17.5 THE OPERATION OF A PACKET SWITCHED NETWORK

17.5.1 What Is Packet Switching?

To best understand the operation of a packet network, it is good to review the workings of statistical multiplexers or stat-muxes for short.

With stat-muxes, it is possible to have the link speed be less than the sum of the terminal speeds. When a network like this is designed, it is assumed that not all terminals are constantly typing simultaneously. In Figure 17.4 (a), x1 can only talk to y1 on the other end, so that each terminal communicates with its respective terminal on the remote end.

Figure 17.4.(b) is a very simple X.25 network, where we have replaced the stat-muxes with packet switches, also called nodes. The terminals are X.25-compatible. With this network, x1 can talk not only to y1 but to any other terminal because a packet switch provides not only statistical multiplexing but also switching. However, x1 must know the address of the terminal it wants to talk to. The links between the nodes, again, are statistically multiplexed, so the aggregate speed of the links can be less than the sum of the terminal speeds.

In Figure 17.5 we have a more usable X.25 network with many links and switches connected in a mesh topology to provide alternate routing and greater reliability. Again, any terminal can connect itself with any other terminal on the network, as long as the addresses are known.

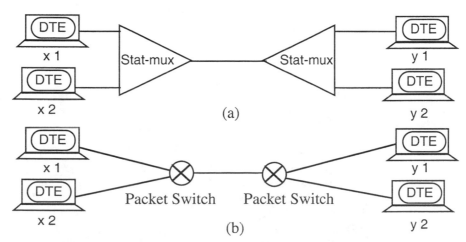

Figure 17.4 (a) In this statistical multiplexing connection, x1 may only link up with y1. (b) In this packet switched connection, x1 may connect with any of the other terminals.

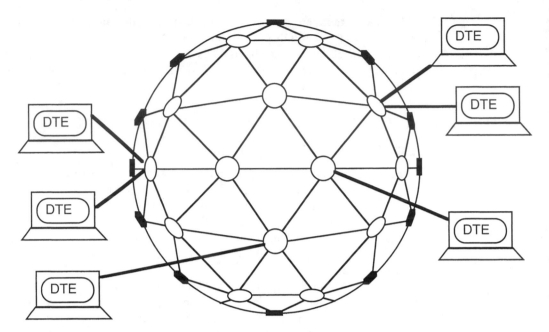

Figure 17.5 A packet switched network provides many alternate paths.

A terminal is designated as a DTE (Data Terminal Equipment) in X.25 terminology. DTEs could be data terminals, mainframes, or anything else where data can terminate or originate. The component of the switch that interfaces with a DTE is called a DCE or Data Communications Equipment (sometimes, Data Circuit terminating Equipment). Many times, a switch or a node serves as a switch as well as a set of DCEs, depending on how many ports it may have. The packet network consists of the nodes, links, and the DCEs, but not the DTEs. Many refer to a packet switched network as the "cloud," for short.

The X.25 standard is defined between the DCE and the DTE. No standard is defined between the nodes, so usually in such a network, one vendor's equipment is used and a proprietary protocol is used inside the cloud.

17.5.2 Protocols Relating to X.25

Many times a DTE is not X.25-compatible, in which case a PAD (packet assembler/disassembler) must be used to get connectivity with the network. A PAD can come with a number of ports, which are synchronous or asynchronous depending on the type of terminals a user wants to connect to the network. The PAD may be located near the terminals if they are located in one place, or if the terminals are not in one location, the PAD may be placed with the DCE.

The services of an asynchronous PAD are specified in X.3, and the interaction between the PAD and the non-X.25 terminal are specified by X.28 by ITU-T. See Figure 17.6. Packet networks can be interconnected or internetworked. In that case,

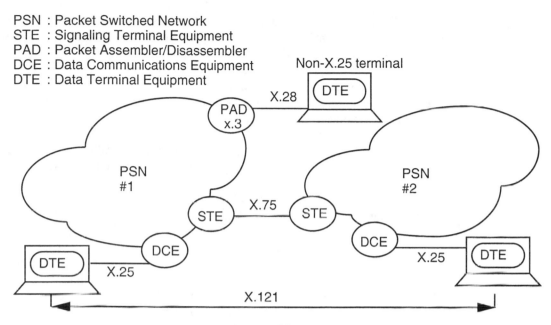

PSN : Packet Switched Network
STE : Signaling Terminal Equipment
PAD : Packet Assembler/Disassembler
DCE : Data Communications Equipment
DTE : Data Terminal Equipment

Figure 17.6 ITU's X.25-related protocols.

X.25-level gateways are needed in each network to communicate with each other. Another name for this gateway is an STE, or a Signaling Terminal Equipment. The ITU-T protocol that is used between STEs is X.75. X.121 is the protocol that provides the proper way of addressing networks that are interconnected. It specifies the country code, network code, and the terminal number.

The international address can be up to 14 digits long plus an optional prefix of a "0" or a "1." For international calls, the prefix of 1 is used. After the optional prefix, the next four digits specify the country and then the PDN within that country. This four-digit field is called the DNIC (Data Network Identification Code). Finally, the last 10 digits identify the DTE that is attached to that network. This way, DTEs can call other DTEs around the world that are not part of the same PDN.

In the international address of "31101234567890," for example, the "31" specifies the United States, the "10" specifies the SprintNet PDN, and "1234567890" identifies the terminal number in SprintNet.

17.6 LAP/B: THE DATA LINK LAYER OF X.25

In the physical layer of X.25, ITU-T recommends using X.21. This has a 15-pin connector with 7 pins that are actually used. The X.21 standard, though part of X.25, is not widely implemented. Most installations use EIA's RS-232 or V.35 standards at the physical level.

For the data link control layer, ITU-T recommends LAP/B or Link Access Procedure/Balanced, which is similar to SDLC or IIDLC. SDLC has already been covered in detail, and as was then noted, there are three types of frames, namely, information, supervisory, and unnumbered. Information and supervisory types of frames were covered at length. Unnumbered frames will be covered now, because they are used in establishing and disconnecting communications links.

At the data link layer three basic modes of operation exist. First is SNRM (Set Normal Response Mode), where a multipoint protocol is used to perform polling and selecting. Then there is SARM (Set Asynchronous Response Mode) which is used for a half-duplex, point-to-point operation. Lastly, SABM (Set Asynchronous Balance Mode) is used for a full-duplex and point-to-point operation. X.25's LAP/B uses this last mode of operation to connect and disconnect a link. When a link is said to be balanced it means that either end can initiate the connection; in LAP/B, this means either the DTE or the DCE.

LAP/B has 5 types of unnumbered frames; they are SABM, UA (Unnumbered Acknowledge), DISC (DISConnect), FRMR (FRaMe Reject), and DM (Disconnect Mode). A UA frame is sent to acknowledge SABM or DISC frames. The SABM frame is used to get a DTE or a DCE in a connect mode and the DISC is sent to put them in a disconnect mode. If information is sent to either a DTE or a DCE that is in a disconnect mode; it will reply with a DM indicating that the recipient isn't connected. Only an SABM frame can get the DCE or the DTE in a connect mode.

An FRMR frame is sent if an illegal frame was received. This is the opposite of the REJ type of supervisory frame, which indicates that there was an error in the data itself. An FRMR frame is sent if an invalid control field was received, an incorrect length frame was received, an invalid Nr was received, or an unexpected ACK was received. FRMR also retransmits the rejected frame's control field to let the receiver know the reason for the rejection.

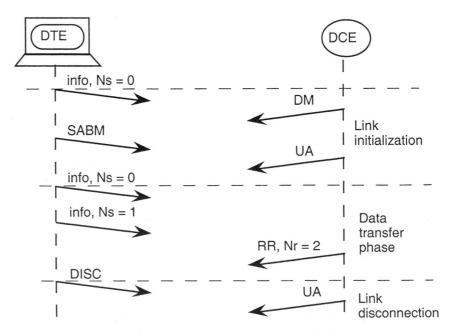

Figure 17.7 Exchange of frames over a DTE-DCE link.

To summarize these points, an example of transmission exchanges is shown in Figure 17.7. The DTE sends an information frame and the DCE replies with a DM frame, notifying the DTE that it is in the disconnect mode. The DTE then brings the DCE into a connect mode by issuing a SABM. The DCE then completes the connection by sending a UA. Then the link goes into a data transfer mode. Here, the DTE sends two frames numbered 0 and 1. The DCE acknowledges that by sending an Nr of 2, indicating that it is expecting to receive DTE's frame number 2. Finally the link is disconnected. The disconnect can be requested by either the DTE or the DCE.

17.7 THE X.25 NETWORK LAYER

17.7.1 The Mechanism of Communications through Layers

When data is sent through a network, it first arrives at the network layer as shown in Figure 17.8. The network layer encapsulates the data into a packet by adding a header to it. The network layer then hands over the packet to the data link layer which then forms an information field out of the packet itself. The packet in the data link layer is called the information field. The information field is then encapsulated into a frame by adding the fields as shown in the diagram. Lastly, the physical layer will transmit the actual bits at the appropriate rate, using correct voltages and so on. The receiving end does this process in reverse.

In Figure 17.9, DTE1 is transmitting to DTE2. The physical layer of DCE1 will receive the raw bits and the data link layer of DCE1 will check and correct the errors on the link with DTE1. The network control layer then receives error-free packets from the data link layer. It then decides from its header how to route the packet so that it is sent in the direction of its destination. When the link is chosen, this same process occurs from the DCE/switch to the next switch. As the packet is sent through the network, this layering process is repeated over each link until the packet reaches the intended DTE. Over each link between devices or packet switches, the physical layer transmits and receives bits, the data link layer controls the errors over the links, and the network layer does the routing of the packets.

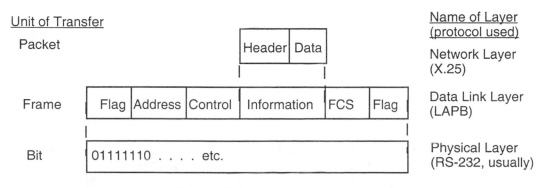

Figure 17.8 The three layers of X.25.

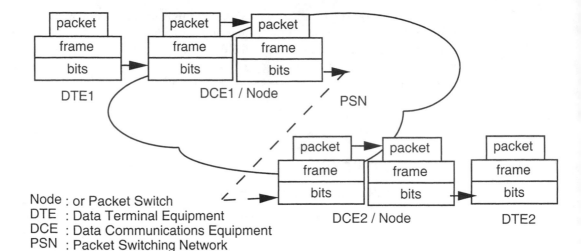

Node : or Packet Switch
DTE : Data Terminal Equipment
DCE : Data Communications Equipment
PSN : Packet Switching Network

Figure 17.9 The transfer of data through a packet network.

17.7.2 Permanent and Switched Virtual Circuits

When a DTE establishes a call, it has to provide the X.121 address of the remote DTE. The switches will find a path through the network using the various links that are available. This bidirectional association between two DTEs across a PSN (Packet Switched Network) is called a virtual circuit.

The physical links between the switches are statistically multiplexed, so that the links are shared by many connections. Each link has about 4096 logical channels available and these logical channels can be assigned to that many data conversations. A logical channel is designated by the LCI (Logical Channel Identifier) and is provided in the packet header. When a switch receives a packet, it will route that packet to the appropriate link depending on its LCI, changing the LCI over the next link.

For example, in Figure 17.10, a packet switching node is receiving three packets. It routes packets with LCIs of 1500 to PSN-A changing the LCIs to 600, and routes the packets with LCIs of 1000 to PSN-B, changing their LCIs to 1100. The PSNs that receive these packets similarly continue this routing procedure, so virtual circuits are defined not only by the physical links they use, but also by which LCIs they occupy over the respective links.

Each node maintains a table specifying which LCIs on which links are routed to which new LCIs and links. New entries are made to these tables during the call establishment phase of calls. This example assumes a virtual circuit implementation of internodal links, but this may not always be true.

There are two types of virtual circuits and they are called PVC for permanent virtual circuit, and SVC for switched virtual circuit. Out of the 4096 channels that are possible, channel 0 is used for network diagnostic purposes. The rest of the channels are assigned in groups of the following: PVCs, incoming SVCs, two-way SVCs, and outgoing SVCs. The LCIs are assigned as calls are made and are freed as calls become disconnected.

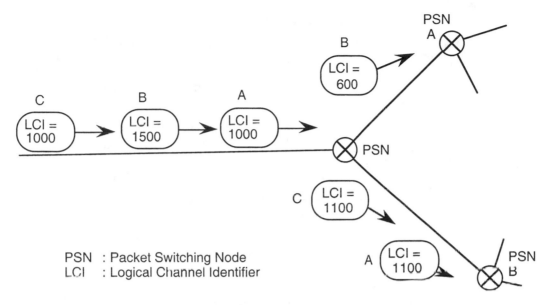

Figure 17.10 Routing of packets through a switch.

PSN : Packet Switching Node
LCI : Logical Channel Identifier

PVCs provide a dedicated channel between two users, and no call set-up phase is required. PVCs oppose X.25's philosophy of bandwidth on demand, so they are not that popular. Switched virtual circuits provide a temporary logical connection between two DTEs and are established when making the call.

17.8 PACKET TYPES

17.8.1 Packet Headers

Data, flow control, and supervisory are three types of packets. The basic header for data packets will be studied first. Figure 17.11 shows a header that is typically 6 nibbles or 3 octets long. The first nibble is the GFI for General Format Identifier, the next three nibbles are the LCI (Logical Channel Identifier) which consists of the LCGN (Logical Channel Group Number) and the LCN (Logical Channel Number). To make life interesting, many refer to the LCI as the LCN. The last two nibbles are the packet type identifier.

The Q or the Qualifier bit in the GFI determines whether the packet is intended for the remote DTE or simply the remote PAD. The D or the Delivery bit specifies whether the acknowledgment is local or end-end.

In Figure 17.12, the difference between these two types of acknowledgments is illustrated. In the local acknowledgment, the ACK or RR (Receiver Ready) is supplied by the local DCE. It confirms that the packet reached the network, but not necessarily the destination. This is similar to when a child drops a letter in a mailbox and comes back to say that the letter was mailed, but cannot confirm that it actually reached its destination. Likewise, local acknowledgment confirms that the packet reached the network, but not the destination.

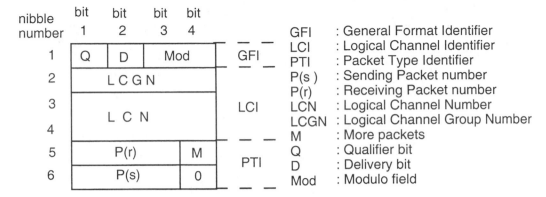

nibble number

	bit 1	bit 2	bit 3	bit 4	
1	Q	D	Mod		GFI
2	LCGN				
3	LCN				LCI
4					
5	P(r)			M	PTI
6	P(s)			0	

GFI : General Format Identifier
LCI : Logical Channel Identifier
PTI : Packet Type Identifier
P(s) : Sending Packet number
P(r) : Receiving Packet number
LCN : Logical Channel Number
LCGN : Logical Channel Group Number
M : More packets
Q : Qualifier bit
D : Delivery bit
Mod : Modulo field

Figure 17.11 The three-octet packet header.

End-end acknowledgment is similar to the "return receipt requested" offered by the postal service. As in the postal service, this type of confirmation takes longer to receive and is more costly.

P(s) and P(r) fields of the PTI are similar to the N(s) and the N(r) fields in SDLC frames except that here, P(s) and P(r) refer to the packet numbers and not the frame numbers. P(s) is the sending packet number and P(r) is the next packet the sender is

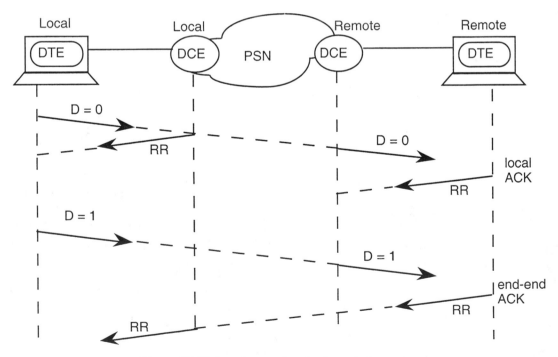

Figure 17.12 Local vs. end-end acknowledgments.

expecting from the receiver. For example, if a DTE is sending a packet with P(s) of 3 and P(r) of 2, that indicates that the DTE is sending its packet number 3 and has received all the packets up to and including packet number 1 from the remote end.

The modulo field of the GFI determines if the transmission mode is normal control or extended. In the normal control mode, the P(s) and P(r) fields are represented using 3 bits each, as shown in Figure 17.11. In the extended mode, 7 bits are used to represent these two fields. In that case, the packet header, unlike that shown in Figure 17.11, would be 4 octets long. The window size, which determines the number of consecutive packets that can be transmitted without requiring a response, is 7 for the normal mode and 127 for the extended mode. The extended mode is more suitable for transmissions with a long delay, such as satellite transmissions.

LCGN, being 4 bits long, allows for 2^4 or 16 numbers of LCGNs. LCN, being 8 bits long, allows for 2^8 or 256 numbers of LCNs. Since every group (or LCGN) out of a possible 16 can each have 256 channels, a total of 4096 channels (LCIs) exist.

Finally, the "more" field simply signals the remote end if additional packets are to be expected or not. This field is used by the upper layers for information unit segmentation (or breaking up of information units into smaller units) and assembly.

17.8.2 Supervisory Packets

Data packets are indicated with a 0 in the 8th bit of the PTI, as shown in Figure 17.11. If the 7th and the 8th bits of the PTI are "01" then the packet type is flow control. Flow control packets are used to positively or negatively acknowledge transmissions.

If the 7th and 8th bits of the PTI are "11," then it is a supervisory type of packet. These packets are used to establish and disconnect connections, and also to bring up circuits in case of problems .

Figure 17.13 not only shows how a connection is made and broken in layer 3, but also summarizes the same for the first two layers. Let us now concentrate on the third layer.

When a DTE needs to establish a call, it provides the address of the DTEs in a CALL REQUEST packet to its DCE. As this packet finds its destination DTE, the address is converted to LCIs on the corresponding links. Once the call is set up the addresses are not needed, only the LCIs. When the packet arrives at the called DCE, it will send an INCOMING CALL packet to its DTE. The called DTE may then send a CALL ACCEPTED packet to its DCE and the calling DTE would receive a CALL CONNECTED packet from its DCE. Now that the call is established, data transfer can occur.

After the data transfer phase, either DTE may disconnect the virtual circuit. This is done by issuing a CLEAR REQUEST. On the opposite end the DTE would receive a CLEAR INDICATION and transmit a CLEAR CONFIRMATION packet. The CLEAR CONFIRMATION packet is also received by the call clearing DTE.

In establishing a call, if the network doesn't want to accept the call, the calling DCE will send a CLEAR INDICATION back to the calling DTE. If the called DTE doesn't want to accept the call, it sends a CLEAR REQUEST packet instead of the CALL ACCEPTED packet.

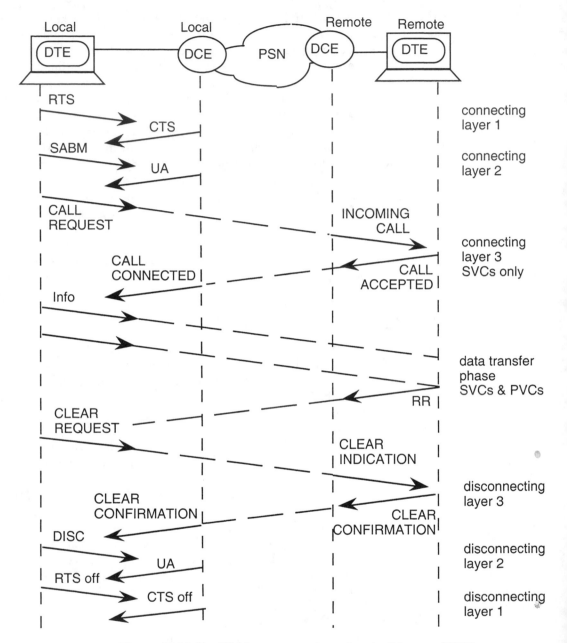

Figure 17.13 Establishing a connection using the 3 layers of X.25.

When abnormal conditions exist during the data transfer phase, there is an ordered set of procedures to follow to bring the circuit up. First an RR is sent to request the remote DTE to respond. If that doesn't work, an INTERRUPT, a RESET, a CLEAR, and as a final resort a RESTART is issued by the DTE. Let us consider them in order.

An INTERRUPT packet is sent during the data transfer phase to obtain an immediate response from the distant DTE. The distant DTE must then send an INTERRUPT CONFIRMATION. This process will synchronize the P(s)s and the P(r)s.

If the INTERRUPT CONFIRMATION is not received, then the DTE knows that there's a problem with the virtual circuit, and it may then issue a RESET. This type of supervisory packet will reset the P(s) and the P(r) counters to zero.

If the RESET CONFIRMATION is not received from the remote end, the DTE may send a CLEAR REQUEST if the circuit is a switched virtual circuit. This request disconnects the virtual circuit and the LCI associated with it is freed.

If the clear is not confirmed, then a RESTART packet may be transmitted as a last resort. This packet will clear all SVCs and PVCs associated by the requesting DTE. All transient data will be lost, so this is primarily done after a power failure. The RESET, CLEAR, and RESTART packets contain a code to indicate the reason for issuing them.

17.9 X.25 FEATURES AND FACILITIES

Just as PBXs provide features in a voice environment, so also does X.25 provide a wide range of features for packet networks. A few examples of such features are described here.

Outgoing Calls Barred: This facility can restrict the DTE from making calls.

Incoming Calls Barred: This restricts the DTE from receiving any calls.

Closed User Groups: This facility creates a virtual network within a larger public network, and DTEs can only talk to others that belong to the same group. However, one DTE can belong to a number of such groups.

Fast Select: This facility is used for credit card authorization. Data is sent in the CALL REQUEST packet to a host, providing the credit card number, amount of purchase, etc. The host will immediately send a CLEAR REQUEST packet instead of the CALL ACCEPTED packet authorizing or not authorizing the purchase. No data transfer phase is used here.

Call Redirection: Similar to the call forwarding feature in PBXs, this allows one DTE to redirect the calls it receives to other DTEs.

Reverse Charging: Similar to a call collect, here a DTE can reverse the charges in a packet network. Dial-up ports on PDNs use this feature extensively.

17.10 INTERCONNECTING X.25 WITH IBM'S NETWORKS

It's common knowledge that IBM is a major vendor of computer equipment and that SNA (System Network Architecture) is IBM's proprietary protocol used to network its computers. SNA networks are most widely used in the business world. The traditional method of connecting SNA networks is by using leased lines for primary links and dial-up lines for backup. However, packet switched networks, public or private, provide an enhanced method of connecting SNA network links. Packet networks are more resilient to failure, provide excellent transmission quality, and are inexpensive, since the costs of the connections are shared among many users. Therefore, many organizations prefer an X.25 network backbone to run their SNA networks.

Let us consider three methods of doing this.

17.10.1 The Software Approach for Implementing SNA over X.25

Figure 17.14 shows one alternative to interconnecting SNA to an X.25 network This involves using a software package called NPSI (NCP Packet Switched Interface). NPSI runs under NCP (Network Control Program) in the front end processors, namely the 3725 or the 3745. NPSI does encapsulation of SNA units into X.25 packets. NCP sends a PIU (Path Information Unit) containing the RU (Request/response Unit) and the SNA headers to NPSI, which in turn adds the packet header and trailers to the PIU. This makes the data ready for the packet network. Encapsulating the data or the RU into a PIU and then again into a packet is called double encapsulation. Packets arriving from the network do this same process, but in reverse.

Now that a packet contains not only X.25 headers but also SNA headers, the maximum size of the data that can be sent becomes smaller. This means that more packets need to be sent and received. The performance of the 3725 is reduced by about 30% and of the 3745 by about 15% because of this overload. Performance can be improved by increasing the packet size from 128 to 256 bytes.

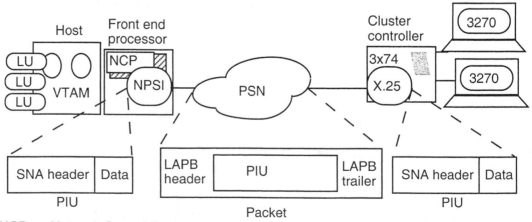

NCP   : Network Control Program   PIU : Path Information Unit
NPSI : NCP Packet Switching Interface   LU : Logical Unit
VTAM : Virtual Telecommunications Access Method

Figure 17.14 Using NPSI to run SNA over X.25.

Similarly, in the tail circuit, an X.25 interface package can be incorporated in the cluster controller. This package is functionally the same as the NPSI, but is designed for the type 2 node.

Simply by adding the appropriate software on both ends, packet networks can be used to transport SNA data streams. This allows the user to preserve his investment in the SNA equipment and still get the benefits of packet networks. Although LU switching is generally done by SNA, PU switching is possible with this software approach. You may recall that PU switching allows everyone on a cluster controller to have access to only one application on one host, whereas LU switching allows everyone on the cluster controller to access any application on any host.

17.10.2 The Hardware Approach

A hardware approach to solve the SNA-X.25 connectivity problem is shown in Figure 17.15. On the host's side, a host PAD or HPAD is connected between the FEP and the network. Also, a terminal PAD or TPAD is connected on the other end. Although this requires extra boxes and cabling, it is less costly than using the NPSI method, and is more popular. One of the key advantages of this method is that it doesn't load down the FEP. Just as the front end relieves the host from doing communications-related processing, the HPAD relieves the FEP from having to assemble and disassemble packets, allowing the FEP to concentrate on the SNA protocol. With NPSI, if the line quality to the network becomes poor, the front end's performance goes down drastically. The HPAD takes care of error correction and frees the front end from having to do it.

HPADs also improve the host's processing time. They provide better network management capabilities and also LU switching. Network changes, such as adding or removing PUs or cluster controllers, are done easily if properly planned in advance.

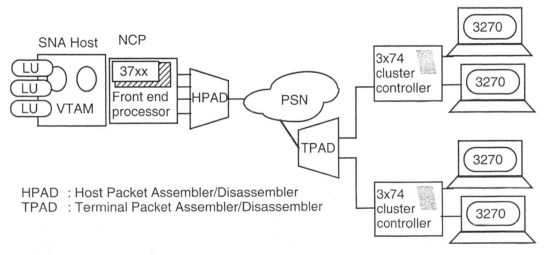

Figure 17.15 Using PADS to run SNA over X.25.

TPADs are functionally complementary to HPADs, but they are designed for the tail end circuits. TPADS provide local polling, so that only the payload goes across the network. TPADs can be used with NPSI residing on the host's end.

Using QLLC (Qualified Logical Link Control), both the software and physical approaches can be combined on one network. This protocol may exist along with NPSI and also in the PADs. QLLC packets convey SDLC commands and responses over the X.25 network, which are converted to SDLC-equivalent frames at the end points.

17.10.3 The XI Approach

Another approach introduced by IBM in the US in 1988 to interconnect X.25 over SNA is called XI (X.25 to SNA Interconnection). Previously we mentioned that X.25 protocol is simply defined between the DTE and DCE and that the protocol used between the DCEs and switches is sometimes proprietary. As shown in Figure 17.16, this proprietary protocol used with XI is SNA's SDLC, and the interfaces between the DTEs and FEPs are still X.25. Using XI involves using a packet network connected by FEPs and SDLC links. All DTEs must be connected to FEPs. XI resides under the FEP's NCP, and all packets must come and go through XI. One copy of XI can provide up to 256 DTE interfaces.

A single LU-LU session exists among the various FEPs or XI nodes, and X.25 virtual circuits are multiplexed on these single LU-LU sessions. This improves performance, because sessions don't have to be created and terminated dynamically. Virtual circuits are transported through the already available sessions. Packet sizes can be as large as 1024 bytes, which also improves the performance of the FEPs. XI also supports NetView, IBM's network management product.

Recently, third-party vendors have introduced communications processors to be used in place of the 37x5 FEPs, which look like a type 4 node to the host. These

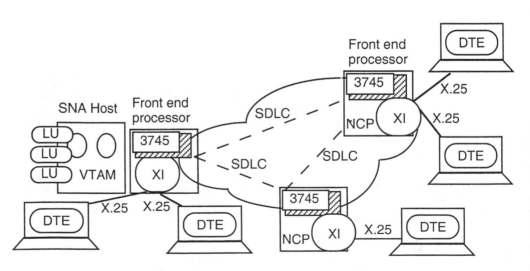

Figure 17.16 Running SNA over X.25 using XI.

processors are designed with X.25 in mind, so duplication of SNA/SDLC and X.25 functions are minimized and provide a nonhierarchical structure to SNA.

17.10.4 Advantages of Using X.25 for BSC Networks

Other advantages of X.25 are apparent when studying a pre-SNA Bisync or BSC network. In Figure 17.17(a), a BSC host is connected with half-duplex multipoint terminals. The highest speed on typical analog lines would be 14.4 kbps. Polling is done from the FEP, making any delays significant. The host is also underutilized, because it can only support one device at a time.

By inserting BSC PADs on both ends of a packet network as shown in Figure 17.17(b), the transmission becomes full-duplex. Transmission is half-duplex only from the FEP to the HPAD and from the TPAD to the terminals, which are the insignificant

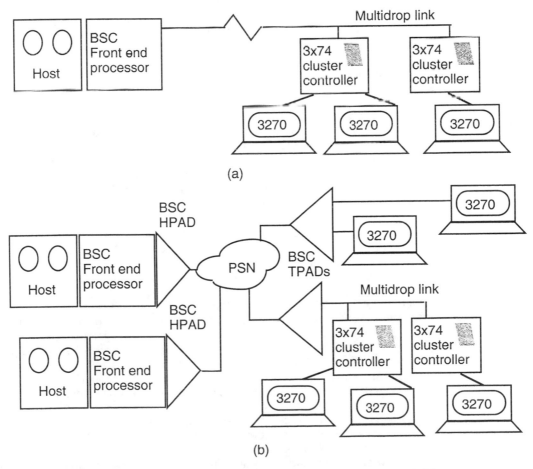

(a)

(b)

Figure 17.17 (a) A typical BSC network. (b) Implementing a BSC network over a packet switched network introduces many new benefits.

parts of the link. Speeds through the packet network can go up as high as 64 kbps from 14.4 kbps. Polling delays are minimized, because polling is done locally from the TPADs and not over the entire network. The terminals are now not restricted to one application on one host, but because of the LU switching provided by the TPADs, they can access any application on any host simultaneously. Similar advantages can be gained for SDLC backbones as well.

EXERCISES

1. A PDN is also referred to as a what?
   - a. LAN
   - b. MAN
   - c. VAN
   - d. WAN
2. Packet switching networks do not provide
   - a. reliability
   - b. security
   - c. low cost
   - d. high transfer rate
3. LAP/B uses which type of transmission mode?
   - a. SNRM
   - b. SARM
   - c. SABM
   - d. SNBM
4. Which field determines the type of acknowledgment requested?
   - a. P(r) and P(s)
   - b. mod
   - c. Q bit
   - d. D bit
5. A call request packet becomes what type of packet on the receiver end?
   - a. call accepted
   - b. call connected
   - c. call acknowledgment
   - d. incoming call
6. Which type of X.25 and SNA interconnection method requires SDLC to be used as the internode link protocol in the network?
   - a. NPSI
   - b. HPAD-TPAD
   - c. XI
   - d. BSC method
7. Which protocol defines the interface between two different packet networks?
   - a. X.25
   - b. X.3
   - c. X.75
   - d. X.121
8. Which X.25 feature doesn't allow a user to make any calls?
   - a. outgoing calls barred
   - b. incoming calls barred
   - c. reverse charging
   - d. call redirection
9. The X.25 standard is specified by which organization?
10. What type of lines incur a flat monthly charge?
11. In LAP/B, which frame acknowledges a DISC frame?
12. When a call is connected between two end points through a packet network, to what is the destination address converted between each link in the network?
13. Which packet is transmitted to initiate a disconnection between two points?
14. Which packet header field determines the window size?
15. NPSI operates in which device and under which protocol?
16. On a BSC network running over a packet network, polling of terminals is done from which device?
17. Discuss the differences between using datagrams and packets.
18. Discuss the differences between dial-up lines and leased lines. Which of these benefits exist in packet networks?
19. How are packet switching and statistical multiplexing similar and how are they different?
20. List the protocols that are related to X.25 and give their purpose.

21. Explain how packets traverse through a network. Give the function of the layers.
22. Draw a four-octet packet header for the extended mode of transmission, giving the reason why the window size is 127 and the number of packet numbers is 128 (0 through 127).
23. Describe the sequence of events that take place when no response is received from the far end in X.25.
24. What are the pros and cons for running SNA traffic using NPSI? Using HPADs and TPADs?

## Chapter 18

SS7

18.1 INTRODUCTION

Back in Chapter 9, the various methods of signaling were introduced, including the differences between per-trunk and common channel interoffice signaling. This chapter is merely a continuation of CCIS, specifically that of SS7. The reader should have obtained an operational overview of SS7 in Chapter 11. The version that is widely used in North America is called CCS7 (Common Channel Signaling number 7), and it differs slightly from the ITU-T's version, which is called SS7. Japan also has its own variant. (These variants differ from each other primarily by their point code sizes and MTPs. ITU-T uses a point code size of 14, USA uses a size of 24, and Japan 16. These terms will be explained later.) Although the discussion will be more based on CCS7, we will simply refer to it as SS7. However, when crossing international boundaries the ITU-T version is used. Hopefully, all these versions will converge sometime in the future.

18.1.1 Advantages

SS7 is a voice network application of packet switched networks, and brings with it many of the advantages of packet switching discussed in Chapter 17. Aside from those advantages and those of CCIS pointed out in Chapter 9, let me point out a few more here.

Probably the most beneficial advantage of SS7 is its flexibility. Since the signaling is software-driven instead of electro-mechanical in nature, new features can be readily implemented in the network by modifying the software and distributing copies of it to all points in the network. This is easier than having to remanufacture new signaling interfaces for all locations every time someone wants to introduce a new signaling function. However, the downside of SS7 is that the programming code for it is quite complex and one bug in it can cripple all communications in one part of the country.

SS7 allows the IXCs, LECs, the international carriers, and soon even equipment for large private networks to talk to one another using one standard language. This allows customers using one 800 number to route calls over different IXCs' networks depending on the time of day, amount of traffic, or tariff structures. Customers will be able to manage their own databases which interact directly with the carrier's signaling network. In short, SS7 opens up a wide variety of creative options to the user.

SS7 predates ISDN and OSI and has been chosen as the interface between switches of carrier networks. SS7 provides many capabilities which ISDN doesn't have to implement, and so SS7 is considered necessary for ISDN to become a reality. ISDN then becomes a user application of SS7. Finally, SS7 provides management signals, through which it becomes easy to maintain, monitor, and administer the network.

Figure 18.1 shows how the various signaling systems coexist in a modern digital environment. Between the end-subscriber and the local CO, ISDN or DTMF may be used for signaling. Q.931 is the standard which specifies ISDN signaling with the subscriber. These protocols are then translated into SS7 at the CO. One should remember throughout this chapter that SS7 has no direct interface with the subscriber. Additionally, "subscriber" is the term used for the person at the phone and "user" is the term used for SS7 nodes, such as the digital switch at the CO.

18.1.2 History

Prior to SS7, ITU-T had specified other signaling systems that were more common in Europe than in North America. SS1 was specified for manually operated ringdown circuits, where one phone is connected to only one other, so that when a phone rings it is always the same phone calling it. SS2 used 600-Hz and 750-Hz tones for supervisory and address signaling. SS3 specified a 2280-Hz signal similar in function to our 2600-Hz SF tone. SS4 (using 2040 Hz and 2400 Hz) and SS5 (using 2400 Hz and 2600 Hz) were variations of SS3.

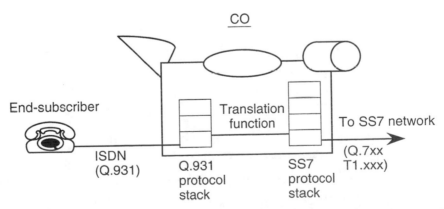

Figure 18.1 ISDN is used for signaling by the end subscriber. The digital switch at the CO is the user of the SS7 signaling network.

These first five signaling systems used CAS (Channel Associated Signaling). CAS is the formal term for what we have so far called per-trunk signaling. Then in 1976 SS6 was introduced in the North American network. It used 2.4-kbps data links in the signaling network, which were later doubled to 4.8 kbps. It provided 800 number services and was designed for analog voice networks.

SS7, on the other hand, was being deployed by the IXCs in the late 1980s. It used 56/64 kbps signaling links and required that stored program control digital switches be used in the voice network.

18.2 TOPOLOGY

18.2.1 Types of Nodes

Figure 18.2 shows the types of nodes existing in an SS7 network. They fall into two categories called SPs (Signaling Points) and STPs (Signal Transfer Points). SPs can be thought of as the end nodes in the network where packets, called messages, originate and terminate, whereas the STPs are the packet switches which route the messages to their proper destinations.

Furthermore, there are three kinds of SPs (Signaling Points) which are called switching points, SSPs (Service Switching Points), and SCPs (Service Control Points). Switching points are the hardware and the software associated in the digital switches that convert the external signaling protocol, such as ISDN or DTMF, into SS7 format messages so that they could be deciphered by the STPs. The switching points are part of the 4ESS, DMS-250, or any such digital switch that is part of the SS7 network. The switches that are not SS7-compliant can have access to the intelligent network through an SSP.

Lastly, the SCP is a database system that is used for credit card authorization, subscriber records for virtual networks, billing information, 800 number conversion tables, and other special services functions. An SCP service can be provided via a separate switch, via an intelligent peripheral connected to an STP, or as an adjunct processor on an SSP/STP.

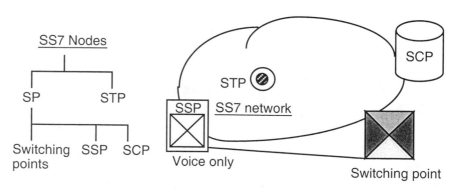

Figure 18.2 Types of SS7 nodes.

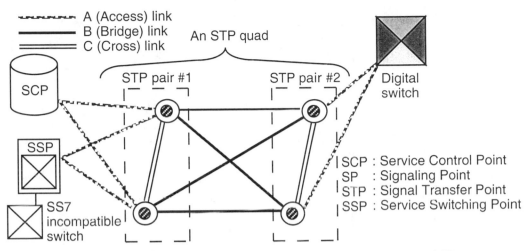

Figure 18.3 An STP quad configuration, showing the three types of SPs and the signaling links that connect them.

18.2.2 Types of Links

Figure 18.3 shows these three types of SPs being connected to STPs. STPs are deployed in what are called mated pairs and they each share the traffic load between them. Two such mated pairs that are interconnected are called an STP quad.

From each SP there are two links to a mated STP pair to which the SP is "homed." These links are called A or access links. The STPs in a pair are connected to each other by C or cross links. Since the traffic between the two STPs is shared, if one fails, the other has enough capacity to accept all of the traffic.

Each STP in a pair is connected to every other pair using B (bridge) links. The redundancy in all of the components of the signaling network makes it less susceptible to failure. Half of the components and links may fail and the network could still remain operational.

Figure 18.4 shows a more general network where the signaling links are fully integrated between an IXC and an LEC network. Notice that the LEC network is shown with a regional STP pair that is a level higher than the local STP pairs. The local and the regional STPs are also called secondary and primary STPs, respectively. The links between such STP pairs are called D or diagonal links.

18.2.3 AIN

Figure 18.5 shows a functional diagram of an AIN (Advanced Intelligent Network). An intelligent network provides an array of data, service logic, and assistance in-service functions in a distributed environment, using SS7. The components of such a network are briefly outlined.

The adjunct is like an SCP that provides geographically localized services to the AIN digital switch. While the SCP provides a centralized source of data to many switches, the adjunct primarily serves only one switch.

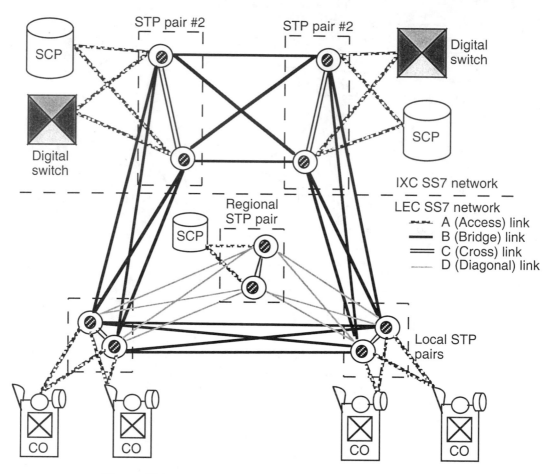

Figure 18.4 A fully interconnected SS7 network between an LEC and an IXC.

Among other services, the IP/SN (Intelligent Peripheral/Service-circuit Node) provides announcements, voice synthesis and recognition, and store-and-forward services for fax transmissions. These services are provided to both the adjunct and the SCP. The IP/SN can be connected to the AIN switch using ISDN.

ABS (Alternate Billing Service) permits customers to charge for calls using collect calling, third number billing, and credit card charging. Information about these details is stored in the LIDB (Line Information Data Base). CLASS (Custom Local Area Signaling Services) provides customers with the following seven services: Return Call, Priority Call, Repeat Call, Select Forwarding, Call Block, Caller ID, and Call Trace.

Triggering allows a switch to query an SCP while processing a call. Examples of triggers are when a caller answers the phone or when a virtual network number is dialed. One can readily see that the simple signaling protocol that was originally set up only to route 800 calls will soon be used to perform much more complex services.

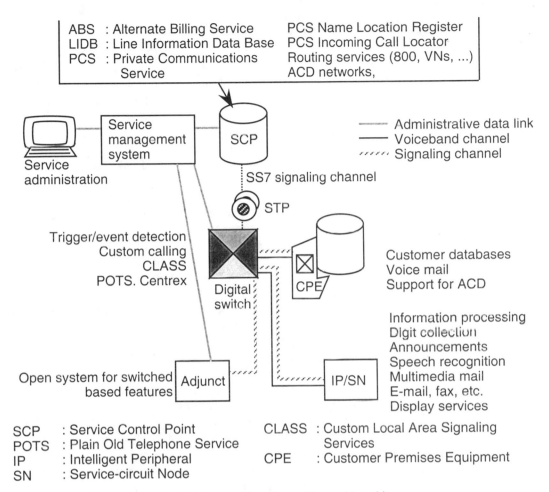

ABS : Alternate Billing Service
LIDB : Line Information Data Base
PCS : Private Communications
        Service

PCS Name Location Register
PCS Incoming Call Locator
Routing services (800, VNs, ...)
ACD networks,

Service management system

Service administration

SCP

—— Administrative data link
—— Voiceband channel
″″″″ Signaling channel

SS7 signaling channel

STP

Trigger/event detection
Custom calling
CLASS
POTS. Centrex

Digital switch

CPE

Customer databases
Voice mail
Support for ACD

Information processing
Digit collection
Announcements
Speech recognition
Multimedia mail
E-mail, fax, etc.
Display services

Open system for switched based features

Adjunct

IP/SN

SCP   : Service Control Point
POTS : Plain Old Telephone Service
IP   : Intelligent Peripheral
SN   : Service-circuit Node

CLASS : Custom Local Area Signaling
         Services
CPE   : Customer Premises Equipment

Figure 18.5 AIN (Advanced Intelligent Network) architecture.

18.3 SS7 PROTOCOL ARCHITECTURE

18.3.1 Comparison with X.25

In X.25 a customer interfaces a DTE with a DCE of the PDN (Public Data Network). Similarly in SS7, a customer's telephone or a PBX interfaces with a switching point. In X.25 a virtual circuit is established prior to sending data between two end DCEs. Similarly, in SS7 a virtual connection, called an SCCP (Signaling Connection Control Part) connection, can be provided between the two end SPs. Think of the SPs as being similar to X.25's DCEs, which provide entry points into the SS7 network. Additionally, the STPs are similar to the packet switches or the transit switches of X.25.

Each network node in an SS7 network has a unique PC (Point Code) associated with it, providing the address of the node. These PCs are implemented by the SCCP layer of SS7, similar to that of the X.25's layer 3 address.

18.3.2 The Layers of the Architecture

Figure 18.6 shows the four layers of SS7 and its various sublayers. Alongside these layers the units of transfer and their headings are shown. Items in this figure will be explained through the remainder of the chapter, so it is not necessary to understand it fully at this time. The figure shows how the four SS7 layers map onto the seven OSI layers. The first layer of SS7 is called MTP-L1 (Message Transfer Part, Level 1) or signaling data link. This is similar to OSI's physical layer, which specifies the electrical and physical properties of the signaling links.

The second layer is simply called the signaling link layer or MTP-L2. It provides error detection and correction across the signaling links. MTP-L3, also known as the signaling network layer, receives messages from the signaling links and, after examining their point codes, determines if the messages should be routed to another link or be handed over to level 4, locally.

SCCP, which is the lower portion of layer 4, provides flow control and sequence control for the messages on an optional basis. Together with MTP, SCCP provides complete network services as the OSI model's first three layers do.

The rest of layer 4 falls into two vertical categories. One category is called ISUP (ISDN User Part) which is used to make an end-to-end call, such as a simple telephone call. It provides the transfer of signaling information between two end users. The other vertical layer is called TCAP (Transaction Capabilities Application Part), and it usually requires a call made to an SCP so that routing information may be obtained for an ISUP call. An example of a TCAP call is when an 800 number is converted to a POTS number. Therefore, it is said that circuit-related functions are needed for an ISUP call while non-circuit related functions are needed for a TCAP call.

ISUP and TCAP layers are further divided into yet other functions. ISUP can exchange messages with MTP-L3 by using the LBL (Link-By-Link) signaling method, or by transferring PAM (Pass-Along Message) messages, or by using SCCP messages. Since SCCP is not always used by ISUP, it is shown to be "chopped off" and not occupying the entire lower layer of ISUP.

TCAP is divided into two sublayers called CSL (Component SubLayer) and TSL (Transaction SubLayer) layers. TCAP is actually a sublayer of TC (Transaction Capabilities) along with ISP (Intermediate Signaling Part). However, because ISP is not currently defined, the scopes of TC and TCAP are identical. More on all this later.

18.4 SIGNALING UNITS

Frames in SS7 are called SUs (Signaling Units). There are three types of SUs as there are 3 types of frames in HDLC. However, their functions do not correspond. The SU types are shown in Figure 18.7.

An MSU (Message SU) encapsulates or carries information from the upper layers. It also sets up and terminates links and provides status for managing the network. The LSSU (Link Status SU) also provides status about the link (whether it is getting congested, or if the link has to be aligned, etc.), but doesn't contain any information from the upper layers. The FISU (Fill-In SU) is transmitted when the link is idle and not carrying any traffic, so that the receiving end knows that the other end is only idle and not out of service.

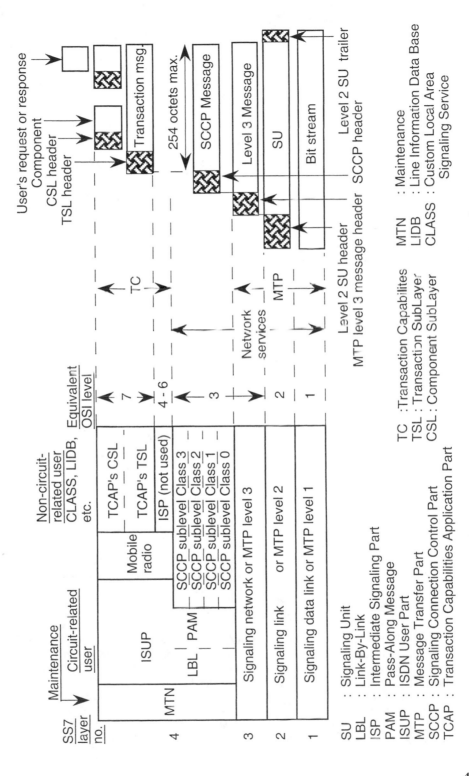

Figure 18.6 The layered architecture of SS7 and the units of transfer.

SU   : Signaling Unit
LBL   : Link-By-Link
ISP   : Intermediate Signaling Part
PAM   : Pass-Along Message
ISUP : ISDN User Part
MTP   : Message Transfer Part
SCCP : Signaling Connection Control Part
TCAP : Transaction Capabilities Application Part

TC   : Transaction Capabilites
TSL   : Transaction SubLayer
CSL   : Component SubLayer

MTN   : Maintenance
LIDB : Line Information Data Base
CLASS : Custom Local Area
          Signaling Service

18.4.1 SU Fields

The first and the last fields of an SU are the '01111110' flag, which requires that the rest of the fields be bit-stuffed, so that the flag doesn't appear anywhere in between. But the activity at this layer is very high and frames are sent one after the other with only one flag between successive frames.

LI (Length Indicator) specifies the length in octets of the SIF (Signal Information Field) for MSUs or the SF (Status Field) for LSSUs. It is set to 0 for FISUs, 1 or 2 for LSSUs, and 3 through 63 for MSUs. If the MSU length is less than or equal to 63 octets, the LI field is set to the actual length. For higher lengths up to 272 octets, this field is still set to 63. This field value is limited to 63, because its length is only 6 bits. The SIF contains information that is being sent by the application user and the SIO (Service Information Octet) specifies which user this information belongs to. The SF field provides the status of the link.

The 16-bit CRC field provides error detection for the SU. FSN (Forward Sequence Number) is the identification number of the MSU being sent while the BSN (Backward Sequence Number) provides the last number of the MSU that was received correctly. FIB (Forward Indicator Bit) indicates that this MSU is being retransmitted if its value is different than the previous FIB that was sent. If the values of the previous and current FIBs are the same, that is an indication that this MSU is being sent for the first time.

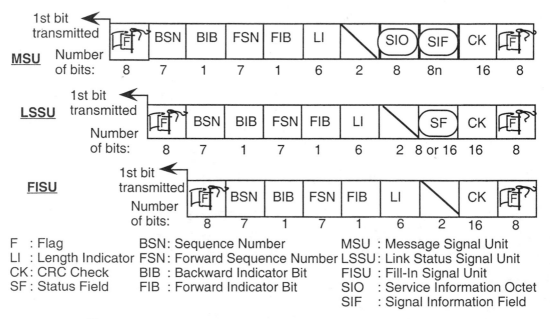

Figure 18.7 The three kinds of signal units are shown. Fields which are unique to one kind of a signal unit are shaded.

If the BIB (Backward Indicator Bit) is opposite in value from the previous one an error is indicated and a request for retransmission is signaled. However, if they are the same then no error is indicated.

18.4.2 An Example of SU Transmission Exchange

Let us look at an example of how these fields are used, and hopefully their functions will become clearer. In Figure 18.8, we have two nodes exchanging a sequence of SUs with each other. An SP and an STP are shown at each end of the link, but they could be any pair of valid SS7 nodes. The types of SUs are shown to be MSU and FISU, but the actual type depends only on whether information is being transmitted or not. Time progresses from top to bottom and for the most part, we'll start the discussion of every SU with a new paragraph.

First, the SP sends a MSU whose number is 1, which is specified in its FSN.

Then a MSU with a number of 2 is sent by the SP.

The STP, which is on the opposite end of this link, sends its MSU number 1. So its FSN is set to 1. At this time, the STP acknowledges the SP's MSU number 2. This is shown by a 2 in its BSN, meaning that the STP received the SP's MSU number 2.

The SP sends its MSU number 3 and acknowledges the STP's MSU number 1 by setting the BSN to 1. Here the FIB is 0 which is the same as the FIB for the previous MSU. Since these FIBs are the same, it further confirms to the STP that MSU number 3 is being sent for the first time. Similarly, since the BIB is 0 for both of these MSUs sent by the SP, it signals no request for retransmission from the STP.

Now the STP sends an FISU to tell the SP that there was an error in its transmission of MSU number 3. An FISU is sent instead of an MSU since it has no signaling information to convey at this time. Let us compare the fields of this FISU with the fields of the MSU sent by the STP. The FSN is still one, since only MSUs increment this field. The BSN is still two, even though the SP transmitted its MSU-3, meaning that MSU-3 was received incorrectly. The BIB has changed, so this indicates to the SP that the STP wants this SU retransmitted.

The SP retransmits MSU-3. The FIB has been changed from 0 to 1, indicating that this SU is being retransmitted. The BSN is still 1, since the last error-free SU received from the STP is 1.

The STP now receives the SP's MSU-3 correctly, which is shown by the 3 in the BSN field. No request for retransmission is given since the BIBs are kept the same as the previous FISU.

The SP sends its MSU-4 and indicates that this is a new MSU by maintaining its FIB at 1.

However, the STP receives this one incorrectly and reverses the BIB bit, requesting a retransmission and maintaining the BSN at 3.

The SP retransmits with the FIB reversed from before and the STP receives it correctly, but now since it has signaling information to send from one of its users, it assembles its MSU number 2. The last MSU sent by the SP in this sequence is 5 and it acknowledges the STP's MSU-2 by setting its BSN to 2.

What we have just shown is a half-duplex communication exchange, but SS7 calls for full-duplex links, running at either 56 kbps or 64 kbps. In this method, all

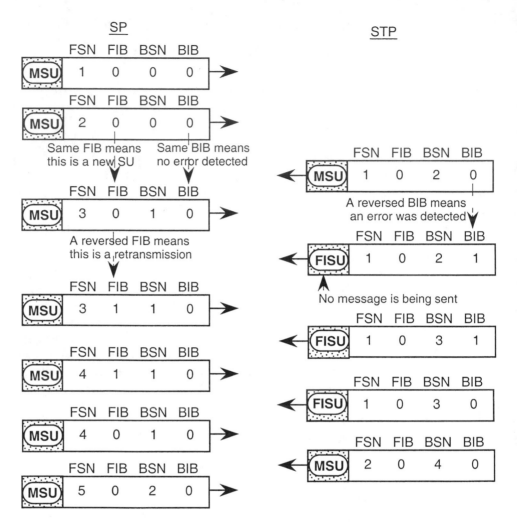

Figure 18.8 An example of exchanges of signaling units.

MSUs are retransmitted beginning from the MSU that caused the error. For satellite links, this would create additional delays and so a different error control method called preventive cyclic retransmission is used.

18.5 MTP LEVEL3

The purpose of the third layer of SS7 is to provide routing, so that a node that receives a message knows whether the message is being handed over to level 4 locally or whether it is being forwarded to another node, and if so, on which link.

The header for this level is 64 bits long for the ANSI standard and 32 bits long for the ITU-T standard. It contains the SLS (Signaling Link Selection), OPC (Origination Point Code), and the DPC (Destination Point Code) fields. Each node in the network, whether SPs or STPs, has a unique point code assigned to it, and it corresponds to the address of the node. However, gateways connecting multiple SS7 networks may have more than one point code associated with them, one for each network.

Between any switching point and an adjacent STP there can be a maximum of 16 links. Because every switching point is connected to two STPs, there are 32 possible links terminating a switching point, 16 per set. For the sake of clarity, Figure 18.9 shows only 3 such links per set.

When a message is to be sent out to an STP, the third layer randomly selects an SLS out of 32 possible values. Each of these values corresponds to one of the possible links. This ensures that the traffic between the two STPs is shared and balanced.

In the figure, messages initiating at the switching point with an SLS of 1, 4, 6, etc., will traverse to the STP which has a point code of 3, and the messages with SLSs of 0, 2, 3, etc., will traverse to the STP which has a point code of 2. In the same fashion, the traffic is balanced as the messages go from one STP pair to the next.

Note that when an application requires that multiple messages arrive in the same order in which they were transmitted, this layer assigns the same SLS for those messages. This will ensure that the messages follow the same path and so are forced to arrive in order.

For instance, all messages with an SLS of 6 will go to point code 3 and then to point code 4. In conclusion, the assignment of SLSs ensures that the load is balanced in the network and that a fixed path can be provided for messages when needed. This fixed path can then be provided without requiring a sequence number field in the level 3 header, as is done in X.25.

Realize that the FSN of layer 2 is used for error control only between two point codes, whereas the SLS remains the same until the message arrives at the DPC (Destination Point Code). Furthermore, layer 3 doesn't provide a virtual connection or datagram service by assigning the same or different SLSs, as it appears to do. This is a function provided by SCCP.

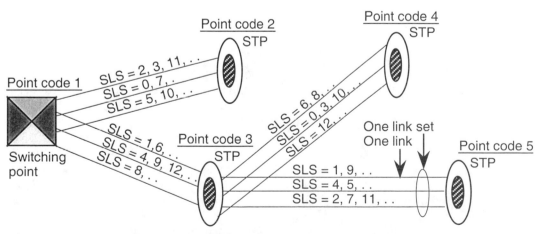

Figure 18.9 The SLS (Signaling Link Selection) field of the MTP level-3 header provides a means of balancing the load in the network and provides a fixed path, if necessary.

18.6 SCCP

18.6.1 The Sublayering of SCCP

Back in Figure 18.6, SCCP is shown to be the lower portion of layer 4 in the SS7 architecture. It is always required by TCAP, the non-circuit-related protocol, and is sometimes required by ISUP, the circuit-related protocol. SCCP segments transmits messages in 279-octet units (MSUs) for the lower-layer protocols and reassembles them into messages at the receiving end.

SCCP is further divided up into 4 sublayers called class 0 through class 3. Classes 0 and 1 are for connectionless transmission of messages. This means that the receiving protocol cannot associate which messages logically belong with the same transmission. With these classes, higher-layer protocols contain fields to identify the transaction in a query-response connection service. However, a class 2 or class 3 level protocol is able to group such units, but not classes 0 and 1.

Classes 0 and 1 both provide connectionless services, but class 1 ensures that the sequence in which the messages were transmitted is maintained.

Class 2 service provides a virtual connection by using a local reference number in the SCCP header. This is similar to X.25's LCI, and similar to X.25, a connection has to be set up between the end points before transmission of data can take place. Lastly, class 3 provides control over data flow and provides data recovery by implementing additional fields.

18.6.2 An Example of a Class 0 Service

Figure 18.10 shows an example of class 0 service provided by the SCCP sublayer. Although this setup is most common in the US, other setups are possible. Let us say that the phone calls 800-123-4567 and the message unit is assembled at the switching point whose point code is 07. The switching point needs to send this message to the SCP that can translate this 800 number into a POTS number. The information about which 800 numbers can be translated by which SCPs is stored at all STPs. Therefore, the switching point sends this message to one of its STPs. The person dialing the number is called an end subscriber, while the applications executing at the SP and the STP are called users.

First, at point code 7, the application layer provides the 800 number and the SCCP also provides the 800 number in its header. The OPC here is 7. The network layer at point code 7 copies the OPC in its header and inserts a DPC of 5. The DPC is inserted after selecting an SLS randomly.

The message unit arrives at point code 5, and here the SCCP layer is invoked since the end point code is equal to 5. After retrieving the 800 number, the STP knows where the SCP is located for this number and selects its DPC (4). The OPC in the SCCP layer stays at 7 since on the return trip, the STP must be able to send the message to the correct SP. However, the OPC in the MTP layer is set to 5, since point code 5 is generating this message.

The message unit may go through another STP such as point code 8, as depicted in the diagram, but doesn't get processed by the SCCP layer. The network layer is utilized, though, in order to select the proper link to the SCP.

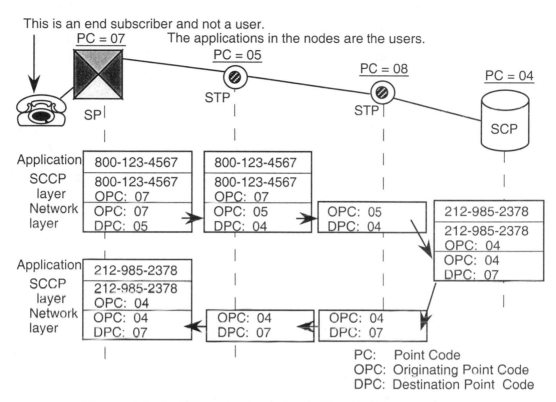

This is an end subscriber and not a user.
The applications in the nodes are the users.

PC = 07   PC = 05   PC = 08   PC = 04

SP   STP   STP   SCP

Application	800-123-4567	800-123-4567		
SCCP layer	800-123-4567	800-123-4567		
	OPC: 07	OPC: 07		
Network layer	OPC: 07	OPC: 05	OPC: 05	212-985-2378
	DPC: 05	DPC: 04	DPC: 04	

				212-985-2378
				OPC: 04
Application	212-985-2378			OPC: 04
SCCP layer	212-985-2378			DPC: 07
	OPC: 04			
Network layer	OPC: 04	OPC: 04	OPC: 04	
	DPC: 07	DPC: 07	DPC: 07	

PC: Point Code
OPC: Originating Point Code
DPC: Destination Point Code

Figure 18.10 An 800 number is sent by the SP to its STP, which then finds the point code of the SCP which has its POTS number and sends the 800 number to be converted. The entire message is sent through each point, but where only the network layer functions are implemented, the network layer headings are outlined. The users are the applications that are running at PC numbers 7, 5, and 4.

At the SCP the message is processed by all of the layers, and the application will convert the 800 number to the POTS number, which is then copied in the SCCP header. Also, the point code of 7 is copied from the OPC of the old SCCP header to the DPC of the new network layer header. On the return trip, the SCCP function is not invoked until it reaches point code 7, since now the end point (DPC = 7) is not any intermediate STP but the SP. Once the POTS number is obtained, the user at the SP must use the ISUP layer to actually connect the circuit for the end subscriber. But first let us take a look into the TCAP layer.

18.7 TCAP

This section outlines the first of the two vertical layers of SS7 as shown in Figure 18.6, namely TCAP (Transaction Capabilities Application Part). The database query example which we looked at in the last section is an example of a non-circuit-related user function. Non-circuit-related functions place a call to an SCP so that routing information can be retrieved from it, which is the general purpose of this layer. Usually, after the TCAP is utilized, the ISUP is needed to complete the call.

18.7.1 Classes of User Requests

Turning our attention back to Figure 18.6, we see that the TCAP layer is divided into what are called the CSL (Component SubLayer) and the TSL (Transaction SubLayer). A TCAP user, or a network application that is executing at a SS7 node, can send either a request or a response to a peer user at another node in the network. The types of requests fall into four classes of operation and they are based on the kinds of responses that are expected.

A class 1 type of request requires that the remote user perform the requested operation and respond whether the operation was successful or not. A class 2 type of request requires the remote node to respond only if the operation failed, whereas a class 3 requires it to respond only if the operation was successful. Finally, class 4 requires no response from the receiving node.

An example of a class 1 request is to convert an 800 number to a POTS number, which always requires a response. An example of a class 2 request is to perform a routine test and respond only if there was some kind of a problem, whereas a class 3 request may broadcast a message to many nodes and only the node to which the message pertains replies. Finally, a class 4 request may simply be a warning that is broadcast to many nodes.

18.7.2 The Two Sublayers of TCAP

Figure 18.6 shows that as a request or a response is being sent down through the layers, it is first processed by the CSL of TCAP. (The unit of a message is called a component.) Then it is sent through the TSL at which time one or more components are assembled into a transaction message. One component may contain only one request or only one response. However, a transaction message may contain several components.

A component may contain a request that is of one of the four class types mentioned, a response stating that the operation was successful or not, or a response stating that the received request (or the response) was not understandable.

The TSL provides a connection-oriented dialogue for the CSL peers to communicate with each other using components. This is done through the connectionless functions provided by the class 0 and 1 layers of SCCP. In other words, using the connectionless services of SCCP, TSL provides a connection for the CSL sublayer.

18.7.3 The CSL Sublayer

There are five kinds of CSL components. The INVOKE component contains one request and only one. The RETURN RESULT-NOT LAST component contains a report of a successful operation and signals that more components are to follow, which belong with this report. The RETURN RESULT-LAST component is the final component in a report containing multiple components. A report may have to be divided into multiple components because a SCCP message is limited to a maximum of 254 octets.

If a requested operation was unsuccessful, a RETURN ERROR component will be sent, and if the received message was not understandable, a REJECT component will be issued.

Each component is identified by a CID (Component IDentifier), so that the returning responses can be associated (or matched) with the requests which were transmitted, even if they were sent by two different applications to the same destination point.

Figure 18.11 shows an example of components being exchanged by the peer users. Initially, the switch wants to translate an 800 number to a POTS number, so it sends an INVOKE component and gives it a CID of 3. A CID is also called an invoke ID.

The SCP upon receiving this request can't provide a response because it needs more information from the switch, let's say, because this 800 number is converted to different POTS numbers depending on what service the customer wants. So the SCP in turn issues another request, stating to dial a 1 to talk to the sales department, and so on. This request, created because of the original request, also becomes an invoke

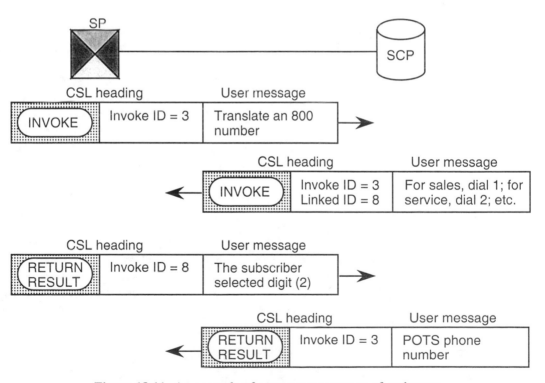

Figure 18.11 An example of component sequence of exchanges.

component at the CSL layer, and receives its own ID of 8. An invoke generated as a result of another is called a linked invoke. Also, a request generated as a result of another request is called a linked operation, as in this case.

The user or the application at the switch receives the correct digit, let us say "2," from its end subscriber. This selection is returned in a RETURN RESULT component with a CID of 8. The SCP user matching the CID of 8 with the linked ID of 8 is now able to provide a RETURN RESULT component (CID = 3) with the correct POTS number. Now the switch is able to complete the call for the process which was initiated with an invoke identifier of 3.

18.7.4 The TSL Sublayer

As noted before, TSL provides an end-to-end connection for the CSL layer using the connectionless services of SCCP. This end-to-end connection is called a dialogue or a transaction. To provide a connection, the TSL message header contains a field, similar to X.25's LCI, called the TID (Transaction IDentifier). Using this TID, users can initiate, maintain, and terminate a dialogue with other users. The CIDs allow the end points to match the receiving responses with the requests that were sent out.

There are five types of TSL messages: BEGIN, END, CONTINUE, UNIDIRECTIONAL, and ABORT. If the BEGIN and CONTINUE messages don't contain any components or upper layer messages, then they are akin to X.25's CALL REQUEST and CALL ACCEPTED packets, respectively.

The END message is similar to the CLEAR REQUEST of X.25, and may be issued by either of the TSL peers. However, unlike X.25, the END message does not get confirmed.

If the BEGIN contains an INVOKE component (that is, of any of the 4 class types) and is replied by an END, then the dialogue as shown in Figure 18.12(a) is similar to X.25's fast select feature. In this case, the END message may be empty, or may contain a class 4 INVOKE, which doesn't require a response, or it may contain a RETURN RESULT, RETURN ERROR, or REJECT component. If a problem occurs and the TSL layer can't maintain the dialogue, then an ABORT is issued with diagnostic information.

Figure 18.12(b) depicts a UNIDIRECTIONAL message which is used to provide a class 4 type of operation. No response is needed here.

As a last example of a simple TSL dialogue, let us look at Figure 18.12(c), where a node may request to have a credit card call authorized. The user may create the request giving the items as shown in the figure, such as the calling party number. The CSL will then encode its header for a class 1 INVOKE, since this operation requires a response. The TSL creates a fast select message out of it and sends a BEGIN. The SCP upon receiving this message validates the call, and may send a class 4 INVOKE requiring that the call be limited to 3 minutes.

18.8 ISUP

ISUP (ISDN User Part) is a protocol providing circuit-related functions between switches. It is the protocol used between ISDN end subscribers supporting voice, data, video, and other applications in a digital environment. TUP (Telephone User Part),

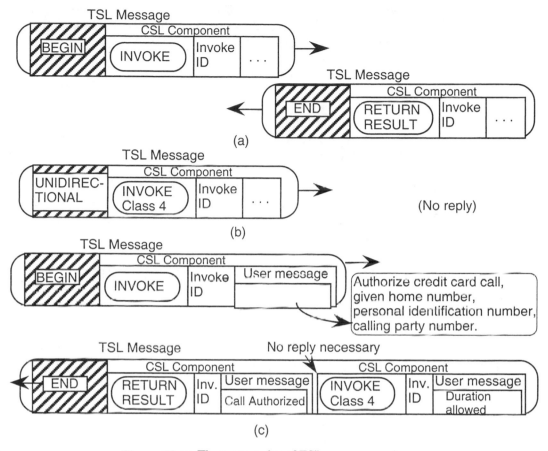

Figure 18.12 Three examples of TSL message exchanges.

which is the predecessor of ISUP, primarily supports voice connections using analog subscriber lines.

18.8.1 Bearer and Supplementary Services

ISUP services are divided into basic bearer services and supplementary services. Bearer services are for the switches which allow them to set up a 64-kbps circuit-switched connection between the end subscribers. They also specify the supervision and the release of such connections. The discussion surrounding Figure 9.1 showed how these functions were provided using CAS (Channel Associated Signaling or per-trunk signaling) in an analog world. These same functions are provided with SS7 in a digital network by the basic bearer services.

Supplementary services are advanced services, provided directly for the end subscriber, which were not available with the CAS signaling methods. They bring a rich variety of services to the ordinary ISDN end subscriber, similar to the kinds of features available with a PBX. Let us outline a few of them here.

Calling Line Identification: Commonly known as caller ID, this service is provided to the called party and it gives the calling party's phone number, and the extension or the subaddress, if it has one.

Calling Line Identification Restriction: This service is provided to the calling party so that his or her phone number may not be presented to the person being called.

Call Transfer: This service enables either end of a connection to establish a connection with a third party and then drop off. If the person doesn't drop off then it becomes a conference call.

Call Forward Busy: This service is used when, while a connection is established between two subscribers, a new call comes in for one of them, and the call is then forwarded to a different predefined number.

Direct Dialing In: Without having to coordinate a call with an attendant, an end subscriber can dial into a PBX and then its extension or subaddress directly through the ISDN.

Closed User Group: Similar to the X.25 feature, subscribers can form a sub-network and users who are not in the group may be restricted to call only members of the group, and/or vice versa. Designated members of a group may have added privileges or restrictions and may belong to a number of such groups.

18.8.2 ISUP Messages

The protocol data unit for ISUP is simply called an ISUP message. The message consists of parameters and information about them. The first two parameters are each an octet and are always needed. They are the CIC (Circuit Identification Code) and the MT (Message Type) parameters. The CIC specifies the 64-kbps physical circuit between two switches that this message pertains to and the MT identifies the type of message or the format for the rest of the message. In the previous analog systems, one trunk carried one voice circuit. Here, the CIC, analogous to one trunk, is not only restricted to voice, but may carry any information the bearer may want to send over a 64-kbps channel.

Other parameters of ISUP messages are categorized into mandatory and fixed length, mandatory and variable length, and optional parameters. The combination of these parameters used in a message define the type of the message. Table 18.1 summarizes the categories and the types of ISUP messages. We will look at a sampling of these shortly.

18.8.3 The ISUP Signaling Connection

Figure 18.13 shows the CIC links between three switches. These are the links over which no signaling is sent but only user information at 64 kbps. From one switch to another a given CIC appears only once. From PC3 to PC4, there is only one circuit

TABLE 18.1 Categories of ISUP Message Types
(Only a few message types are given.)

I. CALL CONTROL
  1. Call Setup
    A) Forward Setup
      IAM   : Initial Address Message
      SAM   : Subsequent Address Message
    B) Backward Setup
      ACM   : Address Complete Message
      CPG   : Call ProGress
      CON   : CONnect
    C) General Setup
      INR   : INformation Request
      INF   : INFormation
      COT   : COnTinuity

  2. Call Supervision
      ANM : ANswer Message
      REL   : RELease
      SUS   : SUSpend
      RES   : RESume
      FOT   : FOrward Transfer
  3. End-to-End Signaling
      PAM : Pass-Along Message
  4. Supplementary Services
  5. In-Call Modification

II. Circuit Supervision
  1. Single Circuit
  2. Circuit Group

with a CIC of 5; however, a CIC of 5 may also exist going to PC2. So the combination of CIC and the DPC (Destination Point Code) uniquely specifies a circuit leaving a switch. The number of CICs between a given pair of switches depends on the demand for traffic.

Figure 18.13 further shows how a circuit-switched connection is being initiated between two end offices, PC2 and PC4. PC3 is an intermediate office through which a connection has to be switched. First the subscriber calls 212-012-3456 and PC2 decides to make the connection through PC3, perhaps because no direct CICs (trunks) are available to PC4. PC4 is the only switch that can complete the connection to the called subscriber.

So PC2 finds a free circuit that has a CIC of 5 connecting to PC3. It generates an IAM (Initial Address Message), listed in Table 18.1, and sends it through the signaling network, via PC5 and PC6 to PC3. The IAM message contains the called party's number and all the required routing information. Layer 3, the network layer, assigns an SLS of 5 and sets the OPC to 2 and the DPC to 3 in its header.

PC3 opens up the ISUP message and realizes that the connection should be made next to PC4. It then finds an idle circuit (CIC = 3) and assembles and sends its own ISUP message to PC4. Layer 3 chooses an SLS of 4 and sends a new IAM message as shown in the figure.

Now, as long as the call is still active, all messages arriving into PC3 from PC2 that have a CIC of 5 and an SLS of 5 are regenerated there and are sent to PC4 with a CIC of 3 and an SLS of 4. This establishes a one-way signaling path. Always having the same SLS between two switches ensures that the messages arrive in the same order that they were sent for that call, while the CIC identifies the circuit that is being used for that call.

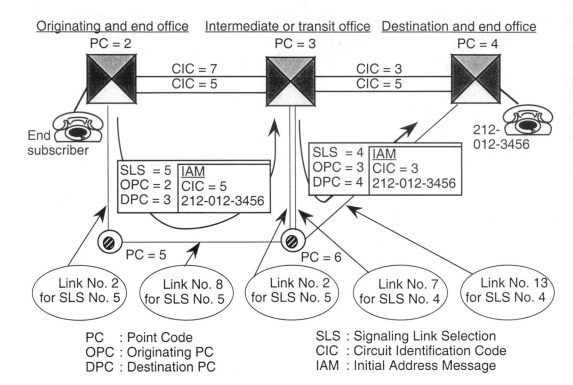

Figure 18.13 Initiating a connection using ISUP.

The figure only shows the signaling path that is established in the forward direction, but one is also established in the reverse direction, using the same set of CICs over the links, but not necessarily the same set of SLSs as were used in the forward direction. Notice that the destination doesn't receive the originating office's PC, but the set of CIC-SLS pairs through intermediate points are used to send messages back to the originating office. An ISUP signaling connection is made up of one such forward and one such reverse signaling path.

18.8.4 ISUP Signaling Methods

What we have just finished describing is the LBL (Link-By-Link) signaling method. Here all the ISUP messages are interpreted and modified by the transit switches. Alternatively, when messages are not interpreted by the transit switches but only by the end offices then it is called end-to-end signaling. End-to-end signaling is achieved either by sending PAMs (Pass-Along Messages) or by utilizing the SCCP connection-oriented or connectionless layers. Figure 18.6 depicts these options, while Table 18.1 lists PAM.

An example of where end-to-end signaling may be needed is when a destination switch, after receiving an IAM, requests and receives more information from the call originating office in order to complete the call. Here the transit switches don't need to know the contents of the information exchange.

When a PAM message, a kind of ISUP message, arrives at a transit switch, it looks only at the MT and CIC parameters. The MT is examined to see that it is a PAM message and the CIC is examined to send the message over the next proper link. But the rest of the contents of the message are not interpreted or regenerated by such switches.

18.8.5 Call Set-up and Release

In conclusion, let us outline how a circuit-switched call may be connected and disconnected using these ISUP messages and the signaling messages sent over the D channel between the subscriber's phone and the switch.

As will be pointed out in Chapter 19, a residential customer's line multiplexes two B channels for sending voice and data simultaneously and one D channel for signaling the switch at the CO. An ISDN phone sends a SETUP message to the switch on the D channel when it goes off-hook, instead of closing the local loop and setting up a DC current as is done with a POTS line. Look at the first three steps as shown in Figure 18.14. It then receives a SETUP ACK message from the switch instead of receiving a dial tone. Similarly, when a telephone number is dialed, an ISDN phone sends an INFO message, and when the phone at the distant end is ringing, it receives an ALERTING message instead of a ringback.

All these signaling messages are sent over the D channel between the subscriber and the switch and are specified in ITU-T's Q.931 protocol. The conversations are carried over the B channels. Although digital messages are being transferred over the subscriber's line, the user still hears the analog signals that were heard with a POTS line. To accomplish this, the dial tone, ringback, and other analog signals are now provided by the subscriber's terminal and not by the local switch. Keeping this user interface consistent on an ISDN phone as it was with a POTS phone allows a smoother transition to ISDN for telephone customers.

Figure 18.14 shows an example of a set-up and a release of a connection over the ISDN. The messages between a switch and a phone are ISDN's layer 3 messages sent over the D channel, while the messages between the switches (via the STPs) are ISUP or Q.931 messages as listed in Table 18.1. Each step is numbered in sequence.

As just mentioned, the telephone and the switch exchange SETUP, SETUP ACK, and INFO messages over the D channel. Then an ISUP message (IAM) is generated and sent to the intermediate switch, which regenerates another IAM which is sent to the destination switch. If more information is to be sent than can be contained in an IAM message, then the originating switch will follow the IAM with a SAM (Subsequent Address Message). A SAM is not shown here. (It appears that the standards committee may have just finished an intense discussion of Dr. Seuss's Green Eggs and Ham when these acronyms were chosen. Apparently, the ham was mistakenly named PAM.)

Figure 18.14 shows that the destination switch needs more information to complete the connection and it sends an INR (INformation Request) message enveloped inside a PAM (Pass-Along Message) back to the call originating switch. The INR may be required to obtain the phone number of the caller to accomplish proper billing, or for other reasons. Step 8 shows that the originating switch replies with an INF (INformation) message, and the destination sends a SETUP message to the distant

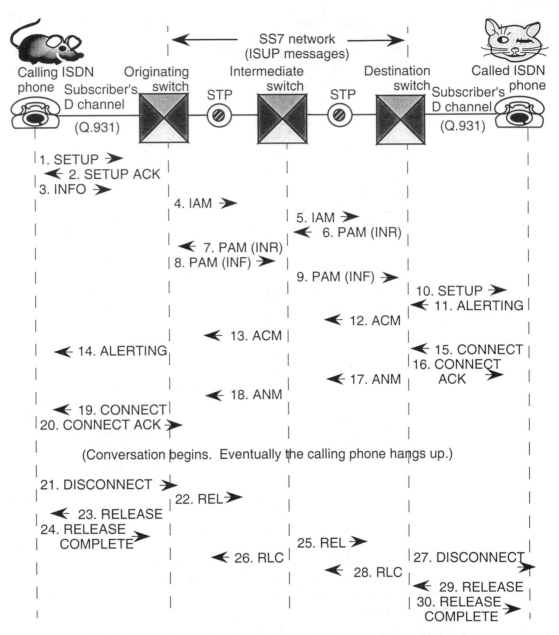

Figure 18.14 A scenario of connecting and disconnecting a call showing the Q.931 messages at the subscriber phones and ISUP messages between the switches.

phone. The phone begins to ring and it sends an ALERTING message over the D channel. Then the switch generates an ACM (Address Complete Message), which then translates into an ALERTING message to the caller.

When the called subscriber picks up the phone, a CONNECT message is sent and the switch sends a CONNECT ACK to the subscriber and an ANM (ANswer Message) through the network. After an exchange of CONNECT and CONNECT ACK at the calling end, the conversation can begin.

The figure shows that the ACM (Address Complete Message) was sent by the switch after it received an ALERTING from the phone. However, it is possible for the switch to send the ACM first before it receives the ALERTING signal. In that case, it will send a CPG (Call ProGress) message upon receiving the ALERTING signal from the phone. It is also possible that the called party may pick up the phone immediately and send a CONNECT without sending an ALERTING message at all.

Finally, either party may hang up first, which generates a DISCONNECT. Here the calling party sends a DISCONNECT which maps into a REL (RELease) to the intermediate switch. At the same time, a RELEASE is sent from the originating switch to the telephone and a RELEASE COMPLETE is received back. The intermediate switch then sends an REL to the destination and an RLC (ReLease Complete) in the reverse direction. Similarly, an exchange of DISCONNECT, RELEASE, and RELEASE COMPLETE occurs on the called party's D channel. Notice that some Q.931 messages such as SETUP, CONNECT, and DISCONNECT can be sent either from the telephone or from the switch.

EXERCISES

1. Why is SS7 more flexible than CAS signaling methods?
   a. It is software-driven.   b. It uses digital switches.
   c. It uses high-speed data links.   d. It uses electromechanical technology.
2. STP pairs are connected to other STP pairs using what type of links?
   a. A-access links   b. B-bridge links
   c. C-cross links   d. D-diagonal links
3. SS7's layer 4 is divided into which major sublayers?
   a. CSL, TSL, and MTP   b. CSL, SCCP, and ISUP
   c. TCAP, SCCP, and MTP   d. TCAP, SCCP, and ISUP
4. Which SU (Signaling Unit) has only the fields that exist in the other two types of SUs?
   a. MSU   b. LSSU
   c. FISU   d. none
5. Which class of operation responds only if the requested operation failed?
   a. Class 1   b. Class 2
   c. Class 3   d. Class 4
6. Which of the following Q.931 messages are sent only from a calling phone?
   a. DISCONNECT   b. SETUP
   c. CONNECT   d. INFO
7. Which ITU-T signaling system corresponds closely with our SF signaling?
8. SCCP and MTP layers are collectively called by what name?
9. In Figure 18.6, if the STP didn't have any information to convey to the SP in the last SU, what type of SU would that have been?
10. If the number of links between two point codes were reduced, would the number of SLSs on each of those links increase, decrease, or stay the same?

11. In Figure 18.8, users (applications) at which PCs provide their services on the "sending trip" and at which ones on the "return trip"?
12. An ISUP signaling path is specified by which pair of items between each pair of switches in the path?
13. Describe the SP and its three types.
14. If the second MSU sent by the STP were received incorrectly by the SP, show the contents of the SUs that would follow in order to resolve that error.
15. What are the three sublayers of TC, and what are their functions?
16. In Figure 18.9, if the SCP could not find the 800 number in its database to convert, what type of CSL component would it send back? Suppose that component had an error in its heading; what type of a component would the SP send? How would the SCP reply then? Draw a diagram outlining this scenario.
17. Which ISUP supplementary service not listed in the text would you like to see implemented? In other words, what would you like to be able to do with your home phone that you think you can't do now?
18. Describe the three methods by which the ISUP can obtain the services of the MTP layer. What is end-to-end signaling? Does it relate to these methods?

Chapter 19

ISDN

19.1 DEFINITIONS

ISDN, although first proposed in 1968 by ITU, didn't become a standard until 1984 when ITU published the Red Books. Since then new recommendations have been published every four years. Like SS7, the North American version of ISDN is driven by ANSI, and is slightly different from that of ITU. This chapter continues where section 5.3.3 left off.

19.1.1 Access Interfaces

There are two methods of accessing the ISDN. The BRI (Basic Rate Interface) access is designed for the residential and small business customers, as well as individuals within a large business. The PRI (Primary Rate Interface) access is primarily for large businesses. BRI is comprised of two B channels, each rated at 64 kbps, and one D channel rated at 16 kbps. The upper-layer protocols for the B channel or the bearer channel are flexible, so that the subscriber may transmit any information in any format that is needed. Using one pair of metallic wires from the CO, an individual can talk on one B channel using PCM encoding and also have a data connection to a different location at 64 kbps on the other B channel.

If voice is compressed at 16 kbps at both end points, then four separate conversations over one B channel are made possible between them. It will be left up to the end points to multiplex, demultiplex, and switch these four channels. It is also possible to send slow motion video, fax, and any other information on the B channel; however, the terminals on the receive end must be compatible with the information that is transmitted. Additionally, a 128-kbps data stream can be fed into an inverse multiplexer and sent over both B channels, where the signal is then recomposed at the distant end back to 128 kbps.

The D, or the delta channel, provides the necessary signaling to set up and disconnect the B channels as required. The messages conveyed over the D channel are defined by ITU's Q.931 and Q.932, or I.451 and I.452, respectively. (When two ITU groups agree on the same set of recommendations, the protocol ends up having two different nomenclatures.) Although the primary purpose of the D channel is to control signaling, it is also used for low-speed packet switching and telemetry, such as having utility metering done automatically. BRI may be configured as 2B + D, B + D, or simply as D.

The PRI access in North America and Japan runs at the T1 rate and in Europe at the E1 rate. PRI's D channel operates at 64 kbps and not at 16 kbps as in BRI. At the T1 rate, it is specified either as 23B + D or as 24B. Unlike T1, the bearer channels are clear with no bits being robbed for signaling purposes. With E1, the PRI can be configured as 30B + D or 31B. Typically, the business customer of PRI will have a PBX or a host connected to its trunk.

Besides the B and D channels, there are H or higher-rate channels as well. H0, H11, H12 channels operate at 384, 1536, 1920 kbps, respectively. These are multiples of 64 kbps. The H4 channel operates at 135.168 Mbps and is capable of carrying standard PCM-based color television signals.

19.1.2 Functional Devices and Reference Points

In order to fully identify the purpose and function of each device, ISDN describes a limited set of devices and the interfaces between them, as shown in Figure 19.1. If these interfaces are implemented correctly, then one vendor's equipment could easily be replaced by another's.

Devices that are not ISDN-compatible are categorized as TE2 (Terminal Equipment 2) devices. These could be analog phones, PCs, 3270 terminals, and so on. To connect a TE2 to the ISDN, a TA (Terminal Adapter) must be used. The TA will allow the TE2 to appear as an ISDN terminal to the rest of the network; conversely, it will allow the rest of the network to interact with the TE2 as if it were an ISDN terminal. The interface between them is called the R reference point, and it will depend on the kind of TE2 that is being connected.

TE1 (Terminal Equipment 1) is a device that is fully ISDN-compatible and is connected to the ISDN using the S interface. This could be a digital telephone, an IVDT, a workstation, or a number of other devices.

NT2 (Network Termination 2) is a device that provides switching, multiplexing, concentrating, or distribution of information for the customer's premises. For example, this could be a LAN server, multiplexer, FEP, or a PBX. Typically, a PRI connection would require an NT2, and a BRI connection would not.

NT1 (Network Termination 1) devices provide proper line termination at the customer's premises. They can provide line monitoring, power feeding, error statistics, and proper timing. Think of them as DSU/CSU devices.

The function of an NT1 can easily be done on a single card, which could then become part of the PBX or a PC. In such a case, the device that functions both as an NT1 and as an NT2 is dubbed an NT12 device. The reference point between these devices is called the T interface. With BRI, without the NT2, the point between the NT1 and the TE is called the S/T interface. In the remainder of this chapter, we'll refer to both the TE1 and the TA-TE2 combinations simply as TE. Furthermore, the term NT

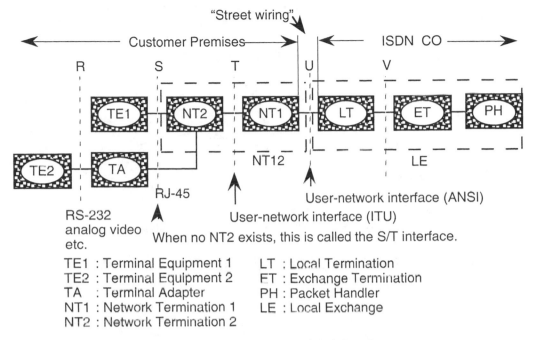

Figure 19.1 Functional groupings and their interfaces.

will be used to mean either the NT1 or the NT2, depending on which one is connected to the TE.

Unlike ANSI, ITU considers NT1 to be part of the local network and doesn't mention the U reference point. However, the FCC designates the NT1 as belonging to the customer, and so the ANSI defines the U interface as the line going to the CO. In ISDN terminology, the CO is called an LE (Local Exchange). The LE itself is comprised of LT (Local Termination), ET (Exchange Termination), and PH (Packet Handler).

The LT complements the functions of the NT1 on the LE side, and is similar to the OCU (Office Channel Unit) described in section 15.4.2. The ET is the ISDN circuit switch and the PH is like a gateway to PDNs.

19.2 TELECOMMUNICATIONS SERVICES

Since ISDN integrates many kinds of services, we need to define what constitutes a service. ISDN does that well by defining services using a limited set of attributes (or distinctive features). By specifying these sets of attributes, what is expected from the ISDN is clearly stated, and all the "pieces" of the ISDN can fit better with fewer misunderstandings among equipment manufacturers, carriers, and users. These attributes are then transmitted on the D channel when requesting a service, such as a telephone connection.

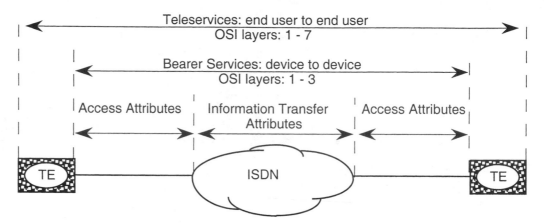

Figure 19.2 Classifications and scopes of telecommunication services.

19.2.1 Types of Services and Their Attributes

Telecommunications services are classified as bearer services, teleservices, and supplementary services, and they are defined in terms of their attributes. Teleservices include bearer services, and supplementary services are provided to both the bearer services and teleservices.

As seen in Figure 19.2 bearer services are network services in that they are characterized by the first three layers of the OSI Reference Model, whereas teleservices provide terminal equipment functions for communications between the end users. These services require the interaction of all 7 layers of the OSI model. The bearer services are categorized into access, information, and supplementary attributes.

Supplementary services have already been outlined in section 18.8.1 in the discussion of the ISUP, and are not discussed any further here.

Table 19.1 shows the three categories of bearer services attributes: information attributes (which specify the capabilities for transmission of information through the ISDN), access attributes (which provide methods of accessing network functions), and general attributes. General attributes are listed as items 10 through 13 in Table 19.1. They include supplementary services, and specify how much delay or what error rate is acceptable and how to interwork ISDN with other ISDN and non-ISDN networks.

19.2.2 Information Transfer Attributes

In this section we will describe the seven information transfer attributes in the order they are listed in Table 19.1.

The first attribute is called the information transfer mode. It identifies one of two mode types: circuit switched or packet switched. The information transfer rate attribute is given in kbps for circuit switched mode and in PPS (Packets Per Second) for the packet mode. The 2 x 64 kbps is provided if a user needs to connect both B channels when establishing a call. In this case, the user has to send both channels over the network separately.

Table 19.1 Bearer Services Attributes	
Attribute	Attribute Description
Information Transfer Attributes	
1. Information Transfer Mode	Circuit Switched Packet Switched
2. Information Transfer Rate	Bit Rate in kbps: 64, 2x64, 384, 1536, 1920, Throughput in PPS
3. Information Transfer Capability	Unrestricted Digital Audio in kHz: 3.1, 7, 15 Speech, Video
4. Structure	Service Data Unit Integrity Unstructured 8 kHz Integrity TSSI, RDTD
5. Establishment of Communication	Demand Reserved Permanent
6. Symmetry	Unidirectional Bidirectional Symmetric Bidirectional Asymmetric
7. Communication Configuration	Point-to-Point Multipoint Broadcast

Table 19.1 (Cont)	
Attribute	Attribute Description
Access Attributes	
8. Access Channel and Rate	D (16kbps) D (64 kbps) B, H0, H11, H12
9. Signaling Access and Information Access	I.430/431 I.451, I.461/462 HDLC, LAPB LAPD, and others
General Attributes	
10. Supplementary Services	Calling Line ID Call Transfer and others
11. Quality of Service	To be defined
12. Inter-working	To be defined
13. Operational and commercial	To be defined

The information transfer capability attribute can be specified as speech for normal voice conversations where data compression can be used. When using a modem, no compression can be requested by specifying this attribute as 3.1-kHz audio instead. 7 kHz is used for transmitting mono radio broadcasts and 15 kHz for transmitting stereo. The default setting for circuit mode transfer is speech whereas for packet switched mode, it is unrestricted. Unrestricted digital information allows any bit pattern to appear anywhere in the data stream. For instance, the service doesn't care if the bits are stuffed or not, as long as they are within SDLC frames.

An unstructured value for the structure attribute means that the boundaries of the octets don't have to be preserved on delivery of the data stream, whereas 8 kHz integrity (the default for circuit mode) requires that the boundaries be preserved so that the 8 bits for each voice sample are kept together.

TSSI (Time Slot Sequence Integrity) requires that information be conveyed to the distant end in the same order as it is delivered to the network for multiple access channels which are sent together, such as the 2 x 64 kbps channels. RDTD (Restricted Differential Time Delay) specifies that the delay through the ISDN be no more than 50 ms, which is necessary with speech.

Communication can be established on demand, where one receives a connection when requested and terminates it when no longer needed, as in dialing a telephone number. A communication can be established in advance using the reserve attribute. Here, the setup and release of a connection is initiated automatically by the network and not by the end user. Lastly, this attribute could be specified as permanent, where a connection is provided, analogous to a leased line, between two points for the duration of time that the service is being subscribed.

If the symmetry attribute is specified as unidirectional, data flows in only one direction, as when a studio is sending a broadcast to a radio transmitter. If it is specified as bidirectional symmetric, the transmission occurs in both directions and at the same rate. A bidirectional asymmetric service transfers information in both directions, but the rates are not the same. This type of symmetry is used when one end is transferring data while the other end replies with an occasional ACK or NACK.

Finally, the communication configuration attribute specifies whether the service involves only two users (as in point-to-point), if it involves two-way communication among several users (multipoint), or if only one point is transmitting to several at once (broadcast).

19.2.3 Access Attributes

The information transfer attributes specify how the information is transferred across the ISDN, and the access attributes, on the other hand, specify how the user accesses the network: with which channels, what rates, and which protocols. Table 19.1 lists several of the values for these attributes. Signaling access protocols describe what signaling methods are used between the user and the network, and information access protocol describes how the information is exchanged from end user to end user.

19.2.4 Teleservices Attributes

These services include not only the bearer services, but also the OSI's higher-layer attributes. These are outlined in Table 19.2, and are not discussed at any length here.

Table 19.2 Teleservices Attributes	
Attribute	Attribute Description
Low-Layer Attributes	
Information Transfer, Access Attributes, and Supplementary Services	Identical to bearer services
High-Layer Attributes	
Type of User Information Layer 4 Protocol Layer 5 Protocol Layer 6 Protocol Resolution (if applicable) Graphic Mode (if applicable) Layer 7 Protocol	Speech (3.1 khz), Sound (15 khz), Text, etc. x.224, T.70 x.225, T.62 T.73, T.61, T.6, T.100 in ppi: 200, 240, 300, 400 Alphamosaic, Geometric, Photographic T.60, T.500

19.3 PHYSICAL LAYER OF BRI

19.3.1 Introduction

As we have said, multiple devices can share the same ISDN interface; that is, many devices can be connected to the same 2B + D interface. In order to accomplish this, ISDN defines three layers similar to OSI's lower three layers: physical, data link, and network layers.

As depicted in Figure 19.3, ISDN recommendations specify the three layers for only the D channel. However, ISDN issues concerning the B channel are limited to only the physical layer. The protocols for layers 2 through 7 for the B channel are the responsibility of the TEs. ISDN simply transfers the bit stream for the B channel over the network. The figure seems to imply that the B and the D channels are physically separated over the line to the LE; however, they are time-division multiplexed over the same physical link.

This figure also shows that ITU defines the network boundary to include the NT1, while ANSI excludes it. In either case, NT1 is part of the customer's premises. In this section, we will look at each boundary individually.

The physical layer, besides providing transmission capabilities for the B and D channels, also provides timing and synchronization. The layer also describes the signaling capabilities for activation and deactivation of terminals, and to gain an orderly access of the D channel.

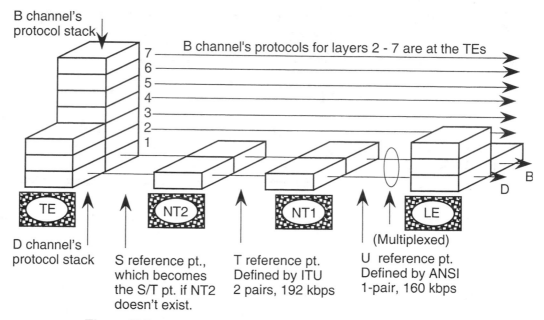

Figure 19.3 ITU's ISDN protocols are specified only at the S and T reference points. Only the D channel is specified for the lower three layers. The B and D channels are simply multiplexed at the physical layer over the same link. ANSI specifies the U reference point, but the difference between it and the S/T points is only at the physical layer.

BRI access can be provided for residential, Centrex, or PBX customers, and with 2B + D configuration (typically, over one pair) each B channel can be assigned its own phone number. Although the local loop would still be the same as before, residential customers would need a sophisticated NT1, the inside wiring may have to be changed to two or three pairs, and the modular jacks may have to be converted to 8-pin jacks, not to mention the cost of the TEs would be higher than today's simple POTS phones.

19.3.2 ANSI's U Reference Point

At this reference point, the NT1 terminates a local loop by providing an 8-pin modular plug called the RJ-45. Out of these 8 pins, only the middle two are used. Since the S/T interface uses 4 wires, NT1 must provide a means of converting the in-house 4 wires to the 2 wires that are used with the LE. To accomplish transmitting and receiving on the same pair without a loss of available bandwidth, echo cancelling is used here. That was covered in Section 3.6.

2B1Q Line Coding: The line code used over the U reference point is called 2B1Q (2 Binary 1 Quaternary) and an example of it is shown in Figure 19.4. The data stream is divided into groups of two bits called quats. There are four possible values for quats, and their voltage levels are given in the accompanying chart. In the data stream shown, notice that the "00" quat is transmitted by sending −3V and the "11" quat by +1V, and so on.

Quat	Approximate value
00	− 3V
01	−1V
10	+3V
11	+1V

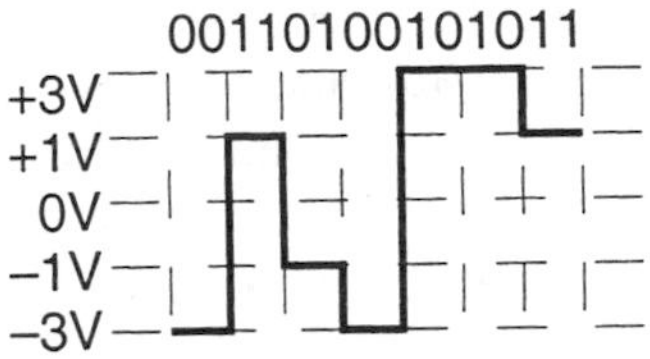

00110100101011

+3V
+1V
0V
−1V
−3V

Figure 19.4 2B1Q (2 Binary, 1 Quaternary) signaling scheme used in ANSI T1.601's U reference point.

However, the problem with this coding is that the line is not balanced for DC voltage. That is, unlike the bipolar format used with T1s, there is not the same number of positive pulses as there are negative pulses. Consequently, a scrambling algorithm is used in the transmitting side and a descrambling algorithm is used in the receive side to achieve DC voltage balancing. By providing DC voltage balancing, the range of the line is extended.

Framing: The bits across the U reference point are sent by using 2B1Q transmission frames. Eight of these frames are combined, as shown in Figure 19.5, to form one superframe. We see that each frame begins with an SW (Synchronizing Word), which has a fixed bit pattern. However, the first frame of a superframe begins with an ISW (Inverted SW) field, which merely complements the SW bits; 1s are set to 0s and 0s to 1s This field is then followed by 12 groups of 2B + D bits. One 2B + D group contains 8 bits for each B channel and 2 bits for the D channel. The frame then ends with 6

Number of bits:	18	8 +8+2	8+8+2		8+8+2	6
2B1Q frame #1	ISW	B1+B2+D	B1+B2+D	. . .	B1+B2+D	M
2B1Q frame #2	SW	B1+B2+D	B1+B2+D	. . .	B1+B2+D	M
2B1Q frame #3	SW	B1+B2+D	B1+B2+D	. . .	B1+B2+D	M
2B1Q frame #4	SW	B1+B2+D	B1+B2+D	. . .	B1+B2+D	M
2B1Q frame #5	SW	B1+B2+D	B1+B2+D	. . .	B1+B2+D	M
2B1Q frame #6	SW	B1+B2+D	B1+B2+D	. . .	B1+B2+D	M
2B1Q frame #7	SW	B1+B2+D	B1+B2+D	. . .	B1+B2+D	M
2B1Q frame #8	SW	B1+B2+D	B1+B2+D	. . .	B1+B2+D	M
	Synchronization word	Group 1	Group 2 . . .		Group 12	Overhead

Figure 19.5 The format for the 2B1Q superframe. One frame contains 240 bits (18 + 18 * 12 + 6), while one superframe contains 1920 bits (240 * 8).

overhead bits called the M field. This field is used to initiate loop backs, get error statistics, and perform other maintenance procedures over the line. The 18 bits for the SW, 216 for the 2B + D groups, and 6 for the M field make the frame 240 bits long.

We can see that this number of bits per frame agrees with the rates which exist at the U reference point by answering this question: If out of a possible 240 bits, only 216 are used for the B and D channels, what is the aggregate rate required to transmit these channels? By setting up the ratios as follows and by solving for the unknown, we get the proper bandwidth of 160 kbps at the U interface.

$$\frac{216 \text{ bits per frame for B and D bits}}{\text{Total of 240 bits needed per frame}} = \frac{144 \text{ kbps for the B and D channels}}{\text{Total rate at the U interface}}$$

19.3.3 ITU's S/T Reference Point

Configurations: Directing our attention now to the other side of the NT, we look at the interface between it and the TEs. Figure 19.6 shows four possible ways of configuring TEs with an NT. The first one is simply called a point-to-point configuration. It allows a maximum length of 1 km between the NT and the TE. In this configuration as well as the others, the propagation delay of the D channel's echo bits (discussed later) constrain the maximum distance and the spacing between terminals.

The next three types are variations of the point-to-multipoint configuration. In each case, up to 8 TEs may be connected. Which terminal can transmit on the bus is decided by the D channel protocol. The S/T interface uses two pairs of wires, which are connected in parallel with the multipoint TEs.

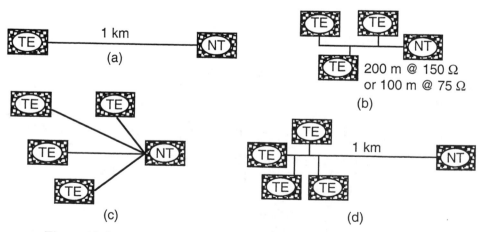

Figure 19.6 Four possible configurations for the wiring on the S/T interface. (a) Point-to-point. (b) Short passive bus. (c) Star. (d) Extended passive bus.

Figure 19.6(b) uses a short passive bus. Aside from the maximum distance between the bus and the terminal being 10 meters, there are no restrictions in how these terminals are placed. However, for a cable with an impedance of 150 ohms, the maximum distance is limited to 200 meters, and for a 75-ohm cable, this distance is 100 meters.

Figure 19.6(d) shows an extended passive bus which increases the distance limitation to 1 km; however, all the terminals must be clustered at the far end of the bus. Here, the distance between them must be kept between 25 and 50 meters. The wiring configuration (Figure 19.6(c)) shows a star topology that is composed of up to 8 point-to-point connections terminating at one card in the NT.

The Connector: Regardless of which configuration is used, the plug is standardized and is called the I.430 connector or the RJ-45. This connector is shown in Figure 19.7. It has 8 pins and is similar to the common RJ-11 jack. A 6-pin connector, when plugged into an 8-pin jack, doesn't make contact with pins 1 and 8. Likewise, a 4-pin connector would not make contact with pins 1, 2, 7, and 8. The chart in the figure shows the pin functions with respect to the TE. These are reversed for functions with respect to the NT. That is, pins 3 and 6 are used for the TE to transmit while for the NT, they are used to receive, and so on.

The RJ-45 is used for PRI as well as BRI. However, over the local loop, the PRI uses two pairs while the BRI uses only one. The assignment of the pin functions, shown in Figure 19.7, are for the S/T interface. This interface only appears with the BRI access and not with PRI. The use of the middle 4 pins is mandatory with both access types.

Figure 19.8 shows how a point-to-multipoint configuration may be set up using these 8 pins. Notice here that the NT's transmission on pins 4 and 5 is received by all of the TEs on the bus. Similarly, all the TEs transmit on pins 3 and 6 while the NT receives over these pins. The D channel bits and its echo bits determine which TE may transmit on the bus at any given time. Now let us look at the complicated yet flexible power distribution scheme that is available at this interface.

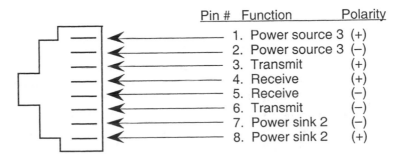

Pin #	Function	Polarity
1.	Power source 3	(+)
2.	Power source 3	(−)
3.	Transmit	(+)
4.	Receive	(+)
5.	Receive	(−)
6.	Transmit	(−)
7.	Power sink 2	(−)
8.	Power sink 2	(+)

Figure 19.7 The function assignments for the pins of an RJ-45 or I.430 connector in reference to TEs. Power 1 is phantomed over pins 3, 4, 5, and 6.

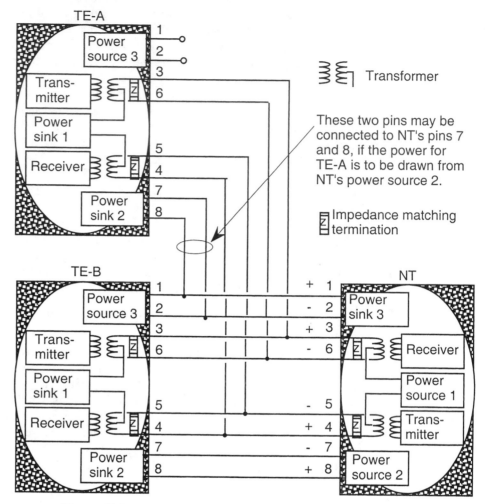

Figure 19.8 An example of a passive bus configuration with its power distribution.

Power Distribution: With POTS, the network (that is the CO) provides the power to operate the telephones. This is advantageous for the user in the event that there is a local power failure, because a CO is better equipped to handle power outages. However, with ISDN, the power may be available from various sources. It could come from the network, NT1, NT2, or the TE. Since the power to drive devices may come from various sources, a portable terminal should not expect power to be available from any jack that it is plugged into.

As seen in Figure 19.8, there are three power sources (and sinks) available. All power is provided at 40 VDC. The NT may provide the power by phantoming it over the 4 required pins (3 to 6). This is called power source 1. Here, the transmitted and received digital signals share the same metallic path as the DC voltage. This power is rated at 1 watt and may be used to drive all of the TEs associated with it. The NT may obtain this power either from the network or from a local AC outlet or a battery.

Power source 2, which is available from an NT on pins 7 and 8, may provide power of up to 7 watts for the TEs. Instead of each device having its own power source it is advantageous to drive them from fewer devices (NT and TEs). This way, fewer power backup systems would be necessary.

The figure further shows that one TE may provide power to other TEs as well as the NT by using power source 3. This source is not part of the ITU recommendations, and its implementation will vary from site to site.

19.3.4 Framing over the S/T Reference Point

For BRI, the signaling over the S/T interface uses what is called pseudoternary coding, which is depicted in Figure 19.9. A logical 1 is transmitted by 0 V and a logical 0 by either +1V or −1V. The polarity of the voltage alternates with every 0 bit and if two consecutive 0s are transmitted with the same polarity, it is called a code violation. Code violations are used on purpose to maintain synchronization.

Figure 19.10 shows the format of the I.430 transmission frame, which is used over the S/T interface. It consists of 48 bits sent in 250 microseconds. The frame format is different from the NT to TE direction as it is from the TE to NT direction. The TE derives its synchronization from the NT, so the TE's transmission is delayed by two bits.

The figure shows all possible pseudoternary values for each bit. Within the 48 bits of each frame, two groups of 8 bits for the B1 channel, and two groups of 8 bits for the B2 channel exist. There are 4 D channel bits per frame. This accounts for 36 bits. Out of the 48 bits per frame, this leaves 12 bits for overhead. Doing the same calculations as were done for confirming the line rate at the U interface, we see that the rate at the S/T interface also corresponds with 192 kbps.

$$\frac{\text{B and D channels' 36 bits}}{\text{Total of 48 bits per frame}} = \frac{144 \text{ kbps for the B and D channels}}{\text{Rate for the S/T interface}}$$

Let us now look at the purpose of the overhead bits, except for the D and E bits, which we'll leave for the next section.

The polarity of the F (Framing) bit is always positive and it marks the beginning of the frame. It is followed by the L (baLancing) bit, which is always negative to provide DC voltage balancing for the F bit. Likewise, the rest of the balancing bits are set to +1, 0, or −1V depending on the settings of the previous bits.

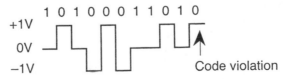

Figure 19.9 Pseudoternary line coding example.

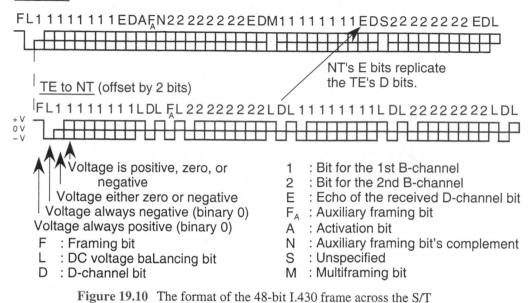

Figure 19.10 The format of the 48-bit I.430 frame across the S/T interface.

In the NT to TE direction, the Fa (Auxiliary Framing) bit is set to 1 in every fifth frame and M (Multiframing) bit is set to 1 in every 20th frame. These bits are set to 0 in all of the other frames. Together these bits help to group multiple frames and keep the line synchronized. The N bit is always set to be the opposite of Fa, so if the Fa bit is 0 then the N bit would be 1.

In the TE to NT direction, the Fa bits are all set to 0 except for every fifth frame. These Fa bits in every fifth frame create a subchannel called Q, whose purpose is not defined yet. Similarly, the purpose of the S bit is also undefined.

The A (Activation) bit is used by the NT to convey to the TE that the interface is active and operational. Figure 19.11 outlines this activation procedure. An INFO 0 signal is shown as being sent by the TE, but it could be sent by the NT as well. This is an absence of any signal and all it indicates is that the line is deactivated. Recall that 0 V corresponds to a binary 1 and a binary 0 is transmitted by either a positive or negative voltage.

The TE's power is then turned on and it sends an INFO 1 signal which is a continuous transmission of "+−111111." This signals the NT that the TE wants to activate the line and so the NT sends an INFO 2 signal with B, D, E, and A bits set to 0. The 0s on the line rapidly alter the polarity of the signal, which enables the receiver to synchronize quickly. Now the TE may send operational data using INFO 3 signals, and so may the NT using INFO 4 signals. Here the A bit would be set to 1 indicating that the line is active.

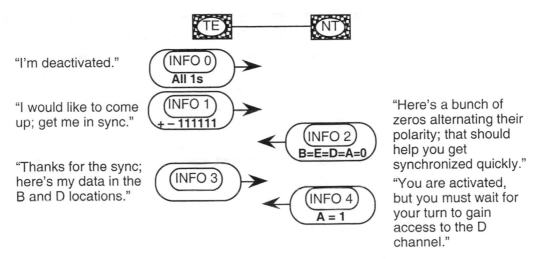

Figure 19.11 An exchange of INFO signals meant to get the TE activated, at which time the A bit is set to 1.

19.3.5 D-channel Access Control

Recall that the D channel is used for signaling and ISDN defines the three layers for its operation. As far as ISDN is concerned, the B channel is a layer 1 issue and it only transports its bits.

With BRI, TEs may be connected in a point-to-multipoint configuration. We saw this in Figures 19.6 and 19.8. The terminals will transmit the B channels on the bus only when they are given access through the D channel, so there is no problem with contention on the B channels. However, this is not the case with the D channel. Problems with contention among the TEs for the D channel have to be resolved. That is, how do we determine which TE may transmit over the D channel at any given time, since the TEs must share the bus to the NT?

The D bits are sent by the TEs as well as by the NT. However, the E bits are echoed back by the NT from the TEs' last D bits. These E bits help the TEs to know whose transmission the NT is getting. If one terminal sends a 0 for a D bit, while another terminal sends 1 for that bit-time, whose bit will the NT receive?

The answer to that question is the TE that sent the zero. Since pseudoternary line coding is used, regardless of what the rest of the terminals are transmitting, if one terminal is transmitting a binary zero then the NT will receive a zero. Remember, a binary 1 provides no voltage on the line while a binary 0 does.

The use of the D channel falls into two priority classes as shown in Table 19.3. Priority class 1 is used for ISDN layer 2 frames which carry signaling information, and priority class 2 is used for frames that carry other information, such as low-speed packet switching, telemetry, etc.

Within each priority class there are two levels specified as normal and lower. The priority class is set to the kind of information that the terminal needs to send to the NT.

Table 19.3 D-Channel Access Priorities		
	Priority Class = 1 Signaling information	Priority Class = 2 Non-signaling information
Normal Lower	8 9	10 11

If a terminal has not sent any level 2 frames yet, it will have its priority level set to normal. And according to the number corresponding to the class and level in the table, the TE will have to count that many successive 1s (or 0V levels) in the E channel it receives from the NT before being allowed to transmit.

After the transmission is complete, the TE will lower its priority level in order to give other TEs a chance to transmit. Once it is able to count as high up as the lower level priority number, then it will know that others who had wanted to transmit have done so. Consequently, it will raise its level back to normal and begin another transmission, if necessary.

Notice that the number of 1s that must be received by a TE that wants to transmit is greater than 6. This is because if some other TE is transmitting on the line, it will have at most 6 consecutive 1s in its second layer frames. Recall from the discussion of SDLC from Chapter 16 that due to bit stuffing, frames are allowed to have at most 6 consecutive 1s, even in the flag field. In the next section, we'll discuss ISDN's second layer which is similar to SDLC. For now, let's look at an example.

Only two terminals, A and B, are shown in Figure 19.12 as sharing the line. Their terminal numbers are called TEIs (Terminal End-point Identifiers) and are shown in the figure. This is part of the second layer's address field which comes after the flag ("01111110") field. The TEIs are 16 ("0010000") and 0, respectively. They have both been activated and have set their priorities to 8, since they both have signaling information to send. Both of them transmit logical 1s (0 V) over the D channel and since no one else is on the line, the NT echoes back these 1s with its E bits.

They both count 8 successive 1s and begin transmission of their level 2 frames. Both of their flag fields are the same, so they both receive the same pattern back on the E channel. Right after these flags, they simultaneously transmit their TEIs and since they differ at the third address bit, B's binary 0 forces a voltage on the line, despite A's binary 1 (0 V). The NT "sees" a binary 0 and echoes it back, but terminal A doesn't get its 1 echoed and so terminates its transmission. However, B doesn't have to restart transmission but continues until it is done, at which time it lowers its priority to 9.

All this time, A has been trying to consecutively count up to 8, but has failed. A can count up only to a maximum of 6 consecutive 1s, due to the number of 1s in B's flags. Actually, 7 consecutive 1s are possible in a frame, which occurs when a frame is being cancelled.

Now that B is done and has to be quiet (no voltage), A is able to count up to 8 and start its transmission. B is unable to transmit now, since it must count up to 9.

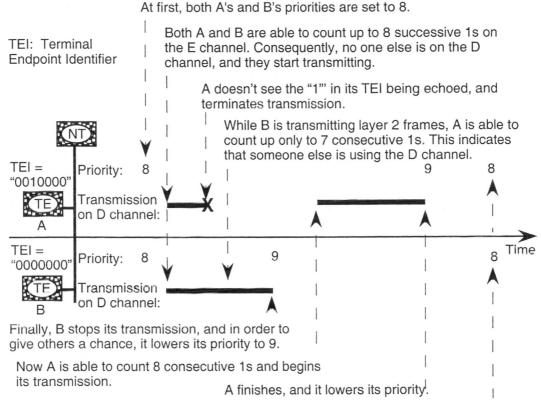

At first, both A's and B's priorities are set to 8.

Both A and B are able to count up to 8 successive 1s on the E channel. Consequently, no one else is on the D channel, and they start transmitting.

A doesn't see the "1'" in its TEI being echoed, and terminates transmission.

While B is transmitting layer 2 frames, A is able to count up only to 7 consecutive 1s. This indicates that someone else is using the D channel.

TEI: Terminal Endpoint Identifier

TEI = "0010000" Priority: 8

Transmission on D channel:

A

TEI = "0000000" Priority: 8

Transmission on D channel:

B

Time

Finally, B stops its transmission, and in order to give others a chance, it lowers its priority to 9.

Now A is able to count 8 consecutive 1s and begins its transmission.

A finishes, and it lowers its priority.

Both A and B can count up to 9 consecutive 1s and so they bring their priority back up to 8. Now either or both may start transmitting again.

Figure 19.12 CSMA/CR (Carrier Sense Multiple Access with Collision Resolution) allows, as shown in this example, for B to continue transmission, even after A detected a collision at point x.

Finally, when B's transmission is complete, it sets its priority to 9. And if no one else is transmitting, then they both can count up to 9 and reset their priorities to 8. This method of gaining control over the D channel is called CSMA/CR (Carrier Sense Multiple Access with Collision Resolution).

19.4 THE PHYSICAL LAYER OF PRI

PRI typically stops at the NT2, so there is no S/T interface defined to the TEs. In other words, PRI provides a trunk connection between, say, a PBX at the customer's site and the local exchange. There are two variations possible at this interface. They are called the 1.544-Mbps and 2.048-Mbps interfaces or ITU's G.703 and G.704 recommendations respectively.

The 1.54-Mbps interface, based on T1, uses the ESF format with clear channel signaling. That is, all of the signaling for the 23 B channels is done over the one D channel operating at 64 kbps. This allows for call-by-call service selection in real time. That is, each channel can be set up for a different service and can be connected to separate destinations. Although this is possible with T1s, it has to be provisioned beforehand, and cannot be configured dynamically, as with PRI. Therefore, the D channel is what gives PRI its appeal. Without the D channel, this interface would be not much different from T1s as described in Chapter 15.

19.5 THE DATA LINK LAYER

19.5.1 Why LAPD?

The second and third layers of ISDN concern only the D channel, as has been said before. The protocol used over the second or the data link layer is called LAPD (Link Access Procedures over the D channel), which is similar to SDLC and LAP/B covered in Chapters 16 and 17, respectively. Please refer back to these chapters when necessary, since this section builds upon that material.

Unlike LAPD, LAP/B is only a point-to-point protocol which is used over the DTE-DCE link. LAPD, on the other hand, can be used between an NT and multiple TEs. It is a full-duplex point-to-multipoint protocol, but so is SDLC. One reason why SDLC wasn't chosen for ISDN, which can operate on multipoint configurations, is that it uses polling, which makes an inefficient use of the available bandwidth. As we have seen in the previous section, CSMA/CR allows multipoint transmission to occur with less overhead and minimum delay. Now only the LAPD issues which differ from those of LAP/B and SDLC will be covered.

19.5.2 Basic Frame Formatting

Figure 19.13 shows the format of the three types of frames which exist: information, supervisory, and unnumbered. After the first flag is transmitted, the EA (Extension Address) bit, whose value is 0, is transmitted indicating that there is another octet in this address field. Eight bits later, an EA bit of 1 is transmitted, indicating that this is the last octet of the address field.

The C/R (Command or Response) bit is set by the user to 0 and is set by the LE to 1, if the transmitting frame is a command. This bit is reversed if the frame is a response to a command frame. All information frames are commands, all supervisory frame types (RR, RNR, and REJ) can be either commands or responses, and out of the unnumbered frames, SABME, DISC, UI are commands; UA, DM, FRMR are responses; and XID can be either.

SABME (Set Asynchronous Balanced Mode Extended), UI (Unnumbered Information), and XID (eXchange IDentification) are the frame types that are new for us. SABME is used for establishing a link which can transfer 127 consecutive frames without requiring a response. UI, as we'll soon see, sends information that doesn't require an acknowledgment and XID is used to automatically set up a data link.

The two S bits give the supervisory frame type and the five M bits give the unnumbered frame type. The P/F bits are used for error control as in SDLC.

(a) Information frame

0	1	1	1	1	1	1	0
S A P I						C/R	EA$_0$
T E I							EA$_1$
N (s)							0
N (r)							P
INFO							
F C S							
0	1	1	1	1	1	1	0

(a)

(b) Supervisory frame

0	1	1	1	1	1	1	0
S A P I						C/R	EA$_0$
T E I							EA$_1$
0	0	0	0	S	S	0	1
N (r)							P/F
F C S							
0	1	1	1	1	1	1	0

(b)

(c) Unnumbered frame

0	1	1	1	1	1	1	0
S A P I						C/R	EA$_0$
T E I							EA$_1$
M	M	M	P/F	M	M	1	1
F C S							
0	1	1	1	1	1	1	0

(c)

SAPI : Service Access Point Identifier
C/R : Command or Response bit
EA$_0$: Extension Address bit = 0
EA$_1$: Extension Address bit = 1
TEI : Terminal Endpoint Identifier
N (s) : Sending frame Number
N (r) : Next Receiving frame Number
FCS : Frame Check Sequence
S : Supervisory function bit
M : Modifier function bit
P/F : Poll or Final bit

Figure 19.13 Three types of LAPD frames: (a) information, (b) supervisory, (c) unnumbered. The fields which are shaded are characteristic of those particular frame types.

19.5.3 The DLCI Field

The DLCI (Data Link Control Identifier) is the combination of SAPI (Service Access Point Identifier) and TEI (Terminal Endpoint Identifier) fields. The TEI identifies the terminal on the interface while the SAPI identifies the access point for the LAPD network layer process in the terminal that is logically connected to its peer process in the LE. Figure 19.14 shows an example of how various terminals and their service-access points may establish logical links with their corresponding entities in the LE. Thus the frame has to specify not only to which terminal it is going, but also to which service-access point of that terminal.

A SAPI of 0 is used to specify the service access point which controls circuit switching procedures, a SAPI of 1 is used for transmission in the packet switching mode, a SAPI of 16 for x.25 communications, and a SAPI of 63 for OAM (Operations, Administrations, and Maintenance) procedures.

There are three types of TEI assignments: broadcast, automatic, and nonautomatic. A TEI of 127, which is all 1s, is the broadcast address, and frames sent with this address are directed to every terminal on the line. Nonautomatic TEIs are hardwired in the terminals, either by encoding the address in ROM (Read Only Memory), by setting switches, or by some other physical method. Before a nonautomatic TEI can be used,

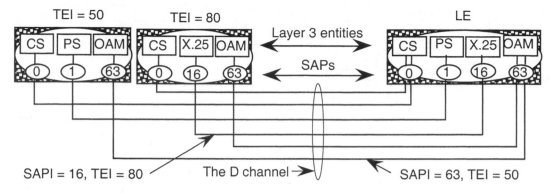

SAPI = 16, TEI = 80   The D channel →   SAPI = 63, TEI = 50

CS   : Circuit switched mode   SAP : Service Access Point
PS   : Packet switched mode   SAPI : SAP Identifier
OAM : Operations, Administration,   TEI   : Terminal Endpoint Identifier
       & Maintenance   LE   : Local Exchange

Figure 19.14 The DLCI (Data Link Control Identifier) consisting of the
SAPI and the TEI provides the address of frames, specifying not only
the terminal, but also the SAP, which provides access to the desired
layer 3 process.

the network side, that is the LE or the NT2, has to approve its use. These TEIs fall in
the range from 0 to 63 whereas automatic TEIs range from 64 to 126.

    Automatic assignment of TEIs is done by the terminal asking the network for a
TEI via the LAPD protocol. Referring to the example in Figure 19.15, we see that this
is accomplished by the terminal first sending a UI frame to the LE. The information in
this frame indicates to the LE that the terminal is requesting a TEI. Because such an

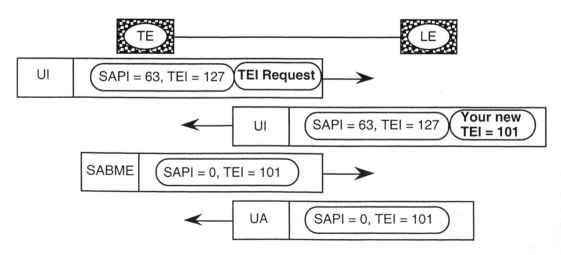

Figure 19.15 Requesting a TEI from an LE, and establishing a link.

operation is an administrative detail, it uses an SAPI of 63 and because the terminal doesn't have a TEI yet, it uses the general TEI of 127.

The LE also replies with a UI frame with the same SAPI and TEI values that it received. However, in the information part of this frame, the LE grants a TEI of 101. Now the TE may exchange data after establishing a logical link by transmitting an

Table 19.4 Network Layer Message Types					
The left two columns specify whether corresponding ACK and REJ message types exist. The right two columns specify if this message is sent by the user, by the network, or both.					
ACK	REJ	Message Type	Brief Description and Purpose	user	netw.
Call Establishment Messages					
* *		SETUP CONNect ALERTing CALL PROC	Request for call establishment Call party answered the call Called phone is "ringing" Call proceeding, received all info.	* * *	* * * *
Call Information Phase Messages					
* *	* *	USER INFO SUSPend RESume	For sending info. to another user Call on hold, but channel connected For resuming a suspended call	* * *	*
Call Clearing Messages					
*		DETach DISConnect RELease REL COM	Call info. saved, channel disconnected Info. saved until REL COM is received Channel and call info. are released Release complete, channel free again	* * * *	* * * *
Miscellaneous Messages					
* * *	* * *	CANcel FACility REGister STATUS CON CON INFOrmation	Request to cancel a facility Request for facility, i.e., call forwarding For facility registration in a database To report conditions of a call For congestion control or flow control To establish a call, and other reasons	* * * * * *	* * * * *

SABME and receiving a UA. Note that an SAPI of 0 corresponds to a circuit switched connection, whereas a TEI of 101 corresponds to the TEI assigned by the LE.

19.6 THE NETWORK LAYER

Because the scope of the D channel network layer is quite complex, we won't study it in much detail. We have already introduced its function in a circuit switched mode while discussing Figure 18.14. There the establishment and the release of a call connection were shown as the D channel network layer interfaced with the SS7's ISUP layer. Table 19.4 summarizes the network layer messages.

The network layer establishes, maintains, and terminates ISDN connections between application processes or entities. It provides a user-to-network layer interface. Addresses to ISDN destinations are composed of three variable-length parts. They are the country code (up to 3 digits), the national significant number (up to 17 digits), and the subaddress (up to 40 digits).

This ends our discussion on ISDN; now let us turn our attention to another important standard called SONET (Synchronous Optical NETwork), which is necessary for building a BISDN (Broadband ISDN).

EXERCISES

1. Which ISDN functional device is used to make non-ISDN devices become part of the ISDN?
   a. TE1   b. TE2
   c. TA   d. NT12
2. A CO's ISDN compatible DMS100 switch corresponds to which functional device?
   a. NT1   b. LT
   c. ET   d. PH
3. Which telecommunications service is provided to both the bearer services and teleservices?
   a. supplementary   b. information transfer
   c. general   d. access
4. What is the bit rate at BRI's U interface?
   a. 144 kbps   b. 160 kbps
   c. 196 kbps   d. 1.544 Mbps
5. The U interface is defined by what standards group?
   a. IEEE   b. ANSI
   c. ITU   d. ISO
6. Which line coding is used at the U reference point?
   a. pseudoternary   b. AMI
   c. 2B1Q   d. unipolar
7. Which station will transmit first if A has a TEI of 12 and a priority level of 9, B has a TEI of 14 and a priority level of 10, C has a TEI of 10 and a priority level of 9, and D has a TEI of 8 and a priority level of 10?
   a. station A   b. station B
   c. station C   d. station D
8. Name the bearer service attribute which identifies whether the connection is circuit switched or packet switched.

9. What pin numbers are used by the NT to transmit data? What pins are used by the NT to provide power to the TEs?
10. How many E bits are sent from the TE to the NT in one frame?
11. Which INFO signal is sent by the NT to the TE to provide it with synchronization?
12. Which fields in the LAPD information frame do not exist in the LAPB information frame?
13. A TEI of 10 tells what about the way the terminal was assigned the TEI?
14. List as many default attributes as possible for an ordinary telephone call.
15. Discuss the various methods of how power source 3 could be used to distribute power and their advantages.
16. What is the difference between activation and access to the D channel?
17. Explain access to the D channel as briefly as possible.
18. What is the advantage of LAPD over LAPB?
19. Explain the parts of the DLCI field and their uses.

## Chapter 20

SONET

20.1 SONET: ISN'T THAT A KIND OF POEM?

T1 was designed by the Bell Telephone Laboratories back in the 1960s to transmit 24 voice channels digitally over metallic wires. T3 technology, which was an extension of T1, was then introduced to support transmission of 672 voice channels over microwave systems. Since T1 and T3 were both based on the transmission of electrical signals, a new technology that was more appropriate for transmission of optical signals was needed. This technology was to be designed so that the problems which were inherent in the T-carrier systems would be minimized, and thus make it easier to network.

In 1985 Telcordia (then Bellcore) provided a solution for these issues in a specification called SONET (Synchronous Optical NETwork). Since then, SONET has become standardized by ANSI and as SDH (Synchronous Digital Hierarchy) by ITU-T. The term "optical" was dropped by ITU-T, because by that time SONET was being transported by other media, such as digital microwave.

SONET is a multiple-level protocol used to transport high-speed signals using circuit switched synchronous multiplexing. It is the only standard for high-speed fiber systems, which can become the vehicle for making future-generation services such as broadband ISDN, ATM (Asynchronous Transfer Mode), and others a reality.

20.2 BENEFITS OF SONET AS COMPARED WITH T3

When a M13 multiplexer receives DS1 signals at its input ports, the DS1s are not necessarily synchronized to a common clock. DS1 signals, instead of being exactly 1.544 Mbps, can have a tolerance so that they may be off by plus or minus 75 bps. Hence, a M13 multiplexer must add extra bits here and there to compensate for these differences in bit rates. This is necessary to properly frame the DS1s into a DS3 frame. The technique of adding these extra bits is called "bit stuffing," which unfortunately is the same phrase as the one used to describe stuffing a 0 after every 5 consecutive 1s.

as is done in SDLC. Because bit stuffing is used in T3, it is said to be asynchronously multiplexed or asynchronously formatted. Note that the use of the asynchronous term here has nothing to do with start and stop bits.

One of the problems with asynchronous multiplexing is that when two points are sending a multiplexed signal to each other, a third location in between them cannot select one channel without first demultiplexing the entire set of channels. This is because with an asynchronous bit stream, bits belonging to a particular channel do not occur at regular intervals, and there are extra bits stuffed depending on the timing of the input sources. So an intermediate node that must drop channels (or add channels for that matter) from a signal stream must have a M13 multiplexer to demultiplex, a patch panel to cross-connect, and another M13 multiplexer to remultiplex the new signal stream. This is difficult to operate and manage, and it requires expensive equipment.

On the other hand, SONET equipment performs synchronous multiplexing, so that no bit stuffing is required. The bytes belonging to each channel are easily identified, which allows SONET to use ADMs (Add and Drop Multiplexer). This device "plucks" (or drops) out only the bits for the channels which are needed and allows the rest of the data stream to pass undisturbed. SONET's synchronous multiplexing also allows channels to be switched or routed from one link to another within milliseconds. Compare this with up to 30 minutes to cross-connect with a T1 DCS (or DACS). Photonic switching, now that it is possible, allows signals to be switched at optical speeds without having to first convert them to electrical signals.

This almost instantaneous switching capability of SONET provides it with what is called APS (Automatic Protection Switching), which can reroute traffic from a link that has failed to another active link without losing any data. With asynchronous networking, as with T1s, APS is possible, but there is a glitch and one loses some data. When bandwidth is required without much advance notice, as in disaster recovery, networks can be automatically reconfigured.

Such management capabilities are some of the most exciting benefits of SONET. But then again these capabilities become even more necessary than for previous methods, since a substantial amount of traffic is depending on these fiber links. Nearly 5% of SONET's bandwidth is used to monitor, control, reconfigure, test, and provision the digital network, compared to 0.5% used in ESF formatting. Furthermore, as we'll see in Figure 20.1, the network management capabilities are provided in layers of hierarchy, allowing the carriers as well as the customers to manage their part of the network. This is done through SONET's OSS (Operation Support System).

With SONET, end-users and carriers don't have to become "hostages" to their vendors as becomes the case when dealing with T3 equipment. This is because T3 formatting is proprietary. On the contrary, SONET is an international standard interface for end-users as well as for carriers and equipment manufacturers. This allows customers to switch vendors and interconnect equipment made by different vendors. This capability is called "mid-span meet." Although proprietary T3 equipment will have to keep its prices up, SONET prices should eventually drop below those for T3, because there will be more vendors providing standardized SONET-based equipment.

Incidentally, SONET rates are standardized to 2,488 Mbps, which is much higher than DS3 rates, and has provisions to go up to 13 Gbps. Yet, SONET has the capability to transport existing signal formats such as DS3, DS1, and E1.

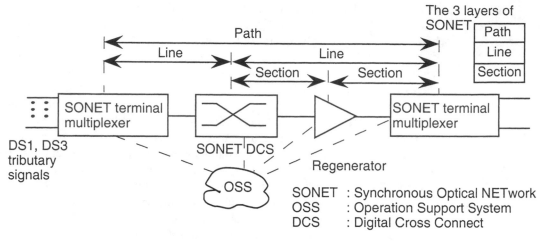

Figure 20.1 The SONET transport.

20.3 SONET RATES AND DEVICES

Table 20.1 shows the popular physical interfaces for SONET. An STS (Synchronous Transport Signal) frame carries data in electrical form while its corresponding signal in optical form is called an OC (Optical Carrier). To produce an OC signal from its STS derivative, the STS signal is scrambled. Notice that because of synchronous multiplexing, STS levels are exact multiples of each other, unlike, for example, the DS3 level (44.736 Mbps) which is not exactly 28 times that of a DS1 signal level (1.544 Mbps).

Figure 20.1 shows three types of SONET devices: the terminal multiplexer, the DCS (Digital Cross-connect System), and the regenerator. The terminal multiplexer serves as a local as well as a long-haul access point to the SONET network. If it is used by the local loop provider, it would be called a DLC (Digital Loop Carrier system). In that case, it would be used as a concentrator of DS-0 signals, which would be connected to the CO switch either locally or remotely.

The DCS provides direct synchronous switching at DS1 and DS3 and other rates. In the figure it could be replaced with an ADM to add or drop channels as necessary. Regenerators are needed every 35 miles for fiber; besides reconstructing the signal, these devices provide error checking, maintenance facilities and other sophisticated services.

Based on the links between these devices, three types of network spans are defined. Corresponding to these spans three layers are defined, the lowest of which is the section layer. It is used for framing, scrambling, and locating faults.

A line exists between two nodes and it is used for multiplexing, synchronization, switching, and cross-connecting SONET signals. It is used for gathering data for network management. Lastly, the end-to-end logical links between customer users is called a path. It is the circuit between two entry points of the SONET cloud. It provides a high degree of maintenance service to the customer. ADM is a path layer device, so that if it replaced the DCS in the figure, there would be two paths present instead of one.

Table 20.1 Popular SONET interfaces				
SONET's Synchronous Transport Signal	SDH's Synchronous Transport Mode	Line Rates in Mbps	Payload Rate in Mbps	Optical Carrier Designations
STS-1	STM-0	51.84	50.112	OC-1
STS-3	STM-1	155.52	150.336	OC-3
STS-12	STM-4	622.08	601.344	OC-12
STS-48	STM-16	2,488.32	2,405.376	OC-48
STS-192	STM-53	9,953.28	9,621.504	OC-192

20.4 SONET TRANSPORT STRUCTURE

In an STS-1 frame, as shown in Figure 20.2, there are 90 columns and 9 rows, totaling 810 bytes. This frame is divided into a transport overhead and an SPE (Synchronous Payload Envelope), which consist of 3 columns and 87 columns, respectively. The order of transmission is such that the first 3 bytes of the transport overhead sent, then the 87 bytes of the SPE, after which the next row of 3 plus 87 bytes is sent, and so on. The transport overhead is further divided into a section overhead and a line overhead, while the SPE is divided into a path overhead and the payload where the tributary data is carried.

Figure 20.3 shows the same frame in more detail. The DC (Data communication Channel) fields in the transport overhead are used for network management information. The payload of the SPE is divided into seven VT (Virtual Tributary) groups and 18 packing bytes. Each VT group is 12 columns wide and may contain one or more VTs of the same type. A VT type is a given block of data that can carry a fixed amount of bandwidth for the user. VT1.5 is used to transport one DS1 signal, VT2 is used to carry one E1 signal, etc., as shown in Figure 20.3. If one entire SPE is used to carry a DS3 signal, then no VTs are needed. So VTs are subdivisions of the SPE and the type of VTs that are used is determined by what the tributary has to send. There are two extra columns of "padding" bytes available to accommodate for multiplexing asynchronous signals.

The SPE is assembled at a terminal node and its path overhead contains the end-to-end management information. For example, the signal label indicates whether the payload contains one DS3 or a combination of lower-rate signals, that is, the type and the number of VTs used. The path overhead stays with the SPE until it arrives at the destination node, hence the term "path." Likewise, the line overhead is processed at all nodes and the section overhead is processed at all nodes as well as at the regenerators.

One of the advantages of SONET is that an entire SONET signal can be handed off in bulk between carriers (LECs or IXCs), without requiring it to be demultiplexed into DS0 levels. However, many carriers use their own stratum one clocks to keep their

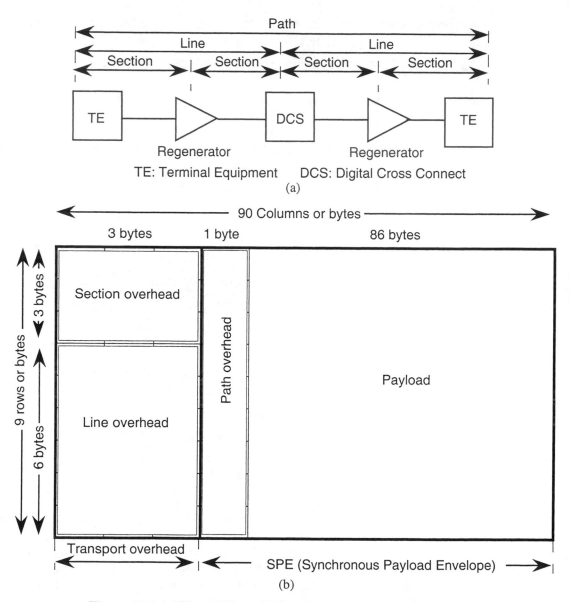

Figure 20.2 (a) Three different kinds of segments present in SONET: path, line, and section. (b) The format of an STS-1 frame with the positioning of the overheads for path, line, and section.

networks in sync and very small differences do exist between these clocks. They are said to be plesiochronous. Instead of using bit stuffing, SONET allows for these clocking differences by permitting the SPE to start anywhere in the STS frame. So SPEs usually start in one frame and end in the next one, as shown in Figure 20.4. This is called "floating the payload."

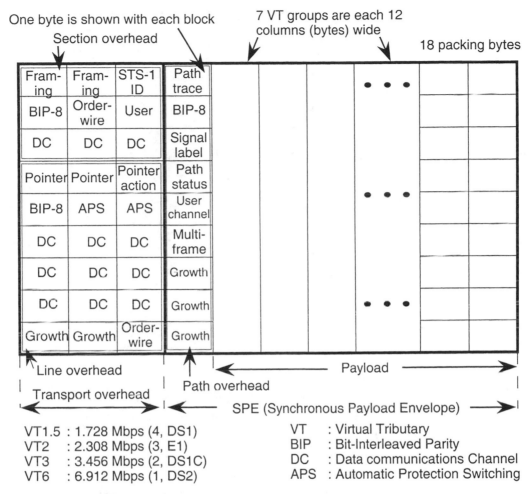

Figure 20.3 The format of the STS-1 frame is shown as being 90 columns by 9 rows. It is 810 bytes long and takes 125 microseconds to transmit; that is, 8000 frames are sent in every second. The payload capacity is 49.54 Mbps. Next to the rates of the VTs, the number of VTs that can fit in one group and the digital signal levels that can be accommodated by the VTs are shown in parentheses.

To notify the receiving node where an SPE starts, pointers are used in the line overhead. A pointer is simply the byte address in the STS frame indicating at which byte the payload begins. As shown in the figure, none of the SPEs start at the beginning of an STS frame, so the pointers contain the byte addresses of where they do begin. In Figure 20.4 SPE3 was loaded into the STS frame too soon, so the pointer action byte is used to contain the data for SPE2, so as to allow SPE3 to start earlier. This is called a "negative stuff." SPE5, on the contrary, came in a little late, so a "positive stuff" byte is inserted in SPE4 to allow for the timing difference in SPE5.

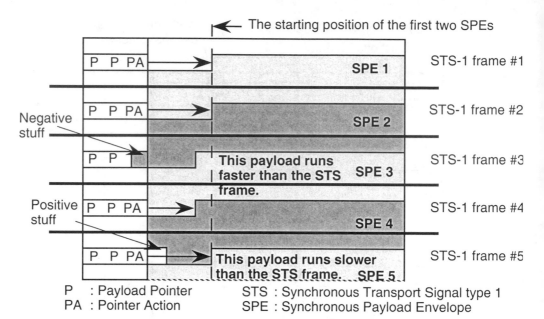

Figure 20.4 The SPEs are floated in the STS frames to compensate for slight timing differences. The starting position of the next SPE may differ by only one octet.

Besides these STS pointers indicating where each SPE begins within the STS frames, VTs may also have pointers indicating where each VT begins within the SPE. Hence the VTs are also allowed to float.

20.5 MAPPINGS

The method by which VTs are loaded into the frames is called a mapping. The types of mappings depend on whether the VTs are floated or not, whether the tributary signals are synchronized with the SONET clock or not, etc. If VTs are floated within an SPE, then additional pointers are required indicating where the VTs begin. Let us look at four popular mappings in the order that they are illustrated in Figures 20.5(a) through (d).

The simplest and inflexible type of mapping is the asynchronous DS3 mapping. It allows the popular DS3 signals to be loaded in the SPE as one "block." Here, the DS3 bits aren't necessarily synchronized with the SONET clock and the DS3 signal can't be synchronously switched, yet it does allow the transport of existing DS3 signals. Notice that the SPE rate of 51 Mbps is less than the DS3 rate. Additional bits have to be added to make up the difference.

Unchannelized floating mode DS1 mapping will allow the VTs to float and the tributary bits may or may not be synchronized with the SONET clock. Here, more sets of pointers have to be processed by the equipment, but synchronous switching of the

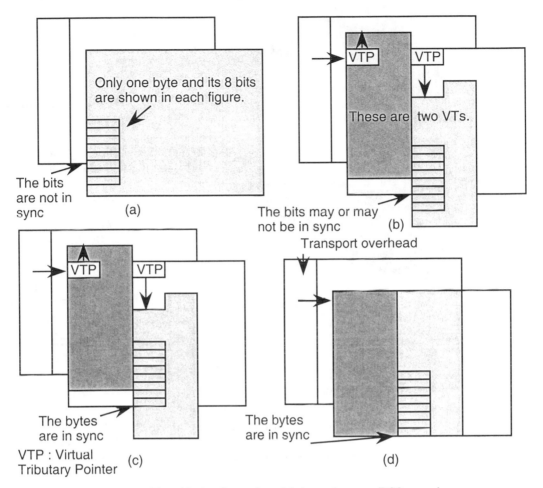

Figure 20.5 Four kinds of mapping: (a) Asynchronous DS3 mapping. (b) Unchannelized floating VTs. (c) Channelized floating VTs. (d) Channelized locked VTs .

VTs is then possible. This means, for example, that a DS1 signal may be addressed and added or dropped "on the fly," but not a DS0 signal.

Channelized or byte-synchronous floating mode DS1 mapping requires that the DS1 signal's bytes be synchronized with those of SONET. Here, not only DS1s, but also DS0 signals can be identified and switched.

Lastly, the channelized or byte-synchronous locked mode DS1 mapping doesn't allow the VTs to float and so requires less pointer processing. However, phase and frequencies have to be maintained in order to benefit from easier cross-connection and switching of DS0 channels. On the down side, the locked mode introduces more delay than the floating mode.

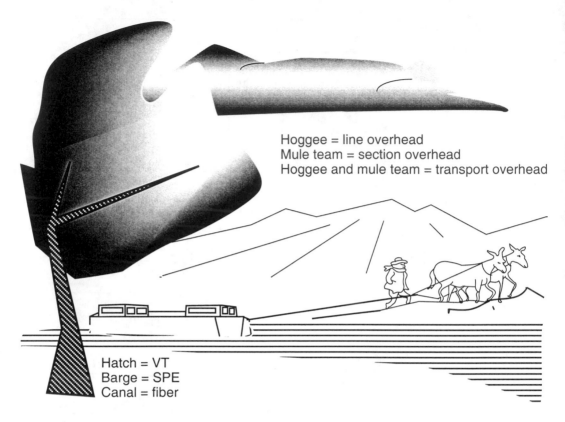

Hoggee = line overhead
Mule team = section overhead
Hoggee and mule team = transport overhead

Hatch = VT
Barge = SPE
Canal = fiber

Figure 20.6 In the 1800s, hauling a barge from Albany to Buffalo took only 9 days at $6 per ton, instead of taking 20 days at $100 per ton using horse wagons.   Now, SONET can haul digital traffic in even less time.

20.6 REVIEW

Let us review the basic SONET concepts by comparing it with the canal system of the 1800s, before trains or cars were invented. This is illustrated in Figure 20.6.

The canal waterway is like the fiber "lightway" of SONET. The barge, along with the mule team and the hoggee driving it, are akin to one STS frame. Consider the barge itself as the SPE and the mule team with its hoggee as the transport overhead. The transport overhead is further divided into a segment overhead (the mule team) and a line overhead (the hoggee). A shipment of goods may be loaded in one barge and continue into the next one just as one SPE may float from one STS frame to another.

The captain who stays in the barge until it reaches its destination, let us say, is the path overhead. He/she knows the barge's contents and their locations within the barge. However, for the sake of our analogy let us assume that the hoggee who is driving the mule team is only going to the next canal intersection. There the barge will get a new transport overhead (mule team and the hoggee) and continue on its journey to the next intersection or its terminal destination.

Between two intersections, the mule team, which is our segment overhead, may need "regeneration" by requiring food and water or rest by being replaced by another team riding in the barge.

We can think of the three big hatches in the barge as analogous to the VT groups. Let us say that each hatch is designated for a specific purpose, for example, one hatch is designated only for food while the others are used only for carrying coal and lumber exclusively. Similarly, the VT groups may carry only one kind of VT. The VTs themselves could be considered as sacks that carry grain or other containers that carry products depending on what the user wants to ship. So in many ways, transporting information over SONET is analogous to transporting goods over a canal system.

20.7 SONET RINGS

Because SONET can carry large amounts of data, a cut in a fiber span or problems in timing can cause disruptions for many customers. In order to plan for such catastrophic failures, SONET is usually deployed in rings.

In Figure 20.7 we see a 2-fiber ULSR (Unidirectional Line Switched Ring). One ring is called the protection ring, which normally doesn't carry any traffic, and the other is the active (or service) ring, which carries all of the traffic. Hence, when NE-A (Network Element)-A communicates with NE-B, it uses only one span. However, NE-B uses four spans in order to communicate with NE-A. This is because traffic flows in only one direction. The delay of traffic in one direction is more than the delay in the other direction. The counterclockwise direction is only used in case of failure as shown in the second diagram.

These types of rings are usually used in a metropolitan area or within cities where the differences in delays are negligible. This is a line switched ring because the entire capacity of one fiber can be transferred from one ring to the other. If it were a path

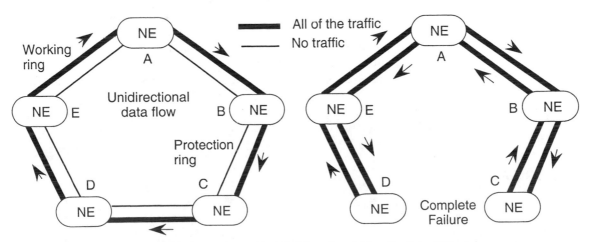

Figure 20.7 2-fiber ULSR (Unidirectional Line Switched Ring) uses one ring in normal operation. If both fibers are cut, the rings are wrapped around.

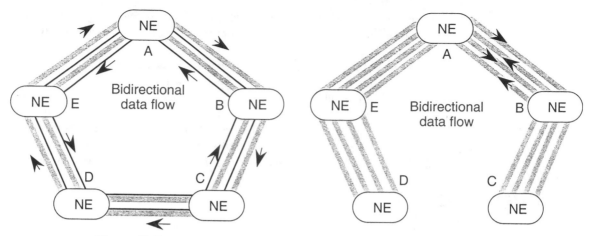

Figure 20.8 4-fiber BLSR (Bidirectional Line Switched Ring) sends half the traffic on each ring. In case of failure, the rings are wrapped around.

switched ring, then only a part of the fiber capacity could be switched on the alternate ring, if necessary. For example, if each link in Figure 20.7 had a capacity of OC-12, then the entire OC-12 would need to be switched, but in a path switched ring, only a portion of that could be switched. For instance, switching could be done at the OC-3 or OC-1 signal level or even at the VT level.

In Figure 20.8 we see a 4-fiber BLSR (Bidirectional Line Switched Ring). In a bidirectional ring, traffic during normal operation flows in both ways. Hence, the delays are the same whether NE-A is transmitting to NE-B or vice versa. Actually, there are four rings present. Traffic travels on only two rings during normal operation while the other two rings are on protection mode.

If only one or two out of the four fiber links become inoperative, perhaps due to equipment failure, then the rest of the ring can still stay intact. In such a case, switching can be done only in the affected span. This is called *span switching*. Unfortunately, if a backhoe is the culprit in the disruption, then chances are that all four fibers on that span would be cut. In that case, *ring switching* would take place as shown in the figure.

The 4-fiber bidirectional rings are more popular with the wide area carriers and IXCs. With such rings, both span and ring switching is possible. With twice as many fibers as 2-fiber rings, these rings provide twice as much protection.

EXERCISES

1. What is SONET's management scheme called?
   a. ADM   b. OSS
   c. APS   d. mid-span-meet
2. Give one difference between SDH and SONET?
3. The payload and the path overhead together are called what in SONET?
4. List some advantages and disadvantages of ISDN over traditional POTS service.

5. What are the advantages and disadvantages of SONET over T3?
6. Is bit stuffing used in SONET? If not, what is used in place of it?
7. Exactly how many OC-3s can fit in a OC-48?
8. Is ADM a path, line, or section level device?
9. Give three types of overheads present in an STS-1 frame. A regenerator would modify which of these overheads?
10. How long is each of the three types of overheads in bytes?
11. List and explain the four types of mappings present in SONET.
12. Give the differences between each of the following types of rings: unidirectional and bidirectional, line switched and path switched, and 2-fiber and 4-fiber.

Chapter 21

Frame Relay

Frame relay network services have seen an almost 50% increase for each of the last seven years. It is a simplified version of X.25 networks that was derived from ITU-T's standards work done on ISDN, and has become an inexpensive way to replace dedicated tie-lines. Many times cost savings have been reduced by 30% and better by converting from tie-lines. Frame relay services are also simple and easy to understand and are well established in the market placed. Although public carriers are replacing their network infrastructure with ATM switches, frame relay has taken a strong foothold and will be with us for some time.

21.1 REVIEW OF SWITCHED NETWORKS

At the end of Chapter 2 we discussed the concept of channel identifiers in a packet switched network. We looked at how these channel numbers along each physical path create a virtual circuit between two end users across such a network. Then in Section 5.1.1 we compared switched circuits with dedicated lines. Table 5.1 summarized their differences. In Table 5.4 and Section 5.3 we also took a first look at PVCs (Permanent Virtual Circuits), SVCs (Switched Virtual Circuits), X.25, frame relay, and ATM. If it has been some time since you studied these sections and tables, it would be a good time for you to review them now. Because the concept of virtual circuits is so central to both frame relay and ATM, the topic of the next chapter, let us take a second look at them before we continue with frame relay.

21.1.1 Virtual Circuits in X.25, Frame Relay, and ATM

Figure 21.1 shows a packet switched network with three packet switches labeled from A through C. They are connected to each other using three tie-lines. Each of the switches have 3 ports, numbered from 1 through 3. One port on each switch is connected to some equipment at the customer's site. This equipment is labeled as CPE (Customer Premises Equipment). Hence three customer sites that are connected by the packet switched network are shown.

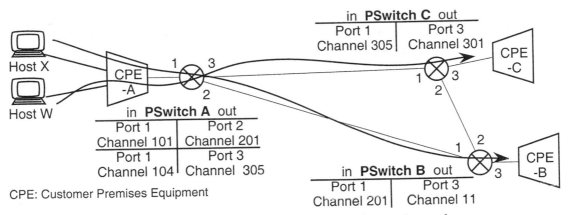

Figure 21.1 Two virtual circuits are established through a packet switched network, each one defined by the packet switching tables.

The packet switched network could be an X.25, frame relay, or ATM network. In the case of an ATM network, the term "packet" is replaced by the term "cell," since the unit of transfer has a fixed length. Data units of variable length at the OSI's third layer are called packets. Frame relay operates primarily at the second layer of the OSI Reference Model, hence the term "frame" is used instead. In any of these cases (packets used in X.25 networks, frames used in frame relay networks, or cells used in ATM networks), the behavior of virtual circuits can be viewed as shown in Figure 21.1. In this section, we will use the terms packets and packet switches to describe any of these three network types.

The packet switched network could be a private switched network. In that case, one organization would own all the switches and lease all the tie-lines connected to them. However, these types of networks are usually public networks in that a network carrier owns the network and its facilities while the private organizations simply connect their equipment to these networks. Hence, the term CPE is used. The CPE is the equipment that the customer connects to the service provider's network.

The CPE, in the case of frame relay networks, would most likely be a router. It could be a PBX as well which provides voice circuit switching for an organization. It could be a multiplexer which combines different types of streams from the customer to the switched network. The CPE could also be called a hub. In any case, the CPE is aware of the protocol that is used at the switch, whether it be X.25, frame relay, or ATM. The CPE must be able to communicate with the packet switch to which it is connected using the specified protocol.

In the case that the customer's equipment doesn't have a frame relay interface, he must buy a FRAD (Frame Relay Access Device). This is a very inexpensive device that connects protocols such as SNA, X.25, etc. to a frame relay network. VFRAD is a special kind of FRAD that connects voice to the network. The CPE in the figure could be one of these FRADs.

In Figure 21.1 PSwitch A is receiving packets on port 1. According to its switching table, those packets which arrive with channel 101 encoded in their packet headers are switched to port 2. The channel numbers for such packets will be changed to 201 in the new packet headers. As the packets travel through a switch, the data portion remains the same: Only the headers change. Here, the channel numbers in the headers are changed according to the switch tables.

These packets arrive at PSwitch B on port 1. According to its table, they are switched to channel 11 at port 3. The CPE-B will then sort out the packets which arrive with a channel 11 from those that arrive from different channel numbers. What happens at the customer's site after the CPE is not our problem right. All we know is that the CPE there will take care of those details. The path through the network, defined by the channel numbers over each physical link, describes a virtual circuit from those two end points. The figure shows also a virtual circuit from Host W that goes through CPE-A and terminates at CPE-C.

You may remember the analogy of a passenger changing flights at a city. The boarding card that he receives at the beginning of each flight is like a header that defines the seat number (channel number) that he will be taking. The passenger is like a data packet which originates from one city and terminates at another. The path that he takes, including the two planes and their corresponding seats, describes a virtual circuit. He could be assigned the same seat number on each leg of his journey, but chances are that he won't be. The same is true with the channel number assignments in our packet switched network.

These channel numbers are called by different names in each of the three technologies we are considering. In X.25, they are called LCIs (Logical Channel Identifiers). Each LCI has two components. One is called the LCGN (Logical Channel Group Number) and the other is called the LCN (Logical Channel Number). Similarly, ATM's channel number is described by its VPI (Virtual Path Identifier) and VCI (Virtual Channel Identifier). Frame relay simply uses one channel identifier called a DLCI (Data Link Connection Identifier). It does not use a pair of channel numbers as the other two technologies do.

You should also remember from previous discussion that multiplexing is done here. Data packets for both Host X and W are sent over one physical link from the CPE-A to PSwitch A. More precisely, statistical multiplexing is done here. That is, if channel 101 is using all of the bandwidth capacity over this link while channel 104 is idle, that is OK. Statistical multiplexing allows sharing of a network link between different sources. It allows more efficient use of the network resource. In some parts of the New Jersey Turnpike, trucks are not allowed to drive in the car lanes. The traffic there is not statistically multiplexed. If the car lanes are practically empty and the truck lanes are congested, there is no way that the car lanes can be shared by the trucks.

21.1.2 PVCs and SVCs

A question that must come to mind is, "How are these tables created in the first place?" How are the entries in the table created to define a virtual circuit through the network? There are two basic ways that this is done. If the circuit is created by some operator manually entering the path at a network management terminal, it is called a PVC (Permanent Virtual Circuit). The circuit is not actually permanent because an operator can manually remove the circuit as well. For this reason, carriers would prefer that we call them "Provisioned Virtual Circuits."

PVCs can be in place for days at a time, and although creating them is a simple matter of adding an entry along the route of the circuit, it can take up to two days for a carrier to provision. It takes more time to fill out the paperwork than to actually make the update at the switches.

When a CPE dials another CPE through a network and creates a virtual circuit that way, it is called an SVC (Switched Virtual Circuit). A phone number pad is not used to do the dialing, but that function is performed by a CPE calling another CPE. To establish an SVC, the CPE must know the address of the destination. Then a signaling protocol proceeds to update the tables and make the connection. This is similar in function to the SS7 protocol used in voice networks,

Currently, frame relay does not provide SVCs, although the carriers are talking about it. Hence, SVCs will not be covered in this chapter. X.25 and ATM do support SVCs, so in the next chapter we will look at how ATM handles signaling.

21.1.3 Advantages of Switched Networks

Suppose that you had a tie-line network as shown in Figure 21.2(a) interconnecting multiplexers from three different sites. Besides the cost to lease these lines, you would need a separate port card for each line, which would not only increase their cost but also increase the complexity of their management.

Then suppose that you needed to bring up a new site on your network as shown in Figure 21.2(b). To have a fully meshed network, or a connection from each site to every other site, you would have to add three additional tie-lines. You would have to add an extra port to each of the existing multiplexers and buy a new multiplexer with three ports. To cut over the new network, you would first have to bring the entire network down and stop production at all sites. While bringing the network up one site at a time, if something fails, you would have to allow enough time to correct problems. In the case that the window of time is exceeded for the cut over, you would have to have a recourse plan in place so you can try again at another time. These adverse effects will only increase as the size of the network increases.

Figure 21.2(c) shows one of the reasons why frame relay has been increasing in popularity in leaps and bounds. Not only does each multiplexer need one port to the network, but when a new one is introduced (Figure 21.2(d)) there is no production impact on the rest of the network. The only thing that needs to be done is to enter the new PVC on a console somewhere. This is usually done by the carrier, or it can be done by the customer if the carrier provides him with the console.

Probably the best advantage about frame relay, or switched networks in general is that the CPE can collect traffic measurements easily. From such statistics, the customer can figure out if he needs more capacity or, for that matter, if he can make further savings by reducing his capacity level through the network.

Costs of switched networks are always less than the tie-line networks by at least 30%. This is because the trunks between the switches are shared among many customers and the carrier can forward those savings to the customers. To the end user, the total complexity of the network is drastically reduced. How the carrier does the switching inside its network is not the user's concern. All that the user cares about is that a virtual circuit originating at one location terminates at the proper one. How many

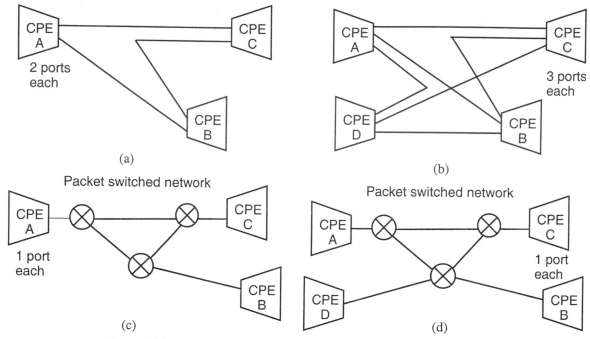

Figure 21.2 (a) A leased line network being expanded (b). (c) A switched network being expanded (d).

hops his traffic takes or which channel numbers it travels on is not of concern to him. The network, as shown in Figure 21.2(c) and (d), is now viewed as nothing but a big cloud into which he can "plug in" as he pleases.

There is better reliability in a switched network due to the vast number of alternate routes which exist. The flexibility of the network is improved. It is not that important to design the network exactly right from the beginning. Adjustments can be made to the capacities and the routes of PVCs. When signing a contract, however, provisions should be made to allow such flexibility without a drastic increase in price.

Many organizations use frame relay networks to connect a corporate office to many regional and branch offices. In this environment, the corporate data center would have a backup data center at another location, geographically. The main and backup data centers would keep their data in synchronization, so if one fails, the other can pick up the load relatively easily.

In a leased line network, you would have to make accommodations for backup lines. With a switched network, however, backup is much easier. PVCs can be entered from all the branch sites to both data centers. Then the customer would agree beforehand that traffic would normally be sent only on the PVCs terminating at the primary data center. The PVCs terminating at the secondary data center would only be used in case the primary center fails. The cost of such backup PVCs is only about 5 to 10% of the cost of the primary PVCs. This is because the carrier knows that you would only use the backup ones occasionally.

Frame Relay

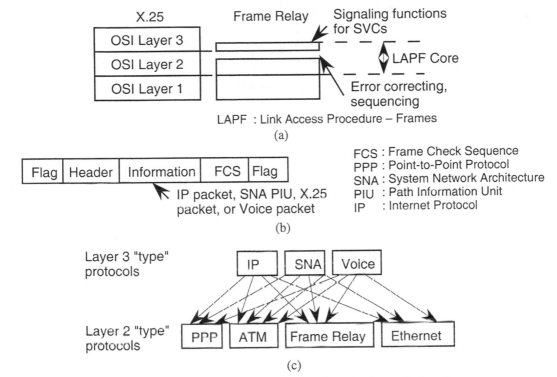

Figure 21.3 (a) Frame relay borrows functionality from all three layers of the OSI model. (b) Basically, frame relay is a layer 2 protocol. (c) Any of the "layer 3" type data units can be encapsulated in the information field of a frame relay frame or, for that matter, of any other "layer 2" type frame.

21.2 THE DIFFERENT VIEWS OF FRAME RELAY

21.2.1 OSI's View of Frame Relay

When we look at frame relay as to how it relates to the OSI Reference Model, we basically see it as a layer 2 protocol. After all, layer 2 uses frames as its basic unit of exchange. However, as Figure 21.3(a) shows, not all of the functions available in layer 2 are incorporated in frame relay. Besides that, some of the layer 3 functions are. These layer 3 functions are all signaling procedures which are needed in SVCs.

The signaling protocol is called Q.933, which is a part of Q.931, the protocol used in the D channel of ISDN. Because SVCs are not currently available in frame relay services, frame relay actually supports only the lower layer-and-a-half of the OSI model.

There are several layer 2 functions which are not supported in frame relay. This makes frame relay a stripped-down version of not only X.25, but also HDLC, the layer 2 protocol of X.25. This makes frame relay services fast, but the price to pay is fewer features than other services. The name of this protocol is called LAPF (Link Access

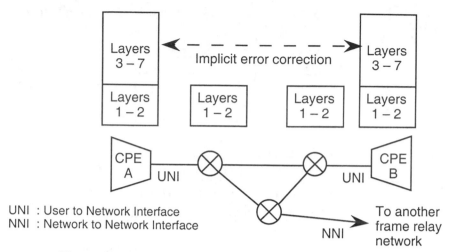

Figure 21.4 At the user's end all seven layers are implemented, but across the network interface and through the network, only the first two layers are implemented.

Procedure – Frames) Core. LAPF Core is a subset of LAPF that is used in SVCs. Currently, LAPF Core is all that is used because PVCs are all that is available from the carriers.

Numbering frames sequentially is a layer 2 procedure that is omitted from frame relay. The lack of frame sequence numbers does not allow a device to ask for retransmissions due to errors. Errors can be detected, but in those cases, the frames are simply discarded without notifying the sender that they were. LAPF Core doesn't provide any flow control, say by using a window field, as is done with HDLC. If data frames arrive much faster than the rate at which they can be handled by a device, then those frames must be discarded.

Figure 21.3(b) shows the basic format of a frame relay or LAPF frame. It looks very similar to SDLC and HDLC, the only difference being in the definition of the fields used in the header. We will look at the header fields later, when we have more time. The information field can encapsulate practically any protocol. We can encapsulate IP packets, SNA packets, etc. For that matter, we can do the same type of layer multiplexing using any other layer 2 protocol. Figure 21.3(c) shows that we can encapsulate IP, SNA, or voice inside a PPP frame, an ATM cell, a frame relay frame, an Ethernet frame, etc.

Figure 21.4 shows the operation of the OSI layers across the entire network. At the end users' sites, the CPEs, all seven layers are implemented, while inside the network only layers 1 and 2 (actually only half of layer 2) are implemented. That means that a packet being transmitted by CPE-A is encapsulated in a LAPF frame and that frame is sent from one switch to another until it arrives at CPE-B. Here, the packet is extracted from the frame and then delivered to the application. Remember, as the frame travels through the network over a PVC, only the DLCIs are changed over each hop, just as the seat numbers of a passenger change when he changes his plane at an airport.

The figure also shows that error correction is a problem of the upper-layer protocols. If the network drops or discards frames without telling anyone, how are such frames retransmitted? This is the problem that occurs when NICs send frames over a LAN and drop frames because of errors. IP does the same thing, and here frame relay does too. In case of IP, we would expect TCP, a layer 4 protocol, to sequence the segments, check and correct errors, provide flow control, and so on. If not TCP, then some other application or software at the end user's location has the responsibility for doing error correction, if error correction is in fact needed. Hence, like IP datagram networks, frame relay networks leave more responsibility to the end points. The network itself is not robust enough to do that. Hence, the phrase "implicit error correction," which means the errors are handled not by the network, but by the end points.

21.2.2 The User's View

As far as the user is concerned, he has a very limited view of the frame relay network and it is mostly based on what he has to pay and what capacity he gets out of the network.

Figure 21.5 shows six items that create the user's view of the network. They are the CPE, access lines, ports, the network itself, the PVCs, and the CIR (Committed Information Rate).

Access Lines: The access lines connect the CPE to the frame relay interface on the first switch. This interface is called the UNI (User-to-Network Interface). The interface from a frame relay network of one carrier to another one is called NNI (Network-to-Network Interface). Both UNI and NNI are shown in Figure 21.4. For example, the interface from AT&T's frame relay network to Bell Atlantic's frame relay network would use the NNI interface. Carriers don't like doing that, however, because management information cannot be transferred quite that easily over the NNI. For customers who need to interconnect to frame relay networks overseas, the carrier may have no choice but to provide such connectivity.

Over the access line, the end user node polls the network every 30 seconds by sending STATUS ENQUIRY messages. This is called a heartbeat poll. The network responds by sending STATUS messages back to the user. These messages specify which virtual circuits are new or are being disconnected, and so on. The absence of either of these messages means that the link is down. This poll is supported by what is called the LMI (Local Management Interface) over the UNI.

Access lines could be 56 kbps, FT1 (Fractional T1), or T1 lines. A nice thing about FT1 lines is that if you need to increase your access speed from, say, 256 kbps to 384 kbps, only the parameters at the end equipment need to be changed. This can be done overnight. If your transmission rate decreases, then to save costs, the access speed can be lowered just as easily.

Access to the IXC's frame relay network could be through an LEC's frame relay network. This configuration is more suitable when there are many nearby locations that need to be aggregated to a long-haul network. But if only one LEC frame relay switch is used to tie in all the nearby locations, that switch could become a central point of failure.

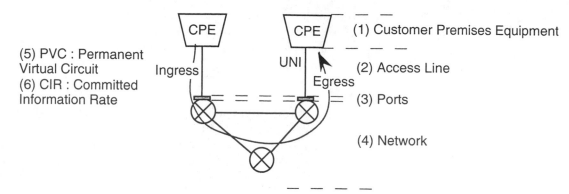

Figure 21.5 The six components of a network as seen by the customer. A PVC is said to start at the ingress side and arrive at the egress side of the network.

You may want to use a dial-up backup to get to your carrier's network. This could be a BRI, PRI, or SW-56-kbps backup line. But care should be taken. If the primary and dial-up line go through the same conduit or come to the same point in your facility, then such backups could become meaningless. Also, remember that your DSU (Data Service Unit and channel service unit) can automatically switch over to an ISDN backup. However, it won't fall back to the primary one automatically when your primary line comes back up. If you forget to switch the DSU back, then you may be hit with a large ISDN bill at the end of the month.

Port Cards: The interface on the first switch is called a port or a port card. This is where the access line is connected. Now the rate of the port could be lower than the rate of the access line. But it doesn't make any sense to lease a port at a higher rate than what can be supported over the access link. Just recently, carriers have started to offer frame relay at DS-3 or 45-Mbps rates. However, conventionally you could only connect to a frame relay network at T1/E1 rates or below down to 56 kbps.

PVCs: Over one access link and through one port, you can have many PVCs (Permanent Virtual Circuits). Each PVC would be identified by its unique DLCI (Data Link Connection Identifier) number over the UNI. How the network carrier switches the circuit through the network is not the end user's concern. In fact, the specifications don't say anything about that. If there are a bunch of telegraph operators sending data frames over the network according to agreed-upon rates, then that is fine as far as the standards are concerned. All that the user cares about is that a particular PVC starting with a certain DLCI at his ingress side arrives with a specified DLCI at his egress side. For that matter, even the distances that the PVCs traverse, other than for international circuits, play no part in their prices. Frame relay pricing is distance insensitive. The switches are too dumb to bother with billing information. This is another reason why frame relay services are fast.

CIR: The user sees frame relay as a *service* and not a *network*. He doesn't care or need to know how the virtual circuits are implemented. He buys PVCs to certain locations running at certain rates and his only concern is that the service provider provides that. The rate at which the carrier agrees to transfer the end user's traffic over a given a PVC is called the CIR (Committed Information Rate). This should be the average amount of traffic that the customer will transmit over the given PVC. If the customer is transmitting at the CIR, there is still no guarantee that the network will be able to transmit all the data. Some frames may have to be dropped due to congestion. On the other hand, if the other customers or PVCs are not transmitting at a given time, the customer can transmit at a rate that is higher than the CIR. This is called *bursting*. The total amount of CIR for an access line should be less than or equal to the speed of the access line. For example, suppose that you had two PVCs with a CIR of 32 kbps from your location. Then the speed of the access line and the rate of the ports should be 64 kbps or above.

21.2.3 The Carrier's View

Basically, the carrier views the network as a service that it provides to its customers, and how the network is connected internally is not something that it has to convey to the customer. When frame relay services were being offered for the first time (around 1992), there were no such things as frame relay switches. Hence, X.25 switches were being used with the new software. Frame relay is basically a software-based protocol. Customers didn't have to know that they were using the old packet switched networks. All that they cared about was that the CIR was being met for all their PVCs.

Afterwards these switches were replaced by switches that were designed to be frame relay switches. All that the customer knew at the time was probably that the performance of the PVCs was increasing. Today, no one makes frame relay switches anymore. Starting around 1998, all the switches in the major carriers have been replaced by ATM switches. Because ATM had a bad reception by the public, however, and was viewed as being nothing more than hype, the carriers didn't advertise their networks as being ATM-based.

Now, the customer brings his traffic to the frame relay interface on the first switch, which is actually an ATM switch. The carrier divides these frames into ATM cells and sends them through its network to the egress ATM switch, which then reassembles the cells into frames and sends them over to the customer. Of course a network carrier cannot utilize all the rich features that its ATM switches can deliver. This is because the UNI does not support that, however, if new specifications come out for the frame relay UNI to support added features, the carriers would only have to change the port cards. Their ATM switches will be ready to transport those features through its network.

In effect, frame relay is being carried over ATM. ATM is never carried over frame relay. By having an ATM backbone network the reliability of the network improves. The carrier is using one network, an ATM network, to carry all the different types of traffic. The ATM network is now carrying not only frame relay traffic but also voice, video, IP, and whatever else it has. This is called *convergence*. By having one ubiquitous network, the costs of the carriers decrease, which hopefully brings the prices down. An added advantage of having an ATM network instead of a frame relay backbone network is that now the trunks between the switches can be upgraded to OC-

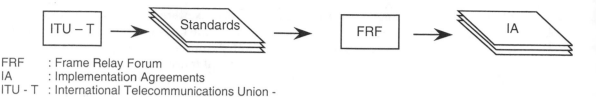

FRF : Frame Relay Forum
IA : Implementation Agreements
ITU - T : International Telecommunications Union -
Telecommunication Standardization

Figure 21.6 The relation of ITU-T and FRF.

3 level transports and above. Frame relay switches until recently could only handle rates of up to T1/E1, and with a high-speed ATM backbone, it's now easier to offer DS-3 interfaces for frame relay services.

Another nice thing about an ATM backbone network that carries frame relay is that the interface between ATM switches is defined and by now well understood. This is not the case with frame relay switches. Therefore, you cannot mix the vendor types of frame relay switches because there is no standard for doing so; however, a carrier can buy ATM switches from different vendors depending on who has the best offer at that time. The competition between ATM switch vendors improves the quality while reducing the costs.

21.2.4 The Standards Bodies' View

As Figure 21.6, frame relay actually started with ITU-T (International Telecommunications Union - Telecommunication standardization sector). This organization created the standards and continues to enhance them. Most frame relay standards' designations begin with the letter "Q," as in Q.933 and Q.922.

These standards are reviewed by the FRF (Frame Relay Forum), which is composed of more than 100 members. These members are carriers and equipment manufacturers. The FRF's job is basically to decide on how to implement the standards so that the services become available as soon as possible. It also reviews these implementation specifications to ensure interoperability of equipment from different vendors. These specifications are called IAs (Implementation Agreements).

21.3 THE FRAME FORMAT

Figure 21.7 outlines the format for a frame relay frame. Like SDLC (and HDLC), the frame begins and ends with a flag and contains an FCS field. The FCS could be used by FR switches to discard, without notification, any frames that are damaged. The fields in the second and third octets are similar to the fields used in ISDN.

The DLCI is like an LCI used in the third layer of X.25, which allows for switching of frames. It is only 10 bits, giving a total of 1,024 channels. There are other variants of the frame relay frame that allow for more DLCIs, but they are not used. The C/R (Command and Response) bit is set by the end system, passed through the network, and read only by the application at the receiving end. The network ignores it. This bit, used mostly by SNA packets encapsulated inside a frame, indicates whether the SNA packet is a command or a response.

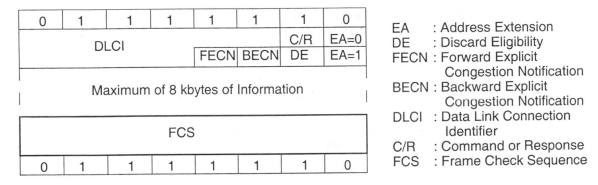

0	1	1	1	1	1	1	0		EA	: Address Extension

Figure 21.7 The frame format for frame relay using the common 2-octet header.

EA : Address Extension
DE : Discard Eligibility
FECN : Forward Explicit Congestion Notification
BECN : Backward Explicit Congestion Notification
DLCI : Data Link Connection Identifier
C/R : Command or Response
FCS : Frame Check Sequence

Previously we said that because frame relay was not limited by the window sizes used in X.25, it allowed for faster relaying of frames through the network. However, removing the windowing mechanism also removes a network's ability to have data flow control. That is, frame relay switches cannot signal the transmitter to throttle back or slow down its transmission because the network is getting congested. This is a major concern in frame relay networks. Let us now consider methods of controlling congestion.

One way this is done is by using the FECN (Forward Explicit Congestion Notification) and BECN (Backward Explicit Congestion Notification) bits. If, for example, a network experiences congestion, partly due to user B transmitting a lot of data to user A, then the congested network switch will set the BECN bit in frames going to B, hoping that user B will slow down its transmission. Likewise, the switch will also set the FECN bit for the frames going to user A, hoping that it will request less data from B. Notice here that the end devices are not obligated to respond to these bits, and if the network cannot handle the traffic load it will simply start discarding some frames.

Ironically, if the routers at the end points do want to help keep the public frame relay network from getting congested, it has no method of telling the LAN applications to stop transmitting momentarily. Additionally, when frames are discarded due to congestion, LAN applications typically retransmit frames, adding to the problem.

On the other hand, when the network discards data, the intelligent end devices may assume that the data is being lost due to congestion and may stop transmitting momentarily. This is called *implicit congestion detection*, since the end nodes are not directly notified of the problem.

The problem with this picture is that, if there are no frames going from A to B, then there is no way to notify the transmitter of the BECN bit. And even if the BECN bit does arrive at the application on the transmitting end, by the time it gets there, the congestion may have disappeared. Similarly, the application at A may not be able to throttle back B from transmitting more frames. Again, by the time this information is conveyed to B, the congestion may have disappeared. In reality then, these two bits are good only for accumulating data monthly reports where you get an idea when and where congestion existed in the network. If these bits are being set at a significant amount, then it might be wiser to increase the CIR of that virtual circuit.

If an end node transmits frames that it doesn't mind losing, such as routing updates, then it can set the DE (Discard Eligibility) bit for such frames to 1. The frames with their DE bits set to 1 will be transmitted if possible; otherwise, they will be the first ones to be discarded. Initially, the idea was to set priority using this bit. If the user was transmitting above his CIR, then the user, realizing some frames might be dropped by the network, could set the DE bit to 1 for the lower-priority frames. However, if there is no congestion through the path of a PVC, then frames with the DE bit set to 0 and 1 both make it through the network. On the other hand, if there is severe congestion then all frames may be discarded, regardless of their DE bit setting. It is only during moderate congestion that the DE bit setting can make a difference in determining which frames are delivered and which ones aren't. Theoretically, that was the intent of the DE bit. However, carriers today disregard the DE bit altogether and it serves no useful purpose, as we'll see shortly in sections 21.4.3 and 21.4.4.

21.4 CONGESTION CONTROL

21.4.1 More on CIRs

We have already mentioned how the carrier can allocate capacity for a user by defining a CIR (Committed Information Rate) for each PVC that is "nailed up" through the network. The amount of traffic that the user expects to transmit over a PVC is defined by the CIR. The carrier will try its best to send traffic at this rate and when the user sends traffic above this rate, that is called bursting. Bursting is allowed and this traffic will be sent through the network, if capacity for it exists. Otherwise, frames will be discarded to leave capacity for other customers who are within their CIR limits. The highest rate at which a user can burst is called the Maximum Negotiated Rate. All frames above this rate will be discarded. Usually, this rate is equal to the rate of the access line but it could be below it.

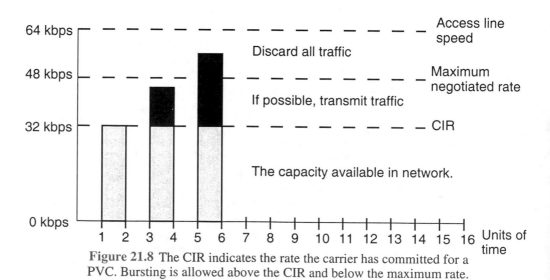

Figure 21.8 The CIR indicates the rate the carrier has committed for a PVC. Bursting is allowed above the CIR and below the maximum rate.

Consider the flow of traffic of a particular PVC as shown in Figure 21.8. The horizontal axis shows units of time, usually as 1-s intervals. The vertical axis shows rates. The customer has negotiated his CIR to 32 kbps but is allowed to burst at rates of up to 48 kbps. The speed of the access line is 64 kbps. Hence, the customer can transmit at that rate, but frames will be dropped.

For example, at time = 1, the user is transmitting at 32 kbps, his CIR. By time = 2, he hasn't increased his rate, so all of his frames are forwarded. This is not true for the times between 3 and 4. During this time, the customer is going above his CIR, and the carrier tries to forward these frames but is not committed to do so for the frames above this rate. Between times 5 and 6, an effort is made for all frames up to 48 kbps, but the frames that arrive at the network toward the end of this period and make the rate go beyond this limit are dropped.

21.4.2 Subscription Levels

On a given access line through a switch port you can have several PVCs provisioned. See Figure 21.9. The ratio of the sum of the CIRs of the PVCs over the maximum port speed is called the *subscription level*. If the sum of the CIRs is more than the port speed, this level is above 100%; otherwise, it is below that. A user can have a subscription level above 100%. All this means is that the user is not transmitting at the full CIR rate for all his PVCs through a port at the same time, but rather the PVCs are taking turns transmitting. On the rare occasions when all PVCs are transmitting at their peak capacity simultaneously, we'll lose some frames. Because that will not happen that often, however, we can live with it. If we consistently lose frames because of this, then we need to reconsider the subscription levels and lower them.

For instance, in Figure 21.9 four locations are shown: a corporate data center, a backup data center, a regional office, and a branch office. In order to keep things simple, only three PVCs are shown, all of which include the corporate center. From

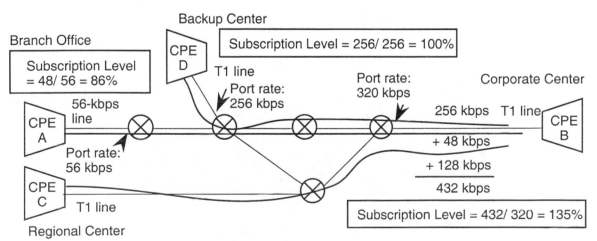

Figure 21.9 Subscription level is the ratio of the sum of the CIRs of the PVCs provisioned at a port over the port speed.

here the CIRs of the PVCs going to the other three locations are 256 kbps, 48 kbps, and 128 kbps. Adding these gives us a total CIR of 432 kbps. If the port speed to the nearest switch is rated at 320 kbps, the subscription level becomes 135%. Similarly, the subscription levels are calculated for two other sites in the figure. Designing such a network properly takes time and planning. One has to know what applications are running at each site and the statistics about how data travels through the network. This can be learned only through experience, but with frame relay service, changes are easy to make as long as they are accommodated for in the initial contract negotiations.

21.4.3 Open Loop Flow Control

Sprint was one of the first carriers to offer frame relay services. This was in the early 1990's. At that time, there were no switches made specifically for frame relay services so Sprint had to use traditional packet switches until frame relay switches became available. These packet switches had no concept of CIR, so Sprint decided to offer services with a CIR of 0. Because of this, all frames became eligible for discarding. The DE bit was set to 1 on all frames. This made the DE bit meaningless. In fact, the delivery rate for all frames was well above 99% for this network. Today, all carriers disregard the value of the DE bit. The method used to control congestion in this network is called open loop flow control.

How the network made an effort to forward all frames through the network is illustrated in Figure 21.10. Here, not only are the switches shown through the paths of the PVCs, but also the states of their buffers. Notice that A is transmitting a lot of traffic to B and the buffers close to B are getting filled up. These switches are draining traffic to B at a slower rate than the rate at which they are getting the traffic from A. As the switches towards B start reaching about 70% capacity, they send a special proprietary signal backwards toward the switches at A, asking them to slow down. This is called a backpressure signal.

As the buffers on the switches in the direction of A start approaching their capacity, they each signal the previous switch to slow down. Finally, when the switch to which A is directly connected reaches 70% capacity, it will send a BECN bit, telling A to completely stop transmitting. This is because not only is its immediate switch

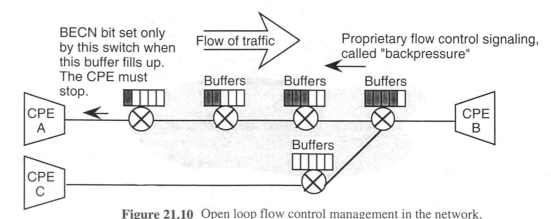

Figure 21.10 Open loop flow control management in the network.

reaching full capacity but also all the switches in the direction of B. This approach to flow control is good when you want to "pump" a lot of traffic into the network or burst for a longer duration. There is no need to slow down. However, when all the switches reach their capacity, you have to completely stop. Also notice that since C is not bursting at all, he can still send traffic even though A is using a lot of network capacity.

Open loop flow control, as used with CIR of 0, provides a high burst capacity. Because more users can send more data, the cost of the network is shared among more customers and the carrier can offer better prices. This type of flow control is very much in line with how IP handles traffic. IP fires packets into the network and lets the routers ahead of the path decide what to do with them. Hence, this type of flow control is more suitable to handle IP.

21.4.4 Closed Loop Flow Control

The other method used for flow control in a carrier network is called closed loop flow control. This is depicted in Figure 21.11. Here, A is transmitting to B. Every time A is transmitting to B, the switch closest to A asks if there is capacity through the network for that PVC. This is done by transmitting a Credit Request signal. If a Credit Granted signal is received back, then this switch can go ahead and send the frames. Here the network is looking ahead to see if there is capacity to send the traffic, then it goes ahead and sends it.

Suppose that A is bursting above its CIR on its PVC: a Credit Request is still sent, but this time, there is a chance that a Credit Denied signal will be received. At this time the switch at A will send a BECN back to A. In this case, instead of completely stopping the transmission, the CPE only needs to slow down to its CIR level. Instead of all DE bits being set to 1, they are all set to 0. This value is still meaningless and is completely ignored by the network switches. When a Credit Granted signal is received back at A's switch, this switch will set the BECN bit back to 0, indicating that A may now burst above the CIR.

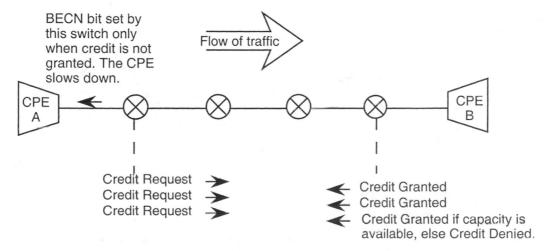

Figure 21.11 Closed loop flow control management in the network.

For closed loop flow controlled networks, the usage is more consistent. The latency is more uniform. There is always some level at which you can transmit. This is more suitable for IBM's SNA networks. SNA networks are time sensitive because there is constant polling going on. For example, an FEP may be asking each controller in a round robin fashion whether they have any traffic to send. SNA expects an answer when polling because it was designed when tie-lines were more common and immediate responses were much more common. These networks have less congestion throughout since the buffers are not getting filled up through a PVC path. For this reason, there is less traffic that the network can accept from fewer users and the pricing tends to be slightly higher.

21.5 MULTIPROTOCOL SUPPORT

21.5.1 SNA Over Frame Relay

Using tie-lines for traditional SNA networks can become expensive. Frame relay networks can save up to 50% of communications costs for such networks. However, as we have already mentioned, SNA is time sensitive and is difficult to run over a frame relay network.

Figure 21.12 shows a crude solution for running SNA over frame relay. The LANs are used to transport SNA packets called PIUs (Path Information Units) over Ethernet frames. The PIUs are encapsulated inside Ethernet frames. The routers shown are acting as bridges and basically encapsulate these Ethernet frames inside frame relay frames. Hence, there are two levels of encapsulation being done, both at the second layer of OSI.

When the FEP (Front End Processor) polls the cluster controller across the WAN, the first router responds for it. On the cluster controller's end, the router polls the controller as if it were the FEP. This far end router collects data from the controller and

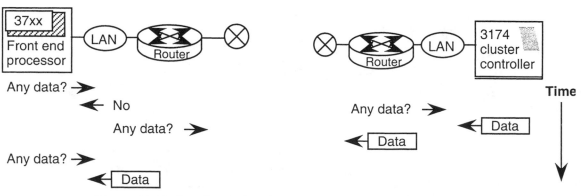

Figure 21.12 Spoofing is done by routers and bridges at the edge of the network to support SNA over frame relay.

Frame Relay

sends it to the router connected to the FEP. When the FEP's router is polled, it forwards the data to the FEP and the FEP thinks it has a direct connection to the cluster controller. This is called *spoofing*.

For small networks this may work fine, but when the size of the network increases, there is too much overhead and delay. The performance of the network drops significantly to the point where it becomes unacceptable for the end users.

To accommodate for these problems, many solutions exist, none of which are totally satisfactory. This is because of the nature of SNA itself which generally cannot tolerate delays. Two of these solutions are shown in Figure 21.13. One is a standard called RFC 1490 and the other is called DLSw (Data Link Switching) and was designed by IBM. In either case, the proper software must be present in the routers at the customers' locations.

Figure 21.13(a) shows that the RFC 1490 solution takes the entire Ethernet frame as it is and sends it across the network after adding its own header and encapsulating it inside a frame relay frame. This method is called RFC 1490 Multiprotocol Encapsulation. The number of bytes used in the header is low, which makes the solution simple. Many routers and frame relay switches support priority of traffic and if that is the case, the SNA frames are sent ahead of the others, resulting in fewer session time-outs.

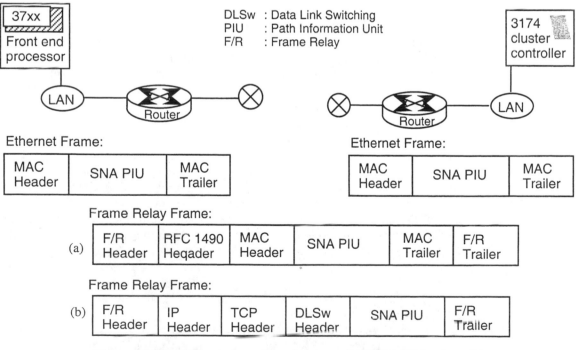

Figure 21.13 (a) The routers add and process the RFC 1490 headers, (b) or they can add and process TCP/IP headers and DLSw headers.

Figure 21.13(b) shows the DLSw solution. DLSw works with any WAN that transports TCP/IP, including frame relay. It does not process any SNA fields inside the PIUs. The TCP layer helps the SNA devices at the far end to manage the connections. DLSw does not work as well over large networks. It uses more bytes in headers than the other solutions require. Neither of these solutions is easy to implement, and both require considerable manual intervention.

21.5.2 VoFR

Running frame relay services over ATM-based networks will make it possible to transport voice. All that will be needed is better interface specifications for this at the frame relay interface. These specifications are called FRF.11 and FRF.13 by the Frame Relay Forum. VoFR (Voice over Frame Relay) can save considerable money, especially across international boundaries. Although carriers presently are investing a lot more in data networks than in voice networks, voice communication is still considerably more expensive than data communication. If carriers ever decide to charge more for data than they do for voice, one wonders if running voice over data services will be as beneficial. Today's data networks are relatively inexpensive, however, and VoFR is a solution that deserves attention.

To do VoFR, you have to over-engineer the PVCs. That is, you should buy more CIR and have a higher port speed than what you would normally have for transporting data. This is because voice packets cannot wait to be delivered. Voice packets are usually smaller than data packets. When a voice packet gets stuck behind a long data packet that is in the process of being transmitted, we have a problem called *head-of-the-line blocking*. To compensate for this, data packets are segmented into smaller blocks, allowing voice packets to be inserted between them. Segmenting of data into smaller blocks makes the interface seem more like an ATM interface.

On the right side of Figure 21.14 we see a VFRAD (Voice Frame Relay Access Device) connected to a PBX. The VFRAD receives voice from the PBX in PCM format and compresses it and packetizes it before encapsulating it inside a frame. Transferring the smaller-sized packets through the network ends up gaining more time than the time taken to compress them. Usually voice frames are between 40 to 80 bytes long.

There might be times when no voice packets are being received from the network into the VFRAD. When there are no frames in the buffer to be played back to the conversation listener, the buffers are said to be *starving*. To minimize buffer starvation, jitter buffers are included in the VFRADs to smooth out the incoming voice.

On the left side of the figure, we see a router connected to the frame relay network. It manages voice frames going to the PBX on the right-hand side and data frames going to some other location not shown in the figure. The router has two local interfaces; one is a LAN card for data and the other is a VFRAD residing in another port card for the PBX. The router will typically segment blocks of data that may cause head-of-the-line blocking. PVCs between these two locations allow voice to be carried from the PBXs through the network.

As with SNA, the FRADs should prioritize voice traffic. Carriers are also starting to support priority for both SNA and voice traffic through their networks. Even with these features, it is tricky to engineer PVCs for voice. We must ensure that the latency

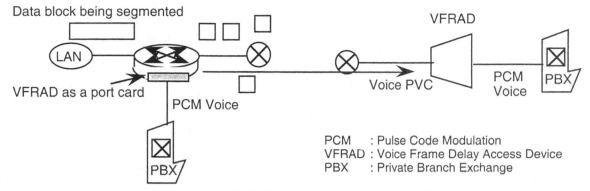

Figure 21.14 A VoFR (Voice over Frame Relay) configuration.

of the packets is acceptable, that the variation of the latency is acceptable, and the speed of the PVC is more than what will be needed on the average. One must take into account the delays that are present because of packetization, depacketization, and the transfer of frames through the network.

EXERCISES

Section 21.1:

1. From Figure 21.15, find out how many PVCs are entered in the switching tables in the packet switched network. Then indicate the origin and the destination of each PVC and the number of switches they go through.
2. The term CPE in a frame relay network could represent which devices?
3. What are the channel numbers called in frame relay networks? In X.25 networks? In ATM networks?
4. What would be a better choice of words for the PVC acronym than what it actually represents? Why?
5. Compare SVCs with PVCs. Why was the discussion of SVCs left for the next chapter?
6. In your own words, give the advantages of switched networks over tie-line networks. Also, give the disadvantages.

Section 21.2:

7. Compare frame relay protocol with the layers of the OSI Model.
8. Which protocols can be encapsulated in the information field of a frame relay frame? How does that compare with what can be encapsulated using ATM cells?
9. Officially, what is a frame called in frame relay?
10. What are the two interfaces defined in frame relay? Which one is less commonly implemented? Why?
11. Who corrects errors in a frame relay service?
12. The rate of traffic that a carrier almost guarantees it will accept from a user is called what? When a user sends more data than this rate, what is that called?
13. What is the danger of using an automatic ISDN backup circuit?
14. Do carriers sell public frame relay networks or services? What is the difference?

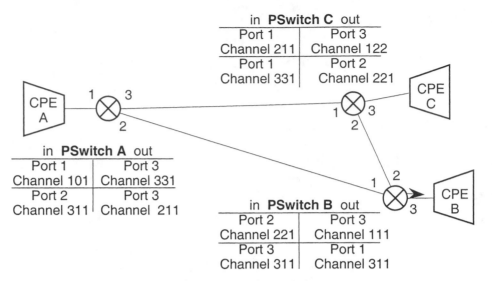

Figure 21.15 Packet switches for Exercise 1.

15. Which term describes the fact that the carriers are using one type of backbone network to transport voice, data, video, etc.?
16. What are the advantages of carrying frame relay frames over an ATM network rather than a frame relay network?
17. Describe the differences between ITU-T and the Frame Relay Forum as far as frame relay standards are concerned.

Section 21.3:
18. What is the purpose of the C/R bit?
19. What was the intended purpose of the DE bit?
20. Are FECN bits set on the frames going to the transmitter or to the receiver?
21. What can the user or the CPE do when frames arrive with their FECN or BECN bits set?
22. How many bytes is the frame relay header?
23. How many possible DLCI values exist?
24. Typically, must each PVC must have its own DLCI?

Section 21.4:
25. The maximum allowable bursting rate is limited by which parameters?
26. Is it possible that all frames sent within the CIR value reach their destination?
27. In Figure 21.9, suppose that another PVC is added going from C to D and the port rate at C's switch is 320 kbps. Recalculate the subscription level at both switches connected to C and D.
28. What are some reasons why you would want a subscription level to be less than 100%? More than 100%?
29. Compare and contrast between open loop flow control and closed loop flow control.
30. In which type of flow control mechanism does the DE bit have significance?

Frame Relay

Section 21.5:

31. Why is running IBM's SNA over frame relay services a tricky task?
32. What is meant by spoofing?
33. Which type of SNA over frame relay services solution transports the entire LAN frame? Which one encapsulates it in an IP frame first?
34. List some points that should be remembered when provisioning a PVC for VoFR.
35. The device which prepares voice to be transferred over a frame relay service is called what?

Chapter 22

ATM

22.1 ATM BASICS

22.1.1 Introduction

This chapter requires an understanding of many sections that we have covered previously. In section 2.5, we saw how packet switched networks were based on virtual circuits, both PVCs and SVCs. In Section 5.3.7, we introduced ATM (Asynchronous Transfer Mode) and discussed its strong points at length. In Chapter 21, we discussed virtual circuits again and explained how they are utilized in frame relay networks. There we also mentioned why ATM provides a better backbone for frame relay networks. By now, you should have some understanding of virtual circuits and ATM networks but not necessarily how ATM is implemented. That is what we'll cover in this chapter.

The whole idea behind ATM is quite simple: Build one network infrastructure to transmit all types of information. Having one network to manage will reduce operating costs. At one time, carriers had one set of circuit switches and transmission facilities to pass voice traffic. This was the carriers' portion of the PSTN. To carry data, they had separate networks completely different from their voice networks. When users started to think about transmitting video and multimedia, neither of these two types of networks proved adequate. But building and managing another network to support these applications seemed wasteful.

Now, carriers are seriously considering creating one network that is based on ATM. All voice, data, video, multimedia, and other information would be transferred through their ATM network. AT&T has already stated that it has installed its last 4ESS switch and is planning to migrate to a network that is based purely on ATM switches and transmission facilities. Frame relay, IP, and whatever new protocol is invented in the future will be transported over this one network. The savings in cost is then expected to be forwarded to the users.

Of course, the requirements of each information type are different. Voice comes in small increments but needs to be delivered isochronously, that is, at a constant rate. A variation in the rate of delivery for voice is not acceptable. Data comes in larger chunks, but normally it is not isochronous. On the other hand, it is more sensitive to errors than voice. Data also comes in bursts. A large file is transmitted and then the data rate drops low or down to zero. Video and multimedia require a lot of bandwidth capacity and are also isochronous.

Even voice and video can be transported in two different ways. One is called CBR (Constant Bit Rate) where the channel is allocated a certain bandwidth, say 64 kbps, whether there is traffic on it or not. This method corresponds to TDM (Time Division Multiplexing) on which T1 circuits are built. A more efficient way to transfer voice and video is first to packetize it. Then when there are no packets from that channel to be transferred, we can insert packets from other channels. Packetizing and compressing voice and video require a service called VBR (Variable Bit Rate).

We are asking one network infrastructure to handle all these types of information, and so we need a network that will be difficult to build; however, placing more intelligence and sophistication in the network makes it easier for the end user to transmit whatever he needs to transmit. Hence, ATM uses a complex set of protocols.

22.1.2 Cells

To meet these requirements, ATM breaks all information PDUs (Protocol Data Units) into cells rather than frames. Cells are of a fixed length while frames come in all sizes. Also, the cell sizes are small compared to those of frames. Variable-length frames arrive with unpredictable delays. A long data frame can delay a voice packet that needs to be delivered immediately. This is called *head-of-the-line blocking*. Cells are smaller in size, and if a voice packet arrives at the network, it can be served almost immediately, minimizing blocking. This provides ATM with statistical time division multiplexing.

Small, fixed-length cells are suitable not only to provide support for voice and video, but also, to be switched in hardware. Processing of frames is generally performed by software. Since cells are of a fixed length, hardware chips can easily process them. The beginning and the end of each cell are easily identifiable. This is not the case with frames. The flag field is used to identify the beginning and the end of each frame. These fields, or SYN fields, are unnecessary with cells. Hardware switching is faster and less expensive than switching that is performed by software.

All ATM switches are cut-through switches. That is, these switches don't wait for the entire cell to arrive in the switch fabric, but almost as soon as the header of the cell is read and while the rest of data is arriving, the cell is directed to the output port of the switch. This type of switching is faster than store-and-forward switching that is used with frames. There, the entire frame is read in the buffer, checked for errors, and then switched to the output port. See Figure 22.1.

Using statistical time division multiplexing, small-sized cells and cells with a fixed length allow ATM to accomplish what it set out to do, that is, to allow one network to carry any type of information over any distance, over a local area or over a wide area. One set of crucial parameters, collectively called QoS (Quality of Service), will also need to be defined. This will specify the level of delay, variation in delay (or amount of jitter), rate of error, and other requirements that are needed on the ATM transmission services.

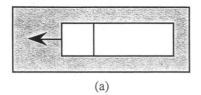
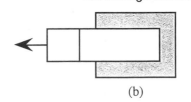

(a)   (b)

Figure 22.1 (a) A store-and-forward switch must read the entire frame before it is directed to the output port. (b) A cut-through switch can forward the cell as soon as the header is read and processed.

22.1.3 ATM Architecture (layers)

Now that we have identified the requirements placed on the ATM network, we need a plan to implement it. This is done by designing its architecture as seen in Figure 22.2. Overall, ATM has three main layers. The physical layer maps to the physical layer of the OSI Reference Model. Above this layer are the ATM cell layer and the AAL (ATM Adaptation Layer). Both of these layers map closely to OSI layer 2. Since the ATM cells are switched in hardware, part of this layer is shown as belonging to OSI layer 1. The function of AAL is to take any kind of information, as shown in the figure, and load it into the ATM cells. The function of the ATM cell layer is to switch the cells and deliver them to their proper destination.

If frames from a LAN are to be transported via ATM cells, the AAL fits under the LLC (Logical Link Control) layer of LANs. LLC is the upper half of the data link layer for IEEE LAN standards, which will be covered in Chapter 23. If IP traffic is to be transported, then the AAL fits under the network layer. ATM requires signaling that provides a connection to the destination end. This signaling is supported by network layer functions and will be covered later on.

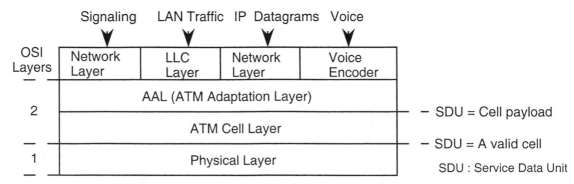

Figure 22.2 The ATM model can be viewed as being part of OSI layers 1 and 2. However, depending on what is being transported through the network, it can interface with applications belonging to different OSI layers. The unit of transfer between these layers is referred to as an SDU (Service Data Unit).

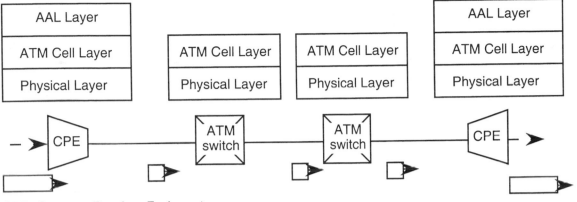

CPE : Customer Premises Equipment

Figure 22.3 The AAL (ATM Adaptation Layer) is an end-to-end protocol and is not implemented in the ATM switches. It divides the application transfer unit into cells which are forwarded through the switches. The AAL at the receiving end will reassemble the cells.

The unit of transfer between the ATM model layers is called an SDU (Service Data Unit) instead of a PDU (Protocol Data Unit). The ATM layer processes ATM cells which are composed of a cell header and its payload. The AAL forwards the payload to the ATM layer when transmitting and receives the payload from the ATM layer when receiving. The physical layer is responsible for providing HEC (Header Error Correction).

Since the AAL gets the information ready to be loaded into cells, its services are required only at the end points of the network. At the receiving end, the cells are reassembled into PDUs (Protocol Data Units) of the user application. This is seen in Figure 22.3. Notice that the only layers which the network switches must process are the physical and the ATM layers.

This three-layer ATM model is further divided into sublayers, as seen in Figure 22.4. The physical layer is divided into the Transmission Convergence sublayer and the Physical Media Dependent sublayer which is mostly implemented through SONET or some other physical transport such as DS3. It provides synchronization and line coding. The Transmission Convergence sublayer, on the other hand, is responsible for cell boundary marking, HEC, framing, multiplexing, and other physical functions. When transmitting a cell, this sublayer adds the HEC field and when receiving a cell, this layer checks for errors. Errored cells are discarded and not forwarded to the ATM layer. This layer adapts the ATM cells to whatever physical media is being used and makes ATM flexible and able to be transported over practically any media.

The AAL is divided into the CS (Convergence Sublayer) and SAR (Segmentation And Reassembly) sublayers. The SAR sublayer divides an application data stream into cells while transmitting and, while receiving, it reassembles them into a data stream compatible to the application. The CS sublayer specifies the requirements for applications. The CS layer protects the unit of transfer from an application before it is segmented by the SAR layer. This layer is further divided into the SSCS (Service

ATM

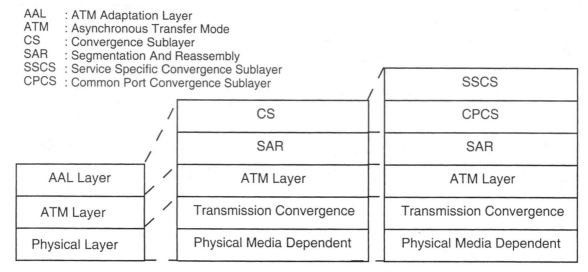

AAL : ATM Adaptation Layer
ATM : Asynchronous Transfer Mode
CS : Convergence Sublayer
SAR : Segmentation And Reassembly
SSCS : Service Specific Convergence Sublayer
CPCS : Common Port Convergence Sublayer

	SSCS
CS	CPCS
SAR	SAR
AAL Layer	ATM Layer	ATM Layer
ATM Layer	Transmission Convergence	Transmission Convergence
Physical Layer	Physical Media Dependent	Physical Media Dependent

Figure 22.4 The three layers of the ATM model can be subdivided into a total of 5 sublayers. The CS sublayer can be divided into further.

Specific Convergence Sublayer) and CPCS (Common Port Convergence Sublayer). The details of these sublayers will be left for a later section in this chapter.

22.2 THE ATM CELL LAYER

22.2.1 Routing of Cells

At the core of the ATM network, cells are transferred by means of virtual circuits. However, instead of defining a virtual circuit only by the collection of virtual channels over each link that the circuit traverses, circuits are defined by using virtual paths as well. Hence, an ATM cell header has two fields identifying over which circuit that cell is going. VPI (Virtual Path Identifier) and VCI (Virtual Channel Identifier) together are needed for a cell to determine its route. As seen with other protocols, ATM supports both PVCs (Permanent Virtual Circuits) and SVCs (Switched Virtual Circuits). As before, PVCs are manually entered and SVCs are established, maintained, and dropped by signaling protocols.

To see how virtual circuits are handled in ATM, consider Figure 22.5. User A has established a virtual path, specified by a set of VPIs, from Switch 1 to Switch 3. It doesn't matter for the sake of this illustration whether it is a PVC or an SVC being described here. If it is a PVC, the connection is permanently available; otherwise, it will be disconnected shortly. The virtual path is defined in the lookup tables at those three switches. This definition is as follows:

Switch 1 transfers all cells with VPI of 100 from User A to Switch 2 with a VPI of 120.

Switch 2 transfers all cells with VPI of 120 from Switch 1 to Switch 3 with a VPI of 110.

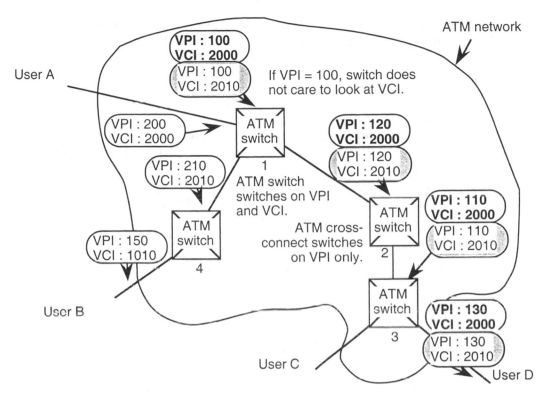

Figure 22.5 All shaded cells belong to one virtual path, which is defined
through switches 1, 2, and 3.

Switch 3 transfers all cells with VPI of 110 from Switch 2 to User D with a VPI
of 130.

Users A and D, and not the switch, worry about the differences between VCIs.
The use of virtual paths is convenient between two locations, if there are many
applications running between them. The user's equipment sorts out which cell belongs
to which application, while the ATM network only has to process the VPIs. This further
increases the speed at which the switches operate. Notice that through a virtual path,
the VCI remains unchanged. In Figure 22.5, the virtual path shown by the cells which
are shaded contain the same VCIs, i.e., VCIs of 2000 and 2010.

What we have just described is called *virtual path switching*. In virtual path
switching the VPIs may change from switch to switch but the VCIs stay the same. VCIs
of 2000 and 2010 traversed the same path from User A to User D. It is like when
passengers of one airplane must get off and board another airplane of the same kind and
take the same seats which they had before.

Virtual path switching can be established permanently by manually entering the
path. This is called PVP (Permanent Virtual Path). An SVP (Switched Virtual Path),
on the other hand, is established through signaling. Carriers would rather sell PVPs
than SVPs because SVPs require more sophisticated signaling mechanisms which may

VPI	: Virtual Path Identifier
VCI	: Virtual Channel Identifier
SVC	: Switched Virtual Circuit
PVC	: Permanent Virtual Circuit
SVP	: Switched Virtual Path
PVP	: Permanent Virtual Path

not be properly implemented. This is true especially if the switches are made by different vendors that are not 100% compatible with each other. (The side figure reviews the basic acronyms used here.)

A customer who has a PVP ready between two sites can then establish SVCs (Switched Virtual Circuits) between the sites through this PVP. The SVCs are sorted out at the customer's premises. This is called *soft PVC* or *switched PVC*. A soft PVC is a PVC through which end points can create and disconnect SVCs as needed. Its implementation is proprietary so the equipment at both ends of the PVC must be from the same vendor. However, no signaling is necessary through the ATM switches. It is a function required only at the end points.

For users who require only one channel rather than a group of channels, the ATM switches must process the VCIs as well. In Figure 22.5, a virtual channel is shown by the unshaded cells going from user A to user B. This is called *virtual channel switching*. Virtual channel switching means that the cell is switched according to the values of VPI and VCI. Here, VCIs are not bundled inside a VPI as in a soft PVC.

Switches that can switch only on VPIs are called ATM DCSs (Digital Cross-connect Systems) and those that can switch on both VPIs and VCIs are called ATM switches.

22.2.2 Network Interfaces

As with frame relay, ATM defines the interface between the user and the first ATM switch. This is called UNI (User-to-Network Interface). If the ATM switch is private, that is, it is owned and operated by the customer, then the interface is called a private UNI. Customers' interfaces to public ATM switches are called public UNIs. Examples of each are shown in Figure 22.6.

Unlike frame relay, ATM does define an interface between its switches. This is called NNI (Network Node Interface). PNNI (Private Network to Network Interface)

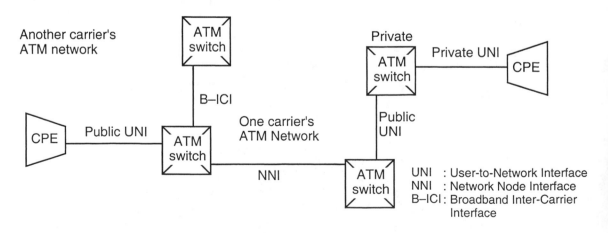

Figure 22.6 ATM switch interfaces.

ATM

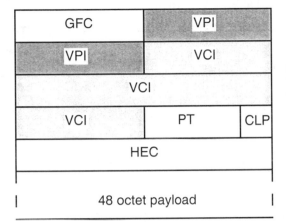

GFC : Generic Flow Control
VPI : Virtual Path Identifier
VCI : Virtual Channel Identifier
PT : Payload Type
CLP : Cell Loss Priority
HEC : Header Error Control

Figure 22.7 The ATM cell uses a 5-octet header and a 48-octet payload. The cell is 53 octets long. The GFC is not used across the NNI but becomes part of the VPI field.

is a specific implementation of NNI. Because NNI is defined, carriers can buy switches from different vendors and do not have to be tied to one vendor. This leverages them to get the best price and service. The interface between ATM networks from different carriers is called B-ICI (Broadband Inter-Carrier Interface).

22.2.3 The Cell Header

As we have already stated, all ATM cells are of fixed length. They are 53 bytes long. The header requires 5 bytes and the payload, the portion that is provided by the AAL, requires 48 bytes.

We have already described VPI and VCI. Their lengths are 8 and 16 bits, respectively. That gives us 256 virtual paths per physical link and 65,536 virtual channels in each virtual path. The side figure shows some VPIs and VCIs that are reserved to provide special functions. When idle, the link continually sends unassigned cells. ILMI stands for Integrated Link Management Interface and provides management information over the UNI, such as address registration. Call signaling will be covered later.

Key Reserved VPIs and VCIs

Description:	VPI:	VCI:
Unassigned cells	0	0
Call Signaling	Any	5
ILMI	0	16
PNNI	0	18

The GFC Field: The first field in the header is called GFC (Generic Flow Control). This field has significance only across the UNI. Once the cell goes inside the network over the NNI, this field is not used. Instead, these bits are used to extend the range of VPI from 8 bits to 12 bits. This field is supposed to provide data flow control or to slow down the transmission of data from the CPE (Customer Premises Equipment) if it is sending cells at a higher rate than what the network can handle. However, it is not currently defined and is always set to all zeros.

Table 22.1 Payload Type Indicator			
Bit 1	Bit 2	Bit 3	Description
0	0	0	User data, no congestion, SDU type 0
0	0	1	User data, no congestion, SDU type 1
0	1	0	User data, has congestion, SDU type 0
0	1	1	User data, has congestion, SDU type 1
1	0	0	Segment OAM F5 flow related
1	0	1	End-to-end OAM F5 flow related
1	1	0	Reserved for future (Traffic management)
1	1	1	Reserved for future

The PT Field: The PT (Payload Type) field identifies the type of cell. It is a three-bit field and in Table 22.1 the bits' meanings are shown. If the first of these bits is a 0 then that indicates that it is a user data cell. If it is a 1 then the cell is understood to be a network information cell. The second of these bits indicates whether or not congestion has been experienced anywhere in the network by the receiving cell. It is also called the EFCI (Explicit Forward Congestion Indicator) bit, and, as in frame relay, the CPE or the edge device is responsible for reacting to congestion.

The third bit is not well defined, except in the case of AAL5. In AAL5, if the cell is not the last cell of a frame, then this bit is set to 0. If it is the last cell of a frame, then it is set to 1. We will cover AAL5 in a later section.

Cell Loss Priority: The CLP (Cell Loss Priority) bit is set by either the CPE or the ingress switch (the first ATM switch that receives a cell from the CPE). The ATM switch will set this bit to 1, making it a lower-priority cell, if the CPE is sending cells at a rate higher than what was agreed. This bit is 0 for high-priority cells and it is 1 for low-priority cells. The low-priority cells are the first ones to be discarded by the network in case of congestion. However, for severe congestion, even the high-priority cells may also be discarded.

HEC: The last field in the ATM cell header is called the HEC (Header Error Control). It provides a means to check for the validity of headers, ensuring that there are no errors in them, and it also provides a means to determine the boundaries of the cells. Basically, it uses an 8-bit CRC algorithm to check for errors. If an error is found in the header, then it is either corrected or discarded. Errors in one or two bits in the headers can be corrected with very good accuracy.

The HEC also allows an ATM device to determine the beginning of each cell. Starting at a particular bit, the device counts off 32 bits (or 4 bytes), assumes the following 8 bits is the HEC, and checks to see if there are no errors. If there is an error, then it assumes that the starting bit wasn't the beginning of the cell. Then it goes to the bit following the first starting bit and repeats the process. Eventually the HEC will check without errors, and then the device assumes that the starting bit marked the beginning of the cell.

In other words, five bytes are counted off starting at consecutive bits assuming that each one is a header. The five-byte block for which the HEC checks out is assumed to be the correct header and the beginning of the cell.

This error checking procedure is repeated for at least two more cells to confirm the beginning and the end of each cell. To further make cell delineation more accurate, the payload may be scrambled so as to make it mathematically less probable that the HEC would be misinterpreted as being inside the payload.

Notice that the cells are not given sequence numbers as is done with level 2 protocols such as SDLC and LAP/B. This is because cells are transferred through only one physical path and hence must arrive in the same sequence as they were transmitted. Another reason why ATM can switch cells faster than a packet switch is that its layer 2 protocol has to process the data to check for errors, whereas an ATM switch only checks the first 5 octets and doesn't process the other 48.

22.3 THE ATM ADAPTATION LAYER

22.3.1 Application Service Classes

Above the ATM layer comes the AAL (ATM Adaptation layer). See Figure 22.2. This layer is not a link-to-link (or a node-to-node) process, but, unlike the ATM layer, concerns itself with only the end points. ATM provides services to different kinds of applications, whether they are images, video, etc. As its name implies, AAL adapts these varying kinds of applications to the single type of transmission mode provided

Application class:	Class A	Class B	Class C	Class D
AAL types	AAL1 & 5	AAL2 & 5	AAL3/4 & 5	AAL3/4 & 5
Type of application	Voice/Video Circuit	Packet Video	Data Frame Relay	Data LANs and IP
Connection mode	Connection Oriented			Connectionless
Rate	Constant	Variable bit rate		
Performance	Low latency		Delay and loss acceptable	

Figure 22.8 ATM defines four classes of service, from A to D, depending on what is required by the application. The AAL types, from 1 to 5, provide standards on how to meet these requirements.

by ATM. AAL provides the same functions that a PAD (Packet Assembler/Disassembler) does in X.25, but with more flexibility. This is the layer that allows ATM to mix different types of information. Because AAL is only implemented at the end points or at the CPEs, and not in the ATM network switches, the network switches only have to concern themselves with routing of cells and do not have to worry about the type of data carried in their payload.

To address the different problems associated with various types of applications running over ATM, the CS sublayer specifies the requirements for those applications. These requirements are divided into Class A, B, C, and D as shown in Figure 22.8. Class A applications require a connection-oriented transfer and a CBR (Constant Bit Rate) service. The amount of latency must be low, which makes this class suitable for voice- and video-based applications.

An application requiring a connection-oriented service, a variable bit rate transfer, and low latency would be classified as a Class B application. Packet video is an example that requires Class B service. In other words, the AAL on the transmitting side would break up the video into cells and require the network to provide Class B service, and when the cells appeared at the receiving end, this layer would reassemble them back into video.

LANs and IP traffic are Class D applications. They are VBR (Variable Bit Rate)-based, connectionless, and not sensitive to delay.

To accommodate these various types of applications, which have their own sets of requirements, ATM has defined a few sets of standards called AAL types. Each AAL type provides a specific implementation of the AAL layer to satisfy these needs. They are also listed in Figure 22.8 and are called AAL types 1 to 5. Although the different classes provide us with a conceptual model of what kinds of services may be required by the applications, the AAL types give us the methods by which they are implemented. Hence, today the AAL types have become more significant than the AAL service classes.

22.3.2 AAL 0

If an application were written using an ATM API (Application Programming Interface), all units of transfer would be exactly 48 bytes long, which would fit nicely into ATM cells. In such a case, there would be no need for the AAL (ATM Adaptation Layer). The application would not need to be adapted to ATM cells: It would make data units which are ready to be loaded into cells. In this case, the AAL is nonexistent and the AAL type is called AAL 0. However, the application must do the segmentation of frames into cells and then reassemble them at the distant end. It's possible in this case that the application could request a retransmission of only one cell rather than the entire frame or packet to which it originally belonged.

On the left-hand side of Figure 22.9, we see an application providing 48-byte units of information to the ATM network. The CS (Convergence Sublayer) and the SAR (Segmentation And Reassembly), which are sublayers of the AAL layer, are not used. Most applications today are not written with ATM in mind, so we need to implement the AAL. Hence, we will see that these layers are implemented in all the other AALs.

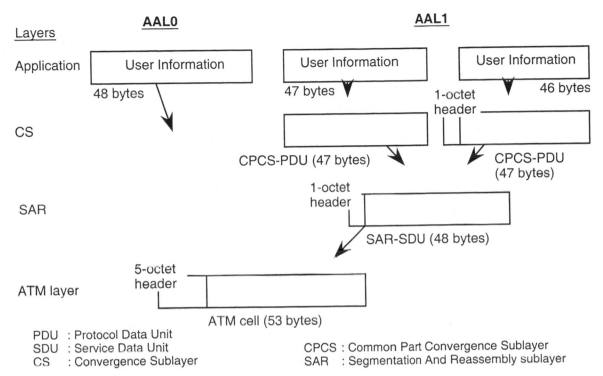

Figure 22.9 AAL type 0 does not use the AAL at all. The application is written with ATM in mind. Applications of AAL type 1 mostly use the SAR layer only. Circuit emulation, DS1, DS3, voice, and real-time video are examples of AAL type 1 applications.

22.3.3 AAL 1

An application that needs to emulate a circuit like DS1 or DS3 may use the AAL 1 format. These applications include voice and real-time video. They run at a constant bit rate and are sensitive to delay.

Figure 22.9 shows an application that is sending a constant bit stream. Every group of 47 bytes are marked, given a SAR header, and placed into a cell. Bit streams which are processed in this manner are said to be "chopped and dropped" into cells. When the beginning of a block of bits needs to be marked, an extra byte of header is used by the CS layer. This is seen on the far right-hand side of the figure. In this case, only 46 bytes of user information is loaded into the CS PDU. For most cells, the CS layer doesn't exist, which gives AAL type 1 low delay. Hence, AAL 1 is appropriate for voice and video.

22.3.4 AAL 2

Originally, AAL 2 was intended to support packetized and compressed voice and video. Later, its implementation was dropped. Today, AAL 3/4 and AAL 5 formats are used for these types of applications.

22.3.5 AAL 3/4

While AAL 1 is more suited for voice and video, AAL 3/4 is more suited for data. Originally, AAL 3 was designed for class C services and AAL 4 for class D services. The difference between them is that class C is connection-oriented while class D is connectionless. For data transfers, low error rate is more important than the connection mode. Therefore, today these two AAL types have been combined into one offering called AAL 3/4.

On the left-hand side of Figure 22.10 we see how user information is loaded into ATM cells using AAL 3/4. Information can arrive in blocks of up to 65,535 bytes into the CS layer. This layer will add a 4-octet header and a 4-octet trailer with padding, if necessary, to make size of the PDU an even multiple of nibbles (or half octets). This unit of transfer is called a CPCS PDU and can be up to 65,544 bytes long. These headers provide a means of detecting if any cells are missing to reassemble the user information. It also provides other types of error checking. Other functions provided by this layer are not much used today.

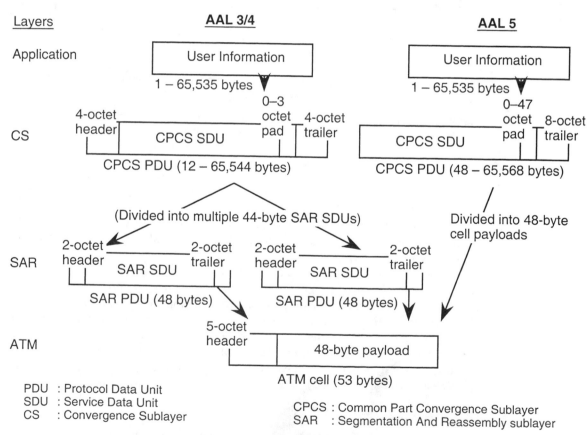

Figure 22.10 AAL 3/4 adds a significant amount of overhead needed for error checking used with data of variable-length packets and frames. AAL 5, on the other hand, is lean and efficient.

The CPCS (Common Part Convergence Sublayer) forwards this PDU to the SAR (Segmentation And Reassembly) sublayer. It does this by chopping the PDU into 44-byte SAR SDUs. This is because the SAR will add its own overhead to each of the SDUs of four bytes before forwarding the PDU to the ATM layer.

Each SAR SDU gets its own 2-byte header and a 2-byte trailer. This layer provides bit error correction for every 44 bytes of data. However, if the application provides error correction itself, then checking and correcting errors may not be necessary. Furthermore, with fiber becoming more and more prevalent, error checking is not as necessary.

The SAR header also provides multiplexing of many data streams over one virtual circuit. This way if an application is idle momentarily, data from another application can be multiplexed over the same ATM connection. This feature is mainly used by SMDS (Switched Multi-megabit Digital Service) which is a service today primarily offered only by Bell Atlantic for high-security circuits. Other than that, SMDS is not much used.

Hence, the most important reason to use AAL 3/4 is to provide error checking on data transfers since retransmissions can be made per SAR PDU rather than of the entire CPCS PDU.

22.3.6 AAL 5

If error control is not crucial to the transfer of data, or, for that matter, voice and video also, then AAL 5 proves to be fast and efficient. Notice from the right-hand side of Figure 22.10, that AAL 5 will add only a trailer of eight bytes and some padding, if necessary, to make the CPCS PDU an even multiple of 48 bytes. The figure shows that the SAR layer is skipped. Actually, the SAR layer will use the third bit of the PT field in the ATM cell header to mark whether or not the cell is the last cell of a given CPCS PDU. Hence, AAL 5 is also called SEAL (Simple and Efficient Adaptation Layer).

There are no headers added by the CPCS layer. There are no headers or trailers added by the SAR layer. This means that there is much less processing that needs to be done by the AAL 5 format. Originally, AAL 5 was designed for transferring IP packets which use TCP to correct any errors. AAL 5 will correct errors, but only at the CPCS layer. This is quite minimum compared to AAL 3/4 where errors are checked on every SAR PDU. AAL 3/4 provides no error checking for the entire CPCS PDU.

Typically, AAL 3/4 has an overhead of about 20%. However, when frame sizes are about 64 bytes this overhead can reach up to 40%. This is about the same as if AAL 5 were used with 64 bytes of information. Hence, AAL 5 has an advantage over AAL 3/4 only when information frames are of larger sizes.

22.4 UNI SIGNALING

In this section we will discuss signaling over the UNI (User-to-Network Interface). The AAL used by signaling is called SAAL (Signaling AAL). It actually uses AAL 5 for the CPCS (Common Part Convergence Sublayer) and the SAR sublayers. Above these layers, SAAL uses the SSCS (Service Specific Convergence Sublayer).

Remember from Figure 22.4 that SSCS and CPCS are sublayers of the CS layer, while CS and the SAR layers are sublayers of the AAL. AAL 5, as we described in the previous section for user data, doesn't use the SSCS layer at all. The SSCS is used primarily by SAAL. The SSCS sublayer provides a reliable transfer of data which AAL 5 lacks.

All ATM end stations and switches must have a unique ATM address within the entire network. ATM addresses are 20 octets long, that is, 160 bits. There are three formats used with ATM addresses, but regardless of the format they all have three basic parts. A prefix part is 13 octets long and identifies the ATM switch. The end system part of the address is 6 octets long and identifies the CPE or the host connected to the switch. The last octet is called the network selector part and its use is determined by the vendor of the end system. The details of the three specific formats are given in

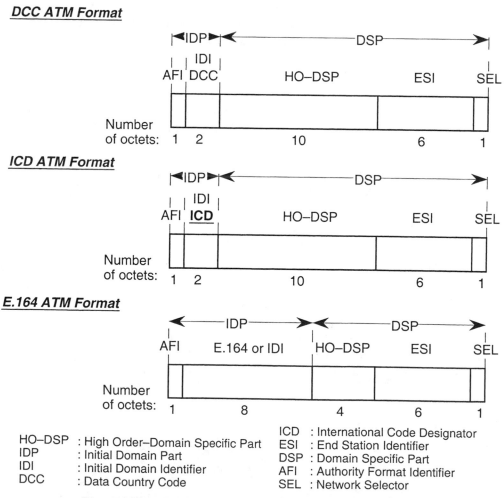

DCC ATM Format

ICD ATM Format

E.164 ATM Format

HO–DSP	: High Order–Domain Specific Part	ICD	: International Code Designator
IDP	: Initial Domain Part	ESI	: End Station Identifier
IDI	: Initial Domain Identifier	DSP	: Domain Specific Part
DCC	: Data Country Code	AFI	: Authority Format Identifier
		SEL	: Network Selector

Figure 22.11 The three addressing formats used in ATM.

Figure 22.11. The name for these addresses is simply AESA (ATM End Station Address).

Figure 22.12 shows how an end station receives its AESA. Typically, using either its MAC address or some other address that is embedded into the hardware, the end station would know its part of the AESA address. These are the last seven octets of the AESA. The administrator of the ATM switch to which the end system is connected would manually enter the 13-octet prefix once, regardless of the number of ports that are available on the switch.

Once the link is connected between them, the end system, using SNMP (Simple Network Management Protocol) commands, will automatically figure out its full address. This dialog occurs on the ILMI (Integrated Local Management Interface) channel. This is always on VPI of 0 and VCI of 16. The end system will tell the switch that it wants to register its address with the switch. The switch will first send the prefix to the end system, and the end system will then formulate its full AESA and register it with the switch.

Once the address is known by the end system, it can bring up the signaling link. No calls can be made until the signaling link is established. This process is outlined in Figure 22.13. The link is established using VPI of 0 and VCI of 5. SSCP sends a Begin frame from the end system to the first point in the ATM network. This frame is replied to with a Begin Acknowledgment frame, which completes the link establishment phase. If the network is not ready at the time it receives the Begin frame, it will send a Begin Negative Acknowledgment frame instead.

Once the link is established, a heartbeat signal is sent across the UNI. This includes a Poll frame sent by the end system and a Status frame sent by the network. These frames confirm from each end that the signaling link is active and ready. When a signaling frame has to be sent across the UNI, Send Data frames are sent. These frames have transmitting and receiving sequence numbers. SSCP accomplishes reliability by the use of these sequence numbers. These numbers are synchronized by both ends during the Poll and Status frame transfers.

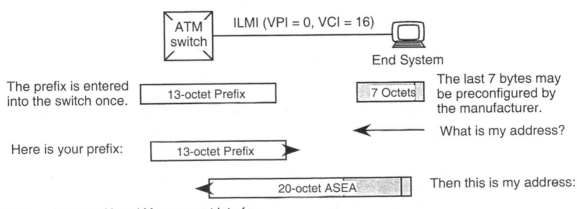

ILMI : Integrated Local Management Interface
AESA : ATM End Station Address

Figure 22.12 Automatic address registration.

ATM

515

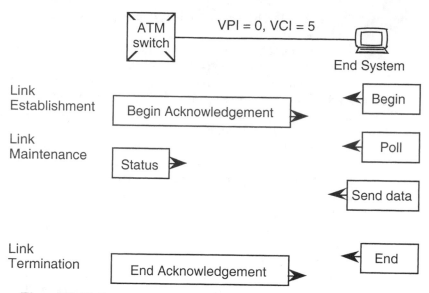

Figure 22.13 Establishing, maintaining, and disconnecting a signaling link over the UNI.

The last portion of Figure 22.13 shows the link being disconnected. The end system sends an End frame and the network responds with an End Acknowledgment frame. All these frames are sent over VPI of 0 and VCI of 5.

Once the addresses are resolved, the signaling link is established, and a call may then be made through the ATM network. This process is illustrated in Figure 22.14. The end system on the left is initiating a call by sending a Setup frame to the first ATM switch. This process is initiated by an upper-layer application. This switch will then perform two tasks. It will use the NNI (Network Node Interface) to negotiate a circuit through the network and return a Call Proceeding frame back to the end system. The Call Proceeding frame will contain the VPI and VCI that are assigned to the end system.

The egress ATM switch, upon receiving the connection request, will also send a Setup frame to the destination end system. This frame will contain the VPI and the VCI that should be used by the end system. If the end system accepts the call, it will send a Connect frame, and eventually another Connect frame will be issued by the ingress ATM switch. Two Connect Acknowledgment frames across each UNI complete the call. Notice that all the frames shown in the figure are across these local interfaces.

Once the call is completed it is time to terminate the connection. This is done by either party sending a Release frame to the ATM switch. This request for termination is sent using NNI over the network until it reaches the switch at the other end. The egress ATM switch will also issue a Release frame. The nodes that received these Release frames will in turn reply with Release Complete frames, thereby dropping the connection.

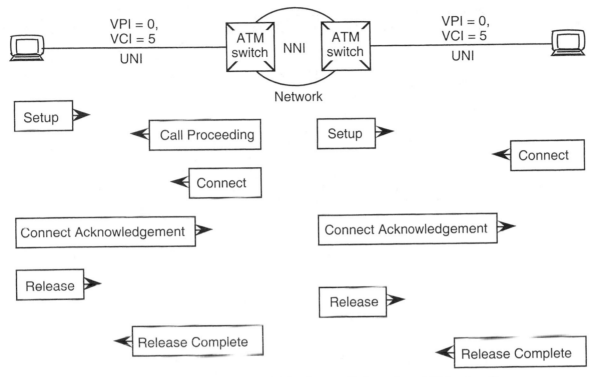

Figure 22.14 Establishing and releasing a call through an ATM network.

EXERCISES

Section 22.1:
1. Which type of traffic is isochronous?

a. video

b. data

b. images

c. LANs

2. Packetized voice uses which type of application service?

a. CBR

c. VBR

b. UBR (Unspecified Bit Rate)

d. ABR (Available Bit Rate)

3. Which of the following is not an advantage of using cells?

a. It allows cut-through switching

b. It produces lower overhead

c. It reduces the amount of head-of-the-line blocking.

d. Switching can be done in hardware instead of software.

4. What is the name for the parameter that determines the amount of delay, the variation in delay, the error rate, and so on?

5. Name the three layers of the ATM architecture, then describe their purpose. Name the layers which are subdivided and also the sublayers.

6. Which layer processes the HEC field in the ATM cell header?

7. Do the switches in the ATM network process the AAL?

Section 22.2:

8. The interface between an end system and the first ATM switch is called what?
   - a. LMI
   - b. NNI
   - c. AMI
   - d. UNI

9. Which bit of the PT field in an header is not much used or implemented?
   - a. 1st
   - b. 2nd
   - c. 3rd
   - d. 4th

10. In what type of switching do the VPIs change from link to link but the VCIs remain the same through a connection?

11. In what type of switching do VPIs and VCIs change from link to link?

12. How is the beginning of an ATM cell determined?

13. How long is the VPI field in UNI? In NNI?

14. What should be the value of the GFC field?

15. Describe how the CLP bit is used and set.

Section 22.3:

16. Which class of service would provide low latency, connection-oriented transfer, and a variable bit rate?
   - a. class A
   - b. class B
   - c. class C
   - d. class D

17. Which AAL is almost nonexistent today?
   - a. AAL 0
   - b. AAL 1
   - c. AAL 2
   - d. AAL 3/4

18. What kind of application would use AAL 0 level services?

19. A voice application that needs to emulate a dedicated circuit would use which AAL?

20. What are the advantages of AAL 3/4 over AAL5?

21. What are the advantages of AAL 5 over AAL 3/4?

22. Suppose that the user information being sent by an application is 80 bytes long. How many CPCS PDUs will be created out of this information? How many bytes long would each of these PDUs be? How many SAR PDUs will be created out of this information? How many bytes long would each of these PDUs be?

Section 22.4:

23. Describe the three parts of AESA and what these parts identify.

24. How many different formats exist for AESA?

25. Describe how an end station registers its address with its ATM switch.

26. Describe how the signaling link is maintained once it is established.

27. Which frame starts establishing an ATM connection?

28. During call establishment, which frames provide the VPI and VCI pairs to be used?

Chapter 23

LANs:
Additional Concepts

In this chapter we take up from where we left off in Chapter 7. In that chapter we had an overview of LANs, but here we will get more details. For example, in Chapter 7 we gave a rough picture of what an Ethernet data frame looks like. Here, we will see that there is more than one kind of Ethernet frame and also how it is formatted. The specifications of various types of Ethernet, Token Ring Networks, and FDDI are also given in this chapter. The chapter ends with descriptions of the new kinds of Ethernet, namely, Fast Ethernet and Gigabit Ethernet.

23.1 SOFTWARE BASICS

In this section we'll turn our attention to the software components needed to build a LAN. We'll assume that the IBM PC is used as a network node, discuss its networking components, and give a brief overview of the Windows 98 networking features. Finally, we will extend our discussion to include the IEEE 802 and proprietary protocols, and show how they relate to each other and the OSI reference model.

23.1.1 NetBIOS

Before we talk about the networking capabilities of the IBM PC, let us briefly look at the roles that BIOS (Basic Input/Output System) and DOS (Disk Operating System) have within a PC.

BIOS and DOS: BIOS (Basic Input/Output System) is a set of machine language routines that are part of a ROM (Read-Only Memory) chip. It physically comes inside the computer. When the power is turned on to the PC, this ROM or BIOS starts a simple program that first checks out what devices are connected to it. This is called POST (Power On Self Test). It checks the CMOS (Channelized Metal Oxide Semiconductor) chip to see how the PC is configured. Because the BIOS uses the CMOS to start up the

519

computer, many people incorrectly think that the BIOS and the CMOS are the same device. CMOS requires a little battery which keeps tracks of the time, stores the password setting, if any, boot sequence, and many other configuration options. After this, the BIOS will look for a boot record on a hard drive or one of the other devices and load in the operating system. Until that time, the BIOS is in charge of the computer.

Unlike the BIOS, DOS (Disk Operating System) comes on a CD or the hard drive and is loaded in the RAM (Random Access Memory) of the computer by the BIOS. DOS uses higher-level instructions than does BIOS. We will use the term DOS to include the Microsoft Windows 98 operating system.

Besides starting up the PC, the primary function of BIOS is to provide software-based control for video displays, keyboards, disk drives, etc., that are connected to the PC. Anytime a person types a character on the keyboard, the BIOS receives it and presents it to the application. Similarly, whenever an application needs to display anything on the screen, it must go through the BIOS, and so on.

DOS provides a higher-level interface for the user or the application. Therefore, it is easier for a user to execute a DOS command than to perform a BIOS call. As shown in Figure 23.1, software applications can perform either BIOS calls or DOS calls. However, BIOS calls are executed faster, since they don't have to go through DOS. Applications that make DOS calls are more portable; that is, they can run over a variety of machines which are emulating the BIOS and using the designated version of DOS. However, at one time, the various versions of BIOS sold by different vendors did not conform to one standard and hence they all worked differently with the same software.

NetBIOS and NOS: To our stand-alone PC, let us now add a NIC to make it part of a LAN. Here, we don't care whether it is a TRN, Ethernet, or whatever other kind of NIC it is. In any case, the machine language code for controlling the NIC resides in the NetBIOS (Network BIOS). In early NICs, NetBIOS resided in a ROM chip on the NIC. Later on, this code was emulated in the network software, whether it was Novell's NetWare or Windows 98. NetBIOS handles all the OSI model's session layer functions, while the NIC itself supports all the layers below and including that layer. See Figure 23.2.

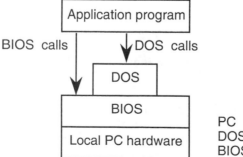

Figure 23.1 An application that makes BIOS calls is more efficient, but an application that makes DOS calls is portable.

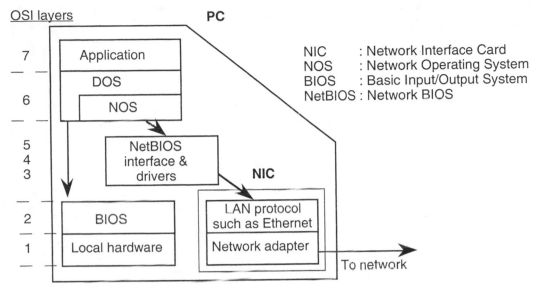

Figure 23.2 DOS can access the local hardware through BIOS or the network devices via NetBIOS.

NetBIOS receives data frames from the local system and transmits them to the network. To interface with NetBIOS, we need an operating system for the LAN called a NOS (Network Operating System). The NOS interacts with the NetBIOS in the same manner as DOS interacts with BIOS.

If the application requires access to a local disk, DOS will gain this access via the BIOS, and if the application requires access to a network disk or resource, the request is directed through the NOS which goes through NetBIOS.

23.1.2 Windows 98 Networking

There are two types of NOS. Windows 98 is an example of a peer-to-peer NOS or simply a peer NOS. These NOSs are usually slower than their server-based NOS counterparts. Server-based NOSs are also called centralized NOSs or client-server based NOSs.

A server-based NOS runs on one machine which is dedicated to be a server, and the network stations or clients access its files. Server-based NOSs are more powerful, because they don't run under DOS, but the NOS takes over the entire server. They are not limited by DOS and can handle many more clients than peer NOSs can.

Nonetheless, a peer NOS allows a low-cost connectivity between the network nodes. Any PC which has a hard drive can be a file server. The network is less dependent on one machine. Anyone can be in anyone else's programs, if it is so desired. However, these small-scale networks do not integrate well with larger, enterprise-wide networks. This makes them difficult to expand. To get an idea of how peer-to-peer networks work, let us briefly look at how Windows 98 can be used for networking.

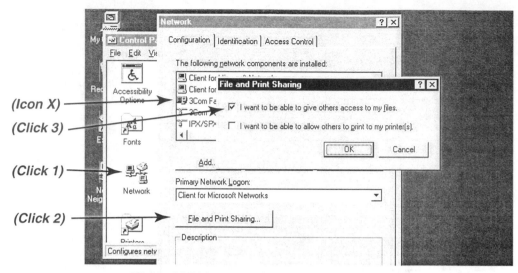
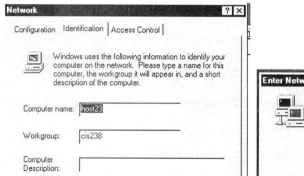

(Icon X)

(Click 3)

(Click 1)

(Click 2)

Figure 23.3(a) Setting up host23 so it can share files.

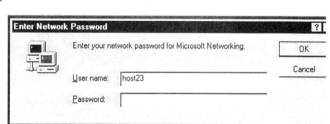

Figure 23.3(b) Confirming host23's identification.

Figure 23.3(c) Signing on host23.

Assume that we have two PCs at home and they are running Windows 98. They each have an Ethernet NIC installed in them, and since only two PCs exist, there is no need for a hub. They are simply interconnected using a Cat-5 crossover cable with RJ-45 modular connectors on each end. We are going to name one PC host23 and the other host2. Instead of using floppies to transfer files from PC to another and to install applications on each PC, we want to be able to share files between each. Let us see how that is accomplished using the peer-to-peer networking software that comes with Windows 98. First, we will go through the steps needed for host23.

On host23, we need to install the drivers for the NIC. Starting with the Start button, we click on Settings, then Control Panel, then the Network icon. The Network window is shown in Figure 23.3(a). This window has three tabs called Configuration, Identification, and Access Control. The Configuration Tab is shown and the 3Com

LANs: Additional Concepts

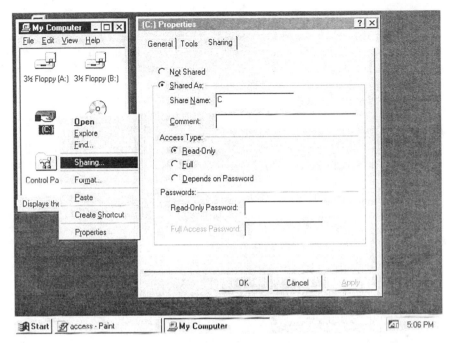

Figure 23.4(a) host23 is *sharing* its C: drive with read-only access.

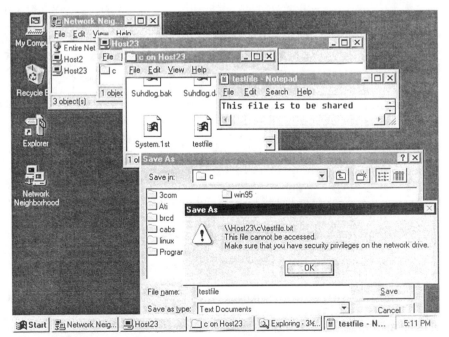

Figure 23.4(b) host2 is *using* host23's testfile, but isn't
allowed to write (or save) over it.

Ethernet card is shown as being installed at the location pointed to by Icon X. If it wasn't installed, select these items in the given order: Start, Settings, Control Panel, Network, Add, Adapter, Have Disk, Browse. Then highlight the driver for your Ethernet card and restart the PC. You may have to restart two times and also go through a Driver Wizard for your PC to recognize the NIC.

Next, we identify our PC as host23 and as being in the workgroup labeled cis238. This is seen by clicking on the Identification Tab. See Figure 23.3(b). For two PCs to be able to share files or printers with each other, they should be in the same workgroup. After identifying the PC, you may have to reboot the PC and it will prompt you to do so. While you are rebooting, you will see a screen like the one shown in Figure 23.3(c). You will see host23 in this screen. Here, don't just close or cancel the box, but click on OK or press Return. Now host23 has been properly configured and identified on the network. Then we do the same steps for host2, our other PC, and get that one also on the network.

Before any resources can be shared, we need to go through the steps outlined in Figure 23.3(a). Getting to the Network box as described before, we click on the File and Print Sharing button. See Click 2 in the figure. That gives us the File and Print Sharing window. Here, we want to specify that we only want to be able to share our files on host23 so we check the box marked as Click 3. Then click on OK and OK again for the Network window. This procedure enables us to share our files with other hosts on the network who belong to the cis238 workgroup. If we had wanted to share our printer then we would have also clicked the other item in the File and Print Sharing window.

host23 will be *sharing* files with other hosts on the network. This means that the files which exist on host23 will become available to others. The only other host we have on this network is host2, but there could be many others. The opposite of sharing is using. host2 will be using the files which host23 makes available for it. In other words, *using* means that the files or resources that exist on other hosts are accessible.

Figure 23.3(a) shows how sharing is enabled for host23 and Figure 23.4(a) shows how the C: drive is made available, in our case, to host2. host 23 could also make other items which are local to it available. These include other drives, folders, or even individual files. Here, the entire C: drive is being shared.

Click on the My Computer icon, then right-click on the C: drive. Here, you will see the menu shown in the figure. Come down to Sharing, and click there. You will see the Properties window. Here, click on the Shared As radio button, and the C drive will appear as shown in the box. We click on the Read-Only radio button. This will not allow host2 to change files, delete files, or create new files on the C: drive. Then click OK. After this you will see a hand under the C: drive's icon, as seen in the figure. This indicates that the C: drive is being shared with others.

Now let us go over to host2. Assuming that its NIC was properly installed and it was correctly configured and rebooted for the network, we should see host2 and host23 in the window obtained by clicking on the Network Neighborhood icon from the desktop. This is seen in the topmost window shown in Figure 23.4(b). This confirms that host2 recognized the presence of itself and host23 on the same network. We want to access host23's C: drive from host2, so from host2 we click on host23. Then the next window labeled Host23 appears, as seen in the figure. Next we obtain the c on Host23 window, as seen in the figure, by clicking on the C: drive folder. There we find the little file called testfile. The testfile was created on host23 before. When we click on testfile, using Notepad, we get the contents of this file which reads "This file is to be shared." We change the file and try to save it. In the Save As message box, we get an error, stating that we don't have rights to save the file on the C: drive on host23. This is because in Figure 23.4(a), we had clicked the Read-Only radio button on host23.

23.1.3 IEEE 802 Standards

In February of 1980, IEEE decided to standardize LANs and, using this year and month number, the 802 project was started. The intention of this project was to standardize the many existing LAN protocols under one "umbrella," called the 802 standards.

For now we will disregard the upper half of Figure 23.5. Let us only look at layers 1 and 2 as they are defined by the IEEE 802 family of protocols.

Toward the top of the 802 stack are the 802.2 specifications, which define the LLC (Logical Link Control) layer. Under it are the MAC (Medium Access Control) and physical layers. The LLC layer and the MAC layer together provide the functions of the data link control layer of the OSI model, while the MAC layer and the physical layer are combined in outlining the details of specific types of LANs. For instance, 802.3 specifies the Ethernet standard, and so on.

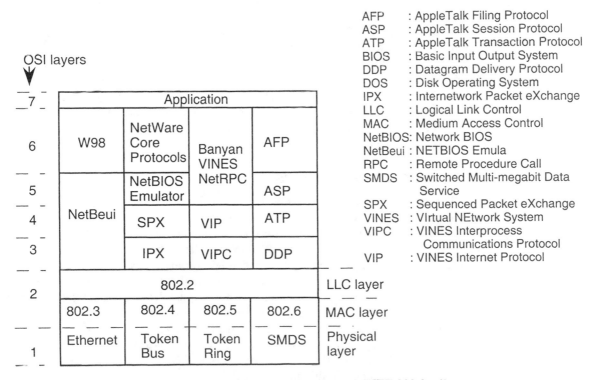

AFP   : AppleTalk Filing Protocol
ASP   : AppleTalk Session Protocol
ATP   : AppleTalk Transaction Protocol
BIOS   : Basic Input Output System
DDP   : Datagram Delivery Protocol
DOS   : Disk Operating System
IPX   : Internetwork Packet eXchange
LLC   : Logical Link Control
MAC   : Medium Access Control
NetBIOS: Network BIOS
NetBeui : NETBIOS Emula
RPC   : Remote Procedure Call
SMDS   : Switched Multi-megabit Data
               Service
SPX   : Sequenced Packet eXchange
VINES   : VIrtual NEtwork System
VIPC   : VINES Interprocess
               Communications Protocol
VIP   : VINES Internet Protocol

Figure 23.5 The proprietary protocols and the IEEE 802 family of protocols as they relate to the OSI reference model.

Because no routing is required on a LAN, in that an intermediate node doesn't have to redirect a received frame over a different link (because there is only one link in a LAN), no network layer is specified by the 802 protocols. When a frame is received by a node, it contains a MAC address and an LLC address called an SAP (Service Access Point). The MAC address specifies the physical node on the network that is physically coded in the NIC.

The SAP address provides the network layer protocol that is being used in the communication. In other words, the SAP provides a logical address to a protocol being addressed in the third or network layer, whereas the network node is specified by the MAC or physical address. For example, a hexadecimal E0 is the SAP address for NetWare, 06 is for IP, and F0 is for IBM's NetBIOS. The LLC layer provides an interface between the network layer and the MAC layer. Additionally, the LLC layer is the same for Token Ring Networks and other type of 802 family of LANs. FDDI, although an ANSI standard, also fits nicely under the LLC layer and is compatible with it.

Figure 23.6 details the functions of the LLC layer further and shows how it fits in the MAC frame. The MAC header and trailer are determined by the specific LAN protocol, such as Ethernet or TRN. The MAC layer treats the data from both the upper layers and the LLC header as information.

The LLC layer manages the LLC header with its 3 fields: the DSAP (Destination SAP), SSAP (Source SAP), and the control field. There are three types of control fields, each determined by the type of LLC frame it is handling. These are information, supervisory, and unnumbered frames. The control field for an unnumbered frame is only 8 bits, while for the other two, it is 16 bits long.

All of the fields shown above have already been discussed in the chapters on SNA and X.25. Lastly, there are two types of LLC services. Type 1 is used for unacknowledged, connectionless, or datagram delivery type of services, and type 2 is used for connection-oriented type of services between the communicating SAPs. The chart depicts the types of unnumbered frames and labels them as either commands or responses. We'll have more to say about LLC shortly in the Ethernet section.

23.1.4 Proprietary Protocols

Directing our attention to the upper half of Figure 23.5, we see a sampling of various proprietary LAN protocols and how they fit in the overall LAN protocol picture. Each of these upper layer (3 to 6) stacks can be implemented over any of the 802.3 through 802.6 layers. Otherwise, they may be implemented over some other proprietary lower-layer protocols. For example, AppleTalk, which is shown in the rightmost column, can run over a proprietary protocol called LocalTalk or it can run over one of the lower-layer protocols shown in the figure. The first stack shown in the figure is Windows 98 which uses IBM's NetBIOS protocol.

Moving across Figure 23.5, we have Novell's NetWare protocol stack. NetWare is based on Xerox's XNS (Xerox Network System). XNS was very influential in defining the OSI model. By the way, Xerox also gave us graphical user interfaces and Ethernet, among other good things.

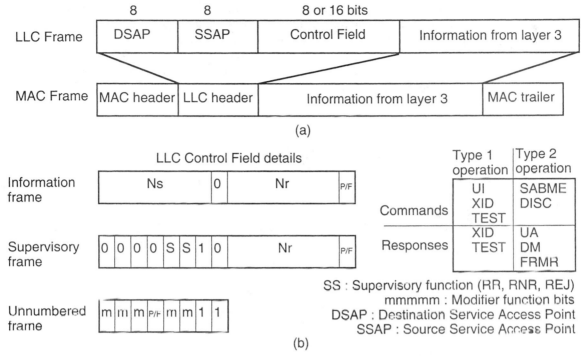

Figure 23.6 (a) As information is accepted by the LLC layer, it adds its own header specifying the protocol type by the SAP. Then the MAC layer adds its own header and trailer. (b) The LLC headers for each of the three types of frames, with modifier functions shown in the table.

Applications can interface with NetWare at various layers. When a network node accesses files on a server using DOS requests, it uses the application layer interface called the Workstation Shell Interface. At the session layer, applications can make NetBIOS-compatible calls, since NetWare's NetBIOS is an emulation of IBM's NetBIOS. A virtual-connection interface is provided at the transport layer for applications which require connection-oriented delivery of packets. This is accomplished by the use of sequence numbers in the SPX (Sequenced Packet eXchange) header. Finally, applications can interface at the network layer for connectionless communications of datagrams. This is provided through the IPX (Internetwork Packet eXchange) protocol.

Banyan Systems Inc.'s VINES (VIrtual NEtwork System) is a NOS based on the Unix operating system. It can be incorporated over various types of networks and platforms. On a DOS platform, the workstation is DOS-based, but on a server, it runs under a Unix kernel. Many of these protocols were originally developed under Unix.

Apple Computer's AppleTalk is used primarily with Macintosh computers. These computers already come with a LocalTalk network interface. At the bottom of the AppleTalk stack is DDP (Datagram Delivery Protocol) which provides communication interface with the appropriate process within the network node.

Although there are several protocols that could be implemented at the upper layers, only the primary ones are shown in the diagram. At the transport layer ATP (AppleTalk Transaction Protocol) provides a sequential and reliable delivery of packets, while ASP (AppleTalk Session Protocol) manages and maintains sessions between sockets (or processes). Lastly, AFP (AppleTalk Filing Protocol) supports file transfers between remote locations.

23.2 ETHERNET

23.2.1 Ethernet Frame Formats

Ethernet was originally created by the Xerox, DEC, and Intel corporations. In 1985, IEEE standardized it as 802.3, which is slightly different from the original de facto standard. In the previous section, specifically in Figure 23.6, we have seen how a header is added to the information received by the LLC layer and forwarded to the MAC layer. Now let us look at the headers and trailers as they are added by the MAC layer in Ethernet. Then when we come to TRN and FDDI, we will go over their MAC standards. The LLC layer is common to them all.

Figure 23.7 shows three types of Ethernet frame formats. In this section, we will refer to the first one simply as Ethernet, although Ethernet II is commonly used. This is the original Ethernet standard. Then come the 802.3 frame format without SNAP (Sub-Network Access Protocol) and the 802.3 with SNAP. The 802.2 frame is encapsulated in the 802.3 frame, as we have mentioned before.

The most common type of Ethernet is the first one shown. It has the simplest structure and so it has won the Ethernet protocol war; however, the 802.3 with SNAP format also exists in some LANs and so it is shown here. This format is best understood by first studying the format without SNAP and hence, that format is also shown here. There are still other Ethernet frame formats that are not shown here. Let us first consider the fields that are common to all formats, then look at how one kind of frame is distinguished from the others.

All frames have a maximum length of 1518 bytes and a minimum length of 64 bytes. The preamble field in Ethernet is 8 bytes long and is not part of the official Ethernet frame. Its purpose is to synchronize the receiving NIC with the transmitting NIC. The preamble has a string of "10"s terminating with a "11." The IEEE frames define a 7-byte preamble and a one-byte SFD (Start Frame Delimiter) field, which together define the same bit pattern as the 8-byte preamble for Ethernet. Due to its many 1-to-0 transitions, this 8-byte string pattern provides synchronization.

The next two fields specify the MAC or physical address of the destination and source nodes. This address field is usually 6 bytes long. The first 3 bytes are administered by IEEE (previously by Xerox) and are assigned to NIC manufacturers. The address bits for the last 3 bytes are assigned and maintained by each manufacturer. So, globally, this physical address is kept unique for all Ethernet cards.

Usually, this address is burned into the ROM of the NIC, but it can also be assigned using a diagnostic diskette. If the physical address needs to be kept the same, then when changing the board, the ROM chip should also be swapped along with it.

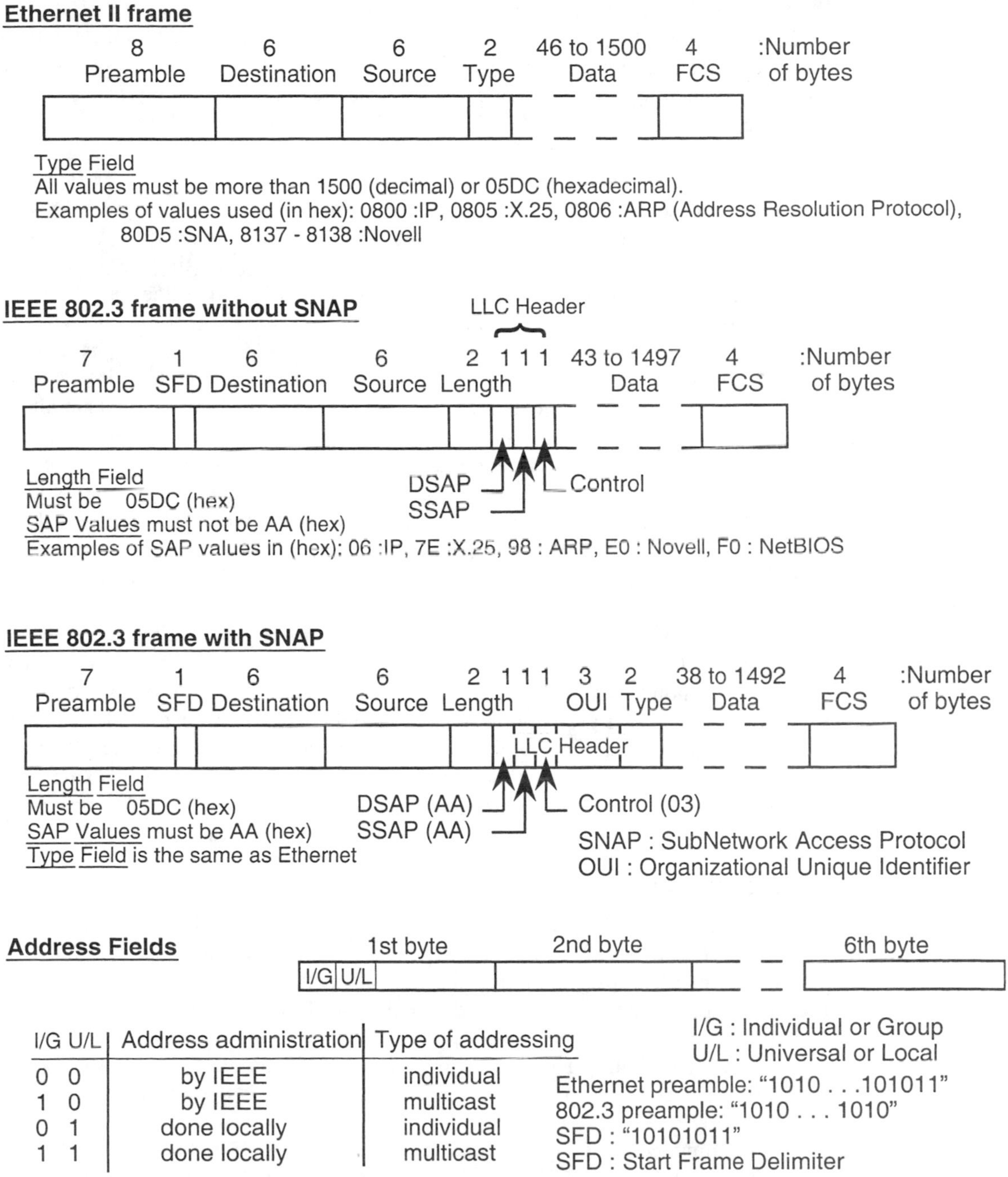

Ethernet II frame

8	6	6	2	46 to 1500	4	:Number
Preamble	Destination	Source	Type	Data	FCS	of bytes

Type Field
All values must be more than 1500 (decimal) or 05DC (hexadecimal).
Examples of values used (in hex): 0800 :IP, 0805 :X.25, 0806 :ARP (Address Resolution Protocol),
80D5 :SNA, 8137 - 8138 :Novell

IEEE 802.3 frame without SNAP

LLC Header

7	1	6	6	2	1 1 1	43 to 1497	4	:Number
Preamble	SFD	Destination	Source	Length		Data	FCS	of bytes

Length Field
Must be   05DC (hex)   DSAP ┘ │ └ Control
SAP Values must not be AA (hex)   SSAP ┘
Examples of SAP values in (hex): 06 :IP, 7E :X.25, 98 : ARP, E0 : Novell, F0 : NetBIOS

IEEE 802.3 frame with SNAP

7	1	6	6	2	1 1 1	3	2	38 to 1492	4	:Number
Preamble	SFD	Destination	Source	Length		OUI	Type	Data	FCS	of bytes

LLC Header

Length Field
Must be   05DC (hex)   DSAP (AA) ┘ │ └ Control (03)
SAP Values must be AA (hex)   SSAP (AA) ┘
Type Field is the same as Ethernet   SNAP : SubNetwork Access Protocol
                                          OUI : Organizational Unique Identifier

Address Fields

	1st byte	2nd byte		6th byte
I/G U/L				

I/G : Individual or Group
U/L : Universal or Local

I/G U/L	Address administration	Type of addressing
0 0	by IEEE	individual
1 0	by IEEE	multicast
0 1	done locally	individual
1 1	done locally	multicast

Ethernet preamble: "1010 . . .101011"
802.3 preamble: "1010 . . . 1010"
SFD : "10101011"
SFD : Start Frame Delimiter

Figure 23.7 The formats of the three types of Ethernet frames and the
MAC address field. In source routing, the I/G bit in the source address is
set to 1; otherwise it is 0.

In both frame types, if the I/G (Individual/Group) address bit is set to 0 by the sender, the frame is sent to only one station, or else it is sent to a group of stations, which is called a multicast transmission. If all 48 bits are set to 1, then it is a broadcast and all stations receive that frame. IEEE frames use the U/L (Universal or Local) address bit to indicate whether the address field conforms to IEEE addressing standards or if it uses some other local scheme of addressing.

The last field in all three formats is the FCS (Frame Check Sequence). It uses the CRC32 scheme to check for errors. Frames with errors that are detected by the NIC are simply discarded. No retransmission is requested by the MAC layer. Upper-layer protocols are responsible for requesting retransmissions for missing frames.

The type field gives the type of Ethernet protocol used in the data field. For example, 0800 is used for IP and 0805 is used for X.25, etc. Notice that the type field doesn't exist in the IEEE frame because the LLC's SAP address provides its function.

The length field in the 802.3 frames gives the length of the data. If this length needs to be conveyed to the receiver in Ethernet, then the upper layers must handle that process. Also, in Ethernet the upper layer must make sure that the data field is at least 46 bytes, while in the IEEE frame, the MAC layer pads additional bytes if necessary.

All valid frame lengths have a value that is less than 1500 in decimal or 05DC in hexadecimal, and all valid type field values are greater than this number. Hence, when a frame is received by a node, the two bytes after the source address are checked. If they are greater than 05DC, the frame is understood as an Ethernet frame; otherwise, as a 802.3 frame.

If the two bytes after the source field are less than or equal to 05DC, the following byte is checked. If its value is AA, then it is understood as an 802.3 frame with SNAP; otherwise, without SNAP. The older version of 802.3 does not use SNAP and so the SAP fields indicate the protocol of the data field that is being transported. Notice that the SAP values differ from the values of the straight 802.3 frame. The 802.3 with SNAP, however, uses the same type field as Ethernet does and there are also more type codes that are possible with this format. From this point on, we'll refer to the IEEE 802.3 standards and the pure Ethernet standards simply as Ethernet.

23.2.2 10Base5

The variations of Ethernet are called 10Base5, 10Base2, 10Broad36, 10BaseT, etc. The first number (10) designates the transmission speed in Mbps over the media and the last number designates the maximum segment length in 100's of meters. The Base or the Broad indicates whether the media uses baseband signaling or broadband signaling. These differences were covered in Chapter 4. For now, let us look at standard Ethernet, which is called 10Base5. This is the original standard that runs at 10 Mbps using 500 meters as the maximum length of segments. It uses a baseband cabling system.

The components of this Ethernet are shown in Figure 23.8. The main cable, or the bus, uses an RG-4 (Radio Grade 4) coax. The impedance of this cable is 50 ohms. On this main cable, there are AUIs (Attachment Unit Interfaces) connected at intervals of 2.5 meters or multiples thereof. These are also called MAUs (Media Access Units) and transceivers. The maximum number of taps on a segment is 100. These AUIs are attached using either a piercing vampire or an inline BNC-type connector.

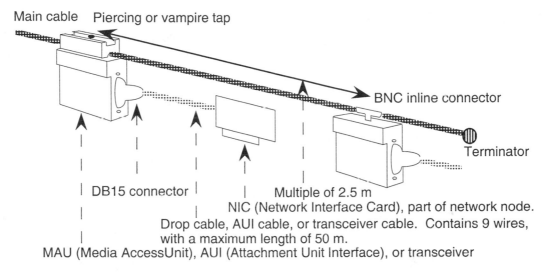

Main cable Piercing or vampire tap

BNC inline connector

Terminator

DB15 connector

Multiple of 2.5 m

NIC (Network Interface Card), part of network node.

Drop cable, AUI cable, or transceiver cable. Contains 9 wires, with a maximum length of 50 m.

MAU (Media AccessUnit), AUI (Attachment Unit Interface), or transceiver

Figure 23.8 The components of a 10Base5 (standard) Ethernet.

From the AUI, the station is connected using an AUI cable, which is also called a drop cable. It is not a coaxial cable but a cable with 9 wires. Its maximum length is 50 meters. It is connected to the transceiver using a DB15 connector, and the other end of it is connected to the NIC inside the workstation. The main coaxial cable must be terminated at both ends with 50-ohm terminators and one of them should be grounded.

The transceiver provides several functions. It can detect if signals are present on the cable and whether or not the cable is available for transmission. If it is, the AUI transmits the signal and backs off if it detects a collision. In the event that the terminal is continuously transmitting (or jabbering), the transceiver will prevent it from transmitting over the line, giving other nodes a chance to communicate. Finally, the AUI provides a heartbeat signal to the terminal, indicating that it is up and operational.

When the performance begins to degrade, due to too many stations on the cable, or because the main cable is exceeding the 500-meter length limitation, the network can be expanded by adding other segments. This is done by connecting repeaters between segments. Repeaters do not eliminate collisions between stations on two different segments; they merely enable the extension of the range of the LAN. In a later chapter we'll see how bridges and routers are able to isolate traffic over individual segments.

The maximum number of repeaters between any two nodes of a network is 4. On the right side of Figure 23.9, a multistory building is shown which has a backbone cable running vertically. Using repeaters, network segments from each floor are connected to this backbone segment. Notice that here nodes from any two floors may communicate with each other using only two repeaters. On the left side of the figure, we have another location on campus that is also connected to this LAN. Typically, a fiber link is preferred over such distances for better quality signals. Here, any station in one building can communicate with another station in the other building using no more than 3 repeaters.

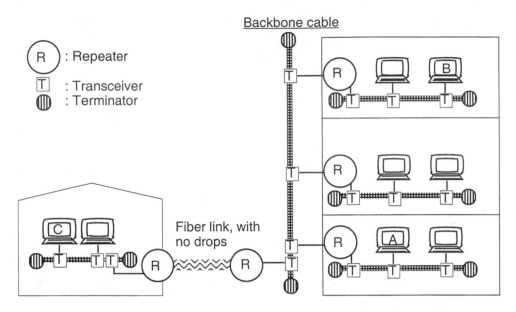

Figure 23.9 The range of an Ethernet network can be extended from 500 meters to 2500 meters using repeaters.

23.2.3 10Base2

In 1985, a less costly version of Ethernet was standardized as 10Base2. Since it uses thin coax, which is easy to install, it is also called ThinNet and CheaperNet. This version still uses the baseband signaling technique with many of the same characteristics as 10Base5. However, 10Base2 has more distance and node placement limitations.

Figure 23.10 shows how typically the NIC is attached directly to the main coax without the use of the AUI cable. The NIC comes with a BNC connector and the circuitry for the transceiver. Attaching the NIC to the main coax is done easily without needing to pierce the coax. The cost per node is also significantly lower than that of 10Base5. Furthermore, the cable designated as RG-58 is only 0.25 inches thick, which makes it not only inexpensive, but also easy to carry and to work with.

Unfortunately, 10Base2 has some limitations. The maximum segment length is only 185 meters. The nodes are attached at 0.5-meter intervals with up to 30 taps per segment. The maximum number of nodes per network, including repeaters, is 1024. This figure is the same as that for 10Base5 and 10BaseT. However, the maximum length of the network using repeaters is only 925 meters, versus the 2500 meters for 10Base5.

23.2.4 10BaseT

Introduction: ThinNet, due to its low cost and ease of installation, became more popular than standard Ethernet very quickly. Because of this immediate success,

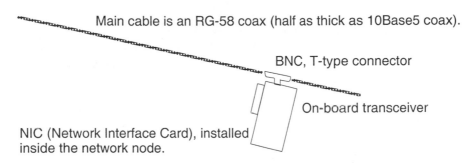

Main cable is an RG-58 coax (half as thick as 10Base5 coax).

BNC, T-type connector

On-board transceiver

NIC (Network Interface Card), installed inside the network node.

Figure 23.10 10Base2 hardware.

another type of Ethernet was introduced that would drive the cost even lower and make installation even easier than before. It is called 10BaseT.

10BaseT uses standard 24 AWG telephone wire instead of coax. This wiring, in many instances, is already in place in existing buildings. Therefore, it needs a minimum amount of installation. Furthermore, 10BaseT can coexist with other types of Ethernet, making it suitable to expand existing networks without having to replace the older technologies.

Initially, 10BaseT was introduced by Synoptics (an offshoot of the Xerox Palo Alto Research Center) as Ethernet over UTP (Unshielded Twisted Pair). In 1990, IEEE adopted it as a standard.

A Hub-Centered LAN: At the heart of the network is a hub. It is also called a concentrator when it is residing in a chassis to which expansion modules can be added. Coming out of the hub (see Figure 23.11) is a standard 50-wire telephone cable which is attached to an old M-66 type punch-down block. This may be done using the standard 50-pin RJ-21 connector. From the punch-down block, the wiring distribution is laid out in the same manner as for telephone circuits.

Each of these circuits from the block would typically go to a wall jack. From there, using a standard RJ-45 connector and a telephone wire, a connection is made to the NIC. Out of the 8 pins available on the RJ-45, 2 are used to transmit, 2 are used to receive, and 4 are not used at all. Since each station uses only 4 wires, a 50-wire cable from the hub can support up to 12 stations.

Notice that this topology, a star-wired bus, is drastically different from the topologies of the other types of Ethernet. Yet it still uses the same type of frame and the CSMA/CD access method as used on the other Ethernets. Collisions occur on the bus inside the hub. When a station transmits, the signal arrives at the hub and after it is repeated, it is retransmitted over all the other ports. This is why the hub is also called a multiport repeater.

The hub constantly monitors the stations on each of its branches by sending test signals to them. The branches that respond to this signal are allowed to communicate with the other branches, while those that don't are shut off by the hub. Status lights over each port on the hub indicate which branches are active and which are not. When an older Ethernet adapter that doesn't respond to this link integrity test signal is connected

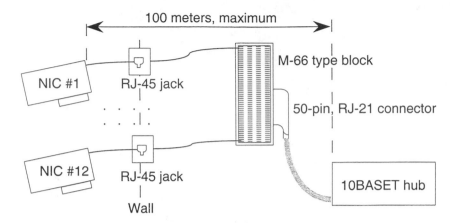

Figure 23.11 As an example, the 10BaseT hub can be connected to a punch-down block using 48 wires of a 50-wire telco cable. From here, connections can be provided for up to 12 network nodes. Each node requires 4 wires.

to a port, its link test can be turned off manually. This allows existing Ethernet segments to be connected to the hub. Typically, the NIC will also have an LED lit to indicate that the link integrity test signal is present. This confirms that the NIC is connected properly to a hub at the other end, but does not confirm that the noise level is acceptable for proper data transfers.

Sometimes with 10Base2, a user may move his workstation by unplugging the T-connector from its back. Because the bus goes through this connector, this operation inadvertently brings down the network. That is because the tap becomes improperly terminated.

On the other hand, with 10BaseT if something does happen to one station or its link, the rest of the network is unaffected. This is because the hub would shut down the defective node since it would fail the link test. This is called partitioning a port. After a hub partitions a defective port, it continues to test this branch to see if it is fixed. When someone does fix the link or its node, the hub notices it due to the continuous testing of the link and will bring that port up automatically.

Jabbering is transmission of excessively long frames. If this occurs over the network, the hub can easily detect which node is doing that and can partition it. This is not as easy on other Ethernets. The hub can also act as a network monitoring device, providing error and collision statistics around the clock for each of its ports. This data can be obtained from a remote location, and easy-to-understand reports can be generated using a software package.

Even though the hub is very attractive in that it provides a means for better management and control of the network, it becomes a crucial element of the network. Care must be taken in selecting and purchasing it, because the reliability of the network becomes very much dependent on it.

First Phase of Expansion: Figure 23.12(a) shows how the standard Ethernet LAN of Figure 23.9 can be expanded to include 10BaseT and Figure 23.12(b) shows the second phase of expanding this network. In Figure 23.12(a), a new LAN with 20 stations is being added to one of the floors and it is connected using an AUI cable to the 10Base5 backbone. First, let us look at the 20-station LAN.

Suppose we have decided to use 12 port hubs for the 10BaseT LAN. Then we would need at least two hubs to accommodate the 20 stations. These two hubs can be cascaded by connecting together a port from each of the two hubs. However, the send pair and the receive pair of these two ports must be crossed, either by using a cable or by flipping a switch on the hub. This would leave us with 22 ports to add stations to.

We have said that the hub acts like a repeater because it retransmits the signal it receives from one port to the rest of the ports. So IEEE specifies that between any two nodes on a network, the signal may go through only 4 hubs. One can easily see that when hubs are connected in series, as in a daisy-chain topology, the number of ports available is much smaller than if they were connected in a tree configuration.

To connect our 20-node 10BaseT LAN to the existing 10Base5 backbone, we simply connect one of the hubs to the backbone. This is done by using an AUI cable from a hub to the transceiver on the backbone.

Second Phase of Expansion: As more new and existing LANs are integrated in the network, concentrators (also called hubs) can be added to every floor. This is shown in Figure 23.12(b) as the second phase of the network expansion project. Here, the old coax backbone is removed and concentrators are interconnected using fiber instead. This is usually installed in redundant pairs routed over different paths.

The chassis of the concentrators are then fitted with the appropriate modules depending on the types of networks existing on each floor. Although the diagram shows all concentrators being configured the same way, they don't have to be. The concentrators allow one to plug and play as requirements change. Lastly, we've added a monitor to perform management functions over the network. As requirements continue to grow, the chassis may be fitted with bridges and routers.

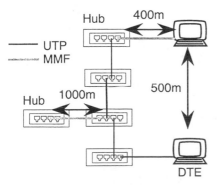

UTP
MMF

Hub 400m
1000m
Hub 500m
DTE

Maximum distances for 10BaseF

23.2.5 10BaseF

In 1987, the FOIRL (Fiber Optic Inter-Repeater Link) was standardized to interconnect Ethernet repeaters using fiber. This helped to increase the distances between repeaters. In 1993, IEEE standardized 10BaseF, which was based on FOIRL. 10BaseF is typically installed using MMF (MultiMode Fiber) with a 62.5/125 μm diameter. As usual, one strand is used to transmit and one is used to receive. The fiber is powered by LEDs and use the ST connectors which were described in Chapter 4.

10BaseF comes in three "flavors" called 10BaseFL, 10BaseFB, and 10BaseFP. Out of these 10BaseFL is the dominant one. With 10BaseFL, the maximum distance between a hub and

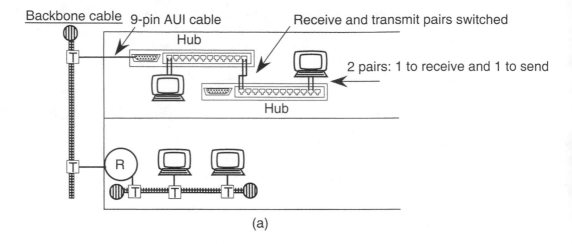

(a)

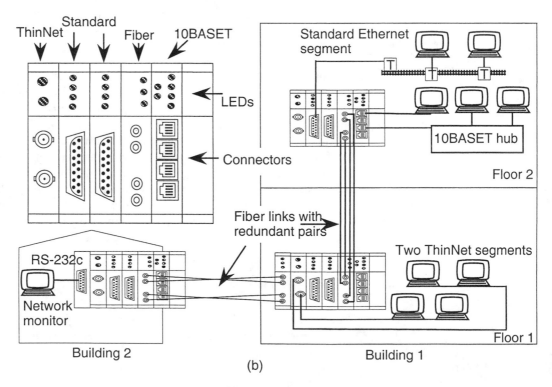

(b)

Figure 23.12 (a) Expanding the network of Figure 23.9 to accommodate up to 22 10BaseT stations. (b) Installing a fiber backbone with concentrators on each floor. An Ethernet concentrator is shown in the inset. Modules of various types of Ethernet can be inserted in the chassis as needed. Typically, fiber is used between floors and buildings. Their transmit and receive pairs are shown to be crossed, since that is necessary.

a NIC is 400 meters, between repeaters it is 1000 meters, and between switches it is 2000 meters. Between two nodes using up to four repeaters and any kind of cable the maximum distance is 500 meters. This is illustrated in the side figure.

23.3 TOKEN-RING NETWORKS

23.3.1 Basic Configuration

TRNs (Token-Ring Networks) use a token passing access method over a ring topology. Just as the hub provides greater management capabilities in 10BaseT networks, TRNs use a wiring concentrator to achieve the same purpose. A wiring concentrator is also called an MAU (Multistation Access Unit). This acronym should not be confused with 10Base5's transceiver which is also called a MAU, which stands for Media Access Unit.

TRN's MAUs typically provide connections for 8 stations as seen in Figure 23.13(a). The figure shows a type 1, data-grade cable. This cable is an STP (Shielded Twisted Pair), since it contains two 22-AWG twisted pairs enclosed in a shield. The shield helps to fend off electromagnetic interference. The connector for this cable is genderless and can be directly connected with another one. The cable is connected to the workstation using a DB9 plug.

Many times, standard telephone UTP (Unshielded Twisted Pair) cabling is also used to connect the workstations with an MAU. This is called type 3 cabling. It uses RJ-45 connectors on both the MAU and the NIC. Because this cable is graded for voice, it has more stringent distance limitations than type 1 cable does.

Physically, the TRN looks like a star, but logically it is a ring. As shown in Figure 23.13(b), when data travels from one node to another, it must first go through the MAU. Therefore, the TRN is called a star-wired ring. Similarly, 10BaseT is called a star-wired bus. The connection from a NIC to the MAU is called a lobe. TRNs operate at either 4 Mbps or 16 Mbps, but to operate at the higher speed, all NICs must be rated for 16 Mbps.

When a station is connected to the MAU and is powered up, it provides a phantom voltage of 5 VDC on the cable. This voltage pulls back a relay at the connector in the MAU, making the node become part of the ring. This is shown for ports 3, 4, and 7 in the figure. If for some reason an NIC from a station can't provide this voltage to the MAU's port, the MAU will keep that node off the ring. This could be because a station is turned off (such as port 1 in the figure), because it is malfunctioning (port 5), or due to a break in the cable.

23.3.2 Extending the Size of the TRN

Figure 23.14(a) shows how a TRN can be easily expanded to more than 8 stations. This is done simply by placing several MAUs in a ring of their own and then connecting the stations to these MAUs. The ring that is created by connecting the MAUs is called the main ring. The MAUs are connected in a ring by placing a cable from one MAU's RI (Ring In) port to another's RO (Ring Out) port. All the MAUs in the main ring may be placed in one rack or they can be placed in different wiring closets. The figure shows the bottom two in one closet and the top one in another.

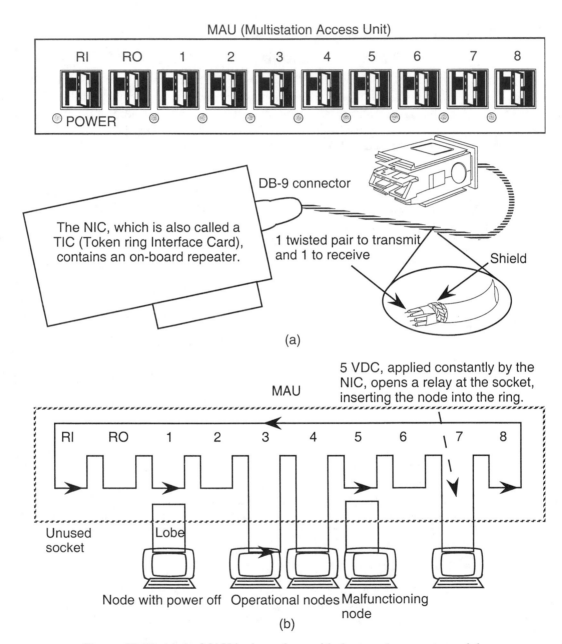

Figure 23.13 (a) An MAU is shown here with the type 1 connector and the STP (Shielded Twisted Pair). (b) The MAU and its stations become a star-wired ring network.

Notice that all nodes now become part of the ring. Each node serves as a repeater; therefore, the maximum length of the lobe for a 4-Mbps network is specified at 300 meters, while for Ethernet, the maximum length of an entire segment is 500 meters. The maximum distance between wiring closets is 200 meters, which can be extended to 730 meters using a pair of repeaters placed at each end of their connecting link. If fiber is used, this range can be extended even further to 3000 meters.

Sometimes only one lobe needs to be extended. In that case, only one repeater is used to increase its range from 300 meters to 610 meters. The maximum number of MAUs and workstations is 33 and 260, respectively. When networks begin to get much larger, they have to be divided into smaller networks which are interconnected using bridges. All the specifications cited above are maximum figures for 4-Mbps networks using type 1 cabling. These limitations become more stringent as the network becomes large, if 16-Mbps speeds are used, or if UTP cabling is used.

Notice in Figure 23.14(a) that as the signal travels from node to node only the outside path is used, and the inside path is not. It is there as a backup. Every station has NAUN (Nearest Active Upstream Neighbor), which is the node from where it receives its signals. In the figure, for example, B is a NAUN to A, since A receives its signal from B.

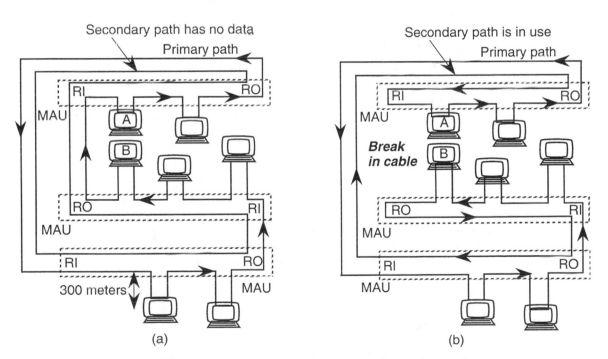

(a)   (b)

Figure 23.14 (a) The two MAUs in the lower portion are in one closet and the top one is in another. They are all interconnected using the RI and RO ports. (b) If one cable between the closets is faulty, then the ring can be restored by utilizing the backup path.

If the cable breaks between the two MAUs, as shown in Figure 23.14(b), a person can remove the connecting cable at both ends and the ring heals itself, using the backup path. On some intelligent MAUs, this healing is done automatically. Here, even if the signal travels through all of the other nodes, B remains as the NAUN for A.

23.3.3 The Active Monitor

When the network is first turned on, the nodes send MAC frames to one another to determine their NAUNs. During this time, they also assign the NIC, typically with the highest address as the active monitor. This special "network overseer" provides synchronization for all the stations. It also buffers up to 24 bits in its shift registers, in order that an entire token, which is 24 bits long, may fit on the ring. This buffering is needed when the ring is too small.

Once the active monitor has been selected, it initializes the ring by purging the ring and generating a new token. This is also done if it doesn't see any activity over the ring at every 10-millisecond interval or if it sees the same high-priority token or frame circulating around the ring more than once. It is able to detect such tokens or frames by setting their monitor bits to 1 every time they come around. The station sending the tokens or frames resets the monitor bit to 0 and if the active monitor notices that this bit is already set, it will restart the ring. Furthermore, the active monitor broadcasts to all nodes that it is still in control, or else a standby monitor will take control of the network.

23.3.4 Signal Encoding

Ethernet uses Manchester encoding to transmit its digital signals. The advantage of this is that it provides a high-to-low or low-to-high level transition with every bit, helping the receiver stay synchronized. Figure 23.15(a) shows this encoding method. A binary 1 is always a low-to-high level transition and binary 0 is just the opposite.

TRNs, on the other hand, use what is called differential Manchester encoding. This requires that a binary 1 start at the same level as the previous bit ended. In other words, at the beginning of a 1, there should not be a level transition and at the beginning of a 0, a transition should occur. See Figure 23.15(b).

Besides providing a method of encoding data bits 1 and 0, TRNs also use two nondata bits called J and K. These bits are differential Manchester code violations, in that they do not have a midpoint level transition. The signal level for J is the same as the previous bit and that for K is not, as seen in Figure 23.15(c).

While we are looking at signal encoding methods, let us look at how FDDI handles it. FDDI uses NRZI (NonReturn to Zero with Invert on 1s) encoding method. Here, both a 0 and a 1 begin at the same level as the end of the previous bit. However, a binary 0 doesn't contain a level transition whereas a binary 1 does. Because of this, FDDI imposes a maximum number of consecutive 0s in its data stream. More on that later.

23.3.5 TRN Frame Format

MAC Frames: The frame for the TRN is more complex than that for Ethernet, as can be seen in Figure 23.16. Yet, it has more features. TRN frames are divided into

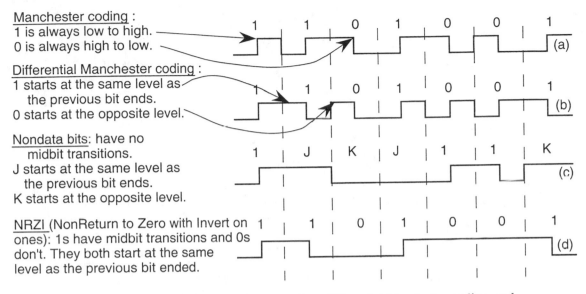

Manchester coding :
1 is always low to high.
0 is always high to low.

Differential Manchester coding :
1 starts at the same level as
    the previous bit ends.
0 starts at the opposite level.

Nondata bits: have no
    midbit transitions.
J starts at the same level as
    the previous bit ends.
K starts at the opposite level.

NRZI (NonReturn to Zero with Invert on
ones): 1s have midbit transitions and 0s
don't. They both start at the same
level as the previous bit ended.

Figure 23.15 Manchester coding, differential Manchester coding, and the non-data bits as used with token-ring networks.

two broad categories called LLC (Logical Link Control) frames and MAC (Medium Access Control) frames. LLC frames are used to send user data and have the same heading as shown back in Figure 23.6. MAC frames, on the other hand, are used to send management and control frames.

The FF (Frame Format) bits in the FC (Frame Control) field indicate whether the frame is an LLC or a MAC frame. The Z bits are used primarily to code various types of MAC frames. For instance, this could be a signal to all the stations to purge the ring or to notify them that the monitor is still present. Beaconing is also coded in here. A beacon MAC frame is sent by a node which hasn't received any signals from its NAUN for a while, maybe because of a break in the cable. When this frame arrives at the NAUN it will take itself off the ring to perform lobe tests. If the tests fail, it will stay off, or else the station that transmitted the beacon will perform self-tests.

The format of the MAC frame is given in Figure 23.16, showing that it has its own header called the LLID (MAC Length ID) followed by a set of fields called subvectors. The reader will be spared from having to learn the details about these fields.

General Frame Formatting: All frames begin with an SD (Starting Delimiter) which is encoded, as shown in Figure 23.16, as "JK0JK000." This field merely marks the beginning of a frame. Similarly, the next-to-last byte is called an ED (Ending Delimiter) and is encoded as "JK1JK1" plus an I (Intermediate frame) bit and an E (Error detected) bit.

The I bit, although rarely used, is set to 1 if more frames are being sent after the present one. Its E bit is set by any node on the ring, if an error is detected as the frame is passing through a node. Hence, error detection is performed on every NIC as the

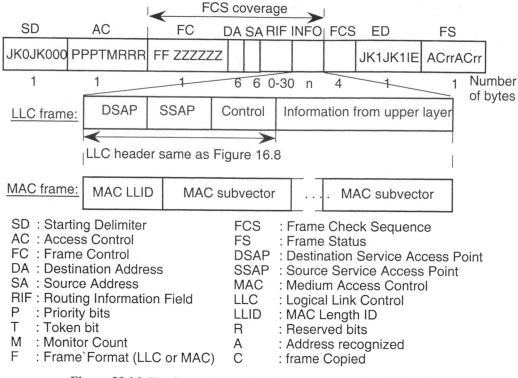

Figure 23.16 The frame format for token-ring networks. If FF = 01, it is an LLC frame, and if FF = 00, it is a MAC frame.

frames traverse around the ring. Each node keeps a record about how often it has set the E bit, making it easy to detect error-prone links.

After the SD field comes the AC (Access Control) field, which contains the M (Monitor count) bit. As we have seen, it is used by the active monitor to detect high-priority frames and tokens which go around the ring more than once. It also contains the token bit which is set to 1 for frames and to 0 for tokens. A token consists of only the SD, AC, and the ED fields, which add up to 24 bits.

Within the AC field, there are also the PPP (Priority) bits and the RRR (Reservation) bits. A token may contain a priority from 0 to 7 and when a token reaches a node that has data to transmit, it will take off the token and transmit the data. It will be allowed to do this only if the priority of the data that is to be transmitted is greater than or equal to the priority given in the token. If this is not the case, the node will set the reservation bits to reserve the token the next time it becomes available, as long as the reservation bits already in the token or frame are not greater than the level of the priority being requested. We will have an example later on to further clarify these fields.

The SA and DA (Source and Destination Address) fields are similar to the address fields of 802.3 Ethernet. However, it is common to interconnect TRNs using source routing bridges. In such cases, the RIF (Routing Information Field) is used to encode the addresses of the bridges. To use the RIF field in a frame, the least significant bit of the SA has to be set to 1. Remember, this is the I/G bit. The RIF contains bridge addresses in the order in which the frame should go in the event the DA is on a different ring than the SA. Source routing is efficient, since the bridges interconnecting the rings don't have to decide on the route. However, the sending node must first investigate the route before it can encode the RIF.

The FCS (Frame Check Sequence) field is used to detect errors. The FS (Frame Status) field contains the C (Copy) and A (Address recognized) bits. These bits are duplicated, since they are not accumulated into the FCS. Both the C and the A bits are set to 0 by the transmitter. The r bits are currently not in use.

The A bits are set by the receiver and the E bit is set by any node except the transmitter. The receiving node acknowledges that it understood that the frame was meant for it by setting the A bits to 1. If the receiver notices that the E bit is 0 and that the FCS checks out, it will copy the data into its buffer and set the C bits to 1.

23.3.6 Example of Operation

Let us next run through Figure 23.17, which illustrates a few concepts of a TRN. We have four stations in the ring, with station 40 being the active monitor. Frames and tokens are moving to the right and then down to the next row. They are shown as they are leaving the respective node and are not shown at all if they remain unchanged. As new concepts are introduced, only the necessary fields are shown, so that they stand out better. The smaller boxes are the tokens (T = 0) and the larger ones are frames (T = 1). Notice that the DA, A, and C fields are not part of the token.

The E, A, and C Bits: At first, node 40 sends a token to node 10. Node 10 doesn't need to transmit, so it sends the token down the ring. Station 20 grabs the token and sends a frame to station 10, setting the E, A, and C bits to 0. The frame goes around the ring until it arrives at 10. Node 10 copies the frame and sets the A and C bits to 1, indicating that it understood the frame was meant for itself and that the frame was copied with no errors. Node 20 then receives this frame back and generates a new token so that others may have a chance to transmit.

At line 3 of the diagram, node 10 then sends a frame to node 30. But while the frame is going through node 20, it detects an error in the FCS field and sets the E bit to 1. So node 30 acknowledges that it understood the frame was meant for it, but indicates an error by leaving the C bit at 0. This frame circulates back to node 10 in line 4, which retransmits that frame. Node 30 gets it error-free and the frame arrives at station 10 at line 5.

The P and R Bits: While this frame was coming back to node 10, node 40 reserved a token to level 2 by setting the R bit to 2. Node 2 now sends a token at P of 2, which prevents other lower-priority stations from grabbing the token before node 40 does. At line 6, node 40 sends its urgent data frame to node 20, which then comes back to node 40, at which time it puts out a token with a priority of 2 at line 7 and node 10 receives this priority token.

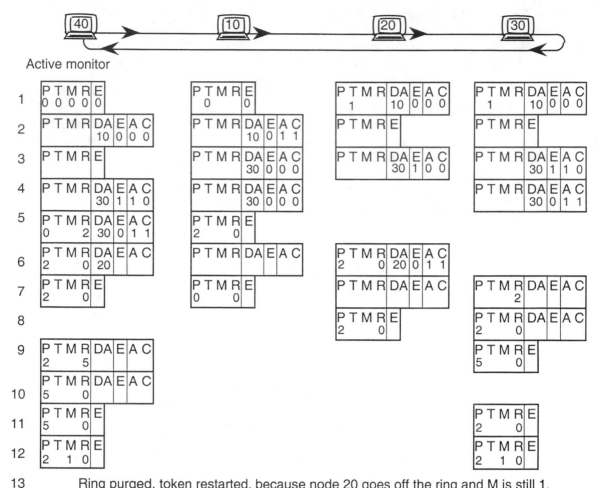

Active monitor

13   Ring purged, token restarted, because node 20 goes off the ring and M is still 1.

Figure 23.17 Frames (larger size) and tokens (smaller size) are shown to be circulating to the right around the ring. If they are not being changed by a node, then they are not drawn here. Also, only the values necessary to understand the concept being explained are shown to keep the figure from being cluttered with unnecessary information.

The station that raises the priority of a token must bring the priority down to the previous level again. So node 10, upon receiving this priority token, sends out a token with the original priority of 0. Node 20 then transmits a frame while node 30 reserves a token for a priority of 2 at the end of line 7.

Bumping Up the Priority Further: At line 8, node 20 sends a token at a P of 2, because it received an R of 2. This allows node 30 to transmit at the higher priority. While node 30 is sending data, node 40 reserves a token for a level of 5 (start of line 9). Node 30 issues a token at a P of 5, which allows node 40 to transmit a frame

544   LANs: Additional Concepts

at P = 5. At line 11, node 40 issues a token with P = 5, which node 30 receives. Node 30 remembers that it raised the priority from 2 to 5, so it now lowers the priority to 2. Eventually, the token of level 2 would arrive at node 20, which should lower the priority to 0, but node 20 shuts itself off.

The M Bit: The active monitor in line 12 sets the M bit to 1 for this priority token, and since node 20 isn't around to lower the priority, this token comes back to the active monitor. It sees that the M bit is still 1 at line 13, purges the ring, and reinitializes the ring.

23.4 FDDI

23.4.1 A Layer-Based Standard

FDDI (Fiber Distributed Data Interface) is a high-capacity LAN standard initially defined by ANSI's X3T9.5 Task Group. This standard operates at 100 Mbps which complements and coexists with Ethernet and other LAN standards. Although copper-based technologies that use FDDI concepts are also being defined, we will concentrate only on the fiber-based standards.

Figure 23.18 shows how FDDI fits neatly in IEEE's 802 family of standards. At the lowest level, PMD (Physical Medium Dependent) is responsible for cables, connectors, and their related equipment.

The PHY (PHYsical layer protocol) defines clocking, encoding, generating signals called symbols, and other functions. Together the PMD and the PHY layers comprise OSI's first layer. Above the PHY is the MAC (Media Access Control) layer responsible for ring initialization, token handling, framing, and addressing. Finally, serving all of the above mentioned layers, the SMT (Station ManagemenT) standard provides managing and monitoring of connections and the ring. SMT is further broken down into components as shown in Figure 23.18.

23.4.2 The PMD Layer

There are four types of PMDs. The first one is called simply PMD and it uses LEDs over a multimode fiber. SMF-PMD uses single-mode fiber and lasers. LCF-PMD

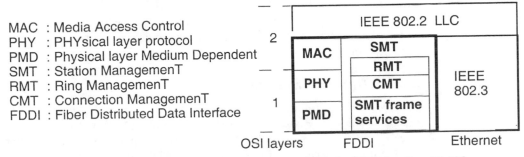

MAC : Media Access Control
PHY : PHYsical layer protocol
PMD : Physical layer Medium Dependent
SMT : Station ManagemenT
RMT : Ring ManagemenT
CMT : Connection ManagemenT
FDDI : Fiber Distributed Data Interface

Figure 23.18 FDDI standards fit nicely within the IEEE family of LAN standards.

uses LEDs over a low-cost multimode fiber, and lastly, TP-PMD standardizes STP and some categories of UTP.

FDDI uses two counterrotating rings, which help it to provide high reliability. The devices that attach to both rings are called dual-attached devices and the ones that attach to only the primary ring are called single-attached devices. Furthermore, devices that allow other devices to attach to the primary ring are called concentrators, while those, such as hosts, which are actually using the network are called stations. By making combinations of these categories, FDDI devices are defined as SAS (Single-Attached Station), DAS (Dual-Attached Station), SAC (Single-Attached Concentrator), and DAC (Dual-Attached Concentrator). For example, a DAS is attached to both rings and doesn't provide direct FDDI ring connections to other devices, while an SAC is attached only to the primary ring of FDDI and does provide ring connections to other devices.

Figure 23.19 shows a dual ring of trees configuration of an FDDI network. Notice that the dual-attached devices are part of both rings, except for the DAS in building 1, which is being used as a SAS. Stations, either SASs or DASs, don't provide ports for other devices to attach, whereas concentrators do, both single- and dual-attached.

Just as in TRNs, if a cable connecting two MAUs breaks, the ring can heal itself. FDDI allows the rings to wrap around, if necessary. It is also possible to install an optical bypass relay at the fiber and device connection. If the device fails, the ring is still intact, because the optical signal would then bypass that device. Because the signal does not get regenerated through a relay, however, the new distance between the neighboring stations may exceed the maximum allowable limit.

Because dual-attached devices are connected to both rings, they are not usually turned off. Turning such a device off would force the rings to wrap around, and turning two such devices off could bring down the network. A dual-attached adapter in a server, bridge, or a router can provide the device with a hot-link to a concentrator and a standby link to a different concentrator, so if one concentrator goes down, the standby link would become connected. This feature is called dual-homing.

An MIC (Media Interface Connector) is used to connect multimode fiber with a station or a concentrator. There are four kinds of these connectors and they are shown in Figure 23.19. They are keyed in such a way that the network can't be configured improperly.

MIC A (or port A) is used to connect the primary ring in ports and the secondary ring out ports of a DAS or a DAC. Locate an MIC of type A in the figure and note that. Port B (or MIC B) complements it. Port M connects a concentrator to another concentrator or a station over the primary ring only. Port S connects a SAS to a concentrator.

23.4.3 The PHY Standard

With FDDI running at high speeds, it is necessary to keep the clocks synchronized. As shown in Figure 23.15, FDDI uses NRZI (NonReturn to Zero with Invert on ones) encoding. This encoding provides level transitions for only binary 1s. Level transitions are necessary for clocks to stay in sync. To keep the receiver's clock synchronized and happy, FDDI doesn't allow more than three consecutive 0s when

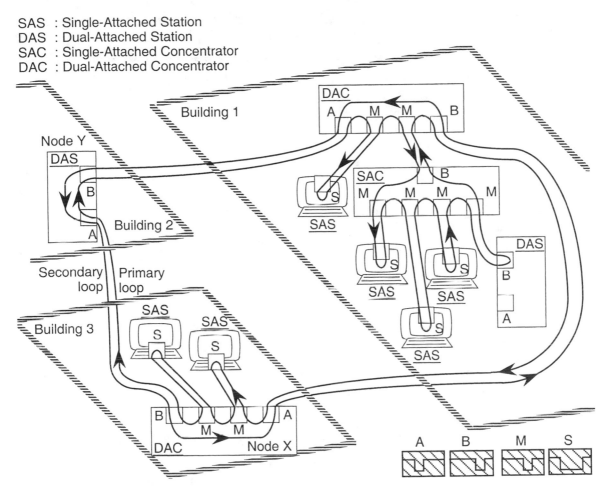

SAS : Single-Attached Station
DAS : Dual-Attached Station
SAC : Single-Attached Concentrator
DAC : Dual-Attached Concentrator

Figure 23.19 FDDI's secondary ring doesn't go through single-attached devices. A DAS could be a minicomputer. Below the diagram, the four types of MICs (Media Interface Connectors) are depicted. The SAC and its stations could be in another building next to building 1.

transmitting information. To ensure that this rule is satisfied, the PHY standard converts every group of 4 data bits (called a symbol) into a 5-bit code group which contains at least two ones. This is called the 4B/5B method of character encoding.

For example, when a data symbol of "0000" is transmitted, it is first converted to a "11110" code group. Table 23.1 shows how 4-bit groups of data are converted into 5-bit code groups. Notice that there are never more than 3 consecutive 0s for any pair of valid symbols. Codes that generate more than 3 consecutive zeros are not implemented and are invalid. Now that we are throwing in extra 1s to help keep the receiver in sync, we must increase the clock speed of FDDI devices to 125 Mbps so that data can be sent at 100 Mbps.

Table 23.1 Code Group Assignments for Symbols							
Code Group	Symbol	Code Group	Symbol	Code Group	Symbol	Code Group	Symbol
00000	Q(Quiet)	01000	invalid	10000	invalid	11000	J
00001	invalid	01001	1(0001)	10001	K	11001	S(set)
00010	invalid	01010	4(0100)	10010	8(1000)	11010	C(1100)
00011	invalid	01011	5(0101)	10011	9(1001)	11011	D(1101)
00100	H(Halt)	01100	invalid	10100	2(0010)	11100	E(1110)
00101	invalid	01101	T	10101	3(0011)	11101	F(1111)
00110	invalid	01110	6(0110)	10110	A(1010)	11110	0(0000)
00111	R(reset)	01111	7(0111)	10111	B(1011)	11111	I(Idle)

Doing this 4-bit to 5-bit conversion not only helps the clocks stay in sync, but also provides 8 extra valid combinations that are used to send control signals between devices. They are J, K, T, R, S, Q, I, and H. For example, if a station receives more than 15 consecutive Q symbols, it assumes that the connection is dead, or if it receives 8 pairs of HQ symbols, that a device is being initialized, etc.

23.4.4 The MAC Layer

Frame Format: FDDI defines a frame format, as shown in Figure 23.20, that is similar to IEEE's 802.5. The maximum length of a frame is 4500 bytes. It begins with a PA (PreAmble) field, which contains 16 consecutive I symbols. This steady stream of 1s gets the receiver in sync quickly. The J and K symbols follow the PA field.

The FC (Frame Control) field contains 8 bits as shown, the first of which is a class bit indicating whether the class of service is synchronous or asynchronous. An asynchronous class of service means that the data is not delay-sensitive, as the transmission of voice would be. In synchronous transmission of services, a station is guaranteed a prespecified fraction of the 100 Mbps of bandwidth for delay-sensitive applications.

The L or the address length bit indicates either a 6-byte or a 2-byte address field. Typically, the address is 6 bytes long. The FF and ZZZZ bits define tokens, SMT, MAC, or LLC frames. SMT frames are used for such functions as passing station addresses and port statuses to create the topology (or the map) of the physical ring. SMT and MAC frames do not cross over bridges and routers to other LANs as LLC frames may.

The ED field contains two T symbols for tokens and one for frames. Finally, the frame status may use R and S symbols to code control indicators. These are the E (Error detected), A (Address recognition), and C (frame Copied) control indicators.

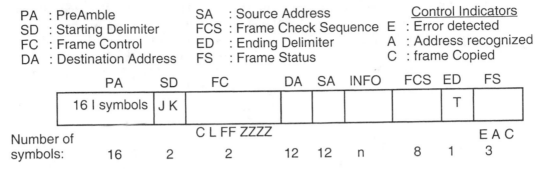

Figure 23.20 FDDI frame format. The token contains only PA, SD, FC, and ED fields, with ED containing two T symbols.

Ring Initialization: Before a ring can be initialized, the SMT components exchange information on port types and addresses over all links between adjacent nodes. Then they run link confidence tests which determine their links' qualities. Once these operations are performed all stations join the ring one by one. This procedure is called establishing a connection with adjacent neighbors and is primarily a function of SMT.

Once this connection is established for all stations on the ring, then the stations bid to determine who is going to send the first token. This is called ring initializing and it is done by a procedure called the claiming process.

Here, all stations issue claim frames giving their SAs and TTRT values. TTRT (Target Token Rotation Time) is equal to one-half the time it takes for a token to arrive back at a station once it has been released. Unlike an auction, where the highest bidder wins, here the station with the lowest value of TTRT wins the right to send the first token.

At first, many claim frames from all stations flood the ring simultaneously. During this time, if a station receives a claim frame whose TTRT is lower than its own, it will pass that claim frame through and stop sending its own claim frames. Eventually, only one station's claim frame makes it all the way around the ring, at which time the winning station issues a token. While this first token goes around the ring, each station copies the TTRT value in its own buffer. On the second pass of the token, stations may send synchronous data and thereafter may send asynchronous data.

Steady-State Operation: FDDI uses the timed-token protocol which differs from 4-Mbps TRN protocol, in that in a 4-Mbps TRN only one frame can exist on the ring at a time. Also, the token is not released until the station transmitting a frame gets it back. However, in FDDI, a station is only allowed to hold on to the token a certain amount of time determined by the THT (Token Holding Timer). So even if a station isn't finished transmitting, it must stop transmitting and release the token for the next user. Notice that the token is released as soon as the frame is sent and doesn't wait until the frame comes back around the ring. This is known as early token release, which allows many frames to exist on the ring at one time. 16-Mbps TRN allows multiple frames to exist on the ring at one time, but both types of TRNs send only one frame per token access, whereas FDDI may send multiple 4500-byte frames per access.

Unlike IEEE's 802.5, where an active monitor maintains the ring, in FDDI this function is distributed and all stations are responsible for ring maintenance. Each station maintains a TVX (Valid Xmission Timer). The "X" is short for "trans" TVX is used to determine if no transmission is occurring on a link. If this timer exceeds, because of noise or a loss of token, it will first start the claim process. Let us go through the steps that node X, an uplink station, and node Y, a downlink station, may take if the link connecting them degrades for some reason. Figure 23.19 shows nodes X and Y.

First Y's TVX will exceed, because it didn't receive any information from X. It will start sending claim frames. Because X can't forward these frames to Y, due to a bad cable, the claim process fails and no token is generated. Now X begins the beacon process. Just as a beacon from a lighthouse warns ships of danger, a beacon frame notifies all nodes that the ring may be broken.

Again, X can't forward the beacon frames to Y. After about 10 seconds, a directed beacon is sent informing the nodes that the beacon is stuck. If this fails, then a trace function is initiated using PHY signaling or line states. The trace message is sent over the secondary ring from Y to X, which forces them to perform self-tests. If the tests are successful, then the nodes will join the ring, or else the ring will wrap itself around, healing itself.

23.5 ETHERNET ABOVE 10MBPS

23.5.1 Introduction

For the rest of the chapter, we continue our discussion from where we left off in Chapter 7. There we have already seen how switches operate and mentioned the advantages of Fast Ethernet and Gigabit Ethernet LANs. Here, we will look at the various standards and provide more details. Figure 23.21 shows some of the Ethernet standards and when they were finalized.

Figure 23.22 shows the motivation for increasing the speed of Ethernet above 10 Mbps. In Figure (a) a simple hub connects a server and other nodes using all 10-Mbps links. This proves to be inefficient, so as a first step, a 100-Mbps NIC is installed in the server and the 10BaseT hub is replaced by a 10/100 Mbps hub. This is seen in Figure (b). This type of hub provides connections at either speed. Since the server can communicate at a higher speed than the rest of the network, it can handle the demand placed on it.

In Figure (c), congestion between two hubs is relieved by adding a 100-Mbps link. Two or more such links can also be added between the same pair of hubs to provide further relief.

In Figure (d), the network has expanded. Many end stations are still running at 10 Mbps, but others, like the CAD/CAM workstations and the servers have been upgraded to run at 100 Mbps. This has now created bottlenecks at the 100-Mbps links.

Figures (e) and (f) show two solutions to this problem. A switch can be added or a Gigabit Ethernet hub can be added to remove the bottlenecks that were experienced at lower rates in the earlier generation of Ethernets.

23.5.2 The Ethernet PHYs

What determines that all the various types of Ethernet can still be called Ethernet? It is the definition of the MAC layer protocol. The MAC layer protocol is common to all the various types of Ethernet, regardless of their speed, the connectors used, or the kind of cable used. In Figure 23.23(a), we see the components of 10-Mbps Ethernet as defined by the standards. The physical medium is the cable that is used. This could be the thick coax used in 10Base5, or the thin coax used in 10Base2, or the UTP used in 10BaseT. The MDI (Medium-Dependent Interface) represents the corresponding connector used with each of these cable types, whether they be a DB15, BNC, or an RJ-45 connector. In 10Base5, the MAU represents the transceiver that is attached to the coax and the AUI (Attachment Unit Interface) represents the drop cable from the transceiver down to the NIC.

With 10Base2, the MAU is built right into the NIC so the AUI interface only becomes an electronic specification onboard the NIC. No AUI cable exists. The MDI here is a BNC connector. Nonetheless, the frames received by the MAC layer in the NIC are the same as with the 10Base5 setup. For 10BaseT, the physical medium is a UTP cable, the MDI is the RJ-45, and again, the MAU and the AUI are onboard the NIC.

With Fast Ethernet, IEEE defines the PHY component. This, you may recall, is the PHY from FDDI. In fact, the development that was accomplished with FDDI has been reused to arrive at the Fast Ethernet standards quickly. The PHY component is shown in Figure 23.23(b). Here, the MDI is still the connector, but a new interface called MII (Media Independent Interface) has been defined instead of the AUI which is used with 10-Mbps Ethernet. Regardless of the type of connector and the media used with Fast Ethernet, the MII specifications ensure that signals arriving at the MAC layer (and being received from the MAC) are consistent.

The PHY is located on each NIC and on each hub or repeater port. For a given media it uses the same electronics. The PHY converts the electrical or the optical signal to the proper electrical signal specific to the MII. With Gigabit Ethernet, the MII is redefined as the GMII (Gigabit MII).

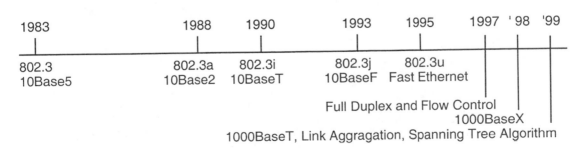

Figure 23.21 The timeline of IEEE standards for Ethernet.

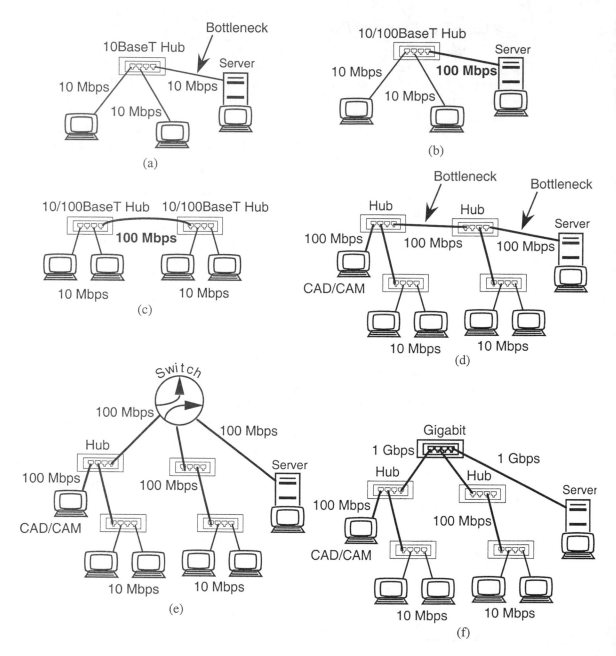

Figure 23.22 (a) A server shared by many nodes becomes a bottleneck. (b) Adding a 100-Mbps link to the server increases performance. (c) Interrepeater links replaced with 100-Mbps links. (d) A tree topology with Fast Ethernet links at the top and standard Ethernet links toward the bottom proves reasonable, but congestion starts to build. (e) A switch or a Gigabit hub (f) solves the problem.

LANs: Additional Concepts

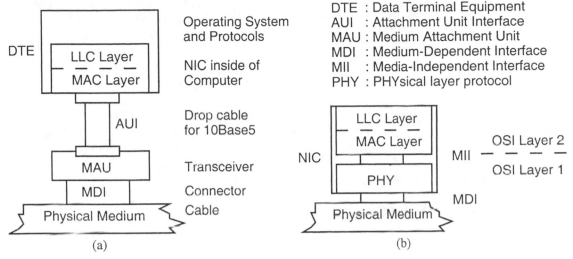

Figure 23.23 (a) IEEE terminology for 10-Mbps Ethernet and (b) for Fast Ethernet.

23.5.3 Full-duplex Operation

With 10Base5 and 10Base2, only half-duplex operation was possible. This was because all the nodes connected to the common cable had to share that cable in order to transmit data. In those environments only one transmission could take place. If one node was transmitting, then no other node could successfully transmit. Hence, a node could not transmit and receive at the same time.

When 10BaseT was introduced as a solution it was noticed that its media was full-duplex capable. The UTP cabling with which it was installed used one pair of wires to transmit and another pair of wires to receive using the hub. By providing separate pairs for the transmission and reception of data, the cable became full-duplex. Now, the only thing left to do was to design full-duplex NICs and hubs.

Actually, full-duplex capability originated with the introduction of switches because unlike hubs, switches provide buffering of frames. In the side figure, the server is busy serving all its clients. By providing it with a full-duplex connection, the congestion is reduced. If all the links shown are running at 10 Mbps, there is a dedicated 20-Mbps capacity between the server and switch. The switch provides buffering on each of its ports, making the switch like a traffic cop at a busy intersection. If any buffers become full, the switch cannot accept any more frames.

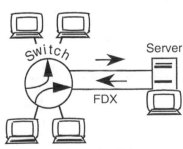

A full–duplex link

From this diagram it becomes clear that to have a full-duplex connection, there must be only two nodes on the link. If there were a third node on such a link, the nodes could not tell if a particular pair is busy is or not. Each pair of pins on a full-duplex cable can only either transmit or receive. The CSMA/CD mechanism is not needed

LANs: Additional Concepts

553

anymore. This means that there is no need for a NIC to listen to the media before it transmits. Also, when used with fiber links, longer lengths between devices are possible. Full-duplex links are also common between two switches.

Full-duplex repeaters have been introduced with Gigabit Ethernet. These devices are also known as *buffered distributors*. Typically a multiport repeater or a hub will retransmit a received signal on all the other ports, but this repeater will receive the entire frame, do an error check, place it in its buffer if necessary, and then retransmit the frame to all the other ports. A switch, on the other hand, will retransmit the frame to only the port to which the destination node is connected. All ports of this device operate at full-duplex and run at 1 Gbps. They have both input and output buffers. The backplane of this device is 1 Gbps so it can only repeat one frame at a time unlike a switch which may manage several connections simultaneously.

23.5.4 Flow Control

In the previous side diagram we saw how a full-duplex link between the switch and the server provided a dedicated 20-Mbps bandwidth between them. In that figure, as more frames are sent to the server from the other nodes, the switch can buffer them and forward them to the server at a rate at which it can receive them. What happens when the buffers of the switch become full? How can the switch tell the other nodes to stop sending frames momentarily? The method in which this is handled is called *flow control*.

With half-duplex Ethernet, that is done simply. If a switch doesn't want to receive any frames from a particular port, it will transmit a frame on that link causing a collision on purpose. The frame contains no real data and its only purpose is to cause the transmitter to back off from sending data. With a full-duplex link, no collisions are possible because CSMA/CD is not existent.

Figure 23.24 shows how the switch forces a collision on a half-duplex link. It also shows how flow control is handled on a full-duplex link. On a full-duplex link, the switch can send special PAUSE frames to the server causing it to refrain from transmitting. The PAUSE times given in these frames tell the server how long to pause.

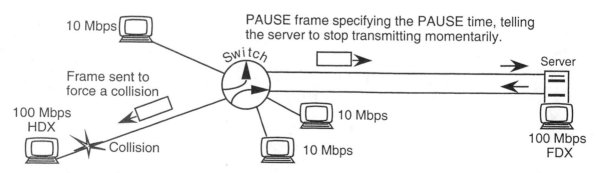

Figure 23.24 The switch creates a collision on a half-duplex link and sends a PAUSE frame on a full-duplex link to slow down the data transfer of the other nodes.

LANs: Additional Concepts

All full-duplex links provide this capability and it is specified by the IEEE 802.3x standard. Notice that the switch in the figure can support ports at various speeds.

23.5.5 Autonegotiation

With all the options that are available with Ethernet, such as, its wire speed (whether it is 10 Mbps, 100 Mbps, or 1 Gbps), full-duplex or half-duplex, and other features which are constantly being added, it becomes necessary for one end of a link to find out what the other end is capable of handling. With 10BaseT, all that existed was the link integrity test which indicated whether the other end of the link was properly connected or not. With newer standards being added to Ethernet, each port also needs to know which capabilities can be supported by the port on the other end of the link. This is called *autonegotiation* and was first specified in the Fast Ethernet standards.

Autonegotiation allows to operate a UTP link using RJ-45 connectors at the highest speed and at full-duplex operation, if possible. If fiber is used, then a decision is made only between half-duplex and full-duplex modes of operation. Fiber ports at present cannot operate at multiple speeds, but copper ports can.

Full-duplex has a higher priority than half-duplex. 1 Gbps has a higher priority than 100 Mbps, which has a higher priority than 10 Mbps. This allows the link to operate at its best capacity. 10BaseT used NLPs (Normal Link Pulses) which we called the link integrity test. This signal allowed each end to verify a proper connection at the other end. Fast Ethernet devices instead transmit FLPs (Fast Link Pulses) continuously. This includes NICs, repeaters, and switches.

This way, for instance, if a 10/100 switch is connected to many 10-Mbps NICs, then those NICs could be replaced by 100-Mbps NICs incrementally as funds become available. If a switch port doesn't get an FLP from a NIC but only an NLP, then it operates at 10 Mbps using half-duplex mode. FLPs are more complex signals than NLPs, indicating the speed and mode of transmission.

Also, on the other hand, if all new NICs bought during the last year or so were both 10 and 100 Mbps-capable, then an old 10-Mbps hub can be replaced by a higher-speed hub or repeater. This type of update can be easily done in a network without having to configure any equipment. The FLPs used in autonegotiation adjust each link to its optimum state automatically.

23.5.6 Link Aggregation

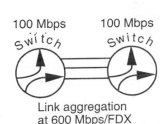

100 Mbps 100 Mbps

Link aggregation at 600 Mbps/FDX

Suppose that two 100-Mbps switches connected together by a single link are running at full capacity. However, the link between them causes a bottleneck. One solution would be to insert a 1-Gbps switch between them, but that might be too costly. By interconnecting multiple ports between the switches, we can relieve some of the congestion and not have to purchase additional equipment. This is shown in the side figure. Three full-duplex ports provide a "fat pipe" of 600 Mbps.

IEEE 802.3ad specifies a standard on how this is accomplished. Theoretically, the standard allows two switches made by different vendors to be linked this way. In a later chapter on interconnecting LANS, the spanning tree algorithm (IEEE 802.1d) used between bridges or switches is described. This algorithm allows for multiple links but allows only one link to be active at any time. The other links are used only for redundancy. The 802.3ad link aggregation standard overcomes this limitation of 802.1d.

23.6 FAST ETHERNET

23.6.1 Fast Ethernet Types

Now that we have seen the various features and advantages that Fast and Gigabit Ethernets provide, let us consider those standards in more detail. There are actually four Fast Ethernet standards that are ratified. However, only two of them have any significance in the marketplace. These are the two pairs over Cat-5 and fiber versions. The two standards that can exist on two-pair and four-pair of Cat-3 cabling are virtually nonexistent. They are called 100BaseT2 and 100BaseT4, respectively. The more common variants of 100BaseT are called 100BaseTX and 100BaseFX. Typically, 100BaseTX is used for horizontal cabling and 100BaseFx is used for vertical and backbone cabling.

100BaseT: 100BaseTX is usually referred as 100BaseT. This version of Fast Ethernet is typically installed using Cat-5 UTP cabling, although it can be installed using the newer grades of UTP cablings, such as Cat-5 enhanced, Cat-6, and up. Type 1 STP can also be used. Cat-5, if properly installed, provides four pairs able to accommodate rates of up to 100 Mbps.

There are many similarities between 10BaseT and 100BaseT. Out of the four pairs available, only two pairs are used, one to receive and one to transmit. They both use the same RJ-45 connector. They both use a star-wired bus topology and use CSMA/CD to gain access of the network. The distance from the hub to the NIC is also 100 meters as with 10BaseT.

100BaseT also shares many characteristics with FDDI, or more appropriately with CDDI, the copper version of FDDI. First, the speed of 100 Mbps is the same for both. We have already seen how IEEE doesn't use the AUI of 10BaseT to define the physical interface to the MAC layer but the MII. Similarly, the MAU no longer exists but is replaced by the PHY. Other accomplishments copied from CDDI include the MLT-3 (Multilevel Threshold-3) method of line signaling and the 4B/5B method of character encoding which we studied in the section on FDDI of this chapter.

We saw that FDDI uses the NRZI method of line signaling. However, CDDI requires a more bandwidth efficient method of line signaling called MLT-3. This method is possible on twisted pair because it uses three voltage levels, but is not possible on fiber which can only have two optical states: either on or off. MLT-3 is needed on copper for the higher speeds, which is more susceptible to noise. You may remember that the operating frequency of FDDI is actually 125 Mbaud giving it an effective rate of 100 Mpbs. If MLT-3 were not used with 100BaseT, then its operating frequency would have to have been 200 Mbaud to give a speed of 100 Mbps at a range of 100 meters. Instead with MLT-3, the operating frequency is only 125 MHz.

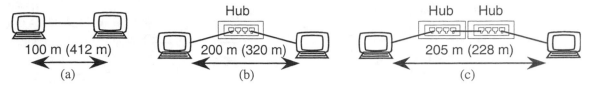

Figure 23.25 Maximum distances are shown for 100BaseT. For 100BaseF, they are shown in parentheses. (a) Between two DTEs. (b) With one hub or repeater. (c) With two hubs.

100BaseF: This fiber version of 100BaseX was also copied and modified from FDDI. 100BaseF uses MMF (MultiMode fiber) with 62.5/125 µm core to cladding diameters. However, SMF (SingleMode Fiber) is also used to extend the range of the cable runs. One strand is used to transmit and another to receive. Originally, the ST connectors were popular but now the SC connectors are becoming more popular.

23.6.2 Expanding the Size of 100BaseX

Originally with 100BaseX, there were two classes of repeaters defined. Class I repeaters never took off because they allowed only one repeater to exist in a collision domain. Class II allows for a maximum of two repeaters, so all further discussion will be based only on Class II repeaters.

Figure 25.25 shows the maximum distances possible using UTP and fiber. The fiber values are shown in parentheses. With UTP, the maximum distance between two DTEs (Data Terminal Equipments) is 100 meters, as seen in Figure 25.25(a). In Figure 25.25(b), a repeater is added, extending the range of the network to 200 meters. Adding two repeaters extends it to 205 meters as seen in Figure (c). Notice that going from a one-repeater network to a two-repeater network increases the range slightly using UTP. However, using fiber, the range decreases by almost 100 meters. Running MMF in a full-duplex mode gives a range of 2 km and running SMF in full-duplex gives a range of 10 km from DTE to DTE.

Figure 23.26 illustrates how a two-repeater network can be increased in size. Figure (a) shows the original network which cannot have more than two repeaters. Figure (b) shows that these hubs can be stacked, making each stack appear as a single hub. The number of hubs that can be stacked depends on its make and model. However, four is a typical number.

Figure 23.26(c) shows that the range of 200 meters (using UTP) can be extended another 200 meters by throwing in a switch (or a bridge). If full-duplex fiber link is added, then a range of 2 km and more is possible.

23.7 GIGABIT ETHERNET

Gigabit was developed from the work that was already done on ANSI's X3T11 standard called the Fibre Channel standard. Fibre Channel runs at 1 Gbaud providing an effective rate of 800 Mbps. The rate of Gigabit Ethernet was increased to 1.25 Gbaud, giving it a data transfer rate of 1 Gbps. The same symbol encoding method used

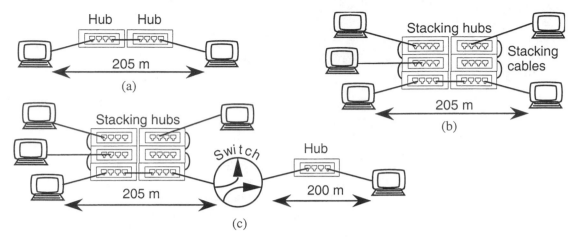

Figure 23.26 (a) A network with two repeaters has seemed to reach its maximum size. (b) At this point, however, more hubs could be stacked, (c) or a switch could be added.

with Fibre Channel, called the 8B/10B method, is used again with Gigabit Ethernet. They both use the GMII (Gigabit Media-Independent Interface) which allows engineers to easily reuse the PHY chips designed for Fibre Channel.

In defining the different types of Ethernet, a parameter called the slot time is specified. The slot time is the minimum amount of time that a NIC may transmit a frame. If Ethernet frames are too small, collisions may go undetected. For that reason, if the frame size is below a certain amount, extra PAD characters are added. You may want to refer back to Figure 23.7 to recall that the minimum Ethernet frame size is 64 bytes, not including the Preamble. The 64 bytes correspond to a slot time of 512 bits or, using the correct unit of measure, 512 bit-times.

When Fast Ethernet was introduced, the speed on the wire was increased tenfold. This meant that small frames could go undetected by other NICs on a large-sized network. Instead of increasing the size of the bit-times, it was decided to reduce the diameter of the network. Hence, we are allowed a maximum of only two repeaters on Fast Ethernet. Reducing the diameter of the network further for Gigabit Ethernet would make the maximum distance between a hub and a NIC 10 meters or less. Hence, for Gigabit Ethernet, the slot time was increased by a factor of 8, or 4096 bit-times. The size of the Ethernet frame remains the same here. Extra carrier extension bits are added at the end of small frames, however, to make known the existence of a frame on the cable.

There are three practical versions of Gigabit Ethernet and they are called 1000BaseSX, 1000BaseLX, and 1000BaseT. The "SX" stands for short wavelength, the "LX" stands for long wavelength, and the familiar "T" stands for twisted pair. 1000BaseSX uses only MMF and short-wavelength (850 nm) optical diodes. Depending on the type of fiber that is used, 1000BaseSX allows runs of up to 550 meters. A slightly costlier version, called 1000BaseLX, uses either MMF or SMF and uses 1300 nm lasers for signal generation. Using SMF (10/125 μm), this version can extend the LAN to ranges of up to 5 km.

To achieve the rate of 1 Gbps over Cat-5, a few technical marvels had to take place. The maximum distance from the hub to the node is still 100 meters. Remember that Cat-5 was originally rated for 100 Mbps, and even at that time, 100 Mbps over UTP seemed impossible. What they have done with 1000BaseT is to use all four pairs to transmit and all four pairs to receive. Echo cancellation, covered in Chapter 3, allows transmission and reception on the same pairs. With earlier Ethernets, it was always one pair to receive and one pair to transmit. The mode of transmission of transmitting and receiving on the same pair simultaneously is called *dual-duplex*. Now each pair is transmitting at 250 kbps and receiving at 250 kbps. 1000BaseT uses a five-level PAM (Pulse Amplitude Modulation) coding system. Each pulse represents two bits (00, 01, 10, and 11). Additionally, FEC (Forward Error Correction) is used to reduce the amount of errors that are possible on twisted pairs. These are the primary reasons why engineers were able to run 1 Gbps on Category 5 cabling.

23.8 VLANs

Figure 23.27(a) shows that every transmission made on one segment of a LAN is repeated over the other segments if only hubs/repeaters are used to interconnect them. Many LAN protocols, except for TCP/IP, generate a lot of broadcast frames over a LAN to either find out who is on the network or tell others on the network that they are still up. This type of overhead traffic is called broadcasting. Segments which are connected by only hubs also repeat all broadcast traffic. The primary method of containing collisions within one segment is to introduce a switch. This is seen in Figure 23.27(b). If we had introduced a router instead of a switch, then we would also have contained broadcasts within one part of the LAN.

VLANs (or Virtual LANs) allow us to define our broadcast domains and our collision domains regardless of where the nodes are physically located. Instead of tying employees to certain locations in a building or a campus setting, with VLAN, they are free to be part of any logical segment (or as we'll see, any subnet). The physical location of employees does not force them to belong to certain organizational groups. If an employee changes departments, he doesn't have to move. That move can be programmed in by a LAN manager on a VLAN-capable switch.

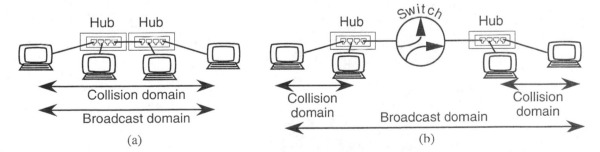

Figure 23.27 (a) A collision or a broadcast made over one hub is transmitted to other hubs. (b) A switch will divide up the collision domains, but not the broadcast domain. Only a router can break up a broadcast domain.

IEEE has defined a VLAN standard as 802.1Q and it uses a 4-byte frame tag to identify each frame. The tag field primarily specifies the VLAN ID and the user priority of the frame. Because the tag field takes up four bytes (which come between the source address and the Type/Length field), the length of the Ethernet frame was increased by another 4 bytes and this is specified by the IEEE 802.3ac standard.

Membership to VLAN groups can be identified either implicitly or explicitly. Implicit membership is derived from the MAC address, Type field, or IP address that is already in the Ethernet frame. Explicit membership is specified by the identification in the tag field. So that the switches know exactly which frames belong to which VLANs and that no duplication IDs exist, all VLAN IDs should be assigned from one management location.

EXERCISES

Section 23.1:
1. What software component in a PC is directly responsible for sending data to the network?
   a. NetBIOS   b. BIOS
   c. DOS   d. application
2. Which of the following terms is NOT associated with a server-based NOS?
   a. client-server based NOS   b. centralized NOS
   c. peer NOS   d. NetWare
3. Which of the following protocol stacks is most closely related to Unix?
   a. NetWare   b. Vines
   c. AppleTalk   d. DOS
4. State the difference between the BIOS and the CMOS.
5. In a peer-to-peer network, describe the difference between sharing and using. What function does a server provide?
6. In Figure 23.4(b), we see an error message. How could this message have been avoided by the person operating host23? By the person operating host2 and still be saving the testfile?
7. Describe the steps to the best of your ability for how host23 could print on host2's printer?
8. Can any of the LAN protocols be used with any of the communications protocols shown in Figure 23.5?
9. Which two layers of IEEE 802 family of protocols make up the OSI's data link layer?
10. Is the MAC header the same for all types of LANs or is the LLC header the same?
11. Which header specifies the node to which the frame is addressed?
12. Which header specifies the network layer protocol of the frame? Which field specifies this information?

Section 23.2:
13. Which field name isn't used in both types of Ethernets?
    a. Type   b. FCS
    c. Preamble   d. SA
14. Which type of Ethernet uses fiber?
    a. 10BaseF   b. 10Base5
    c. 10BaseT   d. 10Base2

15. Which of the following is NOT a name for a transceiver?
    a. AUI   b. MAU
    c. NIC   d. none of the above
16. Without counting the Preamble, what is the smallest Ethernet frame that is possible? Give the answer in bytes.
    a. 18   b. 46
    c. 64   d. 1500
17. In each of the following questions, the bytes of Ethernet headers are shown in hex. Each byte requires two hex digits. Hence, the first 6 groups of two digits represent the destination address and the next 6 groups represent the source address of the NIC. No Preambles are shown. For each question, the destination address, source address, and the 4 bytes following them are shown.
    For each question answer the following:
    i) Which kind of frame is this? Ethernet, 802.3 with SNAP, or 802.3 without SNAP?
    ii) Is the network layer protocol IP, Novell, or unknown?
    iii) Can you determine the length of the frame in hex?
        a) 00 aa 00 01 de e4 00 aa 00 01 df 07 08 00 aa bb
        b) 00 aa 00 01 de e4 00 aa 00 01 df 07 04 00 aa aa
        c) 00 aa 00 01 de e4 00 aa 00 01 df 07 00 aa e0 c0
        d) 00 aa 00 01 de e4 00 aa 00 01 df 07 01 1a 06 06
        e) 00 aa 00 01 de e4 00 aa 00 01 df 07 81 38 aa aa

18. Using only 10BaseT, what is the maximum number of nodes that can be attached to a network. Assume that you don't stack the hubs but cascade them and that there are 8 ports per hub. Sketch the network. Find the longest distance between two nodes.

Section 23.3:
19. How does a MAU know to place a node in its ring or not?
20. What is the station from which all transmissions are received called in a TRN?
21. What type of TRN frame sends data?
22. What are the two special code violations called in TRN?
23. What is the purpose of the RIF field in TRN and how is it used?
24. Give the functions of the active monitor.
25. Draw the Manchester, differential Manchester, and NRZI waveforms for sending 00101110. Assume that the bit before the first one ended with a zero in each case.

Section 23.4:
26. Name the four types of FDDI devices and the four types of FDDI connectors.
27. In FDDI, the station with the lowest ___ value gains the right to send the first token.
28. What are the reasons for converting every 4-bit group of data into 5-bit group codes in FDDI?

Section 23.5:
29. Full-duplex operation doesn't use which of the following characteristics of Ethernet?
    a. MAC header   b. logical bus topology
    c. collision detection   d. a connectionless data transfer
30. Which of the following Ethernets does not use full-duplex operation?
    a. 10Base5   b. 10BaseT
    c. 10BaseF   d. 100BaseT

31. The AUI in 10Base5 is replaced by which interface in Gigabit Ethernet?
    a. transceiver b. PHY
    c. MII d. GMII
32. How is flow control obtained in both half-duplex and full-duplex modes?
33. When two ends of a cable determine in which mode to operate and at what speed, that is called what?
34. If five full-duplex ports are aggregated on two 100-Mbps switches, what is the total bandwidth that is available?

Section 23.6:
35. Which of the following standards were used in developing 100BaseT over UTP?
    a. 10Base5 b. FOIRL
    c. Fibre Channel d. CDDI
36. Once a maximum of two hubs has been achieved with 100BaseT, which procedure is NOT appropriate to add more ports or increase the size of the LAN?
    a. add a repeater b. add a router
    c. add a switch d. stack the hubs
37. Using only two hubs, what is the maximum distance possible with 100BaseT? With 100BaseF?
38. Which characteristics of 10BaseT were copied over to design 100BaseT?

Section 23.7:
39. Which encoding methods are used in Gigabit Ethernet, both in the fiber and copper versions?
40. What were some of the methods by which engineers were able to operate Cat-5 at 1 Gbps when it was standardized at only 100 Mbps.
41. Which technology helped the design of Gigabit Ethernet?
42. What are the fiber versions of Gigabit Ethernet called and how do they differ?

LANs: Additional Concepts

Chapter 24

Bridging and Routing

24.1 INTERNETWORKING DEVICES

As soon as personal computers were connected into LANs, there arose a need for connecting LANs and WANs into complex internetworks. Internetworks, or internets for short, are networks made up of many networks. Many times, internets use a set of protocols based on TCP/IP (Transmission Control Protocol/ Internet Protocol) to "glue" different networks together. The largest of these internets is called the Internet, spelled with a capital "I." The Internet is funded by DARPA (Defense Advanced Research Project Agency) and with over 1,500,000 computers connected, it is the world's largest network. This chapter will outline the devices, protocols, and services related to internetworking.

24.1.1 Adding Bridges to a Network

Back in Figure 7.13, we saw how a LAN could be extended over many floors of a building or even to other buildings in a campus setting by using repeaters. Repeaters boost the signal over the cable so that a LAN is not restricted by being confined to a certain area. With Ethernet, the range of a LAN can be extended from 500 meters to 2500 meters by using up to four repeaters.

When we wanted to use a less expensive LAN technology than 10Base5, we incorporated hubs at various points in the network, as was shown in Figure 23.12. This allowed us to mix the various kinds of LAN technologies. The hubs also provided a point from where signals could be repeated as well as provide better management and troubleshooting capabilities.

Repeaters, however, only repeat the signals, and if we keep adding more stations to the LAN, and add more traffic to it by using it more than before, then eventually our throughput will degrade. This is because the number of collisions will increase. If nodes on both sides of a repeater are simultaneously trying to communicate with each other, then they won't be able to, because repeaters cannot isolate traffic, but simply transfer the signals between each LAN segment.

For example, in Figure 24.1(a), E can't communicate with F at the same time as A is communicating with B. One way to solve this problem is to isolate the segments as shown in Figure 24.1(b). Now A and E may send data simultaneously; unfortunately they can't communicate with each other. So in order to have both capabilities, we add a bridge between these networks. A bridge is capable of filtering; that is, if A is talking to B, it won't pass that frame towards E and G. However, frames sent by A to E will be transferred over. See Figure 24.1(c). In Figure 24.1(a) only one pair of nodes may communicate with each other, since only one communication path exists between all nodes. In Figure 24.1(c), the network is divided into two segments and communication can occur over each segment simultaneously.

However, the decision of where to place a bridge should be done carefully, so that the network is segmented into existing logical groups. That is, the stations on each side of the bridge should communicate primarily among themselves and communicate between each other only occasionally. A general rule of thumb is that 80% of the traffic should be localized within segments, with only 20% of it crossing the bridge. Once these percentages begin to equal each other, more bridges should be added, segmenting the network further. Bridges also allow one to exceed a LAN's distance limitations.

On the other hand, if we are not using our network heavily, repeaters provide a good solution. They are protocol-independent. This means that they don't care about the meanings of the fields in the frames, because they only copy the bits from one side of the bridge to the other. They present only a one- or two-bit delay in the network and, sometimes, they may gain or lose bits. They don't check for errors, because they operate at the OSI's physical layer. The end nodes in a network don't know about their existence, and because repeaters aren't configured, they can always be swapped with other models.

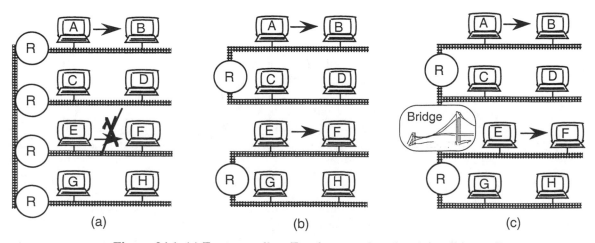

Figure 24.1 (a) E cannot talk to F at the same time that A is talking to B, using repeaters. (b) This is possible by dividing the network, but now A cannot talk to E - H at all. (c) Using a bridge, both things are possible.

Bridging and Routing

24.1.2 Adding Routers to a Network

Bridges are easy to install and can provide a rudimentary level of security at the hardware level. For example, certain users may not be allowed to go out of their own segment. Bridges are easily managed and don't require technical expertise when the network is operating normally. In a bridged network with loops, however, a small problem in one segment can bring the entire network to its knees. Then troubleshooting can become difficult.

Also bridges do not isolate broadcasts (transmission to all nodes) and multicasts (transmission to a group of nodes). There are two types of broadcasts: normal and abnormal. Normal broadcasts are periodic transmissions sent to all nodes in a network by each node, stating their presence on the network. This can take much of the bandwidth on a large network. Abnormal broadcasts are also called broadcast storms; they are due to a failure in a network component. A network with bridges looks like and behaves as one single network.

Once we start adding other networking sites to our internet, especially using WAN links, we will want to form loops in the topology to provide alternate routing. This is shown in Figure 24.2(a). Here, once we start using the network for mission-critical applications, where we want high reliability, a better alternative would be to replace the bridges with routers.

At one time, separate routers and WAN links had to be installed for each type of protocol that needed to be routed. Today, multiprotocol routers handle several protocols simultaneously. They can isolate broadcast and multicast traffic. The type of traffic that exists in different parts of the network can be controlled. Network security and management is much more robust than with bridges, and if the network goes down, the problem can be easily isolated to one port of a router, making it possible to restore the network quickly.

Bridges may not use WAN links efficiently. They are better to use with small distances and typically have only two ports, whereas routers will look at the network layer's header and decide from its internal tables which route seems to be the best. If there is congestion, delay, or extra expense to use one route over another, a router will make the desirable choice. Therefore, routers are more intelligent than bridges.

Bridges are protocol-independent. They operate at the data link layer, unlike routers, which operate at the network layer of the OSI model. Protocols that don't have a third layer, such as DEC's LAT (Local Area Transport) and NetBIOS, can't be routed and must be bridged.

With multiprotocol bridge/routers, one can install them as a bridge, and after seeing how the network performs and grows, they can be configured as routers. They can also be configured to bridge some protocols and route others.

Using Figure 24.2, let us illustrate what is meant by a device operating at the data link layer and the network layer. Suppose we have three networks (numbered 1000, 4000, and 7000) connected to each other. The nodes have three-digit IDs, so a combination of the network ID and the node ID uniquely identifies any node in the network.

Let us say that node 1101 (node 101 on network 1000) is sending a packet to node 4401. In Figure 24.2(a), the node will code the second layer SA (Source Address) and

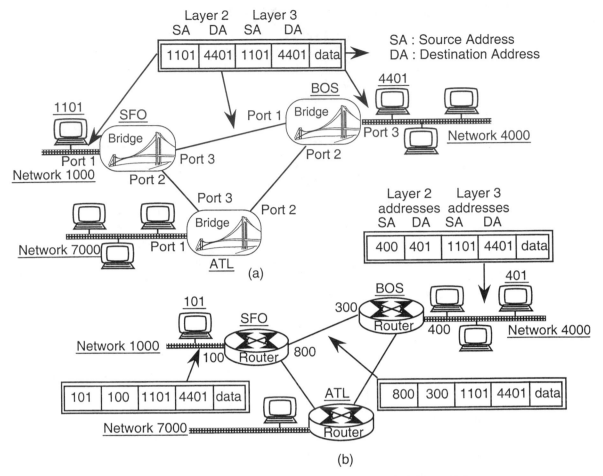

Figure 24.2 (a) The frame remains the same as it goes via bridges. It is one large network. (b) The bridges are replaced with routers. Here, the data link addresses change as the frame goes through them.

DA (Destination Address) to be the same as the third layer SA and DA. In this case, SA and DA are 1101 and 4401, respectively. The SFO bridge, the bridge in San Francisco, will determine from the DA in the second layer that this frame should go over its port 3. Similarly, the BOS (or Boston) bridge will determine that 4401 is on its own network and forward the frame to node 401, using the DA from the second layer.

But, as shown in Figure 24.2(b), in a router-based network, a packet is routed from link to link. First, when node 101 assembles a packet, it sets the SA to 1101 and the DA to 4401 in the third layer header. Using the second layer, it then encloses this packet in a frame with an SA of 101 and a DA of 100, the address of the router's port for network 1000.

Bridging and Routing

The frame reaches the SFO router, which discards the second layer header and trailer after checking for errors. If an error occurs, it requests a retransmission. This router then, after reading the DA in the packet header, decides to send this packet over the direct link to the BOS router. It does this by enclosing the same packet in a new frame which now has an SA and DA of 800 and 300, respectively. This gets the packet to the BOS router.

This router then checks for errors and discards the frame header and trailer. It then decides that this packet can be delivered directly to the recipient. So it encodes the SA as 400 (its own second layer address) and the DA as 401. Finally, node 401 accepts and interprets the data that it receives.

This way, bridges read and process only the data link control information, while routers process the network layer information as well. Because they have less information to process, bridges can send more frames per second than the number of packets routers can send per second. Also, because the frame doesn't get changed as it passes through the bridges, the layout of Figure 24.2(a) is considered to be one large network, while the layout of Figure 24.2(b) is considered as six separate networks.

24.1.3 Collapsing the Backbone

Back in Figure 23.12, we saw how by adding hubs and concentrators on each floor the network was made easy to expand. To allow the network to grow further, we can now add bridge or router cards in these hubs.

However that configuration, with the backbone stretching several floors and buildings, has several problems. If a card fails in one of these hubs, first, a technician may have to carry a LAN analyzer to those various locations, looking for the fault. In the closets where other types of wiring and equipment exist, access to these hubs may be poor. And even if a card is detected to be faulty, the technician may have to come back to the office for a replacement. Having these hubs scattered over various sites prevents a network from coming up in a timely fashion. Furthermore, even during normal operation, file servers on each floor may not be as easy to secure as if they were all located in one room designated solely for such a purpose.

A third-generation hub, or a network with a collapsed backbone, places all components which are critical to the network's operation in one secure room. Let us call it the NOC (Network Operations Center). See Figure 24.3. The backbone, instead of spanning large distances, is totally located in one place and all important network components as well as the segments themselves are connected here. Logically, the hub in the NOC can be thought of as a superhub. The same advantages gained by tying all components on one floor to a "closet" hub can be achieved for the networks themselves by tying them all to one central hub in the NOC.

A LAN analyzer incorporated in a management console gives the network manager full control of the network from one vantage point. At night, to keep the file server data secure, the manager can make sure that all file servers are properly brought down. There is only one room to be kept secure, rather than multiple wiring closets, which have to be shared among other facility services.

If a segment goes down, the manager can isolate the fault quickly from the console. All equipment, including spare devices, is already plugged into the hub,

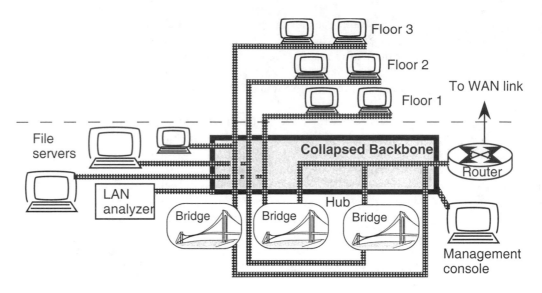

Figure 24.3 An integrated hub with all networking equipment located in the network operations center, shown below the dashed line.

making changes in the configuration possible through the hub's software. If a server or a bridge needs to be swapped temporarily, it can be done using the console instead of physically plugging and unplugging the equipment. Therefore, third-generation hubs can greatly improve the manageability, availability, and control of an extended LAN, but much caution should be taken so that the hub system itself is quite fault-tolerant.

24.2 BRIDGES

24.2.1 Translating and Encapsulating Bridges

Figure 24.4 shows two types of bridges that are not the most commonly found. Figure 24.4(a) shows the operation of what is called a translating bridge. It is used to connect two networks that differ at the first and second layers. A frame on the token ring, if addressed to reach an Ethernet node, is translated by the bridge. It does this by discarding the TRN header and trailer and adding the Ethernet header and trailer. This process is reversed for data traveling in the opposite direction.

Any frame that is addressed to a node on the same network is not forwarded by the bridge. Lastly, the bridge cannot perform fragmentation. Fragmentation is a process which divides large frames into smaller units whenever the data-transporting network cannot handle large-sized frames. Therefore, nodes connected to a translating bridge must be configured so that they do not transmit large frames.

The encapsulation bridge, depicted in Figure 24.4(b), is used over a backbone network, such as the FDDI ring. Here, the protocols of the first two layers of the end systems must be the same and the backbone network encapsulates frames that it

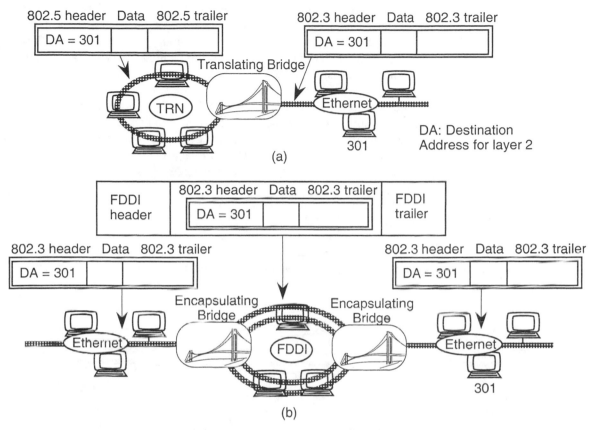

Figure 24.4 (a) A translating bridge converts the layer 2 header and trailer from one format to another. (b) An encapsulating bridge installs one layer 2 frame into another one.

receives from the branch or access networks. The figure shows the left Ethernet LAN transmitting an 802.3 frame that is destined for the Ethernet LAN on the right-hand side. The first bridge encapsulates this frame in an FDDI frame and then the bridge on the right hand side removes the FDDI header and trailer, sending the original Ethernet frame on to its destination.

24.2.2 Transparent Bridges

A translational bridge, as described in the last section, is a special kind of a transparent bridge. Transparency here means that the end systems (or hosts) don't need to know the existence of the bridges in the network. That is, the bridges operate transparently, relative to the nodes. A transparent bridge only passes frames that should be forwarded to another port of the bridge and drops the others. The method by which a transparent bridge finds out the addresses of the nodes connected to its ports is called learning. Figure 24.5 illustrates how this works.

In this figure, there is a cascaded network with two bridges. Units of time are shown on the far left. Under each bridge, its forwarding table is shown as it gets created. As a bridge learns about the existence of the nodes in each segment, these tables become bigger. Each entry in the table specifies on which port which nodes exist and at what time they were last seen there. The bridges use the source addresses in the frames being sent to learn where nodes are located.

At first, when the network is powered up, the bridges don't have anything in their tables. At time = 1, node A sends a frame to G, so bridge X makes an entry in its table noting that A was seen on its port 1 at time = 1. X doesn't know where G is or if it is powered up, so it simply forwards the frame to Y, which processes the frame the same way. This frame is said to flood the network, since no one knows where the destination is located.

Next, F sends a frame to D and just as before, the two tables get updated, but this time, the time is equal to 2. Next, I sends a frame to F. X and Y both receive this frame and filter it. They treat the frame differently from each other. X knows that F is on its port 1, so it forwards the frame to that port. As it does this, it adds I to its table as being on port 2. Y, on the other hand, knows that F is on its port 1 side and drops the frame from going over on its port 2 segment.

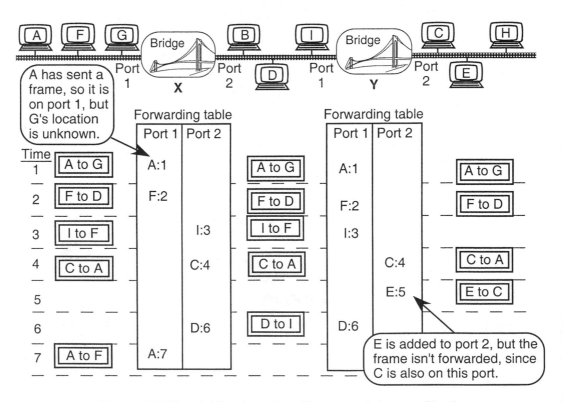

Figure 24.5 How bridges learn the addresses on their ports. The times that the frames were observed are given after the colons.

Then C sends a frame to A, which makes each bridge add C to its forwarding tables. Now both bridges have 4 entries each. Notice that, relative to X, I and C are on the same segment or on the same port. X doesn't know about the existence of Y in this process. If X and Y were routers they would have. Similarly, Y doesn't know on which segment A, F, and I exist; hence X is transparent to Y.

At time = 5, E sends a frame to C. Y has C in its table stating that C is also on port 2, so this frame is dropped and not forwarded. Also, when D sends a frame to I, both bridges drop the frame, because now they know where I is. Lastly, when A sends a frame to F, X updates the time it saw A on port, which is now 7. If the broadcast and the multicast modes were enabled on the bridges, then those messages would be forwarded as well, or else they would be dropped.

24.2.3 Spanning Tree Algorithm

To provide alternate routing and reliability in a network, we know we have to add loops in our network. This way if one link fails, we can use other available links. However, with bridges that introduces a problem.

Consider bridges W, X, Y, and Z connected as shown in Figure 24.7. For now let us look only at the topology shown at the top of this figure and disregard the rest of it. Let us say that a node (call it A) on port 1 of bridge X sends a frame to a node on some other segment. So X notes that A is on its port 1 and forwards the frame to Y, which forwards it to W and Z. Now all four bridges have noted that A is on their port 1 side of the network. What happens when W's copy of the frame arrives on port 3 of Z? Z will note that A has moved from port 1 to port 3 and pass this information to Y. Y will make a note of this change and pass the frame to both X and W. This way, from one frame, many more copies are created and they keep bouncing off each other, keeping the bridges needlessly busy. Hence, the tables never become stabilized.

Therefore, bridges couldn't be placed in loops until Radia Perlman of DEC introduced the spanning tree algorithm. For the sake of reliability, loops are preferred in networks. This method makes bridges pass special configuration messages among themselves to determine the topology of the network. Links are removed, until they are needed again. The bridges place themselves in a logical tree, where only one bridge is the root and the others form the branches of a hierarchical structure. This way, the problem of looping in a bridged network is eliminated.

A configuration message, among other fields, contains a root bridge ID, a cost, and a sending bridge ID. All bridges have a unique 48-bit address. When a bridge sends a configuration message, the bridge which it thinks is the root and the number of hops it is away from that root are encoded in the message. Periodically, bridges pass these messages among themselves to eliminate any loops that may have been introduced in the network. If a link goes down where alternate paths are available, then those paths or links will be reactivated by this algorithm.

When a bridge receives a configuration message on its ports, it will determine the best message out of these that it can send. The best message is the message that has the smallest root ID. If root IDs are the same, then the cost field is used as the tie breaker. If these are also the same, then the sending bridge ID is used to determine the best configuration message.

If the best configuration message is received on one of the ports, that port is considered the root port, and if the bridge in question can send the best message, it considers itself as the root bridge. If there are any ports to which the bridge cannot send a better message than what was received on it, those ports are blocked. But if there are ports to which the bridge can send better messages, then those ports are included in the spanning tree. When a port is included, data is received and forwarded over that port, and when it is blocked it isn't. In either case, configuration messages are received and forwarded.

For example, Figure 24.6(a) shows a bridge, with an ID = 70, having six ports. The best configuration messages arriving at each port are also shown. The bridge then determines that port 4 has the best message, since 40-2-80 (representing the root ID, cost, and the sending bridge ID) is less than any other message. Messages from ports 1, 5, and 6 are worse, because their root IDs are greater than 40. Port 3 is also worse, because even though the root is 40, its cost is higher than 2. And port 2 is also worse than port 4, because its sender ID is larger. Port 4 is then referenced as the root port, because costwise it is closest to the bridge which it thinks is the root.

This bridge then determines that the best message it can send is 40-3-70. This has a hop count of one more than what it received on port 4. Since this message is better than what it received on ports 1, 5, and 6, it will send 40-3-70 on these ports. See Figure 24.6(b). However, 40-2-90 and 40-3-30 from ports 2 and 3 are better than what this bridge can send, so those ports are pruned or blocked. Although it will continue to read the configuration messages from these ports, no data will be read from them or forwarded to them.

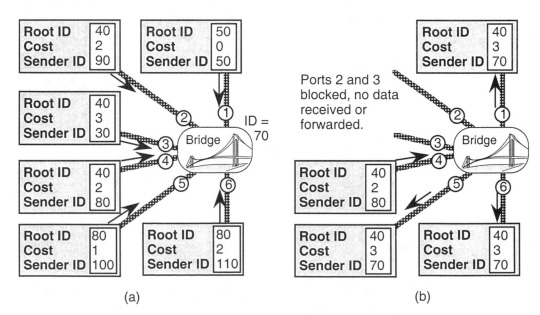

(a)   (b)

Figure 24.6 (a) The bridge shown has an ID of 70. It receives configuration messages from other bridges on its six ports. (b) After it applies the spanning tree algorithm, it decides that port 4 is closest to the root and that ports 2 and 3 would form loops.

Figure 24.7 illustrates how a bridged network removes its loops by the use of this algorithm. Let us say at first that X thinks it is the root and sends the 20-0-20 message over both of its ports. Y realizes that its own ID of 40 is worse than 20. So it sends a message of 20-1-40 over its other two ports. This message indicates that bridge 40 is 1 hop count away from the bridge it thinks is the root. Y also labels port 1 as the root port, because it learned that X is the root from its port 1. Likewise, Z also sends a similar message over its ports 1 and 3.

W, upon receiving these messages from Y and Z, considers itself better than either of them, because its own ID is 10. W then sends 10-0-10 to Y and Z. They make a note that the root is changed to 10 and the root is 1 hop count away from them. X receives 10-1-40 from Y and 10-1-30 from Z. X picks Z as being closest to the root and determines that the best message it can send is 10-2-20. This is worse than what it receives from 40 (10-1-40), so it blocks port 2 and considers port 1 as the root.

Y also blocks its port 2, since the message that it can send (10-1-40) is worse than what it receives on that port (10-1-30), but continues to send its 10-1-40 on its port 1. Z can send a better message (10-1-30) than what it receives on either ports 1 and 2, so it does.

Now the map of the network is redrawn in Figure 24.7(b). The final root is 10 and all of the loops are removed. In the event W goes down, it will stop sending messages and the other bridges will determine that too much time has passed since W made its presence known. They will then time out W and the entire process will be repeated without W in the new configuration. But if W comes back up, then the configuration will be restored as shown, automatically, without any human intervention.

24.2.4 Source Routing Bridges

Unlike transparent bridges which maintain forwarding tables, source routing bridges rely on the source of the frame to provide the path over the bridges. When an end system (host) sends a frame that must travel over several bridges, it encodes the bridge addresses in the proper order in this field to specify the route it must take. This way, each bridge knows which port to forward the frame to.

Source routing bridges are used primarily with TRNs (Token-Ring Networks). Referring back to Figure 23.16, notice that the 802.5 frame allows the use of an RIF field. Recall that if the I/G bit (Figure 23.7) of the source address is set to 1, an RIF (Routing Information Field) is used and if it is 0, it is not used in the frame. This bit is available to indicate the presence of the RIF field, because even if a frame could have a multicast destination address, it can't have a source address of several stations.

If a device doesn't know the route to the desired destination point, it must first find out that route. This is done by the device sending an explorer frame, which is also called a route discovery frame. This frame is flooded in the network as each bridge forwards it to all the others. Before a bridge forwards a frame over its ports, it copies its own address in the frame's RIF field. Eventually, a number of these explorer frames appear at the destination, which then decides which is the best path between the two end points. Usually this is determined by the explorer frame which arrives first. The receiver then sends only one frame back to the sender, who then copies the addresses which define the path to that destination for future reference. Then it sends its message.

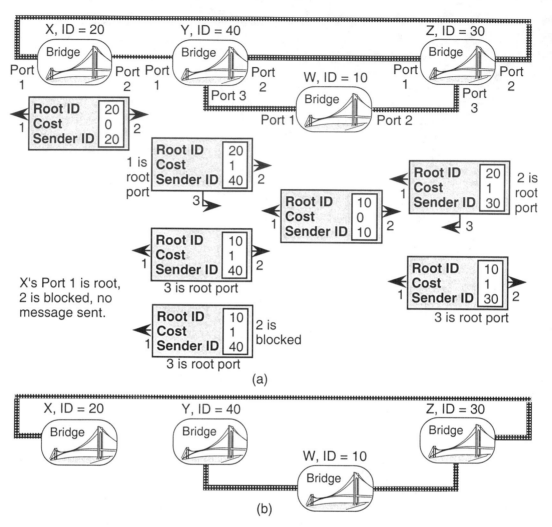

Figure 24.7 (a) The process of sending configuration messages in the spanning tree algorithm. (b) The final network after trimming out all of the loops.

If this machine is turned off and comes back on line, it has to go through this process again. One can see that route exploration performed by each station on every network can generate excessive traffic over large extended LANs.

There are two types of explorer frames. One type sends these frames in all directions and is called the All paths explorer. The Spanning tree explorer frame, on the other hand, sends out these frames only along the branches of a spanning tree. Hence, it is necessary to define three types of RIF fields. One type is where the route is known and is explicitly specified as to its destination. The other two types correspond to the two types of explorer frames, where the addresses of the bridges are collected in this field.

Some of the differences between transparent bridges and source routing bridges are that, with transparent bridges, the network appears as one single network to the end nodes. That is, the bridges are transparent to the end nodes. However, source routing bridges are not transparent to the end nodes. The end nodes have to know about their existence and must be able to handle source routing. Even if source routing bridges may cost less, the cost of the more intelligent end nodes outweighs the savings. Transparent bridges can typically be swapped, but source routing bridges must be configured by assigning every segment and bridge a unique number. The problem of finding a route is calculated by the end systems in source routing bridges, and is done by the bridges when using transparent bridges.

Lastly, an SRT (Source Route Transparent) bridge is a bridge which can function as either type. According to IEEE, all bridges must be transparent and they can add source routing as an added feature. The SRT bridge merely observes the multicast bit in the source address of a frame to determine whether this frame should be bridged transparently or be bridged using the source routing method.

24.3 ROUTING PROTOCOLS

24.3.1 Routing, Routing Protocols, and Routed Protocols

In this section we will discuss routing protocols and the methods in which they operate. Routing protocols, routed protocols, and routing itself are all dissimilar terms. Routers are the type of packet switches which are used in internetworking LANs. They contain routing tables which determine how incoming datagrams (or packets) will be forwarded to their next destination. This is called routing. Routing is simply the act of looking through the routing table to direct the datagram to the next router or end system.

The procedure used for routing is trivial compared to the procedures used to create the tables in the first place. The method in which these routing tables are created and updated is called a routing algorithm and the specific implementation of it is called a routing protocol. Routing protocols exist and operate only in routing devices whereas network protocols such as IP (Internet Protocol), NetWare, or DECnet, which are routable through routers, are called routed protocols. Now, let us discuss the details of RIP, OSPF, and BGP, which are routing protocols.

24.3.2 Distance Vector Routing and RIP

Basic Algorithm: The first routing protocol which became widely used is called RIP (Routing Information Protocol). Originally, it was used in XNS in 1980 and it is currently available in most implementations of Unix as "routed," pronounced as "route Dee." RIP falls in a class of routing algorithms called distance vector routing. The best path to a destination is determined by the least number of hops. However, the best path may be determined by some other metric than the number of hops. Since RIP is a routing protocol which specifies how routing tables are built, let us consider how RIP handles that process.

The basic idea behind RIP is that each router first determines who its neighbors are. Then they transmit an update message to only their neighbors every 30 seconds.

Every time a router receives an update message from one of its neighbors, it looks at the addresses and their respective distances that its neighbors can reach. If the neighboring router can reach a destination that is currently unreachable, it will add that destination as being reachable. In this table, it will also maintain the distances to reach the various nodes. The distances to the destinations are measured in the number of hops.

If another neighbor can reach a destination with fewer hops, it will enter that route in the table instead. If the distance necessary to reach a destination is more than 15 hops, it will not enter that destination in its table and assumes that it is unreachable. Therefore, RIP is only good for networks where the number of routers between any two nodes is 15 or less. After the "diameter" of the network exceeds this amount, one must resort to other protocols. Let us look at an example of how RIP works and then make refinements to this basic description as we encounter problems.

An Example: Figure 24.8(a) shows four networks, A through D, internetworked by three routers (R1 through R3). This example illustrates how RIP builds the routing tables in each of the routers by having the routers pass update messages to each other. The tables are shown as having four columns under the routers and the update messages are shown under the networks which they travel.

Initially, the routing tables are empty, except for the networks that are directly connected to them. For example, R1 has entered a distance or a cost of 0 to reach networks A and B, since they are directly connected to its ports. R1 doesn't yet know that C and D exist.

After 30 seconds, all routers send update messages to their neighbors. R1 tells R2 that it can reach A and B at a cost of 0 hops each. R2, after analyzing this message, disregards the fact that R1 can reach B directly, because R2 can also. However, R2 learns that R1 can reach A at a cost of 0. So it adds A to its table and enters the cost to be one more than the cost from R1, since R2 is one hop away from R1. Now R2 can also reach A at a cost of 1. Hence, after the transmission of the first round of update messages, R2 can get to all four networks, but R1 and R3 can get to only three of them.

Not until another 30 seconds have passed and R2 sends another set of update messages do R1 and R2 find out that they can reach the networks on the far ends. In other words, R1 learns from R2 that R2 can reach network D at a cost of 1, so it adds D to its table, making the cost equal to 2. Similarly, R3 adds A to its table at a cost of 2. Now the network is said to be converged. That is, all routers have the proper information about how to reach all reachable destinations in the network.

Counting to Infinity: Now what if R3 fails? How will R1 be notified? If R1 is not notified, it will send datagrams to R3, unnecessarily using the network bandwidth. To avoid this problem, RIP requires that the update messages be sent every 30 seconds, even if the sender's database hasn't been changed. This way, all routers keep their tables current and keep a timer for each entry.

If a router fails to receive a confirmation from a network that is already in its table for 180 seconds, it will set the hop count to 16, indicating that this network is

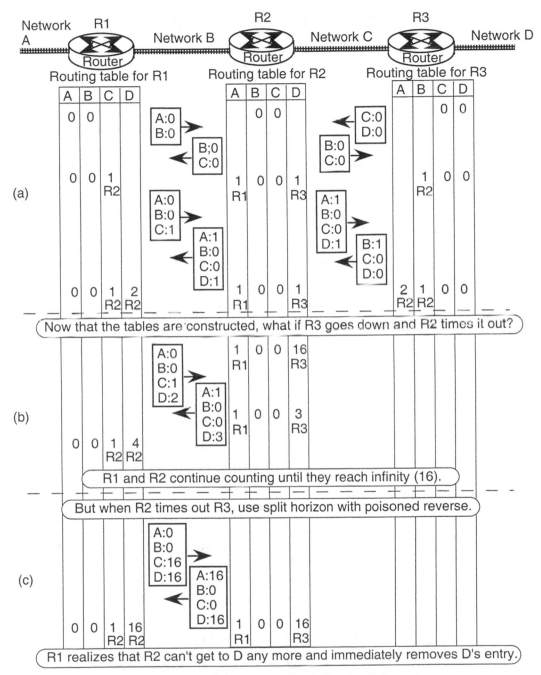

Figure 24.8 (a) The basic operation of RIP (Routing Information Protocol). (b) The problem of counting to infinity. (c) Convergence occurs quickly using split horizon with poisoned reverse.

unreachable. After another 120 seconds, if it still doesn't receive a message, it will remove that entry from the table altogether. This is called garbage collection. Garbage collection prevents "I can't reach this network" messages from taking up network bandwidth, which becomes unnecessary after a while.

Referring to Figure 24.8(b), we see another problem that arises if R3 goes down. Let us say if R3 goes down, R2 will not receive any entries from R3. After 180 seconds it will set the cost of D to 16, or unreachable. Next time R2 sends a message to R1, it indicates its cost to D as 16, also considered to be infinity in RIP. However, R2 learns that R1 can get to D with a cost of 2. So R2, not realizing that R1 considers reachability through R2, merely updates its own database, entering a route to D with a cost of 3. This is one more than the assumed cost from R1.

Then R1 learns from R2 that R2's cost to D has gone up to 3. Therefore, R1 updates its cost to D to become 4. Then R2 ups its cost to 5 until the entries for D at both routers reach 16 and they time out. This is called "counting to infinity" and is caused by a routing loop. Here, the network has converged or stabilized slowly, because R1 thought it could get to D via R2 and R2 thought it could get to D via R1. Therefore, RIP has purposely set the infinity count to a low 16.

Split Horizon: To avoid routing loops, a technique called split horizon is used. This prevents a router from sending update information to a neighbor from whom it received that information to begin with. For instance, R1 should never send reachability information for D to R2, since R1 received that information from R2 in the first place. So if R3 goes down as it did at the beginning of Figure 24.8(b), instead of sending a cost of 16, R2 will not send an entry for network D at all and let R1 time out D. Hence, unreachability for a node is determined at every router.

RIP actually uses a mechanism called split horizon with poisoned reverse. This is illustrated in Figure 24.8(c). Here, instead of R2 not sending an entry for D at all, it will send an entry with a cost of 16. R1, upon noticing that R2's cost to D has gone to infinity, and that its route was learned from R2, will consider 16 as "poison" and delete that entry for D immediately. This way, convergence is achieved quickly and prevents R1 from transmitting wrong information to other nodes. Also, note that R2 sends a cost of 16 for A to R1 since R2 learned that information from R1 to begin with.

However, routing loops do exist in RIP for other configurations as when R1 thinks it can get to D via R2 and R2 thinks it can get to D via R3 and R3 thinks it can get to D through R1. Here, a mechanism called triggered updates will send new information learned about the topology almost immediately, reducing the looping problem. When even this technique doesn't work, unreachability can still be achieved by counting to infinity.

24.3.3 Link State Routing and OSPF

Link State Protocols: There are two types of link state protocols. They are OSPF (Open Shortest Path First) and IS-IS (Intermediate System to Intermediate System). Although each has its benefits and drawbacks, we will concentrate primarily on OSPF. Again, giving details of one and not the other in no way implies that one is better than the other. It only allows us to study the pertinent concepts in more depth.

In the distance vector algorithm, we saw how each node transmits its entire routing table to only its neighbors. This makes the network converge slowly because two routers that are many hops away from each other will not know about their existence until the intermediate routers have updated and forwarded their tables, one router at a time.

With link state routing protocols, this is not the case. Each router, instead of transmitting its entire database to only its neighbors, transmits the information about its neighbors to all of the other nodes in the internet. While the intermediate routers between two distant end routers are creating their tables, the information for the end routers to create their tables is already in transit. This causes the network to converge rapidly. Furthermore, if a change occurs, only that change, rather than the entire database, is transmitted to all nodes. OSPF is a routing protocol that implements this link state routing algorithm.

Unlike in RIP, where the cost between two routers is the number of hops, OSPF allows one to choose a preferred route based on a number of link characteristics, called metrics. These metrics can be specified in terms of reliability, delay, bandwidth, cost of the link, load of the link, and other such items. Many of these metrics are dependent on one another, depending on the configuration of the network. And while for one instance reliability may be the most important metric, for others it may be cost or some other factor. With OSPF one can choose the cost between two points based on these metrics rather than just on the number of hops.

OSPF Routing Tables: In Figure 24.9, we have a mesh network of routers, using point-to-point links. It is important for the routers to know who their neighbors are. This is accomplished using the Hello protocol. At the beginning, each router will send a Hello Packet to each of its neighbors giving its own router address. These Hello Packets are sent periodically to detect changes in their adjacent links and they are not forwarded by the receiving routers. For example, R1 will send Hello Packets over each of its interfaces to R2 and R3. When they in turn send their Hello Packets back with R1's address, R1 will have established two-way communications with them. At this time, the cost of the links will be established.

Once each router has determined its neighbors, the adjacent pairs synchronize their databases. LSAs (Link State Advertisements) are then flooded throughout the network. These are packets of information sent by each router specifying its link state at that time.

In the figure, four LSAs are shown as they are sent by each router after the links are initialized. R1, for instance, broadcasts its database (which specifies that R2 and R3 are 4 and 1 units away, respectively) to all nodes. Therefore, even though R4 is not directly connected to R1, it will soon also receive that LSA. These LSAs are flooded in all directions simultaneously. However, for the sake of explanation, let us assume that each LSA arrives at each of the other routers one at a time. This will help us see how the "shortest path" routing tables are built.

Initially, R1 doesn't know about R4's existence, but when it receives R2's LSA, it computes the cost to R4 to be 7, 4 to R2, and then 3 to R4. R2, upon receiving R1's LSA, notes that the cost from R1 to R3 is only 1, so it chooses the shortest path to R3

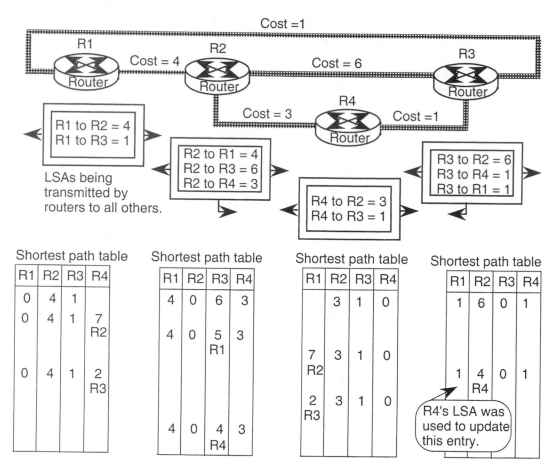

Figure 24.9 As the LSAs (Link State Advertisements) from the various sources reach their multiple destinations, the shortest path tables for each of the routers are built . The router numbers under table entries denote that the path is not direct and that this is the next hop router designation. In this example, it also indicates the router whose LSA was used to update that particular table entry.

as being through R1, because 5 (or 4 + 1) is less than the cost to R3 directly (which is 6).

Let us say that R4 receives R2's LSA first and notes that R1 is now also accessible at a cost of 7. Then R3, upon receiving R4's LSA, updates its cost to R2 to be 4 (or 3 + 1) via R4, which is less than the cost to R2 directly. Similarly, R1, using R3's LSA, adjusts its cost to R4 to be 2 and R4 does likewise. Finally R2 adjusts its cost to R3 to be 4, via R4.

What has happened here is that every router has created an identical link state database, which describes the topology of the network. Using this database, each router, relative to itself, has created a routing table that is based on the shortest path tree. Each router's path tree is derived with itself being the root of the tree.

Multiaccess Networks: In the last section, over every network or link only one pair of routers could communicate with each other. Consider Figure 24.10. Over the Ethernet, R4, R5, and R6 can communicate with each other, and using the PSN (Packet Switched Network), they can communicate with the rest of the routers. Both the Ethernet and the switched network are considered to be multiaccess networks. Note that these are not the same as multidrop networks, where each point has only direct access to one controller. In a multiaccess network, every router can communicate directly with any other. Switched networks are typically nonbroadcast and Ethernets are broadcast types of multiaccess networks.

In multiaccess networks, instead of each router establishing adjacency with every other router, based on their IDs, they elect what is called a DR (Designated Router). They also elect a BDR (Backup DR) to take over in case the DR fails. Next, each router establishes adjacency with only the DR. This eliminates one-to-many combinations with each router, which reduces the amount of unnecessary protocol traffic over the network. The DR then assigns a name to its network that includes its own name. In the figure, R4 has been elected the DR for both networks, and it has assigned the switched network the address of R4.1 and the Ethernet the address of R4.2. The DR now sends LSAs on behalf of the network as well as for itself. So each router that is not a DR advertises that it only has a link to its network, rather than to all the other routers in its network.

The chart in Figure 24.10 shows that a link to the R4.1 network is advertised by R1 through R4 and a link to R4.2 is advertised by R4 through R6. R4.1 advertises that it has links to R1 through R4 and hosts H1 and H2. Similarly, R4.2 advertises a list of its routers and hosts. The transmission of LSAs for R4, R4.1, and R4.2 are all handled by R4.

Now, if R1 receives an LSA from its WAN link, which must be forwarded to all the routers in the switched network, R1 will multicast this LSA to the DR and the BDR. The DR will then multicast it for R1 to R1 through R3 and wait for an explicit

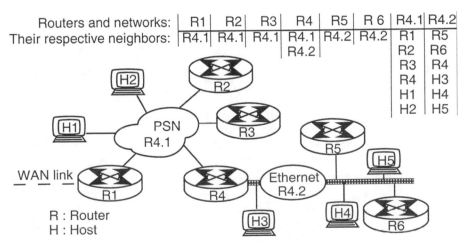

Figure 24.10 Establishing neighbors in a multiaccess network.

acknowledgment of that LSA. For a router that doesn't provide an acknowledgment, R4 will retransmit the LSA using the data link layer.

OSPF Areas: When more and more routers are added to an internet, routing traffic between routers can increase sharply, consuming a large amount of bandwidth on the network. Regardless of the algorithm chosen, it eventually becomes necessary to divide up the internet into smaller internets, called areas. Then a copy of the routing protocol can run independently in all areas and much of the routing traffic can be localized within the areas.

All routers in one given area maintain their own database. If a change occurs, that change is propagated to all routers only in that area. This restricts the flooding of LSAs only to the area of concern, reducing the interarea traffic. This is the description of level 1 areas.

However, to provide access to routers outside of level 1 areas, a level 2 area is used to interconnect them. Figure 24.11 shows a level 2 area (called a backbone area) that is used to interconnect two level 1 areas hierarchically. Although each of these routers may run the OSPF protocol, they can be classified into 4 types of routers. The figure shows the kind of router that each router is.

An internal router has no direct connection to any other area, except for its own area (R2, R5, R6, R8, R9, and R10). A backbone router is a router with an interface to the backbone (R1 through R4, and R7). An area border router is a type of a backbone router that is connected to at least two areas (R1, R3, R4, and R7). And finally, an AS (Autonomous System) boundary router is one that attaches to other higher-level areas called ASs. ASs will be covered shortly.

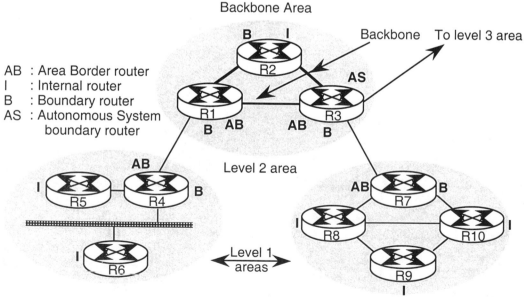

Figure 24.11 Types of OSPF routers.

IS-IS: OSPF was actually derived from IS-IS and so the two are very similar to each other. An IS is OSI's cool way of referring to a router whereas an ES (End System) refers to an end host node. While OSPF routes only the IP protocol, because it is encapsulated in IP datagrams, IS-IS routes all routable protocols. It was designed by researchers at DEC headed by Radia Perlman for OSI's CLNP (ConnectionLess Network Protocol).

If an area is partitioned, say because of a loss of a critical link, IS-IS can automatically repair it using a virtual link, whereas with OSPF, a virtual link must be manually configured. With IS-IS, every link has separate passwords to transmit and receive for authenticating packets, but with OSPF only one password is used. Because OSPF routes only IP datagrams, it is optimized for routing, while IS-IS is optimized for minimizing storage and processing requirements. In any case, choosing a routing protocol involves making tradeoffs on such issues. Lastly, IS-IS can be used for inter-AS and intra-AS routing, but OSPF can be used only for intra-AS routing.

24.3.4 Autonomous Systems and BGP

Back in the early days of the Internet, ARPANET served as the backbone network over which long-haul traffic was transported. The backbone network was called the Internet core and its routers were called the core gateways. Hierarchically attached to these core gateways were other routers called external gateways. External gateways were the entry points into other network areas called ASs (Autonomous Systems). See Figure 24.12(a).

Because an AS is a large collection of networks and routers which is administered by a single authority, such as a university, it is typically maintained and paid for by one entity. It tries to shield itself from routing problems which may occur in other ASs. One must apply to the NIC (Network Information Center) of DDN (Defense Data

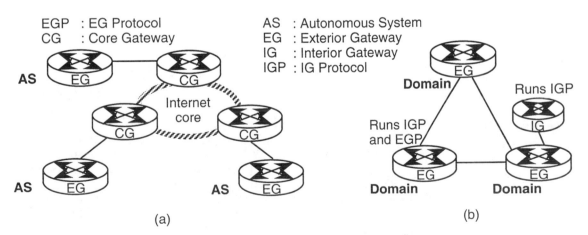

Figure 24.12 (a) Traditionally, when the ASs were connected to the core, the Internet was structured hierarchically. (b) Currently, the ASs are also called domains, which access each other directly.

Bridging and Routing

Network) to obtain an AS number. Within an AS, there may be level 2 and level 1 areas, as discussed in the section on OSPF. In that case, the routing between ASs can be thought of as level 3 routing.

Traditionally, inter-AS routing was done via the core. But as the Internet grew, the core became too crowded and hard to manage. Now, the core as we once knew it no longer exists. The ASs are being connected directly to each other, making this high layer of the network topology flat rather than hierarchical. Although the term AS is still used, the correct term is domain, as shown in Figure 24.12(b).

The routers used to exchange traffic between domains are called interdomain routers (or gateways). They use a family of routing protocols called interdomain routing protocols or EGPs (Exterior Gateway Protocols) for short. The protocols used within a domain are called intradomain routing protocols or IGPs (Interior Gateway Protocols). RIP and OSPF are examples of IGPs.

Examples of EGPs include BGP (Border Gateway Protocol) and a protocol that is itself called EGP. EGP, therefore, may refer either to a set of interdomain protocols or to a protocol named EGP.

BGP is a distance vector algorithm. With it, all the exterior gateways between two adjacent domains are joined using a fully connected mesh topology. They use TCP (Transmission Control Protocol) to send reliable messages between each other. BGP provides a more powerful method of authentication of packets than does OSPF. This in fact is better, since the method of maintaining security on each network can be kept confidential.

BGP uses source routing in the sense that the routing information block, when being transmitted, lists the AS numbers in its routing path. All messages have a 16-byte field called the marker in its header. It is reserved for authentication, possibly employing a mechanism for digitizing signatures. BGP uses the OPEN, UPDATE, NOTIFICATION, and KEEPALIVE messages.

The OPEN message is used when two routers are first connected. Besides the header's marker used for authentication, this message itself has another 13 bytes reserved for future implementation of an authentication scheme. It also provides the AS number and specifies the hold time. This is the time interval in which the receiver should expect to get messages from its neighboring gateway. When a router has no messages to send, it will send a KEEPALIVE message which contains only a 19-byte BGP message header. This will prevent the connecting router from timing out the transmitting router.

The UPDATE message is used to transfer routing information. It specifies whether this information came from the interior gateway protocol or if it was learned from BGP or by some other means. Along with other attributes, it also specifies the AS_Path and the address of the next router in the path. Finally, when one router wants to terminate a connection with its neighbor, it will send a NOTIFICATION message providing the reason for it.

24.4 ROUTER CONFIGURATION

Let us now change our emphasis from algorithms and protocols to setting up a router in real life. Let us outline the configuration of a Cisco M-Chassis type router

584

with two ports. This is by no means a training tutorial, but only an overview of some of the tasks that are done in configuring a typical router. Again, we will discuss one specific product to make the explanation meaningful. The reader should be warned that using a Cisco router doesn't imply that other routers are inferior. In fact, each vendor has its own unique set of features and services that one must carefully evaluate before forming an opinion. Here it is assumed that illustrating how one specific product operates makes learning products from other vendors much easier.

This router with its two ports will connect an existing, isolated Ethernet LAN to the Internet. So, for its installation, we need two Internet addresses (one for each port) from our network administrator. First, we will configure it on the bench connecting an ASCII terminal to its terminal port and nothing to its Ethernet ports. Then we will take it to the site and install the two Ethernet connections and power it up, after which it will run Cisco's proprietary IGRP routing protocol, and if everything goes well, we won't need to do anything else to it.

This router has two Ethernet interfaces on its back panel, which are connected to the Ethernet board inside it. The router has to also come with a processor board. The processor board will typically have a jumper at pin pair 9 and if the router is going to be booted up locally, there should also be a jumper on pin pair 1. If the booting is done off the network, then pin pair 3 should be jumped instead (for a CSC3 processor card). There are dip switches on the Ethernet board, which have to be set according to the slot position the board will go in the chassis. Let's turn on the box!

The connected terminal will display:

```
CSC3 (68020) processor with 4096k bytes of memory.
1 MCI controller (2 Ethernet, 0 Serial)
2 Ethernet/IEEE 802.3 interface
32k Bytes of non-volatile configuration memory
4096k bytes of flash memory on MC+ card (via MCI)
```

This information shows that the box (or the router) uses the Motorola 68020 microprocessor with 4 kbytes of RAM. It supports two Ethernet interfaces. It also has 32 kbytes of nonvolatile memory and 4 kbytes of flash EPROM memory. Flash EPROMs can be programmed while they are in the box, without having to be removed.

Then it will ask:

```
Would you like to enter the initial configuration dialogue? [yes]:no
```

The default setting is shown in brackets; we chose "no" this time. Then a prompt with the router's name for user access appears. User access is shown by ">." Typing "enable" gives us a privileged access, shown by "#." This can be password protected at a later time. Then we type "setup" and we can go through the configuration dialogue as shown below.

```
Router>enable
Router#setup

Configuring global parameters:

Enter host name: matchbox
Enter enable password: matchhead
```

```
Enter virtual terminal password: matchstick
Configure SNMP Network Management? [yes]: no
Configure IP? [yes]:
    Configure IGRP routing? [yes]:
        Your IGRP autonomous system number [1]:
Configure DECnet? [no]:
Configure XNS? [no]:
Configure Novell? [no]: yes
Configure AppleTalk? [no]: yes
  Multizone network? [yes]:
Configure CLNS? [no]:
Configure Vines? [no]:
Configure bridging? [no]:

Configuring interface parameters:

Configuring interface Ethernet0:
    Is this interface in use? [yes]:
    Configure IP at this interface? [yes]:
        IP address for this interface: 128.6.1.1
        Number of bits in subnet field [0]: 8
        Class B network is 128.6.0.0, 8 subnet bits;
            mask is 255.255.255.0
    Configure Novell on this interface? [yes]:
        Novell network number [1]:
    Configure AppleTalk on this interface? [yes]:
        Extended AppleTalk network? [yes]:
```

The setting of global parameters determines which protocols we will be prompted for as we set up each interface. For example, since Novell was set to "yes" in the global settings, we were asked about it while setting up Ethernet interface 0. The meaning of IP addresses and masks was covered in Chapter 8. In the same fashion as this interface is set up, Ethernet interface 1 will also be set up. At the end of the dialogue session, we will be asked the following:

```
Use this configuration? [yes/no]: yes
```

Now this image is stored in the nonvolatile EPROM. It is stored as a command script, which will be used every time the box boots up. Of course, it can be changed. These parameter names and their settings, as they were generated in the setup dialogue are stored in a file called the command script file. This script can be viewed by simply typing:

```
matchbox#write terminal
```

Notice that the prompt shows the router's name as it was given during the setup dialogue. If we type the following, we will be shown information about what has transpired on that particular interface:

```
matchbox#show interface ethernet 0
Ethernet 0 is administratively down, line protocol is down
```

```
Hardware is MCI Ethernet, address is 0000.0c03.e1f8
MTU 1500 bytes, BW 10000 kbit, DLY 1000 usec, rely 255/255,
load 1/255
Encapsulation ARPA, loopback not set, keepalive set (10sec)
ARP type: ARPA, ARP timeout 4:00:00
Last input never, output 0:27:17, output hang never
Last clearing of "show interface" counters never
Output queue 0/40, 0 drops, input queue 0/75, 0 drops
Five minute input rate 0 bits/sec, 0 packets/sec
Five minute output rate 0 bits/sec,
        0 packets/sec 0 packets input, 0 bytes, 0 no buffer
        Received 0 broadcasts, 0 runts, 0 giants
        0 input errors, 0 CRC, 0 frame, 0 overrun, 0 ignored,
            0 abort
        26 packets output, 5193 bytes, 0 underruns
        0 output errors, 0 collisions, 1 interface reset,
            0 restarts
```

Notice that this interface is down. Its MAC address is 0000.0c03.e1f8. This hardware address can be stored on a network server which can map its MAC address with the IP address using ARP (Address Resolution Protocol). The last input field indicates the time when data was last received into this interface and the last output indicates when data was last transmitted. These are useful when debugging a problem. Other fields provide other data pertaining to the activity over this interface.

If we type configure, we can bring up this interface as shown here.

```
matchbox#configure
Configure from terminal, memory, or network? [terminal]:
Enter configuration commands, one per line.
Edit with DELETE, CTRL/W, and CTRL/U; end with CTRL/Z
interface ethernet 0
no shutdown^Z

matchbox#
```

Now, if we type "show interface ethernet 0," we will see that Ethernet 0 is not administratively down and that the line protocol is up. This is because we did a "no shutdown." The configure command changes settings in the RAM, but not for booting up purposes. If booting up is to be done from the nonvolatile memory, then typing "write memory" will save those changes there.

Basically, we are finished. Now we can connect the box at the site and hope it works. If problems occur, then we can telnet to the box from our shop and log onto it as if we were there physically and perform the tasks similar to the ones we have just described.

EXERCISES

1. Which device operates at the physical layer of the OSI model?
   a. repeater   b. bridge
   c. router   d. gateway

2. Which device doesn't isolate traffic from two segments?
   a. repeater
   b. bridge
   c. router
   d. gateway
3. When passing through which device does the second layer header of a frame change?
   a. repeater
   b. bridge
   c. Ethernet switch
   d. router
4. What disadvantage does collapsing the backbone present?
   a. poor security
   b. poor maintenance
   c. single device dependence
   d. poor management
5. Which type of bridged network requires the transmitting node to know the addresses of the bridges along the path?
   a. learning bridge
   b. encapsulating bridge
   c. source routing bridge
   d. translating bridge
6. Which intradomain routing protocol requires each node to transmit its information about the network to its neighbor?
   a. RIP
   b. OSPF
   c. IS-IS
   d. BGP
7. Which intradomain routing protocol requires a node to transmit the information about its neighbors to all nodes?
   a. RIP
   b. IS-IS
   c. EGP
   d. BGP
8. Which type of second layered device will convert one frame format to another one?
9. Which type of second layered device will perform both circuit switching and packet switching?
10. The act of looking through the tables and routing a packet to the correct router is called what?
11. How often does RIP send update messages, and in number of hops, what is the largest network diameter possible?
12. In RIP, what is it called when two nodes keep adding the number of hops to a failed destination until they reach 16?
13. Give two examples of link state routing protocols.
14. Which routing protocol uses source routing, in a sense?
15. Before configuring a router, one must obtain which addresses?
16. What are some advantages of bridges over routers?
17. What are some advantages of routers over bridges?
18. Name the types of bridges covered and describe each using one or two sentences.
19. List the advantages of collapsing the backbone.
20. Describe how the spanning tree algorithm removes loops in a bridged network.
21. What is split horizon?
22. What is the purpose of creating OSPF areas?

Bridging and Routing

Chapter 25

TCP/IP:
Additional Concepts

25.1 INTRODUCTION AND REVIEW

In 1974, Vinton G. Cerf and Robert E. Kahn proposed a design for a set of protocols in an article published in *IEEE Transactions of Communications*. This set of protocols would be able to internetwork many types of networks, regardless of the network access protocols or the vendors of their equipment. The DoD (Department of Defense) had a need to interconnect networks belonging to various organizations, such as NSF (National Science Foundation), NASA, and research and educational institutes. So the DoD through DARPA (Defense Advanced Research Projects Agency) provided funds to BBN (Bolt, Beranek, and Newman) to implement a set of protocols based on the article.

TCP/IP was first implemented in BSD (Berkeley Software Distribution) Unix and so the Unix operating system still plays an important role with TCP/IP. Although these protocols are now implemented in many operating systems, this chapter is primarily based on Unix. Unlike other operating systems, Unix is written in a high-level language, which makes it portable to various types of hardware platforms. Furthermore, Unix lends itself to networking more than any other operating system.

In Chapter 8 we have already studied TCP/IP in quite some detail. We saw how this architecture is divided into four layers, as shown in Figure 25.1. These are the network access, internet, transport, and application layers. If the protocol used in the physical layer is Ethernet then the Type field in its header, if 0800 (hex), will determine that its data portion is an IP datagram. The IP header's protocol number determines whether its data portion should be forwarded to ICMP, TCP, UDP, etc. Finally, the port number in the TCP or UDP header determines which application is being carried in the data portion. The relation of these protocols to each other and their characteristics was covered in quite some detail.

In this chapter we will avoid redundancy and hope if you cannot recall something that you will to go back and review that material. We will start at the network access layer and climb up through the protocol stack, covering material that wasn't covered in

589

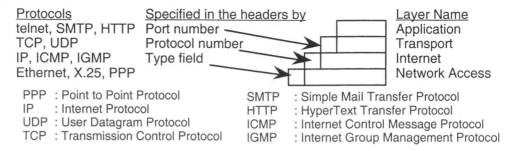

Protocols	Specified in the headers by	Layer Name
telnet, SMTP, HTTP	Port number	Application
TCP, UDP	Protocol number	Transport
IP, ICMP, IGMP	Type field	Internet
Ethernet, X.25, PPP		Network Access

PPP : Point to Point Protocol   SMTP : Simple Mail Transfer Protocol
IP   : Internet Protocol   HTTP : HyperText Transfer Protocol
UDP : User Datagram Protocol   ICMP : Internet Control Message Protocol
TCP : Transmission Control Protocol   IGMP : Internet Group Management Protocol

Figure 25.1 The TCP/IP network architecture.

Chapter 8. This time, we will study all of the fields in the major protocols and see how they are used.

25.2 THE NETWORK ACCESS LAYER

25.2.1 ARP and RARP

RFCs 826, 903, and 1700 describe these two protocols in detail. RARP (Reverse Address Resolution Protocol) is used with diskless workstations or X terminals. These devices don't have an IP configuration file to read from a hard drive as other hosts do. They cannot come up on the network without knowing their IP address. What such a station does is first read the MAC or hardware address from its NIC and then broadcast it over the network to all hosts. "Who knows my IP address?" would be the meaning of its broadcast packet. This would be the RARP Request.

There would be one server that has a list of the IP addresses for each MAC address on the network. This server would then send a unicast RARP Reply to the diskless workstation, providing it with its correct IP address. Then the workstation could boot up.

Figure 25.2 shows the format for either the ARP or RARP packet. The left column shows the number of bytes taken by each field. The next column gives their names and the last two columns give examples and descriptions of these fields. We will try to keep this format as we describe protocol headers.

Number of Bytes	Field Name	Example	Description
2	Hardware Type	0001	Is this Ethernet, LocalTalk, etc.?
2	Protocol Type	0800	Is this to map IP or some other address?
1	Hardware Length	06	Length of the hardware address in bytes.
1	Protocol Length	04	Length of the protocol address in bytes.
2	Operations	0001	Is this ARP or RARP, request or reply?
variable (6)	Source HW Address.	00aa0001bfdc	
variable (4)	Source IP Address	abcdef02	
variable (6)	Target HW Address	000000000000	
variable (4)	Target IP Address	abcdef01	

Figure 25.2 The fields of the headers for ARP and RARP. The numbers in parentheses are the number of bytes when used in Ethernet.

The Ethernet frame header is not shown. Its frame type in hex would be 0806 for ARP or 0835 for RARP. ARP and RARP can be used not only with Ethernet and IP but with other protocols as well. The type of hardware is given in the first two bytes of the header. For Ethernet, it is 1, for IEEE 802 protocols it is 6, and for frame relay it is F.

The type of protocol is 0800 for IP. In the example packet shown in Figure 25.2, we see that the hardware type is Ethernet and the protocol type is IP. Hence, the hardware address length is 6 bytes. That's 48 bits which matches the length of Ethernet. The protocol length for IP addresses is 4 bytes or 32 bits.

Next, the Operation field signals the type of packet this is. For an ARP Request packet this code is 1. For an ARP Reply, it is 2, for an RARP Request it is 3, and for an RARP Reply it is 4. Finally, the addresses of hardware and IP are provided. Since this example packet has an Operational code of 1, it is an ARP Request packet. In such a packet, the source host is trying to find the hardware address of the target. Therefore, for now the Target HW Address field is basically garbage.

25.2.2 Proxy ARP

Proxy ARP is a fairly simple, but subtle, means of determining the network gateway between the local host and the requested remote host, a host not on the same subnet as the local host, i.e., a way of avoiding a lot of static routes.

"Proxy" ARP is a method (not a protocol) for responding to ARP requests. It is currently defined as correct and appropriate behavior.

In Proxy ARP, if a gateway sees an ARP request for an IP address that is not on the local cable, *and* it knows how to get to that IP network, it will respond with an ARP response. But instead of the remote host's Ethernet address, it will put its own in there on behalf of the remote host. Hence the term "proxy" is used. Essentially, the gateway tricks the querying host into thinking that it (the gateway) is the remote host.

This is done on the hosts by what is now a standard Unix routing entry:

```
route add default <my_own_ip_address> 0
```

implying that the entire world is attached to the local Ethernet, and that everything is 0 hops away. The "route add" command will be covered in more depth later.

Now what happens is that whenever an ARP request for a remote address is issued, a gateway will respond with (essentially) "send it over here" and will forward the packet correspondingly. For all intents and purposes, the host believes that the gateway is the remote system.

Consider the following terminal dialogue executed from a host called pilot at Rutgers University. The ping command merely checks to see if a host is active or not.

```
%arp -a
. .
(no entry for foghat or vax003.stockton.edu systems)
%ping foghat
foghat.rutgers.edu is alive
%ping vax003.stockton.edu
vax003.stockton.edu is alive
%arp -a
```

```
  .   .
foghat.rutgers.edu  (128.6.13.13) at aa:0:4:0:98:f4
vax003.stockton.edu (134.210.1.6) at aa:0:4:0:98:f4
```

Notice, according to their IP addresses, foghat is on subnet 128.6.13.0 and vax003.stockton.edu is on subnet 134.210.1.0. Pilot, however, is on neither of these subnets. Yet, by observing foghat's and vax003's Ethernet addresses, pilot sees both as having lil-gw's Ethernet address. lil-gw happens to be on subnet 128.6.7.0. It is acting as the proxy server for foghat and vax003.

Of course, this results in a larger ARP table, but ARP entries are supposed to time out (be expired). This avoids having lots of route entries in the routing table.

A route tells the host to which gateway a packet should be sent in order to access a remote system. At Rutgers, we have 150 active subnets—obviously, static routes for all networks would produce a huge routing table. The average size of the ARP tables tends to be about 20 entries, since hosts always tend to talk to a "closed set" of other hosts.

Also, note an odd side effect. If you have a route entry for a specific gateway, and that gateway goes down, you're out of luck. All your packets will fall on deaf ears.

If you're using proxy ARP, you'll time out waiting for a response, purge that ARP entry in your table, and re-ARP again. If there is more than one gateway on the local Ethernet, then the other gateway will answer (if it knows how to get to the intended remote network), and the IP session will recover. This allows you to dynamically switch between gateways, while never losing connectivity.

Generally, ARP tables provide the addresses of hosts and routers on the local subnet, that is, the systems that are directly connected on the same LAN. On the other hand, routing tables provide the addresses for systems that are not connected to the local subnet. So, what is the purpose of proxy ARP?

Suppose a host uses routing tables to access a remote host which goes down. By the time the routing tables are updated by the routing protocol, the TCP sessions with that host will become disconnected. Using proxy ARP, however, the ARP tables are updated before TCP sessions have a chance to become disconnected.

25.2.3 PPP

RFC 1661 describes PPP (Point-to-Point Protocol). PPP allows packets of various protocols to be sent over a serial link, either dedicated or dial-up. The older protocol for serial links is called SLIP (Serial Line IP), which only supports IP. PPP, on the other hand, supports a number of protocols other than IP. It also provides CRC (Cyclic Redundancy Check) for error detection and dynamic allocation of IP addresses over the serial link. These advantages over SLIP makes PPP more attractive. Of course, to provide these benefits and flexibility, PPP has more overhead in terms of number of added fields per frame as well as the presence of more control frames during transmission.

The basic frame format for PPP is shown in Figure 25.3(a). Like SDLC, this frame starts and ends with a flag that marks the beginning and the end of the frame. See Chapter 16 on SNA for the discussion of SDLC frames. Bit stuffing must occur during the rest of the frame so that the flag doesn't appear anywhere inside it. After the flag, the Address always has the same value since there is only one host on the opposite end to address. Also, since there is a special set of control protocol frame types, the Control field is not used either. Most of the time, these two fields are omitted during initial link negotiation. The checksum field checks for errors in the header and the data. Although the data field is shown to be 1500 bytes, it may be reduced down as far as 296 bytes for interactive traffic. The smaller frames over a low-speed link would provide better response time for real-time applications.

When the link is inactive, PPP is said to be in the *Dead* state. When one host wants to make a connection with another over the serial link, LCP (Link Control Protocol) packets are transferred to configure and establish the link. This is called the link *Establish* state. As seen in the third column of Figure 25.3(b), LCP protocol ID is c021. Once the link has been established, authentication may occur if it is set. This occurs during the *Authentication* state. The default is not authentication. PAP (Password Authentication Protocol) and CHAP (Challenge Handshake Authentication Protocol) are two of the popular methods used for authentication.

Next comes the *Network* state. During this state, NCP (Network Control Protocol) packets are transferred for the protocol over which communication must occur. For IP, this is 8021 according to the middle column of Figure 25.3(b). Now data can be transported over this link using the protocol IDs listed in the left column. For IP datagrams, this is 0021. Finally, in the *Terminate* state, LCP packets allow for the link to achieve the Dead state.

In summary, LCP provides for graceful transition from one state to the next. NCPs allow for a network protocol to be initialized, and data for that protocol is sent using the protocol IDs listed in the far left column.

Number of Bytes	Field Name	Example	Description
1	Flag	7e	Always 0111 1110.
1	Address	ff	Always 1111 1111. May be omitted.
1	Control	03	Always 0000 0011. May be omitted.
2	Protocol Type	0021	Protocol. May be reduced to 1 byte in length.
0-1500	Data	---	Data
2	Checksum	024a	Error checking
1	Flag	7e	Always 0111 1110

(a)

Protocol IDs		NCP (Network Control Protocol) IDs		Link Control Protocol IDs	
0021	IP	8021	IP - NCP	c021	LCP : Link Control Protocol
0023	X.25	8023	X.25 - NCP	c023	PAP : Password Authentication Protocol
002b	Novell IPX	802b	IPX - NCP	c025	LQR : Link Quality Report
0201	802.1d	8031	Bridging - NCP	c223	CHAP : Challenge Handshake Authentication Protocol

(b)

Figure 25.3 (a) Frame format for PPP resembles SDLC or HDLC. (b) The various Protocol Types can basically be divided into three categories.

Number of *BITS*	Field Name	Example	Description
4	IP Version	4	Version of IP protocol
4	IP Header Length	5	Length of the IP header only
8	Type of Service	00	Service quality requested
16	Total Datagram Length	05dc	Length of the datagram
16	Datagram Identification	890c	Number of the datagram used in fragmentation
3	Flags	0	Flags are also used in fragmentation
13	Fragment Offset	0	Byte number of where the fragment begins
8	Time-to-Live	fd	Number of hops left for the datagram to travel
8	Protocol	01	ICMP, IGMP, TCP, or UDP
16	Header Checksum	902a	Error checking on only the header
32	Source IP Address	b081d01	IP address of the host who sent the datagram
32	Destination IP Address	09cd00a	IP address of the target host
variable	Options	-	Rarely used options
variable	Padding	-	Forces the header to end at a 32-bit boundary.

Figure 25.4 The IP datagram header is normally 20 bytes.

25.3 IPv4

IP is described in RFC 791 by Postel. The only fields we have mentioned so far in the IP datagram header are the protocol and IP address fields. As seen in Figure 25.4, there are a lot more fields in this header. Let us go through the rest of them in order. You may want to refer back to Figure 8.14 to see how the fields of an IP header are decoded by the Ethereal LAN Analyzer. In Figure 25.6(a) the header is drawn in a block format.

The first four bits of the header specify the version number of the datagram. In the example shown, it is 4. In IPv4, most IP datagram headers are only 20 bytes long so the header length, given in number of 32-bit words, is usually 5. The only time that the header could become larger than 5 words is if options are used. Since this is a four-bit field, the largest header length can only be 60 bytes. This is obtained by converting 1111 from binary to decimal yielding 15 words or 60 bytes. To find out if the header has options or not, look at this field.

Data Precedence
(Bits 1 to 3 of TOS)
111 National Network Control
110 Internetwork Control
101 CRTIC/ECP
100 Flash Override
011 Flash
010 Immediate
001 Priority
000 Routine Delivery

Type of Service: This field could become important if it were implemented in routers. Currently, it is rarely used except by the DoD. It is divided into two parts. The first part is 3 bits long and is called precedence. The rest of the 5 bits belong to a part called service bits. Typically, the value of precedence is set to 000 for routine datagram delivery. However, if set to 111 (in binary), it would give the datagram the highest priority. These priority datagrams allow diagnostic and management packets to get through a network when it is congested or having other problems. In such cases, these packets would get through first, even if it means that lower-priority packets get dropped. The list of these priorities is given in the side figure.

TCP/IP: Additional Concepts

Users with a high precedence code can transmit at the flash level. Those who have an even higher code, called the flash override, can bump the users who are at the flash level. Levels above the flash override levels are for network control purposes.

The next four bits are called service bits and they are used more commonly. But again, many routers don't implement these bits so setting them doesn't serve any useful purpose. The last bit is always 0. Out of the four service bits, only one bit can be set at any given time. They represent minimum delay, high throughput of data, high reliability, and minimum cost. Telnet and other interactive protocols would require minimum delay. FTP and SMTP data transfers would require high throughput. SNMP (Simple Network Management Protocol) and OSPF routing protocol packets would require high reliability. The minimum monetary cost bit is rarely used, but could be used by OSPF when making a routing decision to send the datagram on the lowest-cost link. These service bits are summarized in the side figure.

Service Bits (Bits 4 to 8 of TOS)

00000	Normal service
10000	Low delay request
01000	High throughput request
00100	High reliability request
00010	Low monetary cost

(Other combinations not used)

The total length of the datagram in bytes, including the lengths of the header and the data, is given in the datagram length field. Although, the largest datagram could be 2^{16} or 64 kbytes long, this high value is not used. All hosts, however, are expected to accept 576-byte datagrams. If larger datagrams are to be sent, that value must first be verified. That value is called MTU (Maximum Transfer Unit). To find out how many bytes the data occupies in a packet, the IP header length should be subtracted from this field. For example, if the IP header length is 5 and the total datagram length is 100 in decimal, 5 times 4, or 20, is the length of the header, and subtracting this from 100 gives 80. Then the data carried in the datagram is 80 bytes long.

The minimum amount of data for an Ethernet frame is 46 bytes. If the data is actually less than that, padding bits are added to make the data at least 46 bytes long. In such a case, the total datagram length field will indicate how many of the bytes are real data and how many are just padding. In the datagram example shown in Figure 25.4, the value of 05dc is shown for this field. This is 1500 bytes, the maximum size of data that Ethernet can carry. With 20 bytes for the header, this datagram has 1480 bytes of IP data. The 1480 bytes of IP data actually has an ICMP packet due to the given protocol of 1. It contains 4 bytes of ICMP header and the ICMP data. For an 802.3 frame, the maximum value would be 05d4 or 1492 bytes, since 3 bytes are used by the LLC and 5 bytes are used by the SNAP header.

Fragmentation: The rest of the IP header fields are affected by what is called *fragmentation*. When a large datagram is transferred from one network to another network that accepts only smaller-sized frames (or smaller-sized MTUs), the router may have to divide the datagram into fragments. This is done so that the fragment can be transported by the network of the smaller-sized MTU.

If a datagram can be divided into fragments, the destination host must reassemble them back into a datagram. If there are fragments derived from many datagrams how can a host know which fragment belongs to which datagram? The answer is the datagram *Identification* field. Each datagram is given a unique identification number by the transmitting host. Hence, all the fragments created from the same datagram have the same identification. Two datagrams arriving from different hosts possibly could

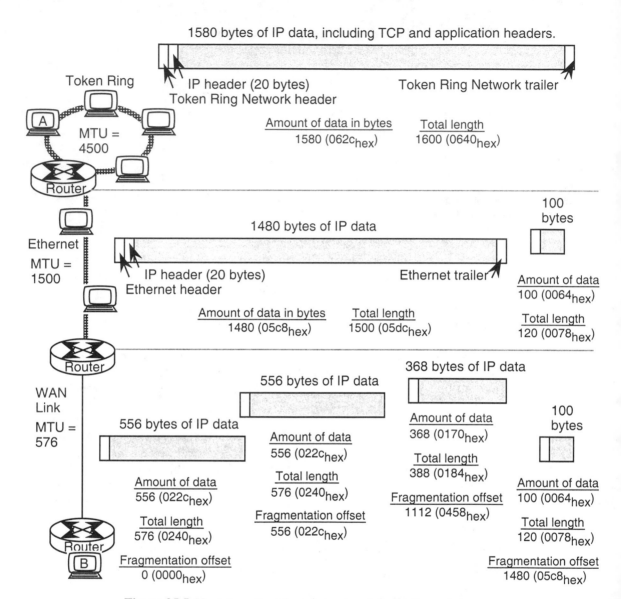

Figure 25.5 Host A on the token ring network is sending a datagram to Host B. The router must break the datagram into two fragments so that the data in the Ethernet frame doesn't exceed its maximum MTU (Maximum Transfer Unit) of 1500 bytes. The first of these fragments must be refragmented so that the amount of data doesn't exceed the WAN link's MTU of 576 bytes.

have the same identification. However, in such cases, the different values for *Source IP Addresses* will determine that they are different datagrams. This field is sufficiently large (16 bits), so that two datagrams arriving from one host cannot have the same

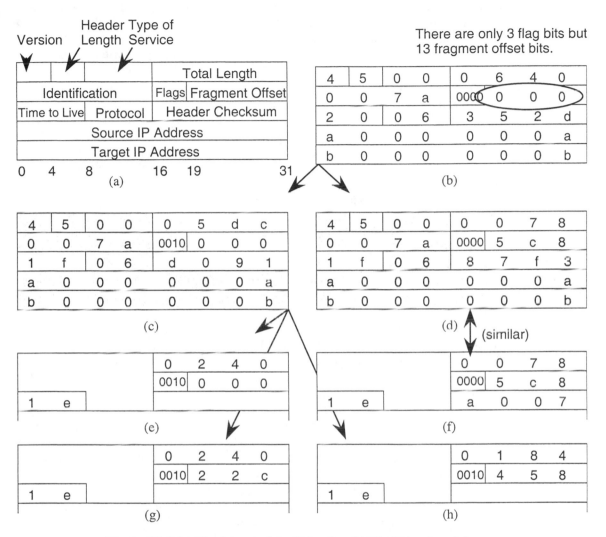

Figure 25.6 (a) The format of the IP header. (b) The IP header of the original datagram being transported over the token ring network. (c and d) First, the datagram is divided into two fragments. Values of all shaded fields are exactly the same as the original datagram and will be the same for the headers of the WAN link's fragments. (e, g, and h) The three fragments that were created by dividing up the first Ethernet fragment. (f) The second Ethernet fragment doesn't have to be refragmented.

identification at any given time. Let's go through an example of fragmentation to better understand the purpose of these fields.

At the top of Figure 25.5, we see 1580 bytes of data being placed in a datagram which is 1600 bytes long by Host A. This datagram is transported to the first router over a Token Ring Network, which allows frames to carry up to 4500 bytes of data.

Therefore, 1600-byte-long datagrams can easily be transported over this network. Notice, the decimal numbers of 1580 and 1600 are converted to hex in the figure since we will need these numbers to synthesize the datagram header. To create the other headers that we will need in this figure, other bytes are also converted to hex.

Now this datagram is routed to an Ethernet LAN that can only support data of 1500 bytes. This requires that the router fragment the 1600-byte datagram into a 1500-byte fragment and a 120-byte fragment. The second IP header requires an additional 20 bytes. Hence, the 1580 bytes of data is divided into two fragments each carrying 1480 bytes and 100 bytes, respectively.

Next, the lower router on the Ethernet LAN must route these two packets over a WAN link. It may not know the largest-sized packet that the receiving host can accept. According to specifications, the smallest figure for this is 576 bytes, including the header. Hence, the router may refragment into packets of data as large as 556 bytes. The first fragment is then divided into two 576- and one 388-byte fragments. Adding 556, 556, and 368 gives 1480 bytes of data arriving in the first Ethernet frame. The second Ethernet frame doesn't need to be refragmented. This way, one datagram is divided into four fragments.

Only the receiving host will reassemble these fragments. If they come out of sequence, how can it know the order in which to reassemble them. The *Fragmentation Offset* field provides this function. Notice, from the bottom part of Figure 25.5, that this offset is given as 0 for the fragment on the far left, indicating that this is the first fragment. The next fragment's offset is 556, indicating that the previous bytes from 0 through 555 are in a preceding fragment. 556 plus 556 is 1112, which would then be the offset for the third fragment. Lastly, the offset for the 120-byte packet is 1480, the number of bytes preceded that packet. Using these numbers, the target host can reassemble the fragments. With the hex conversions done for these numbers, we are armed with enough information to create the IP headers for each packet. Notice that a datagram can be called a packet and so can a fragment. Fragments can travel from link to link, but a datagram transmission is an end-to-end delivery. In our example, the destination host received one datagram encoded into four packets.

Its time to code the headers for all these IP packets. You will want to refer to Figure 25.5 as we go over the headers in Figure 25.6. In Figure (a), the IP header is given again. In Figure (b), we see the header of the datagram in the Token Ring Network. The *Flags* field uses three bits, but the *Offset* field uses the following 13 bits. Notice here that the version is set to IPv4. The length of the header is 5 words. The default value of 0 for Type of Service is used. Next, the *Total Length* of 640_{hex} is given.

The datagram identification is $007a_{hex}$. Next comes the 3-bit *Flags* field. Here, the first bit is always 0. The next bit indicates that this datagram may be fragmented. If it were 1, then the datagram could not be fragmented. In that case, it would just be discarded and an ICMP error message would be sent to the source host indicating that this happened. The third flag bit is also 0 indicating that there are no more fragments following this packet. See the side figure.

At the beginning of the third word, we see that the *Time to Live* field is set to 20_{hex}. This is actually the number of hops this

Flag Bits

000 Fragmentation allowed and
no more fragments to follow
001 Fragmentation allowed and
more fragments to follow
010 Fragmentation not allowed and
no more fragments to follow

TCP/IP: Additional Concepts

packet can travel before it is discarded. This means that after this packet can go through a maximum of 32 routers. This prevents a packet from going through infinite loops in a network. The upper-layer protocol is 06 or TCP and the *Header Checksum* is calculated to be $352d_{hex}$. (This is not an actual calculation.) The last two words give the source and destination IP addresses.

Now let us look at the headers of the two fragments which are sent over the Ethernet. They are shown in Figures (c) and (d). All the fields that are copied over from the datagram are shaded. The non-shaded fields are the fields which we will now discuss. In Figure (c), the *Total Length* field is $05dc_{hex}$ which is the length shown for the first fragment in the Ethernet LAN in Figure 25.5. The last *Flag* bit is set to 1, indicating that one or more fragments are following this one. The offset is 0 indicating that this is the first fragment and the hop count is reduced from 20_{hex} to $1f_{hex}$. This indicates that this packet has gone through one router. The checksum for the header is going to be different than the checksum for the packet header in the Token Ring Network.

For the header shown in Figure (d), the Total Length is 0078_{hex}. The offset is $5c8_{hex}$, indicating that this many bytes have preceded this fragment. The more fragments to follow flag is 0, indicating that this is the last fragment for this datagram and the checksum calculation will be different than for any of the other packets.

This brings us to the four packets which will travel over the WAN link. These are shown in Figures (e) through (h). In Figure (h), the 120-byte-long packet header is almost the same. The only field that has changed is *Time to Live*, because we have gone through one more router. It has been decremented by 1 to $1e_{hex}$. This makes the checksum for the header also change. These two fields change for the same reason for the first three packets. The lengths of the header and the offset values are simply copied from Figure 25.5. Notice, however, that all the fragments have a 1 for the more fragments flag bit except for the last fragment.

25.4 IP Address Shortages

When TCP/IP was first developed it was supposed to have been a temporary solution for the Department of Defense until OSI became finalized. Hence, the IP addresses of 32 bits were thought to be sufficient. However, TCP/IP became too popular for its own good and now we don't have enough IP addresses to go around. IP version 6 provides 128-bit addresses. But other solutions for the IP address shortage problem have been surfacing, some of which are temporary.

25.4.1 CIDR

CIDR (Classless InterDomain Routing) is described in RFCs 1518 and 1519. The country of China, for example, has applied six times to get a class B network and have been denied each time since no more class B addresses exist. There are still class C network addresses available and so they are being given out instead of class A or B addresses. The problem with a group of class C addresses instead of one class B address is that the group of network addresses increases the size of the routing tables. A separate entry must exist in the routers for each class C network. What CIDR does is disregard the network and host bit boundaries for the different classes and make this

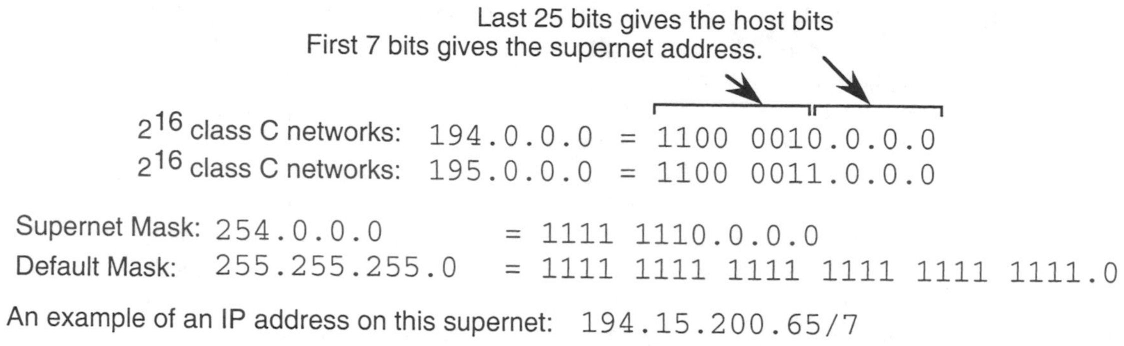

Last 25 bits gives the host bits
First 7 bits gives the supernet address.

2^{16} class C networks: 194.0.0.0 = 1100 0010.0.0.0
2^{16} class C networks: 195.0.0.0 = 1100 0011.0.0.0

Supernet Mask: 254.0.0.0 = 1111 1110.0.0.0
Default Mask: 255.255.255.0 = 1111 1111 1111 1111 1111 1111.0

An example of an IP address on this supernet: 194.15.200.65/7

Figure 25.7 Two 2^{16} class C networks are combined into one super-network. With 7 network bits, the mask becomes 254.0.0.0 instead of 255.255.255.0. The last line shows how the mask is written with the IP address.

bit boundary more flexible. This allows many class C networks to be routed using one routing table entry rather than many. Many networks can now be routed using one table entry.

When routing is done using classes, the network and host bit boundaries are fixed and known by all routers. For example, for a class C network, there are 24 bits used to code the network address and 8 bits used to code the host address. However, since the network and host bit boundaries can vary with CIDR, we need to convey where the boundary exists with each IP address. Older routing protocols do not support a variable-length boundary. OSPF and RIP-2, however, do. The network and host bit boundary is provided in what is called the supernet mask and the collection of the class C networks that are grouped together is called a *supernet*.

When aggregating several class C networks together into a supernet, it is best to locate them in the same geography or topology. Class C networks belonging to the same supernet, should all be in the same region or belong to the same ISP or organization. This way, when a router belonging to the supernet gets any packet for itself, it can route it quickly toward the correct destination. Let us look at an example.

Figure 25.7 shows all the class C networks that begin with 1100 001 in binary. There are 2^{17} of these networks each with 256 host addresses. All these networks can be supernetted by defining the supernet mask to be 254.0.0.0 instead of the natural or default mask of 255.255.255.0 for class C networks. When the IP address is given, its supernet mask of 7 bits is also given by using "/7." For example, the IP address of 194.15.200.65/7 indicates that this address uses 7 network bits and 25 host bits. Only an additional 5 bits are needed to transmit the supernet mask with its IP address.

This range of addresses are all located in Europe. In USA, only one router entry needs to be available for all of the 2^{17} networks for those packets to be forwarded toward Europe. Without CIDR, we would have needed 2^{17} routing table entries. Notice, non-classless addresses can also be written using the "/" notation. For example, the IP address of 72.9.0.34 can be written as 72.9.0.34/8 since class A addresses use 8 network bits.

25.4.2 DHCP

RFC 1541 describes DHCP (Dynamic Host Configuration Protocol). Before DHCP, each host in a LAN would be assigned its own IP address. This address was static and was entered in the configuration files of the host. During the booting up process, that IP address was assigned to that host. Even with RARP, if the diskless workstation didn't know its IP address, it obtained its fixed IP address from a RARP server. In any case, each host (or each MAC address) used a given IP address.

If a host was communicating only within its own LAN and didn't need an IP address, then that IP address was wasted. Furthermore, if a host was idle or powered off, then again its assigned IP address was not being used. For everyone to have an IP address when they needed it, they had to keep an IP address for always. DHCP addresses this problem by assigning IP addresses dynamically, as they need them. Suppose that you had only one class C network with 254 usable addresses. Without DHCP you could support only 254 hosts in the LAN. However, with DHCP, now you can provide Internet support for perhaps 500 hosts. The number of hosts that can be supported depends upon the usage of IP addresses. To support 500 hosts, we are assuming that only up to 254 of them require an IP address at any given time and that the others are idle or accessing the local network.

The concept of DHCP is rather simple. It uses a DHCP server which manages all of the IP addresses that are going to be assigned dynamically. When a host needs an IP address, it will ask the DHCP server for an IP address, then when it is finished using the IP address, the host will give it back to the DHCP server. This way the returned IP address becomes available for some other host to use. Notice, each time a host requests an IP address from the DHCP server, it may not get the same address. This becomes a problem for DNS service which must map hostnames with IP addresses. If a host can have several IP addresses during the course of a day, it becomes difficult for DNS to track that. For this reason, many servers are given fixed IP addresses because they are in use all the time. However, DHCP proves to be more advantageous for clients.

DHCP's roots go back to RARP. RARP provides IP address resolution for each LAN segment. Every segment separated by a router in a LAN required its own RARP server. To avoid this requirement, the BOOTP protocol was created, which uses UDP and is routable. RARP is a network access layer protocol while BOOTP and DHCP are TCP/IP applications. In a multisegment, only one BOOTP server is needed for diskless workstations to obtain their IP addresses. However, with BOOTP, each physical address maps to one IP address. A DHCP server manages a pool of IP addresses and leases them out to whichever host needs them.

Figure 25.8 outlines the header for a DHCP message. Aside from the Flags and Options Area fields, this format is the same as that of a BOOTP message. An example of a request with an Operation Code of 1 and a response with an Operation Code of 2 are shown. The request message is sent by the client to the DHCP server asking for a lease of an IP address. The response message is sent by the DHCP server.

The Hardware Type and Hardware Length fields are the same as we encountered in the ARP and RARP frames. See Figure 25.2. The Number of Hops field specifies through how many routers this message may pass. The Transaction ID is used to match the reply message with the request message. The amount of time passed since the request was made by the client is coded in the Seconds field.

Number of _bytes_	Field Name	Request Example	Reply Example	Description
1	Operation Code	01	02	Request or Response
1	Hardware Type	01	01	Ethernet, Token Ring, etc.
1	Hardware Length	06	06	MAC Address Length
1	Number of Hops	01	01	Number of routers allowed
4	Transaction Id	3f00910a	3f00910a	Identification of request
2	Seconds	0000	0010	Time elapsed since request
2	Flags	0000	0000	Only leftmost bit used
4	Client IP Address	00000000	00000000	IP Address, usually not known
4	Your IP Address	00000000	a10045b8	Address received from server
4	Server IP Address	00000000	a10045b9	Address of the DHCP server
4	Gateway IP Address	00000000	a10045b9	Address of default gateway
16	Client Hardware Addr.	b081d01..	b081d01..	MAC Address
64	Server Hostname	0000000..	0000000..	DHCP server name
128	Boot Path & Filename	0000000..	0000000..	Initial configuration information
variable	Options Area	0000000..	0000000..	Vendor-specific information

Figure 25.8 The DHCP message format.

If the far left bit in the Flags field, the only one used currently, is set to 1, the client is asking that the response be sent using a hardware broadcast. In the example this is a 0. Hence, the response will be sent using a unicast frame only to the client. Because the client doesn't know its IP address, this field is set to 0. In the response message from the DHCP server, the client's IP address is provided in the Your IP Address field. Also, the IP addresses of the DHCP server and the default router are provided in the next two fields. The hostname of the server can be encoded, if known. However, like the rest of the fields, if the value for a field is not known, it is filled with zeros.

25.4.3 Private IP-based Networks

A private enterprise, such as General Electric, can decide to create its own private internet using TCP/IP. An organization such as this can have its own set of routers and leased lines interconnecting its LANs and WANs. Such a network is called a private internet, with a lower case "i." It would own and operate the infrastructure of such an internet. Although costly to maintain, it would have more security control. It could use any IP address because it would not be connected to the public Internet, with an uppercase "I."

A private internet may want to connect to the public Internet, but then it would need registered IP addresses. In such a case, it would need to reassign the IP addresses for all its internal hosts, if it can get authorization for that many. A better solution for this problem would be, to begin with, to assign designated private IP addresses to the internal hosts. Then when a connection needs to be made with the Internet, it would get official registered IP addresses and insert a NAT (Network Address Translation) device at the boundary.

Class	Range of Addresses		Number of Addresses Available
Class A:	10/8	(10.0.0.0 - 10.255.255.255)	2^{24}
Class B:	172.16/12	(172.16.0.0 - 172.32.0.0)	2^{20}
Class C:	192.168/16	(192.168.0.0 - 192.168.255.0)	2^{16}

Figure 25.9 Private IP address ranges which are not routable through the public Internet.

The designated private IP addresses can be used by any private network. This is because these addresses are not routable over the Internet. Whenever an IP packet with a private IP address arrives at any Internet router, it discards it. Hence, if you want to connect to the Internet, you can use any of these private addresses without having to register them, but you won't be able to send packets over the Internet.

RFC 1918 identifies three sets of private network IP addresses, one in each class of A, B, and C address space. They are listed in Figure 25.9 and are 10/8, 172.16/12, and 192.168/16. In the next chapter on Linux, we use addresses from this group for our hosts in the lab.

To begin with, if the organization can get registration for public IP addresses, then when the time comes for them to be connected to the Internet, the conversion is easier and local host addresses do not need to be reassigned. Using private IP addresses is the next best solution.

25.4.4 NAT (Network Address Translation) Devices

Figure 25.10(a) shows a private internet using the 172.16/12 addresses being connected to the Internet using a NAT device. The NAT addresses or the registered addresses are shown to be on the 201.117.30/24 network. Every time a host needs a public connection, the NAT box finds an unused public IP address and dynamically creates a translation table entry for that address and the local IP address. Then during the session, every time the internal host sends out an IP packet, the NAT box converts its source address to the translated public address. Similarly, when a packet arrives for that NAT (or public IP) address, the NAT box converts its destination address to the private address.

This is shown in Figure 25.10(b). An IP packet comes from the Internet into the NAT box destined for 201.117.30.33. The NAT box looks at its internal translation table and changes that address to 172.16.10.111 in the IP header of that packet. There are only 2^8 public addresses available to be shared by up to 2^{20} private hosts. However, since not all private hosts will be accessing the Internet at the same time (and many will be accessing the hosts within the private network anyway) this solution is acceptable. In the event that there are no more public addresses available in the pool, the NAT device will return an ICMP error message stating that the destination address is unreachable.

It turns out that NAT devices are useful for other purposes. If a customer wants to change their ISP but to keep their original IP addresses from the previous ISP, then an NAT device managed at the previous ISP can redirect packets to the new ISP. Also,

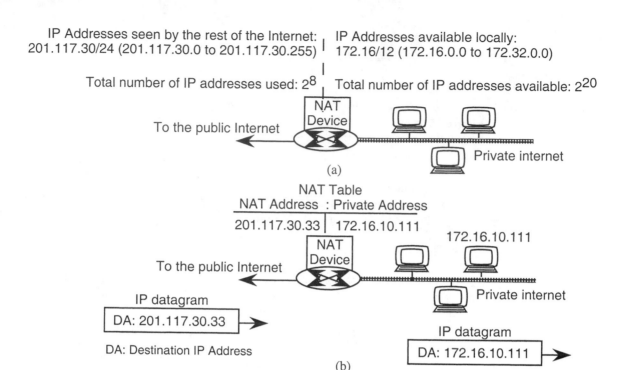

IP Addresses seen by the rest of the Internet: | IP Addresses available locally:
201.117.30/24 (201.117.30.0 to 201.117.30.255) | 172.16/12 (172.16.0.0 to 172.32.0.0)

Total number of IP addresses used: 2^8 | Total number of IP addresses available: 2^{20}

To the public Internet

NAT Device

Private internet

(a)

NAT Table
NAT Address : Private Address
201.117.30.33 | 172.16.10.111

172.16.10.111

To the public Internet

NAT Device

Private internet

IP datagram

DA: 201.117.30.33

DA: Destination IP Address

IP datagram

DA: 172.16.10.111

(b)

Figure 25.10 (a) A NAT (Network Address Translation) device can
serve more local hosts than the number of registered IP addresses it has.
(b) For example, the NAT device converts the IP address of an incoming
IP packet from a registered IP address to a private, local IP address.

when two companies merge and need to merge two sets of private internets, NAT
devices placed at the boundaries of the two networks can provide a solution.

NAT adds some control to security by eliminating spoofing of IP addresses.
Hackers can send packets into your network with source IP addresses belonging to your
own set of IP addresses, making your network think that they are local packets. This
is called address spoofing. However, if you have private IP addresses, then this is not
possible. Routers in the public Internet will drop packets that contain such addresses.

This is the first time in IP history that devices have changed IP addresses in the
headers of IP packets. When this is done, the checksum has to be recalculated for each
header. All this slows down the routing of the packets.

25.4.5 Proxy Servers

A NAT box will share a pool of public IP addresses with many local hosts. On
the other hand, a more specialized NAT box called a *proxy server* will share only one
IP address with several local hosts. In Linux, this is called *IP masquarading*.

Looking at Figure 25.11, we see a proxy server with one official address of
201.117.30.33. This one address can provide connections to multiple local hosts on the
private internet simultaneously. In Linux, the default maximum limit is set to 4096

hosts. Instead of mapping IP addresses, the proxy server uses port numbers to differ-entiate the connections. These port numbers are used from the TCP headers.

In our example shown in the figure, an incoming IP packet arrives destined for port number 61001. Port numbers above 61000 are used for proxy servers. The server looks up in its table and finds that this port maps to the local address of 172.16.10.111 and port 4190. Then the IP packet is converted and sent to this host. Notice that not only is the IP header altered but also the transport or TCP header. The figure also shows how an outgoing packet is converted by the proxy server using the table.

Typically, proxy servers are used for smaller private networks, while NAT devices are used for larger networks. That is, it is said that NAT devices scale better. However, since all local hosts hide behind one public IP address and security can be configured in all layers of a proxy server, a proxy server provides better security than a NAT device. Plus, it's easier to get one IP address than several. These differences are summarized in Table 25.1.

A major drawback of NAT devices or proxy servers is that they do not support a new protocol called IPsec (IP Security). This protocol requires that data encryption be an end-to-end issue and that no devices in the path of IP packets alter them in any way. Other emerging protocols will also not work with NAT devices without adding more software to them, making them application layer gateways. Doing this will only slow down the packets further, making streaming multimedia unacceptable. Another protocol called RSIP (Realm Specific IP) is being developed currently to address the problems with NAT and proxy servers.

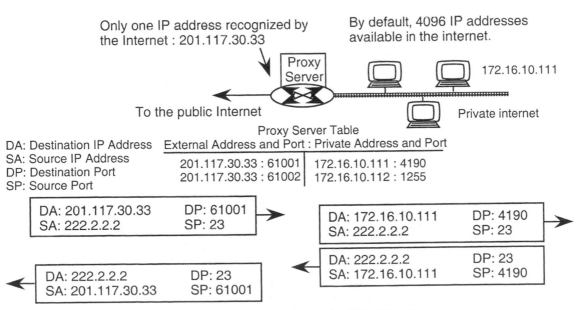

Figure 25.11 A proxy server uses only one official IP address to connect multiple local hosts. In this example, all the local hosts hide behind the IP address of 201.117.30.33. The port number is used to identify each local host.

	NAT Server	Proxy Server
Table 25.1 Comparison of NAT and Proxy Servers		
Original intent	Convert addresses	Provide security
Is the IP address converted?	Yes	No
The external network sees how many addresses?	A pool of them	Only one
How are connections identified to internal hosts?	IP Addresses	Ports
Level of security?	Marginal	At all layers
Used with what size networks	Larger	Smaller

25.4.6 IPv6

History repeats itself. TCP/IP was created as an interim solution for the DoD until OSI became the standard method of internetworking. Instead TCP/IP became the de facto standard. Similarly, the methods that we have mentioned in the previous sections to overcome the problem of IPv4 address shortage were created as interim solutions until IP version 6 became finalized. At the time of this writing implementation of IPv6 looks like it is going to take longer than was first anticipated.

IPv6 extended IPv4 address lengths from 32 bits to 128 bits. That is enough addresses to fit 50 addresses on every square inch of land that exists on earth. But there are other advantages for IPv6. Primarily they include extensions for authentication and

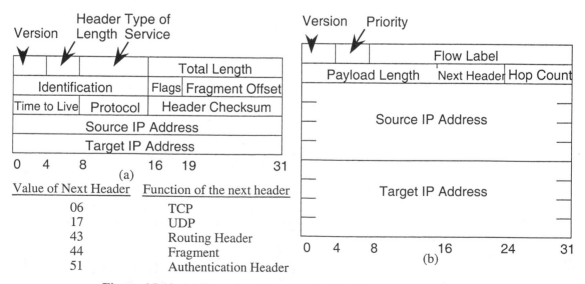

Figure 25.12 (a) IP version 4 header. (b) The IP version 6 header. The table shows some values of the Next Header field and how they are used.

TCP/IP: Additional Concepts

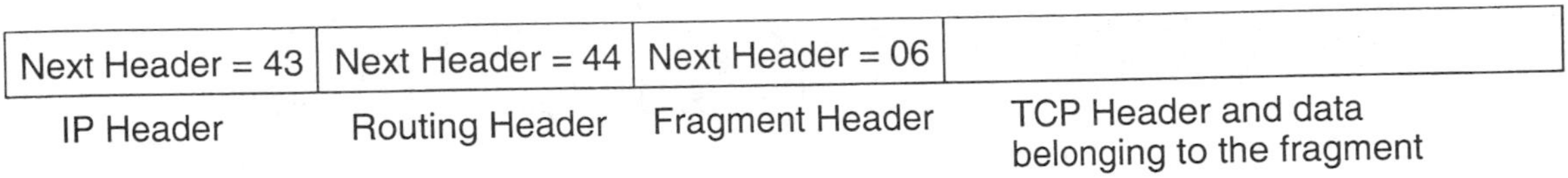

Next Header = 43	Next Header = 44	Next Header = 06	
IP Header	Routing Header	Fragment Header	TCP Header and data belonging to the fragment

Figure 25.13 An example of an IP packet with one IP header and two extension headers.

encryption extensions for better security, privacy, and integrity. More levels of addressing hierarchy are present than just network, subnet, and host portions. Flow labelling provides better QoS (Quality of Service) for real-time applications. This field is shown in Figure 25.12(b). Improved and efficient routing support for a wider base of IP addresses is achieved by regional cluster addressing and a simpler header format.

In Figure 25.12(a) and (b) the headers for IPv4 and IPv6 are shown. Remember the 3-bit Flags field and the 13 bit Fragment Offset field of IPv4? Well, they don't exist in the new header format. All fields as you can see delimit at 4, 8, 16, 24, and 128-bit boundaries. This makes it is easier for routers to process packets. Additionally, there are fewer fields to examine. Instead of calculating the length of the data as was done with IPv4, the length of the data is placed directly in the header. The Hop Count field of IPv6 is used exactly as the Time to Live field of IPv4.

Although the header is simplified for most cases, an IP packet may have several headers. The value given in the Next Header field specifies whether or not there are additional headers appended to the current IP header. As shown in the figure, if the value of the Next Header field is 17, then the header following this one is a UDP header. In this case, this field functions as the Protocol field of IPv4. Additional headers between the IP header and the transport layer header are called extension headers.

For an example, see Figure 25.13. Here, the Next Header field of the IP header signals that the next header is a routing header. From the chart in Figure 25.12, we see that a value of 43 represents a routing header. This is the first extension header. In this header the value of 44 signals that the next header is a fragment header. Hence, a fragment header appears next. This is the second extension header. The fragment header also has its own Next Header field, whose value of 06 signals that the next header is a TCP header. Therefore, a TCP header and its data is shown next.

25.5 ICMP

In Chapter 8, we introduced ICMP and UDP. Here, we will extend that discussion to include their header formats. In Figure 25.14, the format of the ICMP message is shown. It has a 32-bit-long header which includes the Type, Code, and Checksum fields. An ICMP message, besides having a header, may also contain data of a varying length. The data is determined by the values of the ICMP Type and Code. A checksum is calculated using the entire ICMP message, including the header and data.

There are many possible Type values and they are shown in Table 25.2. Each message type has an associated meaning, and is either a query message or an error message, and that is also shown in the table. An error message cannot generate another error message. An ICMP message type can have several codes. For instance, notice that the Destination Unreachable message has 16 possible Code values. Each code, in this instance, represents the reason why the IP datagram wasn't delivered. Hence, the Type

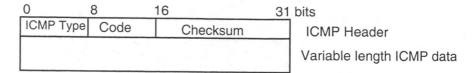

Figure 25.14 The format of an ICMP message.

gives you what is wrong and the code gives you the reason for it. However, there are only four Type values which have more than one code.

Depending on the type of the message, data will be placed in the ICMP message. This data may contain IP addresses or, when reporting a problem, may contain entire IP headers plus 64 bytes of data. This 64 bytes of data will help the receiving host examine the transport and application layer headers to determine the cause of the failure. Examples of some of these messages will be studied later when using the ping and the traceroute commands.

25.6 UDP

The UDP header is shown in Figure 25.15. It is only 8 bytes long compared to 20 or 24 bytes for TCP. The Length field gives the length of the entire UDP datagram and similarly, the Checksum is calculated for the entire UDP datagram. The Checksum field is verified only by the destination host.

Table 25.2 ICMP Message Types			
Type (in decimal)	Number of codes for this type	Query or error message	Meaning of this message type
0	1	Query	Echo reply used with ping
3	16	Error	Destination is unreachable
4	1	Error	Source quench
5	4	Error	Redirect for host, network, or TOS
8	1	Query	Echo request used with ping
9	1	Query	Router advertisement
10	1	Query	Router solicitation
11	2	Error	Time exceeded used with traceroute
12	2	Error	Parameter problem or bad IP header
13	1	Query	Timestamp request
14	1	Query	Timestamp reply
15	1	Query	Information request (obsolete)
16	1	Query	Information reply (obsolete)
17	1	Query	Address mask request
18	1	Query	Address mask reply

TCP/IP: Additional Concepts

0	8	16	31 bits
Source Port		Destination Port	
Length		Checksum	

Figure 25.15 The UDP header. The length is the length of the entire UDP datagram, including the header. Also, the Checksum is calculated over the entire datagram.

The Destination Port identifies the application to which the rest of the data is to be forwarded. On the other hand, the Source Port field is optional and can be filled with zeros. Some server applications choose to do this.

25.7 TCP

25.7.1 The TCP Header Format

TCP is described in RFC 793. For now let us go over the individual fields of the TCP header. After this we will go over examples of data exchanges to better appreciate their purpose and how they are used. Figure 25.16 shows the format of the TCP header. Typically its length is five 32-bit words because the Options and its necessary Padding fields are not used. In such cases, the Header Length field is coded as 5. In rare cases where Options are used, the Header Length is 6.

The most common option is the maximum segment size option. It normally occurs only once while establishing a TCP connection. The sending TCP module indicates to the receiving TCP module the maximum size of the segment it is willing to accept. Several TCP segments may be sent, but the maximum size of each one should not exceed this limit.

In Chapter 8 we have already come across the Source and the Destination Port fields. As used in the UDP header, these fields provide the addresses of the applications.

When a TCP module sends data, it numbers or sequences each byte of data. The number of the first byte of data in the TCP segment (which comes right after the TCP header and may be part of the application header) is placed in this field. This field doesn't specify how many bytes there are in the segment, only the sequence number of the first byte of data it contains. To find out how much data exists in a TCP segment, you must subtract the IP and TCP header lengths from the Total Length Field given in the IP header. When a connection is being established the very first byte number is derived from the internal clock and is hardly ever 0.

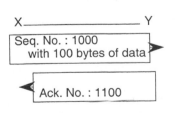

The Acknowledgement number is valid only when the ACK flag is set to 1. The Flags are shown next to the Reserved field in the figure. (The Reserved field is not used.) The Acknowledgement number specifies the next sequence number of the transmitting TCP module that is expected by the receiver. For example, in the side figure we see that X is sending 100 bytes of data to Y. The number of the first byte is 1000, hence the number of the last byte is 1099. Because from 1001 to 1100 there exist 100 numbers, from 1000 to 1099 there also exist 100 numbers. Because

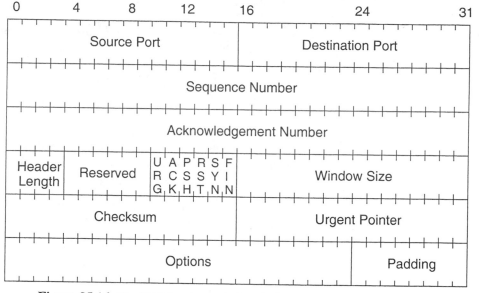

Figure 25.16 The TCP header includes six flags shown next the Reserved field.

Y has received byte numbers up to 1099 without errors, Y is expecting byte number 1100 next and codes the Acknowledgement field with 1100.

The first Flag we see is the URG (Urgent) flag. If this is set, that is, if its value is 1 the Urgent Pointer field is valid and is being used. Similar to the ACK flag, when it is set, the Acknowledgement Number field is valid and is being used. The purpose of the Urgent Pointer is to identify the location in the data that should be processed before any of the rest of the data. This field is an offset, which means to count off this many bytes from the first byte of the data in the TCP segment. Exactly how this field is used depends upon each implementation.

The PSH (Push) flag when set means that the data should be sent immediately before the rest of the data is assembled. For example, in a chat session where two terminals are communicating in real time, every time the return key is pressed, the data is "pushed" through the network. This makes the segment sizes small.

The RST (Reset) flag when set means to reset the entire connection immediately. The receiving TCP module will clear all buffers, and all data that is still being sent is considered lost.

The SYN (Synchronize) flag is used to establish a TCP connection. Similarly, the FIN (Finish) flag is set to terminate a connection. When a host sets the FIN flag that means that it has no more data to send; however, it will accept data until the other end sets its own FIN flag.

The Checksum field in the IP header only checks for errors in the IP header, but here it checks for errors in the TCP data as well as the TCP header, or the entire TCP segment.

TCP/IP: Additional Concepts

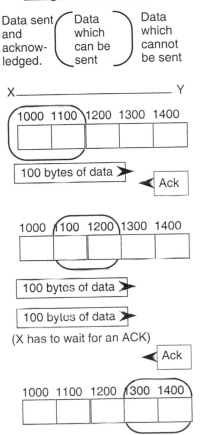

Using the Window field

Data sent and acknowledged.

Data which can be sent

Data which cannot be sent

X————————————Y

1000 1100 1200 1300 1400

100 bytes of data ➤   ◄ Ack

1000 1100 1200 1300 1400

100 bytes of data ➤

100 bytes of data ➤

(X has to wait for an ACK)

◄ Ack

1000 1100 1200 1300 1400

The Window Size field is used by TCP to achieve flow control. If a receiving module wants to accept a maximum of only 200 bytes of data into its buffer that is unacknowledged, this field will be encoded with 200. The receiver can change this value during the life of a connection and be able to accept a greater or lesser amount of unacknowledged data.

In the top of the side diagram a shaded window is shown. This window is imaginary and is placed as if over all the data as it is being transmitted. All data to its left has been sent and acknowledged, all data within the window still has to be sent, for which an acknowledgement has to be received, and all data to the right of the window cannot be sent. Once some data is acknowledged by the receiver, the window can be moved to the right. Let us look at an example.

In the side diagram we see X has 1500 bytes of data to be sent to Y. The size of the window which Y has advertised to X is 200. Hence X is free to sent 200 bytes of data and wait for an acknowledgement. It sends 100 bytes and gets an ACK from Y. Now the window moves 100 bytes to right because of the ACK.

X then sends two segments, each with 100 bytes of data, and waits for an ACK. If it doesn't receive an ACK for the first of these segments in a certain amount of time, it will retransmit it. If it doesn't receive an ACK for the second one either, then it will retransmit that one too. However, before the timeout period, X receives an ACK for the second segment, which means that Y received the first one without errors also. Now X moves the imaginary window over by 200 bytes and continues sending data in the window.

25.7.2 An Example of TCP Exchange of Segments

Using only selected fields of the TCP segments header, Figure 25.17 shows how TCP establishes a connection, transfers data by maintaining a reliable data stream, and then removes the connection. Instead of numbering segments as other protocols number their frames, TCP numbers the individual bytes of data. The Sequence number of a segment identifies the number of the first byte in the segment being transmitted. The Acknowledgment number identifies the byte number of the sender that the receiver is expecting next. The ACK, SYN, FIN fields are one-bit flags that are part of the TCP header.

The Connection Phase: In Figure 25.17, the first segment sent by Host A has its SYN (SYNchronize) bit flag set to 1 and the Sequence number to 5. This tells the TCP module in Host B that A is numbering its segments starting at 5. The Acknowledgement number is 0, indicating that this is the first segment being used in establishing a connection, since Host A doesn't know B's starting segment number yet. Also, since the SYN flag is set and the ACK flag isn't, that is also an indication that the connection

TCP/IP: Additional Concepts

is being established. Host A may at this time indicate its Maximum Segment Size by encoding it as an option and making the Header Length equal 6 instead the typical 5. A can also indicate its Window size at this time, but since in our example only Host A is transmitting to B, this field is not shown.

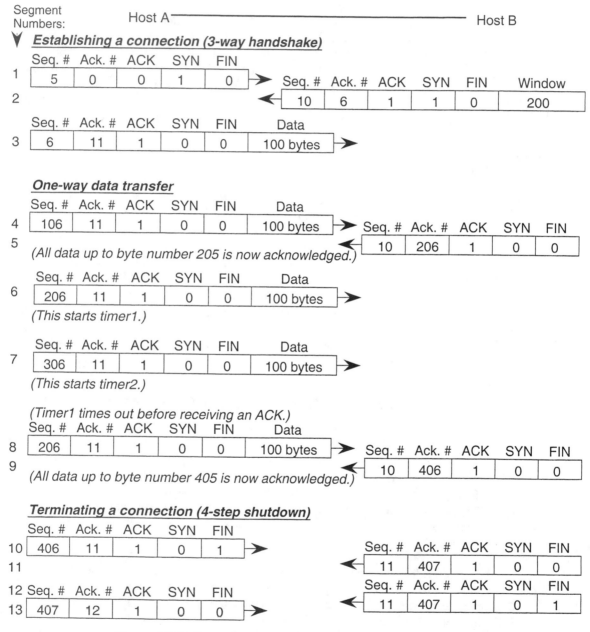

Figure 25.17 Establishing a TCP connection, transferring data, and terminating a connection.

In Segment 2, Host B generates its own Sequence number of 10. It will set its SYN bit to 1, meaning that it also needs a connection established the other way. Also, it will set the ACK bit to 1, indicating that the Acknowledgment number is valid and acknowledging that it is willing to provide a connection to A. The Acknowledgment number is 6, indicating that Host B has received all of A's data bytes up to 5 correctly. Although in the connection phase, this just means that A's first byte of data should actually be numbered at 6. Host B has also set its Window size to 200, signaling A that it can only accept up to that many octets in its buffer during this transmission. This enables B to control the amount of data transmitted from A so it isn't sent too fast for B.

In Segment 3, Host A then acknowledges B's acceptance of the connection by setting the ACK flag to 1 and the Acknowledgment number to 11. If Host B were to send data, which it won't in this example, it would number its first byte of data as 11. Host A sends its first stream of data, starting its Sequence number at 6. This completes the connection using a three-way handshake and now either host is ready to transmit.

Data Transmission Phase: A chose to send 100 octets of data in the first segment, so it has already sent bytes numbered from 6 through 105. In Segment number 4, A sends bytes numbered from 106 through 205. Again 100 bytes of data are sent. Notice that A has sent 200 bytes without receiving an ACK. In Segment number 2, B has indicated its Window size as 200 so A cannot do anything at this time but wait for an ACK for certain time period.

In Segment number 5, Host B acknowledges all 200 bytes of the data that was outstanding by setting the Acknowledgment number to 206 and setting the ACK flag.

Using Segments number 6 and 7, Host A is now free to send another 200 bytes. A is limited to this due to B's Window size. Every time a new segment is sent, A will start a timer specifically for that segment. Hence, one timer is started for Segment number 6 and another one for Segment number 7. Host A is waiting for a response from B and it doesn't arrive.

The timer for Segment 6 goes off. Hence, that segment is retransmitted as shown in Segment number 8. There are a number of reasons why Host A did not receive an ACK from B. Maybe there was an error in the data when Segment 6 arrived at B. This would be checked by B's TCP module using the Checksum field. When a segment arrives with an error, it is simply discarded and it is left to the transmitting host to time out and retransmit that segment.

Another reason why Host A did not receive an ACK is maybe because Host B received the segment late (but correctly). In this case, Host A would end up transmitting Segment 6 again and Host B would receive duplicate frames. From the Sequence number of the segments, B would be able to identify them as duplicates and drop one. It is also possible that the ACK sent by Host B arrived late or was lost. Again, A would need to retransmit Segment 6 as shown in Segment 8.

Finally, Host B sends Segment 9 acknowledging all bytes up to 405. This ACK acknowledges both segments.

The Disconnection Phase: Segment 10 is the first segment used to disconnect the connection. Setting the FIN bit to 1 indicates that Host A is initiating termination.

Either host could do this. Host B acknowledges the request for termination by incrementing the Acknowledgment number by 1 and setting its ACK bit to 1. This is seen in Segment 11. Host B could send data at this time if it wished, but instead it also initiates the termination to Host A by setting its FIN flag to 1 in Segment 12. In Segment 13, A acknowledges B's request for termination.

25.7.3 Connections

Being able to transfer data between two hosts, as we have just seen, is not sufficient. The host must also know what data belongs to which process. For example, in Figure 25.18, there are two users, Users A and B, which are telneting to a single remote host. Telnet allows users to log on to remote hosts and access their services. The internetwork must know which transmission belongs to which user.

From Chapter 8, we know that IP accesses TCP by setting the protocol to 6 and TCP accesses telnet by setting the port number to 23. The protocol and port numbers are specified in the datagram and segment headers.

When a user wants to telnet to a host, a copy of telnet is provided to the user that first initiates a connection. The connection is provided by assigning the user a port number (4016 for user A) by the operating system of the originating host. The remote host is continuously running a program which listens for connection requests on port 23. In Unix such programs that run continuously in the background are called daemons and this one in particular is called intelnet.d. Once the connection is established

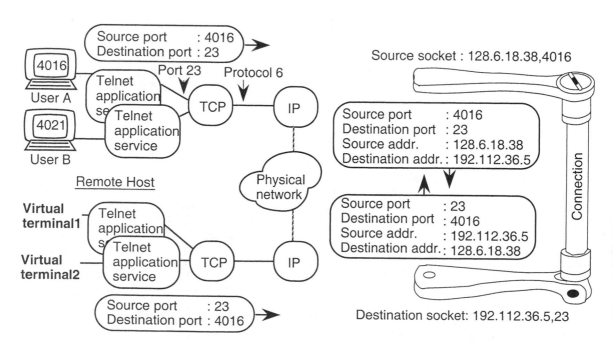

Figure 25.18 A connection between a user and a host is specified by their pair of sockets.

between the user and the remote host, the two telnets communicate using the telnet protocol.

In Figure 25.18, A is given the port number of 4016 and B is given the number of 4021. These port numbers help TCP to distinguish between the data streams for the two users. Figure 25.18 shows how data is exchanged between the remote host and user A. When A sends a data stream, its source port is 4016 and the destination port is 23. Upon its arrival at the host, TCP knows to direct this transmission to telnet from the port number of 23. In the reverse direction, when data is received by TCP at the user's end, TCP knows the user by noting the destination port number.

IP addresses uniquely identify hosts in the Internet. The combination of the source port number and the source IP address is called the *source socket*. In Figure 25.18, the source IP address is 128.6.18.38 and the source port number is 4016. The combination of these two numbers is the source socket. Similarly, the combination of the destination IP and port addresses is called the *destination socket*. Lastly, the communication (or in OSI terminology, the session) between these two sockets is called a *connection*. This pair of sockets uniquely defines a connection in the entire Internet.

25.8 APPLICATION LAYER

25.8.1 SMTP

The Basic Protocol: Electronic mail is probably the most popular application of TCP/IP networks, and it is essentially a special type of memoranda forwarding protocol. The protocol used on top of TCP/IP for mail transfers is SMTP (Simple Mail Transfer Protocol), and it is essentially a "chat" protocol for establishing certain information about the mail message. Chat protocols use 7-bit ASCII codes to exchange communication control messages, unlike protocols which use binary numbers. ASCII-based messages, such as "message number 220" or "MAIL FROM: . . ," make these protocols easy to write and debug. On the other hand, FTP is written in binary codes. One must know how to work with the hexadecimal numbering system in order to interpret its commands.

There are essentially two primary parts to a mail message: (1) The "envelope" and (2) the "body." The "envelope" contains the "To:" and "From:" fields, which indicate the obvious. The "body" portion is passed as data, and is never inspected as part of the protocol. SMTP uses TCP as the substrate for the SMTP session. The SMTP session, after the TCP session is established, would look something like this:

```
%mail -v ramteke@pilot.njin.net
220 pilot.njin.net, Sendmail 5.59/SMI4.0/RU1.5/3.08
HELO hercules.rutgers.edu
250 pilot.njin.net Hello hercules.rutgers.edu, nice to meet you
MAIL FROM: <brisco@hercules.rutgers.edu>
250 postmaster... Sender ok
RCPT TO: <ramteke@pilot.njin.net>
250 <ramteke@pilot.njin.net>... Recipient ok
DATA
```

```
354 Enter mail, end with a "." on a line by itself
[data is transferred]
.
250 ok
QUIT
221 pilot.njin.net closing connection
```

Here mail is the command used to send mail. The "–v" asks the mailer to let us see the SMTP conversation. All lines starting with a number are from the remote or receiving host; all lines starting with characters are from the local or sending host. Note that the entire protocol is 7-bit ASCII characters, and the protocol elements correspond nicely to English words. The "HELO" statement identifies the local machine to the remote machine. The "MAIL FROM:" specifies the sender of the mail. The "RCPT TO:" specifies to whom delivery should ultimately occur (it need not be local). The "DATA" statement puts the remote system into data collection mode, and it will continue to collect the body of the mail message until a "." is seen as the only character on a line. The "QUIT" statement terminates the SMTP session.

Interpreting Responses: The lines with leading numbers make it easy for the sending program to understand the returned statements, and the English comments following it make it easy for humans to read. The SMTP response codes are in five different classes:

100 series messages are positive preliminary replies. The command has been accepted, but the requested action is being held in abeyance pending confirmation.

200 series messages are positive completion replies. The requested action has been successfully completed.

300 series messages indicate a state of change. The command has been accepted, but is being held in abeyance, pending receipt of further information.

400 series messages indicate a temporary error. The command was not accepted, and the requested action did not occur. Try again later.

500 series messages indicate a permanent error. The command was not accepted, and the requested action did not occur. Do not try again.

Considering some examples of these message types should give a better idea of how they are classified. 100 series messages are uncommon. One may encounter this message type when sending mail through a network other than the Internet. This would indicate that the mail was sent, but whether it reached its destination can't be confirmed.

The purpose of 200 and 300 series messages is evident from the SMTP output provided above. In that output, "250 Recipient OK" could be replaced by a 400 series message which says "420 File system is full." This would indicate that the recipient doesn't have room in his file system to receive mail and that the sender should try later. In that same location "520 No such user" could be substituted, if the address or the name of the user were incorrect. This 500 series message tells the sender not to try this same user again.

Depending on the first digit, the sending program can decide whether to supply additional information (i.e., proceed with sending the message), save the message for later retransmission (for temporary errors), or return the message to the user (for permanent errors). The other digits also have similar significance, but are not discussed here. The reader is referred to RFC 821 for complete discussion of SMTP.

Parts of the Protocol: Fortunately, users of electronic mail need not memorize the entire SMTP protocol (there are more response codes than those mentioned above). Most mailer systems can conceptually be broken into three different parts: (1) The MUA (Mail User Agent), (2) the MTA (Mail Transfer Agent, and (3) the MDA (Mail Delivery Agent). These three programs can model any type of electronic message passing system.

Typically the MUA worries about things like collecting particular information from the user, such as for whom the message is intended, what the subject is (which is passed as data), any CCs, BCCs (Blind Carbon Copies), and FCCs (File Carbon Copies), and (of course) the body of the message. From the CC, BCC, TO, and FROM fields one can really tell that the electronic mail was modeled after memos. Often the MUA will provide features other than those listed above, but it need not necessarily do so.

The MTA is the element that typically takes a file (which contains the electronic mail) and parses enough of it to determine the originator and recipient of the message; it then has the SMTP session with the remote system. The MDA takes care of delivering the mail message to the appropriate user (it accounts for things like quotas, available disk space, etc.) on the system once it is received from the MTA.

Usually, there is a program for each of these three agents, but this need not necessarily be the case. In some cases, particularly with Unix systems, the MTA and MDA are often the same—this is the case with sendmail. Sendmail also has the ability to discern the different methods for delivering mail used over networks other than the Internet.

Other electronic mail protocols, such as MIME (Multipurpose Internet Mail Extensions), have been developed to support 8-bit binary information and multimedia information as well as plain 7-bit ASCII text.

25.8.2 Telnet

RFC 854 defines the telnet protocol. This is an old term referring to a dial-up connection over a TELephone NETwork. It is a flexible protocol in that terminals of different types can be used to communicate with a remote host as if they were native to that host. In order to provide compatibility over a wide range of terminal types, options are set by either end of the connection. If one end cannot support a particular telnet option then the other end is forced not to. On the other hand, a terminal with many features can still use those features even if low-end terminals can't.

In Figure 25.18, we saw that each user (or client) had a telnet session with a virtual terminal at the remote host, the server. The clients and the host communicate with each other using what are called NVT (Network Virtual Terminal) commands. These commands can be sent during the lifetime of a connection and don't have to be initiated only while the connection is being established. To distinguish data from NVT commands, all NVT commands begin with a hex FF, indicating to the other end to interrupt the data stream and that an NVT is coming. RFCs 854 through 861 and others specify these options and commands. We won't bother giving their details in hex.

Table 25.3 Six Possible Methods of Options Negotiation

Command	Description	Response	Description
DO	Sender wants the other end, the receiver, to enable this option	WILL	Receiver agrees to enable this option.
		WON'T	The receiver doesn't enable this option.
WILL	The sender itself wants to enable this option	DO	The receiver gives the sender permission to do so.
		DON'T	The receiver doesn't allow the sender to enable this option.
DON'T	The sender wants the receiver to disable this option	WON'T	The receiver has no choice but to agree.
WON'T	The sender wants to disable this option for itself.	DON'T	The receiver must comply.

There are only four commands and responses and they are listed in Table 25.3. They are DO, WILL, DON'T, and WON'T. Any of these can be commands or responses and they must be sent with a specified option. They can be issued by either a client or a server.

When an option is sent with the DO command, the receiver of the command is asked to enable that option. It has two choices: It can either enable it by returning a WILL response or keep it from being enabled by responding with a WON'T. These responses are listed in the first two rows of Table 25.3.

In the following row it is shown that a sending station can notify the other end that it wants to enable a certain option. In that case, the sender sends a WILL command. The receiving station, which could be a server or a client, can respond positively by sending a DO, or negatively by sending a DON'T.

The sender may wish the other end to disable a certain option by sending a DON'T. In this case, the receiver has no option but to reply with a WON'T. Similarly, when a sender wants to disable an option for itself, it will send a WON'T, which forces the receiving end to send a DON'T. These are the signals that are used to enable and disable options, which makes the telnet protocol flexible enough to remotely log on to practically any kind of a host. Let's look at an example.

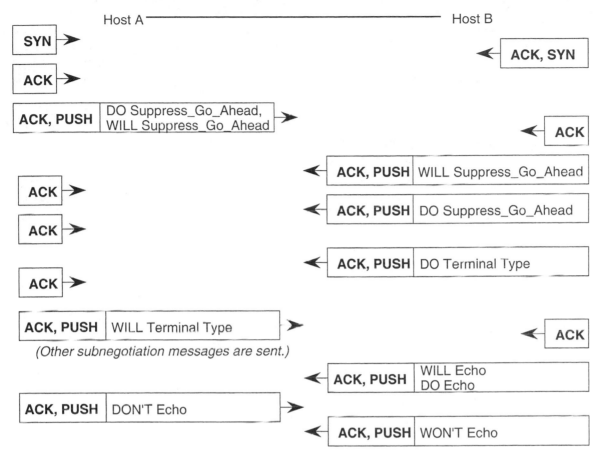

Figure 25.19 An example of a telnet session exchanging NVT (Network
Virtual Terminal) commands and responses. TCP segment headers and
key flag settings are shown in shaded boxes.

Look at Figure 25.19. First, we see the three-way handshake to open a TCP
connection. All TCP headers are shown to be shaded and their flags, which are set, are
also shown within these headers.

Then Host A sends a DO and a WILL for the option called Suppress_Go_Ahead.
The Go_Ahead option means that after each transmission a "Go ahead" signal is to be
sent, as users say "over" with CB radio, making it a half-duplex channel. Suppressing
this option means to make the channel full-duplex. Notice that the PUSH flag is sent
so that this command is sent right away.

When A is sending the DO Suppress_Go_Ahead command, it is asking B to
enable this option, and when it is sending the WILL, it is telling B that it (or A) is about
to enable this option.

Host B acknowledges A's segment. Then it may send two individual telnet
responses back to A. B's WILL is a response to A's DO and B's DO is a response to
A's WILL. The two ACKs follow from A and now the connection is full-duplex.

Next, Host B wants to set the terminal type option with A and A agrees. After this they agree on the details of the terminal type to be used. This is called a subnegotiation and these messages are not shown in the figure. Next, Host B wants to enable the Echo option for itself and also wants A to enable it. A responds by sending a DON'T. Now B is forced not to use that option and responds with a WON'T. The ACKs for these last messages are omitted from the diagram. All these messages can be sent between the two hosts before the user even gets a login prompt.

25.9 EXPLORING THE EXISTING NETWORK

25.9.1 Network Interfaces

What we want to do now is change gears and explore a TCP/IP network. We will be using a server where I have an account at Rutgers University. Its address is pilot.njin.net. We want to start poking around pilot and see what other machines are connected to it and then see what is connected beyond the local segment. Let's start by looking at the ARP table. Although we will be using commands in Unix, other operating systems provide similar information.

```
% arp -a
plinius (128.6.18.45) at 08:0:20:9:3e:be
hardees (128.6.18.2) at 08:0:20:9:43:dd
lil-gw (128.6.7.5)  at aa:0:04:0:98:f4
waller (128.6.7.41) at 00:0:0c:1:08:38
```

In this display, the host names are given along with their IP addresses and their corresponding 6-byte Ethernet addresses in hex. The first three bytes of an Ethernet address identify the manufacturer of the Ethernet card. The first three bytes of plinius and hardees are 8:0:20, which identify their manufacturer to be Sun Microsystems. lil-gw is running DECnet, which requires it to have a DEC Ethernet address, and waller, our terminal server, is manufactured by Cisco.

We at pilot can now construct a partial network map as shown in Figure 25.20. However, we are told (which we will soon verify) that the host pilot is also acting as a gateway between the 128.6.18.0 and 128.6.7.0 subnets. When a host is connected between two or more subnets it is also acting as a gateway. Hence, all gateways are hosts, but not all hosts are necessarily gateways. We are using the term gateway here to mean a router since that is done commonly.

In case of problems on the network, this information about manufacturers should agree with what we physically know about the systems, i.e., that waller is indeed a Cisco host. If, for example, waller's address started with 0:0:c, then we could suspect that the ARP table has become corrupt.

It is also possible, when someone configures a host, that they give it an incorrect IP address used by someone else. For example, if plinius is configured with an incorrect IP address of 128.6.18.2, which is also hardees' address, then hardees may log an error message that 8:0:20:9:3e:be (plinius) was sending a duplicate IP address. Such messages may be found in /usr/adm/messages at hardees.

Also, by using the `arp -a` command on pilot, we could verify that plinius was indeed advertising the wrong IP address. It is, of course, best to reconfigure plinius

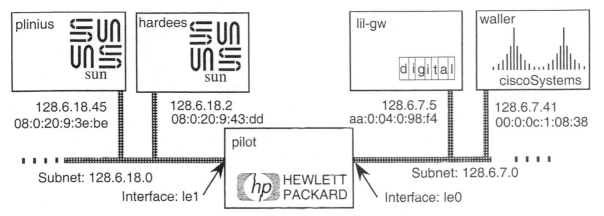

Figure 25.20 Drawing a partial network map using some of the entries from pilot's ARP tables.

with its correct IP address and then let the ARP tables be automatically updated. However, we could also manually delete the wrong ARP entry for hardees and add the correct one by entering the following at pilot:

```
#arp -d hardees
hardees (128.6.18.2) deleted
#arp -s hardees 8:0:20:9:43:dd
```

The pound sign (#), also called the tic-tac-toe or the musical sharp sign, indicates that this command can only be done from the superuser's account. The command with the –d option deletes hardees from the table and the command with the –s option adds hardees back to the ARP table with the correct ARP address. Manually adding an entry to the ARP table prevents it from being updated automatically. In other words, plinius won't be able to make pilot think that it has hardees' IP address anymore. hardees would never see packets from plinius, because plinius has the wrong MAC address for hardees. Therefore, the problem with plinius should be corrected anyway.

As shown in Figure 25.20, we can verify that we have two network interfaces available on pilot by using this netstat command:

```
pilot%netstat -ain
Name  Mtu       Net/Dest      Address  Ierrs Opkts Collis Queue
le0   1500      128.6.7.0     128.6.7.38   .   ..     ...
le1   1500      128.6.18.0    128.6.18.38  .   ..     ...
lo0   1536      127.0.0.0     127.0.0.1      .    ..         ...
```

The –i option in this command asks for the displays of the interfaces that are configured. The –a option requires that all of these interfaces be displayed. And the –n option makes the addresses be displayed using the numeric format. If we left out the –n option, our display would be:

```
pilot%netstat -ai
Name  Mtu       Net/Dest           Address Ipkts Ierrs Opkts
le0   1500      BROAD-7-0.RUTGERS.EDU pilot .  ..    ...
```

TCP/IP: Additional Concepts

```
le1    1500        broad-18-0.rutgers.edu pilot   .  ..   ...
lo0    1536        loopback              localhost  .     ..
```

The order of the entries in both of these displays is the same: The only difference is whether numeric addresses or names are given. Let us disregard the fields shown with dots. They are not necessary to understand basic interface configurations. From these two displays we see that the names of the configured interfaces are le0, le1, and lo0. "Le" is used to denote Ethernet interfaces, of which we have two: le0 and le1.

The lo0 interface exists on all hosts and is called the local interface or the loopback interface. The le interfaces are on our network map of Figure 25.20, but the loopback interface is internal and doesn't appear on such maps. A loopback interface is used to do loopback tests by the local host to see whether or not it is fit to be connected to the external networks. By default, the loopback address for all hosts is 127.0.0.1.

The address field of these two displays specifies the IP address assigned to each interface, which corresponds to its 6-byte Ethernet address. The Network/Destination field displays the network or the host which is accessible from this interface. Because these addresses end with a ".0" for both Ethernet interfaces, we can say that these are subnet addresses and not host addresses. If, for example, an le2 was added to pilot, whose Net/Dest address was configured to be 128.6.10.1, we could say that this interface is connected to only one host whose address is 128.6.10.1. In this case, this would be a point-to-point link with access to only one computer, unlike le0 and le1, which have access to entire subnets.

25.9.2 Subnet Masking

Now that we have verified that we have two network access interfaces on pilot, let us verify that the subnetting is done, using the last octet of the IP address. We have already found the names of the available interfaces from the `netstat -ain` command. Using these interface names we can see how they are configured using the following three commands:

```
%ifconfig le0
le0: flags=63<UP,BROADCAST,NOTRAILERS,RUNNING>
     inet 128.6.7.38 netmask fffff00 broadcast 128.6.7.255

%ifconfig le1
le1: flags=63<UP,BROADCAST,NOTRAILERS,RUNNING>
     inet 128.6.18.38 netmask fffff00 broadcast 128.6.18.255

%ifconfig lo0
le0: flags=49<UP,LOOPBACK,RUNNING>
     inet 127.0.0.1 netmask ff000000
```

Here, again, we see the IP addresses assigned for each interface, but now we can also make sure that the masking is properly set. Notice that the netmasks are given in hex. Also, notice for le0 and le1, the first 3 octets are masked for the subnet and the last octet for the host number. The broadcast address matches correctly with how the subnet mask is set up. Subnetting was covered in Chapter 8.

TCP/IP: Additional Concepts

If the subnet mask is set incorrectly, then a host may be able to communicate with hosts on its own subnet and with remote hosts, but not with hosts on other local subnets. Shortly, we'll see how to configure a subnet mask.

25.9.3 Routing Tables

The next thing we want to see is pilot's current routing tables. This is done using the `netstat` command with the –r option for routing. Again, let us see the display using both the host and network names and their numeric addresses.

```
%netstat -r
Routing tables
Destination            Gateway                Flags      Inter
localhost              localhost              UH         lo0
igor.rutgers.edu       nb-gw.rutgers.edu      UGHD       le0
okapi.rutgers.edu      lil-gw.rutgers.edu     UGHD       le0
default                pilot                  U          le0
broad-18-0.rutgers.    pilot                  U          le1
BROAD-7-0-RUTGERS.E    pilot                  U          le0

%netstat -nr
Routing tables
Destination            Gateway                Flags      Inter
127.0.0.1              127.0.0.1              UH         lo0
128.6.13.26            128.6.7.1              UGHD       le0
128.6.11.3             128.6.7.5              UGHD       le0
default                128.6.7.38             U          le0
128.6.18.0             128.6.18.38            U          le1
128.6.7.0              128.6.7.38             U          le0
```

Again, the order of the entries in these two displays is the same. From their last columns, we recognize our three familiar interfaces: lo0, le0, and le1. The destinations for the last two routes are 128.6.18.0 and 128.6.7.0. They both end with a ".0" so these are routes to subnets and not to individual hosts. If a destination ends with a nonzero number, then it typically specifies a route to a host assuming that subnetting is being done on a 8-bit boundary. This can also be seen by noticing that the H(Host) flag is set for host routes and not for subnet routes.

As we have seen before, the last two entries are the routes to two subnets to which pilot is directly connected. These entries state that the gateway to either of these subnets is pilot. In one case it is the le1 interface (128.6.18.38) and in the other case, it is the le0 interface (128.6.7.38). Apparently, all routes are up and running, since the U(Up) flag is set for them all.

The loopback interface provides a route to the local host and it is always in the routing table. The default route specifies to which gateway packets must be sent if the route is not found in the table. This entry helps the table from becoming too long. So, for instance, if we want to send data to NIC.DDN.MIL (192.112.36.5), which is not listed in the table, then the data packet is sent to the default gateway to route the packets.

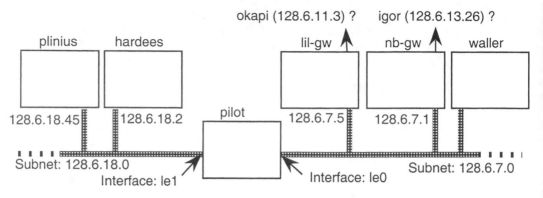

Figure 25.21 Discovering the existence of igor and okapi. We would like to know how many hops they are away from pilot.

Lastly, we come across two routes, one to igor and the other to okapi. Both of these routes use remote gateways, that is, gateways connected to other subnets. This is indicated by the G flag being set for them. In the first case, the remote gateway which provides access to igor is called nb-gw and in the second case, the remote gateway which provides access to okapi is called lil-gw. These routes also have their D flags set, meaning that these routes were added due to ICMP redirects.

From the display of `netstat -nr`, we see that the address for nb-gw is 128.6.7.1 and that for lil-gw is 128.6.7.5. This means that both of these gateways are on the 128.6.7.0 subnet, which is connected to le0 of pilot. Now our updated network map looks like that shown in Figure 25.21.

25.9.4 Tracing Routes

How do we know if igor and okapi are directly on the other sides of nb-gw and lil-gw or if there are other gateways in between them? This can be easily answered by using the `traceroute` command as shown. Let's first do a traceroute to igor.

```
%traceroute igor
traceroute to igor.rutgers.edu (128.6.13.26), 30 hops max,
    40 byte packets
1. nb-gw.rutgers.edu (128.6.7.1) 4ms 2ms 2ms
2. monster.rutgers.edu (128.6.4.3) 2ms 2ms 2ms
3. igor.rutgers.edu (128.6.13.26) 3ms 2ms 2ms
```

What is happening here is that pilot is sending 40-byte UDP packets to the destination specified in traceroute. The packets are sent with an illegal port number of 33434. The first UDP packet is sent with the TTL (Time To Live) field set to 1. The TTL field is part of the IP datagram header. When the first gateway along the route to igor gets this packet, it decrements the TTL by 1 and cannot forward the packet to its destination. See Figure 25.22(a). It sends an ICMP message back to the source, stating that the time to live for that UDP packet has exceeded.

Pilot will notice who sent the ICMP message from its IP datagram source address. In this case, it is nb-gw. Pilot will also measure the time it took for this round trip transmission of packets to occur. This procedure with the TTL set to 1 is repeated three times and the time is measured each time. In our display, these times were 4ms, 2ms, and 2ms.

Now in Figure 25.22(b), pilot will perform the same procedure, but this time with the TTL field set to 2. nb-gw decrements TTL by 1 and routes the packet to monster. monster, however, decrements the TTL to 0 and can't forward the packets any further. So it sends an ICMP time-exceeded message back to pilot. Now pilot knows the gateway for the second hop and its round trip delay.

Finally, in Figure 25.22(c), pilot sends out UDP packets with a TTL of 3 and this time doesn't receive a time-exceeded message, because it reaches its destination address. Instead, it sends a port-unreachable message. Pilot knows it has reached the final destination. The port number in the UDP packet was set on purpose to an illegal number so as to induce this ICMP message. Notice that each of the three UDP packets sent with a TTL of 2 took 2ms each and the ones sent with a TTL of 3 took 3ms, 2ms, and 2ms.

Now we know that to get to igor, there exists one other gateway called monster. Similarly, when we do a traceroute to okapi, we come across another gateway called waks-gw, which is a gateway between lil-gw and okapi. This time, let us use the numeric address of okapi to do the following traceroute:

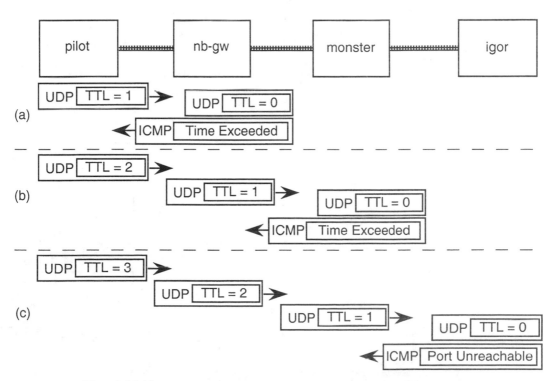

Figure 25.22 When doing a traceroute to an address, pilot will repeatedly send UDP packets, increasing the TTL (Time To Live) by one, until it receives a port unreachable message back.

```
%traceroute 128.6.11.3
traceroute to 128.6.11.3 (128.6.11.3), 30 hops max,
    40 byte packets
1 lil-gw.rutgers.edu  (128.6.7.5)  9ms 2ms 2ms
2 waks-gw.rutgers.edu (128.6.12.3) 5ms 3ms 3ms
3 okapi.rutgers.edu   (128.6.11.3  3ms 3ms 4ms
```

Datagrams travel different routes and independently from each other, so the times shown in the traceroute displays may not always seem consistent. Now, compiling all the information from our traceroutes, our new network map is as seen in Figure 25.23.

Figure 25.24(a) shows a more interesting traceroute to rins.st.ryukoku.ac.jp, a host located in Japan. The .jp designates the address as being in Japan. Many of the gateways along the route are named using the cities where they are located. It is easy to see, for instance, that the route goes through Chicago, San Francisco, and Hawaii, before reaching the last three gateways in Japan. Also, notice the significant jumps in times when reaching the first gateway in Hawaii or in Japan. Depending on the delays associated with links, these measured times can vary.

Figure 25.24(b) shows an unsuccessful traceroute. Here, a set of three asterisks is shown after ru-alternet-gw, indicating that the problem lies between that point and the next. The asterisks are repeated up to 30 times.

A better way to check to see if a host is up and running is to simply do a ping. It does not use up as much network bandwidth as traceroute does. Here's an example where a ping is done two times to a host in Australia, using 56 bytes of data:

```
%ping -s csuvax1.murdoch.edu.au 56 2
PING csuvax1.murdoch.edu.au
64 bytes from csuvax1.murdoch.edu.au (134.115.4.1):
    icmp_seq=0. time = 3299 ms
64 bytes from csuvax1.murdoch.edu.au (134.115.4.1):
    icmp_seq=1. time = 2975 ms
2 packets transmitted, 2 packets received, 0% packet loss
```

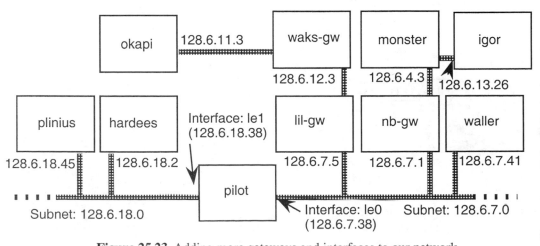

Figure 25.23 Adding more gateways and interfaces to our network.

```
%traceroute rins.st.ryukoku.ac.jp
traceroute to rins.st.ryukoku.ac.jp (133.83.1.1), 30hops max, 40byte packets
 1  lil-gw (128.6.18.30)  3 ms  2 ms  2 ms
 2  ru-alternet-gw (128.6.21.8)  2 ms  3 ms  2 ms
 3  Washington.DC.ALTER.NET (137.39.18.1)  11 ms  9 ms  10 ms
 4  ENSS136.t3.NSF.NET (192.41.177.253)  14 ms  12 ms  12 ms
 5  t3-1.Washington-DC-cnss58.t3.ans.net  (140.222.58.2)  14 ms  13 ms  16 ms
 6  t3-3.Washington-DC-cnss56.t3.ans.net  (140.222.56.4)  17 ms  13 ms  16 ms
 7  t3-0.New-York-cnss32.t3.ans.net  (140.222.32.1)  18 ms  20 ms  19 ms
 8  t3-1.Cleveland-cnss40.t3.ans.net  (140.222.40.2)  34 ms  34 ms  41 ms
 9  t3-2.Chicago-cnss24.t3.ans.net  (140.222.24.3)  44 ms  46 ms  40 ms
10  t3-1.San-Francisco-cnss8.t3.ans.net  (140.222.8.2)  83 ms  83 ms  80 ms
11  t3-0.San-Francisco-cnss9.t3.ans.net  (140.222.9.1)  81 ms  85 ms  84 ms
12  t3-0.enss144.t3.ans.net  (140.222.144.1)  83 ms  83 ms  84 ms
13  ARC2.NSN.NASA.GOV  (192.52.195.11)  93 ms  96 ms  87 ms
14  imp.Hawaii.Net (132.160.249.1)  141 ms  141 ms  148 ms
15  menehune.Hawaii.Net (132.160.1.1)  138 ms  146 ms  144 ms
16  132.160.251.2 (132.160.251.2)  257 ms  409 ms  392 ms
17  jp-gate.wide.ad.jp (133.4.1.1)  392 ms  341 ms  251 ms
18  wnoc-kyo.wide.ad.jp (133.4.7.2)  336 ms  351 ms  331 ms
19  rins.st.ryukoku.ac.jp (133.83.1.1)  355 ms  373 ms  484 ms
```

(a)

```
%traceroute rins.st.ryukoku.ac.jp
traceroute to rins.st.ryukoku.ac.jp (133.83.1.1), 30hops max, 40byte packets
 1  lil-gw (128.6.18.30)  3 ms  2 ms  2 ms
 2  ru-alternet-gw (128.6.21.8)  2 ms  3 ms  2 ms
 3  *  *  *
 4  *  *  *
 .   .
30  *  *  *
```
                                              (b)

Figure 25.24 (a) Doing a traceroute to a host in Japan. (b) An unsuccessful traceroute.

Obviously, if pings were done for all possible addresses on subnet 128.6.12.0, then we could find out all the hosts connected on the other side of lil-gw and could extend the network map beyond what is shown in Figure 25.23. Similarly, other subnets could be explored, but your network administrator could just as easily provide you with a network map for your installation and prevent you from using up network bandwidth.

25.10 INSTALLING A NEW SUBNET

25.10.1 Configuring the Interfaces

Let us now expand our network by adding a new subnet labeled 128.6.101.0. On this subnet, we need to add a workstation called pascal (128.6.101.2) and interconnect it to subnet 128.6.18.0 using the gateway called ada. See Figure 25.25 for these addresses given to us by our network administrator. First, let us configure the interfaces for pascal, then for ada.

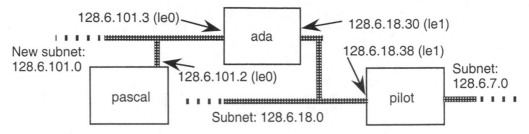

Figure 25.25 Adding a new subnet (128.6.101.0).

On pascal's /etc/rc.boot file used for booting up purposes, we add these lines: (The slash is the continuation character for extending a command over multiple lines.)

```
ifconfig      lo0 127.0.0.1
ifconfig      le0 128.6.101.2 netmask 255.255.255.0 \
              broadcast 128.6.101.255
```

This way, every time pascal is booted up, the loopback interface and the le0 interface are properly configured. Subnetting is done on the last octet boundary as before, as seen by the subnet mask and the broadcast address. Notice that for all interfaces on a subnet, the netmask and broadcast addresses must be the same.

If for some reason we need to disable the le0 interface from the network, we could enter:

```
#ifconfig le0 down
```

And to bring it back up, we would enter:

```
#ifconfig le0 128.6.101.2 up
```

Likewise, for ada's bootup file, we would add these lines:

```
ifconfig lo0 127.0.0.1
ifconfig le0 128.6.101.3 netmask 255.255.255.0 broadcast \
              128.6.101.255
ifconfig le1 128.6.18.30 netmask 255.255.255.0 broadcast \
              128.6.18.255
```

25.10.2 Configuring Static Routing

After executing these ifconfig statements, our routing tables on pascal look like:

```
%netstat -nr
Routing tables
Destination          Gateway          Flags  ...      Interface
127.0.0.1            127.0.01         UH              lo0
128.6.101.0          128.6.101.2      U               le0
```

Notice, since only the router to its own subnet is given, pascal can't get to pilot yet.

```
%ping pilot
Sendto: Network is unreachable
```

To add an explicit route to pilot from pascal, we could do the following:

```
#route add 128.6.18.38 128.6.101.3 1
```

This would add 128.6.18.38 to pascal's routing table, making 128.6.101.3 the le0 interface on ada as the gateway. The 128.6.101.3 must be a gateway on the same subnet that pascal is on. Such a gateway must be one hop away. The 1 at the end of the line states that the metric for the number of hops is 1, since the gateway is one hop away.

However, why add only a host route? Let us, instead, add a subnet route of 128.6.18.0. This will give pascal access not only to pilot but also to all the hosts on that subnet.

```
#route delete 128.6.18.38
#route add    128.6.18.0 128.6.101.3 1
```

The route delete command will delete the route to pilot, and the route add will add a route to subnet 128.6.18.0. Now, let us go even a step further and make ada the default gateway for all other routes. This is done by entering:

```
#route -n add default    128.6.101.3 1
add net default: gateway 128.6.101.3
```

So now pascal's routing tables should look like:

```
#netstat -rn
127.0.0.1          127.0.0.1          UH        lo0
default            128.6.101.3        UG        le0
128.6.101.0        128.6.101.2        U         le0
```

The following command will make pilot the default gateway for ada:

```
#route -n add default 128.6.18.38 1
```

So ada's routing tables will be:

```
#netstat -rn
127.0.0.1          127.0.0.1          UH        lo0
default            128.6.18.38        UG        le1
128.6.101.0        128.6.101.3        U         le0
128.6.18.0         128.6.18.30        U         le1
```

25.10.3 Configuring Dynamic Routing

Instead of configuring ada for static routing, a better choice would be to configure it for dynamic routing. This means having the gateway run a routing protocol. In our case, since we are connecting only two subnets, RIP would be sufficient. If, on the other hand, we were interconnecting to a different domain, then we might want to run EGP or BGP, as well. The routing daemon used to run RIP is called routed and the daemon used to run RIP, Hello, EGP, and BGP is called gated (Gateway Routing Daemon).

To run routed, simply enter:

```
#routed
```

When starting routed from the setup file, routed will look in the /etc/gateways file to see if any routes are predefined. On ada, we may want to specify the default route in this file as follows:

```
net 0.0.0.0 gateway 128.6.18.38 metric 1 active
```

Here, the net identifies this address as a network address. If it were an address to a host, then the line would begin with the keyword host. A network address of 0.0.0.0 denotes the default route. The address following the keyword gateway specifies 128.6.18.38 as the gateway for that route. The metric of 1 indicates the number of hops to the destination and active means that RIP may update this route if necessary. If update messages are not received for the allotted time frame, then RIP may delete it as well. It also means that this gateway may send update messages to others. A passive route, on the other hand, makes the designated route a static route that can't be updated or deleted by RIP.

25.11 DOMAIN NAME SERVICE

25.11.1 Purpose and Operation

So far we have been using host names and addresses interchangeably. However, we have not mentioned how a name is converted to its IP address, which must be done in order to generate a datagram. For example, in Figure 25.24 when we asked pilot to do a traceroute to rins.st.ryukoku.ac.jp, how did it find its IP address to be 133.83.1.1? This is done by a service called DNS (Domain Name Service). It allows people to use host names, which are easier to remember than IP addresses. It is the responsibility of DNS to convert a name into its correct IP address.

The way DNS handles this is by using a distributed database containing host names and addresses information, organized hierarchically. See Figure 25.26. At the top of the hierarchy is one root domain. This domain is served by a set of name servers which store information only for the top-level domain servers. Examples of top-level domains are net, mil, etc. The servers in the top-level domains, in turn, only have information about the servers in the second-level domains, and so on. Each server stores information about the servers that are in the domain below it. This makes it unnecessary to maintain one large file that contains the names and addresses of all the million or so hosts on the Internet.

Now, if a local server, for example pilot.njin.net, wants to find the address of the host, rins.st.ryukoku.ac.jp, it will first look in its cache (or memory). If it isn't there, then it will search for the address of a server of one of the subdomains in the given host name. If none of these addresses is found in the cache, it will query a root domain server, which will give the address of a server in the jp domain. This server will do the same and provide a server address for the ac.jp domain to pilot. This is done repeatedly until pilot receives the IP address of rins.st.ryukoku.ac.jp.

TCP/IP: Additional Concepts

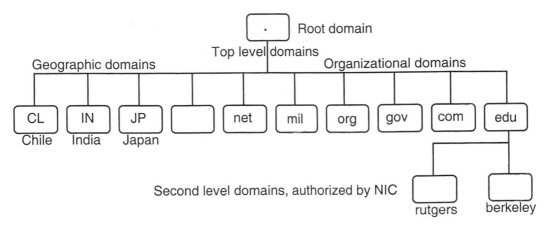

Figure 25.26 The domain hierarchy.

The local server will then store the address of the host as well as the addresses of all the domain servers it had to encounter. This is done for future reference. Then if it needs to find the address of another host in the st.ryukoku.ac.jp subdomain, it knows the server that would have that. Notice that the dots separate each subdomain in a name. For example, ac is a subdomain in jp and ryukoku is a subdomain in ac, etc. Also, notice that subdomains and subnetworks are not necessarily related.

25.11.2 DNS Servers

To run DNS, most Unix systems use the BIND (Berkeley Internet Name Domain) software. This basically uses a client and server model. Figure 25.27 shows that all computers can act as a client that can direct queries to servers. A server can provide the answer to a client's question. If it can't, it can at least provide the address of another server that can, or the name server can forward the request to a name server who can answer the query. This is how caching name servers learn new addresses. In BIND, a client is called a resolver and a server is a name server.

As shown in Figure 25.27, there are three types of servers. A primary server loads the information for the domain from a local disk. This information is called the zone file. Here, the word "zone" is being used for domain. This zone file is maintained by the domain administrator and contains the most up-to-date information about the domain. From the primary server, other servers receive their information. There is only one primary server per domain.

Secondary servers act as a backup to the primary and they receive their information by performing zone file transfers, periodically, from the primary server. Both the primary and the secondary servers are considered to be authoritative or master servers.

Then there are caching-only servers, which are not authoritative. The only way they inherit domain information is when a resolver queries them for information which they don't have. Then they ask other servers who may have the answer or know who does. Upon acquiring the information, they cache it, and that information is then available for future reference.

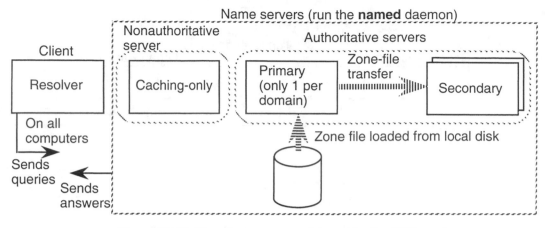

Figure 25.27 The client-server model used by the DNS service.

To configure a resolver, one needs only the /etc/resolv.conf file. This file is used as necessary by the BIND library of routines. Servers, however, use a daemon called named, which is configured by the following five files: named.boot specifies where domain information is available; named.ca specifies where the root domain servers are; named.local specifies the local loopback domain; and named.hosts and named.rev are the zone files, which convert host names to IP addresses and vice versa.

The named.boot file contains configuration commands, while the other four files store information using resource records. Resource records are written in a standard format and each record is categorized by its record type. Some of these record types are shown in Table 25.4.

25.11.3 Nslookup

Next, let us use a tool called nslookup to get better acquainted with DNS. Let us follow the dialogue as shown in Figure 25.28.

Table 25.4 Resource Record Types Used in DNS		
Type	Type meaning	Function
A	Address	Maps a host name to an IP address
CNAME	Canonical Name	Host nickname or alias
HINFO	Host Information	CPU and operating system name
MINFO	Mailbox Information	Mail list or mailbox information
MX	Mail Exchanger	Domain's mail exchanger host name
NS	Name Server	Domain's authoritative name server
PTR	Pointer	Maps an IP address to a host name
SOA	Start of Authority	Parameters which specify zone implementation

TCP/IP: Additional Concepts

We start off by typing nslookup. This command is not found in the current path. We ask the system where it is and it finds it in the /usr/etc directory. Using that path, we execute nslookup again and we are in that program.

The first thing it does is list the default server as being pilot. This is the name server that will handle all our queries, until we change it. Then we query it for the IP address of a host (hardees), and it finds it. This is because the record type is set to A

```
%nslookup
nslookup: command not found
%whereis nslookup
/usr/etc/nslookup
%/usr/etc/nslookup

Default Server: pilot.njin.net
Address:        128.6.7.38

>hardees.rutgers.edu.    (Default record
non-authoritative answer:  type is A.)
Name:   hardees.rutgers.edu
Address: 128.6.18.2

>set type=NS
>.
Default Server: pilot.njin.net
Address:        128.6.7.38

non-authoritative answers:
(root) nameserver = NS.NIC.DDN.MIL
(root) nameserver = Terp.UMD.EDU
(root) nameserver = NS.NASA.GOV
   :        :          :
authoritative answers can be found from:
NS.NIC.DDN.MIL inet addr. 192.112.36.4
Terp.UMD.EDU    inet addr. 128.8.10.90
NS.NASA.GOV     inet addr. 128.102.16.10
   :        :          :
>server terp.umd.edu.
Default server: terp.umd.edu
Address:        128.8.10.90

>nasa.gov.
Default server: terp.umd.edu
Address:        128.8.10.90
non-authoritative answers:
nasa.gov nameserver = NS.NASA.GOV

authoritative servers can be found from:
NS.NASA.GOV inet addr. 128.102.16.10
NS.NASA.GOV inet addr. 192.52.195.10
   :        :          :
```

```
>berkeley.edu.
   :        :          :
authoritative servers can be found from:
Vangogh.cs.Berkeley.edu  addr = 128.32.130.2
VIOLET.Berkeley.EDU inet addr =
128.32.136.22
UCBVAX.Berkeley.EDU inet addr =
128.32.133.1

>server vangogh.cs.berkeley.edu.
Default Server: vangogh.cs.berkeley.edu
Address:        128.32.130.2

>cs.berkeley.edu.
   :        :          :
ucbvax.berkeley.edu inet addr. = 128.32.130.12
ucbvax.berkeley.edu inet addr. = 128.32.149.36
vangogh.cs.berkeley.edu addr. = 128.32.130.2

>set type=A
>ls cs.berkeley.edu > ourfile
>view ourfile          (Security concern: ls)
CS      128.32.131.12
CS      server = ucbvax.Berkeley.edu
CS      server = vangogh.cs.berkeley.edu
acacia  128.32.131.120
adder   128.32.130.64
al      128.32.131.144
   :        :          :

>al.cs.berkeley.edu.
Default server: cs.berkeley.edu
Address:        128.32.131.12

Name:    al.cs.berkeley.edu
address: 128.32.131.144

>set query=HINFO  (Security concern: HINFO)
>al.cs.berkeley.edu.
Default server: cs.berkeley.edu
Address:        128.32.131.12

al.cs.berkeley.edu  CPU= ti/explorer, OS=lisp
```

Figure 25.28 An example of a session with **nslookup**.

by default in nslookup and this type of record maps a host name to its address. See Table 25.4.

We can change the record type by using the set command, as is done next. Here we change the record type of NS (Name Server) and it will stay as such until we change it again.

Now we enter the root domain by simply typing a dot. Because the type was set to NS, we will be given the servers for the root domain. You may want to refer to Figure 25.26. In these displays we will not show all the servers. Using the server command, we now change our default name server from pilot to terp.umd.edu, a root domain server found in the previous list.

Next, we come down the hierarchy of domains by listing the servers for the domain named nasa.gov. Then we do the same for berkeley.edu. Here, we change the default server to one of the berkeley.edu domain servers and then find the servers for the subdomain cs.berkeley.edu.

Now, we reset the record type to A and use the ls command as shown. This transfers the information (or resource records) for the cs.berkeley.edu domain into a file called ourfile into our account at pilot. Using the view command, we can see the contents of that file. This file shows the entire list of host names and their addresses in the cs.berkeley.edu subdomain; this may be necessary if we can't remember the correct spelling of the host in that subdomain.

Of course, if all we needed was the address of a particular host in the cs.berkeley.edu domain, we could have simply queried the cs.berkeley.edu server, without having to transfer the entire list. The query could have also been answered by pilot itself. This is done next. Lastly, we set the query to host information and find the kind of CPU and the operating system used by al.cs.berkeley.edu.

25.11.4 Walking through a DNS Lookup

For a final illustration, let us sit in DNS's "driver seat" and look up information as DNS would. This will show how each domain delegates control and authority to its subdomains' name servers, without requiring any name server to maintain full knowledge of the entire network. If we ask DNS to give the IP address of al.cs.berkeley.edu, it will give it to us directly. Let us walk through the steps which DNS would take to obtain its IP address.

At the top of Figure 25.29, we set the record type to NS (Name Server). This will display only such records for all queries that are made. As in Figure 25.28, we enter the root (".") domain and we are given its name servers.

Then we enter "edu.", which provides us with the name servers for the "edu" domain. These name servers are the same as they are for the root domain. Note the dot (".") after the "edu." Out of the list provided for us, we choose ns.nic.ddn.mil as our name server for the edu domain by using the "server" command.

From this name server, we ask for the name servers for the berkeley.edu domain. Out of the handful, we choose vangogh.cs.berkeley.edu as our server for the berkeley.edu domain. Then we query vangogh.cs.berkeley.edu for the name servers for the cs.berkeley.edu domain and we are given ucbvax.berkeley.edu as one of the choices. Now we make it our name server to be queried and ask for the information about al.cs.berkeley.edu.

Here, we get an error message, because the record type is still set to NS from before and al.cs.berkeley.edu is not a domain, so it doesn't have name servers. It is a host. Changing the record type to "any" we are then given the IP address among other information for that host. To end, we exit nslookup.

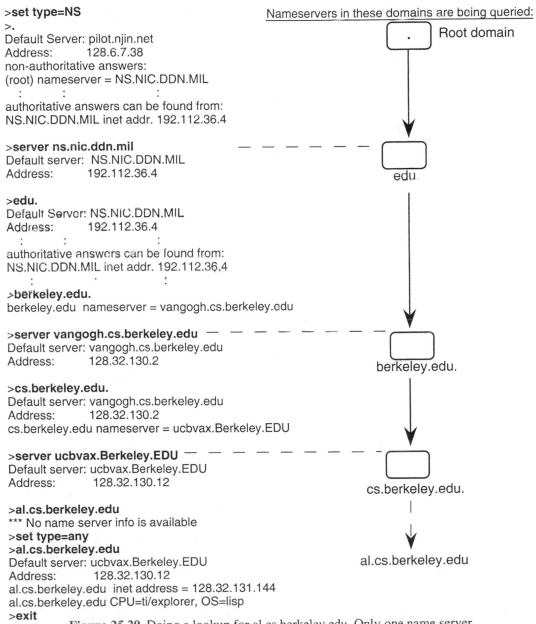

```
>set type=NS
>.
Default Server: pilot.njin.net
Address:        128.6.7.38
non-authoritative answers:
(root) nameserver = NS.NIC.DDN.MIL
     :          :
authoritative answers can be found from:
NS.NIC.DDN.MIL inet addr. 192.112.36.4

>server ns.nic.ddn.mil
Default server:  NS.NIC.DDN.MIL
Address:        192.112.36.4

>edu.
Default Server: NS.NIC.DDN.MIL
Address:        192.112.36.4
     :          :
authoritative answers can be found from:
NS.NIC.DDN.MIL inet addr. 192.112.36.4
     :       .      :
>berkeley.edu.
berkeley.edu  nameserver = vangogh.cs.berkeley.edu

>server vangogh.cs.berkeley.edu
Default server: vangogh.cs.berkeley.edu
Address:        128.32.130.2

>cs.berkeley.edu.
Default server: vangogh.cs.berkeley.edu
Address:        128.32.130.2
cs.berkeley.edu nameserver = ucbvax.Berkeley.EDU

>server ucbvax.Berkeley.EDU
Default server: ucbvax.Berkeley.EDU
Address:        128.32.130.12

>al.cs.berkeley.edu
*** No name server info is available
>set type=any
>al.cs.berkeley.edu
Default server: ucbvax.Berkeley.EDU
Address:        128.32.130.12
al.cs.berkeley.edu  inet address = 128.32.131.144
al.cs.berkeley.edu CPU=ti/explorer, OS=lisp
>exit
```

Nameservers in these domains are being queried:

. Root domain

edu.

berkeley.edu.

cs.berkeley.edu.

al.cs.berkeley.edu

Figure 25.29 Doing a lookup for al.cs.berkeley.edu. Only one name server is shown per query.

```
>set type=any                                    >server ns.adelaide.edu.au
>.                                               Default server: ns.adelaide.edu.au
Default Server: pilot.njin.net                   served by:
Address:        128.6.7.38                          MUNNARI.OZ.AU
authoritative answers can be found from:            128.250.1.21
NSINTERNIC.NET inet addr.  198.41.0.4
    :        :           :                       >4.115.134.in-addr.arpa.
>server 192.112.36.4                             Default server: ns.adelaide.edu.au
Default server: [198.41.0.4]                     served by:
Address:        198.41.0.4                          MUNNARI.OZ.AU
                    ___(Don't forget this dot.)     128.250.1.21
>in-addr.arpa.  ◄                                4.115.134.in-addr.arpa
Default server: [198.41.0.4]                        nameserver=csuvax2.csu.murdoch.edu.au
Address:        198.41.0.4
*** No any type information is available . . .   >1.4.115.134.in-addr.arpa.
                                                 Default server: ns.adelaide.edu.au
>134.in-addr.arpa.                               served by:
Default server: [198.41.0.4]                        MUNNARI.OZ.AU
Address:        198.41.0.4                          128.250.1.21
                                                 1.4.115.134.in-addr.arpa.
                                                    hostname=csuvax1.murdoch.edu.au
>115.134.in-addr.arpa.
Default server: [198.41.0.4]                     >exit
Address:        198.41.0.4
115.134.in-addr.arpa
   nameserver=ns.adelaide.edu.au
```

Figure 25.30 Doing a reverse lookup for 134.115.4.1

25.11.5 Reverse Lookups

Looking up a host's name based upon its IP address is a function very similar to normal host name lookups. In Figure 25.30, we are looking for the host name that has an IP address of 134.115.4.1, a host in Australia. To find the name associated with the address 134.115.4.1, the name server library would form the name "1.4.115.134.IN-ADDR.ARPA." Note that the address is reversed, and is looked up under the domain IN-ADDR.ARPA—the "IN-ADDR" is "Internet Address."

When looking up the "IN-ADDR" name, a name server checks its cache for an address for the IN-ADDR.ARPA name server. If it's not there, it would contact the root name server. In the session with the IN-ADDR.ARPA name server, the local name server would request the name server for the 134.IN-ADDR.ARPA name server. When the local name server requests the name server for 115.134.IN-ADDR.ARPA, it would receive an "edu.au" address, since authority for the network 134.115 belongs to "edu.au." The local name server would continue on down to the 4.115.134.IN-ADDR.ARPA name server. When it asked for the namerserver for the 1.4.115.134.IN-ADDR.ARPA name server, it would get an error—since there is no name server for it. It would then ask for the "PTR" record, and receive the information that 1.4.115.134.IN-ADDR.ARPA (the 134.115.4.1 address) has the name "csuvax1.murdoch.edu.au."

Just as there is a defined hierarchy for finding the addresses of machines when given the names, there is a mirror hierarchy for finding the names of machines when the address is known.

TCP/IP: Additional Concepts

EXERCISES

Section 25.2:
1. Suppose that you are looking at an Ethernet frame header. How can you tell whether the frame contains an ARP packet or an RARP packet?
2. By looking at the packet itself, by considering the value of which field can you tell whether it is an ARP/RARP request or reply?
3. What is the purpose of proxy ARP?
4. Does ARP work only with IP? What about PPP? What about SLIP?
5. Which field of the PPP frame is not used?
6. Match the following PPP states with their proper descriptions:

Authentication State	A. LCP packets are sent.
Network State	B. The idle state
Dead State	C. PAP or CHAP could be used here.
Establish State	D. Data can be transferred during this state

Section 25.3:
7. Which field in the IPv4 header is used to determine whether or not options are used?
8. Which field in the IPv4 header is used to control how many hops the datagram may travel through?
9. All hosts are expected to accept datagrams of what maximum size?
10. If a router cannot pass a large datagram, what may it do with it?
11. All fragments derived from the same datagram have which fields the same?
12. Can fragments be reassembled into a datagram by intermediate routers or by the end host?
13. How do you calculate the length of the data field in a datagram?

Section 25.4:
14. Suppose that we want to supernet the addresses in the range of 196.0.0.0 through 199.255.255.255.
    a. How many bits would be used for the supernet address?
    b. How many host bits would be used?
    c. What would be the supernet mask?
    d. How would you write the IP address 198.183.20.34 using the "/" notation?
15. Which routing protocols work with CIDR?
16. DHCP was derived from what other protocol?
17. How do each of the following conserve IP addresses: CIDR, DHCP, NAT servers, and proxy servers?
18. Which field in the DHCP frame determines whether Ethernet is being used?
19. When creating your own IP-based network, what are the advantages and disadvantages of using designated private IP addresses as specified in RFC 1918?
20. Compare and contrast NAT servers and proxy servers.
21. What are some reasons you can give to convince someone to convert to IPv6 from IPv4?

Sections 25.5 and 25.6:
22. How long is a UDP header? An ICMP header?
23. Which fields in a TCP header also appear in a UDP header?
24. Which ICMP message type has the most codes? What is the decimal code for this type? Can you determine some reasons why you may get this error message?

Section 25.7:
25. If the TCP layer in a host receives an error in a segment, what does it do?
    a. It sends a NAK.
    b. It requests the transmitting process to reduce the window size.
    c. It simply waits until the segment is resent.
    d. It sets the ACK flag to 0.
26. How would Host A acknowledge that it received from Host B all data bytes numbered up to 1000? State the fields and their values.
27. How would Host A slow down the data transfer from Host B?
28. How can Host A make sure the TCP segment gets sent through the network immediately?
29. By the value of which other field can it be determined if the Acknowledgement Number field is valid? If the Urgent Pointer field is valid?
30. The SYN flag is set by which host during what phase?
31. The FIN flag is set by which host during what phase?
32. How can one determine the length of a TCP segment's data?
33. A source socket is a combination of which two fields?

Section 25.8:
34. SMTP uses which port? Which transport layer protocol does it invoke?
35. Which series of SMTP messages indicate a permanent error?
36. By what hex sequence can a host know to interrupt the data stream and read the next byte as a NVT command?
37. Which two NVT commands require that the receiver comply with the sender's request?
38. What mechanism does telnet use to achieve flexibility in serving differing terminal types?

Sections 25.9 and 25.11:
39. Which command shows the state of the routing tables?
40. Which command lists the gateways to a distant host?
41. What are some flags that may be given when displaying a routing table and what do they mean?
42. Explain what the loopback address is.
43. What are the server types used in the BIND software?
44. What are some similarities and some differences between subnetworks and subdomains?

TCP/IP: Additional Concepts

Chapter 26

Linux Administration

26.1 INTRODUCTION

Throughout this book we have been studying networking concepts. There is no better way to truly understand these concepts than to experience them in a working network. In this chapter we'll install a network and do basic administrative tasks to better appreciate TCP/IP-based networks. We will create accounts for other users, send and receive e-mail from others, share files, create a mini worldwide web, and do other such tasks. We'll also perform some network administrative tasks, such as create subnets, tighten security, and even do a little DNS configuration. Of course, this chapter cannot be a comprehensive guide to administration, but will focus on the key topics to help you understand some of the details that are necessary.

From this chapter, you can easily design your own set of labs and a fully operational "playing ground" for a real network. The tasks outlined here are primarily geared for a lab environment that does not connect with the Internet. You should not try these tasks on servers that are actually in use without further research on your own part. However, the commands and operations performed on fully connected and operational servers are the same as the ones described here for the self-contained lab.

The reason why I chose Linux for my labs was because it was practically free. There are no licensing fees for clients to access the servers. Soon, however, it was evident that there were other more important reasons to select Linux. Of these the primary one is that the source code for Linux is open. If there is a problem or a bug in the operating system, there are programmers around the world who can look at the code and get it fixed. Users are not dependent on the expertise of the programmers in the company that owns the operating system. Furthermore, if the company that owns the operating system is large, they may not care for the features you want to add to their operating system. With open source, you can add features and make improvements yourself. Linux is a variant on Unix, which has had over twenty years to mature. It is stable and reliable. These advantages of Linux are much more important than its low costs, both initial and operating costs.

Although the heart of Linux, or the kernel, is the same among different distributions, its distributions differ from each other by what software packages are included and the directories where they are stored. For most purposes, they provide the same services. The Red Hat and Caldera distributions of Linux provide technical support. Red Hat is easy to use because it has user-friendly administrative tools. I have chosen Slackware 4.0, which is better for educational purposes. Instead of clicking buttons on a GUI-driven menu, you manually do the tasks and see more about what is happening "behind the scenes." However, for a Linux server on which an organization is depending for its business operation, the other distributions may be better because they provide full technical support.

Slackware costs only four dollars plus shipping for on-line orders from www.cheapbytes. com. The official four-CD set can also be purchased from Walnut Creek at 1-800-786-9907. Good resources for Linux on the web are sunsite.unc.edu/ LDP, www.linux.org, and www.linux-howto.com. You will find that people are willing to help you more with Linux and other free software than with other operating systems.

To do the install, we will only need the first CD from either set and two floppy diskettes. In the lab, instead of dedicating a PC to each group of students, I use removable IDE hard drives. This way a group is assigned a hard drive for a semester and the same PC can be shared by several lab sections. A problem created by one group on their hard drive doesn't affect students from other sections. Additionally, the PCs can be used for other purposes and by other courses which have their own set of removable hard drives.

26.2 INSTALLATION

26.2.1 Preparation

Installation Outline
1. Create space on the hard drive
2. Create two installation diskettes
3. Boot the PC under Linux
4. Repartition the hard drive
5. Enter setup
   Format the swap partition
   Format the native partition
   Install disksets
   Create a boot diskette
   Install LILO
   Configure the network
6. Reboot and shutdown

For your hardware, choose components which have been proved to be "tried and true." Selecting hardware that is the "latest and greatest" is not a wise choice because there may not be support for it in the distribution you get. At the time when a CD is created, a new device may not have hit the market yet and so it may not include support for it. Remember that ISA components can't share interrupts but PCI components can. Also, PCI cards are easy to configure and run at a faster speed. We will be using a 2.3-GB hard drive that already has Windows installed. On this hard drive space will be allocated for the Slackware 4.0 distribution of Linux.

Once we are done with the installation, we'll have all services available to us. There will be nothing left to be installed.

The side figure shows the outline of what we need to do. The first step is to create space on the hard drive, which currently is all occupied by Windows. The next step is to create two installation disks from Windows. We will use these disks to boot the PC under Linux (or Unix).

Then we can repartition the hard drive. Partitioning allows us to specify how much hard drive space should be allocated for each operating system. It also allows us

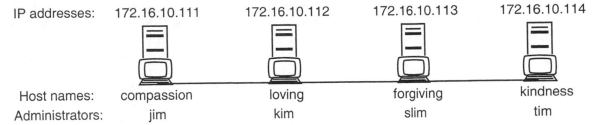

IP addresses: 172.16.10.111   172.16.10.112   172.16.10.113   172.16.10.114

Host names: compassion   loving   forgiving   kindness
Administrators: jim   kim   slim   tim

Figure 26.1 A small Ethernet network of Linux servers. The domain which they are in we'll call lab.small.edu.

to specify the partition's file system. Windows requires only one partition, but Linux requires at least two. One is called the swap partition. This partition will be used to extend the range of RAM to include this portion of the hard drive. It is also called virtual memory. The other partition is called the Linux native partition. This is where the operating system resides. We will use one large partition to make things simple. The swap partition will be designated as /dev/hda1 and the native partition as /dev/hda2. The "hd" stands for hard drive, "a" for the first hard drive and numbers 1 or 2 stand for the partition numbers for the first hard drive.

Once the partitions are created on the hard drive, we are ready to start the setup utility. During this process, we will be formatting the partitions and will be prompted for which disksets we want to install. Then the basic installation is complete. After that, we can create a boot diskette that will allow us to boot the server in case some of the file systems on the server become corrupt. Then we install LILO (LInux LOader), which will allow us to dual boot the server, either under Windows or under Linux. After this, we configure the server by giving information about the server and its network environment. Finally, we reboot the system and see if we are ready for network communication.

Figure 26.1 shows the small Ethernet network that we will install and work with in this chapter. There are only four servers here. Each one has an IP address and a wacky hostname. The names of the students who will be acting as their administrators are also shown for them. The installation process is the same for all four. We will observe jim as he gets his server ready.

26.2.2 Partitioning the Hard Drive

Before we partition the hard drive for Linux, we must make space for it because it already has Windows on it. This can be done by using a program called fips or Partition Magic. Partition Magic has to be purchased but fips comes with the Slackware CD. If you will be installing only Linux or installing Windows all over again, then you don't have to reduce an existing partition using one of these programs. You can go directly to the step where the diskettes are created, partition the hard drive, and do the install. If you will also be installing Windows, then you should create the diskettes, partition the hard drive, install Windows, then install Linux. In this run, Jim already has Windows installed and we will use fips to repartition the hard drive.

Using fips: First and foremost, we back up all the important files we may have under Windows in case the repartition process fails and we lose everything on the hard drive. The fips program doesn't come with a guarantee. This is shown in Step 1 of Figure 26.2. Step 2 shows how to find how much disk space is available on the hard drive while in Windows. Then we defragment the hard drive through Windows, which moves all free space to the end of the hard drive for Linux. In Step 3 of the figure, we create a DOS system disk that will enable us to boot the PC in DOS. Then from the CD we copy the files fips.exe, restorrb.exe, and errors.txt to the floppy. I have taken the e: drive as the CD-ROM drive and the a: drive as the floppy drive. This is probably a good time to read the readme file to make sure we didn't miss anything.

Removing the CD and inserting the floppy we restart the PC and then the fips.exe utility. Throughout this chapter, we will need only the first CD.

As seen in the figure, one partition is shown on the screen. It starts at cylinder 0 and ends at cylinder 299. The "0Bh" indicates that this is a FAT-32 type partition which is used on Windows 95. We are prompted for which partition we want to split and since only one exists, we enter a 1. Then fips makes a backup of the boot sector in case it encounters problems and needs to reinstate the booting mechanism for the

1. Save the registry and backup the Windows system.
2. MyComputer -> Right Click on C: drive -> Properties ->
   a. General Tab -> find amount of free disk space.
   b. Tools -> "Defragment now . . ."
   c. General Tab -> find amount of free disk space.

3. Go to MS-DOS prompt and insert CD (my e: drive)
   c:\> format a: /s   *(Create a DOS boot disk.)*
   c:\> copy e:\install\fips-20\fips.exe a:
        (Also copy restorrb.exe, errors.txt to a: drive.)
4. With floppy in a: drive, restart PC and run fips.
   a:\> fips.exe

Partition Table		Start			End			Start	Number of	
Part	Bootable	Head	Cyl	Sector	System	Head	Cyl	Sector	Sector	Sectors	MB
1	yes	1	0	1	0Bh	254	299	63	63	4779437	2351

```
Which partition do you want to split (1/2/3)? 1
Do you want to make a backup copy of your root and boot sector? y
Enter start cylinder for new partition (157-299):
Use cursor keys to choose cylinder,  <enter> to continue

Old Partition   Cylinder    New Partition
1222            157         1129  ◄────── The first suggested divisions for partitions.

1313            167         1038  ◄────── Pressing the down arrow once,
                                          gives this division.
```

New Partition Table		Start			End			Start	Number of	
Part	Bootable	Head	Cyl	Sector	System	Head	Cyl	Sec.	Sector	Sectors	MB
1	yes	1	0	1	0Bh	254	166	63	63	2669247	1313
2	no	0	167	1	0Bh	254	299	63	2669310	2110190	1038

```
Ready to write the new partition scheme to disk. Proceed (y/n)? y
Windows is restarting
```

Figure 26.2 Running fips to repartition the hard drive.

Linux Administration

```
C:\> format a:                          E:\> cd rootdsks
C:\> chkdsk a:                          E:\ROOTDSKS> rawrite color.gz a:
(Insert the Slackware CD in drive.)     Track 74 . . .
C:\> E:                                 done
E:\> cd \bootdsks.144
E:\BOOTDSKS.144>rawrite net.i a:        E:\ROOTDSKS> rawrite rescue.gz a:
Track 35 . . .                          Track 76 . . .
done                                    done
```

Figure 26.3 Creating the boot, root, and rescue diskettes from Windows.

hard drive. This booting information is stored by fips as the file rootboot.000 on the floppy. This is a safety feature.

Because Windows takes up the first 156 cylinders on the hard drive, it asks whether we want to start the new partition at 157. According to the figure, this would leave us with 1.222 MB for Windows and 1.129 MB for Linux. By pressing the down arrow, the next set of numbers are shown. Here the new partition would start at 167. We press the up and down arrows to select the size and we settle for the choice that starts the Linux partition at 167 and press Enter. Now the new partition table is shown and the partition table is written on the hard drive once we enter y for yes.

Creating the Boot Images: Now in the DOS prompt through Windows, create three floppies. Label them as "Boot," "Root," and "Rescue." The first two will be used for the installation. The boot and the rescue diskettes will be used whenever there is a problem starting your server. Figure 26.3 shows how the three disks are created. Each rawrite command requires you to place in another diskette. Rawrite creates Unix-formatted diskettes through DOS. Diskettes should first be formatted and checked for bad sectors because rawrite can't verify what is written.

The boot image contains the kernel that is needed to boot the Linux system. Because we will be using a network, net.i will allow us to get on the network after the install. Otherwise, the kernel would have to be recompiled. There is also the scsi.i boot image, which is used for SCSI cards, and the bare.i boot image, which contains the bare basic IDE support that is included in all images. Read the readme file in the bootdsks.144 directory for more information.

The color.gz file is a ramdisk image. It allows the RAM in the PC to boot up as a hard drive. It contains the root file system. For laptops, use the pcmcia.gz file. Save the rescue disk for when you may have problems booting up later on.

Partitioning the Hard Drive: Once you have these diskettes ready, shut down the PC using Windows. Place the boot diskette in the floppy drive and turn on the PC. If you are using removable hard drives, first make sure you have the proper hard drive in the PC. Follow Figure 26.4 as we describe the process. Soon you will get a boot: prompt. Press Enter. After a while, you will be prompted to insert the root diskette. Do so and you will get a slackware login prompt. Login as root or superuser. No password will be required. Now the PC is running under Linux and we are ready to fdisk the hard drive. Enter the fdisk command shown in the figure. This command allows you to partition the hard drive.

```
(Insert installation boot diskette and power up the PC.)
boot: (Press enter)
VFS: Insert root disk      (Insert root diskette and press enter.)
slackware login: root
# fdisk /dev/hda                        (Enter the fdisk utility.)
Command (m for help): m
d     delete a partition           q    quit without saving changes
n     add a new partition          t    change a partition's system id
p     print the partition table    w    write table to disk and exit

Command (m for help): p        (Notice that we already have a Win95 partition.)
Device Boot    Start    End     Id    System
/dev/hda1      1        166     b     Win95 FAT32

Command (m for help): n        (Create the swap partition.)
Command action:    e    extended,    p    primary partition (1-4)p
Partition number (1-4): 2
First cylinder (167-524, default 1): 167
Last cylinder or +size or +sizeM or +sizeK (1-524, default 524): 186

Command (m for help): n        (Create the native partition.)
Command action:    e    extended,    p    primary partition (1-4)p
Partition number (1-4): 3
First cylinder (187-524, default 101): 187
Last cylinder or +size or +sizeM or +sizeK (187-524, default 524): 299
Command (m for help): p
Device Boot    Start    End     Id    System
/dev/hda1      1        166     b     Win95 FAT32
/dev/hda2      167      186     83    Linux native
/dev/hda3      187      299     83    Linux native

Command (m for help): t     (Set the correct partition type for the swap partition.)
Partition number (1-4): 2
Hex code (type L to list codes): L
0   Empty             c   Win95 FAT32 (LB  63   GNU HURD        a6   OpenBSD
1   DOS 12-bit FAT    e   Win95 FAT16 (LB  64   Novell Netware  a7   NEXTSTEP
2   XENIX root        f   Win95 Extended   65   Novell Netware  b7   BSDI fs
6   DOS 16-bit >=32  17   Hidden OS/2 HPF  82   Linux swap      e1   DOS access
7   OS/2 HPFS        1b   Hidden Win95 FA  83   Linux native    e3   DOS R/O
8   AIX              40   Venix 80286      85   Linux extended  eb   BeOS fs
b   Win95 FAT32      52   Microport        a5   BSD/386
Hex code (type L to list codes): 82
Changed system type of partition 2 to 82 (Linux swap)
Command (m for help): p
Device Boot    Start    End     Id    System
/dev/hda1      1        166     b     Win95 FAT32
/dev/hda2      167      186     82    Linux swap
/dev/hda3      187      299     83    Linux native

Command (m for help): w      (Write the new partition table to the hard drive. )
#
```

Figure 26.4 Using Linux's fdisk to partition the hard drive.

The first thing that we try is the "m" command which shows a list of commands which fdisk will accept. Only a few common ones are shown. Throughout this chapter, we will not show all of the lines of text that are displayed on the screen for two reasons. One reason is to simplify the understanding of what is going on and the other is to save space on the printed page. Hence, all the screen displays are not accurate, but are correct enough to help you understand the process.

As noted by the "m" command, the "d" command allows you to delete a partition, "n" allows you to create a new one, the "t" command allows you to change the type of the partition, and so on. If you end up messing up the partition table while in the fdisk utility, simply enter "q" to quit the program without saving. On the other hand, "w" will allow you to write the new partition table to the hard drive when done.

One of the first things we do is to press "p" to see the current partition table. This shows us that a Windows partition already exists. Next, we press "n" to create a new partition, indicate that it will be the second partition, and have it occupy cylinders 167 to 186. This will be the swap partition. Usually about 64 to 100 kB is sufficient for it. In the same manner we create the Linux native partition from cylinder 187 to cylinder 299. When we print the table again, we notice that the default partition type is Linux native. Both of the new partitions were created as Linux native partitions.

Hence, we change the type of partition number 2. Using the "t" command, we enter "L" to list all the types of partitions that Linux can create. There are more partition types than what are shown here. We change the type to Linux swap, print the table one more time, and then write the table to the hard drive. Now we are ready to do the install.

Installing the OS: Right at the # prompt, enter setup. The # prompt indicates that you are a superuser and should be careful of what you do. It is a privileged account. Insert the CD in its drive and follow the steps shown in Figure 26.5 as we install the OS. In this figure, each new screen is shown with an equals sign (=) at the beginning of a line. The next equals sign at the end of a line indicates the end of the screen. At the bottom of each screen a prompt is shown such as <Yes> or <Exit> or whatever. The correct prompt to pick is shown after the second equals sign. So let's start.

After typing setup, you will see the first screen. Choose ADDSWAP. This will format and configure the swap partition. Then the installation process prompts you into formatting the native partition. During these steps you may see a handful of messages in black and white. Ignore them unless you get errors. If you get errors, you may want to select a format type where bad blocks are checked instead of selecting the format type shown in the figure. In that case, you may want to repartition the hard drive and use cylinders that do not contain bad blocks or just get a new drive.

Because the hard drive we are using already has a Windows partition on it, we get the FAT PARTITION IS DETECTED message. When prompted if we want to make this partition visible from Linux, we choose NO. This way, the files on Windows are not accessible from Linux.

Since we already have the CD inserted, we let setup scan for it automatically and choose the normal Slackware install. Then we are asked which packages or disksets we want to install. By using the up and down arrow keys and the space bar you can change

```
#setup                                          = Insert Install boot disk = <OK>
== SLACKWARE LINUX SETUP                         = Copying . . .
      HELP              KEYMAP                    = Make Boot Disk
      ADDSWAP ◄───      TARGET                       Continue             = <Ok>
      SOURCE            SELECT                    = Continue                = <Ok>
      INSTALL           CONFIGURE                 = Modem Configuration
      EXIT                        == <OK>             no modem            = <No>
                                                  = Screen Font Configuration = <No>
= Swap space detected= <YES>                      = LILO Installation
= Formatting Swap Partition...                        simple              = <Ok>
= SWAP SPACE CONFIGURED = <EXIT>                  = SELECT LILO DESTINATION
= CONTINUE WITH INSTALLATION?    = <Yes>              MBR                 = <OK>
= Select Linux installation partition            = CONFIGURE NETWORKING?    = <Yes>
    /dev/hda2      Linux Native  = <Ok>           = Configuration Network   = <ok>
= Format Partition                               = Enter Hostname (Use lower case.)
      Format         Quick format  = <Ok>            [compassion]
= SELECT INODE DENSITY FOR /dev/hda2             = Enter Domain Name
      4096 1 inode per 4096 bytes  = <Ok>            [good.stuff.edu]
= Formatting /dev/hda2 ...                       = IP ADDR (Don't use number pad.)
= Done Adding Linux Partition   = <Exit>             [172.16.10.111]
                                                  = Eneter Netmask
= FAT/FAT32/HPFS PARTITIONS DETECTION                [255.255.255.0]        = <Ok>
  would you like to make these                   = GATEWAY
  partitions visible for linux?  = <No>              [172.16.10.1]
= Continue? = <Yes>                              = Use a Name Server       = <yes>
= Source Media Selection                         = IP address for Name server
    1 Install from Slackware CD  = <OK>              [172.16.10.111]       = <Ok>
= autoscan                       = <Ok>          = NETWORK SETUP COMPLETE   = <ok>
= Place disk in CD ROM drive     = <Ok>          = MOUSE CONFIGURATION
= Scanning . . .                                     ps2                   = <Ok>
= CHOOSE INSTALLATION TYPE                       = GPM configuration       = <yes>
    Slackware Normal             = <Ok>          = Sendmail
= Continue?                      = <Yes>             SMTP+BIND             = <ok>
= PACKAGE SERIES SELECTION                       = TIMEZONE CONFIGURATION
  [X] Base                                           US/Eastern            = <Ok>
  [X] Apps           . . . etc.                  = Warning: Would you like to
  (Use the default selections.)    = <Ok>            set root password?    = <No>
= Continue?                      = <Yes>         = Setup Complete           = <ok>
= Select Prompting Mode                          = Slackware Linux Setup
    FULL                         = <Ok>              EXIT                  = <ok>
=                                                # reboot
    Bootdisk                     = <OK>         # shutdown -h now
 (Insert the install boot disk.)
```

Figure 26.5 Menus and screens seen while installing Linux. The "=" sign at the beginning of a line indicates a new screen and the "=" sign and the prompt at the end of it indicates the response selected for that screen. The prompts are shown in angle brackets < >.

the default selections. If you have enough disk space, it's just as easy to install all the default selections. Choose the FULL prompting mode and wait for a few minutes as you see all the software that gets installed.

Now its time to get the kernel from the installation boot disk and copy it on the hard drive. Remove the root diskette and replace it with the boot disk. Now the kernel is copied to the hard drive so that the hard drive is self-bootable. In Figure 26.5, for the Make Boot Disk menu, I have decided to skip this step by selecting Continue. You may, however, want to make a boot disk. In that case, at this menu get another diskette (now it becomes the fourth one) and label it "Running Boot." Then at this menu, select Format, 1.44 kB, Simple, and Continue. Then we are at the Modem Configuration. I choose No.

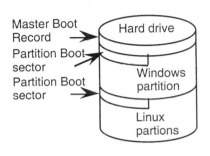

Master Boot Record

Partition Boot sector

Partition Boot sector

On a hard drive there is one MBR (Master Boot Record) which has the partition table on it and a boot loading program. Also, each partition has its own boot sector which helps it to boot up the PC using that partition's operating system. See the side figure. When Windows is installed, a standard DOS MBR file is loaded in the MBR and when the BIOS starts up the PC, the DOS MBR and the program from the Windows partition boot sector is used. In this case, the Windows partition is tagged as active. We want a dual boot system, so we will replace the DOS MBR by the LILO (LInux LOader) program in the MBR. LILO will enable us to choose which partition boot sector we want to use to boot up the machine. Hence, we choose a simple LILO installation in the figure. It can be modified later.

Now we come to the part of the install where we configure the network. Here, the hostname, IP address, subnet mask, and the router or the gateway's IP address are provided. This information is obtained from Figure 26.1. We also make ourselves a DNS or a name server. We can always come to this part and change these items by typing netconfig and rebooting the PC. The netconfig utility will walk you through all the steps from CONFIGURE NETWORKING? to NETWORK SETUP COMPLETE as shown in the figure.

```
:~# cat /etc/lilo.conf
# LILO configuration file
# generated by liloconfig
# Start LILO global section
boot = /dev/hda
message = /boot/boot_message.txt
prompt
timeout = 60
vga = normal

#Linux partition config begins
image = /vmlinuz
root = /dev/hda2
label = Linux
read-only

# DOS  partition config begins
other = /dev/hda3
label = DOS
table = /dev/hda

:~# lilo
Added Linux *
Added DOS
:~#
```

Last, we provide the mouse type and the timezone and don't bother setting the root password yet. After coming to the first menu shown for setup, we exit. Now we can enter reboot at the root prompt. We could have also done a CTL-ALT-DEL to reboot, but this signal is good only on Linux and can be used to power down the server. The way to power down most Unix servers is using the shutdown -h now command.

Modifying LILO: While we reboot, we come across the LILO menu asking whether we want to boot under DOS (or Windows) or Linux. If we just press the enter key, the default is DOS, but we would like to change the default to Linux. Furthermore, by default the delay is set to 120 seconds and we would like to reduce it down to 6 seconds. This way we won't have to even press the enter key at the menu prompt. If we just let the PC sit there for 6 seconds, LILO will automatically boot the PC under Linux.

To make these two changes, change your directory to `/etc`. Then edit the `lilo.conf` file. For some tasks, the use of the `vi` editor is required. Here, the `pico` editor will suffice. Use either one to edit this file so that it is as shown in the side figure. Comments begin with a hash mark. There are three sections to our file. One is a global section, and then there are two sections, one for each bootable partition.

In the global section, we have changed the timeout from 1200 to 60. This will make the PC boot up using the default partition without pressing the enter key in 6 seconds. Then the five lines (including the comment line) belonging to the Linux partition configuration are moved from the bottom of the file to the top. These lines are placed above the DOS partition configuration. Placing the Linux configuration first makes the PC start under Linux by default.

In pico, doing a CTL-K five times, moving the cursor to the proper place, and doing CTL-U once will move those five lines which were deleted. It is better to make a copy of an important file like this before you edit it. Then if you make a mistake, you can always go back to the original version. After you edit the `lilo.conf` file, you must run lilo to install LILO on the boot sector. This is shown at the end of the side figure on the previous page. With the command `liloconfig` you can configure LILO and install it as you did during setup.

26.3 GETTING ACQUAINTED WITH OUR SERVER

Follow Figure 26.6 as we explore the server setup. (If you need to learn or review basic Unix commands, you should get the text called Unix By Experimentation, Prentice Hall. To make sure it was good, I had to write it!) The first thing that we do after booting up is to use the `ifconfig` command to check our network interfaces. The local loopback interface shows that its IP address is 127.0.0.1 and that it is up and running. If our server cannot communicate with this interface, it won't be able to communicate with the network. This interface allows our host to make sure there is no problem with itself.

The eth0 interface is our Ethernet interface. If we didn't get this interface, then we would have to recompile the kernel. However, the net.i boot image allows us to get this interface immediately since we are using a common Ethernet card by 3Com. The hardware address shows the NIC address in hex and the information entered during network configuration.

Next, we will be in the `/etc` directory for a while so we change the directory there. We want to see if kim has finished installing Linux on her server and so we do a ping. She is up, but if we use her server name of loving, our host (or rather jim's host) doesn't recognize loving's IP address. Doing a `more` on the file called hosts reveals that our host only knows its own IP address. The IP address of loving is not entered. Hence, we use `pico` again and add to it the IP addresses of all the other three servers. The command `cat /etc/hosts` confirms to us how this file was updated. Now, when we do `ping loving`, our server finds the IP address from the `/etc/hosts` file and the ping succeeds. This confirms that our host compassion is network ready.

Before we start doing other network-related tasks, let us see some basic configurations for our server. Go to Figure 26.7. Here, we see that the file called `/etc/HOSTNAME` has the full hostname. Everything up to the first dot is called the base

```
compassion:~#  ifconfig
eth0       Link encap:Ethernet  HWaddr 00:50:04:D3:DE:13
           inet addr:172.16.10.111  Bcast:172.16.10.255  Mask:255.255.255.0
           UP BROADCAST RUNNING MULTICAST  MTU:1500  Metric:1
           RX packets:301 errors:0 dropped:0 overruns:0 frame:0
           TX packets:7 errors:0 dropped:0 overruns:0 carrier:0
           collisions:0 txqueuelen:10  Interrupt:10 Base address:0x1000
lo         Link encap:Local Loopback
           inet addr:127.0.0.1  Mask:255.0.0.0
           UP LOOPBACK RUNNING  MTU:3924  Metric:1

compassion:~#  cd /etc
compassion:/etc#  ping 172.16.10.112
64 bytes from 172.16.10.112: icmp_seq=0 ttl=255 time=0.5 ms
64 bytes from 172.16.10.112: icmp_seq=1 ttl=255 time=0.2 ms
compassion:/etc#  ping loving
ping: unknown host loving
compassion:/etc#  more hosts
127.0.0.1              localhost
172.16.10.111              compassion.good.stuff.edu compassion

compassion:/etc#  pico /etc/hosts
compassion:/etc#  cat hosts
172.16.10.111         compassion.good.stuff.edu compassion
172.16.10.112         loving.good.stuff.edu    loving
172.16.10.113         forgiving.good.stuff.edu forgiving
172.16.10.114         kindness.good.stuff.edu  kindness
compassion:/etc#  ping loving
64 bytes from 172.16.10.112: icmp_seq=0 ttl=255 time=0.3 ms
64 bytes from 172.16.10.112: icmp_seq=1 ttl=255 time=0.2 ms
```

Figure 26.6 Getting acquainted with the network environment.

hostname and after it is the domain in which it belongs. The command hostname also gives the name of the host. This command can also be used to change the hostname. We can change it to winter, for instance. Then, using pico, we can change it back to compassion. Depending on your personal tastes or to get a more descriptive name, you might want to change the name of your server. After logging out or rebooting, the word change will be shown at the command prompt.

If you change ISPs, you have to change your IP address. The /etc/rc.d/ rc.inet1 file contains your network configuration. Now this is a critical startup file, so before updating it in any way, you should first make a copy of it and give it an extension of "orig." This indicates that it is the original file. First, we do ls rc.inet1.orig to make sure the version of this file created during the installation does not already exist. If some other administrator altered this file and also backed up the .orig file then we would be overwriting it. Hence, an ls is done first. This confirms that the .orig file is not there to begin with, so we proceed to make it.

Doing an ls -l on these files shows us that they are both overwritable. To protect the .orig version we use chmod 400 and another ls -l to show that the .orig file is protected from being overwritten inadvertently. Now, using pico or any other

```
compassion:/etc#  more HOSTNAME
compassion.good.stuff.edu
compassion:/etc#  hostname
compassion
compassion:/etc#  hostname winter
compassion:/etc#  pico HOSTNAME
compassion:/etc#  more rc.d/rc.inet1
IPADDR="172.16.10.111"
NETMASK="255.255.255.0"
NETWORK="172.16.10.0"
BROADCAST="172.16.10.255"
GATEWAY="172.16.10.1"

:~#  cd /etc /rc.d
:/etc/rc.d#  ls rc.inet1.orig
:/etc/rc.d#  cp rc.inet1 rc.inet1.orig
:/etc/rc.d#  ls -l rc.inet1*
-rwxr-xr-x    Nov 24  rc.inet1
-rwxr-xr-x    Nov 24  rc.inet1.orig
:/etc/rc.d#  chmod 400 rc.inet1.orig
:/etc/rc.d#  ls -l rc.inet1*
-rwxr-xr-x    Nov 24  rc.inet1
-r--------    Nov 24  rc.inet1.orig
:/etc/rc.d#  pico rc.inet1
```

```
compassion:~#  dmesg | grep eth0
eth0: 3Com 3c905B 00baseTx 0x1000,
00:50:04:d3:de:13, IRQ 10
compassion:~#  uname -a
Linux compassion 2.2.6 #2 Tue May 4
21:50:43 CDT 1999 i686 unknown
compassion:~#  cd /proc
compassion:/proc#  cat interrupts
 10:        360            XT-PIC  eth0
compassion:/proc#  cat ioports
0000-001f : dma1
compassion:/proc#  cat pci
  Bus  0, device  15, function  0:
    Ethernet : 3Com 3C905B 100bTX.
compassion:/proc#  ps
 PID TTY          TIME CMD
 188 ttyp0     00:00:00 bash
 202 ttyp0     00:00:00 ps
compassion:/proc#  ps -aux
USER     PID   START    TIME COMMAND
root       1   13:38    init [3]
root     203   13:48    ps -aux
compassion:/proc#  cat /etc/fstab
/dev/hda1    swap   swap defaults   0    0
/dev/hda2    /      ext2 defaults   1    1
none         /proc  proc defaults   0    0
```

Figure 26.7 Changing your network configurations and observing other
server settings.

editor, the file can be updated to include the correct network configurations. The safest
way to change a hostname or any of the network addresses, is to use netconfig as
explained during the setup procedure.

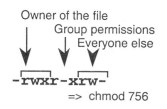

Owner of the file
Group permissions
Everyone else
-rwxr-xrw-
=> chmod 756

r	w	x	chmod
-	-	-	0
-	-	x	1
-	w	-	2
-	w	x	3
r	-	-	4
r	-	x	5
r	w	-	6
r	w	x	7

The side figure reviews Unix file permissions. The first dash in ls -l
indicates that this entry is a file and not a directory or a link. Then the
permissions of file owner, group, and public are given as triplets. To change
the permissions as shown, you would need to use chmod 756 on the file in
question. The r, w, and x represent read, write, and executable privileges,
respectively.

Starting at the top of the second column of Figure 26.7, we come
across the dmesg command. This command displays all the messages
which scrolled off the screen during bootup. I just want to see what kind of
Ethernet card I have, so we pipe dmesg into the grep command, looking
for the string eth0. This reveals that we have a 3c905B card. Next, the
uname -a command reveals we are running kernel version 2.2.6 of Linux.

In the /proc directory, there are a few interesting files. The interrupts file shows how the interrupts are configured. Again, only one line
of the output is shown for the sake of brevity. Next, the I/O ports and the
recognized PCI cards are shown. The ps command shows which processes

related to your login are running and the `ps  -aux` command shows all of the processes.

When the server is started up, the /etc/fstab file is read. This is called the file system table. This file determines which file systems are mounted during the boot process. Here, we see that the swap partition and the Linux native partitions are mounted as /dev/hda1 and /dev/hda2. There is also a file system labeled as "none." This is not a real file system but a directory called /proc. It is necessary on all Linux systems and should never be modified.

The second column in the display shows the mount points. Swap and / are the mount points for these two file systems or partitions. Swap and ext2 are the types of file systems and the next column shows that the default options are set. The last two sets of numbers indicate when the file systems are checked.

26.4 USER ACCOUNTS

26.4.1 Password Protecting the Root Account

The first thing that Jim should do is password protect the root account. This he can do at the superuser prompt (#) by simply entering the simple command: `passwd`, then entering a good password. In every class there is someone who forgets his root password. When this happens, use the procedure outlined in Figure 26.8.

We will need to use some commands and files that we will get to eventually. Right now if you forgot your root password, you just want to get into the server.

Place the installation boot diskette, which you made to start fdisk, in the floppy drive and start the PC. At the boot prompt, press Enter. When asked to enter the root diskette, place the rescue diskette that you made in Figure 26.3 in the floppy drive. Then do the `e2fsck` command on the correct hard drive partition. This will check and clean the file system. If prompted, just press Enter. Other options probably will not

(Insert installation boot diskette and power up the PC.)
`boot:` *(Press Enter.)*
`VFS: Insert root disk`   *(Insert rescue diskette and press Enter.)*
`slackware login: root`
`# /sbin/e2fsck /dev/hda2`   *(e2fsck may be under /bin instead.)*
`# mount -t ext2 /dev/hda2 /mnt`
`# vi /mnt/etc/shadow`

:set showmode	Shows whether you are in command or insert mode
ESC key	Go to the command mode
i	Go to the insert mode
:wq	Write the file and quit
:q!	Quit without saving file

`# cat /mnt/etc/shadow`
`root::9805`   *(Rest of the line is not shown.)*
`# reboot`   *Remove all the cryptic password characters between the first set of colons by using either the Del key or the x key in the command mode.*

Figure 26.8 Nulling out the root password using the rescue diskette.

make any sense. Then mount the hard drive using the `mount` command. This basically makes the hard drive accessible through the `/mnt` directory.

Now use `vi` to edit the shadow password file on the hard drive. Here is some motivation to learn vi. To review, this editor has two basic modes and you should know which mode you are in. To get into the command mode, press the ESC key. In the command mode, you can provide commands. To enter text, press the i key; then you will be in the insert mode and you will be able to enter characters. I like to see in which mode I am. Hence, I always start my vi session by pressing the ESC and the colon (:) keys, then entering set showmode. This shows the mode while I am editing. If I make a mistake and want to start over again, I enter ESC, :q!. To save and quit, I enter ESC, :wq.

What we need to do is to remove all the characters between the first set of colons for the root account. If the file was updated correctly, the start of the entry for the root account will be as shown in the figure. All commands in the root login should be done carefully and without rushing. Now remove the diskettes and reboot. You will be able to log in as root without being required to provide a password. Then reset the password.

26.4.2 Creating an Account

Now it is time to create an account for ourselves. We are sitting with Jim and even though he is the administrator for compassion, he needs an account for himself. His username will be jim. When he needs to do administrative tasks he will log in as root, and when he needs to telnet to other servers, check his personal e-mail, or just monitor what is happening with his server, he can log in as jim. Doing all his daily tasks under the root login is not wise. What if he inadvertently deletes an important file while he is logged under root? So he logs under root only when absolutely necessary and logs under jim at other times.

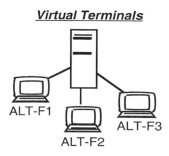

Virtual Terminals

ALT-F1

ALT-F2

ALT-F3

Instead of logging under one account, logging out, and then logging under another account repeatedly, it is better to have two windows open. We haven't yet configured X Windows, a GUI (Graphical User Interface) for Unix, but Linux provides another option. Using the ALT and function keys, we can simulate additional terminals attached to our server as shown in the side figure. We can use the server console to simulate up to six virtual terminals. Then we would not need additional physical terminals.

The first time that we log on, we are on the first virtual terminal. To start another login session, we only have to press ALT-F2. That is, we press the ALT and the F2 keys simultaneously. The left-hand column of Figure 26.9 shows jim logged on as root using the ALT-F1 terminal and the right-hand column shows him switched to the next terminal by pressing ALT-F2. On ALT-F2, Jim is testing the account that he created for himself. Notice that on the ALT-F1 session, he has all hash marks for the prompt sign, indicating that he is logged on as root, and on the ALT-F2 session he has the dollar sign, indicating that he is just a common user on his server.

Having two logins like this is very convenient. This way, while Jim is telneting to another server and someone comes over to him and asks him for a user account or

```
compassion:~# adduser                    compassion login: jim
Login name for new user []:   jim        password: jim  (Password is not echoed.)
User id [ defaults to next available]:   compassion:~$ who
Initial group for jim [users]:           root    tty1    Nov 24 14:04
Additional groups for jim []:            jim     tty2    Nov 24 14:04
jim's home directory [/home/jim]:        compassion:~$ grep jim /etc/passwd
jim's shell [/bin/bash]:                 jim:x:1000:100:Prof. Jim Thomas,,,:
Account expiry date (YYYY-MM-DD) []:                    /home/jim:/bin/bash
Changing the user information for jim    compassion:~$ grep jim /etc/shadow
Enter the new value, or press return     /etc/shadow: Permission denied
        Full Name []:  Prof. Jim Thomas  compassion:~$ pwd
        Room Number []:                  /home/jim
        Work Phone []:                   compassion:~$ telnet loving
        Home Phone []:                   loving login:  jim
        Other []:                        Password:
Changing password for jim                loving:~$ more /etc/passwd
New password:  jim                       kim:x:1000:100::/home/kim:/bin/bash
Bad password: too short.   jim           jim:x:1001:100::/home/jim:/bin/bash
Warning: weak password.                  slim:x:1002:100::/home/slim:/bin/bash
New password:  jim                       loving:~$ more /etc/shadow
Re-enter new password:  jim              /etc/shadow: Permission denied
Done...                                  loving:~$ telnet compassion
compassion:~# cat /etc/passwd            compassion login:  jim
root:x:0:0::/root:/bin/bash              Password:
operator:x:11:0::/root:/bin/bash         compassion:~$ who
guest:x:405:100::/dev/null:/dev/null     root    tty1    Nov 24 14:04
nobody:x:65534:100::/dev/null:           jim     tty2    Nov 24 14:04
jim:x:1000:100:Prof. Jim Thomas,,,:      jim     ttyp1   (loving.good.stuf)
              /home/jim:/bin/bash        compassion:~$ logout
compassion:~# grep jim /etc/shadow       Connection closed by foreign host.
jim:kDPngBVvSnjrs:10919:0:99999:7:::     loving:~$ logout
compassion:~# ls -l /etc                 Connection closed by foreign host.
-rw-------  1 root  367 /etc/shadow      compassion:~$ logout
-rw-r--r--  1 root  611 /etc/passwd      compassion login:
compassion:~#
```

Figure 26.9 Creating an account and testing it.

some similar task, all he has to do is switch over to the ALT-F1 session. Then when he is done serving that user, he can do an ALT-F2 to proceed with his previous session.

Jim enters the `adduser` command to create a user account. The first thing he enters is the username which is jim. We will use all lowercase usernames. Then we are prompted for a number of items for which we just press the Enter key. The default values are shown in square brackets [ ]. To make things simple, Jim gives himself the same password as his account name. Since, we are not on the Internet and we are in an educational setting, we can live with this. Otherwise, using weak passwords is definitely a bad idea.

After Jim finishes giving himself an account, we look at the `/etc/passwd` file. Here are stored all the users who have accounts. The account for jim is also here. Each new user will get a one-line entry in this file. Fields on each line are separated by colons. The first field is the username, jim. The next field is supposed to be his password, in encrypted form. For security reasons, Slackware has a separate file where the users' encrypted passwords are stored, and this file is called the `/etc/shadow` file.

The `/etc/passwd` file is readable to anyone who has an account on the server, but the `/etc/shadow` file is not. This way it becomes harder for someone to download the password file and run a program called crack to find out users' passwords.

The field after the password is the uid or user identification. Jim's uid is 1000. The next field is the gid (group identification) which is 100. When we study the /etc/ group file using Figure 26.13, we will see that the name of this group is users. This is his default group. Then comes his full name because he had entered one. After this his login directory and shell are given.

The next command shows that Jim can see his encrypted password using the `grep` command and the shadow password file. He can do this because he is logged in as root. The encrypted password is completely different from the actual password of "jim." The `ls` command shows that the passwd file is readable by anyone, but the shadow file is only readable by root.

Now, moving to the right-hand column of Figure 26.9, we see that Jim has gone to another virtual terminal by pressing ALT-F2. Here, we see the familiar login prompt for our server, compassion. Jim logs himself and does a who. We see that root is logged from tty1 (or ALT-F1) and jim is logged in from tty2 (ALT-F2). The `/etc/passwd` file is readable for the public and Jim now falls into that category because he is not in a superuser session. Hence, he can read that file, but not the `/etc/shadow` file. He gets an error message: "Permission denied."

Now let's see if Kim has given Jim an account on her machine called loving. Jim telnets over to loving, makes a connection, and then logs in. He wants to see who else Kim has given accounts to on her server so he looks at the `/etc/passwd` file on loving. It looks like Kim has given herself an account and also one to slim. He tries to get to the shadow password file on loving, but again, he has no permission to do that.

From lovely, Jim can telnet back to his own server. He does so and logs in. Now he sees himself logged in twice on compassion using the who command. The first login session is on tty2 and the other one is from loving. Then he logs out of compassion and gets back to loving. Then he logs out of loving and gets back to compassion. After logging out of compassion for the second time, the ALT-F2 terminal displays the familiar login screen.

26.4.3 A Review

I would like to now summarize many of the concepts we have just encountered by adding bugs in our network. Jim and Kim have both added bugs on their servers and we have to find out what they are from Jim's perspective. Follow Figure 26.10.

From compassion using the ALT-F2 terminal, we log in as jim without a hitch. We try to telnet to loving but can't. Then we try to ping there. If ping doesn't work and if it wasn't disabled for security reasons, then of course telnet or any higher-layer protocol will not work. When we do a ping using the IP address, that doesn't work

```
                        jim on compassion ALT-F2
compassion:~$ telnet loving
loving: Host name lookup failure           (Problem, can't telnet to loving.)
compassion:~$ ping loving                  (Can't ping loving either.)
ping: unknown host loving                  (Can't recognize host name, loving.)
compassion:~$ ping 172.16.10.112           (Can't ping using IP address either.)
PING 172.16.10.112 (172.16.10.112): 56 data bytes
7 packets transmitted, 0 packets received, 100% packet loss
                                           (Boot up loving. It was turned off.)
compassion:~$ ping 172.16.10.112           (Start the ping while it is booting up.)
PING 172.16.10.112 (172.16.10.112): 56 data bytes
64 bytes from 172.16.10.112: icmp_seq=31 ttl=255 time=0.6 ms
64 bytes from 172.16.10.112: icmp_seq=30 ttl=255 time=1000.7 ms
31 packets transmitted, 2 packets received, 87% packet loss
compassion:~$ telnet loving                (Can't recognize host name again.)
loving: Host name lookup failure
compassion:~$ grep loving /etc/hosts       (Entry for loving is commented out.)
# 172.16.10.112           loving.good.stuff.edu     loving

                        root on compassion ALT-F1
compassion:~#pico /etc/hosts               (jim as root removes the comment.)

                        jim on compassion ALT-F2
compassion:~$ grep loving /etc/hosts       (jim checks the file to be ok.)
172.16.10.112       loving.good.stuff.edu     loving
compassion:~$ telnet loving                (Now he can telnet to loving.)
loving login: jim
Password:                                  (However, he cannot log in.)
Login incorrect
                        root on loving ALT-F1 for kim
loving:~# grep -i jim /etc/passwd          (kim checks and finds that jim does
jim:x:1001:100:,,,:/home/jim:/bin/bash       have an account, so she resets
loving:~# passwd jim                                  jim's password.)
                        jim on compassion ALT-F2
compassion: telnet loving
loving login: jim
password:
loving:~$                                  (Finally, jim can log on loving.)
```

Figure 26.10 Correcting many problems as Jim tries to log onto his account on loving.

either. So we go over to loving and find that it was powered down. Hence, we power it back up.

While it is being powered up, we do a ping command and let it sit. when it finally comes up, we start getting ping packets back. Without looking at the loving server, we now know that loving is up. Doing a CTL-C will stop the ping. Notice that 31 packets were transmitted but only 2 were received because 29 packets were lost while loving was getting started.

Now that loving is up, we try to telnet to it, but find that there is a host name lookup failure. Looking at the `/etc/hosts` file we grep for loving, and find that Jim added a hash mark at the beginning of the entry for it. This made the line into a comment and so it was not recognized. Therefore, we do an ALT-F1 and from the root logon, remove the comment for loving using pico.

We are now back to jim's login session and we check to make sure the comment is indeed removed. Now we can make a telnet connection to loving, but we can't log on. Hence, we go to Kim's machine and first check to see if jim has an account there. The – i option makes grep ignore the case of the string for jim. Jim has an account with the expected spelling. Now we ask Kim to reset the password for jim. This time, Jim can log in.

26.4.4 E-mail

Now that the accounts are set up and working, let us do some basic networking functions. We'll start with e-mail. In Figure 26.11 we see Jim logging into loving and creating a .forward file there. This file contains the e-mail where all mail for Jim should be forwarded. The forward address is jim@[172.16.10.111], or jim@compassion. Now if anyone sends Jim mail at loving, it will get forwarded to him at compassion. This allows Jim to check his mail from only one server, although he may have accounts

```
compassion:~$ telnet loving
loving login: jim
loving:~$ echo jim@[172.16.10.111] > .forward
loving:~$ cat .forward                (The dot-forward file is created.
jim@[172.16.10.111]                        on loving.)
loving:~$ logout

compassion:~$ telnet loving 25        (Telneting to SMTP of loving.)
Connected to loving.good.stuff.edu.
220 loving.good.stuff.edu ESMTP
helo compassion                       (Identification of compassion's SMTP)
250 loving.good.stuff.edu Hello jim@compassion,
pleased to meet you
mail from:<jim@compassion>            (Mail from jim@compassion.)
250 <jim@compassion>... Sender ok
rcpt to:<jim@loving>                  (Mail for jim@loving)
250 <jim@loving>... Recipient ok
data                                  (Data for mail to follow.)
354 Enter mail, end with "." on a line by itself
Dear Jim,
     I am testing the .forward file.
Jim
.                                     (Finished entering data for mail.)
250 LAA00201 Message accepted for delivery
quit                                  (Terminate the SMTP session.)
221 loving.good.stuff.edu closing connection
Connection closed by foreign host.
You have mail in /var/spool/mail/jim
compassion:~$
```

Figure 26.11 Creating a .forward file on loving to forward jim's mail to compassion, then testing it by manually sending mail to jim on loving. This is confirmed by the "You have mail . . ." message at the end of the session.

on many servers. He could have created the .forward file on compassion to forward his mail to loving.

After he creates the file, he logs off at loving and now is back in the compassion session. To check to see if the forwarding of mail works, he sends himself mail. He could have sent mail to himself by using pine or any other mail program. Instead he telnets to loving at port 25. This starts an SMTP session with loving. The first thing he does is identify the SMTP server at loving that he is sending mail from compassion. This is done with the helo command. Then he indicates that the mail is from jim@compassion and it is being sent to jim@loving. This is done using the mail and rcpt commands, respectively. Then he enters the data for the mail using the data command and terminates the data file by entering a dot on a line by itself. Finally, he quits the SMTP session. This is an example of sending e-mail manually.

As soon as the mail is delivered to loving, it is forwarded back to compassion and since Jim is logged in as himself, the message pops on his screen. A CTL-L will clear the screen and he can read the mail later or delete it using a mail utility. This confirms that his .forward file was created correctly.

26.4.5 FTP

Now we will test out ftp. In Figure 26.12, Jim creates a file called local.file on compassion using the echo command. The content of this file is "This is a file on compassion." Then he telnets to loving and similarly creates a file called remote.file with the contents of "This is a file on loving."

To transfer the local.file to loving and the remote.file to compassion, he enters ftp. First, he logs in as himself and he now has an ftp session open with loving. When he does a get from loving, he gets an error because local.file doesn't exist on loving. Similarly, since remote.file doesn't exist on compassion, he gets an error when he tries to put it on loving.

However, he can do get remote.file and put local.file without errors. In fact, going to the top of the second column in Figure 26.12, he can now also do get local.file, whereas before this command generated an error. This is because now local.file also exists on the remote server or loving. He cannot do the cat command and many of the shell commands. The ftp program doesn't allow you to do all the shell commands, but it allows you to transfer files between servers. On the other hand, the telnet program allows you to do all of the shell commands, but doesn't allow you to transfer files. After Jim quits ftp, he checks to see that both files were indeed transferred between the two servers.

26.4.6 Sharing Files in Groups

Next, Tim and Slim come to Jim and ask him to place them in a group so that they can share files with each other, but prevent others from doing so. Tim and Slim want their group to be called netgroup.

Following Figure 26.13, Jim checks to see if Tim and Slim both have accounts on his server and they do. Kim also has an account and so does Jim, as seen from the /etc/passwd file. Jim enters the pico editor and carefully adds another group called netgroup. He should have made a backup of the /etc/passwd file just in case

```
compassion:~$ echo This is a file on compassion > local.file
compassion:~$ cat local.file
This is a file on compassion
compassion:~$ telnet loving
loving login: jim
loving:~$ echo This is a file on loving > remote.file
loving:~$ cat remote.file
This is a file on loving
loving:~$ logout

compassion:~$ ftp loving                ftp> get local.file
 220 loving FTP server ready.            200 PORT command successful.
 Name (loving:jim):                      150 Opening BINARY mode connection.
 331 Password required for jim.          226 Transfer complete.
 Password:                                29 bytes received
 230 User jim logged in.                ftp> cat local.file
ftp> get local.file                      ?Invalid command
 200 PORT command successful.           ftp> quit
 550 local.file: No such file.           221 Goodbye.
ftp> put remote.file
 local: remote.file: No such file       compassion:~$ ls
ftp> get remote.file                    local.file   remote.file
 200 PORT command successful.           compassion:~$ telnet loving
 150 Opening BINARY mode connection.    loving login: jim
 226 Transfer complete.                 loving:~$ ls
  25 bytes received                     local.file remote.file
ftp> put local.file                     loving:~$ cat local.file
 200 PORT command successful.           This is a file on compassion
 150 Opening BINARY mode connection.    loving:~$ cat remote.file
 226 Transfer complete.                 This is a file on loving
  29 bytes sent
```

Figure 26.12 Creating files on two servers and using ftp to transfer them. Finally, we verify that they were transferred.

it is corrupted by mistake. By using the tail command, we see the last three lines of the file including the line that was added for netgroup.

The name of the group comes first and then the gid or group identification. The gid is 1001. Low numbered gid's should be reserved for the system groups. Hence, we start numbering our groups starting at 1001. Tim and Slim are the only members of this group. Notice that the group called users has a gid of 100. This is the primary group for all regular users and is indicated in the /etc/passwd file. Hence, usernames are not provided for this group in the /etc/passwd file.

Once Jim tells Tim and Slim that he created the group, Tim logs on compassion and using echo creates a file called netgroupfile. The content of this file is "echo This file is executable." Tim displays the file using cat and does a long listing. From the permissions, Tim notices that the file can be read by anyone, even Kim who doesn't belong to his group. In fact, the file belongs to the users group instead of netgroup. To correct these two problems, he sets the permissions to 740 using the chmod command and corrects the group using the chgrp command. Another long listing confirms that these changes were done correctly.

From these permissions, Tim who is the owner of the file should be able to read, write, and execute it. Slim, who is a group member, should only be able to read the file and Kim, who is neither, should not be able to even read the file. Tim first checks his permissions.

jim on compassion creating the group netgroup
```
compassion:~# tail /etc/passwd
jim:x:1000:100:Prof. Jim Thomas,,,:/home/jim:/bin/bash
kim:x:1001:100:,,,:/home/kim:/bin/bash
slim:x:1002:100:,,,:/home/slim:/bin/bash
tim:x:1003:100:,,,:/home/tim:/bin/bash
compassion:~# pico /etc/group
compassion:~# tail -3 /etc/group
users::100:games
nogroup::-2:
netgroup::1001:tim,slim
```

tim on compassion creating the netgroupfile
```
compassion:~$ echo echo This file is executable > netgroupfile
compassion:~$ cat netgroupfile
echo This file is executable
compassion:~$ ls -l
-rw-r--r--   1 tim        users        29 Dec 17 11:49
netgroupfile
compassion:~$ chmod 740 netgroupfile
compassion:~$ chgrp netgroup netgroupfile
compassion:~$ ls -l
-rwxr-----   1 tim        netgroup     29 Dec 17 11:49
netgroupfile
compassion:~$ echo date >> netgroupfile
compassion:~$ cat netgroupfile
echo This file is executable
date
compassion:~$ netgroupfile
This file is executable
Fri Dec 17 11:51:31 EST 1999
```

slim on compassion checking netgroupfile's permissions
```
compassion:~$ whoami
slim
compassion:~$ grep netgr /etc/group
netgroup::1001:tim,slim
compassion:~$ cd ~tim
compassion:/home/tim$ cat netgroupfile
echo This file is executable
date
compassion:/home/tim$ echo hostname >> netgroupfile
bash: netgroupfile: Permission denied
compassion:/home/tim$ netgroupfile
bash: ./netgroupfile: Permission denied
```

Figure 26.13 Jim creating a group, Tim creating a file to be shared with the group, and Slim reading the file.

Using the echo command, he appends the date command to netgroupfile. Then using the cat command, he displays the file and finally, by simply entering the file name, he executes each line of the file.

Next comes Slim. He first checks the `/etc/group` file to make sure he belongs to netgroup. He changes the working directory to Tim's home directory. When he does cat netgroupfile, it is displayed. However, when he tries to append to the file or execute it, he gets a `Permission denied` message. If Kim had tried doing these three operations on the file, she would have been denied because of the file permissions set by Tim. (Testing of permissions by Kim is not shown in the figure.)

26.5 BASIC SECURITY

26.5.1 Remote Login for Superuser

Suppose that Jim has become a systems administrator for a server at work and he would like to log in from home and do his administrative tasks. He would like to enable superuser privileges while he is telneting from home, but he doesn't want others who do not have the authority to be able to do that. Figure 26.14 shows Jim logging into loving from compassion. The loving server will act as Jim's PC at home from where he wants to gain supervisor access into compassion.

He logs into compassion directly as root since he knows the root password. There are two problems with this setup. If the root password leaks out, then root access is gained. It would be better if the person needed to break into at least two passwords. The second problem is that compassion cannot make an entry in its log files as to who gained root access. It could be anyone. It would be better if the person had to identify who he was before being granted root access. Of course, a good hacker would delete the log files anyway, but it is good to keep a record as to who got in, just in case he doesn't.

To correct these problems, Jim switches over to his root session using ALT-F1. He goes to the /etc directory and notices the terminals from where root is allowed to log in. To save space, they are condensed. We have seen some of these tty's (terminal types) in Figure 26.9. Toward the end of that session Jim did the who command and saw himself logged in on some of these tty's. tty1 through tty6 are the six virtual terminals obtained using ALT-F1 through ALT-F6, ttys's are for serial connections, and the ttyp's are for remote telnet connections. We have to remove ttyp0 through ttyp3 to disable direct root login using telnet. Jim does that using pico and by using the tail command he sees that these entries have been properly removed.

Jim then switches to his session on loving and tries to directly log in as root. He can't. That's good. He must first log in as himself and then do the su – command which enables him with superuser privileges. At least this time, compassion knows who did an su (SuperUser access).

Going to the top of the second column of Figure 26.14, we see that Jim pretends to be slim and logs into compassion. He then finds out that even slim can do the su – command and become a superuser. This means that anyone who has an account and has found out the root password can get in. Let us tighten the security further.

jim on compassion: ALT-F2
```
compassion:~$ telnet loving
loving login: jim
loving:~$ telnet compassion
compassion login: root
Password:
compassion:~# logout
```

jim on compassion as root: ALT-F1
```
compassion:~# cd /etc
compassion:/etc# cat securetty
console   tty1      tty2      tty3
tty4      tty5      tty6      ttyS0
ttyS1     ttyS2     ttyS3     ttyp0
ttyp1     ttyp2     ttyp3
compassion:/etc# pico securetty
compassion:/etc# tail -5 securetty
tty6
ttyS0
ttyS1
ttyS2
ttyS3
```

jim on compassion: ALT-F2
```
loving:~$ telnet compassion
compassion login: root
Password:
Login incorrect
loving:~$ telnet compassion
compassion login: jim
compassion:~$ su -
Password:
compassion:~# exit
logout
compassion:~$ logout
```

```
loving:~$ telnet compassion
compassion login: slim
compassion:~$ su -
Password:
compassion:~# exit
logout
compassion:~$ exit
Connection closed by foreign host.
```

jim on compassion as root: ALT-F1
```
compassion:/etc# grep SU_W login.defs
SU_WHEEL_ONLY no
compassion:/etc# pico login.defs
compassion:/etc# grep SU_W login.defs
SU_WHEEL_ONLY yes
compassion:/etc# pico group
compassion:/etc# grep jim group
root::0:root,jim
wheel::10:root,jim
compassion:/etc#
```

jim on compassion: ALT-F2
```
loving:~$ telnet compassion
compassion login: slim
compassion:~$ su -
You are not authorized to su root
compassion:~$ exit
logout
loving:~$ telnet compassion
compassion login: jim
compassion:~$ su -
Password:
compassion:~# exit
logout
compassion:~$
```

Figure 26.14 Securing the server for remote superuser login.

Switching over to his root session, Jim finds the line in the /etc/login.defs file that has to do with SU_WHEEL_ONLY. This is set to no. Using pico, Jim changes the no to yes and this is confirmed in the second grep command. Then he modifies the /etc/group file so that he is placed in the root and the wheel groups. These two edits ensure that only members of the wheel group are allowed to do the su – command.

Jim then masquarades himself as slim and logs into compassion from loving. Slim is not allowed to su. That's what he wanted. Then he logs as himself into compassion and finds out that he can enable root privileges without problems.

Security is a big issue on servers that are on the public internet. As soon as some holes are fixed, others start surfacing. One should always keep up to date with the latest security bugs. The fixes that were just illustrated were done with Slackware 3.6. With newer versions of Slackware, some of these fixes may not be necessary because the newer installs are more secure than the previous ones.

26.5.2 Blocking Certain IP Addresses

In the event that you are getting bombarded with e-mail to your server from a certain IP address, you want to be able to block services to that IP address. Let us see now how that would be done.

A daemon is a process that is always running in the background of a server to see if anyone is requesting any service. There is a telnet daemon called telnetd in Unix that is always listening to see if any client wishes to telnet to that server. There is also a process called smtpd that is always listening to see if anyone is trying to send e-mail to it and so on. There is also a master daemon that oversees all the individual daemons and it is named inetd. Its configuration is given in the file called /etc/inetd.conf. A line from this file is as follows:

```
telnet stream tcp nowait root /user/sbin/tcpd wu.telnetd
```

This line shows that during startup, inetd will start up /user/sbin/tcpd and use wu.telnetd as an argument. This then runs as a process started by root. The file called /etc/services will have the port numbers for each of the TCP applications listed.

Now if we add this line without any spaces to the /etc/hosts.allow file:

```
in.telnetd:172.16.10.115:DENY
```

all telnet requests from this IP address will be denied by this server. To deny all hosts whose address begins with 128.117.100, you would simply drop the 115 in the line. Specifically, it would be:

```
in.telnetd:172.16.10.:DENY
```

26.5.3 Blocking Anonymous ftp

Anonymous ftp allows anyone who doesn't have an account on a server to download files that are readable by the public. This type of ftp doesn't require a password. Many administrators feel that this is a security hazard. Hence, if they need files that are available to the general public, they set up a server that is dedicated to only provide anonymous ftp. This way, private files can have better protection.

We can disable anonymous ftp simply by adding this line to the /etc/ftpusers file:

```
anonymous
```

You will find that root and a few other accounts are already listed in the file, meaning that these accounts cannot do file transfers. By adding anonymous, now this account cannot do file transfers either.

26.6 USING X WINDOWS

26.6.1 Configuring X Windows

X Windows is a free GUI (Graphical User Interface), developed through MIT, which over the years has become popular for all versions of Unix. Let us get our server ready for X Windows. We will do this by following Figure 26.15 as we outline how X

```
compassion:~#  SuperProbe                      Your monitor definition:     asdf
WARNING - THIS SOFTWARE COULD HANG            Enter the vendor name:    asdf
YOUR MACHINE.                                 Enter the model name:    asdf
First video: Super-VGA
 Chipset: ATI 264GT3 (3D Rage III)           Now we must configure video card.
 Memory:   8192 Kbytes                        Database about the chipset.
 RAMDAC:   ATI Mach64 integrated              Do you want to look at the database?    n
        15/16/24/32-bit DAC w/clock
 Attached graphics coprocessor:               Determine which server to run.
        Chipset: ATI Mach64                    3   The XF86_SVGA server.
        Memory:  8192 Kbytes                   4   The accelerated servers.
                                              Which of these screen typess(1-4)?    3
compassion:~#  xf86config
                                              The server is selected by changing the
This program creates aXF86Config file,             symbolic link 'X'.
Press enter to continue.   <ENTER>            Want me to set the symbolic link?    y
                                              Want to set it in /var/X11R6/bin?    y
First specify a mouse protocol type.
 1.  Microsoft compatible                     Information about your video card.
 2.  Mouse Systems (3-button protocol)         1   256K
 3.  Bus Mouse                                 2   512K
 4.  PS/2 Mouse                                3   1024K
 5.  Logitech Mouse                           Enter your choice:    3
Enter a protocol number:    4
                                              Enter a few identifications
Want to enable Emulate3Buttons?    n          Identifier for your video card:    asdf
                                              Vendor name of your video card:    asdf
Now give the full device name                 Model name of your video card:    asdf
Pressing enter will use the default.
Mouse device:   <ENTER>                        1   Chrontel 8391
                                               2   ICD2061A and compatibles
Do you want to use XKB?   n                   Clockchip setting (1-12)?    <ENTER>

If you want non-ASCII characters. . .         Want me to run 'X-probeonly' now?    n
Want to enable these bindings?    n
                                               1   Change the modes for 8pp
Now we want to set the monitor.                2   Change the modes for 16bpp
Press enter to continue.    <ENTER>           Enter your choice:    1

You must indicate the horizontal sync.        Select modes from the following list:
 1   31.5; Standard VGA,                        1   "640x400"
 2   31.5 - 35.1; Super VGA                      2   "640x480"
 3   31.5, 35.5; 8514 Compatible                 3   "800x600"
 4   31.5, 35.15, 35.5; Super VGA                4   "1024x768"
 5   31.5 - 37.9; Extended Super VGA           Which modes?   3
Enter your choice (1-11):    4
                                              Do you want a virtual screen ?   n
You must indicate the vertical sync.           4   Change the modes for 32bpp
 1   50-70                                      5   The modes are OK, continue.
 2   50-90                                     Enter your choice:    5
 3   50-100
 4   40-150                                    Shall I write it to /etc/XF86Config?    y
Enter your choice:    4                        compassion:~#  startx
```

Figure 26.15 An outline of setting the X Windows configuration.

Windows is configured. Although many lines have been deleted and many lines have been shortened from this dialog, all of the entries are present and none have been deleted.

To start, we can get some information about our display by running the SuperProbe software. We have a Mach64 card which is a good card at this time. The settings that we will choose will not use the full capability of this card, but once we get X Windows running minimally, we can always reconfigure it with better resolution and features. There are 8 Mbytes of RAM on this card.

To start the configuration, we type xf86config. The first thing it asks us is what type of mouse we have. We choose a PS/2 mouse by entering a 4. Then we choose not to use foreign characters from our keyboard or extended keyboard mappings.

Then we begin setting the monitor. First, we choose a Super VGA monitor and pick a modest vertical sync setting. Other choices were given but they are not shown in the figure. This takes us to the top of the second column of Figure 26.15. Here, we could have just pressed Enter three times, but here we enter a dummy name: "asdf."

Now that the monitor is configured, we continue by configuring the video card. We pick a Super VGA server and let the system specify the link to that server. Again, we provide some dummy identifiers and names. This time it is for the card. Then we use the default clock chip setting and decide not to run X-probe. We don't want a virtual screen. This is when the screen is larger than the physical screen. We indicate that the modes for the screen are fine by entering 5. Finally, we write the configuration to the XF86Config file and start running X Windows.

Notice, to run X Windows on your machine you need information about your system. The more information you have about your PC, the easier it will be to pick the correct choices in this dialog. Remember, SuperProbe can also give you a good amount of information about your video setup. Even after gathering all this information, you may still have to run the xf86config command a few times, each time trying settings that are slightly different. After some trial and error, you should be running X Windows on your server. A little patience is all that is needed, but having a GUI to work with afterwards will make it worth it.

26.6.2 The Apache Web Server

Once X Windows is set up, we can start Netscape which comes with the Slackware distribution. When we installed Linux, the Apache web server was installed by default. Since then we have had a web server running with our hosts, but we never accessed it as such. To access your own web server, simply enter your IP address in the browser as shown:

```
http://172.16.10.111
```

The example above shows how Jim can view his own home page from his browser. To add a link to kim's host, Jim can add this line in his index.html file which is located in the /var/lib/apache/share/htdocs directory:

```
<A HREF="http"//172.16.10.112/">loving</A>
```

Now Jim's page has a link to kim's machine. This way, additional links can be added among the other web servers in the lab, recreating a mini-WWW environment.

26.7 NETWORK ADMINISTRATION

26.7.1 DNS

Now let us configure compassion as a DNS server. We will have loving access compassion as a DNS server instead of having it use the /etc/hosts file to resolve IP addresses from host names.

To do that we will need six files on compassion. The contents of these files are shown in Figures 26.16(a) and (b). Two files will be set up in the /etc directory and four in the /var/named directory. The named subdirectory will need to be created under the /var. Specifically, these files are called /etc/named.conf, /etc/resolv.conf, /var/named/named.local, /var/named/root.cache, /var/named/good.stuff.hosts, and /var/named/

/etc/named.conf

```
/* A simple BIND 8 configuration */
options {
        directory "/var/named";
};
zone "good.stuff.edu." in {
        type master;
        file "good.stuff.hosts";
};
zone "10.16.172.in-addr.arpa." in {
        type master;
        file "good.stuff.rev";
};
zone "." in {
        type hint;
        file "root.cache";
};
zone "0.0.127.in-addr.arpa." in {
        type master;
        file "named.local";
};
```

/etc/resolv.conf

```
search good.stuff.edu
nameserver 127.0.0.1
```

/var/named/named.local

```
@   IN   SOA  compassion.good.stuff.edu.
                 hostmaster.good.stuff.edu. (
                 1986012101 ; Serial
                 3600       ; Refresh
                 300        ; Retry
                 3600000    ; Expire
                 14400 )    ; Minimum

    IN   NS   compassion.good.stuff.edu.
1   IN   PTR  localhost.
```

/var/named/root.cache

```
; formerly NS.INTERNIC.NET
.                       3600000  IN  NS  A.ROOT-SERVERS.NET.
A.ROOT-SERVERS.NET.     3600000      A   198.41.0.4

.                       3600000      NS  B.ROOT-SERVERS.NET.
B.ROOT-SERVERS.NET.     3600000      A   128.9.0.107

.                       3600000      NS  C.ROOT-SERVERS.NET.
C.ROOT-SERVERS.NET.     3600000      A   192.33.4.12
```

Figure 26.16(a) Four of the six files required on compassion, our DNS server.

Linux Administration

665

/var/named/good.stuff.hosts

```
@               IN      SOA     compassion.good.stuff.edu.
                                hostmaster.good.stuff.edu. (
                                19991124         ; serial
                                10800            ; refresh 3 hours
                                3600             ; retry 1 hour
                                3600000          ; expire 1000 hours
                                86400)  ; minimum 24 hours

                IN      NS      compassion
                IN      MX      10 compassion
                IN      MX      50 loving

compassion      IN A    172.16.10.111
loving          IN A    172.16.10.112
```

/var/named/good.stuff.rev

```
;/var/named/good.stuff.rev
;
@       IN      SOA     compassion.good.stuff.edu.
                       hostmaster.good.stuff.edu. (
                       19991123         ; serial
                       10800            ; refresh 3 hours
                       3600             ; retry 1 hour
                       3600000          ; expire 1000 hours
                       86400)  ; minimum 24 hours

        IN      NS      compassion.good.stuff.edu.

111     IN      PTR     compassion.good.stuff.edu.
112     IN      PTR     loving.good.stuff.edu.
```

Figure 26.16(b) The rest of the files on our DNS server, compassion.

good.stuff.rev. Every comma, parenthesis, etc. has to entered exactly as shown. The files are simplified as much as possible. They could be even more simplified if no connection to the public Internet was made. However, these files, as listed, are sufficient to resolve IP addresses over the Internet.

We will not labor over the syntax of these files at this time since studying the man pages would help one understand them. In Figure 26.17 we see the only file that loving would need to access compassion as a name server. This file is called /etc/resolv.conf.

```
loving:# cat /etc/resolv.conf
search good.stuff.edu
nameserver 172.16.10.111
```

Figure 26.17 The only file for DNS needed on loving.

(Notice that /etc/hosts has commented out the IP address for compassion.)
```
loving:/etc# grep 111 hosts
#172.16.10.111 compassion.good.stuff.edu compassion
```

(Therefore, the IP address for compassion is resolved from the DNS server.)
```
loving:/etc# ping compassion
PING compassion.good.stuff.edu (172.16.10.111): 56 data bytes
64 bytes from 172.16.10.111: icmp_seq=0 ttl=255 time=0.3 ms
```

(Renaming resolv.conf prevents loving to get the IP address from the DNS server.)
```
NOW RESOLV.CONF DOESNT EXIST AND PING DOESNT RESOLVS
loving:/etc#mv resolv.conf resolv.conf.old
loving:/etc#ping compassion
ping: unknown host compassion
```

(Restoring resolv.conf allows to resolve IP addresses again.)
```
loving:/etc# mv resolv.conf.old resolv.conf
loving:/etc# ping compassion
PING compassion.good.stuff.edu (172.16.10.111): 56 data bytes
64 bytes from 172.16.10.111: icmp_seq=0 ttl=255 time=0.2 ms
```

```
loving:~# nslookup
Default Server:  compassion.good.stuff.edu
Address:  172.16.10.111
```

```
> compassion
Server:  compassion.good.stuff.edu
Address:  172.16.10.111
Name:     compassion.good.stuff.edu
Address:  172.16.10.111
```

```
> 172.16.10.112
Server:  compassion.good.stuff.edu
Address:  172.16.10.111
Name:     loving.good.stuff.edu
Address:  172.16.10.112
```

```
> exit
loving:~#
```

Figure 26.18 Accessing the DNS server for loving.

Starting at the top of Figure 26.18, we see that on loving, we have commented out the entry for compassion in its /etc/hosts file. Therefore, when we ping compassion, we must be resolving our IP address through the /etc/resolv.conf file which points loving to compassion. To confirm that, we rename the resolv.conf file using the mv command. Now we can't ping compassion. Renaming it with its original name allows us to ping compassion and resolve its IP address again. Then the nslookup command is checked to make sure the DNS server is configured properly and it is.

26.7.2 Static Routing

Another experiment we can do is to configure one of our servers as a router. Let's make loving a router. For that, we'll need to install another Ethernet card inside it. Figure 26.19 shows that we have used two hubs to create two subnets. The server compassion and one Ethernet card of loving are on one subnet and forgiving and the other Ethernet card of loving are on another subnet. This is seen in the figure. We could have just used two crossover cables and connected the cards directly, but then we could not add other servers to the subnets.

To configure loving as a router we must modify its /etc/rc.d/rc.inet1 file. This is also shown in Figure 26.19. Here, we have defined variables in all capital letters, such as IPADDR and IPADDR2. Each interface of loving will need its own IP address, its own subnet mask, its own network address, etc.

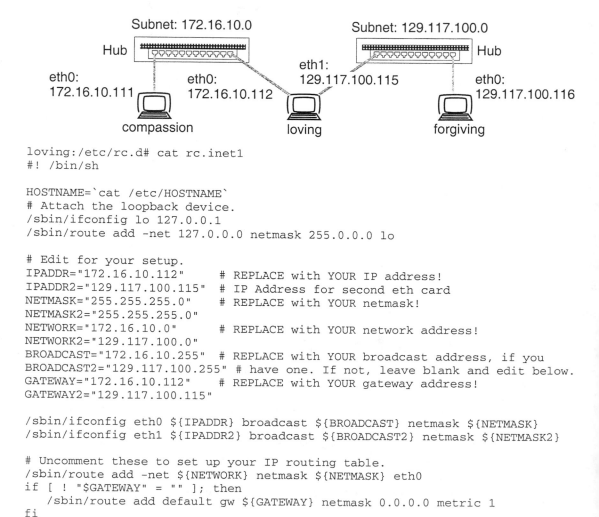

```
loving:/etc/rc.d# cat rc.inet1
#! /bin/sh

HOSTNAME=`cat /etc/HOSTNAME`
# Attach the loopback device.
/sbin/ifconfig lo 127.0.0.1
/sbin/route add -net 127.0.0.0 netmask 255.0.0.0 lo

# Edit for your setup.
IPADDR="172.16.10.112"      # REPLACE with YOUR IP address!
IPADDR2="129.117.100.115"   # IP Address for second eth card
NETMASK="255.255.255.0"     # REPLACE with YOUR netmask!
NETMASK2="255.255.255.0"
NETWORK="172.16.10.0"       # REPLACE with YOUR network address!
NETWORK2="129.117.100.0"
BROADCAST="172.16.10.255"   # REPLACE with YOUR broadcast address, if you
BROADCAST2="129.117.100.255" # have one. If not, leave blank and edit below.
GATEWAY="172.16.10.112"     # REPLACE with YOUR gateway address!
GATEWAY2="129.117.100.115"

/sbin/ifconfig eth0 ${IPADDR} broadcast ${BROADCAST} netmask ${NETMASK}
/sbin/ifconfig eth1 ${IPADDR2} broadcast ${BROADCAST2} netmask ${NETMASK2}

# Uncomment these to set up your IP routing table.
/sbin/route add -net ${NETWORK} netmask ${NETMASK} eth0
if [ ! "$GATEWAY" = "" ]; then
   /sbin/route add default gw ${GATEWAY} netmask 0.0.0.0 metric 1
fi
```

Figure 26.19 Configuring loving to be a router between two subnets.

Notice the two /sbin/ifconfig commands in the file. They configure each of the two Ethernet interfaces: eth0 and eth1. The string, ${IPADDR}, provides the value of that variable which we defined above. Below these lines is a /sbin/route add command. This will add only the first subnetwork to the routing table. We will add the other subnet manually.

In Figure 26.20, we boot up loving and notice that both the eth0 and the eth1 interfaces are configured. We check the addresses to make sure they are correct. A netstat -nr command shows that the first subnet is entered in the routing table, but not the other subnet. Hence, we do a route add command to add the other subnet to the routing table. The word "gw" stands for gateway. The interface 129.117.100.115 is the gateway for the 129.117.100.0 subnet. From loving, our router, we can ping servers on both subnets.

```
loving:~# ifconfig
lo        Link encap:Local Loopback
          inet addr:127.0.0.1  Bcast:127.255.255.255  Mask:255.0.0.0
          UP BROADCAST LOOPBACK RUNNING  MTU:3584  Metric:1

eth0      Link encap:Ethernet  HWaddr 00:50:04:D3:D9:98
          inet addr:172.16.10.112  Bcast:172.16.10.255  Mask:255.255.255.0
          UP BROADCAST RUNNING MULTICAST  MTU:1500  Metric:1

eth1      Link encap:Ethernet  HWaddr 00:10:4B:70:9A:C6
          inet addr:129.117.100.115  Bcast:129.117.100.255  Mask:255.255.255.0
          UP BROADCAST RUNNING MULTICAST  MTU:1500  Metric:1

loving:~# netstat -nr
Kernel IP routing table
Destination     Gateway         Genmask         Flags   MSS Window  irtt Iface
172.16.10.0     0.0.0.0         255.255.255.0   U       1500 0         0 eth0
127.0.0.0       0.0.0.0         255.0.0.0       U       3584 0         0 lo

loving:~# route add -net 129.117.100.0 gw 129.117.100.115

loving:~# netstat -nr
Kernel IP routing table
Destination     Gateway         Genmask         Flags   MSS Window  irtt Iface
172.16.10.0     0.0.0.0         255.255.255.0   U       1500 0         0 eth0
129.117.100.0   0.0.0.0         255.255.255.0   U       1500 0         0 eth1
127.0.0.0       0.0.0.0         255.0.0.0       U       3584 0         0 lo

loving:~# ping 129.117.100.116
PING 129.117.100.116 (129.117.100.116): 56 data bytes
64 bytes from 129.117.100.116: icmp_seq=0 ttl=64 time=0.3 ms
64 bytes from 129.117.100.116: icmp_seq=1 ttl=64 time=0.2 ms

loving:~# ping 172.16.10.111
PING 172.16.10.111 (172.16.10.111): 56 data bytes
64 bytes from 172.16.10.111: icmp_seq=0 ttl=255 time=0.3 ms
64 bytes from 172.16.10.111: icmp_seq=1 ttl=255 time=0.2 ms
```

Figure 26.20 Adding a new route to loving.

```
compassion:~#  netstat -nr
Destination     Gateway         Genmask         Flags   MSS Window  irtt Iface
172.16.10.0     0.0.0.0         255.255.255.0   U         0 0          0 eth0
127.0.0.0       0.0.0.0         255.0.0.0       U         0 0          0 lo
0.0.0.0         172.16.10.112   0.0.0.0         UG        0 0          0 eth0

compassion:~#  ping 172.16.10.112
PING 172.16.10.112 (172.16.10.112): 56 data bytes
64 bytes from 172.16.10.112: icmp_seq=0 ttl=64 time=0.3 ms
64 bytes from 172.16.10.112: icmp_seq=1 ttl=64 time=0.2 ms

compassion:~#  ping 129.117.100.116
PING 129.117.100.116 (129.117.100.116): 56 data bytes
64 bytes from 129.117.100.116: icmp_seq=0 ttl=63 time=0.6 ms
64 bytes from 129.117.100.116: icmp_seq=1 ttl=63 time=0.5 ms
```

Figure 26.21 Testing loving as a router.

But do we have a route from compassion to forgiving through loving? To check that out, we turn to Figure 26.21. Here, we add the default route to compassion the same way we added a route to loving. From compassion, we can ping to both loving and forgiving, confirming that loving is now configured as a router between the two subnets. A similar check from forgiving to compassion proves that the reverse path is configured as well.

EXERCISES

Section 26.1:
1. Which of the following is NOT a distribution of Linux?
   a. Red Hat   b. Open BSD
   c. Slackware   d. Caldera
2. Comment on the advantages of Linux? There is much written about this in various sources.
3. What item is the same among the different distributions of Linux?

Section 26.2:
4. What are the names of the utilities which allow you to repartition a hard drive?
5. How many partitions were needed for Linux? What was each partition called and what were they used for?
6. The specification for /dev/hdb3 indicates which hard drive and which partition?
7. Which diskettes are needed for installing Slackware?
8. Describe LILO and what it does.
9. Which fdisk command allows you to do each of the following: see the partition table, change the partition type, remove a partition, and create a new partition?
10. Which command allows you to change the IP address and/or host name?
11. What is the proper way to shutdown a Unix server?

Section 26.3:
12. Which files are updated when changing the IP address? When changing the host name?
13. Under which circumstances would you need to change the IP address?

14. Which file allows you to address a host by its host name and not its IP address?
15. Which command allows you to see each of the following?
    a. The interfaces that are currently running on the server.
    b. The messages which were displayed on the screen while the server was booting up.
    c. The file system table.
    d. The type of CPU used in your server.

Section 26.4:
16. Which diskettes are needed to remove the root password?
17. Give the command to do each of the following tasks.
    a. Find out who has accounts on a server.
    b. Create a new user
    c. Find out whether james has an account.
18. Jim would like to read his e-mail only on forgiving and he has accounts on forgiving, loving, and compassion.
    a. On which server(s) should he create which file(s)?
    b. Show the contents of one of these file(s).
    c. Every time someone sends him e-mail on loving or compassion, what must Jim do (if anything)?
19. Explain the difference between ftp and telnet.
20. Explain the difference between got and put.
21. What command will not allow the owner to do anything with the file, the group members to only write to the file, and everyone else to read and execute the file? Use file1 as the file name.

Section 26.5:
22. To prevent login into root directly using telnet, which tty's were removed from which file(s)?
23. What command allows one to enable superuser privileges?
24. To enable only himself to enable superuser privileges, Jim had to add himself to which groups and modify which file in which way?

Linux Administration

VPNs

In the early 1990s when the first edition of this text was written, virtual networks over the PSTN were in the forefront. At the present time, virtual networks over the Internet have taken their place in a big way. Instead of stating "at the time of this writing" at every turn, let us assume that to be the case throughout this chapter. You may not want to include this chapter since VPNs (Virtual Private Networks) are changing so rapidly. Then again, VPNs have become so important that they deserve some explanation rather than none at all.

27.1 INTRODUCTION TO VPNs

27.1.1 What are VPNs?

In Section 5.1.4, we discussed the differences between PSTN-based VPNs and Internet-based VPNs. Today, when VPN is mentioned, it is assumed to refer to Internet-based VPNs. In fact, we can have VPNs over frame relay or ATM networks as well. In a broad sense, a *virtual network* is creating a private network using public network facilities such as the Internet, PSTN, frame relay, etc. Virtual networks simulate a private network, while sharing the resources of public networks. This looks just as if you have the network to yourself or have direct connections between the various sites.

The introduction of intranets was the first step in the evolution of VPNs over the Internet. An *intranet* is nothing more than a network consisting of TCP/IP devices and links all belonging to one organization. Here, the organization wants to create its own internet but doesn't want to risk security by going on the Internet. (The public Internet is spelled with a capital "I" while a private internet is spelled with a lowercase "i.") Figure 27.1(a) shows an example of an intranet that spans three cities.

When an organization wants to have connectivity to the Internet, so that its members have access to the public world and the public can access its intranet, it may use a firewall to connect itself to the Internet. This is shown in Figure 27.1(b). The firewall can be configured to filter packets, allowing certain packets to exit the intranet and preventing others from doing so. It can also filter some packets from entering the

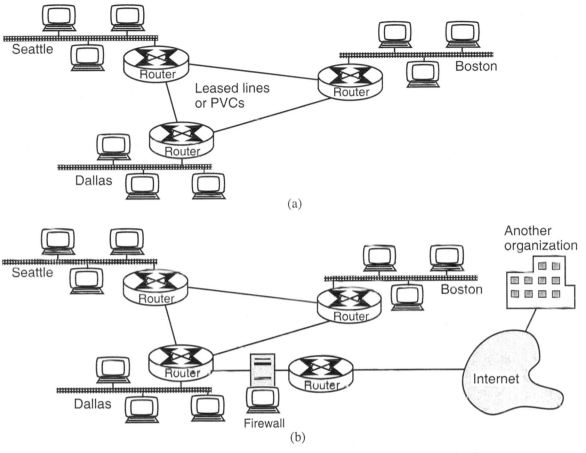

Figure 27.1 (a) An intranet is a TCP/IP network where one organization owns or leases all equipment, connnections, and leased lines to which others have no direct access. (b) Using a firewall, an intranet can be connected to the public Internet, which is then seen as an extranet to other public users.

intranet while allowing others to enter. There are many ways to determine these policies. The intranet as viewed by others on the Internet (depicted by "Another organization" in Figure 27.1) is called an extranet. When the Internet is used to carve out a communication link between two sites, the link is called a *tunnel*. We described tunneling and encapsulation at the end of Chapter 2.

27.1.2 Classifying VPNs by User Type

VPNs come in many flavors and so we will describe some of them. We can do that by classifying them into groups. There are basically two methods in which this can be done. Figure 27.2 outlines them both. We can classify them by the manner in which they are used by the end users or we can classify them according to the OSI layers.

<u>Classifying VPNs using user-types:</u>

Access VPNs: Remotely located users can access corporate networks.

Intranet VPNs: Sites belonging to one corporation can access each other.

Extranet VPNs: Sites belonging to different corporations can access each other.

<u>Classifying VPNs using the OSI layers:</u>

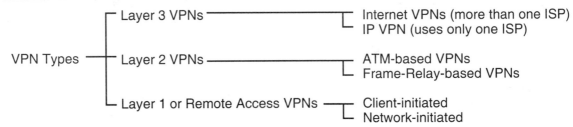

Figure 27.2 Two methods of classifying VPNs.

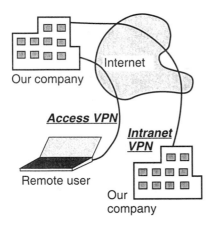

If we classify them by the types of users involved, then we have access, intranet, and extranet VPNs. When a salesperson is temporarily in a hotel or visiting some customer's site and needs access to the network back at his home office, they need what is called *remote access VPNs* or access VPNs, for short. See the side diagram. When two sites belonging to the same organization can connect to each other using the Internet, this called *Intranet VPN*. This is also shown in the side diagram.

An organization may need to get into the intranet of another organization to get purchase orders or what not. The type of VPN that gives one organization access to another organization's network through the Internet is called an extranet VPN. See the side diagram.

27.1.3 Classifying VPNs by OSI Layers

The second method of classifying VPNs as shown in Figure 27.2 involves using the OSI layers. Let us start at the second layer. At this layer, we have frame relay and ATM networks which can be used as VPNs. These networks are secure because you can have PVCs (Permanent Virtual Circuits) created between your sites. No other traffic ever goes over your PVCs and so you not only get better security but also can determine its QoS (Quality of Service). Because these types of VPNs are not taking over the press that much, we will not mention them again except to say that if you do

VPNs

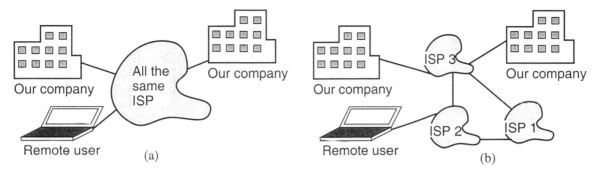

Figure 27.3 (a) IP-VPN. (b) Internet-VPN.

have a choice of getting a VPN between two sites using either the Internet or layer 2 VPNs, you should seriously consider these layer 2 VPNs. If you can trust the carriers with your data over leased lines, then you should be able to do the same with frame relay and ATM.

At OSI layer 3, we have two more kinds of VPNs called Internet-VPNs and IP-VPNs. These VPNs are based on the IP protocol which does routing or a layer 3 protocol. They both use the Internet as seen in Figure 27.3. However, when a company uses one ISP (Internet Service Provider) to connect to the Internet, it is called IP-VPN or single-ISP VPN. See Figure 27.3(a). If a company is spread across the country, then an ISP which has a nationwide presence is necessary. All traffic between the sites can be made to travel on the Internet backbone belonging to that ISP. Only when packets need to be transferred between other companies, which may be using different ISPs, are connections made to other ISPs.

Having one ISP transport all the traffic between the sites enables the ISP to provide better security. The ISP can provide contracts called SLAs (Service Level Agreements). SLAs provide business customers guarantees of what level of service they will get from their ISP. The availability of service, the amount of throughput and delay, the mean time to repair, prioritization of traffic, and QoS are some characteristics by which SLAs can be guaranteed. If more than one ISP is involved in creating the VPN, then one cannot expect any prespecified level of service. However, now that we can specify the level of QoS, voice and video can also be transferred between sites at acceptable levels of performance.

As more ISPs are involved in providing connectivity between distant sites as shown in Figure 27.3(b), no specific guarantees can be expected. These types of VPNs can be labeled as Internet-VPNs. However, with Internet-VPNs, we can have coverage around the globe and in many more locations. No one ISP can have a presence everywhere that easily.

Figure 27.4(a) shows a client-initiated remote access VPN and Figure 27.4(b) shows a network-initiated remote access VPN. In a client-initiated remote access VPN, the end user must have VPN access software installed on his laptop by the IT technicians at the corporate office. This software must be compatible with the software installed on the corporate network. Then VPN connections can be created from the end

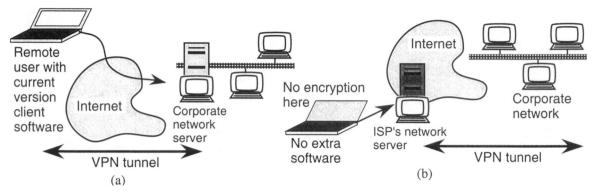

Figure 27.4 (a) With client-initiated remote access, the remote user dials directly into the corporate network, creating a VPN tunnel from end to end. (b) With network-initiated remote access, the remote user dials a single given number into a network server. The network server from the ISP then creates a VPN connection to the corporate network.

user to the corporate office. The end user can dial from anywhere into any ISP on the Internet.

In a Network-initiated VPN the user does not need VPN software installed on his machine, nor does it have to be compatible with the VPN software at the corporate office. The user simply dials to a prespecified phone number, which connects him to a special network server at the ISP designated as the VPN network server for that company. There is no encryption between these two points.

Now the ISP's network server will create a VPN connection on behalf of that user through the Internet. One problem with this setup is that if the remote user is far from the network server, the phone connection charges may become significant. Users dialing into an 800 number around the country can be prohibitive. On the other hand, when users are located in a metropolitan district, then this type of VPN can be more suitable.

27.2 VPN ADVANTAGES

We have already discussed how better service can be achieved through IP-VPNs. Initially, VPNs were created because of the reduction in operating costs that they provide. However, their advantages don't end there. Internet access is becoming more common from more locations each day. Access from many more locations is possible if the Internet is used. If a company needs a temporary connection, with a leased line you may have to wait well over a month depending on the carriers involved. In other words, VPNs provide better connectivity to your network than other methods.

Of course, security has been a big concern for VPN users all along. But over the years a lot of research has been done to get good security, and now transferring sensitive data securely over VPNs has become possible. Hence, not only can your employees access their data from practically anywhere, but they can now access it securely. Your customers can access your web sites and transfer credit card information without being concerned about anyone else getting it. Your corporate sites can access each other using secure VPN tunnels. You can also go into other companies' VPNs and exchange funds securely.

In the mid-1990's no one thought of the web becoming a major marketing front. Those who have made their presence known over the web are now able to draw higher profits. The same is true with VPNs. Creating a VPN will position your company to opportunities that would not be available otherwise. That is probably the biggest reason to install a VPN. As new applications are created, companies with VPNs will able to capitalize on them and increase their growth.

27.3 SECURITY ISSUES

27.3.1 Identifying Security Requirements

Ensuring security is a major issue in implementing VPNs. Hence, instead of taking the definition of security for granted, let us itemize what is meant by security so we can determine whether we have achieved security or not. We will find out that no one encryption scheme alone will allow us to do this and that we need several encryption schemes.

Authentication: When you go to a web site such as www.prenhall.com and you are about to give your credit card number so that you can purchase a book, how do you know that you indeed have this site on the other end and not some kid in a foreign country? How can you be sure that no third party is masquerading as this site before you send in your credit card number? (This is also called spoofing.) Authentication is the ability to make sure you have the party on the other end which claims to be that party and no one else. That is, they are who they say they are.

Message Integrity: How can you be sure that the message that was sent from the source was not modified by someone else while it was in transit? Message integrity allows us to secure the message so that we can be sure that it was not altered.

Non-Repudiation: Someone sends an e-mail to his stock broker asking him to buy a large number of stocks for him. Then the next day the price of that stock plunges. How can the stock broker protect himself in the event that his customer claims that he never requested that purchase in the first place? Non-repudiation will provide a means of proving that a given message came from the party which had sent it.

Confidentiality: How can we be sure that the message was not being "sniffed" while it was in transit? You may not care that much if someone reads your e-mail about what course section you are signing up for next semester. However, for some people, some messages being sniffed by the unauthorized people may be disastrous. Confidentiality gives us the privacy which may be required.

Authorization and Audits: Is the person on the other end of the connection authorized to submit purchases? Authorization gives us the ability to determine this.

Also, we may need to prove the hands through which a document or a transaction has gone. Audit enables us to maintain such an "electronic paper trail."

27.3.2 Cryptography

Hashing: As we have said before, to meet all these requirements for achieving security, we will need more than one encryption scheme. Hashing is one such scheme. It allows us to basically achieve message integrity. Hashing uses no keys at all. It is also called one-way encryption. This is because hashing takes cleartext and converts it to what is called ciphertext or encrypted text. Once the ciphertext is created, the cleartext cannot be extracted from it. Hence, the term one-way.

Examples of hashing functions are HMAC, MD2, MD4, MD5, and SHA. For illustration purposes, we will use a much simpler function that uses the modulus function. The modulus function returns the remainder after dividing a number by a predefined number. That is, 40 mod 37 is 3 and 77 mod 37 is also 3. The remainder after dividing 40 or 77 by 37 is 3 in either case. Given the ciphertext of 3, we cannot derive the 40 because there are many other numbers which will return a remainder of 3 after dividing them by the predefined number of 37.

Figure 27.5 shows that the data being transmitted is 6249. After applying the hash function of modulus 37, we get 33 as the remainder. We append the 33 after the data (6249). At the top right-hand side of this figure, suppose that we end up receiving 6248 as the data portion instead of 6249. How would we know that a third party somewhere in our connection altered this message?

We would be able to determine this by applying the hashing function to our data. 6248 mod 37 gives us 32. The result from the hashing function (32) does not match the 33 we received in the hash field. Hence, we can tell that integrity has been compromised.

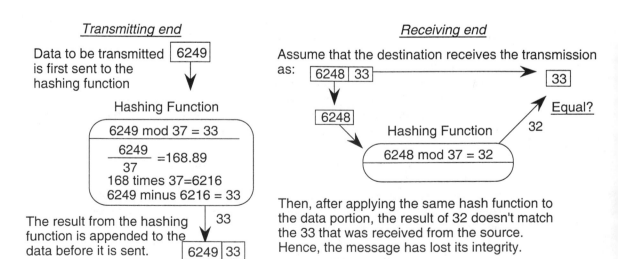

Figure 27.5 How hashing checks for message integrity.

Convert these digits: 0 1 2 3 4 5 6 7 8 9
respectively to these: 5 2 9 4 1 3 7 0 6 8

(a)

To transmit this message: 8533   These digits are received: 6344
These digits are sent: 6344   which are interpreted this way: 8533

(b)

Figure 27.6 (a) The key which is used by both ends. (b) A message is encrypted before transmission and at the receive end, it is decrypted.

Secret Key Cryptography: This method of key encryption is called two-way or symmetric cryptography. Using SKC (Secret Key Cryptography), the sender can convert cleartext to ciphertext and at the receive end, the ciphertext can be converted back to cleartext. SKC is basically used to achieve confidentiality or privacy. Examples of SKC algorithms are DES, 3DES, IDEA, CAST, RC4, and RC5. As before, we will use a much simpler method of illustrating SKC. This is shown in Figure 27.6.

SKC works in the same manner as when two children create a secret code for which only they have the same piece of paper with the code. Figure 27.6(a) shows such a code. A 0 is converted to a 5, a 1 to a 2, and so on. Figure 27.6(b) shows the message 8533 being encrypted with this code so that the data actually transmitted is 6344. The 6344 is then decoded by the receiver using the same key.

Public Key Cryptography: With PKC (Public Key Cryptography), keys come in pairs. One key is called the private key and other is called the public key. The public key is published to everyone who needs to authenticate messages coming from the person holding the private key, because only the person with the private key can send messages that are decipherable using the matching public key. By the same token, messages that are encoded by anyone using a particular public key can be interpreted only by the one person holding the private key.

When distributing these keys, either key can be the private key or the public key. However, once the keys are assigned, it is very important to keep the private key secure so that no one else knows what it is. When a message is encrypted using the private key, that message can be decrypted by any person knowing the public key. The receiving person, when decrypting the message, can decrypt only the message and not the private key with which it was encrypted.

Diffie and Hellman from Stanford were the first ones to prove that such a system is possible and Rivest, Shamir, and Aldeman from MIT followed them to create the RSA (named after them) public key system. The longer the length of the key, the more secure the encrypting scheme, but the longer it takes to decrypt the message. Hence, PKC is mostly used to exchange the secret keys for SKC, which are generated randomly during a session. PKC is also used for authentication and non-repudiation.

There are two examples of PKC that we will illustrate. One is not actually used but very simple and the other outlines how RSA works. Figure 27.7 shows how ignore the carries works. In this figure, there are two keys: 3 and 7. We can assign either one as the private key, and then the other would be the public key. Here, we have chosen

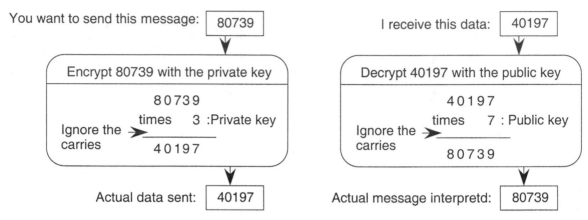

Your public key is 7 and your private key is 3.
Everyone knows your public key (7),
but only you know your private key (3).

You want to send this message: | 80739 |

Encrypt 80739 with the private key

80739
times   3 :Private key
Ignore the → ―――――――
carries   40197

Actual data sent: | 40197 |

I receive this data: | 40197 |

Decrypt 40197 with the public key

40197
times   7 : Public key
Ignore the → ―――――――
carries   80739

Actual message interpretd: | 80739 |

Figure 27.7 Public key encryption.

7 as your public key and 3 as your private key. Then you tell everyone that 7 is your public key, but you keep the number 3 secret.

Suppose you want to send a message, 80739. You multiply these digits with 3, ignoring any carries you get as seen in the figure. The result is 40197. If you send this encrypted message to me, I can decrypt that message using your public key of 7. Of course, anyone who has your public key and gets that message can decrypt it. However, we know that the message must have come from you because only you hold your private key to encrypt the message in the first place.

RSA is much more sophisticated and so we will look at a simplified version of it. RSA uses a pair of prime numbers for the private and public keys. Figure 27.8 gives the method for calculating the keys, shows an example of it, and then shows an example of encrypting and decrypting a message. Let us first look at how the keys are calculated.

First pick two prime numbers, p and q. We picked 5 and 3. Then multiply them and call this number n. n is 15. Then find s which is the product of $p - 1$ and $q - 1$. We get 8. Then find a prime number that doesn't divide evenly into s, such as 11, and call it e. Next, find an integer, d, so that $((e)(d) - 1) / s$ is an integer. We come up with d being 3. We have these two keys at our disposal: (n, e) and (n, d). We will pick n and e or 15 and 11 as the private key and n and d or 15 and 3 as the public key.

To encrypt a message use this formula:

$$C_i = M_i^e \bmod n, \text{ or } C_i = M_i 11 \bmod 15,$$

where M_i are the cleartext characters and C_i are the ciphertext characters; and to decrypt the message use this formula:

$$M_i = C_i d \bmod n, \text{ or } M_i = C_i 3 \bmod 15,$$

Basic Rules for finding the keys	Example

Pick two prime numbers called p and q. $p = 5$ and $q = 3$
Find their product and call it n. $n = 15$
Find the product of $p-1$ and $q-1$ and call it s. $s = (4)(2) = 8$
Find a number that doesn't divide evenly into s and call it e. $e = 11$
Find an integer and call it d so that this division is an integer: $d = 3$

$$((e)(d) - 1) / s = \text{an integer}$$

$((3)(15) - 1) / 8 = 32 / 8 =$
an integer

Now use this formula to encrypt each digit:

$$C_i = M_i{}^e \bmod n$$

Encrypting and decrypting the digit 3

where M_i is each digit to be encrypted

If M_i is 3, then 3^{11} is 177,147.

and C_i is the encrypted digit.

177,147 mod 15 is 12,
     the remainder after dividing
     177,147 by 15

To decrypt a message use this formula:

$$M_i = C_i{}^d \bmod n$$

Hence C_i is 12.

The private key is n and e
and the public key is n and d

If C_i is 12, then 12^3 is 1728

and 1728 mod 15 is 3.
Hence M_i is 3.

The conversion chart for encryption

M_i: 0 1 2 3 4 5 6 7 8 9

C_i: 0 1 8 12 4 5 6 13 2 9

The conversion chart for decryption

C_i: 0 1 2 4 5 6 8 9 12 13

M_i: 0 1 8 4 5 6 2 9 3 7

Figure 27.8 The method for finding the public and private keys used in RSA.

If M_i is 3, for instance, then C_i would encrypt as 12, and if C_i is 12, then M_i would be decrypted as 3. The chart for all the digits is shown in the figure. Notice, some digits don't encrypt well. For example, 4, 5, 6, and 9 are all the same. If we pick very large prime numbers generated by a computer, the encryption method is much better.

An Example: All of the above mentioned methods can be used to send a message, achieving the requirements needed for a secure transmission. Let us see an example of how this can be done.

Suppose that I want to send you some data. Follow Figure 27.9 as we describe the encryption process. To simplify the explanations we'll use the same algorithms and keys we have described before. I know my private key to be (15, 11) and your public key to be 7, and I want to transmit the message, 8533, to you securely.

The first thing I must do is randomly generate a session key used with SKC. Let us say that we came up with the same key, as shown in Figure 27.6, where a 0 was replaced with a 5, a 1 with a 2, etc. I take the data and the session key and apply my SKC algorithm to get 6344. This is my encrypted message, which I will send to you.

Next, I take my message and hash it. The result is shown to be 23. This will allow you to make sure that my message was not altered by any person in the middle when it comes to you. Then I take my private key, (15, 11), and apply my public key algorithm to this hashed value. This will become (8, 12), which is called the *digital*

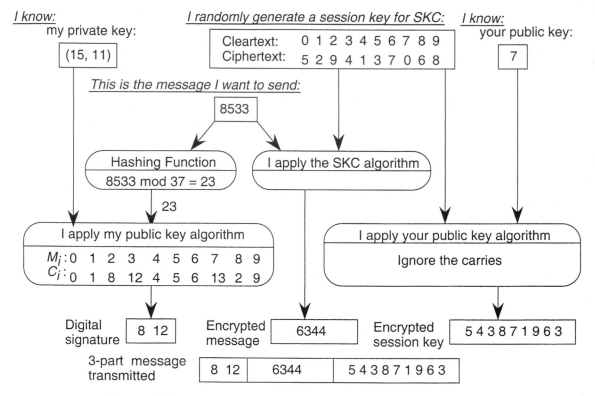

Figure 27.9 An example of how all three methods of encryption are used in transmitting a message securely.

signature. Applying my public key algorithm to the hashed value will allow you to make sure that the hashed value came from me and no one else.

Now, you won't be able to decipher my message unless I also send you my randomly generated session key. I do that by taking your public key, 7, and applying your public key algorithm to the session key. 5 times 7 is 35, and I ignore the 3 and send you the 5. 2 times 7 is 14, and I ignore the 1 and send you the 4, and so on. From this, the encrypted session key is generated. Because only you have your private key, only you can decrypt this session key. Then all these three parts are sent to you together.

You get the data and can delimit or separate these three parts from each other. As seen in Figure 27.10, you know my public key and your private key. The first thing that you can do is use your private key, 3, to decrypt the session key. This is seen as 5, 2, 9, etc. in the figure. This assures you that the message was meant for you. Using this session key, you can now decrypt the message from 6344 to 8533. At this point, you still have to make sure that no one altered my message along the way and that this message did, in fact, come from me.

To make sure of these two things, you must first hash the message into 23. Then you must apply my public key and my public key algorithm to find out the signature. Last, you must check to see if the signature that you received in the data stream and the signature that you calculated are the same or not. If the signatures are the same, as

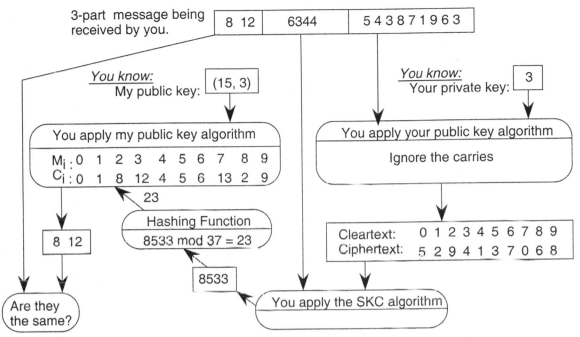

Figure 27.10 How the data sent from Figure 27.9 is being decrypted.

implied in the figure, then you can be assured that my message arrived to you securely. If they are not the same, then you can assume that the message was not received securely.

Of course, all this has to be done without the user knowing it is being done. If a browser is being used, then these procedures have to be built into the browser. Also, which SKC, PKC, and hashing algorithms are being used has to be decided upon before the message is transmitted. There is also a lot of overhead in the amount of data that is sent so data is first compressed, then it is encrypted.

27.3.3 Certificates

Public keys are freely distributed, either using insecure e-mail or by placing them on a web server somewhere. Now suppose that a person needs to securely communicate with other companies' extranets: That person would need the public keys for each company. If only a few companies are required, then only a few public keys would be needed. As soon as the number of companies with which secure communication takes place increases, the number of public keys would become unwieldy. We need a better method of communicating with a large number of companies and not have to keep track of all of their individual keys.

Public key certificates allow us to do this and more. They allow us to make sure that the public key belongs to the person claiming that that key belongs to them. They allow us to make sure that the public key did not expire or was revoked. They also allow us to find the public key reliably.

Certificates provide a means of identifying a person or entity (like a business). They state who issued the certificate, when it expires, what the serial number is, and the restrictions in how the key may be used. For example, a credit card, a driver's license, and a passport are all examples of certificates (although not the kind being discussed here). They all identify the holder of the certificate. There is an expiration date associated with them, a serial number, and information on what you can do with them. A credit card, for instance, specifies how much credit is remaining on the card, a driver's license specifies whether a motorcycle can be driven with it and if wearing glasses is required, and so on.

Certificates can be issued by anyone. How reliable the information on the certificate is depends on the certificate issuing authority. For example, the identity of a person carrying a passport that is issued by the federal government is trusted more than the identity of a person holding a credit card or a card issued by a grocery market.

The nature of *digital certificates* is specified by ITU-T's X.509 standard. They contain the same items that we have stated come with certificates in general. For instance, they contain the expiration date, the issuer's name and public key, the name of the entity holding the certificate, and their public key. They also contain what can be done with the certificate and its class. There are four classes for certificates and they represent how much the certificate authority made you go through to prove who you are before the certificate issuing authority would vouch for your identity. For example, a card issued by a grocery market would represent a class 1 certificate, while a passport would represent a class 4 certificate.

A CA (Certificate Authority) is anyone who issues a certificate. How much a CA is trusted depends on their certificate issuing policies and the class of the certificate. A CA must be able to issue and revoke keys. They must be able to identify and register an identity using a policy statement. They must be able to provide a list of serial numbers to identify which certificates are now invalid.

Hospitals can issue certificates to their patients or colleges can issue them to their students. There are also companies who specialize in issuing certificates because their certificate issuing and maintenance practices are trusted by others. Such companies include the U. S. Postal Service, VeriSign, GTE CyberTrust, etc.

These companies ship their certificates in the web browser and you can look them up. For instance, in Netscape Communicator 4.7, click in the following order to find out which certificates are present in your browser: Tools -> Security Information -> Signers. Then select one of the certificates, click on Edit, view its public key in hex, and when done, click Cancel.

Certificate chains allow one entity or organization to identify itself securely. Suppose that you are on Prentice Hall's web site and you are about to make a purchase by giving your credit card number to them. How do you know that the party on the other end is really Prentice Hall and not some teenager in a foreign country? Certificate chains allow you to confirm that without you requiring to keep the public keys of all the retail merchants with which you will engage in business.

Let us see how this is accomplished by using an example. We have already mentioned that all browsers ship with the public keys of root CAs. Root CAs are CAs that are trusted in the PKI (Public Key Infrastructure) and who vouch for other

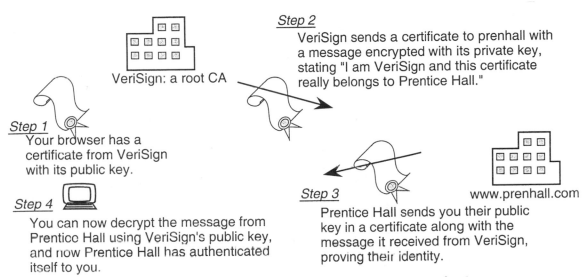

Step 2
VeriSign sends a certificate to prenhall with a message encrypted with its private key, stating "I am VeriSign and this certificate really belongs to Prentice Hall."

VeriSign: a root CA

Step 1
Your browser has a certificate from VeriSign with its public key.

Step 4
You can now decrypt the message from Prentice Hall using VeriSign's public key, and now Prentice Hall has authenticated itself to you.

Step 3
Prentice Hall sends you their public key in a certificate along with the message it received from VeriSign, proving their identity.

www.prenhall.com

Figure 27.11 A certificate chain is where a root CA vouches for the identity of another party.

companies or organizations. The certificates from root CAs which are in your browser are shown as Step 1 of Figure 27.11.

Before you actually give out your credit card number to Prentice Hall, you would like Prentice Hall to authenticate itself to you. (You never authenticate yourself to such a retailer.) As shown in Step 2 of the figure, a root CA, which we'll assume to be VeriSign, sends a certificate to Prentice Hall with a message that is encrypted using its private key. This message basically verifies Prentice Hall's identity.

Then Prentice Hall sends a certificate to you with this message from VeriSign, giving you its own public key. This is seen in Step 3. You can verify that this is indeed Prentice Hall and no one else because you have VeriSign's public key in your browser with which you can decrypt that message. See Step 4.

If you don't trust VeriSign, you can go to your browser and check off the items for VeriSign so the certificate from Prentice Hall is not checked against VeriSign's certificate, but with some other root CA. Now Prentice Hall will send you certificates with messages from several root CAs. Now you are ready to give your credit card number. At this time, you may get a dialog box warning you. You will notice that you are running https (not http) with port number 443 (not 80). This uses what is called SSL (Secure Sockets Layer). Remember also that all VeriSign has proved to you is that Prentice Hall was on the other end of your communication session. It did not assure you that Prentice Hall was trustworthy. You had to determine that when you gave them your credit card number.

27.4 IPSec

The first RFC that you should check for IPSec is RFC 2401. At the time of this writing there are many protocols being used in VPNs. However, we'll primarily concentrate on IPSec (IP Security protocol). The idea behind IPSec is that instead of building security in each of the Internet applications one at a time, we should build security in IP itself. Because all traffic has to go through IP anyway, that will ensure our communications throughout the Internet will be secure. By making IP secure, we have made the Internet secure.

One of the key advantages of IPSec is that it is a framework that does not specify exactly how it should be implemented. How IPSec is to be implemented depends on what demands are placed by the applications. Therefore, IPSec is flexible. As newer forms of security methods are invented, they can be easily made available through IPSec. Also, IPSec will be compatible with IPv6 whenever that becomes more widely used.

There are three parts to IPSec and they consist of AH (Authenticated Header), ESP (Encapsulation Security Payload), and IKE (Internet Key Exchange). AH and ESP protocols add headers to the IP packets.

Authentication means to prove identity and the AH does just that as well as provide integrity or the assurance that the data was not altered. For many applications this level of security will be enough, but for those who also need to add encryption by scrambling the data, using ESP is necessary instead of using AH. ESP adds a level of security that is not available with AH. AH uses HMAC with MD5 (RFC 2403) or

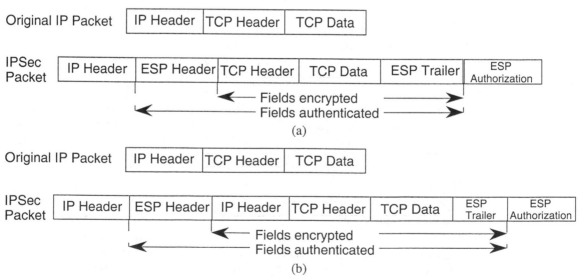

Figure 27.12 (a) ESP being used in the transport mode. (b) ESP being used in the tunnel mode.

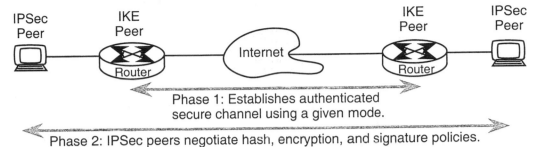

Figure 27.13 IKE uses two phases to exchange keys and to negotiate protocols.

HMAC with SHA1 (RFC 2404). ESP uses these same protocols but also adds DES-CBC (RFC 2405) for encryption.

IKE is a security policy negotiation protocol that is flexible. IKE allows you to select authentication, encryption, and hashing methods for a given communication session. Other parameters needed for secure communications are also provided through IKE.

ESP can be used in either in transport mode or in tunnel mode as shown in Figure 27.12. In the transport mode an ESP header is added between the IP and TCP headers as shown in Figure 27.12(a). At the end of the datagram an ESP trailer is also added. The entire packet is authenticated except for the IP header. The TCP header, data, and the ESP trailer fields are encrypted.

In the tunnel mode, as shown in Figure 27.12(b), the entire IP packet is kept together and an ESP header and trailer are added. A new IP header is also added that has the IP address of the security gateway in it. This way, a hacker sniffing the packet in the network will find only the address of the gateway and the end point where the packet is ultimately going. All the fields from the ESP header to the trailer are authenticated and those from the old IP header to the trailer are encrypted.

Figure 27.13 shows roughly how IKE (Internet Key Exchange) works. The two routers shown are some type of security gateways, which create a secure channel using keys or certificates. They can do this by using either one of two modes called the main mode and the aggressive mode. Main mode is more secure while the aggressive mode is faster. A connection can start in the main mode and then go into the aggressive mode.

After the security gateways create this secure tunnel between them, the end hosts negotiate which encryption, signature, and hash policies to use. This is shown in phase 2 of the diagram.

SSL: Using SSL (Secure Sockets Layer) is a different approach to securing an application over the Internet. This is a protocol that is inserted between an application and the TCP protocol. To TCP, it looks like an application. Its port number, for instance, is 443 and its name on the locator of a web browser is https. SSL is then implemented on both the client and the server side of the secure connection. It can be used with http, telnet, ftp, etc.

SSL uses the SSL Handshake Protocol for initial negotiation and uses the SSL Record Protocol to transfer data. They provide privacy and integrity of messages with authentication between the client and server. For banking transactions, an extension of SSL called SGC (Server Gated Cryptography) is used with 128-bit-long keys.

EXERCISES

Section 27.1:

1. A private network that is carved out of a public network is called what?
2. A private network that uses TCP/IP devices is called what?
3. When an organization has access to another organization's private network through the Internet, that private network is viewed as what kind of network?
4. Which type of layer 3 VPN is considered more secure and why? What are some of the limitations of this kind of VPN?
5. Are layer 2 VPNs considered more secure than layer 3 VPNs? Why? What added benefit is there to this kind of VPN?
6. In which type of layer 1 VPN is there encryption along the entire path of the connection? Is this type of VPN more suitable for users located within a certain geographical region? Why?

Section 27.2:

7. Give reasons to install a VPN.
8. List the concerns you might have about installing a VPN and how they might be overcome.

Section 27.3:

For the following five questions, choose the correct security issue from the following list.

a. authentication	b. audit
c. integrity	d. confidentiality
e. non-repudiation	f. authorization

9. Finding out where a given transaction got lost.
10. Being able to tell whether the party on the other end has permission from his company to make a purchase order.
11. Being able to transfer data so that no one can tap into it.
12. A method in proving the identity of a party.
13. Being able to prove the identity and the contents of a message.

For the following seven questions, give the type of cryptography being described. Choose from this list:

a. hashing	b. SKC	c. PKC

14. DES and Triple DES are examples of this type of security.
15. RSA is a common algorithm used for this type of security.
16. MD (Message Digest) and SHA (Secure Hash Algorithm) are examples of this method.
17. It is used to provide integrity of data.
18. This type of cryptography always provides the same length result regardless of the length of the original text.
19. This type of cryptography is used to exchange keys since it takes time.
20. This is asymmetric cryptography.

21. Using the ignore the carry method of encryption shown in Figure 27.7, give the ciphertext if the cleartext is 3859.
22. Using all the same keys and algorithms given in Figure 27.8, construct the three-part encrypted message to be transmitted if the cleartext is 5091.
23. Decrypt the message obtained in the above problem using the method shown in Figure 27.8.
24. Rearrange the diagram shown in Figure 27.8 so that validity is not checked by verifying the digital signatures but by verifying the hash values.
25. What is the advantage and the disadvantage of having longer key lengths?
26. What is the disadvantage of improving technology by having computers operate at higher and higher speeds?
27. What do certificates prove and not prove about a party?
28. Describe how certificates are used.
29. In your browser, which CA has the most the most number of certificates?

Section 27.4:
30. List the three main parts of the IPSec protocol and their purpose.
31. Give two advantages of IPSec.
32. What are the two phases used in IKE?
33. What advantage does running ESP in the tunneling mode provide as opposed to running it in the transport mode?
34. Although problems were found in SSL in 1998, what approach does it use to provide security as opposed to IPSec?

Appendix

The Alphabet Dance

2B1Q	2 Binary, 1 Quaternary
4WTS	4-Wire Terminal Set
AA	Automated Attendant
AAL	ATM Adaptation Layer
AAR	Automatic Alternate Routing
Abis	BSC-BTS Interface
AC	Alternating Current
AC	Authentication Center (wireless)
ACD	Automatic Call Distributor
ACK	ACKnowledgement
ACM	Address Complete Message
ACP	Action Control Point
ACS	Automatic Call Sequencer
ADM	Add-and-Drop Mux
ADPCM	Adaptive Differential PCM
ADSL	Asymmetric DSL
AESA	ATM End Station Address
AFT	Analog Facility Terminal
AH	Authentication Header
AIN	Advanced Intelligent Network
AMI	Alternate Mark Inversion
AMPS	Advanced Mobile Phone Service
ANI	Automatic Number Identification
ANSI	American National Standards Institute
AP	Adjunct Processor (MCI)
AP	Action Point (SDN)
API	Application Program Interface
APPC	Advanced Program-to-Program Communications
APPN	Advanced Peer-to-Peer Networking
APS	Automatic Protection Switching

ARIN	American Registry for Internet Numbers
ARP	Address Resolution Protocol
ARPANET	Advanced Research Projects Agency NETwork
ARS	Automatic Route Selection
AS	Autonomous System
ASCII	American Standard Code for Information Interchange
ASIC	Application-Specific Integrated Circuit
ASR	Automated Speech Recognition
AT&T	American Telephone & Telegraph Co.
ATM	Asynchronous Transfer Mode
ATP	Application Transaction Program
ATU-C	ADSL Terminal Unit - CO
ATU-R	ADSL Terminal Unit - Remote
AUI	Attachment Unit Interface
AWG	American Wire Guage
B8ZS	Binary 8-Zero Suppression
BBN	Bolt, Beranek, and Newman
BCM	Bit Compression Mux
BECN	Backward Explicit Congestion Notification
Bellcore	BELL COmmunications REsearch
BGP	Border Gateway Protocol
BIB	Backward Indicator Bit
B-ICI	Broadband Inter-Carrier Interface
BIND	Berkeley Internet Name Domain
BIOS	Basic Input/Output System
BISDN	Broadband ISDN
BIU	Basic Information Unit

BLSR	Bidirectional Line Switched Ring		CMA	Communications Managers Association
BLU	Basic Link Unit		CMB	Credit Manager Bandwidth
BOC	Bell Operatin Company		CMC	Communications Management Center
BPV	BiPolar Violation		CMOS	Channelized Metal Oxide Semiconductor
BRI	Basic Rate Interface (2B + D)		CNAR	Customer Network Administration Report
BS	Base Station			
BSC	BS Controller		CNI	Common Network Interface
BSC	Binary Synchronous Communications		CNOS	Change Number Of Services
BSN	Backward Sequence Number		CO	Central Office
BT	British Telecom		Codec	Coder-Decoder
BTA	Basic Trading Area		COS	Class Of Service
BTS	Base Transceiver Station		CP	Cable Pair number
BTU	Basic Transmission Unit		CPCS	Common Port Convergence Sublayer
C/I	Carrier-to-Interference ratio		CPE	Customer Premises Equipment
CA	Certificate Authority		CPI	Computer-PBX Interface
CAD	Computer-Aided Design		CPI	Common Programming Interface
CAP	Competitive Access Providers		CPU	Central Processor Unit
CAP-QAM	Carrierless Amplitude/Phase and Quadrature Amplitude Modulation		CRC	Cyclic Redundancy Check
			CS	Convergence Sublayer
CAS	Centralized Attendant Service (PBX)		CSL	Component SubLayer
CAS	Channel-Associated Signaling		CSMA/CA	Carrier Sense Multiple Access with Collision Avoidance
CAT-5	CATegory 5 cabling			
CATV	CAble TeleVision		CSMA/CD	CSMA with Collision Detection
CBR	Constant Bit Rate		CSMA/CR	CSMA with Collision Resolution
CCIR	International Radio Consultative Committee		CSS	Center-Stage Switch
			CSU	Channel Service Unit
CCIS	Common Channel Interoffice Signaling		CTDR	Customer Traffic Data Report
CCITT	Comité Consultatif Internationale de Telegraphiqué et Telephoniqué		CTI	Computer Telephony Integration
			DA	Destination Address
CCK	Complementary Code Keying		DAC	Dual Attached Concentrator
CCR	Customer-Controlled Reconfiguration		DACS	Digital Access and Cross-connect System
CCS7	Common Channel Signaling 7			
CD	Compact Disc		DAL	Dedicated Access Line
CDMA	Code Division Multiple Access		DAP	Data Access Point
CDPD	Cellular Digital Packet Data		DARPA	Defense Advanced Research Projects Agency
CDR	Call Detail Recording			
CEPT	Conference on European Posts & Telecommunications		DAS	Dual Attached Station
			DATTS	Direct Access Trunk Test System
CIC	Circuit Identification Code		dB	Decibel
CICS	Customer Information Control System		DC	Direct Current
CID	Component IDentifier		DCE	Data Communications Equipment
CIDR	Classless InterDomain Routing		DCP	Data Communications Protocol
CIR	Committed Information Rate		DCR	Dynamic Controlled Routing
CISC	Complex Instruction Set Computing		DCS	Distributed Communications System
CLASS	Custom Local Area Signaling Services		DCS	Digital Crossconnect System (or DACS)
CLEC	Competitive Local Exchange Carrier		DDD	Direct Distance Dialing
CLNP	ConnectionLess Network Protocol		DDN	Digital Data Network
CLNS	ConnectionLess Network Service		DDN	Defense Data Network
CLP	Cell Loss Priority		DDS	Digital Data Service
CM	Configuration Management			

DDS	Dataphone Digital Services
DE	Data Eligibility bit
DEC	Digital Equipment Corporation
DECT	Digital European Cordless Telecommunications
DHCP	Dynamic Host Configuration Protocol
DIA	Document Interchange Architecture
DID	Direct Inward Dialing
DINA	Distributed Intelligent Network Architecture
DIP	Dual In-line Package switch
DISA	Direct Inward System Access
DISC	DISConnect
DLC	Digital Line Carrier
DLCI	Data Link Control Identifier
DLL	Dynamic Link Library
DLSw	Data Link Switching
DM	Disconnect Mode
DMI	Digital Multiplexed Interface
DMT	Discrete Multitone Transmission
DNHR	Dynamic NonHierarchical Routing
DNIC	Data Network Identification Code
DNIS	Dialed Number Identification Service
DNS	Domain Name Service
DoD	Department of Defense
DOD	Direct Outward Dialing
DOS	Disk Operating System
DOV	Data Over Voice
DPC	Destination Point Code
DQDB	Distributed Queue Dual Bus
DR	Designated Router
DS-0	Digital Signal, level 0
DS-1	Digital Signal, level 1
DSAP	Destination SAP
DSL	Digital Subscriber Line
DSLAM	Digital Subscriber Line Access Module
DSP	Digital Signal Processing
DSSS	Direct Sequence Spread Spectrum
DSU	Digital Service Unit
DSX-1	Digital System cross-connect 1
DTE	Data Terminal Equipment
DTMF	Dual Tone MultiFrequency
DTW	Dynamic Time Warping
DVCC	Digital Verification Color Code
DWDM	Dense Wave Division Multiplexing
E&M	Ear and Mouth signaling
EA	Extension Address
EAMPS	Extended AMPS
ECS	Enterprise Communications Server
EFCI	Explicit Forward Congestion Indicator

EGP	Exterior Gateway Protocol
EIA	Electronics Industries Association
EKS	Electronic Key System
EMI	ElectroMagnetic Interference
EMS	Element Management System
EN	End Node
EO	End Office
EPN	Expansion Port Network
ES	End System
ESF	Extended Super Frame
ESN	Electronic Serial Number
ESP	Encapsulation Security Payload
ESS	Electronic Switching System
ETN	Electronic Tandem Network
FACCH	Fast Associated Control CHannel
FCC	Federal Communications Commission
FCS	Frame Check Sequnce
FDDI	Fiber-Distributed Data Interface
FDL	Facility Data Link
FDM	Frequency Division Multiplex
FDMA	Frquency Division Multiple Access
FDX	Full DupleX
FEC	Forward Error Correction
FECN	Forward Explicit Congestion Notification
FEP	Front End Processor
FIB	Forward Indicator Bit
FID	Format ID
FISU	Fill-In Signal Unit
FLP	Fast Link Pulse
FMH	Function Management Header
FOIRL	Fiber Optic InterRepeater Link
FOT	Fiber Optic Terminal
FR	Frame Relay
FRAD	Frame Relay Assembler/Disassembler
FRF	Frame Relay Forum
FRL	Facility Restriction Level
FRMR	FRaMe Reject
FSN	Forward Sequence Number
FT1	Fractional T1
FTP	File Transfer Protocol
FX	Foreign eXchange
FXO	Foreign eXchange, Office
FXS	Foreign eXchange, Subscriber
GDS	Generalized Data Stream
GE	Gigabit Ethernet
GFC	Generlc Flow Control
GFI	General Format Identifier
GMMI	Gigabit MMI
GMSC	Gateway Mobile Switching Controller

The Alphabet Dance

GPS	Global Positioning System
GSM	Global System for Mobile communications
GUI	Graphical User Interface
HDLC	High-level Data Link Control
HDSL	High-speed Digital Subscriber Line
HEC	Header Error Correction
HEHO	Head-End Hop-Off
HIVR	Host-Interactive Voice Response
HLR	Home Location Register
HMDF	Horizontal Main Distribution Frame
HMM	Hidden Markov Modeling
HPAD	Host Packet Assembler/Disassembler
HTML	HyperText Markup Language
HTTP	HyperText Transfer Protocol
I/G	Individual/Group bit
I/O	Input/Output
IANA	Internet Assigned Numbers Authority
IBM	International Business Machines Corp.
ICMP	Internet Control Message Protocol
IDDD	International DDD
IDF	Intermediate Distribution Frame
IDSL	ISDN DSL
IEC	InterExchange Carrier
IEEE	Institute of Electrical and Electronics Engineers
IETF	Internet Research Task Force
IGMP	Internet Group Management Protocol
IGP	Interior Gateway Protocol
IKE	Internet Key Exchange
ILEC	Incumbent Local Exchange Carrier
ILMI	Integrated Link Management Interface
IMS	Information Management System
IMT	InterMachine Trunk
IMTS	Improved Mobile Telephone Service
IMUX	Inverse MUltipleXer
INMS	Integrated Network Management Systems
INSITE	Integrated Network System Interface and Terminal Equipment
IP	Internet Protocol
IPsec	IP Security protocol
IRTF	Internet Research Task Force
IS	Intermediate System
IS-IS	IS to IS protocol
ISDN	Integrated Services Digital Network
ISO	International Organization for Standardization
ISOC	Internet SOCiety
ISP	Internet Service Provider
ISSI	Inter-Switching System Interface
ISUP	ISdn User Part
ITU	International Telecommunications Union
ITU-R	ITU Radio communication sector
ITU-T	ITU Telecommunications standardization sector
IVDT	Integrated Voice/Data Terminal
IVR	Interactive Voice Response
IXC	IEC
JAIN	Java Api for Integrated Networks
JTAPI	Java Telephony API
JES	Job Entry Subsystem
KSU	Key System Unit
LAN	Local Area Network
LAP/B	Link Access Procedure/Balanced
LAPD	Link Access Procedures over the D Channel
LAPF	Link Access Procedure - Frames
LAT	Local Area Transport
LATA	Local Access and Transport Area
LCI	Logical Channel Identifier
LCP	Link Control Protocol
LCR	Least-Cost Routing
LE	Local Exchange
LED	Light-Emitting Diode
LEN	Low-Entry Networking
LESA	Local Exchange Switched Access
LILO	LInux LOader
LLC	Logical Link Control
LMDS	Local Multipoint Distribution Services
LMI	Local Management Interface
LMU	Line Monitor Unit
LOA	LOcal Address
LORAN-C	LOng RAnge Navigation-C
LPC-RPE	Linear Predictive Encoding with Regular Pulse Excitation
LSA	Link State Advertisement
LSB	Least Significant Bit
LSSU	Link Status Signaling Unit
LT	Local Termination
LU	Logical Unit
MAC	Media Access Control
MAN	Metropolitan Area Network
MAU	Media Access Unit (Ethernet)
MAU	Multistation Access Unit (TRN)
MCI	Microwave Communications Inc.
MCR	Mapped Conversation Record
MDA	Mail Delivery Agent
MDF	Main Distribution Frame

MF	MultiFrequency
MFJ	Modified Final Judgment
MFS	Metropolitan Fiber Systems
MFT	Metallic Facility Terminal
MIC	Media Interface Connector
MID	Message ID
MMDS	Multipoint Multichannel Distribution Services
MMF	MultiMode Fiber
MMI	Media-Independent Interface
MS	Mobile Station
MSB	Most Significant Bit
MSC	Mobile Switching Center
MSU	Message Signal Unit
MTA	Mail Transfer Agent (SMTP)
MTA	Major Trading Area (wireless)
MTP	Message Transfer Part
MTS	Message Telecommunications Service
MTSO	Mobile Telecommunications Switching Office
MTTR	Mean Time To Repair
MTU	Maximum Transfer Unit
MUA	Mail User Agent
MUX	MUltipleXer
MVS	Multiple Virtual Systems
NACK	Negative ACKnowledgement
NANPA	North American Numbering Plan Administration
NAT	Network Address Translation
NAU	Network Addressable Unit
NAUN	Nearest Active Upstream Neighbor
NCP	Network Control Program (SNA)
NCP	Network Control Point (PSTN)
NEMOS	NEtwork Management Operation support System
NetBIOS	Network BIOS
NETCAP	NETwork CAPabilities manager
NFS	Network File System
NIC	Network Interface Card
NID	Network Interface Device
NIMS	Network Information Management Systems
NIU	Network Interface Unit
NLP	Normal Link Pulse
NNI	Network-Network Interface
NNMC	National Network Management Center
NOC	Network Operations Center
NOS	Network Operating System
NPSI	NCP Packet Switching Interface
NRA	Network Remote Access

NRAMS	NRA Monitoring System
NRZI	Non-Return to Zero Inverted
NSC	Network Service Complex
NSF	National Science Foundation
NT	Northern Telecom
NT1/2	Network Termination 1 and 2
NTI	Northern Telecom Inc.
OAI	Open Architecture Interface
OAM	Operations, Administrations, and Maintenance
OC-1	Optical Carrier, level 1
OCU	Office Channel Unit
OE	Office Equipment designation
OLTP	On-Line Transaction Processing
OPC	Origination Point Code
OPX	Off-Premise Extension
OSI	Open Systems Interconnection
OSPF	Open Shortest Path First
OSS	Operation Support System
OUI	Organizational Unique Identifier
OVSF	Orthogonal Variable Spreading Factor
PAD	Packet Assembler/Disassembler
PAM	Pass-Along Message
PAP	Public Access Profile
PBX	Private Branch eXchange
PC	Personal Computer
PCM	Pulse Code Modulation
PCS	Personal Communications System
PDN	Public Data Network
PDU	Protocol Data Unit
PHY	PHYsical layer protocol
PIU	Path Information Unit
PKC	Public Key Cryptography
PKI	Public Key Infrastructure
PLCP	Physical Unit Control Point
PLU	Primary Logical Unit
PMD	Physical Medium Dependent
PN	Pseudorandom Noise
PNNI	Private Network-to-Network Interface
POP	Point of Presence
POTS	Plain Old Telephone Service
PPN	Processor Port Network
PPP	Point-to-Point Protocol
PPS	Packets Per Second
PRI	Primary Rate Interface (23B or 30B + D)
PSN	Packet Switched Network
PSTN	Public Switched Telephone Network
PT	Payload Type
PTT	Postal, Telephone, and Telegraph

The Alphabet Dance

PU	Physical Unit
PUC	Public Utility Commission
PVC	Permanent Virtual Circuit
PVP	Permanent Virtual Path
QCELP	Qualcomm Code Excited Linear Prediction
QLLC	Qualified Logical Link Control
QoS	Quality of Service
RAM	Random Access Memory
RARP	Reverse Address Resolution Protocol
RBOC	Regional BOC
RDPS	Reverse Direction Protection Switching
RFC	Request For Comments
RFI	Radio Frequency Interference
RH	Request/response Header
RIF	Routing Information Field
RIP	Routing Information Protocol
RISC	Reduced Instruction Set Computing
RJ	Register Jack
ROM	Read-Only Memory
RSA	Rivest, Shamir, and Aldeman
RSIP	Realm-Specific IP
RTNR	Real-Time Network Routing
RU	Request/response Unit
SAAL	Signaling AAL
SABM	Set Asynchronous Balanced Mode
SABME	SABM Extended
SAC	Serving Area Concept (PSTN)
SAC	Single Attached Concentrator (FDDI)
SACCH	Slow Associated Control CHannel
SAP	Service Access Point
SAPI	SAP Identifier
SAR	Segmentation And Reassembly
SAS	Single Attached Station
SBS	Satellite Business Systems
SC	Stick-and-Click fiber connector
SCCP	Signaling Connection Control Part
SCM	Service Control Manager
SCP	Service Control Point
SCPMS	SCP Management System
SDDN	Software-Defined Data Network
SDH	Synchronous Digital Hierarchy
SDLC	Synchronous Data Link Control
SDN	Software-Defined Network
SDNCC	SDN Control Center
SDSL	Single-pair DSL
SDU	Service Data Unit
SEAL	Simple and Efficient Adaptation Layer
SF	Single Frequency
SFD	Start Frame Delimiter

SIO	Service Information Octet
SIP	SMDS Interface Protocol
SIVR	Speech-Independent Voice Recognition
SKC	Secret Key Cryptography
SLA	Service Level Agreement
SLC-96	Subscriber Line Carrier
SLS	Signaling Link Selection
SLU	Secondary LU
SMDR	Station Message Detail Recording
SMDS	Switched Multi-megabit Digital Service
SMF	Single-Mode Fiber
SMS	Service Management System
SMTP	Simple Mail Transfer Protocol
SNA	Systems Network Architecture
SNADS	SNA Distributed Services
SNF	Segment Number Field
SNI	Subscriber Network Interface
SNID	Smart NID
SNMP	Simple Network Management Protocol
SOHO	Small Office/Home Office
SONET	Synchronous Optical NETwork
SP	Signaling Point
SPARC	Scalable Processor ARChitecture
SPC	Stored Program Control
SPE	Synchronous Payload Envelope
SRDM	SubRate Data Multiplexing
SRT	Source Route Transparent bridge
SS	SMDS Switching system
SS7	Signaling System 7
SSAP	Source SAP
SSCP	System Services Control Point
SSCS	Service-Specific Convergence Sublayer
SSL	Secure Sockets Layer
SSMA	Spread Spectrum Multiple Access
SSP	Signal Service Point
ST	Stick-and-Twist fiber connector
STE	Signaling Terminal Equipment
STM	Synchronous Transmission Mode
STP	Signal Transfer Point (PSTN)
STP	Shielded Twisted Pair (LANs)
STS	Synchronous Transport Signal
SU	Signaling Unit
SVC	Switched Virtual Circuit
SVP	Switched Virtual Path
TA	Terminal Adapter
TAPI	Telephony API
TAT	TransATlantic cable
TCAP	Transaction Capabilities Application Part

TCP	Transmission Control Protocol
TDM	Time Division Multiplex
TDMA	Time Division Multiple Access
TE	Terminal Equipment (1 or 2)
TEHO	Tail-End Hop-Off
TEI	Terminal Endpoint Identifier
Telco	TELephone COmpany
TFTP	Trivial File Transfer Protocol
TG	Transmission Group
TH	Transmission Header
THT	Token Holding Timer
TIA	Telecommunnications Industries Association
TIC	Token Ring Interface Card
TID	Transaction IDentifier
TMPA	Tapi-to-tsapi MAPping
TN	Terminal Number
TP	Transaction Program
TP	TeleProcessing
TPAD	Terminal PAD
TPC	TransPaCific cable
TRN	Token Ring Network
TSAPI	Telephony Services API
TSL	Transaction SubLayer
TSO	Time Sharing Option
TSSI	Time Slot Sequence Integrity
TTL	Time To Live
TTRT	Target Token Rotation Time
TTS	Text-To-Speech
TVX	Valid Transmission Timer
U/L	Universal or Local
UA	Unnumbered Acknowledge
UCD	Uniform Call Distributor
UDP	User Datagram Protocol
UDSL	Universal aDSL
UI	Unnumbered Information

ULSR	Unidirectional Line-Switched Ring
Um	Air Interface
UN	United Nations
UNI	User-to-Network Interface
UNMA	Unified Network Management Architecture
UTP	Unshielded Twisted Pair
VAC	Volts AC (Alternating Current)
VAN	Value-Added Network
VBR	Variable Bit Rate
VC	Virtual Circuit
VCI	Virtual Channel Identifier
VDC	Volts DC (Direct Current)
VDSL	Very high DSL
VFRAD	Voice-FRAD
VINES	VIrtual NEtwork System
VLAN	Virtual LAN
VLR	Visitor Location Register
VLSI	Very Large Scale Integration
VMDF	Vertical MDF
VoFR	Voice over Frame Relay
VoIP	Voice over IP
VPDS	Virtual Private Data Service
VPI	Virtual Path Identifier
VPN	Virtual Private Network
VR	Voice Recognition
VSAT	Very Small Aperture Terminal
VSELP	Vector Sum Excited Linear Prediction
VT	Virtual Tributary
VTAM	Virtual Telecommunications Access Method
WAL	WATS Access Link
WAN	Wide Area Network
WATS	Wide Area Telecommunications Service
WDM	Wave Division Multiplexing
WWW	World Wide Web
XID	eXchange IDentifier

The Alphabet Dance

Index